THE
THOUGHT AND CULTURE OF THE
ENGLISH RENAISSANCE

THE
THOUGHT & CULTURE OF THE
ENGLISH RENAISSANCE

An Anthology of Tudor Prose
1481 — 1555

EDITED BY
ELIZABETH M. NUGENT

AND INTRODUCED BY
DOUGLAS BUSH   ELOISE L. PAFORT
W. GORDON ZEEVELD   GERTRUDE ANNAN
W. E. CAMPBELL   F. S. BOAS
H. S. BENNETT

CAMBRIDGE
AT THE UNIVERSITY PRESS
1956

PUBLISHED BY
THE SYNDICS OF THE CAMBRIDGE UNIVERSITY PRESS

London Office: Bentley House, N.W.I
American Branch: New York

Agents for Canada, India, and Pakistan: Macmillan

Printed in Great Britain at the University Press, Cambridge
(Brooke Crutchley, University Printer)

PREFACE

By reprinting portions of the writings of early Tudor authors, I hope that this anthology, in some measure, will aid in confirming an opinion which has long been emerging from European and American critiques, namely, that the Renaissance of continental Europe and England was the gradual flowering of the seeds of Western culture sown in the Middle Ages. A reason for this new critical approach has been offered by Professor Leicester Bradner while praising the recently founded Renaissance Society of America. He points out that the 'popular myth' which envisioned the Renaissance as 'the revival of light and joy after the bleak darkness of the Middle Ages' has been 'exploded by the better understanding of the great achievements of the twelfth and thirteenth centuries'.

Professor Bradner's remarks are especially applicable to the English Renaissance. And it is conceivable that a more widespread knowledge of the authors of the early Tudor period, men of enduring faith and high learning, standing midway between Chaucer and Shakespeare, will bring about an even deeper understanding of the issues—spiritual, social, and political—that mark the great eras of these poets.

I had in mind a rather slim volume when dispatching an outline for the project to Professor Douglas Bush in the spring of 1941. In his gracious reply, he commended the 'enterprise' because 'the early Tudor age is commonly enveloped in mist'. In his enthusiasm for the period, he named some six or more authors and works that he would like to see included, but 'with the hesitation of one who has made an anthology and knows how hard it is to please everybody'. So the number of authors began to grow, and not a few names were added by the late Rev. William J. McGarry, S.J., Professor Karl Young, and Professor John Archer Gee.

As the list increased, so did my problems. My gratitude goes forth to the many who have aided me, especially my collaborators whose names accompany their introductions or translations. It has been a privilege to know and work with each of them. Their contributions give authority and vigour to the volume.

Acknowledgements to scholars in the biographical sketches and notes will not, I trust, be overlooked. With them I also wish to thank the Very Rev. Monsignor Vincent J. Flynn, the Rev. George W. Shea, Dr James McManaway, Professor Laura Hibbard Loomis, the Rev. Joseph C. Plumpe, Mother Margaret Williams, R.S.C.J., the Rev. William La Verdière, S.S.S., Professor A. C. Krey, the Rev.

Eckart Koehle, O.S.B., Professor Eden Sarot, Professor A. S. Salter, Professor E. G. R. Taylor, the Rev. W. A. Hinnebusch, O.P., and Professor George Sarton.

In their former administrative capacity at University College, Seton Hall University, I extend my sincere thanks to the Rev. Daniel A. Murphy and Dr Charles H. Elliott. For many thoughtful considerations I wish to express my gratitude to the Right Rev. Monsignor John L. McNulty, President of Seton Hall University. Finally, for her enduring patience and enthusiasm that has helped the book into print, I am grateful to my mother, Florence Burkley Nugent.

I wish to pause here to pay tribute to University Microfilms, that extraordinary project which eased immeasurably the burden of research. For expediting my use of the films I am indebted to Mr A. P. DeWeese and his assistants in the Main Reading Room of the New York Public Library; also, for their kind help my thanks are due to Mr L. M. Stark and Mrs Philomena Houlihan in the Rare Book Room, and Dr J. D. Gordan and his assistants in the Berg Collection. To the many librarians and their staffs whom space does not permit me to name, I extend my sincere appreciation for their labours in my behalf. Among these are Miss E. L. Pafort and Dr Curt Bühler of the Pierpont Morgan Library; Miss L. M. Stubblefield, Miss A. H. Bonnell and Miss M. R. Burns of Butler Library, Columbia University; the staff of the General Theological Seminary Library; and the Rev. Charles Murphy and Mrs Mary Cooper Kaiser of Seton Hall University Library. I have had special courtesies at the British Museum and Corpus Christi College Library, Oxford.

I wish to acknowledge the kindness of the Rev. Canon Edward Charles Rich for permission to reprint portions of Lily's Grammar from the Peterborough Cathedral Library. I am also indebted to those publishers who have generously given permission for reprints. Except for a portion of Miss Annan's article, taken from *Ciba Symposia*, vol. XI, no. 9, the publisher of each work is mentioned at the end of the selected passage. For efficient and cheerful services in preparing the manuscript, I am indebted to Dr Helen Bannerman and Miss Virginia McCauley.

I wish to make personal acknowledgement to the Syndics and staff of the Cambridge University Press who have been most cooperative and helpful in every way and have given generously of their time in discussing editorial points that have arisen while the book has been in the press.

At first it was intended to keep the old spelling. However, the advisability of this was questioned, since most Renaissance spelling is close to the modern, and revision would not involve etymological changes. Though the scholars whose opinions were sought did not all agree on a modernized text, the majority felt it would have wider appeal and would not essentially mar the charm and piquancy of early Tudor prose.

Changes in capitalization have been necessary, though there are instances where it has been thought advisable, in some letters and school statutes for example, to retain the old form. Care has been taken to avoid changes in punctuation except where necessary for clarity. The slanting bar is replaced by the comma, and the colon, when need be, gives way to the semicolon.

E. M. N.

New York
31 May 1954

CONTENTS

PART I

TUDOR HUMANISTS

PART II

THE POLITICAL AND SOCIAL ORDER

TRADITION AND EARLY TUDOR MEDICINE

PART III

SERMONS AND RELIGIOUS TREATISES

PART IV

CHRONICLES AND HISTORIES

PART V

ROMANCES AND TALES

PART I

TUDOR HUMANISTS

TUDOR HUMANISTS[1]

INTRODUCTION BY DOUGLAS BUSH

THE BEGINNINGS OF THE ENGLISH RENAISSANCE

Modern historians, while making the spirit of the Renaissance spread from Italy over the rest of Europe, have regularly contrasted the aesthetic, irreligious neo-paganism of the South with the sober Christian piety of the North. The fundamental change that humanism underwent in crossing the Alps was presumably due to the invincible moral constitution of the northern nations, which were profoundly stimulated by an impulse they rejected. Such a view, so congenial to the Nordic and especially the Anglo-Saxon belief that the Latin peoples are inevitably immoral, has its measure of truth, but even our brief glance at Italian humanism may serve as a qualification. All that we can safely assert is that the religious, ethical and civic motives of Florentine humanism in particular were in the North even more pure and predominant than they were in Italy as a whole. If northern humanism grew up largely in the service of the Reformation, we should remember that much of the energy of Italian humanism was devoted to the support or the revival of medieval religious orthodoxy. When we read in Bacon and Milton that the Reformation, with its appeal to ancient authority, brought about the classical Renaissance, we may say that these men, lacking our long perspective, put the cart before the horse, yet their view is much nearer the truth than that of modern historians who consider the Renaissance essentially irreligious.

The real character of English humanism did not definitely emerge until the end of the fifteenth century, though it might have been predicted much earlier. Nearly all the Englishmen who went to Italy to study or had connexions with Italian humanists were churchmen, and the increasing strength of the classical revival did not fundamentally alter their religious habits of life and thought. They sometimes show a veneer of literary aestheticism, but it is only a veneer. Whatever neo-paganism flourished in Italy, these men did not seek it or acquire it. Most of the fifteenth-century English travellers came home with their books and lecture-notes and planted themselves in their ecclesiastical furrows, to make the earth fruitful, or, perhaps, merely to vegetate. In the early fifteenth century Poggio was able to sneer at barbarous Englishmen. Some

---

[1] Reprinted in part from *The Renaissance and English Humanism*. The Alexander Lectureship. University of Toronto Press, 1939.

eighty years later Erasmus rejoices in being welcomed by a group of English humanists which has no superior in Europe, and Aldus recognizes, in the person of Linacre, the international authority of English scholarship. We cannot take account here of the early phases of humanism in England—they have been illuminated by Professor Schirmer—but logic as well as history would prevent us from regarding as a sudden phenomenon the appearance of that distinguished circle which included Grocyn, Colet, More, Linacre, Latimer, Lily, and others. And these names indicate the character of English humanism in its first maturity, a thoroughly religious and ethical character which had its Catholic and Protestant phases and then passed into such divergent channels as learned puritanism and Cambridge Platonism.

Except More, who early in life took Pico as his model, all of these men studied in Italy, and Italy only confirmed and ripened a humanism more positively religious and practical than that of their somewhat shadowy predecessors. The oldest of the group, William Grocyn, seemed to younger admirers the very incarnation of Christian humanism. Though a theologian of the old school, Grocyn came to accept Valla's proof that 'Dionysius the Areopagite' was not a writer of the apostolic age. From Italy Colet brought back something of Savonarola's ascetic rigour and a new or enlarged knowledge of the Christian Platonism of Ficino and Pico. If Italian humanism taught Colet an historical approach to the Epistles of St Paul, it—and a nearer view of the Papacy—also fortified his zeal for a simplified theology, for the inward reformation of the universal church and its individual members on the pattern of Christ himself. Lily was the first head of Colet's school of St Paul's. Linacre, while less actively devout than Colet and More, was a great exemplar of both philological and scientific humanism. Almost all the men of this circle were able Grecians as well as Latinists, and most of them, like Erasmus, studied Greek in order to have the key to the New Testament, to drink of the unadulterated fountain of Christianity. Linacre's motto was also 'ad fontes'. His Greek scholarship (like that of Rabelais some years later) was applied to purifying the great works of classical science and medicine from medieval accretions.

One topic must be emphasized, though briefly. We cannot overestimate the importance of the Platonic strain in English humanism. In two groups of men it manifests itself with special power, in Colet, Erasmus, More, and Elyot in the early sixteenth century, and in the Cambridge Platonists in the middle of the seventeenth; in the intervening period the irrigating stream had not dried up. This Platonism was, of course, eclectic, drawn, in varying proportions, from Plato and Plotinus, Augustine and Dionysius, Ficino and Pico. It appeared in diverse forms, in political and educational thought, in truly religious mysticism and in amatory pseudo-mysticism, in doctrines of rational ethics and of supra-rational poetic inspiration. But everywhere it had a fertilizing, broadening, and sweetening influence. In the history of thought one could name many narrow, dogmatic Aristotelians; it would be hard to name a narrow, dogmatic Platonist. In England, in an age of puritan strictness, Platonism gave to rules of Christian piety and virtue a rational sanity and an idealistic ardour which inspired not only religious thinkers but poets like Spenser and Milton. In an age of sectarian conflict it made for charity and tolerance, for the belief that, as a living Platonist has said, the grace of God is not distributed denominationally....

THE SPIRITUAL AND INTELLECTUAL
FORCES OF HUMANISM

But our concern must be with the spiritual and intellectual quality of humanism, not with its history. The great change from Catholicism to Protestantism meant that the older humanistic ideal of a universal church as the channel of a purified universal faith gave way to a more national outlook on national questions. That Cheke and Ascham are of smaller stature than Colet and More, Mr Chambers would doubtless explain by saying that they were not angels but Anglicans. Although we should not ascribe all differences in individual character and endowment to a general change in religion, we might, without pressing the parallel, put Colet and Ascham beside Newman and Kingsley. There is something of Kingsley in the simple, sturdy, English faith of the prefatory verses to Ascham's *Toxophilus*:

> Reioyse Englande, be gladde and merie,
> Trothe ouercommeth thyne enemyes all.
> The Scot, the Frencheman, the Pope, and heresie,
> Overcommed by Trothe, haue had a fall:
> Sticke to the Trothe, and euermore thou shall
> Through Christ, King Henry, the Boke and the Bowe
> All maner of enemies, quite ouerthrowe.

While in the middle decades of the century Truth, as embodied in the Church of England, is something of a chameleon, the Protestant humanists, like their Catholic predecessors, are men of sober piety— though it has been observed that Ascham's censure of dicing betrays a rather minute knowledge of technique. If Ascham has a less intense and less philosophic spirituality than Colet, he only reveals more clearly the plain moral puritanism which was a large element in the Catholic divine. On the other hand, while Colet had been afraid of ancient pagan literature, Ascham lived with the classics and constantly celebrated them as a treasury of wisdom second only to the Bible.

For in their fervently didactic faith in the classical authors as the supreme guides, outside of revelation, to life and conduct as well as the arts of expression, the Protestant humanists shared a traditional orthodoxy which was an even more universal bond than Catholicism. The first formal defence of poetry written in the Tudor age, that of the Catholic Sir Thomas Elyot, is essentially the same in spirit as John of Salisbury's. The function of poets is to teach, and even Plautus and Terence, Ovid and Martial, have good counsel mixed with their licentious matter. Ascham is never weary of proclaiming the creed he holds with his friend and preceptor, Cheke:

> These books be not many, nor long, nor rude in speech, nor mean in matter; but next the majesty of God's Holy Word, most worthy for a man, the lover of learning and honesty, to spend his life in. Yea, I have heard worthy Mr Cheke many times say; I would have a good student pass and journey through all authors both Greek and Latin. But he that will dwell in these few books only; first, in God's holy Bible, and then join with it Tully in Latin, Plato, Aristotle, Xenophon, Isocrates, and Demosthenes in Greek, must needs prove an excellent man.

One need not multiply documentary proof of the indissoluble marriage of virtue and good letters. And while the great end of education is virtuous discipline, that does not mean indifference to the aesthetic appeal of ancient literature; it does mean emphasis on moral and philosophic substance, on values immediately applicable to life. Of much modern study of the classics, and literature in general, we might say what has been said of the New Testament, that we make up for not believing in Christ by admiring His style. In the sixteenth century, veneration for the ancients as a superior race of beings might, of course, lead to slavish subservience, but that was the only occasional defect of a saving faith in high standards. If we want to be like the ancients, devout humanists said, we must imitate even their gestures, and, rightly understood, that is not an ignoble creed. Continental humanists, from Petrarch to Sturm, echoed Cicero's doctrine that eloquence is nothing but articulate wisdom, and that eloquence without wisdom is a weapon in the hand of a madman. The same faith in good Latin, and the same warning, are repeated in England not merely by a professional classicist like Ascham but by a divine like Thomas Becon. Good Latin, as the instrument of God-given reason, is the symbol of religious, ethical, and social solidarity. When we think of the Renaissance humanist's limitless faith in the possibilities of education, we may remember among other things that that faith was not annually sapped by the spectacle of alumni reunions.

The broad aim of Tudor humanism was training in virtue and

good letters; the practical aim was training for the active Christian life, especially public life. For humanism was not only religious, it was also both aristocratic and utilitarian. The mere title of Elyot's book, *The Governour*, indicates its object. It continues the long tradition of European treatises on the education of a Christian prince, a tradition carried on in many similar documents down to Milton's *Of Education*. And we do not need to limit ourselves to pedagogical works, for the same motive inspires the heroic romances of Sidney and Spenser. This is a basic element in Tudor humanism which Phillimore and Mr Chambers apparently do not understand. The idea that the failure of later Tudor England to produce great works of pure scholarship is a mark of arrested development betrays a misconception of the vital spirit of English humanism. More had no desire to rival Scaliger, nor did Erasmus—if we may count him as partly English—envy the reputation of Budé. Erasmus and More and their followers did not investigate the coinage or the grammar of the ancients, they sought to make the rational wisdom of antiquity supplement the teaching of Christ. The *Praise of Folly* and *Utopia*, *The Governour* and *The Scholemaster*, remain living books. All the English humanists, like the majority of Continental ones, regarded classical learning as a means, not an end, and their energies were given to education. They wished to produce citizens and statesmen, not scholars. It was these Tudor humanists who established what was to be the ruling motive of English classical study down to the days of 'the Jowett mind'. From More to Milton the writings of English humanists are chiefly on public affairs, education, and religion. William Cecil might have remained a college don and crowned his life with an edition of Aristotle's *Politics*; instead he applied ancient wisdom (not without help from Machiavelli) to practical statesmanship. Classical scholars pure and simple have always been rare accidents in England. A. E. Housman believed that the function of a classical scholar in our time was the emending of texts, preferably of bad poets. That was not the belief of More and Elyot and Cheke and Ascham and Sir Thomas Smith and Thomas Wilson. If Housman belongs, in learning and temper, to the tradition of J. C. Scaliger, the modern descendants of these Tudor humanists are men like Dean Inge and Gilbert Murray, Sir Alfred Zimmern and Sir Ronald Storrs.

We might think Christian humanism was so firmly rooted as a working faith, as a final educational and moral discipline, that nothing, not even religious and political unrest, could shake it for ages to come. But I wish to review some of the causes, internal and external, which led to what may be called the break-up of the Renaissance synthesis. In using such a phrase I do not mean, of course, that Christian humanism was ever completely dominant or that it was ever completely extinguished. Yet in the sixteenth century humanism is a relatively universal and recognizably definite frame of religious and cultural philosophy, a tower of strength which has many zealous defenders and, in England, few formidable enemies. It is, to change metaphors, the one great highway along which men march toward the city of God....

THE RISE OF SCEPTICISM AND THE CHRISTIAN HUMANISTS

The two great philosophic enemies of religion and morality, and hence of Christian humanism, were sceptical and naturalistic doctrines. Even within the scholastic tradition the early divorce between reason and faith opened the way for those two extreme positions of the Renaissance, anti-Christian rationalism and anti-rational fideism. In the thirteenth and fourteenth centuries Aristotle had been the patron saint not only of scholastic theology and ethics but of irreligious rationalism and naturalism. In the fifteenth and sixteenth centuries, notably at the University of Padua, the doctrines of Aristotelian commentators were further developed and pro-pagated, and they were now strongly reinforced by increased know-ledge of ancient sceptics, from Lucretius to Lucian. Even Cicero, another patron saint of orthodoxy, was, on the strength of the *De Natura Deorum* and *De Divinatione*, constantly invoked by ration-alists. In the sixteenth century, and especially in England, religion and ethics, politics and economics, were inseparably united, and on all fronts Tudor humanism formed a solid bulwark of orthodox thought. While on the Continent, in spite of the Inquisition and the Sorbonne, sceptical ideas circulated pretty freely—Pomponazzi and Vicomercato enjoyed the protection of cardinals—in England, what-ever some men's private thinking or behaviour might be, public utterances were all of one kind. It is not till the end of the century that we encounter Raleigh's 'school of atheism'—which was not atheistical—and such young rebels as Marlowe and Donne. Up till then we infer the knowledge of heretical doctrines mainly from the frequent attacks on them....

To the modern-minded this whole account of Christian humanism, with its frequent repetition of such uninspiring words as 'orthodoxy', may seem only too obviously medieval and tame, a homely loaf of brown bread compared with the brandy of bold speculation and rebellion. But to the zealous humanist apparent platitudes could be living realities—there is, after all, no unbridgeable gulf between the Polonian faith and the Apollonian—and this simple creed, directly or indirectly, provided much of the solid ideological foundation for the golden age of our literature, the late sixteenth and earlier seven-

teenth centuries. One might point out the more or less strongly
Christian humanism of such men as Sidney and Spenser, Daniel and
Chapman, who preach rational control of the sensual impulses, and
who in larger ways represent the tradition by virtue of their concern
with aristocratic culture, with humane values and the good life, and
their upholding of the established order. Even the more complex
and impersonal Shakespeare is no less attached than the most
orthodox humanist to constituted authority, and no less scornful of
the mob. Humanistic ideas and ideals in various kinds of imaginative
and reflective writing must not be ignored entirely. Two major
premisses of the serious writers of this age must be mentioned, and
they may be distinguished as ethical and metaphysical.

In his famous discourse on the dignity of man Pico della Mirandola
had proclaimed the completeness of human freedom and self-
direction, but, like other Christian humanists, he had been conscious
of man's frailty as well as of his greatness. Pico imagines the Creator
concluding an address to man:

'Thou shalt have power to decline unto the lower or brute
creatures. Thou shalt have power to be reborn unto the higher, or
divine, according to the sentence of thy intellect.'
Thus to man, at his birth, the Father gave seeds of all variety
and germs of every form of life.

It is that simultaneous double vision of man which gives the literature
of the English Renaissance its ethical strength and centrality, its
heights and depths of tragic emotion. It is, to be sure, the mark of
the greatest writers of all ages, especially the ancients, but the
Christian religion exalted man's sense of his divinity and deepened
his sense of bestiality; the distance between the two extremes is
greater than it is in the most religious and philosophic of the classical
authors. We may think, for example, of the difference in the range
of feeling, of nobility and degradation, between Virgil's Aeneas and
Shakespeare's Antony; the difference between Dido and Cleopatra
is another matter.

While Renaissance writers look out upon a world which offers
the widest tragic contrasts, the most appalling horrors, they themselves commonly stand in the centre, not on or beyond the margins,
of the normal and ethical. Excess is excess and sin is sin—not self-
expression. But in some later ages, when religion has lost its hold,
the beast has been forgotten, and we have the literature of sentimental optimism. We may remember that a romantic has been
defined as a person who does not believe in the fall of man. And
in other ages, such as our post-war period, the god has been forgotten, and we have the literature of sentimental pessimism. We
may remember that realism has been defined as romanticism on all

fours. But in the great literature of the Renaissance man is both a god
and a beast and the greatest writer of the age is close enough to the
Christian and classical traditions to see always with both eyes:

> What a piece of work is a man, how noble in reason, how
> infinite in faculties, in form and moving, how express and admirable
> in action, how like an angel in apprehension, how like a god: the
> beauty of the world; the paragon of animals; and yet to me,
> what is this quintessence of dust?

These familiar words will serve to recall the whole texture of
Shakespeare's thought and feeling, and one might add that hardly
less familiar sentence in which Sir Thomas Browne plays magnificent
variations on the double theme:

> But man is a noble animal, splendid in ashes, and pompous in
> the grave, solemnizing nativities and deaths with equal lustre, nor
> omitting ceremonies of bravery in the infamy of his nature.

The other concept of the Renaissance mind, the metaphysical, is
the macrocosmic complement of the ethical. Not only the soul of
individual man, but the whole world is the battle-ground between
God and Satan. *Macbeth* is not simply a drama of human ambition
and human crime brought to an end by human resistance; hell and
outraged heaven play a part. Macbeth and Lady Macbeth have
leagued themselves with the powers of darkness, and Malcolm and
Macduff are the conscious instruments of the powers above. It might
be said that such a concept springs from purely Christian tradition,
yet the Greek dramatists even more than the Elizabethan link earth
with heaven and hell. Orestes, like Hamlet, is not merely a son
avenging his father's murder, he is an agent of Apollo in righting
wrong (though Aeschylus goes on to invoke a higher ideal of
justice).

The essential difference between the medieval and the modern
mind, if I may violate my own past warnings against such large
terms, is that for the one the universe and human life constitute a
divine order with a divine purpose, while for the other the universe
and human life are either an ordered or a haphazard mechanism.
And there is no doubt to which category the Renaissance mind
belongs. Shakespeare does not simply reflect 'the mixed and muddled
scepticism of the Renaissance'. His sense of man's life as part of a
supernatural world grows directly out of the medieval religious
tradition, which was strong enough to absorb even the heroic pagan
tradition. Shakespeare may have been sufficiently withdrawn from
religion to see the natural man acting in a natural world, yet he is
not so far withdrawn, in time or in temperament, that medieval
religious concepts have lost their imaginative and emotional power

over him. While most of his contemporaries are more obviously and firmly Christian, and he has often been regarded as a great heathen, even his imaginative world is conditioned by the religious and ethical values of Christian humanism.

It is the loss of that religious view of life which makes the modern literature of social forces and other merely mundane and human motives seem, in comparison, such a small pinched thing. No proletarian background, no dark inner world of the unconscious, can take the place of a stage which includes God and Satan, heaven and hell. Authors of the immediate present talk a good deal about a faith in Life as the sole and all-sufficient creed for the artist. He is to take a brave stand on

> The fact of life with dependence placed
> On the human heart's resource alone,
> In brotherhood bonded close and graced
> With loving-kindness fully blown,
> And visioned help unsought, unknown.

Such an attitude is doubtless better than the defeatism which preceded it, yet the instinctive craving for something more appears in the effort of many recent writers to make a religion out of Marxism. Of course we cannot even if we would bring back a general belief in a supernatural world—though it is odd that our scorn for theology is equalled only by our eager acceptance of the infallible and successively self-contradictory dogmas proclaimed by science, psychology, and economics—but at any rate a glance over the last three centuries inspires doubts of the future adequacy of humanistic optimism cut loose from a sobering faith in something like original sin. Indeed, it would be hard to name a modern expression of this optimistic faith in Life which could be put beside two poems that owe their fundamental power to a medieval belief in sin and a medieval *contemptus mundi*, that is, *The Waste Land* and *Ash Wednesday*.

WILLIAM GROCYN
1446?-1519

The encouragement of Christian humanism was the life work of William Grocyn, referred to in his own day as the 'Patriarch of English Learning'. In the absence of biographical data, this early Tudor scholar, educator, lecturer, and parish priest has remained a shadowy figure. Only one of his letters is extant; all that is known about him has been gleaned from the letters of his friends, Thomas Linacre, John Colet, Sir Thomas More, and the Venetian printer Aldus Manutius.

Grocyn's long association with Oxford University began in 1465 when he matriculated at New College. His life there is obscure until 1481. In that year he was appointed Divinity Reader in Magdalen College, and he took part in theological debates before Richard III. About 1488 he left to study in Italy, spending his time in Florence and Rome where he studied Greek with Demetrius Chalcondyles and Politian. When Grocyn returned to England in 1491, he was ordained to the priesthood. About this time he began the public teaching of Greek at Exeter College, Oxford, numbering Thomas More and Erasmus among his students.

It was the custom for scholars to support students studying at the universities. From his small income, Grocyn aided Erasmus, whose letters are filled with brief sketches of the humanists whom he met during his first visit to England. He calls Grocyn 'the patron and preceptor of us all' and 'a man of the most severe and chaste life, exceedingly observant of ecclesiastical rules, almost to the point of superstition, and to the highest degree learned in scholastic theology; while he was, at the same time, a man gifted by nature with the most acute judgment and exactly versed in every description of educational knowledge'.

During a course of lectures on the Ecclesiastical Hierarchy *by Dionysius, the pseudo-Areopagite, in St Paul's Cathedral in 1503, Grocyn was the first to question his identity, deciding that he was probably a fourth-century philosopher, as had long been contended by Lorenzo Valla.*

When Grocyn left London in 1506, Archbishop Warham appointed him master of the collegiate church of All Hallows in Maidstone, where he remained until his death in 1519. He left a small estate and a library of 105 printed books and 17 MSS. which was catalogued by his executor Thomas Linacre. Over half of the works are by the early and medieval Church Fathers. The rest are equally divided between the Greek and Latin classics and the writings of contemporary Italian authors. Works by St Augustine and Cicero are most numerous.

None of Grocyn's sermons or works on philosophy is extant. His will and a letter to Aldus Manutius are the only writings that have survived. The 'elegant' letter which Aldus 'thought it well' to insert in his edition of Linacre's translation of Proclus's De Sphaera *(1499) confirms not only the breadth of Grocyn's learning but also his gracious and sincere appreciation of the scholarship of his friends.*

Letter to Aldus Manutius

TRANSLATED BY SAMUEL A. IVES

William Grocyn of Britain sends greetings to Aldus Manutius of Rome:

Thomas Linacre, my very esteemed friend and yours, also, my dear Aldus, has recently returned to England safe and sound, thank Heaven! By telling me in the greatest detail of all your services to him, he has easily endeared you to me in a remarkable way if only for this reason alone. Hence whatever you have done for him, I consider as a personal favour to me, for the interests of friends should be common. And yet I cannot deny that you have done me a certain personal service, both in public and private, so that I now find myself indebted to you for three reasons: for what you have done for my friend, for me, and for the public at large which last embraces all your services.

And now to speak a bit of this latter service to all, it is one that seems to me so unusual that I scarcely know what to admire or praise most: your talent or your good judgment, your perseverance or your ability, your good fortune or your courtesy. For without extraordinary talent, you could not have invented that marvellous device expressly designed for the printing of Greek letters. Yet unless you were possessed of a very keen judgment in selecting the authors whose works you desired to print, you would not have placed Aristotle before Plato, contrary to Cicero's opinion.

And in this decision I am in entire agreement with you, being myself one who considers that there is as much difference between the great philosophers Aristotle and Plato as between a man of much learning and a man of much lore, if I may so put it. Without incredible perseverance you would not have pursued so lofty a project in the face of the great hardships of our day; while without your amazing diligence, you would not amid so many hindrances have followed to a successful completion the task that you commenced. Finally, what is more fortunate than that you should consider all learned men worthy of this your service, or what more courteous than that you should wish them so to be?

Wherefore since this great and distinguished work of yours is now so widespread that you have practically laid the whole world under obligation to you in everlasting remembrance of your noble deed; and since your personal favour, closely joined to your public service, has reached even us Englishmen so segregated from the rest of the world, I consider that if we would appear at all grateful, we must be accounted as indebted to you not only in company with the others, but even more than the others. For although the extent of your service far surpasses any possible thanks we may offer you, yet we will be no more reluctant in receiving it than you will regret having given it, which we shall surely see never happens.

My friend Linacre has also told me that you are now engaged in a far more amazing task, and one on which you had formerly decided, namely, printing parallel the books of the Old Testament in Latin, Greek, and Hebrew, and those of the New, in Latin and Greek, a truly difficult undertaking, and one especially worthy of a Christian. If only you be enabled to complete this work, you will far surpass not only all those who ever attained fame in this kind of endeavour but your own former efforts as well.

And so, my dear Aldus, may you at length embark upon this great enterprise and at the same time produce that which you have so long contemplated and planned, for I cannot be led to suppose that such a divine labour be without the utmost success. As for myself, I shall in no way neglect anything that may be helpful in this project.

Regarding the debt that I owe you personally, do not worry. I have seen to it that you shall soon be recompensed.

LONDON,

27 August 1499

The Will of William Grocyn

In the Name of God, Amen. The second day of June, the year of Our Lord, a thousand five hundred and nineteen, and the eleventh year of the reign of King Henry the Eighth, I William Grocyn, Clerk, Master of the College of All Hallows of Maidstone in the county of Kent, being of whole mind and in good memory, laud be unto Almighty God, make and ordain this my present testament and last will in manner and form following, that is to say:

First, I bequeath and recommend my soul to Almighty God, my Maker and Redeemer, to the most glorious Virgin, His mother Our Lady Saint Mary, and to all the holy company of heaven: and my body to be buried at the stall end in the high choir of the College of Maidstone aforesaid. *Item*. I will that all my debts the which I owe of right or of conscience to any manner person or persons be well and truly contented and paid by mine executor or else ordained for so to be paid. *Item*. I bequeath to my godson William Lily a hundred pounds. *Item*. I bequeath to William Capper, my godson, one hundred and twenty pounds. *Item*. I bequeath to Sir William Page, priest, upon condition that he will take upon him the oversight of the execution of this my present testament and last will, my gown of violet ingrain,[1] furred with black cony.

Item. I bequeath to Alice Linacre my scarlet gown with the hood, thereto belonging, lined with sarcenet.[2] *Item*. I will that Thomas Tayllour, my servant, shall have to him, his heirs and assigns forevermore all that my messuage, or tenement, with garden and other appurtenances set, lying and being in Stone Street of Maidstone, aforesaid, the which I late purchased and bought of one John Clere. And I will that all and every such person and persons as stand and be enfeoffed and seised of and in the said messuage or tenement with garden and the appurtenances, shall from henceforth stand and be enfeoffed and seised of and in the same messuage or tenement and garden with the appurtenances to the use and behoof of the said Thomas Tayllour and of his heirs and assignees.

The residue of all my goods and chattels and debts, after my debts paid, my funeral expenses performed, and these my legacies contained in this my present testament and last will fulfilled, I give and bequeath to Master Thomas Linacre, clerk; he to bestow such part thereof for the weal of my soul and the souls of my father, mother, benefactors, and all Christian souls, as it shall please him. The which Master Thomas Linacre of this my present testament and last will, I make and ordain mine executor. And of the execution of the same, I make and ordain the foresaid Sir William Page, overseer: and I utterly revoke and annul all and every other testaments, wills, legacies, bequests, executors, and overseers by me before this time in any wise made, named, willed, and bequeathed.

And I will that this my present testament and last will and the legacies, bequests, executor, and overseer, contained in the same, shall stand and abide for my very testament and last will, legacies, bequests, executor, and overseer, and none other.

In witness whereof to this my present testament and last will, I have set my seal. Given the second day of June and year above said. These witnesses, Thomas Homson, clerk, and Robert Ward, clerk.

[signed] WILLIAM GROCYN

Copied from the Principal Probate Registry (Ayloffe, 30).

---

[1] *ingrain*, dyed.   [2] *sarcenet*, fine silk.

THOMAS LINACRE
1460?–1524

Through his devotion to science and the Greek and Latin classics, Thomas Linacre urged English scholarship toward the goal of universal learning that had been the aim of earlier Oxford scholars, particularly John Free, William Grey, Robert Flemming, John Gunthorp, and John Tiptoft. Linacre was born in Canterbury in 1460. He attended Christ Church monastic school there under the direction of the noted Greek scholar, Prior William Selling. With his aid, Linacre entered Oxford in 1480, and four years later he was elected Fellow of All Souls College. When Selling was sent to Italy in 1485, as ambassador to the Papal Court, Linacre resigned his fellowship and accompanied him as far as Bologna. In Florence he began his Greek studies under Politian who was then tutoring the younger son of Lorenzo de Medici, Giovanni, the future Pope Leo X. A lasting friendship sprang up between Giovanni and Linacre.

After several years he went to Rome, where he spent his time reading and collating Greek manuscripts in the Vatican library. Later in Venice he met the great Venetian printer Aldus Manutius, and became interested in translating the works of Aristotle, Proclus, and Galen. From an allusion to Linacre in Aldus's preface to his great edition of Aristotle's works, printed between 1495 and 1497, it is probable that the English scholar helped to edit them.

A natural bent for science led Linacre to Padua to study at the university's famed School of Medicine which stressed the teaching of the ancient Greek medical authorities, Hippocrates and Galen. He took the degree of Doctor of Medicine at Padua, studying further at Vincenza under Nicola Leonicus who wrote the first treatise on syphilis and edited the first complete Greek edition of Galen's works.

Before the close of the century Linacre returned to England, and was among the first to teach Greek at Magdalen College, Oxford. With William Grocyn and William Latimer he began making a Latin translation of Aristotle's works. According to Erasmus, who was among his first students, only Linacre's section was finished. Neither this nor his lectures on Aristotle's Meteorologica, which Sir Thomas More attended in London in 1505, are extant.

Linacre's last teaching posts were in the royal household as tutor to Prince Arthur in 1500, and again in 1509 to Princess Mary, the daughter of Katherine of Aragon and Henry VIII. At some time during his stay in London, Linacre was ordained to the priesthood.

In spite of his arduous work as lecturer, translator, and tutor, Linacre practised medicine after his return from Italy. Early in the reign of Henry VIII, he became the king's personal physician and encouraged him to aid in founding the Royal College of Physicians of London. After its establishment in 1518, Linacre served as its first president, helping to write the charter which permitted the College to regulate the practice of medicine in London and its environs.

During his latter years, Linacre held ecclesiastical posts in churches in Kent, Wells, Westminster, and York. He lived frugally, and used his ample means to establish three lectureships in medicine, two at Oxford and one at Cambridge. His property and extensive library were willed to the College of Physicians. Linacre died in London in 1524, and was buried in St Paul's Cathedral.

Except for his grammars, discussed in another section of this book, Linacre's extant works are all Latin translations of Greek classics. They include Proclus's De Sphaera (1499), dedicated to Prince Arthur; Galen's De Sanitate Tuenda (1517) and Methodus Medendi (1519), both dedicated to Henry VIII; and De Temperamentis (1521), printed by Siberch at Cambridge and dedicated to Pope Leo X. The dedicatory Epistle of the latter work reveals not only the strong friendship that existed between the papal scholar and Linacre, but also shows the general esteem for Leo X as a patron of learning.

Dedicatory Epistle of Galen's De Temperamentis[1] *to Pope Leo X*

TRANSLATED BY SISTER MARIA WALBURGA, S.S.J.

To you, most Holy Father, on whom rests the guidance of the whole Christian state, I present this little volume. I offer it not as a fitting tribute to your studies, but in the hope that it will be helpful to students. If it can be of use to them, I do not doubt that it will please you. I am mindful, too, of your recent munificence when you not only made me happy but each of those who were once your fellow-students. And, indeed, I wish to declare by at least some tribute of my labours that I am not unappreciative.

The one talent by which I can hope to accomplish this is in the field of literature. And as my ability is thus limited and you are eminent in letters, this seems especially fitting.

Galen's little work [*De Temperamentis*] belongs to the literary field, being no less essential for philosophers than for doctors. Since the text is brief, my task will soon be accomplished, and it will give you an opportunity to judge my ability as a translator. I confess that

---

[1] The full title reads: *Galeni Pergamensis: De temperamentis et de inaequali intemperie.* [Galen of Pergamos: On temperaments (humours) and their unequal mixture.]

this *opuscule* is quite out of proportion to your great bounty and unworthy of your sacred Highness. But you are the Vicar on earth of Him who praised the 'two mites' of the poor woman:[1] and you know that according to tradition they who could not afford incense offered the 'salted cake'.*

I have more and greater writings at hand which, my health and duties permitting, will be finished and dedicated to you unless I know that it will displease or harass you in any way. My poor craftsmanship forbids me to think that these works will bring you any renown, but they will receive honour and prestige through the inscribing of your name, revered by all men of letters. If anyone benefits from my work, it will be due to the kindness of your Holiness and your evident interest in my studies.

I pray God to keep you and prosper all your undertakings.

London, the fifth of September, in the year of the Christian Redemption, fifteen hundred and twenty-one.

COLOPHON: *Galeni Pergamensis:...T. Linacro interprete: apud Cantabrigiam per J. Siberch, 1521.*

MARGARET BEAUFORT, COUNTESS OF RICHMOND AND DERBY
1441–1509

Though Margaret Beaufort, Countess of Richmond, was one of the most learned and deeply religious women of her day, her enforced political role in uniting the houses of York and Lancaster, which placed her son Henry Tudor on the English throne, has overshadowed her philanthropy and her interest in education and literature.

Born in 1441 at Bletshoe, Margaret Beaufort was a direct descendant of John of Gaunt and the only child of the wealthy John Beaufort, Duke of Somerset, and his wife, formerly Margaret Beauchamp. At her father's death, in 1444, she became heir to his great fortune. With her two half-brothers, children of her mother's second marriage, she was educated by private tutors. She had a fluent knowledge of French, but regretted that she knew little Latin. At fifteen she married Edmund Tudor, later Earl of Richmond, a half-brother to King Henry VI through the marriage of the dowager Queen Katherine to his father, Owen Tudor. He died the following year, and Margaret's only child, Henry Tudor, was born, on St Agnes' Day, 28 January 1457, in Pembroke Castle in South Wales.

Three years later, Margaret Tudor married Henry Stafford. The political unrest of the times kept them self-exiled in Wales and away from

[1] Mark xii. 42. Scriptural references are to *Biblia Sacra* throughout.

the royal claimants to the English throne, to many of whom she was closely related. Most of her time during the next fifteen years was spent in supervising the education of her son and in translating various devotional works from French. Her quiet way of life was disturbed in 1471 when Henry Tudor, then fourteen, was forced to flee to France from the supporters of Edward IV, who feared his 'natural' claims to the throne. Margaret's life after that was a series of sorrows and disappointments. Her husband died in 1481, and her son was exiled fourteen years in France.

For expediency rather than a desire to wed again, in 1482 Margaret became the wife of the Yorkist Thomas Lord Stanley, later Earl of Derby, believing he could aid in freeing her son. Though Stanley openly supported the house of York, he quietly sympathized with the Lancastrian cause, and through his financial backing and the marriage of his ward Princess Elizabeth, daughter of Edward IV, to Henry Tudor, he and Margaret were instrumental in bringing the Wars of the Roses to an end.

Margaret Beaufort sought complete retirement after her son Henry VII came to the throne in 1485. Her determination to lead a secluded life was revealed after her death in the Month's Mind sermon preached by Bishop John Fisher, her spiritual adviser. He relates that she 'obtained license in her husband's days long before he died' for a formal separation, and made a vow before Richard Fitzjames, afterwards Bishop of London, to spend the rest of her life in prayer and penance. A copy of the written promise was later given to Bishop Fisher and was deposited by him in the archives of St John's College, Cambridge.

These last years of Margaret Beaufort's life were spent in Surrey in a house provided for her by her devoted son. Most of her public benefactions were made at this time and attended to by Bishop Fisher. It was at his suggestion that she founded Christ's College, Cambridge, in 1505, and also St John's College, Cambridge, the latter completed by Fisher after her death. She established in perpetuity two professorships in divinity, one at Cambridge and another at Oxford. Bishop Fisher's efforts to encourage preaching led her to establish a preachership at Cambridge. Besides her interest in education, Margaret Beaufort supported many poor scholars at both universities and founded homes for the indigent and aged.

At her death in 1509, she had outlived her closest relatives. She was buried in Westminster Abbey, and her epitaph was written by Erasmus. Skelton praised her, and Shakespeare in Richard III recognizes her sanctity.

Margaret Beaufort was among the first patrons of English printers. Wynkyn de Worde, her official printer, issued for her Bishop Fisher's sermons on the Penitential Psalms, and Walter Hilton's Scala Perfectionis (1494) was 'Englyshed and printed' at her request. De Worde's edition of the Imytacion of Christ (1503) included her translation of the fourth book on the Holy Eucharist to which she was deeply devoted. He also printed her translation of The mirroure of golde for the synfull soule (1522). Caxton dedicated to her The History of King Blanchardine and Eglantine (1484).

The Statutes of Christ's College, Cambridge, *the only known work attributed to Margaret Beaufort, were written in 1505. It is probable that Fisher assisted her in drawing them up, and translated them into Latin. The* Statutes *are based on those of God's House, of which Christ's College was a refoundation. This earlier college was founded in 1439 by William Bingham, a London priest, and was intended to train the head-masters of grammar schools. In 1442 King Henry VI enlarged and endowed the college.*

In compiling the Statutes *for her new foundation, Margaret Beaufort stressed the broad aims of the Renaissance, which included the student's spiritual welfare. The emphasis placed on the study of Greek and Latin is attributed to her friend Erasmus, who as guest of Bishop Fisher visited Christ's College in 1506.*

Statutes of Christ's College, Cambridge

TRANSLATED BY H. RACKHAM

To the honour of Christ Jesus and the increase of His Faith, in the year of Our Lord 1506, the following Statutes were put forth by the Princess of excellent piety, Margaret, Countess of Richmond and Derby, and mother of the most illustrious King Henry VII, for Christ's College at Cambridge, which at no small expense the Princess herself lately completed, although it had before been in some measure begun by Henry VI of blessed memory, formerly King of England. We, Margaret, Countess of Richmond and Derby, and mother of the most illustrious King Henry VII:

PREFACE[1]

When we consider the various offices of each person within this College, which we have already named Christ's College in Cambridge, the whole number of these persons presents itself under the plan of one body, of which the Master or Keeper is the head; the two deans, the arms; the steward and the prefect of the Common Chest, the two hands; the Fellow scholars, the solid and principal members of the body itself; the reader, the member deputed to the procreation of new offspring; the pupil scholars, a most suitable *seminarium*; and, lastly, the hired servants are, as it were, the feet at the base of all. We shall therefore appoint concerning each severally, distinguishing what pertains to each, and following the order now given, to the end that each Statute may be the more easily and with-

[1] Chapter 1.

out great labour found when wanted; and this we shall do with the assent of John Siklyng, the present Master, and the rest of the Fellows of the same College, as will appear at the foot hereof below.

OF THE AUTHORITY OF THE MASTER OR KEEPER[1]

And since it is proper to begin with the head, by which it is fitting that the other members should be ruled and controlled, we shall first appoint concerning the Master or Keeper, whom we wish to be, as it were, the head of all scholars. We therefore assign to John Siklyng (who has already been appointed by our command as master and keeper of the aforesaid College), and also to all the rest of his successors, each for his time, authority over all the scholars of the same College, both Fellows and pupils, to govern, rule, punish, and remove the same: and to administer the domestic affairs of the whole College, in accordance with the Ordinances and Statutes lately put forth by us, which follow below.

Nevertheless it shall not be allowed to the same John, nor to any of the future keepers, without the declared consent of the majority of the Fellow scholars, by himself or by the agency of any one else, to engage in any quarrel, plea, or other action in the name of the College; nor to alienate or let to farm any lands, tenements, tithes, oblations, or other possessions, whether temporal or spiritual, already bestowed or hereafter to be bestowed upon it; nor to grant to any one any office, fee, or pension out of the property of the College; nor to bestow the advowsons or presentations of those churches which belong to the patronage of the aforesaid College; nor, finally, to enter upon any business from which discredit or detriment might arise to the said College, without summoning together all the Fellows, and save with the consent of the majority of them. But if they give their consent, then we will and appoint that any action of the Master, that does not conflict with our Ordinances and Statutes, shall be deemed valid and acceptable: Provided, nevertheless, that they shall admit no one as bailiff, receiver, or tenant who has not given to the College a sufficient security for its indemnity.

OF THE STIPEND OF THE MASTER[2]

And in order that the Master may not undertake all these onerous duties for nothing and without emolument: we will and appoint that the Master or Keeper of the said College, each for his time, shall receive for the trouble of his administration, besides weekly commons and a yearly grant for clothing, six pounds, thirteen shillings and fourpence, to be paid to him in equal portions at the customary four quarter-days; and for yearly clothing, twenty shillings each

---

[1] Chapter II.　　　　[2] Chapter IX.

year, and for weekly commons, twelve pence each week; and the
same shall be allowed, in accordance with a dispensation obtained
by us from the Supreme Pontiff Julius II, to hold not more than two
benefices with cure[1] besides the Mastership itself; besides such and
so many benefices without cure as may be; Provided that, if he
exceed this number of benefices with cure, we will that he be *ipso
facto* deprived of all right and title to the Mastership of the College.
But on the aforesaid John Siklyng, we bestow all the emoluments
of the benefice of Fen Drayton in the county of Cambridge, without any man's gainsaying; and with these emoluments (so far as
concerns his stipend) we desire him to be content, and not to claim
anything more for himself in our College aforesaid.

OF THE SCHOLASTIC EXERCISES OF THE FELLOWS[2]

After the worship of God, we will that they shall all devote themselves to the study of learning. And since the increase of the faith
(which we desire above all things) takes its start from theology, we
specially commend theology to all of them, that they may set it
before them as the goal of their studies. Nevertheless we wish each
of them to be initiated and instructed according to the custom of the
University in philosophy and the Liberal Arts, by which theology
is approached and without which it cannot be acquired.

Every week, therefore, we wish them to hold two disputations
in the College Chapel, one in philosophy, the other in theology;
in which each shall be opponent and respondent in his course and
order, so far as his attainments and learning allow. We wish the
same to apply themselves, each according to his degree, to hearing
or performing all the lectures, responsions, and oppositions which are
enjoined upon them by the Statutes of the University; and to ascend
from degree to degree, as soon as possible, in accordance with the
custom and practice of the University. None of the Fellows after he
has incepted in Arts shall be a Regent for more than four years,
unless in the following fifth year he shall be either Proctor of the
University, or Public Reader in the same, or at least domestic
Reader within the College; and in that case we wish that no one shall
abdicate that Regency at his own discretion, except with the advice of
the Master and the majority of the Fellows.

At table every day at dinner they shall diligently and attentively hear
the Bible or the writings of the holy Fathers, until the Master or his
locum tenens[3] shall order the Bibler to stop. And they shall always use
the Latin language as long as they are within the bounds of the College,
except in their rooms only; unless the solemnity of a feast prevent, or
other lawful reason to be approved by the Master or his *locum tenens*.

---

[1] pastorate.   [2] Chapter xxx.   [3] *locum tenens*, deputy.

OF THE VICIOUS MANNERS FORBIDDEN TO EVERY FELLOW[1]

But because it is of little avail to be learned, unless they are good and adorned with virtuous manners, we, therefore, will and appoint that none of the same Fellows shall frequent public taverns, suspected houses, or any place of ill fame; none shall take part in drinking bouts, ingurgitations, or the bearing of arms, or secular commerce forbidden to clerks; none shall engage in secret colloquy with loose women, especially within any rooms of the said College; which we desire that no woman shall enter, unless she be thoroughly honest, and very rarely, excepting at a time of sickness one known and approved by the Master or his *locum tenens*.

None, moreover, shall be a night-walker, or shall lie for the night outside the said College in any place within three miles from the same, or shall venture at all to be outside the circuit of the College after nine o'clock of any night from the feast of St Michael to the feast of Easter, or after ten o'clock from the feast of Easter to the feast of St Michael, unless he have a lawful reason to be approved by the Master or his *locum tenens*.

None, moreover, shall keep dogs, or birds of prey, or play at dice or cards, except at the time of the Nativity of Christ for the sake of relaxation; and then we do not permit that game on any account to take place elsewhere than in the Hall.

Finally, none shall show disrespect to his senior; but shall give place to him both at home and abroad, in chapel and at table, in the schools and in the streets, unless, perchance, he be of some higher scholastic degree: for unless his degree prevents, we desire that every senior shall always take precedence of his junior in all places.

OF THE READER AND HIS OFFICE[2]

We notice that this body still lacks an essential member, whereby new offspring may be procreated and generated. We, therefore, will and appoint that one of the Fellows shall be chosen by the Master and the major part of the Fellows as domestic Reader, which office no one elected thereto shall refuse under pain of losing his Fellowship, but shall be bound to perform it with diligence, as long as the Master and the majority of the Fellows think fit. On every day not a feast day, in accordance with the custom observed in the scholastic hostels within the University, in each quarter of the year, after the Mass of the day, when the bell has been rung, the Reader shall publicly deliver in the hall of the said College, for the space of two hours, four lectures; one, in sophistry, the second, in logic, the third, in philosophy, and the fourth, from the works of either the poets or

[1] Chapter XXXI.   [2] Chapter XXXVI.

the orators. But we leave to the Master and the deans to decide, as they may judge most profitable for the actual audience, what book he shall expound in each of these faculties.

Moreover, he shall be present at all the scholastic exercises of the pupils from the beginning to the end; which we wish to be such in number as has been customary in the hostels of scholars elsewhere within the University: viz. every Monday and Thursday from twelve to one, oppositions; every Monday, Wednesday, and Thursday from three p.m. to five, a sophism; likewise every Monday from the end of supper to seven, a problem in logic; also every Friday, from three p.m. to five, a problem in philosophy; and likewise from nine a.m. to eleven, a disputation in grammar, unless perchance on the same day one has been held in the public schools; while during the long vacation, besides all these exercises, every Monday, Wednesday, and Thursday, there shall be sophisms from eight to ten; in all of which exercises he shall use his diligence and industry in such manner as he may hope will be of profit to his audience.

Margaret Beaufort, *Early Statutes of Christ's College, Cambridge*, ed. with introduction, translation, and notes, by H. Rackham (Cambridge, 1927.)

RICHARD FOX
1448?–1528

Richard Fox began his long career as a churchman, diplomat, and educationalist during the reign of Henry VII, whom he helped gain the English throne. Born in Lincolnshire about 1448, Fox was the son of Thomas and Helena Fox. It is likely that he attended Winchester grammar school and went on to study at Magdalen College, Oxford, and Cambridge. There is no record of his having taken a degree from either university. It is probable that he was ordained to the priesthood at the University of Paris, where he studied and, it is thought, took the degrees of Bachelor of Arts and Doctor of Canon Law. While in France, Fox met Henry Tudor, Earl of Richmond, and espoused his cause against Richard III. He was with the earl when he landed at Milford Haven in 1485, and also at the battle of Bosworth on 22 August 1485.

After the coronation of Henry VII, Fox was made a member of the king's Council, and later Secretary of State and Lord Privy Seal. As the king's envoy, Fox's genial manner aided him on diplomatic errands in France, Flanders, and Scotland. He was entrusted with carrying out the arrangements for the marriage of the king's eldest daughter, Margaret, to James IV of Scotland; and he attended to the preliminary plans for the wedding of Prince Arthur to Katherine of Aragon in 1501. With Bishop Fisher, Fox served as executor of the will of Henry VII.

Though best known as Bishop of Winchester, Fox had previously been nominated to three other sees, Exeter, Wells, and Durham. Despite his busy life, he was a zealous prelate. His letters to Cardinal Wolsey are earnest appeals to be released from official duties in order to care for his diocese.

Both universities recognized his interest in education. Cambridge made him Chancellor in 1501. After serving three years, he relinquished the office to Bishop John Fisher. In 1507 he was appointed visitor of Magdalen College, Oxford. Shortly after, he wrote the new statutes for Balliol College.

The greatest work of Fox's life came in 1516 when he founded and endowed Corpus Christi College, Oxford. Freed from cares of public office, which were assumed by his lifelong friend Cardinal Wolsey, Fox devoted his time to the new foundation, which became the centre of humanistic and theological studies in the university. John Claymond, President of Magdalen College, an outstanding scholar and saintly priest, was chosen by Fox to be the first president of Corpus Christi. Among the lecturers, readers, and fellows appointed by the founder were Luis Vives, Nicholas Kratzer, Reginald Pole, John Fox, Thomas Lupset, Nicholas Udall, Edward Wotton, and John Clement. Twenty years after Fox's death, when Henry VIII appointed Nicholas Harpsfield first Regius Professor of Greek, it was a choice that would have pleased the founder. During his life, Fox was generous in his gifts of books and funds to the library. He willed the college his crozier, chalice, and paten, which are its most cherished possessions. The portrait of Fox that hangs in the college hall was made in 1521 by Joanus Corvus of Bruges, and shows him aged and blind.

A capable architect, Fox drew the plans for his college. He also designed Henry VII's Chapel in Westminster Abbey and the Gothic Chapel in Winchester Cathedral.

Corpus Christi College was not, however, Fox's only venture in the field of education. He founded two grammar schools, one in 1522 at Taunton, the other in his home town, Grantham, a few months before his death on 5 October 1528.

Like many prominent men of his time, Fox had bitter enemies. But among his friends he numbered Bishop John Fisher. Two years before Fox's death, the saintly Fisher dedicated to him his book against Oecolampadius, On the truth of Christ's Body and Blood in the Eucharist (1526). In the dedicatory epistle Fisher's tribute to Fox does much to refute the harsh criticism often levelled at him, making him a shrewd and conniving politician. 'Ever since our acquaintance', Fisher declares, 'your lordship had taken so affectionate an interest in me that I felt myself impelled most ardently both to learning and to virtue.'

Fox's only extant writings are his letters and statutes for Corpus Christi College. He translated the Rule of seynt Benet (1516) for 'the devout, religious women', of his diocese 'vnto the moders tonge, comune playne rounde English, easy and redy to be understande by the sayd devoute religiouse women'. A human and friendly side of Fox's nature is revealed in his letters, and they also give an account of the severe trials that beset his young college.

The Statutes of Corpus Christi College are Fox's plan for the teaching of Christian humanism in English universities through a curriculum based on a firm foundation of scholastic theology and philosophy—the Greek and Latin classics serving as channels of culture. Fox established the first Greek Readership at Oxford. The Reader was one of the principal officers of the College, and all 'the fellows, scholars and students, even the masters' were obliged to attend his lectures.

In demanding the study of Greek, Fox states that it was in accord with the sacrosancti canones or 'holy ordinances' of the Church. He referred to the ruling of the oecumenical council held in 1311–12 at Vienne. Describing this ruling, Professor R. Weiss writes in Bibliothèque d'Humanisme et Renaissance (1952) that the Council 'assembled at Vienne issued a decree quite remarkable in its scope and outlook. This decree (text in Corpus Juris Canonici, ed. E. Friedberg, vol. II, Lipsiae, 1881, cols. 1179–80) enacted that teaching posts in Hebrew, Chaldean (by which was meant the Syriac language), Arabic and Greek, should be established forthwith at the Papal Court and at each of the four principal studia generalia of Christendom, that is to say, at Paris, Oxford, Bologna, and Salamanca'. Professor Weiss points out that each university was to have two teachers for each language, whose duties were not only to lecture, but also prepare Latin versions of works they were teaching. At Oxford the salaries of these professors were to be paid through ecclesiastical taxation.

Though there had been several earlier attempts, the Council's ruling was successfully carried out for the first time at Corpus Christi College. The opposition that Fox met with is shown in Sir Thomas More's letter to Oxford University in which he reminds the most reverend fathers of the Council's decree when he states that 'Greek is a subject required in every place of learning by the Church Universal'.

Letter to Cardinal Wolsey

WINCHESTER
23 April 1516

My very singular good Lord,

In my most humble wise I recommend me to your good lordship. And where I understand by my fellow William Purde that of late your said lordship divers times asked of him when I intended to be there, and that, finally, ye commanded him to send to me for my coming thither: my lord, if my impediments and the causes of my absence from you were not both reasonable and necessary, and that I had not the King's license to be occupied in my cure, whereby I may do some satisfaction for twenty-eight years negligence, I were greatly to be blamed; and to your good lordship I should be unkind, considering and remembering your great goodness of time past.

And as I have said to yourself, and to some other also, I had never better will to serve the King [Henry VII] that was my maker (whose soul God pardon) than I have to serve the King, his son, my sovereign lord, that now is: And, specially, since your good lordship hath had the great charge that ye have in your hand; perceiving better, straighter, and speedier ways of justice and more diligence and labour for the King's rights, duties, and profits to be in you than ever I see in time past in any other. And that I, myself, had more ease in attendance upon you in the said matters than ever I had before. Albeit, I trust, I gave you such attendance as ye will not complain of me.

But, my lord, to serve worldly with the damnation of my soul and many other souls whereof I have the cure, I am sure ye will not desire. And as it shall please God to give me grace, I shall endeavour me to do both God and the King some service. And so I tenderly beseech you, mine own good lord, to be contented.

I assure you, my lord, my absence from you is neither to hunt, nor hawk, nor to take none other worldly pleasure, nor for ease of my body, nor yet for quietness of mind which is troubled night and day with other men's enormities and vices more than I dare write. Whereof I remember ye showed me, ye had some knowledge when ye were Bishop of Lincoln. And of them, I assure you, there is plenty here with much more. But I have provided the medicine which, I trust, shall do good service. Nor verily, my lord, I seek no lucre of money. I pray God, I may *lucrari animas* [enrich souls].

Also, my lord, I consider well that ye have as much labour of body and business of mind as ever had any in your roumes,[1] and more; and never none had less help. But of great weighty cause, hear I none. And so the Emperor [Maximilian] and the Swiss speed well* (whereof I have as great desire to hear as of any matter), I trust ye shall have no great troublous matters. But your pains be, nevertheless.

And I require you, and heartily pray you, lay apart all such business from six of the clock in the evening forthward: which, if ye will use it, shall after your intolerable labours greatly refresh you. And, good my lord, when the term is done, keep the counsel with the King's Grace wheresoever he be. Thus, my lord, I presume *docere Minervam* [to teach Minerva]: but I write it of good mind and

---

[1] *roumes*, official positions.

to good intent, Our Lord be my Judge. Thus, my lord, I humbly and heartily beseech you to spare me of my coming up yet: and pluck me not from the necessity that I am in till I have finished it. And I shall make all diligence possible.

And for further declaration of my mind in this behalf and to the entent I do you no more encumberance with this my long, tedious letter (whereof I beseech you, my lord, of pardon), it may please you to give credence to William Purde and benignly to consider all that he shall show you on my behalf. And I shall as heartily daily pray for you as any priest living.

At Winchester, the 23rd day of April, with the hand of your assured priest and beadman.   R. WYNTON

To my lord Cardinal of York.

Letter to John Claymond

ESHER

25 February 1517(?)

Brother Master President,

I have received your letter by your servant, this bearer, for the which I heartily thank you; for it was to my great comfort and, in manner, revived me out of many dumps and perplexities that I was in by reason that I had no sooner writing from you. I was in great doubt that the Prior [John Burton] by some envious counsel had changed his mind;* but now I thank God and your diligent and wise ways, I am brought into good surety of the power, ground, and site of our college. And by Humphrey Coke, which shall be here with me upon Sunday and depart toward you upon Monday, ye shall receive the Foundation [statutes]* under my seal. And therewith, and in the same, a grant of the said site with a letter of attorney to the Warden of the New College [William Porter] and the President of Magdalen College [John Hygdon] to bring you and your company into the possession thereof.

And whereas ye sent me at this time the names and order of such as shall be Fellows and Scholars of our college, whereof two be Masters of Art and one Bachelor, this order doth far vary from the names that ye left with me, and that ye wrote yourself in the *minutiae* of the Foundation. And of them there is none named, neither Master of Art nor Bachelor; and as ye left them with me, and in the same order, they be written in the Foundation without naming of any of them Master or Bachelor. And this ye must take in worth at this time. And to save our honesty in that behalf, ye must cause such a discreet person to read the Foundation at the time of the possession taking as by your good instruction may and can subvert the order, and read them, as ye have ordered them, with their additions of Masters and Bachelors—saving that it shall be no great inconvenience to read my poor kinsman in the same order that he is now in in the Foundation. And as soon as ye may, cause ye the Foundation to be new written with a good large substantial hand. And therein ye may order the names of the said Fellows with their additions of Masters and Bachelors, dioceses and shires in the same form that ye sent them to me at this time, saying that I will that my said kinsman [Thomas Fox] be the first.

And in this new writing, add the child that my lord of Winchecombe [Richard of Kidderminster] writeth to you for, called Kenelme Aden of Gloucestershire, if ye find him able therefore, and else not. And if he be too young or otherwise unable to be a Fellow, leave him out and reserve him for a disciple, and so take him in to you when ye list, so he be able. And by him ye may excuse you to Sir Robert Poynes for his child, saying that he can have but one for Gloucestershire.

And when ye have new written the said Foundation, send it to me with the other, and I shall seal it and send it to you again. And to excuse you to my lord of Winchecombe for the Master of Art that he writeth to you for, ye may say that by the Foundation there be no Masters of Art eligible, which is true. And as for those Masters that ye have now taken in, ye may say ye have so done of necessity to make them officers. And to make your saying true, I pray you make them either deans or bursars, and take no more Masters of Art to you hereafter. For from henceforth, I will that in that point ye observe the Statutes which be not yet ready; and, I think, it will be yet fifteen days or I can send them to you.

And let your company begin commons seven or eight days before your departing into the North country. And I shall send you more money by Humphrey Coke, for they must yet for a season live upon my purse. And in your absence I doubt not your vice-president [Robert Morwent] will order them accordingly; and bid him as he shall need anything that he write and send to me, and so soon will I do to him.

The barge departed from Westminster upon Friday last with your kitchen stuff and other things: and with it cometh to you Robert, bailiff of Savoy, which shall deliver you one part of the indenture containing the particulars of the said stuff. And at my coming to Winchester, which shall be about the latter end of the next week, I shall send you more stuff. And, I pray you, depart no sooner northward than ye shall be enforced to do of pure necessity, for

I would gladly that before your departing, ye see your company somewhat meetly established. And certify me of such of your matters as there shall be from time to time occurant. And thus fare ye well.

At Esher, the 25th day of February.

Your loving brother
R. WYNTON

To Master John Claymond, President of Corpus Christi College in Oxford.

―――――――――

Letter to John Claymond

WINCHESTER
17 July 1517

Brother Master President,

I commend me heartily to you. And to exhort you to take patiently the great tempest* that hath lately been among your company; I can no better say than to desire you to take it as I have ever used to take such things myself, *videlicet, speravi semper me felicem habiturum exitum, ubi durum et grave erat principium* [namely, I have always hoped to have a happy ending when the beginning was hard and unpleasant]. And, also, I would ye should think that in this case God proveth you *et tunc beatus vir qui suffert temptationem*[1] [and blessed, then, is the man that endureth temptation]: And as touching myself, since it hath pleased God to leave me your person, I will give Him double thanks: the one is that He hath left me yourself, and the second is that He hath so proved you, and in the same proof taken to His mercy my poor kinsman [Thomas Fox], your disciple, while he was, as I trust, in the state of grace.

As touching the procurates[2] that ye have sent me, they be not sufficient for so great matter. And, therefore, Mr Myles shall be with you shortly to accept more large constitutions. And then he shall show you the specialties of the matters. And when the said Mr Myles cometh to you, I shall send you more money for your building. And thus fare ye heartily well.

At Winchester, the 17th day of July.

Your loving brother
R. WYNTON

To my brother, the President of Corpus Christi College in Oxford.

Letters of Richard Fox, ed. P. S. and H. M. Allen, (Oxford, 1929.)

―――――

[1] Jas. i. 12.   [2] *procurates*, proxies.

Statutes of Corpus Christi College, Oxford

The Foundation Statutes of Bishop Fox given to Corpus Christi College, Oxford, 1517

TRANSLATED BY G. R. M. WARD

In honour of the most precious body of Our Lord Jesus Christ, and of His most Holy Mother, and of all the other saints, patrons of the cathedral churches of Winchester, Durham, Bath and Wells, as also of Exeter, We Richard Fox, by Divine Vocation, Bishop of Winchester, founder, builder, and endower of the College of Corpus Christi in the University of Oxford, first invoking the most dread name of the most holy and undivided Trinity, have framed our Statutes for the same college, and have written them in this original book, in order to their constant and everlasting remembrance and establishment: and We, the aforesaid, have set our seal thereto in manner following:

THE PREFACE CONCERNING THE FOUNDATION[1]

'We have no abiding city here,' as saith the Apostle, 'but we seek one to come'[2] in heaven at which we hope to arrive with the greater ease and dispatch if while we travel in this life, wretched and death-doomed as it is, we rear a ladder whereby we may gain a readier ascent. We give the name of virtue to the right side of the ladder, and that of knowledge, to the left, and between these two sides lie steps; for either side hath rounds of its own by which we may either soar on high, or sink into the lowest depths. We, therefore, Richard Fox, by Divine Providence, Bishop of Winchester, being both desirous ourselves of ascending by this ladder to heaven and of entering therein and being anxious to aid and assist others in a similar ascent and entrance, have founded, reared, and constructed in the University of Oxford, out of the means which God of his bounty hath bestowed on us, a certain bee garden which we have named the College of Corpus Christi, wherein scholars, like ingenious bees are by day and night to make wax to the honour of God, and honey, dropping sweetness, to the profit of themselves and of all Christians.

We appoint and decree by these presents that in this bee garden there shall dwell forever a president, to hold authority over the rest; twenty scholars or fellows; the same number of disciples; three lecturers to be therein employed, each in his office and order; and, moreover, six ministers of the chapel, of whom two must be priests,

---

[1] Chapter I.   [2] Heb. xiii. 14.

two, not priests, but clerks and acolytes, or, at the least, initiated by the primary tonsure, and the two remaining, choristers.

OF THE PUBLIC LECTURERS[1]

The bees make not honey of all flowers without choice, but from those of all the sweetest and best scents and savours which are tasted and distinguishable in the honey itself; hence the kinds of honey in different regions are various according to the diversity of the flowers; and neither Britain, Attica, or Hybla can produce honey so long as the honey-bearing flowers are far away. We, therefore, are resolved to constitute within our bee garden forever three right skilful herbalists, therein to plant and sow stocks, herbs, and flowers of the choicest, as well for fruit as thrift, that ingenious bees swarming hitherward from the whole gymnasium of Oxford may thereout suck and cull matter convertible, not so much into food for themselves as to the behoof, grace, and honour of the whole English name and to the praise of God, the best and greatest of Beings.

Of the above three, one is to be the sower and planter of the Latin tongue, and to be called the Reader or Professor of the Arts of Humanity who is manfully to root out barbarity from our garden, and cast it forth, should it at any time germinate therein; and he must on all common days and half-holidays throughout the year during an entire hour, or a little more, beginning at about eight o'clock in the forenoon, publicly lecture in the Hall of our College, or elsewhere at some public place in the University if it seem good to the President and a majority of the seven Seniors, and clearly interpret some part of the underwritten authors: namely, on Mondays, Wednesdays, and Fridays, Cicero's *Epistles*, *Orations*, or *Offices*, Sallust, Valerius Maximus, or Suetonius Tranquillus at the will of the President and Seniors. But when his hearers have made such progress in the above authors that they wish and are able to mount to higher things, and it seems good to the President and Seniors and the majority of the auditors also, then we permit Pliny, that luminary in natural history, Cicero's *De Arte*, *De Oratore*, or *De Partitionibus*, the *Institutiones Oratoriae* of Quintilian, or the *Declamations*, or some such exalted writer to be read and explained in the room of the above mentioned authors and works. But on Tuesdays, Thursdays, and Saturdays, Virgil, Ovid, Lucian, Juvenal, Terence, or Plautus are to be explained by him. And on every feast day in the afternoon, at any hour to be assigned by the President and Seniors, at a full meeting of all, he is publicly to read and explain Horace or Persius. Nor, however, do we forbid him to change these lectures with the consent of the President and Seniors and to explain on consecutive days what

[1] Chapter XXI.

we have hinted at for reading on alternate days; and, besides, to interpret on the same day some part of a poet, together with an orator.

Furthermore, three times during every week of the year and four times only at his own election, during the excepted periods of the vacations, on days and at hours to be limited by the President and Seniors, he is to read privately in some place of our College, to be appointed by the President, to all of the household who wish to hear him, either the *Elegancies* [*Elegantiae* (1471)] of Laurentius Valla, or the *Attic Lucubrations* [*Noctes Atticae* (A.D. 165?)] of Aulus Gellius, or the *Miscellanies* [*Miscellanea* (1489)] of Politian, or some such author, at the pleasure of the President and the majority of the auditors.

But the second herbalist of our apiary is to be, and to be called, the Reader of the Grecists and of the Greek Language, whom we place in our bee garden expressly because the holy ordinances have established and commanded most suitably for good learning and Christian literature especially, that such a one should never be wanting in this University of Oxford in like manner as in some few other most famous places of learning. Yet we would not for this reason have those persons excused who ought at their own charge to support a Greek Readership therein; but this lecturer of ours is on all common or half-holidays throughout the year publicly to read and clearly to explain, beginning at ten o'clock in the forenoon, or a little earlier, some portion of two of the underwritten authors for an entire hour, or somewhat longer in the Hall of our College. He is, therefore, to read on Mondays, Wednesdays, and Fridays, some part of the *Grammar* [γραμματικῆς εἰσαγωγή (1495)] of Theodorus [Gaza], or some other approved Greek grammarian, together with some part of the speeches of Isocrates, Lucian, or Philostratus; but on Tuesdays, Thursdays, and Saturdays, he is to read Aristophanes, Theocritus, Euripides, Sophocles, Pindar, or Hesiod, ...together with some portion of Demosthenes, Thucydides, Aristotle, Theophrastus, or Plutarch; but on holidays, Homer, the *Epigrams*, or some passage from the divine Plato, or some Greek theologian. Also, thrice every week and four times only at his own option during the excepted periods of the vacations, he shall read privately in some place of our College, to be assigned for the purpose by the President, some portion of the Greek Grammar or Rhetoric, and also of some Greek author, rich in various matter, to all of the household of our College who wish to hear him....But all the fellows, scholars, and students of our College, even the masters, not being divines, who are present in the University, are to hear throughout these public lectures, as well Greek as Latin, in the order above given. And whosoever shall be absent from any one of these lectures, or not present as soon as any one of them is begun, and does not remain till its conclusion...shall be punished in the same manner as if he had been absent on a feast day from the divine offices.

Lastly, a third gardener, whom it behoves the other gardeners to obey, wait on, and serve, shall be called and be the Reader in sacred Divinity, a study which we have ever holden of such importance as to have constructed this our apiary for its own sake, either wholly, or most chiefly; and we pray and, in virtue of our authority, command all the bees to strive and endeavour with all zeal and earnestness to engage in it according to the Statutes. This our last and divine gardener is, on every common and half-holiday through-out the year, beginning at two o'clock in the afternoon, publicly to read and profoundly to interpret in the Hall of our College, during an entire hour, some portion of Holy Writ, to the end that those wonder-working jewels which lie remote from view and latent may come forth to the light; and this is to be done with the exception of eight weeks only, that is, three about Christmas, two at Easter, one at Pentecost, and two in autumn, during which we by these presents give to the President and the majority of the seven Senior Fellows the power of dispensing with his reading. Nevertheless, we do not forbid that on very urgent cause, first approved of by the persons above mentioned, he may, even in term time, be absent for a little while, or forbear to lecture, provided only he substitutes some other person of competence in their judgment who meanwhile is either to carry on the same reading, or, at least, some other to be assigned by the parties above mentioned. But in alternate years, that is, every other year, he is to read some part of the Old Testament and some part of the New which the President and the major part of the Seniors appoint; and he must always in his interpretation, as far as he can, imitate the holy and ancient doctors, both Latin and Greek, and especially Jerome, Austin, Ambrose, Origen, Hilary, Chrysostom, Damascenus, and others of that sort—not Liranus,[1] not Hugh of Vienne, and the rest, who as in time, so in learning are far below them, except where the commentaries of the former doctors fail.

Also, we will that all the Fellows of our College by us designed for divinity, saving the Doctors, shall be bound to attend these theological lectures, in the same manner as we have above bound the Bachelors of Arts, the Masters who are not Divines, and the others, to attendance at the other lectures. Now we will that the Lecturer himself should be always bound by oath, diligently to perform all the above acts with all his might in the same way as the rest of the Lecturers. Moreover, we will that each of the above gardeners shall empower their hearers, after their lectures, to question without

[1] Liranus, Nicholas de Lyra.

great or unseemly debate what either the gardeners have not sufficiently explained during their reading, or what has caused scruple or doubt to the hearers themselves; and, so far as they can, shall resolve and clear up their questions and difficulties....And if no person in our College shall be found competent in the judgment of the President and the electors for the office of any lecturer vacating, or if any person in our College be found competent, and yet a stranger shall be found much more learned...then we will that he shall be preferred to that office and as public lecturer before all the fellows and scholars of our College...provided only he is born in England, Greece, or Italy, beyond the Po.

Richard Fox, *The Foundation Statutes of Bishop Fox for Corpus Christi College now first translated into English with a Life of the Founder*, G. R. M. Ward (London, 1843).

JOHN COLET
1466–1519

John Colet completes the trio that included William Grocyn and Thomas Linacre whose efforts helped to encourage Christian humanism in England. An old Dutch engraving of Colet shows his deeply ascetic countenance and gaunt body worn thin by abstemious habits. Throughout his life, Colet was the spiritual confidant of many of his contemporaries who loved him and admired his scholarship and ability as a teacher.

The Colets were a distinguished London family, having considerable prestige because of aid given to Henry VII during the Wars of the Roses. John Colet, the eldest and only one of Sir Henry and Lady Christian Colet's twenty-two children to survive infancy, was born in London in 1466. Disliking the political career of his father, who was twice Lord Mayor of London, John Colet entered Oxford in 1483 and directed his studies toward the ministry. He excelled in mathematics and philosophy, devoting most of his time to the works of Plato. About 1490 he took a Master of Arts degree and left for a few years' stay on the Continent, visiting Italy and France.

Possibly in Florence or Rome, Colet studied Greek under Politian, as did Grocyn and Linacre. Erasmus states that Colet spent his days studying the works of the early Church Fathers, Origen, Cyprian, Ambrose, and Jerome, and he gave much time to the treatises of Dionysius the pseudo-Areopagite. In France Colet met Robert Gaguin, the French historian, and Guillaume Budé, who were destined to bring about Colet's lifelong friendship with Erasmus.

Soon after Colet returned to London in 1496, he was ordained to the priesthood. During the next ten years, he delivered gratuitously at Oxford his famous Latin lectures on St Paul's Epistles. In describing these lectures to his friend John Sixtus, Erasmus declares, 'He spoke not only with his voice but with his eyes, his countenance, and his entire being.' In 1505, the year before he finished his lectures, Henry VII appointed him Dean of St Paul's Cathedral.

Colet's great civic work was the founding of St Paul's free grammar school for boys. An account of the school is given by Erasmus in a letter written in 1520 to Justus Jonas, the German reformer who had requested him to write a short account of Colet's life. In complying with the request, Erasmus became Colet's first biographer. The facts were gathered through his long association with Colet together with data obtained from Thomas Lupset, who from his earliest years had been under the Dean's care at St Paul's School and at Oxford.

In his letter, Erasmus calls the founding of St Paul's School, in 1510, a civic duty determined upon by Colet when he inherited a considerable fortune at the death of his father. If Colet had hoarded his wealth, Erasmus states that it 'might have had a corrupting influence on his life; and he spent a great part of the money in building a new school in the churchyard of St Paul's, dedicating this splendid structure to the Child Jesus. He added a large dwelling in which the two masters lived, and for whom he provided an adequate salary so they might teach free of charge, but the enrolled students should never exceed a specified number. He divided the building [the over-all measurements were one hundred and twenty-two feet by thirty-three] into four parts. The first, the entrance hall, is for cate-chumens; and no child can be admitted unless he can already read and write. The second part is for those who are under the sur-master, and the third, for those under the headmaster. A curtain separates these divisions and can be drawn at will. Over the master's chair is a beautiful image of the Child Jesus, seated in a teaching posture. As the students enter and leave the school, they salute it with a hymn. Above it hangs a representa-tion of God the Father, saying: Hear ye him. This inscription was placed there at my suggestion. At the far end is a small chapel in which divine service is held. The entire school has no bays or recesses; nothing resembling a dormitory or a dining room. Each boy has his place on a bench, and these are so arranged that they rise slightly one above the other. There are sixteen boys in each class, and the boy who is first in his class has a little desk raised higher than the rest. Boys who wish to enter the school are not chosen promiscuously, but are selected according to natural capacity and ability.'

The school was built of stone and the following inscription was carved across the front: Schola Catechizationis Puerorum in Christi opt. Max. Fide et Bonis Literis. Anno Christi MDX. [*School for the instruction of boys in the faith of Christ, the best and greatest, and in good literature. In the year of Christ, 1510.*] *Colet rewrote the* Statutes *in 1518, and he ordered his hand-written copy to be preserved in the School. He chose*

William Lily as the first headmaster. Both Lily and Colet wrote Grammars expressly for the school and Erasmus sent 'as a small literary present', De copia verborum ac rerum *(1512) which he dedicated to Colet.*

Henry VIII, like his father, continued to honour the Dean of St Paul's. In 1511 the king made him a member of the Board of Examiners that licensed physicians to practise surgery in England. The same year he was appointed chaplain and preacher in ordinary to the king.

Never in robust health, owing to his self-imposed fasting and strenuous life, Colet retired from London, in 1518, leaving his school in charge of the Mercers' Guild. Intending to enjoy a quiet 'retreat', he stayed at the small house that he had built near the Carthusian monastery at Sheen. But his health continued to fail, and he died the following year in London at the home of his mother, Lady Christian Colet, then over ninety. Throughout his life he had been deeply devoted to her, and, according to Erasmus, who knew her, she was one of the most charming and intellectual women of her day. Colet was buried in St Paul's Cathedral. An epitaph on his tomb was written by William Lily.

Only a few of Colet's Latin lectures are extant. These are on the Epistles of St Paul. His English translations of the pseudo-Dionysian works, Heavenly Hierarchy, Ecclesiastical Hierarchy, Concerning the Sacraments of the Church, *and* On the Divine Names, *have been lost. Among his English works that have survived are* Grammatices Rudimenta *(1527) of which William Lily was co-author;* Statutes of Paul's School *(1518);* The sermon of Doctor Colete made to the conuocation at Paulis *(1530); and* A ryght frutefull monycion *(1534).*

Colet's lectures were first translated and printed by John H. Lupton, in 1869, from MSS. in the libraries of Cambridge University and St Paul's School.

Statutes of Paul's School

I John Colet deliver this little book into the hands of Master Lily, on the 18th day of June in the year of Our Lord Christ, 1518, in order that he may keep and preserve it.

PROLOGUE

I John Colet, the son of Henry Colet, Dean of Paul's, desiring nothing more than the education and bringing up of children in good manners and literature, in the year of Our Lord a thousand five hundred and twelve, builded a school in the east end of Paul's Church for 153 [boys] to be taught free in the same: and ordained there a master and a surmaster and a chaplain with sufficient and perpetual stipends ever to endure, and set as patrons and defenders, governors and rulers of that same school, the most honest and faithful fellowship of the Mercers of London. And for because nothing can continue long and endure in good order without laws and statutes, I, the said John, have here expressed and showed my mind what I would, should be truly and diligently observed and kept of the said Mercers, governors of the school, that in this book may *apparere*[1] to what intent I found this school.

CONCERNING THE HIGH MASTER[2]

In the grammar school founded in the Churchyard of Paul's at the east end, in the year of Our Lord, a thousand five hundred and twelve, by John Colet, dean of the same church, in honour of Christ Jesus in *pueritia* [boyhood] and of his Blessed Mother Mary, in that school shall be first a high master. This master in doctrine, learning, and teaching shall direct all the school. This master shall be chosen by the wardens and assistants of the Mercery; a man, whole in body, honest and virtuous and learned in the good clean Latin literature and also in Greek; if such may be gotten, a wedded man, a single, or a priest that hath no benefice with cure neither service that may let his due business in the school. The Mercers shall assemble together in the school-house with such advice and counsel of well[3] literature and learned men as they can get: [and] they shall choose this master and give unto him his charge, saying unto him on this wise:

'Sir, we have chosen you to be master of this school to teach the children of the same not only good literature but also good manners, certifying you that this is no room[4] of continuance and perpetuity but upon your duty done in this school. And every year at Candelmas when the Mercers be assembled in the school-house, ye shall submit you to our examination; and found doing your duty, according ye shall continue. Otherwise, reasonably warned, you shall content you to depart ye. And ye of your part, not warned of us but of your mind in any season willing to depart, ye shall give us warning twelve months before, without we can be shortlier well provided of another.

'Also, being master, ye shall not absent yourself but upon license of the surveyors for the time being.

'Also, if any controversy and strife shall be betwixt you and the surmaster or the chaplain of the school, ye shall stand at the direction of the surveyors being for that year'.

And if the chosen master will promise this, then admit him and name him to it and stall him in his seat in the school and show him his lodging, that is to say, all cellars beneath and the hall, the kitchen, and buttery; and, over that, all the whole story and chambers; and

---

[1] *apparere*, appear.　　[2] Chapter I.　　[3] *well*, good.　　[4] *room* [roume], position.

in the house roof, the little mid-chamber and the gallery in the southside. As touching all the story of chambers next underneath the galleries, he shall nothing meddle withal; and they shall give him the implements of his house by indenture.

All these lodgings he shall have free without any payment; and in this lodging he shall dwell and keep household to his power.

His wages shall be a mark a week and a livery gown of four nobles, delivered in cloth.

His absence[1] shall be but once in the year and not above thirty days, which he shall take *conjunctim* or *divisim* [consecutively or separately].

If the master be sick of sickness curable, yet, nevertheless, I will he shall have his wages; and in such sickness if he may not teach, let him reward the under-master for his more labour somewhat according.

If the master be sick of sickness incurable or fall into such age that he may not conveniently teach, and hath been a man that long and laudably hath taught in the school, then let another be chosen: and by the discreet charity of the Mercery let there be assigned to the old master a reasonable living of ten pounds, or otherwise, as it shall seem convenient, so that the old master after his long labour in nowise be left destitute.

If the under-master be in literature and in honest life according, then the high master's room vacant, let him be chosen before another.

The high master shall have the tenement in Stebenhithe, now in the hands of Christopher Middleton, to resort unto; which tenement the Mercers shall maintain repair.

THE CHILDREN

There shall be taught in the school, children of all nations and countries indifferently to the number of 153, according to the number of the seats in the school.

The high master shall admit these children as they shall be offered from time to time; but first, see they can[2] their catechism, and, also, that he can read and write competently, else let him not be admitted in no wise. *De admissione puerorum* [Concerning the admission of boys]

A child at the first admission, once forever, shall pay four pence for writing of his name. This money of the admissions shall the poor scholar have that sweepeth the school and keepeth the school clean.

In every form one principal child shall be placed in the chair, president of that form.

---

[1] *absence*, vacation.   [2] *can*, know.

The children shall come into the school in the morning at seven of the clock, both winter and summer, and tarry there until eleven and return again at one of the clock and depart at five; and thrice in the day prostrate, they shall say the prayers with due tract[1] and pausing, as they be contained in a table in the school, that is to say, in the morning, at noon, and at evening.

In the school in no time in the year they shall use tallow candle in no wise, but only wax candle at the cost of their friends.

Also, I will they bring no meat nor drink neither bottles; nor use in the school no breakfasts nor drinkings in the time of learning in no wise; if they need drink, let them be provided in some other place.

I will they use no cockfighting, neither riding about victory, neither disputing at Saint Bartholomew's, which is but foolish babbling and loss of time. I will, also, they shall have no remedies;[2] if the master grant any remedies, he shall forfeit forty shillings *toties quoties*[3] except the king or any archbishop or a bishop, present in his own person in the school, desire it.

All these children shall every Childermas Day come to Paul's Church* and hear the Child Bishop's sermon; and, after, be at High Mass, so each of them offer one pence to the Child Bishop, and with the masters and surveyors of the school.

In general processions when they be warned, they shall go twain and twain together soberly and not sing out, but say devoutly, twain and twain, seven psalms with litany.

To urine they shall go thereby to a place appointed, and the poor child of the school shall see it conveyed away from time to time and have the vaile[4] of the urine: for other causes, if need be, they shall go to the water side.

If any child after he is received and admitted into the school go to any other school to learn thereafter the manner of that school, then I will that such child for no man's suit shall be hereafter received into our school, but go where he list, where his friends shall think is better learning; and this I will, be showed unto his friends or others that offer him at his first presenting into the school.

WHAT SHALL BE TAUGHT

As touching in this school what shall be taught of the masters and learned of the scholars, it passeth my wit to devise and determine in particular, but in general to speak and somewhat to say my mind: I would there were taught always the good literature, both Latin and Greek, and good authors such as have the very Roman eloquence joined with wisdom, specially Christian authors that wrote their

---

[1] *tract*, length of time.   [2] *remedies*, half-holidays.
[3] *toties quoties*, as often as.   [4] *vaile*, money.

wisdom with clean and chaste Latin, other in verse or in prose; for my intent is by this school specially to increase knowledge and worshipping of God and Our Lord Christ Jesu and good Christian life and manners in the children; and, for that intent, I will the children learn first, and above all, the Catechism in English; and after, the *Accidence* that I made, or some other, if any can be better to the purpose to induce children more speedily to Latin speech, and then *Institutum Christiani Hominis*, which that learned Erasmus made at my request, and the book called *Copia [Verborum]* (1512) of the same Erasmus.

And then other authors Christian, as Lactantius, Prudentius, and Probus and Sedulius and Juvencus and Battista Mantuan and such others as shall be thought convenient and most to purpose unto true Latin speech: All barbary, all corruption, all Latin adulterate which ignorant blind fools brought into this world, and with that same hath disdained and poisoned the old Latin speech and the very Roman tongue which in the time of Tully and Sallust and Virgil and Terence was used, which also Saint Jerome and Saint Ambrose and Saint Augustine, and many holy Doctors learned in their times—I say that filthiness and all such abusion which...more rather may be called blotterature than literature, I utterly abanish and exclude out of this school and charge the masters that they teach always that is the best, and instruct the children in Greek and Latin in reading unto them such authors that hath with wisdom joined the pure chaste eloquence.

Joannes Colet fundator novae scolae manu sua propria.[1]

John Colet, *Die Schriftsprache in der Londoner Paulsschule.* Ed. S. Blach (Halberstadt, 1905).

SEBASTIAN BRANT

1457–1521

When Sebastian Brant, a professor of law at the University of Basel, wrote the Narrenschiff *(1494), the stern satire of his short metrical sermons' caught the popular fancy on the Continent and in England. With the words of the psalmist, ' They that go down to the sea in ships, doing business in the great waters' (Douay, cvi. 23), as a caption for the first of the poem's famous woodcuts, Brant launched his attack. ' All is folly and*

[1] John Colet, founder of the new school, with his own hand.

every man is a fool', was his sharp dictum to the people who had endured a century of wars and plagues. And throughout, the woodcuts show a motley crew—kings, clergy, lawyers, doctors, merchants, scholars, crafts-men—rich and poor, climbing aboard his Ship. Continental translators helped to spread his message, but their versions lacked Brant's simple style and earnest plea that people reform their lives according to Christian principles.

The first, and also the worst, offender among the translators was Brant's own student Jacob Locher, the German humanist. In his Latin version Stultifera Navis (1497), Locher polished away the charm and vigour of Brant's German proverbs, substituting classical allusions that failed to catch the timely satire of the original. Translations in various European languages followed Locher's version, and twenty-four editions of the poem were printed before 1509. Among these was Pierre Riviere's verse paraphrase La nef des folz (1497). Two years later, Jehan Drouyn, 'bachelier en loix et en decret', based a prose version, Nef des folles (1499), on Riviere's work.

Henry Watson, translator in the employ of Wynkyn de Worde, made the first English version, The shyppe of fooles (1509), in prose. Drouyn's translation served as his text, and since it is a free rendering, Watson's prose bears little resemblance to Brant's famous work. Unlike Alexander Barclay whose Shyp of folys (1509) appeared in polished verse form within the same year, Watson knew neither Latin nor German and so could not compare Drouyn's text with Brant's or Locher's. As Drouyn had retained Locher's marginal notes, so did Watson, using also the French translator's own preface. The prelude and the Argument in the English version are Brant's with some additions made by Drouyn, Riviere, and Locher.

In a comparative study of The English Versions of The Ship of Fools, Aurelius Pompen, O.F.M., doubts that Watson was, as he declares, urged to translate the work by Lady Margaret Beaufort. It was more than likely that De Worde pushed it, knowing that his friendly rival Richard Pynson was about to print Barclay's version.

The value of Watson's translation is his effort to anglicize the satire, showing the universality of Brant's genius. The Shyppe also reveals the influence that the French language and literature had on the English vocabulary and the nation's reading taste during the early Renaissance.

Of Watson's life, little is known except that he served as a professional translator for De Worde. His most ambitious work is his translation of the French romance, The Hystorye of Olyuer of Castylle (1518).

The Ship of Fools

TRANSLATED BY HENRY WATSON

PROLOGUE

Thereafter followeth the prologue of the translator of this present book entitled, *The Great Ship of Fools of this World*.

Knowing that *Melius est habundare quam deficere*:* It is better to have abundance of divers things than to have necessity, wherefore I have put myself to translate this present book, called *The Great Ship Of Fools*, out of French into English because that this book hath been first made in the Allemayne[1] language; and out of Allemayne, it was translated into Latin by Master Jacques Locher, and out of Latin into rhetoric French. I have considered that the one delighteth them in Latin, the other in French, some in rhyme, and the other in prose; for the which cause I have done this, moreover, considering this that Terence saith: *Tot capita*; *tot sensus*:* Also, many heads; also, many opinions. And then considering the saying of Vergil: *Trahit sua quemque voluptas*:* Everybody will do after their voluntees[2] and will accomplish them; but as Vergil saith, moreover, *Nescia mens hominum*:* The voluntees of men is unknown. Wherefore they that will have Latin, take it; the French, rhyme or prose; or Allemayne or English. Who will have the moral sense take it; who that will have the literal sense, take it. 'And who will have all, take all,' as Aesop says.*

To the honour of the right high and right sacred Trinity, Father, Son, and Holy Ghost in one essence, and of the right glorious Mother of God, and of all the saints of paradise, I have begun to make this translation for to exhort the poor humans, the which by imbecilities[3] and pusillanimites[4] have ensued the fools of this present world and their works. And to the end that they may eschew all mundanes[5] and fools, I pray them that they have regard unto this present book, and that they comprehend the substance to the end that they may wisely govern themself in the time to come, and that through their labour, they may be of the number of the saved. For when a man debateth, the shame that it be not vanquished multiplyeth his force. And the good conscience also multiplyeth virtues in man.

Considering also that the prose is more familiar unto every man than the rhyme, I Henry Watson, indigne[6] and simple of understanding, have reduced this present book into our maternal tongue of English out of French at the request of my worshipful master

[1] *Allemayne*, German.   [2] *voluntees*, whims.
[3] *imbecilities*, folly.   [4] *pusillanimites*, timidity.
[5] *mundanes*, worldly people.   [6] *indigne*, unworthy.

Wynkyn de Worde through the enticement and exhortation of the
excellent Princess Margaret, Countess of Richmond and Derby, and
grandame unto our most natural sovereign lord King Henry VIII,
whom Jesus preserve from all encumbrance. If that I have added
anything in any place, I have not done it by arrogance, but for to
apply unto the Scripture and because that it came unto purpose.
I have not willed to change the name of the book, the which hath
been called by the first composer *The Ship of Fools*. He hath figured
a ship full of fools fleeting upon a sea.

By the ship we may understand the fools and errors that the
mundanes are in; by the sea, this present world; the fools being in
the ship, are the sinners; for we are in this world as pilgrims fleeting
from one country to another, and after our operations we shall be
remunerate at the port of salute.[1] Since that it is so, we must search
in this book, the which may well be called 'The Doctrinal of Fools',
for there may be founden good and healthful doctrines contained as
well in the holy pagan works as in those of the saints and prophets and
of laws and of the decrees of holy Fathers, the which have rowed so
well in this world that they are arrived at a good port, that is, in the
glory eternal, to the which will conduct us, the Father, the Son, and
the Holy Ghost. Amen.

You lecturers, humbly I require you for to pardon me if that I have
erred in anything, for the tenderness of my years hath so affusked[2]
me that I have not applied me unto the letters as I ought to have done:
the language is not authentic to the end that everybody may understand some thing, for folks unlettered demandeth not things obscure.

ARGUMENT IN 'THE SHIP OF FOOLS OF THIS WORLD'

For the felicity and salute of all the human gendre[3] is compiled and
directed the *Ship of Fools* of this transitory world, in the which
ascendeth all they that vageth[4] from the way of truth and from the
plain exhortation of the intellective understanding in transmutable
and obscure thoughts of the frail body. Wherefore this present book
may be called satire, notwithstanding that the first author did delight
him in the new intitulation of this present book, for right so as by the
poesies and fictions the ancient poets did correct the vices and
frailities of mortal men. Semblably, this present pagyne[5] specifyeth
before their sight the estate and condition of men to the end that, as
a mirror, they behold the *moeurs* and rectitude of life. Nevertheless,
think not, ye lecturers, that I have word by word direct and reduced
this present book out of French into our maternal tongue of English,
for I have only (as reciteth Flaccus) taken entirely the substance of

---

[1] *salute*, salvation.　　[2] *affusked* (*offusque*), obfuscated.　　[3] *gendre*, kind.
[4] *vageth*, wander.　　[5] *pagyne*, pageant.

the Scripture in *espérance* that mine audacious presumption should be pardoned of the lecturers, having aspect unto the capacity of my tender years and the imbecility of my little understanding in leaving the egressions,[1] poetiques,[2] and fabulous obscurtees[3] in achieving the work in facile sentence and familiar style [and] in supplicating all the readers to have me for excused if that I have failed in anything.

Hereafter ensueth the first chapter.

OF BOOKS INUTILE[4]

The first fool of the ship: I am certain
That with my hands [I] dress the sails all.
For to have books I do all my busy pain,
Which I love not to read in special
Nor them to see, also, in general.
Wherefore it is a proverb all about:
Such thinketh to know that standeth in doubt.

Young folks that intend for to know divers things, approach you unto this doctrine, and [let] it revolve in your mind's organics[5] to the end that ye may comprehend and understand the substance of it, and that ye be not of the number of the fools that vageth in this tempestuous flood of the world. And, you, also, the which have passed the flowering age of youth to the end that and[6] ye be of the number of the fools mundanes, that ye may learn somewhat for to detray you out of the Ship *Stultifere*.

Wherefore understand what the first fool saith, being in the great Ship of Fools: 'I am the first in the ship, vagaunte with the other fools. I turn and hoist the cords of the ship, sailing farforth in the sea. I am founded full evil in wit and in reason. I am a great fool for to affye[7] me in a great multitude of books. I desire always and appetiteth new inventions, compiled mystically, and new books in the which I cannot comprehend the substance nor understand nothing. But I do my busy cure for to keep them honestly from powder and dust. I make my lectrons and my desks clean right often. My mansion is all replenished with books; I solace me right often for to see them open without anything compiling out of them. Ptolomeus was a rich man,* the which constituted and commanded that they should search him through every region of the world the most excellent books that might be founden. And when they had brought them all, he kept them for a great treasure. And that notwithstanding he ensued not the ensignments[8] nor the doctrine

---

[1] *egressions*, digressions.　　　　[2] *poetiques*, literary devices.
[3] *obscurtees*, obscure words.　　　[4] Chapter I.
[5] *organics*, mechanism.　　　　　[6] *and*, if.
[7] *affye*, trust.　　　　　　　　　[8] *ensignments*, lessons.

of the divine sapience, howbeit that he could dispose nothing of the life without it, what books somever he had, nor compose anything to the release of his body at that time.

'I have read in divers books, in the which I have studied but a little while, but oftentimes I have passed the time in beholding the diversities of the coverings of my books. It should be great folly to me to apply by excessive study mine understanding unto so many divers things where through I might lose my sensual intelligence, for he that procureth for to know overmuch and occupyeth himself by excessive study is in danger for to be extraught[1] from himself; also everyone is dispensed, be he a clerk or understand he nothing, yet he beareth the name of a lord. I may as well commit one in my place, the which thinketh for to learn science for him and for me. And if that I find myself in any one place in the company of wise men, to the end that I speak no Latin, I shall condescend unto all their propositions for fear that I should not be reproached of that that I have so evilly learned.'

O doctors, the which beareth the name and can nothing of science, for to eschew great dishonour come never in the company of learned men: our ancient fathers, herebefore, did not learn their resplendishing science in the multitude of books, but of an ardent desire and of a good courage. They had not their spirits so unsteadfast as the clerks have at this present time: it were more propice[2] for such folks for to bear asses' ears than for to bear the names of doctors and can nothing of cunning.

OF STUDY INUTILE[3]

> Who will not exercise study,
> But run about from place to place,
> Is replenished with folly,
> And is deject from all good grace,
> For no science he will purchase.
> Wherefore he shall repent him sore,
> Because he would not learn no more.

You foolish students, come into this place and you, young scholars, also, that passeth your time in running from town to town and trifling in the university, dispending your fathers' goods foolishly without any studying, living like beasts in having no regard to the time future nor to recover the time that ye lose study in this chapter and leave your running about in the streets, for it shall profit you much.

You students, that wear long gowns and hoods,* also—as who saith, ye be excellent clerks and prudent men, and yet ye be incensive fools, for when ye should be at your lessons and in your studies, ye

---

[1] *extraught*, distraught.   [2] *propice*, appropriate.   [3] Chapter XXVII.

be at the tavern or among naughtypackes,[1] passing your youth in vicious operations. They imagine new reasons, saying that they be not subject to right reason, for their flesh is frail. They go from street to street, seeking the night, and [they] will learn nothing nor follow the teaching of wise and prudent men. They resemble not to the discreet men nor to them that be their masters, the which for to learn science did watch divers times and took great pain and solicitude. And yet there be divers fools that will learn four or five sciences without having perfect intelligence of their grammar that is the foundation of all sciences. They go running unto logic and maketh a great sort of argument and of crooked sophisms, and have ever in their mouth sortes[2] of Plato, [showing] how well that by logic and subtle arguments an obscure thing may well be clarified.

Nevertheless there be some that fixeth their study thereon without any other ensignment. They resemble unto croaking frogs by their murmurations, for they tarry not on fair authorities, and, the meanwhile, youth passeth away in taking his natural course without any tasting of delectable science, and so they remain always replete with vices. Foolish legists and decretists, that studieth in codices and in institutes and that readeth the lessons of doctors, ye wene to be more expert than a great advocate, and yet ye can nothing because of the great vainglory that holdeth you by the head. They that run to many towns, as to Vienne, Arsonde, Orleans, Paris, Poitiers, Pavia, Padua, Toulouse, Louvain, Montpelier; in Basel were they nourished; they can tell something of Barbary; of the sea of Gaul; and they have seen the city of Rome, of London, of Naples, of Milan, of Avignon and of York; and when they return home again, they be all too ragged and can nothing. They be not set by because they would not follow good doctrine; but notwithstanding that they have long gowns full of pleats and hoods, seeming great clerks, yet they are but beasts. They go to dinners and banquets where they be set most highest, wenyng[3] to the assistants that they be great clerks. The others be players at tennis, at cards, at dice, bourdellers,[4] and pillars of taverns, running night and day for to break doors and windows and doing other evils infinite. And their friends hath great pain for to assemble goods for them, wenyng that such rioters be good clerks; but they sell all for to go on rioting.

COLOPHON: Thus endeth the *Shyppe of Fooles* of this world. Imprinted at London in Fleet Street by Wynkyn de Worde, printer unto the excellent Princess Margaret, Countess of Richmond and Derby and grandame unto our most natural sovereign lord King Henry VIII.... 1509.

[1] *naughtypackes*, bad companions.
[2] *sortes*, chance selections of passages from an author's work .
[3] *wenyng*, feigning.   [4] *bourdellers*, jesters.

CUTHBERT TUNSTALL

1474–1559

The notable career of Cuthbert Tunstall spanned the Tudor period, beginning in the reign of Henry VII and closing the year after Elizabeth I came to the throne. As his first biographer, Charles Sturge, describes him, Tunstall was 'a classical scholar of European fame, a mathematician of repute; close friend of More and Erasmus; judge, diplomatist, statesman, administrator, theologian; bishop successively of two famous sees, London and Durham, at a time of religious crisis; eloquent, witty, and withal of a nature so humane and lovable as to win warm praise from men of very dissimilar creed and outlook'.

Tunstall was born in 1474 in Yorkshire and belonged to the Tunstall family of Thurland Castle. He studied at Oxford and Cambridge and at the University of Padua under Nicola Leonicus. Back in England in 1505, he served with several embassies sent to the Continent by Henry VII. During the reign of Henry VIII, Tunstall became the king's most successful envoy to the courts of Europe, serving several times with Sir Thomas More. But like other courtiers of Henry VIII, Tunstall was soon compelled to take sides on the momentous issues—the king's divorce and the Oath of Royal Supremacy. He accepted the king's demands on both. But more of a conservative than a reformer, Tunstall fought against an outright denial of the doctrine of transubstantiation in the Six Articles (1539) and The Boke of Comon Praier (1549). His persistent leanings toward Catholic doctrine led, however, to his imprisonment in the reign of Edward VI.

Queen Mary released Tunstall from prison in 1553, and he recanted. She restored his see, and he remained Bishop of Durham until deprived of it by Elizabeth I, with whom he dared argue for the old faith. She was anxious for him to break again with Rome since he was the sole surviving pre-Reformation bishop. His refusal made him virtually a prisoner under the charge of Archbishop Matthew Parker in Lambeth Palace. He died there on 18 November 1559.

Besides his theological works on the Eucharist and predestination, Tunstall wrote two Latin works in the classical tradition: De arte supputandi (1521) and Compendium in decem libros Ethicorum Aristotelis (1554). The latter was printed in Paris shortly before his death. Tunstall's De arte, that has been called 'the most classical work which was ever written on the subject in Latin', was dedicated to Sir Thomas More. The first book of its kind printed in England, it is divided into four sections: Numerations, Fractions, Profit and Loss, and Ratio. Tunstall believed that no subject equalled 'the mastery of numbers' as a mind trainer.

His only English work, Palm Sunday Sermon (1539), is a vigorous attack on Papal supremacy. A great portion of it, however, is a plea for 'penance and repentance by the amendment of our sinful lives'.

Dedicatory Epistle to De Arte Supputandi

TRANSLATED BY JAMES EDWARD TOBIN

Cuthbert Tunstall, to Thomas More, greetings:

Several years ago, friend More, when I was involved with the usurers, and we could not sufficiently agree on the means by which I could escape the fraud which I had long and seriously suspected, I was forced to give close attention to the still not fully settled problem and to master all over again the complexities of computing which had so bored me as a young student. When, by this study, I had extricated myself from the web spun by crafty men, I concluded that there would be no small reward for me during the rest of my life if I maintained a ready skill in figuring; so that, as long as I kept this at my finger-tips, I would not be deceived by any sharper again.

Accordingly to gain an even more thorough knowledge of mathematics, I read thoroughly every single book written on the subject—scholarly, incomplete, Latin, foreign, in any language in which I was competent (for there is scarcely a nation which does not have something on the subject, written in the vernacular). And, so that I should not have to re-read often and not without distaste entire volumes, many pages of which were occasionally unappealing —if it can be said that there was anything in these books which was exactly pleasing—I made notes as I went along. The result was that I gathered for myself many remarks from the writings of many men: and since they were piling up about me in my room for some time, I concluded that it might prove profitable if, by translating them into Latin, I could make them a little clearer.

While I was striving to do that, and the work was proceeding all too slowly, drugged by fatigue I often cast aside the books, abandoning hope that I could complete what I planned, both because the content in itself was obscure, and because many problems often arose which, it seemed, could not be expressed in Latin—or even with clarity. On the other hand, I was ashamed to surrender to difficulties and to abandon what I had begun under favourable circumstances. There-upon I tried to see whether going over the problems would bring any solution. I gained pleasure from occasionally joining in strife with them and, although they proved bothersome to some extent— on the other hand this was not always the case—at least they did increase my determination to persist in the task. I sometimes thought, after I was unable to obtain a solution for which I had especially hoped, since everything depended on a kind of inspiration, that the task would not be useless if what was barbarous through lack of polish, I rendered less rough.

Thus, at last, made assured in my resolve, I overcame the tedium and, having surmounted numerous difficulties, I noted down the many remaining problems from various sources, which I had been diligently collecting for some time, and thought that, sometime in my leisure, and after the example of the bear, I would lick my shapeless offspring into form. Now, however, although a man most unworthy of the honour, through the kindness of the King, who is deserving well of all good men and of myself far more than I can say, I have been appointed to the vacant see of London, and, since I am about to devote the rest of my life to sacred letters, I have thought that all profane writings should be set completely aside.

I have especially determined to separate myself from those commentaries on the science of mathematics that I had gathered together in my house, considering that they are more worthy of the strongbox of Vulcan than of Minerva. I did not think that they were finished enough to come into the hands of scientists, nor did I think it right that any part of my future career should be taken from devotion to sacred letters to polish them further. Yet it occurred to me that something not without use to those approaching mathematics could be gained from my papers; and that it would not be considered a wise action if I merely committed to the flames what I had learned through so many nights of arduous study. But I could not bring myself to dedicate so rough and unpolished a work to a King, educated far beyond the usual fortune of rulers and deserving, beyond all mortals, only the best from men, lest I should interfere with the business of the realm while he took time to read these trifles and lest I should seem to have won for myself by a minor service a favour which there is not the slightest hope of repaying.

And so, while I was searching for the most likely of my many friends to whom I might dedicate this collection, you, because of our closeness and your largeness of heart, seemed to be the best suited of all, because you would be amenable, if there were anything attractive in this work, to consider it a favour; if it were childish, to find in it some good; if it were blundering, to forgive. For whom can these things be more fitting than for you who, engaged fully in examining accounts, hold first place in the King's Treasury, after the Prefect; and who can pass them on to be read by your children whose education in the discipline of the liberal arts you have directed. These notes will be especially profitable for them, if they are worthy of being read at all, for the wits of youth are quickened by nothing so much as by the mastery of numbers. Farewell.

COLOPHON: *In aed. R. Pynsoni.* 1522.

GIOVANNI FRANCESCO PICO
DELLA MIRANDOLA
1469–1533

The mystical and philosophical writings of the late Italian Renaissance that so impressed English scholars who studied on the Continent were chiefly the works of the eminent humanists, Savonarola, Ficino, and Giovanni Pico della Mirandola. Of the three, the most influential was probably Pico. He was born in 1463, the son of Gianfrancesco Pico, Prince of Mirandola, a small territory near Ferrara. After studying at several universities and at Florence, Pico began to write on questions in philosophy and theology. His inquisitive mind, together with his ascetic way of life and interest in clerical reform, led to his friendship with Savonarola, whose encouragement to have him enter the priesthood went unheeded.

Pico attracted wide attention for his stand against astrology, then popular in Germany and Italy. By 1486 he had compiled nine hundred questions, covering all the branches of philosophy. Some of his views were considered heretical, and the book was prohibited by Innocent VIII. The ban was removed in 1493 when Pico presented an elaborate Apologia. *He died the following year in Florence.*

It was to dispel the controversy that raged over his works a few years before his death that his nephew Giovanni Francesco wrote his uncle's life. Also well known as a philosopher and humanist, the younger Giovanni wrote extensively. Besides writing his uncle's life Vita per Joannem Franciscum *(1496), he wrote the life of Savonarola and a plea to the Lateran Council, held in 1512, for clerical reform,* Joannis Francisci Pici oratio ad Leonem X et concilium Lateranense de reformandis Ecclesiae moribus *(1535). It was dedicated to Willibald Pirkheimer, the Nuremberg humanist. Francesco died a tragic death at the hand of his nephew Galeotti in 1533.*

It was probably through John Colet that Sir Thomas More became interested in translating Giovanni's Lyfe of J. Picus Myrandula *(1510). When he began to work on it, More had just finished his law studies at Lincoln's Inn and was 'propounding' to himself 'as a pattern of lyfe, a singuler layman John Picus, Erle of Myrandula'. In spite of the cares of a growing family and his duties as a member of Parliament, it was finished and dedicated to his young cousin Joyeuse Leigh, a nun of the Poor Clares, in a convent outside of London. He sent it to her as a New Year's gift, writing in the dedicatory epistle, More's first extant English letter, 'whereas the gifts of other folk declare that they wish their friends to be worldly fortunate, mine testifieth that I desire to have you godly prosperous'.*

Two editions of More's translation were printed, the first by Wynkyn de Worde about 1510, and the second by John Rastell before 1520.

The Life of John Picus

TRANSLATED BY SIR THOMAS MORE

Here is contained the *Life of John Picus*, Earl of Mirandola, a great lord of Italy, an excellent cunning man in all sciences and virtuous of living: With divers epistles and other works of the said John Picus, full of great science, virtue, and wisdom, whose life and works be worthy and digne to be read and often to be had in memory.

OF HIS PARENTS AND TIME OF HIS BIRTH

In the year of Our Lord God, 1463, Pius II being then the general Vicar of Christ in His Church, and Frederick, the third of that name, ruling the Empire, this noble man was born, the last child of his mother Julia, a woman come of a noble stock, his father hight John Francis, a lord of great honour and authority.

OF HIS SETTING FORTH TO SCHOOL AND STUDY IN HUMANITY

Under the rule and governance of his mother he was set to masters and to learning, where with so ardent mind he laboured the studies of humanity that within a short while he was (and not without a cause) accompted among the chief orators and poets of that time; in learning marvellous swift and of so ready a wit that the verses which he heard once read, he would again, both forward and backward to the great wonder of the hearers, rehearse; and over that, would hold it in sure remembrance: which in other folks [is] wont commonly to happen contrary, for they that are swift in taking, be oftentimes slow in remembering; and they that with more labour and difficulty receive it, more fast and surely hold it.

Wit receiveth; remembrance holdeth

OF HIS STUDY IN PHILOSOPHY AND DIVINITY

After this, as a desirous ensearcher of the secrets of nature, he left these common trodden paths and gave himself wholly to speculation and philosophy, as well human as divine. For the purchasing whereof (after the manner of Plato and Apollonius) he scrupulously sought out all the famous doctors of his time, visiting studiously all the universities and schools, not only through Italy but also through France. And so indefatigable labour gave he to those studies that, yet a child and beardless, he was both reputed, and was indeed, both a perfect philosopher and a perfect divine.

Travelling from place to place wonderfully increaseth knowledge

OF HIS LEARNING UNIVERSALLY

But because we will hold the reader no longer in hand, we will speak of his learning but a word or twain generally. Some man hath shone in eloquence, but ignorance of natural things hath dishonested him; some man hath flowered in the knowledge of divers strange languages, but he hath wanted all the cognition of philosophy; some man hath read the inventions of the old philosophers, but he hath not been exercised in the new schools; some man *All cunning* hath sought cunning, as well philosophy as divinity, for *and know-* praise and vainglory and not for any profit or increase of *ledge in* Christ's Church. But Picus all these things with equal *bounded in* study hath so received that they might seem by heaps as *J. Picus* a plenteous stream to have flowed into him. For he was not of the condition of some folk (which to be excellent in one thing, set all other aside), but he in all sciences profited so excellently that which of them soever ye had considered in him, ye would have thought that he had taken that one for his only study. *J. Picus his* And all these things were in him so much the more *own master* marvellous in that he came thereto by himself with the strength of his own wit, for the love of God and profit of His Church, without masters; so that we may say of him that Epicurus, the philosopher, said of himself, that he was his own master.

JOHN PICUS, EARL OF MIRANDOLA, TO ANDREW CORNEUS, GREETING:

Ye exhort me by your letters to the civil and active life, saying that in vain and, in manner, to my rebuke and shame, have I so long studied in philosophy, but if I would at the last exercise that learning in the entreating of some profitable acts and outward business. Certainly, my well-beloved Andrew, I had cast away both cost and labour of my study if I were so minded *A monstrous* that I could find in my heart in this matter to assent unto *persuasion* you and follow your counsel. This is a very deadly and *touching the* monstrous persuasion which hath entered the minds of *philosophy* men, believing that the studies of philosophy are of estates and princes, either utterly not to be touched or, at leastwise, with extreme lips to be sipped; and rather to the pomp and ostentation of their wit than to the culture and profit of their minds to be little and easily tasted. The words of Neoptolemus they *Felicity* hold utterly for a sure decree, that philosophy is to be studied either never or not long; but the sayings of wise men they repute for japes[1] and very fables, that sure and steadfast felicity

---

[1] *japes*, jests.

standeth only in the goodness of the mind; and that these outward things of the body or of fortune little or naught pertain unto us.

But here ye will say to me thus: 'I am content, ye study, but I would have you outwardly occupied also. And I desire you not so to embrace Martha that ye should utterly forsake Mary. Love them and use them both, as well study as worldly occupation.' Truly, my well-beloved friend, in this point I gainsay you not; they that so do, I find no fault in nor I blame them not, but certainly it is not all one to *say* we do well if we do so, and to *say* we do evil but if we do so. This is far out of the way to think that from contemplation to the active living—that is to say, from the better to the worse—is none error to decline, and to think that it were shame to abide still in the better and not decline.

Contempla-
tion

Shall a man then be rebuked because that he desireth and ensueth virtue only for itself; because he studieth the mysteries of God; because he ensearcheth the counsel of nature; because he useth continually this pleasant ease and rest, seeking none outward thing, despising all other thing, since those things are able sufficiently to satisfy the desire of their followers? By this reckoning it is a thing either servile, or, at the leastwise, not princely to make the study of wisdom other than mercenary. Who may well hear this; who may suffer it? Certainly he never studied for wisdom which so studied therefor that in time to come either he might not or would not study therefor. This man rather exercised the study of merchandise than of wisdom.

The study
of wisdom
never to be
omitted

Ye write unto me that it is time for me now to put myself in household with some of the great princes of Italy, but I see well that, as yet, ye have not known the opinion that philosophers have of themselves, which, as Horace saith, 'repute themselves, king of kings';* they love liberty; they cannot bear the proud manners of estates; they cannot serve. They dwell with themselves, and be content with the tranquillity of their own mind; they suffice themselves and more; they seek nothing out of themselves; the things that are had in honour among the common people, among them be not held honourable.

Philosophers

All that ever the voluptuous desire of men thirsteth for or ambition sigheth for, they set at naught and despise. Which while it belongeth to all men, yet, undoubtedly, it pertaineth most properly to them whom fortune hath so liberally favoured that they may live not only well and plenteously but also nobly. These great fortunes lift up a man high and set him out to the show; but oftentimes as a fierce and skittish horse, they cast off their master. Certainly always they grieve and vex him, and rather tear him than bear him. The golden mediocrity, the mean

High estate

Mean estate

estate, is to be desired, which shall bear us, as it were, in hands more easily; which shall obey us and not master us.

I, therefore, abiding firmly in this opinion, set more by my little house, my study, the pleasure of my books, the rest and peace of my mind, than by all your kings' palaces, all your common business, all your glory, all the advantage that ye hawk after, and all the favour of the court. Nor I look not for this fruit of my study, that I may thereby hereafter be tossed in the flood and rumbling of your worldly business, but that I may once bring forth the children that I travail on; that I may give out some books of mine own to the common profit which may somewhat savour if not of cunning yet, at the leastwise, of wit and diligence. And because ye shall not think that my travail and diligence in study is anything remitted or slackened, I give you knowledge that after great fervent labour with much watch[1] and indefatigable travail I have learned both the Hebrew language and the Chaldean, and now have I set hand to overcome the great difficulty of the Arabic tongue. These, my dear friend, be things which do appertain to a noble prince, I have ever thought and yet think.

The right fruit of study

Written at Paris the 15th day of October, the year of grace, 1492.

COLOPHON: Imprinted...by me, Wynkyn de Worde [1510].

DESIDERIUS ERASMUS
1466–1536

Erasmus was well on the way to fame before he published his great satire, Moriae Encomium *in 1509. At the time he finished it, he was a guest at the home of Sir Thomas More in Bucklersbury. It was his third visit to England. On two previous visits, in 1498 and 1506, he had studied at Oxford and Cambridge and made lasting friendships with More, Bishop Fisher, and John Colet, Dean of St Paul's Cathedral. The Universities of Turin, Louvain, and Paris had already conferred degrees on him; he was a recognized Greek and Latin scholar; and he was known as a grammarian. His two early works,* Adagia *(1500) and* Enchiridion Militis Christiani *(1502), had been well received in England. He had travelled in Italy, and lightened the editorial burdens of his friend, the Venetian printer Aldus Manutius.*

When Erasmus left England, in 1515, he had determined to settle at Basel; and there on 7 March 1516 he published Novum Instrumentum, *a thousand-page folio containing his Latin translation of the New Testament,*

---
[1] *watch,* vigilance.

his own Greek version of it, and Annotations, *all of which had taken sixteen years to complete. At intervals between 1516 and 1536 he printed his Latin version of the works of the early Church Fathers.*

Still under the monastic vows he took in 1489 at the Augustinian house in Steyn, Erasmus's petition to Pope Leo X to be released from the rule was granted in 1517. This gave him unrestricted freedom to travel. But his extensive literary labours, which included his espousal of the Church's cause in the Lutheran controversy, kept him close to Basel. It was not until 1526, when the city became the centre of 'bloody conflicts between the nobles and the peasants', that he moved to Freiburg. Ten years later, he was back again in Basel, living with Jerome Froben, son of his good friend, John Froben.

Throughout his life, Erasmus consistently refused to accept honours. His old friend Cardinal Farnese, who was elected Pope Paul III in 1534, was anxious to raise him to the College of Cardinals, but Erasmus refused. He spent his last years finishing books that he had begun long before, particularly the treatise on the art of preaching, Ecclesiastes, sive Concionator Evangelicus *(1535).*

His health began to fail in 1535; and he became greatly depressed over the news of the trials and death of his old friends, Bishop John Fisher and Sir Thomas More. Believing a change of climate would benefit him, Erasmus determined in the spring of 1536 to go to Besançon with his protégé, the young canon Lambert Coomans. But he was too weak to make the journey, and died on 11 July. He was buried in the Cathedral of Basel under the altar of the Blessed Virgin Mary.

Fifteen of Erasmus's works, including Moriae Encomium, *were translated into English before 1550, and the first half-century of Tudor prose reflects his principles of Christian humanism. None of his works was more widely read than the* Moriae Encomium. *His satire strikes a mean between that of Lucian and Sebastian Brant, having some of the brilliance of the Greek satirist, but none of his paganism. It is more bluntly spiritual in the manner of Brant. People in every walk of life smarted under Erasmus's quipping—high churchmen, perhaps more than others. Just how serious he meant to be may be inferred from his comment to Sir Thomas More, to whom* Moriae Encomium *was dedicated: 'Nothing is more amusing than to treat trifles in such a way as to show yourself any-thing but a trifler.' Though the work was popular all over Europe and enjoyed by Pope Leo X, it was bitterly denounced by many, including Martin von Dorp of Louvain, who accused Erasmus of attacking dogma. Sir Thomas More wrote a short theological treatise in the form of a letter to Dorp, pointing out that Erasmus's satire was aimed at the lax morals of Christians and not at Christian doctrine.*

The first English translation of Moriae Encomium *was made by Sir Thomas Chaloner, who published his version,* The Praise of Folie, *in 1549. Chaloner, who belonged to a Welsh family, was born in 1521. He attended both Oxford and Cambridge Universities though there is no* record of his having taken a degree. During the reign of Henry VIII, Chaloner began a diplomatic career, and was sent as ambassador to the court of Charles V. In 1541 he was appointed first clerk of the Privy Council, in which service he gained the friendship of the Duke of Somerset and Sir John Cheke. Chaloner retired during the reign of Mary I, but when Elizabeth I came to the throne, he again took up his duties as an envoy, serving for short periods at the court of the Emperor Ferdinand I and at the court of Spain. He died in 1565, a year after his return to England.

Besides The Praise of Folie (1549), Chaloner translated Sir John Cheke's Latin version of Two Homilies of St John Chrysostom (1543) and An homilie vpon that saying of S. Paul: Brethren I wold not haue you ignorant, what is becom of those that slepe (1544). His poem, 'How the Lorde Mobray...was...banyshed the Realme', appeared in the first edition of A Myrroure for Magistrates (1559). Chaloner's The Praise of Folie is especially notable for his use of a sturdy vernacular which keeps the tone close to that of the early Tudor speech.

The Praise of Folly

TRANSLATED BY SIR THOMAS CHALONER

CHALONER TO THE READER

A folly it may be thought in me to have spent time in Englishing of this book entitled The Praise of Folly whereas the name itself seemeth to set forth no wisdom or matter of gravity unless perhaps Erasmus, the author thereof, delight to mock men in calling it one thing and meaning another. To this I answer that Folly in all points is not (as I take it) so strange unto us but that her name may well be abidden as long as will-we-or-nil-we, she will be sure to bear a stroke in most of our doings. Howsoever, a certain sect of fault-finders condemn all things that fully square not with their own rules; yea, twice blind in this, that among the common errors and infirmities of mortal men, they will bear nothing with their brethren as who saith they were demi-gods, and not more than one or two ways linked in Folly's bands.

I have therefore bestowed an English livery upon this Latin book, as well as I could, not so much to please all men as rather to show how even this Folly toucheth all men. Wherein I would not be noted as a carper of any man particularly (for what more unfitting than in books or plays to touch men by name?); nor that herein I seek to have any kind of men noted for their trade of life, otherwise than the abuse thereof deserveth, but only my meaning is such as Erasmus in this book shall express for us both.

He of his modesty is content to set no great face upon it, nor would be noted to have spent great labour in making thereof, saving as in pastime to have assayed whether ought might be spoken in praise of Folly, whereas wisdom, the virtue, can praise itself. And therefore he imagineth that Folly should be a goddess who before all kinds of men assembled, as to a sermon, should declare how many benefits they receive at her hands: and how without her access nothing in this life is delectable, commodious, or tolerable unto us—no, not even our own life. This brave boast might well come from Folly: and seeing that wiser men are wont to take in worth what is said by a fool, therefore is Erasmus also the bolder to put that tale in Folly's mouth, which under another person he would have made more courtesy to have spoken.

So what excuse he maketh, the same I require may serve for me—that things spoken foolishly by Folly may be even so taken and not wrested to any bitter sense or earnest application. For surely if the crabbedest men that be, are wont to take a fool's words as in sport for fear lest others might reckon they would not wince without a galled[1] back, then how much more is a dumb book written generally to be borne withal, namely, where the title pretendeth no gravity, but rather a toy to stir laughter without offence in the book if the reader bring none offence with him. For then, truly, he may chance to see his own image more lively described than in any painted table. But if [in] that ways he mislike the deformities of his counterfeits, let him much more mislike to be such one, in deed.

And seeing the vices of our days are such as cannot enough be spoken against, what know we if Erasmus in this book thought good between game and earnest to rebuke the same and chiefly to persuade (if it might be) a certain contention in every man to hold him agreed with such lot and state of life as ariseth to him. For which purpose was I also soonest moved to English it—to the end that mean men of baser wits and condition might have, [in] a manner, comfort, and satisfaction in themselves inasmuch as the High God who made us all of one earth hath, nevertheless, chosen some to rule and more to serve: Whereat not so much lacketh that the inferiors should repine as rather set in the meaner degree they should thank God the more without aspiring to things above their reach, which should draw more trouble and perils than if they abstained therefrom and gave place to others who had greater gifts of God and were called by authority of their prince or country to wield the same.

For, surely, if a man of the poorer sort whose eyes are dazed in beholding the fair gloss of wealth and felicity, which the state of a great lord or councillor in a commonwealth doth outwardly represent, did inwardly mark the travails, cares, and anxieties which such

[1] *galled*, sore.

one is driven to sustain (doing as he ought to do) in serving his master and country, whereby he is nothing less than his own man, now, I believe, he would not much envy his state, nor choose to change conditions of life with him.

But this were even the chiefest point of wisdom, though fools (as Folly calleth them), that is to say, vulgar folk, are those that un-witting of their treasure do indeed enjoy this sweet quietness and greatest good turn. And weighing this foolish book after this sense, I ween a profit also may arise therethrough to the readers besides the delectation, being so pithily piquant as it is.

For as Erasmus in all his works savoureth of a lively quickness and spareth not sometime in grave matters to sprinkle his style, where he may snatch opportunity, with merry conceited sentences, so in this book, treating of such a theme and under such a person, he openeth all his bouquet: So, farforth, as by the judgment of many learned men, he never showed more art nor wit in any the gravest book he wrote than in this his *Praise of Folly*. Which the reader, having any considerance, shall soon espy how in every matter, yea, almost every clause, is hidden, besides the mirth, some deeper sense and purpose. Indeed, I again say not but he maketh Folly to speak at random without sparing of any estate of men: but yet, indifferent ears will hear their faults patiently as long as they may choose whether they will take the fault upon them or not, or be aknown to be those whom Folly noteth.

But even this frankness of Folly's taunting I have presumed in some points to itch to the best, namely, in two or three places which the learned reader, comparing with the Latin book, may easily perceive how either I have slipped over a line or two, or eased the sour sense of the Latin with some mannerlier English word: Wherein I chose rather to be counted a scant true interpreter than otherwise to touch things which were unsaid as long as it hurted not the grace of the book though they were omitted.

Likewise in all my translation I have not pained myself to render word for word, nor proverb for proverb, whereof many be Greek, such as have no grace in our tongue, but rather marking the sense, I applied it to the phrase of our English. And where the proverbs would take no English, I adventured to put English proverbs of like weight in their places, which may be thought by some cunning translators a deadly sin. But I stick not, for all that, in this foolish book to use mine own foolish taste. And if it be mislike, I pass not greatly though I lose the praise of my Folly.

FOLLY SPEAKETH

Howsoever men commonly talk of me (as pardie, I am not ignorant what lewd reports go on Folly, yea, even among those that are veriest fools of all) yet that I am she, I only (I say) who through mine influence do glad both the gods and men. By this it may appear sufficiently that as soon as I came forth to say my mind afore this your notable assembly, by and by all your looks began to clear up, unbending the frowning of your brows and laughing upon me with so merry a countenance as, by my troth, meseemeth even that all ye whom I see here present do fare as if ye were well whittled[1] and thoroughly moisted with the nectar wine of the Homerical gods, nor without a portion of the juice of that marvellous herb nepenthes which hath force to put sadness and melancholy from the heart; whereas before, ye sat all heavy and glooming as if ye had come lately from Trophonius' cave or Saint Patrick's Purgatory.*

A fool's presence stirreth laughter

But like as when Phoebus displayeth his golden bright rays upon the earth, or when after a sharp stormy winter, the new primetide flourisheth with his calm sweet western winds then, lo, a new likeness, a new hue, and a new youth, as it were, returneth unto all things: even so as soon as I appeared, ye all began to look up lustily.

So what thing these cunning rhetoricians for all their long and forepenned orations can hardly bring about (I mean to drive care and pensiveness out of the hearers' minds) that have I with my only look and presence accomplished. And now ye shall wit to what entent at this time in this so strange an apparel, I am come forth amongst you, upon condition ye will not think much to bestow on me your cares awhile. I mean not those cares that ye carry with you to sermons, but those ye give to players, to jesters, and to fools. Yea, those (hardily) wherewith my friend Midas whilom hearkened to the rural god Pan in preferring his rustical song before Apollo's far finer melody.

To trifles better care given than to graver matters

For I purpose a season to become a sophist. Mistake me not, I pray you, as if I said sophister, such as nowadays drive into children's heads certain tangled trifles with more than women's stubbornness and scolding in their disputations. But I mean the other who to the end they might shun that presumptuous name of *sophi* or wisemen did rather take upon them to be called Sophists, whose study and profession it was to advance and set forth in their writings the praises both of the gods and of men also, such as were famous and worthies here in earth.

Ye shall hear, therefore, the praise set forth not of Hercules nor yet

[1] *whittled*, drunk.

of Solomon, but rather of mine ownself, that is to say, of Folly. In which point, a straw for all these cankard philosophers and sages who say it is a most outrageous folly and presumption for one to praise himself. For truly, let them make it as foolish a part as they list so long as they cannot deny it to be congruent. And what, I pray you, may be more apt or better fitting than Dame Folly to praise herself and be her own trumpet? For who can livelier describe me than I myself? Unless, perhaps, some be better acquainted with me than I myself am.

Notwithstanding even this my self-praise, as meseemeth, I may well take upon me with a more shamefast grace than to do as commonly these great and learned men use, *Orators and poets* who suborn some glossing orator or vain-spoken poet, hired also for meed, to dilate and blast forth their praises or, rightlier to say, pointed lies.

And yet shall one of those shamefast, maidenly men not stick then to display his peacock feathers and rouse himself while such shameless flatterers do go about to make him, being a man less worth than naught, coequal yet unto the gods in blasoning him for a paragon and absolute example of all manner virtues from which he knoweth himself to be as far wide as from hence to the man in the moon, namely, while those glorious glossers would deck the crow with other birds' feathers or pain them to wash away a Moor's blackness, or labour of a sely[1] fly to make an elephant.

For short, I follow in this point the common proverb which saith that he may rightly praise himself whom none other body will. Albeit, to say the truth, I cannot but marvel at men's ingratitude, should I call it, or negligence, that where with one assent they all so frankly do observe me and gladly peruse my commodities, yet hath not one of them, now so many revolutions of years passed, undertaken with some thankful oration to set forth the praises of me, Folly; Whereas some of them have not wanted, who with solemn styles and much loss of sleep and candle showed at least their folly, whatever their matter was, in commendation [of] some of this notable tyranny, some of that, some in praise of the fever quartane, others in setting forth what commodities be in a fly, in baldness, or such like hateful things. But at my hand ye shall hear an unadvised and sudden tale told, though so much, perhaps, the truer.

Which I would not ye should think were said of me for a colour[2] to advance thereby the ripeness of my wit, as commonly these learned men do, who putting forth (as ye know) *The vain glory of* some book more than whole thirty winters had in cul- *learned men* ling, yea, and, that sometimes none of their own doing, will swear yet that they made it but for a recreation of their graver

---

[1] *sely*, poor.   [2] *colour*, excuse.

studies, or rather as fast as pen could run. For, truly, it hath ever best liked me to speak straight whatsoever lay on my tongue's end....

Here now I reck not much to pass over untouched; how no manner act or noble deed was ever attempted nor any art or science invented other than of which I might fully be held first author. For as touching war, the very head and spring of all great enterprises which so commonly are praised and enrolled by historians, is it not (trow ye), a foolish practice to begin such variance as ever both parties receive more damage than profit by. For of those that leave their carcasses in the field, as did the Megarians, never count is made. But yet when armies join together and trumpets blow up bloody notes, to what stead, I pray you, can these good father sages serve, who soaked up with long study, lean and cold of blood, may scantly draw their wind? Nay, then must fat and lusty bloods do the feat, having boldness with the most and wit with the least. Unless, perchance, some would choose such a soldier as was Demosthenes who, following Archilochus,* the poets read, scarce looking his enemies in the face, threw down his shield and ran away, as cowardly a warrior as he was a wise orator.

But counsel in wars, they say, is of great importance. And as for that, I stick not much that counsel in a captain is requisite so it be warlike and not philosophical. For commonly, they that bring any valiant feat to pass are good bloods, venturers, companions, swasshes,[1] dispatchers, bankrowtes, with such like, and none of these philosopher candlewasters: Who how unmeet they be to serve for any common affair or purpose among men, we may be taught by the example of Socrates himself, the only wise man, but unwisely judged by Apollo's oracle. That whereas on a time he went about to have said his mind in a certain matter to the commons of Athens, he left off suddenly, being all laughed to scorn.

Howbeit, this Socrates as in one point, meseemeth, was not all wise in that he would not take upon him the name of a wise man, but rather ascribed the same unto God only; and thought it best for a wise man not to busy himself or meddle with matters of the commonweal. Unless, perhaps, he might have said more rightly that who so would be taken among the number of men should not meddle too much with wisdom. For, I pray you, what drove Socrates upon his arraignment to drink poison for the death he was condemned to, saving only that his excellent, that is, his goodly quality of wisdom? Because while whole days together he trifled out the time in disputations upon the clouds, upon ideas, and by geometry pained himself to mete a fly's feet, discussing also how a gnat, being so little a vermin, might yield so great a sound, he

Marginal notes: Folly, author of all noble acts and arts · War

---

[1] *swasshes*, bullies.

never applied himself to learn things pertaining to this common trade of life.

But now cometh Plato, his disciple, to defend his master at the bar: a gay advocate, I promise you, who, being offended with the noise of the people thronging about him, could scant make an end of the first clause of his tale. And what say you by Theophrastus who taking upon him to speak unto a great assembly as soon as he stood up by and by could say never a word, as if he had seen a wolf at unaware.* And how should he then have encouraged soldiers to fight? Or else Socrates, who of a certain natural timorousness durst never afore audience open his lips? Marcus Tullius, the father of Roman eloquence, ever with an unseemly trembling began his orations, as it were, a sobbing child, which Quintilian interpreteth* to be the sign of a wary and wise orator who pondered well the weightiness of his matter. But when he saith so, doth he not plainly confess wisdom to be an obstacle against any bold feat?

Wise men dastards, either to fight or speak in a press

For what will such shrimpish bodies do, trow ye, when it cometh to handstrokes, that are almost dead for fear when they strive but with bare words? And yet after all this, in God's name, is that worthy saw of Plato's* much commended, 'How those commonweals most happily should flourish that were governed by philosophers or whose governors applied themself to philosophy.' No, no, if ye look in histories, ye shall find no rulers were ever more pestilent to a commonweal than if the same at any time fell into the hands of such one as was given to any sect of philosophy. For proof whereof, I allege unto you the two Catos: the one, whereof with his heady and frantic accusations disturbed greatly the quiet of Rome city; the other, in going about over-wisely to protect the same, did utterly subvert it. And join ye hardily to them both, Brutus and Cassius with the two Gracchi, yea, and Cicero, himself, for as pestilent a citizen among the Romans as Demosthenes was to the Athenians' commonweal.

Likewise, what trow ye by Marcus Aurelius? I admit he was a good emperor, and yet could I wrest that praise also from him because his too much philosophership made him odious and hateful to the people. But admit, I say, he was good, yet truly more pernicious was he to the commonweal in leaving so ungracious an imp as Commodus was for successor in his state than ever he was profitable through his own good wielding of the same.

For commonly this kind of men that are bookish and give themselves to such peevish disciplines, like as in other things so also in child-getting have very ill luck, as if nature of pity (I ween) provided that this plague, this disease (I say) of wisdom, should not spread over largely among men. So Cicero had a son far unlike him in conditions. And Isocrates,

Wise men's children commonly fools

that wise man, had children 'liker to their mother than their father', as one writeth merrily, that is to say, they were fools.

Now though these wise men be as unapt for all public offices and affairs 'as an ass is to finger a harp', yet might it so be abidden if they were not also as untoward in any private duty pertaining to this life. For bid once one of these sages to dinner, and either with his silent glooming or his dark and elvish problems he will trouble all the board. Desire him to take hands in a ball—ye will say a camel danceth. Bring him to a midsummer watch, or a stage play, and even with his very look he will seem to disdain the people's pastime so that wise Don Cato must be fain to avoid the place because he cannot forbear it frowning.

Wise men unfit for any function of this life

Let him light on a knot of good company talking merrily, and by and by every wight holds his peace. If he must buy anything, make a bargain, or, briefly, do ought of those things without which this common life cannot be lead, then sooner will ye take him for a block than a reasonable creature. So much lacketh, lo, that he may stand his country or his friends in profitable stead, who neither is skilled in things daily inured and much differeth from the common opinion and manners of the other people. Perconsequent whereof he must needs deserve their hatred and displeasure through great diversity of livings and dispositions atwixt them.

Wisdom breedeth hatred

For, and if ye list to judge indifferently, is there ought done here among mortal men not full of folly, both by fools and afore fools? So that if one only wight would take upon him to kick against all the rest, him would I advise that, as Timon [of Athens] did, he should shrink into some desert, there to enjoy his wisdom to himself.

COLOPHON: Imprinted at London in Fleet Street in the house of Thomas Berthelet....1549.

ST THOMAS MORE
1478–1535

Over a hundred biographies and many sketches of the life of Sir Thomas More have been written since 1534, the year of his trial in Westminster Hall, when the twelve jurors of the King's Bench found him, once Chancellor of the kingdom, guilty of treason for refusing to take the Oath of Royal Supremacy demanded of each subject by Henry VIII. But More will always be his own best biographer. He unwittingly summed up his life clearly and aptly in the few last words that he spoke on the scaffold 6 July 1535, when according to the account of his execution that appeared shortly after in the Paris News Letter, *More referred to himself as 'the King's good servant, but God's first'.*

Born in London in 1478, the son of Sir John More and his wife Agnes, Thomas More from an early age showed exceptional ability as a student. After attending the usual grammar school and serving as a page in the house of John, Cardinal Morton, More attended Oxford where he came under the direction of Grocyn and Linacre. Taking a Bachelor of Arts degree in 1494, he then began his law studies at Lincoln's Inn. A short interval in More's early manhood was spent in the London Charterhouse determining whether to embrace the contemplative life of the Carthusians. Deciding he had no religious vocation, he married Jane Colt, who bore him three daughters and a son. After her death in 1511, he married Alice Middleton, a widow, who survived him.

More's political career moved swiftly. He was a member of Parliament at twenty-four; in 1518, Privy Councillor; in 1521, sub-treasurer of the Exchequer; in 1523, Speaker of the House of Commons; and in 1525, Chancellor of the Duchy of Lancaster. When Wolsey was forced to resign, Henry VIII, who had long been a friend and admirer of More, appointed him Lord Chancellor in 1529. The English Reformation which came on rapidly in the next few years climaxed More's career. On the fourth centenary of his death, 1935, More was canonized by Pope Pius XI.

Though his life was intensely bound up in the political and social problems of the time, More's interest in the humanities never waned. His part in the controversy over the teaching of Latin and Greek at Oxford is an early example of it. The immediate events which provoked his letter to the authorities at the university ended almost twenty years of dissension in the colleges over the desirability of the study of the classics.

If a letter written by Erasmus can be taken literally, the affair came to a head in the spring of 1518 when Henry VIII was staying at Abingdon, near Oxford, to avoid the sweating sickness then raging in London. With the king were his secretaries, Richard Pace and Thomas More. At this time, Erasmus states, More's protégé and future son-in-law, John Clement, was attending Oxford, and reported to him that a theologian of the university had preached against the pagan influences that follow the study of the classics. Within a short time, according to Erasmus, another theologian preached before the king, continuing the attack on Latin and Greek.

Erasmus turns his letter into a dialogue, reporting the debate that followed the sermon when the king summoned the theologian to court. Both Pace and More took part, and through their pleas caused the theologian to apologize and retract his statements. In commenting on the incident, John Stapleton in his biography of More says his luculenta oratio so impressed the king that he commissioned it to be written in letter form *and sent to the governing body of Oxford University of which William Warham, Archbishop of Canterbury, was then Chancellor.*

Stapleton further relates that the letter was translated into English by one of More's daughters. But the only extant copy of the letter is the Latin edition, printed at Oxford by John Lichfield in 1633.

Letter to Oxford University

TRANSLATED BY T. S. K. SCOTT-CRAIG

Thomas More to the Most Reverend Fathers, the Vice-Chancellor, Proctors, and Faculty of the University of Oxford, greetings:

I have been wondering, gentlemen, whether I might be permitted to communicate to scholars of your distinction, certain conclusions to which I have recently come. Yet I have hesitated in approaching so brilliant a group, not so much on the ground of my style, as on that of seeming to give an exhibition of pride and arrogance. Who am I, the possessor of little prudence and less practice, a scholar of mediocre proportions, to arrogate to myself the right to advise you in anything? And how can I dare to offer advice in the field of letters especially, when any one of you is fitted by his wisdom and erudition to give advice in that field to thousands?

At first sight, Venerable Fathers, I was therefore deterred by your unique wisdom. But, on second thought, I was encouraged; for it occurred to me that only ignorant and arrogant fools would disdain to give a man a hearing, and that the wiser and more learned you were, the less likely you would be to think highly of yourselves or to scorn the advice of others. I was further emboldened by the thought that no one was ever harmed by just judges, such as you are above all, simply on the ground that he offered advice without thinking of the consequences. On the contrary, loyal and affectionate advice, even if imprudent, has always deserved praise and thanks.

Finally, when I consider that, with God's help, I ought to offer you whatever slight learning I have acquired, since it was at your University that my education began, it seems the duty of a loyal friend not to pass over in silence what I deem it serviceable to bring to your attention. Since, then, the only danger in my putting pen to paper seemed to lie in the fact that a few might deem me too audacious, while I know that my silence would be condemned by many as ingratitude, I have preferred that the whole world should condemn my audacity rather than that anyone should have the chance to say that I showed myself ungrateful to your University, the honour of which I feel myself bound to defend to the uttermost.

Moreover, no situation has, I believe, arisen in recent years, which, if you desire to maintain the honour of that institution, more urgently requires your serious attention.

The matter is as follows: When I was in London recently, I rather frequently heard that some members of your faculty, either because they despised Greek, or were simply devoted to other disciplines, or most likely because they possessed a perverse sense of humour, had proceeded to form a society named after the Trojans. The senior sage christened himself Priam; others called themselves Hector, Paris, and so forth; the idea, whether as a joke or a piece of anti-Greek academic politics, being to pour ridicule on those devoted to the study of Greek. And I hear that things have come to such a pass that no one can admit in public or private that he enjoys Greek, without being subjected to the jeers of these ludicrous 'Trojans', who think Greek is a joke for the simple reason that they don't know what good literature is. To these modern 'Trojans' applies the old saw, 'Trojans always learn too late.'

The affair aroused much comment, all very critical; and I myself felt somewhat bitter that even a few academics among you had nothing better to do in their spare time than to cast slurs on their colleagues' subjects. But I kept in mind that one could not expect the whole crowd of academics to possess wisdom, temperance, and humility; and so I began to dismiss the matter as a triviality. However, since I have been here in Abingdon in attendance at the court of His Victorious Majesty [Henry VIII], I have found that the silliness is developing into a form of insanity. For one of these 'Trojans', a scholar in his own estimation, a wit of the first water in that of his friends, though slightly deranged in that of any one observing his actions, has chosen during Lent to babble in a sermon against not only Greek but Roman literature, and finally against all polite learning, liberally berating all the liberal arts.

His whole performance was of a piece. Perhaps such a body of nonsense could not be preached on the basis of any sensible text; in any case, he followed neither the old custom of elucidating a whole passage of Scripture, nor the recent one of expounding some few words of Scripture; instead he elaborated on some stupid British proverbs. So I have no doubt that his frivolous sermon very deeply disturbed those who heard it; since I see that all who have heard fragmentary reports of it are unfavourably impressed.

What man in the audience, in whose breast burned even a spark of Christianity, would not groan at this degradation of the royal office of sacred preaching, which gained the world for Christ—above all at the hands of those whose supreme duty it was to protect it with the authority of their office? Who could possibly have devised a more outrageous insult than for an avowed preacher,

during the most solemn season of the Church's year, in the presence
of a large Christian congregation, in the sanctuary itself, from the
elevation of the pulpit (as it were from the throne of Christ), and in
view of the Sacred Body of Christ, to turn a Lenten sermon into
Bacchanalian ravings? What a look must have been on the faces of
the audience, who had come to hear spiritual wisdom, and saw the
laughable pantomime he put on in the pulpit! They had expected
to listen in reverence to the Word of Life; when they departed, all
they could record they had heard was an attack on humane letters
and a defamation of the preaching office by a fatuous preacher.

It would have been no reproach to secular learning if some good
man, who had retired from the world to the monastic life, suddenly
returned and used this speaker's phrases: 'much in watchings, much
in prayer' or 'the path to be trod by those who seek for heaven' or
'other matters, like humanistic education, trivial if not a positive
hindrance to the spiritual life', or 'simple country folk, and the
unlettered, flying quicker to heaven', etc., etc. All this could have
been borne from such a man. His simplicity would have been
pardoned by his audience. They would have generously admitted his
saintliness, and given serious consideration to his piety, devotion, and
righteousness. But when they saw a man with the academic ermine
over his shoulders, step on to the platform in the midst of a gathering
composed solely of academics, and calmly proceed to rant against
all humane learning, one would have had to be stone-blind not to
notice a signal pride and wickedness, a positive hatred of the higher
arts. Many must have wondered indeed how such a man could get
the idea that he had to preach either about Latin, of which he did not
know much, or about the liberal arts, of which he knew less, or
about Greek—in which he could not even grunt that it was 'all
Greek' to him!

If such an abundance of material had been supplied by the seven
deadly sins, an altogether suitable theme for sermons, who would
have believed him totally inexperienced therein! Though, as a
matter of fact, what is it but sloth, when one is in the habit of
denouncing rather than of learning that of which one is ignorant?
And what is it but hatred, when one defames those who know what
one deprecates but does not comprehend? And what is it but
supreme pride, when he wishes no kind of knowledge to be prized
save what he has falsely persuaded himself that he knows, and when
he even—not from modesty, as might be the case with other people—
arrogates more praise to himself for his ignorance than for his
knowledge?

Now as to the question of humanistic education being secular.
No one has ever claimed that a man needed Greek and Latin, or
indeed any education in order to be saved. Still, this education which

he calls secular does train the soul in virtue. In any event, few will question that humanistic education is the chief, almost the sole, reason why men come to Oxford; children can receive a good education at home from their mothers, all except cultivation and book-learning. Moreover, even if men come to Oxford to study theology, they do not start with that discipline. They must first study the laws of human nature and conduct, a thing not useless to theologians; without such study they might possibly preach a sermon acceptable to an academic group, without it they would certainly fail to reach the common man. And from whom could they acquire such skill better than from the poets, orators, and historians?

Moreover, there are some who through knowledge of things natural [i.e. rational] construct a ladder by which to rise to the contemplation of things supernatural; they build a path to theology through philosophy and the liberal arts, which this man condemns as secular; they adorn the queen of heaven with the spoils of the Egyptians! This fellow declares that only theology should be studied; but if he admits even that, I don't see how he can accomplish his aim without some knowledge of languages, whether Hebrew or Greek or Latin; unless, of course, the elegant gentleman has convinced himself that there is enough theology written in English or that all theology can be squeezed into the limits of those [late scholastic] 'questions' which he likes to pose and answer, for which a modicum of Latin would, I admit, suffice.

But really, I cannot admit that theology, that august queen of heaven, can be thus confined. Does she not dwell and abide in Holy Scripture? Does she not pursue her pilgrim way through the cells of the holy Fathers: Augustine and Jerome; Ambrose and Cyprian; Chrysostom, Gregory, Basil, and their like? The study of theology has been solidly based on these now despised expositors of fundamental truth during all the Christian centuries until the invention of these petty and meretricious 'questions' which alone are today glibly tossed back and forth. Anyone who boasts that he can understand the works of the Fathers without an uncommon acquaintance with the languages of each and all of them will in his ignorance boast for a long time before the learned trust his judgment.

But if this foolish preacher pretends that he was not condemning humanistic education in general but only an immoderate thirst for it, I can't see that this desire was such a sin that he had to deal with it in a public assembly, as if it were causing society to rush headlong to ruin. I haven't heard that many have gone so far in such studies that they will soon be overstepping the golden mean. Further, this fellow, just to show how immoderate *he* could be in a sermon, specifically called students of Greek, 'heretics'; teachers of Greek, 'chief devils'; and pupils in Greek, 'lesser devils' or more modestly and facetiously as he thought 'little *devils*'; and the zeal of this holy man drove him to call by the name of devil one whom everybody knows the Devil himself could hardly bear to see occupy a pulpit. He did everything but name that one [D. Erasmus], as everybody realized just as clearly as they realized the folly of the speaker.

Joking aside—I have no desire to pose as the sole defender of Greek learning; for I know how obvious it must be to scholars of your eminence that the study of Greek is tried and true. To whom is it *not* obvious that to the Greeks we owe all our precision in the liberal arts generally and in theology particularly; for the Greeks either made the great discoveries themselves or passed them on as part of their heritage. Take philosophy, for example. If you leave out Cicero and Seneca, the Romans either wrote their philosophy in Greek or translated it from Greek.

I need hardly mention that the New Testament is in Greek, or that the best New Testament scholars were Greeks and wrote in Greek. I am but repeating the consensus of scholarship when I say: however much was translated of old from Greek, and however much more has been recently and better translated, not half of Greek learning has yet been made available to the West; and, however good the translations have been, the text of the original still remains a surer and more convincing presentation. For that very reason all the Doctors of the Latin Church—Jerome, Augustine, Bede, and a host of others—assiduously gave themselves to learning Greek; and even though many works had already been translated, they were much more accustomed to reading them in the original than are many of our contemporaries who claim to be erudite; nor did they merely learn it themselves, but counselled those among their successors who wanted to be theologians, above all to do the same.

So it is not as if I were just giving your Worships good advice about preserving the study of Greek. I am rather exhorting you to do your duty. You should not allow any one in your university to be frightened away from the study of Greek, either by public assemblies or private inanities, since Greek is a subject required in every place of learning by the Church Universal. Common sense is surely enough to convince you, that not all of your number who give themselves to the study of Greek can be blockheads; in fact, it is in part from these studies that your university has acquired its pedagogical prestige both at home and abroad.

There seems to be an increasing number of cases where Oxford has benefited from the presence of men nominally studying Greek only, but really taking the whole liberal arts course. It will be a wonder if their enthusiasm for you does not evaporate when they realize that so serious an enterprise is held in such contempt. Just think, too, what they are doing at Cambridge, which you have always outshone; those who are *not* studying Greek are so moved by common interest in their university that they are actually making large individual contributions to the salary of the Greek professor!

You see what I mean; and much more could be said to the point by men with better minds than mine. All I am doing is warning you of what others are saying and thinking, not telling you what it behoves you to do. You see much better than I that, if wicked factions are not suppressed at birth, a contagious disease will spread, and the better half be slowly absorbed by the worse, and that outsiders will be forced to take a hand in helping the good and wise among you. Any former student of the university takes its welfare as much to heart as you who are its living members. And I am sure that the Reverend Father in Christ who occupies the See of Canterbury, [William Warham], who is the Primate of all our Clergy and who is also the Chancellor of your university, will not fail to do his part. Whether for the clergy's sake or yours, he rightly feels interested in preventing the decay of learning; and learning will perish if the university continues to suffer from the contentions of lazy idiots, and the liberal arts are allowed to be made sport of with impunity. And what about the Reverend Father in Christ, the Cardinal of York, [Thomas Wolsey], who is both a patron of learning and himself the most learned of the episcopate? Would he endure patiently if aspersions were cast in your university on the liberal arts and the study of languages? Will he not rather aim the shafts of his learning, virtue, and authority at these witless detractors from the arts?

Last but not least: What of our Most Christian King? His Sacred Majesty has cultivated all the liberal arts as much as ever a king did; indeed, he possesses greater erudition and judgment than any previous monarch. Will his wisdom and piety suffer him to allow the liberal arts to fail—through the interests of evil and lazy men—in a place where his most illustrious ancestors wished that there be an illustrious seat of letters, a place which is an ancient nursery of learning, whose products have been an ornament not only to England but to the whole Church, a place which possesses so many colleges that have perpetual endowments specially designated for the support of students (in which respect there is no university outside the kingdom that can compare with Oxford), a place in which the aim of all its colleges and the purpose of all its endowments is none other than that a great body of academics, delivered from the necessity of earning their daily bread, might there pursue the liberal arts?

I have no doubt that you yourselves will easily in your wisdom find a way to end this dispute and quiet these stupid factions; that you will see to it not only that all the liberal arts may be free from derision and contempt but that they shall be held in dignity and honour. By such diligence in intellectual pursuits you will reap benefit for yourselves; and it can hardly be said how much you will gain favour with our Illustrious Prince and with the above-mentioned Reverend Fathers in Christ. You will forge an almost miraculous bond between yourselves and myself, who have thought that all this had to be written now in my own hand out of my deep personal affection for you. You know that my services are at the disposal of each and all of you. May God preserve your glorious seat of learning unharmed; and may He grant that it flourish continually in virtue and in all the liberal arts.

29th March [*1518*]

COLOPHON: *Oxoniae*. J. Lichfield, imp. T. Huggins, 1633.

JUAN LUIS VIVES
1492–1540

Literary relations between Spain and England were strengthened when Henry VIII invited the Spanish humanist Juan Luis Vives to the English court. The invitation may have been prompted by Erasmus, who had encouraged Vives to supervise an edition of St Augustine's De Civitate Dei *and dedicate it to Henry VIII. Shortly after it was printed, in 1522, Vives was invited to England to tutor Princess Mary, the king's daughter, for whom he wrote* De ratione studii puerilis epistolae duae (*1523*).

Within the next few years Vives accepted Richard Fox's invitation to lecture at Corpus Christi College, Oxford. The degree of Doctor of Laws was conferred on him by the university.

Among the many scholars who came from the Continent to England during the sixteenth century, few had greater influence on the educational and social policy of the country. His treatise De institutione feminae Christianae (*1529*), *encouraging the education of women of all classes, was dedicated to Queen Katherine of Aragon. Two other works on education followed:* De Disciplinis (*1531*), *perhaps the greatest Renaissance study on the principles of teaching, and* Exercitatio linguae Latinae (*1538*), *a Latin grammar that became very popular because of its clear and simple presentation of the rudiments of the language. Each of these works went through more than forty editions.*

Vives's treatise on social reform, De subventione pauperum (*1526*), *was revolutionary for its time, encouraging state aid for hospitals, schools for foundlings, and help for the aged poor. His commentary on Aristotle's* De anima et vita (*1538*) *is one of the first modern works on psychology, preceding Francis Bacon's theory of inductive reasoning.*

Two of Vives's treatises were translated into English: The Instruction of a Christen Woman *(1529) and* An Introduction to Wysedome *(1540). The latter, a devotional treatise, was translated by Sir Richard Morison, who used it as a weapon to force a broad social pattern for all classes.*

The Instruction *was translated into English by Richard Hyrd, one of the younger humanists, who took his Bachelor of Arts degree at Oxford in 1519. He refers to Sir Thomas More as his 'bringer-uppe' which suggests that he may have lived with the Mores at Chelsea, possibly as tutor to the More children, succeeding William Gunnell. Hyrd assisted More's daughter Margaret Roper with her translation of Erasmus's* Treatise upon the Pater Noster *(1526), and he wrote a preface for it, urging the education of women. Henry VIII sent Hyrd and Stephen Gardiner to Spain in 1528 to obtain opinions on the royal divorce from the Spanish universities, but Hyrd died during the journey.*

The Instruction of a Christian Woman

De Institutione Feminae Christianae which book whoso readeth diligently shall have knowledge of many things wherein he shall take great pleasure, and specially women shall take great commodity and fruit toward the increase of virtue and good manners.

A very fruitful and pleasant book called *The Instruction of a Christian Woman* made first in Latin and dedicated unto the Queen's good grace by the right famous clerk Master Luis Vives, and turned out of Latin into English by Richard Hyrd.

RICHARD HYRD'S PREFACE

Unto the most excellent princess, Queen Katherine, the most gracious wife unto the most noble and mighty prince, King Henry the .VIII., her humble beadman and orator Richard Hyrd, praying good prosperity and welfare.

Were it not, most excellent Princess, that the consideration of your great goodness and benignity did as much encourage and bold me as the respect and regard of mine own ignorance retardeth me and holdeth back, I never durst presume to dedicate and present unto the majesty of your noble Grace, this my rude and simple translation, so much the more uncomely and unmeet to be offered in your high presence in how much the eloquence of the author staineth and defaceth the rude speech of the translator. For had I, most gracious Princess, that gift of erudition and utterance that I were able in our English tongue to give this book as much perspicuity, light, life, favour, grace, and quickness, as Master Luis Vives hath given it in Latin, then durst I boldly put it forth to your grace not without good hope of thanks, considering the matter to be such as neither a more profitable nor more necessary can lightly come in hand.

For what is more fruitful than the good education and order of women—the one half of all mankind, and that half also whose good behaviour or evil tatchis[1] giveth or beareth the other half almost all the whole pleasure and commodity of this present life, besides the furtherance of or hinderance, further growing thereupon, concerning the life to come. And surely for the planting and nourishing of good virtues in every kind of women—virgins, wives, and widows— I verily believe, there was never any treatise made, either furnished with more goodly counsels; or set out with more effectual reasons; or garnished with more substantial authorities; or stored more plenteously of convenient examples; nor all these things together more goodly treated and handled than Master Vives hath done in his book. Which book when I read, I wished in my mind that either in every country women were learned in the Latin tongue, or the book out of Latin translated into every tongue. And much I marvelled, as I often do, of the unreasonable oversight of men which never cease to complain of women's conditions. And yet having the education and order of them in their own hands, not only do little diligence to teach them and bring them up better, but also purposely withdraw them from learning by which they might have occasions to wax better by themselves.

But since this fault is too far gone and over largely spread to be shortly remedied, I thought at the leastwise for my part it would do well to translate this book into our English tongue for the commodity and profit of our own country. Which when I had secretly done by myself, I showed it unto my singular good master and bringer-up, Sir Thomas More, to whose judgment and correction I use to submit whatsoever I do or go about that I set any store by: Who not only for the matter itself was very glad thereof, but also for that (as he then showed me) he perceived that it should be to your noble Majesty (for the gracious zeal that ye bear to the virtuous education of the womankind of this realm whereof Our Lord hath ordained you to be Queen) so great and special pleasure that he had intended, his manifold business notwithstanding, to have taken the time to have translated this book himself. In which he was (as he said) very glad that he was now prevented—not for eschewing of his labour, which he would have been very glad to bestow therein, but for because that the fruit thereof may now sooner come forth than he could have found the time.

---

[1] *tatchis*, traits.

Howbeit, as I answered him, it were better to bring forth dates in a hundred years (for so long it is or that tree bring forth his fruit) than crabs in four years. And though he reckoned himself eased of the translating, I besought him to take the labour to read it over and correct it. Which he right gladly did. Whereby I have been the more encouraged to put forth unto your most noble grace this translation: To whose Majesty since the original work was dedicated, I was of very duty, methought, bound to dedicate the translation.

Wherefore if there be, as I well wote there is, any good in the matter, thank be to Master Vives, the maker. If anything be well in this translation, thank be to the labour of my good master. For nothing in this work claim I for mine own but the show of my good zeal to do good to others and service to your noble grace: Whom with the sacred majesty of the most excellent Prince, your dearest spouse, and your noble issue, with increase of more, Our Lord long preserve unto the weal of yourself, your realm, and all Christendom besides.

OF THE LEARNING OF MAIDS[1]

Of maids some be but little meet for learning, likewise as some men be unapt. Again some be even born unto it, or at least not unfit for it. Therefore they that be dull are not to be discouraged; and those that be apt, should be hearted and encouraged. I perceive that learned women be suspected of many, as who saith the subtlety of learning should be a nourishment for the maliciousness of their nature. Verily, I do not allow in a subtle and crafty woman such learning as should teach her deceit, and teach her no good manners and virtues. Notwithstanding, the precepts of living and the examples of those that have lived well and had knowledge together of holiness, be the keepers of chastity and pureness, and the copies of virtues, and pricks to prick and to move folks to continue in them.

Aristotle asketh a question,* why trumpeters and minstrels that play at feasts for wages and at resortings and gatherings of people, whom the Greeks call in their language, as ye would say, Bacchus' servants, be ever given unto pleasures and no goodness at all, but spend out their thrift and their life in naughtiness. He maketh answer himself: that it is so because they be ever among voluptuousness and pleasures and banqueting, nor hear any time the precepts of good living, nor regard any man that liveth well. And therefore they can live none otherwise than they have learned, either by seeing or hearing. Nor have they heard nor seen, neither used anything but pleasure and beastliness among uncomely crying and shouting, among dancers and kissers, laughers and eaters, drunkards and spewers, among folk drowned in exceeding overmuch joy and

---

[1] Book I, Chapter IV.

gladness; all care and mind of goodness laid apart, therefore [they]
must needs show such things in their conditions and all their life

But you shall not lightly find an ill[1] woman except it be such one
as either knoweth not, or, at leastway, considereth not, what chastity
and honesty are worth; nor seeth what mischief she doth when she
forgoeth it; nor regardeth how great a treasure, for how foul, for
how light and transitory an image of pleasure she changeth; what
a sort of ungraciousness she letteth in what time she shutteth forth
chastity; nor pondereth what bodily pleasure is; how vain and foolish
a thing which is not worth the turning of a hand, not only unworthy
wherefore she should cast away that which is the most goodly
treasure that a woman can have. And she that hath learned in books
to cast [away] this and such other things, and hath furnished and
fenced her mind with holy counsels, shall never do any villainy
For if she can find in her heart to do naughtily, having so many precepts of virtue to keep her, what should we suppose she should do,
having no knowledge of goodness at all?

And, truly, if we would call the old world to remembrance and
rehearse their time, we shall find no learned woman that ever was
ill:[1] where I could bring forth an hundred good as Cornelia, the
mother of [the] Gracchi, which was an example of all goodness and
chastity and taught her children her ownself. . . . Also Sulpitia, wife of
Caleno, left behind her holy precepts of matrimony that she had used
in her living herself, of whom the poet Martial writeth* on this wise:

> Readeth Sulpitia all young women,
> That cast your mind to please one man.
> Readeth Sulpitia also all men,
> That do intend to please one woman.
> Of honest and virtuous love doth she tell,
> Chaste pastimes, plays, and pleasure.
> Whose books, who so considereth well
> Shall say, there is none holier.

There hath been seen in our time the four daughters of Queen
Isabella,* of whom I spake a little before, that were well learned all
It is told me with great praise and marvel in many places of this
country that Dame Joan, the wife of King Philip, mother unto Caro
that now is, was wont to make answer in Latin, and that without any
study, unto the orations that were made, after the custom in towns
unto new princes.

And, likewise, the Englishmen say by their Queen [Katherine]
sister unto the said Dame Joan. The same saith everybody by the
other two sisters which be dead in Portugal. The which four sister
there were no queens by any men [held] in remembrance more

---

[1] *ill*, bad or evil.

chaste of body than they; none of better name; none better loved of their subjects; none more favoured nor that kept both them and all theirs better without spot of villainy; there were none that more hated filthiness and wantonness; none that ever did more perfectly fulfil all the points of a good woman.

Now if a man may be suffered among queens to speak of more mean folks, I would reckon among this sort the daughters of S.T.M.Kn.,* M.E. and C. and with them their kinswoman M.G: Whom their father not content only to have them good and very chaste, would also they should be well learned, supposing that by that mean they should be more truly and surely chaste. Wherein neither that great wise man is deceived, nor none other that are of the same opinion. For the study of learning is such a thing that it occupieth one's mind wholly and lifteth it up unto the knowledge of most goodly manners, and plucketh it from the remembrance of such things as be foul. And if any such thought come into their mind, either the mind well fortified with the precepts of good living avoideth them away, or else it giveth none heed unto those things that be vile and foul when it hath other most goodly and pure pleasure wherewith it is delighted. And, therefore, I suppose that Pallas, the goddess of wisdom and cunning, and all the Muses were fained in old time to be virgins.

And the mind set upon learning and wisdom shall not only abhor from foul lust, that is to say, the most white thing from soot and the most pure from spots, but also it shall leave all such light and trifling pleasures wherein the light fantasies of maids have delight, as songs, dances, and such other wanton and peevish plays. 'A woman', saith Plutarch, 'given unto learning will never delight in dancing.' But here, peradventure, a man would ask, 'What learning a woman should be set unto; and what shall she study?' I have told you, the study of wisdom: that which doth instruct their manners and inform their living and teacheth them the way of good and holy life.

WHAT BOOKS BE TO BE READ AND WHAT NOT[1]

Saint Jerome writing unto Laeta* of the teaching of Paula commandeth thus: 'Let her learn to hear nothing nor speak but if that appertaineth unto the fear of God.' Nor there is no doubt but he will counsel the same of reading. There is a use nowadays worse than among the pagans, that books written in our mothers' tongues [and] that be made but for idle men and women to read, have none other matter but of war and love. Of the which books I think it shall not need to give any precepts.

I speak unto Christian folks. What need I to tell what a mischief is

---

[1] Book I, Chapter V.

toward when straw and dry wood is cast into the fire. Yea, but these be written, say they, for idle folk, as though idleness were not a vice great enough of itself without firebrands be put unto it wherewith the fire may catch a man altogether and more hot. What should a maid do with *amour* which once to name were a shame for her? I have heard tell that in some places gentlewomen behold marvellous busily the plays and joustings of armed men, and give sentence and judgment of them; and that the men fear and set more by their judgment than the men's. It cannot likely be a chaste mind that is occupied with thinking on *amour* and tourney and man's valiance. What place among these be for chastity, unarmed and weak! A woman that useth those feats drinketh poison in her heart. Of whom this care and these words be the plain sayings: This is a deadly sickness, nor yet ought to be showed of me, but to be covered and held under lest it hurt others with the smell and defile them with the infection. . . .

Wherefore I wonder of the holy preachers that when they make great ado about many small matters many times, they cry not out on this in every sermon. I marvel that wise fathers will suffer their daughters, or that husbands will suffer their wives, or that the manners and customs of people will dissemble and overlook that women shall use to read wantonness. It were fitting that common laws and officers should not only look upon the courts and matters of suit, but also manners both common and private. Therefore it were convenient by a common law to put away foul, ribald songs out of the people's mouths: which be so used as though nothing ought to be sung in the city but foul and filthy songs that no good man can hear without shame nor no wise man without displeasure.

They that made such songs seem to have no other purpose but to corrupt the manners of young folks; and they do none otherwise than they that infect the commonweal with poison. What a custom is this, that a song shall not be regarded but it be full of filthiness? And this, the laws ought to take heed of and of those ungracious books such as be in my country in Spain: *Amadis, Florisande, Tirante, Tristan,* and *Celestina*, the bawdy mother of naughtiness; in France, *Lancelot du Lac, Paris and Vienne, Ponthus and Sidonia,* and *Melusine*; in Flanders, *Flor and Whitfleur, Leonel and Canamour, Curias and Floret, Pryamus and Thisbe*; in England, *Parthenope, Genarides, Hippomadon, William and Meliour, Libius and Arthur, Guy, Bevis,* and many other; and some translated out of Latin into vulgar speeches, as the unsavoury conceits of Poggio and Æneas Silvius' *Eurialus and Lucrece*, which books but idle men wrote, unlearned and set all upon filth and viciousness. In whom I wonder what should delight men but[1] the vice pleaseth them so much. As for learning, none is to be looked for in those men which saw never so much as a shadow of learning themself. . . .

[1] *but*, except.

Now what books ought to be read. Some everybody knoweth, as the gospels and the Acts and the Epistles of the Apostles, and the Old Testament, St Jerome, SS. Cyprian, Augustine, Ambrose, Hilary, [and] Gregory; [also] Plato, Cicero, Seneca, and such other. But as touching some, wise and sad men must be asked counsel of in them. Nor the woman ought not to follow her own judgment, lest when she hath but a light entering in learning, she should take false for true; hurtful instead of wholesome; foolish and peevish for sad and wise. She shall find in such books as are worthy to be read, all things more witty and full of greater pleasure and more sure to trust unto; which shall both profit the life and marvellously delight the mind.

Therefore on holy days continually and sometime on working days, let her read or hear such as shall lift up the mind to God, and set it in a Christian quietness and make the living better. Also, it should be best afore she go to Mass to read at home the gospel and epistle of the day, and with it some exposition if she have any. Now when thou comest from Mass and hast overlooked thy house, as much as pertaineth unto thy charge, read with a quiet mind some of these [books] that I have spoken of if thou canst read, if not, hear. And on some working days do likewise, if thou be not letted with some necessary business in thy house and thou have books at hand, and specially if there be any long space between the holy days.

For think not that holy days be ordained of the Church to play on and to sit idle and talk with thy gossips, but unto the intent that then thou mayest more intentively and with a more quiet mind think of God and this life of ours and the life in heaven that is to come.

COLOPHON: Imprinted at London in Fleet Street in the house of Thomas Berthelet near to the conduit at the sign of Lucrece [1529?].

THOMAS LUPSET
1498?–1530

Thomas Lupset was born in London about 1498, not far from St Paul's School, which was to have an important bearing on his life through its founder, John Colet. He was the son of prosperous middle-class parents, Thomas and Alice Lupset. A member of the Company of Goldsmiths, Lupset had ample means to afford his son a good education. In his early youth the younger Lupset went to live in the household of Dean Colet, who was probably a friend of his parents, and attended St Paul's School, where his talents were recognized by William Lily. In 1513 Lupset went to

Pembroke Hall, Cambridge, at the suggestion of Colet, but he disliked it, and left after a few months.

During his short stay, he met Erasmus, who was teaching Greek at the university, and aided him in preparing several Greek MSS., particularly the New Testament, Novum Instrumentum. *Preparing manuscripts for the press was a congenial task for Lupset, and by 1520 he had helped Thomas Linacre with his editions of Galen, and had journeyed to Paris to attend to the second edition of Sir Thomas More's* Utopia.

On his return to England, Lupset entered Corpus Christi College, Oxford, taking a Master of Arts degree in 1521. With the recommendations of Linacre and More, he was immediately appointed a Wolsey Lecturer in the College. Though he was very popular, Lupset resigned the post in 1523, leaving for Italy to study at the University of Padua. While there he stayed with Reginald Pole, whom he had probably known in London, and their friendship is immortalized in Thomas Strachey's Dialogue between Pole and Lupset.

In the next seven years, the last of his life, Lupset crowded writing, teaching, and editing. Precocious and eager to get ahead, according to his first biographer George Lily, in Elogia virorum, *Lupset took the various tasks that came his way: he travelled to Trent as secretary to Richard Pace; he helped a group of Venetian scholars edit the first Greek edition of Galen's works. He returned to England in 1527, and was sent to Paris to urge Pole to aid the king's divorce; he served as secretary to Cardinal Wolsey; he tutored two youths, Edmund Withipole and Christopher Smith, sons of London merchants; and he found time during his last two years to write three treatises. Taxing his strength and following Colet's example of keeping to an abstemious diet that weakened his health, Lupset died of tuberculosis in London in 1530.*

His writings are: A treatise of charitie *(1533);* A compendious treatyse, teachyng the waye of dyenge well *(1534); and* An exhortation to yonge men *(1535). Each of them was printed posthumously. The first work is a moral treatise, based on the Epistles of St Paul. It ends with a short dialogue between a brother and sister, discussing the full meaning of the word 'charity'. A compendious treatyse follows the pattern of the* Ars Moriendi. *In An exhortation Lupset proposes a way of life for the Christian humanist who while obeying St Paul should profit by the advice of Plato.*

Besides these treatises, Lupset wrote a dialogue, not extant, mentioned by George Lily, and three letters in Epistolae aliquot eruditorum. *He translated* A sermon [of Chrysostom]; that no man is hurted but of hym selfe *(1542), and probably Colet's* Convocation Sermon *(1530?).*

In his critical study of Lupset, John Gee claims a high place for the young English scholar among the writers of early Tudor prose because of the 'strong and direct influence', which his writings show 'of humanistic and patristic thought; and of the general manner of expressing that thought in literary form'.

An Exhortation to Young Men

An Exhortation to Young Men persuading them to walk in the pathway that leadeth to honesty and goodness: written to a friend of his by Sir Thomas Lupset, Londoner.

TO MY WITHIPOLE

It happeneth at this time (my heartily beloved Edmund) that I am in such a place where I have no manner of books with me to pass the time after my manner and custom. And though I had here with me plenty of books, yet the place suffereth me not to spend in them any study. For you shall understand, that I lie waiting on [Thomas Wolsey] my Lord Cardinal, whose hours I must observe to be always at hand lest I be called when I am not by: the which should be straight taken for a fault of great negligence. Wherefore, now that I am well satiated with the beholding of these gay hangings that garnish here every wall, I will turn me and talk with you.

For you must know that my mind hath long coveted to show what affection I bear toward you: the which hitherto, peradventure, I never uttered unto you so plainly that you might take thereof any perfect knowledge. And that I so did keep in such outward tokens, whereof when you were with me you should have perceived my love, the cause was none other but that, indeed, I loved you. For long I have been taught, that the master never hurteth his scholar more than when he uttereth and showeth by cherishing and cokering[1] the love that he beareth to his scholars. I think you lacked with me no cherishing, but of cokering you had very little, because I was loth to hurt you: the which lothness came, I say, of that I loved you. *How masters hurt their scholars most*

But now inasmuch [as] you be of age, and also by the common board of houseling[2] admitted into the number of men, to be no more in the company of children, and specially forasmuch as my rule over you is ceased, I will not defer any longer the expressing of mine heart that no less loveth and favoureth you than if nature had made you either my son or my brother. For this always is my mind: if I have a friend in whom I find such faith and honesty that I inwardly joy in heart with him, I reckon *True friendship* straight that all his be mine without exception: So that in very deed I take to my care as my own all things that be in my friend's care. This mind had I to my friend Andrew Smith whose son Christopher, your fellow, I ever took for my son: and now I think plainly that he is so in very deed.

---

[1] *cokering*, pampering. [2] *houseling*, reception of the Eucharist.

This strength hath true love in friendship, the which hath likewise joined your father in such manner to my heart that, methink, you should be no more his son than you be mine. And though I can suffer your father to take the rule of you more than I do, yet I cannot suffer that he should care more for your profit than I do. For as I desire and wish that you never have need of me, so surely if you ever should have, it should well then appear that as nature hath given you one father, so your father's friendship hath provided for you another father. Wherefore, good Edmund, reckon no less affect[1] in me to do you good than is in your own father, whose only study and care is to see you grow and prosper toward the state of an honest man: and I, to further you to the same am as desirous as he is: and as much as I can, I will help you, both with my counsel and power, such as I have.

If you will call to your mind all the frays that have been between you and me, or between me and Smith, you shall find the causes ever depended of a care I had for your and his manners when I saw certain fantasies in you or him that jarred from true opinions: the which true opinions, above all learning, I would have masters ever teach their scholars. But now that you be of better ability to take counsel, I will begin to show you my mind in staying you for the whole course of your life, that you may in time learn what is to be done to be a good and honest man.

True opinions

You be yet in the first entry of your life, and now is the time to have a guide that may faithfully conduct you in the right way. For there be so many paths, and, for the most part, all bypaths be more worn with the steps of your foregoers than is the very true path of living, that if you go alone, you may, peradventure, long wander out of the straight way....

Wherefore, my good Withipole, take heed to my lesson. I am in doubt whether you have any other lover that can and will show you a like tale: but well I am assured that you have none that can thus teach you with a better will or have you take profit by him than I do: and of me—how long you shall have this use, it is in God's will to determine. As much as lieth in me, I will now procure and provide that these letters shall keep to your use the sum of my counsel; by the which if you order your will, I put no doubt but, first, the grace of God shall be rooted in you; and next, you shall live with a merry heart; and, finally, never to lack the commodities requisite for the short time in this world. In the which case you shall obtain the worship and dignity of a good and an honest man whose conditions I had rather see you have with poverity than in great abundance to be a man of small honesty. You may be good, honest, and rich: and

[1] *affect*, desire.

so study to be, or else think never of riches: for otherwise you shall deceive yourself, and do contrary to that way that as well worldly wisdom as the truth of our faith showeth you. But now hear what I say.

First and last (mine own good Withipole), remember earnestly to have in your mind three certain things, the which be of such value that he that forgetteth either their dignity and nature or else the degree and order of them, he cannot please neither God, nor himself, nor the world. I say, in all the course of your life there be three things to be looked so upon that the first of them must be first of you regarded; the second, next after; and the third, in his place after the two. Beware, as of deadly poison, that you ruffle not them without care, one before the other, as to take the third in the place of the first, or the second after the third, or both the second and the third before the first....

There lieth more weight and value upon the knowing and keeping of this tale, that I shall tell you, than if I could show you the way within a few months to be a man of great power, both in exceeding abundance of riches and also in passing authority of rule. Therefore, as well for the fruit that followeth, if you do after mine exhortation, as for the infinite hurts that you cannot escape if you should forget that I say, I warn and warn you again, hear this lesson with a glad ear, and print the same in your mind to execute with lively diligence the effect of this counsel wherein is contained your life and death, your joy and sorrow, as well in this world as in that shall be hereafter.

These three things be: the soul, the body, and the substance of this world. The first place hath, by good reason, the soul,   Soul seeing it is a thing immortal that is created and made after the figure and shape of Almighty God. The next, and second room, hath the body as the case and sepulchre of the soul   Body and nearest servant to the secrets of the spirit. The third room occupieth the riches and goods of this world as the necessary instruments or tools for the body, the which cannot want nor lack such things. Let then the eye of your inward   Goods of mind first and chiefly ever behold the first thing in you;   this world that is, your soul. Next thereto, have a respect to your body; and thirdly, consider the world. Care for your soul as for your chief jewel and only treasure. Care for your body for the soul's sake. Care for the world for the body's sake. Beware above all things that you go not backward as he doth that careth first to be a rich man; next, to be a healthy man; and thirdly, to be a good man: where he should do clean contrary; first, to study for goodness; next, for health; and then, for wealth.

You see so great blindness among men that some folk so careth for riches that very little they look for the health of the body, and nothing at all they mind the state of the soul. I say to you, some folks do thus. I would to God, I might not truly report, that for the most part all men, in manner nowadays, do no otherwise. Look upon either the spiritual sort or the temporal, and much ado you shall have in the great swarming multitude of this blind sort to find out them that first above all things care for their soul; next, for their body; and thirdly, for goods of this world. You shall see merchants spare no travail nor jeopardy of the body to get these goods. They be, to say the truth, so occupied in the study of this third thing that scant they have time to care for the second; and as for the first, they pass nothing thereupon. It seemeth a thing least in their thoughts: where of conveniency the same care, study, and thought that they give to the obtaining of these worldly goods, they should spend it all in the maintenance of the first thing, that is, the soul. And the small little regard that they take for the first, should be bestowed for the third: and more than they do, they should cherish the second.

The same confusion is with us scholars: for our first study is to get promotion, to get these goods, to live wealthily. In this care we busily be occupied continually. Somewhat more we cherish our bodies than doth the merchant; but our cherishing is for the longer use of these goods; not, as it should be, for the soul's sake. And as for the soul, we have as little regard as other men have, although we speak thereof more than, peradventure, other men do....

Scholars

More particularly in writings, you shall learn this lesson, if you would sometime take in your hands the New Testament, and read it with a due reverence. For I would not have you in that book forget with whom you talk. It is God that there speaketh; it is you, poor creature of God, that readeth. Consider the match,[1] and meek down your wits. Presume not in no case to think that there you understand aught. Leave devising thereupon. Submit yourself to the expositions of holy Doctors. And ever conform your consent to agree with Christ's Church. This is the surest way that you can take, both before God and man. Your obedience to the universal faith shall excuse you before God, although it might be in a false belief: and the same obedience shall also keep you out of trouble in this world, where you see how foolish meddlers be daily sore punished, both to their own undoing and also to the great sorrow and lamenting of their lovers and friends.

New Testament

Surely, the trouble is, as I have said, that it is your part to obey and to follow the Church. So that both for your soul's sake and for your bodily quietness with the comfort of your friends, I exhort you to meddle in no point of your faith otherwise than the Church shall

[1] *match*, association.

instruct and teach you. In the which obedience read for your increase
in virtue the story of our Master Christ that lively expresseth the
whole course of a virtuous life.[1] And there you shall hear the Holy
Ghost command you to 'seek first afore all things the kingdom of
heaven; and then (saith the Spirit of God) all other things appertaining to the body and world shall by themself follow without
your care'.[2]

In reading the gospels, I would you had at hand Chrysostom and
Jerome, by whom you might surely be brought to a perfect understanding of the text. And hereafter at leisure, I would
you read the *Ethics* of Aristotle, either under some expert   Reading the
philosopher, or else with comment of Futtiratius.* And   gospels
let Plato be familiar with you, specially in the book, that he writeth,
De Republica. Also you shall find much for your knowledge in the
moral philosophy of Cicero, as in his books, *De Officiis* [*Of Moral
Duties*]; *De Senectute* [*Of Old Age*]; *De Fato* [*Of Fate*]; *De Finibus*
[*Of Ends*]; *De Academicis* [*Of Academic Philosophers*]; *Questio de Thusc.*
[*Tuscalan Disputations*]. Specially read with diligence the works of
Seneca, of whom ye shall learn as much of virtue as man's wit can
teach you. These works I think sufficient to show you what is virtue,
and what is vice; and by reading of these, you shall grow into a high
courage to rise in a judgment above the common sort to esteem this
world according to his worthiness, that is, far under the dignity of
the virtues, the which the mind of man conceiveth and rejoiceth in.
These books shall lift you up from the clay of this earth and set you
in a hill of high contemplation from whence you shall look down
and despise the vanity that foolish men take in the deceitful pomp of
this short and wretched life. More books I will not advise you for
your soul's study and to read than these, except it be *Enchiridion* that
Erasmus writeth, a work, doubtless, that in few leaves containeth an
infinite knowledge of goodness.

Think not, my good Edmund, that I over charge you. For I know
what pleasure you have in reading; and in better books you cannot
bestow your pleasure than in these, the which be in number but few,
and yet they shall do you more good than the reading here and there
of many other. I would to Jesus, I had in your age followed like
counsel in reading only these works, the which now at last by a great
loss of time in reading of others, I have chosen out for my purpose
to refresh with them the rest of my life. And I counsel you now to
begin to do the same when time and convenient leisure shall be given
you to read any book.

The second care is for the body; the which you must   Bodily
cherish, as much as may stand with the service of your   health
former thought and study, for your chief treasure. Have a respect

[1] Matt. vi.   [2] Luke xii. 31.

to keep your body in good health, the which resteth in the air and in your diet. Abide not where corruption or infection is: Eat not nor drink not out of time or measure; nor yet of such meats and drinks as be more delicate and pleasant than wholesome. Know the measure of your stomach before you overload your belly. Choke not your appetite; but feed your hunger. Drown not your lust, but quench your thirst; and ever for your soul's sake, keep you from gluttony. Fast sometime, both for devotion and also for your health. Sleep rather too little than too much: as much as you take from sleep, so much you add to your life. For sleep is death for the time. Exercise you continually; for in labour, your body shall find strength; and lustiness is gotten by the use of your limbs. Let never the sun rise before you: you shall have to all your affairs the longer day. And ever for your soul's sake, flee from idleness; the which is not only in him that doth nothing, but also in him that doth not well: and idle you be, when you be not well occupied.

Corrupt air. Diet

Fast

Sleep

Exercise

Idleness

Be temperate in your lusts touching the bodily pleasure. The time shall not be long till your friends, by God's grace, will provide you of an honest mate. In the mean season let the fear and love of God keep you in chastity, the which appertaineth to your chief care, for needs you must so do, seeing that otherwise lechery shall sore defile your soul, the which you must regard before the body's appetite. For this part I would you read, as your leisure shall be, a little work of Galen, *De bona valetudine tuenda* [On keeping good health]. And in the works aforenamed, you shall find many things that shall instruct you well for this part also and likewise for the third; the which third, ever hath occupied men's stomachs more than either the first or the second. Wherefore as well in Holy Scripture as in the other philosophers, and especially in Seneca, you shall find many lessons that appertain to the third care. This third care is for the goods in the world....

Yet before I leave this third care, I will show you my mind; what is chiefly in this part to be cared for as the best portion of worldly riches. Surely I reckon no possession of lands, nor yet no substance of merchandise, nor yet no abundance of money to be comparable to a good friend. Therefore above all things in this world, procure to have plenty of friends and make of them your compte as of your best and most precious goods. Always your friend shall be more profitable to you than any treasure, or power besides, can be. How you shall know them that be worthy to be your friends, and by what means, and what way friends be both gotten and also kept, ye shall best learn in Cicero's little book *De Amicitia* [On friendship]. I cannot say

Temperance

A good friend

in this thing any point that is left of him, wherefore I remit you to that work.

Another point touching this care of worldly goods is to use accordingly your wife, when the time shall come that you shall have one. For to obtain substance of goods, it lieth as much in the wife to keep *that* you bring home as in your travail   Housewife to bring home. And surely unless she be the keeper and sparer, the husband shall little go forward in his labour of getting. And the very truth is that there is no evil housewife but for her faults the good man is to be blamed. For I am utterly of this opinion that the man may make, shape, and form the woman as he will. I would go farther with you in this thing, and show somewhat of the way to order your household if I saw not this matter so largely intreated of divers philosophers of whom ye shall hear as much as may be said on this thing.

Specially I would you read with most diligence the proper book that Xenophon writeth hereof. It is called *Oeconomicus**: that is to say, 'the craft to order and keep a house', where this author giveth such counsel for all the course of an honest man's life in this world to grow in riches under the means of discretion and wisdom that no man, in my mind, can say more therein or better. The which judgment of mine I doubt not but you will approve when you have read the said work. It is translated out of Greek into Latin by one Raphael [Maffei]. But in his translation the work loseth a great part of the grace that it hath in the Greek tongue, and also his translation in many places is false. And it plainly appeareth that Raphael understood not well what Xenophon wrote in Greek. I have therefore, for divers of my friends' sake, translated the same work out of the Greek tongue into English; and you shall have the same with my good will when your pleasure is to read it....

To confirm you the faster in these right opinions, I would you read the little book of Epictetus, entitled his *Enchiridion*, well translated into Latin by Angelo Politian. But, to say the truth, the work is so briefly and darkly written that without a comment or a good master you shall not perceive the fruit of the text. I am in mind, if I may have thereto leisure, to translate the comment of Simplicius* upon the said work: and then shall you find such sweetness in that book that I believe it will ravish you into a higher contemplation than a great sort of our religious men come to. And one thing, believe me, my good Withipole, that in reading of these old substantial works, the which I have named unto you, shall, besides the perfection of knowledge, gender a certain judgment in you that you shall never take delight nor pleasure in the trifles and vain inventions that men nowadays write to the inquieting of all good order; by reason that the most part of men that read these new

flittering[1] works lack perfect judgment to descry a weighty sentence
from a light clause, the which judgment cannot be gotten but by a
long exercising of our wits with the best sort of writers. And to me,
it is a pitiful thing to behold the foolish dreams of these young clerks
in men's hands, and to see these noble old works of the holy fathers
and philosophers lie untouched. Where if these new writers speak
anything well, it is piked[2] out of these ancient books. But whatsoever these petty clerks pike out nowadays, for the most part, it is
defaced and brought out of good fashion with their evil handling

I will now make an end. It is sufficient to a willing mind, such as,
I trust, is in you to have with a friend's finger the way appointed
where you must walk if you will proceed in virtue: the which is only
the thing that maketh a man both happy in this world and also
blessed in the world to come. Believe you my counsel, and see
the same; or else hereafter you will, peradventure, bewail your
negligence.

                         Fare ye well

At More, a place of my lord Cardinal's, on the feast of Saint
Bartholomew. 1529.

COLOPHON: *Londoni in aedibus Thomae Berthelet....1535.*

SIR THOMAS ELYOT
1490?–1546

*Sir Thomas Elyot was one of the few in his circle of learned friends—
Linacre, More, Colet, Lily, and Cranmer—who did not attend either
Oxford or Cambridge. The son of Richard and Alice Elyot, he was born
in Somersetshire about 1490. His only sister Margery married Robert
Puttenham, reputed author of* The Arte of English Poesie *(1589).*

*The elder Elyot was a successful lawyer, and held several lucrative
positions in London courts. Shortly after he was appointed Judge of the
Common Pleas Court, in 1513, Henry VIII knighted him. He made a
constant companion of his young son, and supervised his law studies.
Thomas Elyot declares that after his twelfth year he had no formal education. What he knew of Greek and Latin was learned under the personal
guidance of Thomas Linacre, 'a worshipfull phisition and one of the
most renouned at that tyme in Englond'.*

*In 1511 the position of clerk of the Assize of the Western Circuit was
vacant, and Elyot was appointed through the aid of his father. This was*

---

[1] *flittering*, fluttering.   [2] *piked*, pirated.

the first in a series of political appointments that included clerk of the Privy Council, sheriff of Oxfordshire and, later, Cambridgeshire, and ambassador to the Court of Charles V. He was elected to Parliament from Cambridge in 1542.

In spite of the many difficult tasks that Elyot performed for Henry VIII and Cardinal Wolsey, he claimed that neither of them gave him adequate pay. In 1530 he declared that he was 'discharged Clerk of the Council without any recompence', and rewarded only with the 'order of Knighthode, honorable and onerouse having moche lasse to lyve on than bifore'. His principal revenue came from estates in Oxfordshire and Cambridgeshire left him by his father.

Between 1531 and 1535, when Elyot served as English ambassador to Charles V, England was smarting under the religious and political upheaval caused by the Reformation. His first task at the emperor's court was to help Stephen Vaughan, the king's special envoy, track down the English heretic William Tyndale, who was then living in Antwerp. The term 'heretic' was soon to confront Elyot himself. As a close friend of Sir Thomas More, Bishop John Fisher, and Cardinal Wolsey, he was suspected of favouring the old faith. To settle the matter, he took the Oath of Supremacy in 1535. And through his duties as ambassador to the court of Charles V, he managed to keep out of England during the height of the Reformation fury.

Before 1540 Elyot retired from the king's service, and his last participation in a public affair was at the reception for Anne of Cleves at Blackheath. His name appears among the noblemen who were ordered 'to receive the Ladie Anne Cleave and wait on the Kinge'.

Elyot married Margaret Abarrow of Hampshire soon after his father's death in 1523. They had no children, and little is known of his married life. He died on 26 March 1546.

Duties of public office did not keep Elyot from undertaking arduous literary tasks. His most important work is The boke named The gouernor (1531). Other of his major works are discussed elsewhere in this volume. Among his lesser writings are three short dialogues; Pasquil the playne (1532); Of the knowledeg whiche maketh a wise man (1533); and The defence of good women (1545). His last work, A preseruatiue agaynste deth (1545) is a devotional treatise based on Scriptural texts and written 'as well for myn owne erudicion as for the remembrance of other men'.

The Gouernor, considered the earliest English treatise on the theory of education, consists of three books, two of which contain over thirty chapters. Though his vigorous insistence on reforms in the Tudor system of education caused considerable antagonism, the work won immediate recognition. He believed that the foundation for high moral training lay in a thorough knowledge of the Greek and Latin classics.

The plan of the Gouernor follows such medieval treatises as John of

Salisbury's Polycraticus; De Regimine Principum, *begun by St Thomas Aquinas and finished by Bartholemeus de Lucca; Castiglione's* Il Cortegiano (*1518*); *Francisco Patrizzi's* De Regno et Regis Institutione (*1518*); *and Erasmus's* Institutio Principis Christiani (*1516*). *The last work is the only one that Elyot acknowledges as a source. The* Gouernor *was reprinted seven times before 1580.*

_____

The Governor

The Book named the Governor devised by Thomas Elyot, Knight

THE PROHEME

The proheme of Thomas Elyot, knight, unto the most noble and victorious prince, King Henry the Eighth, King of England and France, Defender of the true Faith, and Lord of Ireland.

I, late considering, most excellent Prince and mine only redoubted sovereign lord, my duty that I owe to my natural country with my faith, also of allegiance and oath wherewith I am double bounded unto your majesty, moreover the accompt that I have to render for that one little talent delivered to me to employ, as I suppose, to the increase of virtue, I am, as God judge me, violently stirred to devulgate or set forth some part of my study, trusting thereby to acquit me of my duties to God, your Highness, and this my country.

Wherefore taking comfort and boldness partly of your grace's most benevolent inclination toward the universal weal of your subjects, partly inflamed with zeal, I have now enterprised to describe in our vulgar tongue the form of a just publicweal. Which matter I have gathered as well of the sayings of most noble authors, Greeks and Latins, as by mine own experiences—I being continually trained in some daily affairs of the publicweal of this your most noble realm almost from my childhood. Which attempt is not of presumption to teach any person, I, myself, having most need of teaching, but only to the intent that men which will be studious about the weal public may find the thing thereto expedient compendiously written.

And forasmuch as this present book treateth of the education of them that hereafter may be deemed worthy to be governors of the publicweal under your Highness (which Plato affirmeth* to be the first and chief part of a publicweal; Solomon saying, also, Where governors be not, the people shall fall into ruin),[1] I, therefore, have

[1] Prov. xi. 14.

named it, *The Governor*, and do now dedicate it unto your Highness as the first fruits of my study. Verily, trusting that your most excellent wisdom will therein esteem my loyal heart and diligent endeavour by the example of Artaxerxes,* the noble King of Persia, who rejected not the poor husbandman which offered to him his homely hands full of clean water but most graciously received it with thanks, esteeming the present not after the value, but rather to the will of the giver. Semblably, King Alexander retained with him the poet Cherilus* honourably for writing his history, although that the poet was but of a small estimation. Which that Prince did, not for lack of judgment, he being of excellent learning as a disciple to Aristotle, but to the intent that his liberality employed on Cherilus should animate or give courage to others much better learned to contend with him in a semblable enterprise.

And if, most virtuous Prince, I may perceive your Highness to be herewith pleased, I shall soon after (God giving me quietness) present your grace with the residue of my study and labours: wherein your Highness shall well perceive that I nothing esteem so much in this world as your royal estate, my most dear sovereign lord, and the publicweal of my country. Protesting unto your excellent Majesty, that where I commend herein any one virtue or dispraise any one vice, I mean the general description of the one and the other without any other particular meaning to the reproach of any one person. To the which protestation I am now driven, through the malignity of this present time all disposed to malicious detraction.

Wherefore, I most humbly beseech your Highness to deign to be patron and defender of this little work against the assaults of malign interpreters which fail not to rent and deface the renown of writers, they, themselves, being in nothing to the publicweal profitable: Which is by no man sooner perceived than by your Highness, being both in wisdom and very nobility equal to the most excellent princes whom, I beseech God, ye may surmount in long life and perfect felicity. Amen.

THE SECOND AND THIRD DECAY OF LEARNING AMONG GENTLEMEN[1]

The second occasion wherefore gentlemen's children seldom have sufficient learning is avarice: for where[2] their parents will not adventure to send them far out of their proper countries, partly for fear of death, which, perchance, dare not approach them at home with their father; partly for expense of money which they suppose would be less in their own houses or in a village with some of their tenants or friends, having seldom any regard to the teacher, whether he be well

---

[1] Book I, Chapter XIII.　　　　[2] *for where*, wherefore.

learned or ignorant. For if they hire a schoolmaster to teach in their houses, they chiefly inquire with how small a salary he will be contented, and never do insearch how much good learning he hath, and how among well learned men he is therein esteemed: Using therein less diligence than in taking servants whose service is of much less importance, and to a good schoolmaster is not in profit to be compared.

A gentleman ere he take a cook into his service, he will first diligently examine him: how many sorts of meats, potages, and sauces he can perfectly make; how well he can season them that they may be both pleasant and nourishing. Yea, and if it be but a falconer, he will scrupulously inquire what skill he hath in feeding, called diet, and keeping of his hawk from all sickness; also, how he can reclaim her and prepare her to flight. And to such a cook or falconer whom he findeth expert, he spareth not to give much wages with other bounteous rewards. But of a schoolmaster, to whom he will commit his child to be fed with learning and instructed in virtue, whose life shall be the principal monument of his name and honour, he never maketh further inquiry but where he may have a schoolmaster and with how little charge. And if one be, perchance, founded well learned but he will not take pains to teach without he may have a great salary, he then speaketh nothing more, or else saith, 'What, shall so much wages be given to a schoolmaster which would keep me two servants?' To whom may be said these words: that by his son being well learned, he shall receive more commodity and also worship than by the service of a hundred cooks and falconers.

The third cause of this hindrance is negligence of parents, which I do specially note in this point there have been divers, as well gentlemen as of the nobility, that delighting to have their sons excellent in learning have provided for them cunning masters who substantially have taught them grammar and very well instructed them to speak Latin elegantly, whereof the parents have taken much delectation; but when they have had of grammar sufficient, and be comen to the age of fourteen years and do approach or draw toward the estate of man, which age is called mature or ripe (wherein not only the said learning continued by much experience shall be perfectly digested and confirmed in perpetual remembrance, but also more serious learning contained in other liberal sciences, and, also, philosophy, would then be learned), the parents, that thing nothing regarding, but being sufficed that their children can only speak Latin properly or make verses without matter or sentence, they from thenceforth do suffer them to live in idleness, or else, putting them to service do, as it were, banish them from all virtuous study or exercise of that which they before learned. So that we may behold divers young gentlemen who in their infancy and childhood were wondered at for their aptness to learning and prompt speaking of elegant Latin which now being men not only have forgotten their congruity (as is the common word) and unneth[1] can speak one whole sentence in true Latin. But that worse is, hath all learning in derision; and in scorn thereof will of wantonness speak the most barbarously that they can imagine.

Now some man will require me to show mine opinion if it be necessary that gentlemen should after the age of fourteen years continue in study. And to be plain and true therein, I dare affirm that if the elegant speaking of Latin be not added to other doctrine, little fruit may come of the tongue since Latin is but a natural speech; and the fruit of speech is wise sentence which is gathered and made of sundry learnings. And who that hath nothing but language only, may be no more praised than a popinjay, a pye,[2] or a stare[3] when they speak featly.[4]

There be many nowadays in famous schools and universities which be so much given to the study of tongues only that when they write epistles, they seem to the reader that like to a trumpet they make a sound without any purpose, whereunto men do hearken more for the noise than for any delectation that thereby is moved.

Wherefore they be much abused[5] that suppose eloquence to be only in words or colours of rhetoric. For, as Tully saith, 'What is so furious or mad a thing as a vain sound of words* of the best sort and most ornate, containing neither cunning nor sentence?' Undoubtedly, very eloquence is in every tongue where any matter or act done, or to be done, is expressed in words clean, propitious, ornate, and comely: whereof sentences be so aptly compact that they by a virtue inexplicable do draw unto them the minds and consent of the hearers—they being therewith either persuaded, moved, or to delectation induced.

What eloquence is

Also every man is not an orator that can write an epistle or a flattering oration in Latin: whereof the last (as God help me) is too much used. For a right orator may not be without a much better furniture: Tully saying that to him [an orator] belongeth the explicating or unfolding of sentence with a great estimation in giving counsel concerning matters of great importance: Also to him appertaineth the stirring and quickening of people languishing or despairing, and to moderate them that be rash and unbridled....

Wherefore inasmuch as in an orator is required to be a heap of all manner of learning which of some is called 'the world of science', of others 'the circle of doctrine', which is in one word of Greek, encyclopedia, therefore at this day may be found but a very few orators. For they that come in message from princes, be, for honour, named

[1] unneth, scarcely.   [2] pye, magpie.   [3] stare, starling.
[4] featly, cleverly.   [5] abused, deceived.

now orators if they be in any degree of worship: only poor men, having equal or more learning being called messengers. Also they which do only teach rhetoric—which is the science whereby is taught an artificial form of speaking wherein is the power to persuade, move, and delight, or by that science only do speak or write without any adminiculation[1] of other sciences—ought to be named rhetoricians, declamators, artificial speakers, named in Greek, *logodedali*, or any other name than orators.

Semblably they that make verses, expressing thereby none other learning but the craft of versifying, be not of ancient writers named poets, but only called versifiers. For the name of a poet, whereat now (specially in this realm) men have such indignation that they use only poets and poetry in contempt of eloquence, was in ancient time in high estimation: insomuch that all wisdom was supposed to be therein included, and poetry was the first philosophy that ever was known: Whereby men from their childhood were brought to the reason how to live well, learning thereby not only manners and natural affections but also the wonderful works of nature; mixing serious matter with things that were pleasant: As it shall be manifest to them that shall be so fortunate to read the noble works of Plato and Aristotle, wherein he shall find the authority of poets frequently alleged. Yea, and what more is, in poets was supposed to be science, mystical and inspired. And therefore in Latin they were called *vates*, which word signifieth as much as 'prophets'.

And therefore Tully in his *Tusculane Questions** supposeth that a poet cannot abundantly express verses sufficient and complete, or that his eloquence may flow without labour—words well-sounding and plenteous without celestial instinction: Which is also by Plato ratified. But since we be now occupied in the defence of poets, it shall not be incongruent to our matter to show what profit may be taken by the diligent reading of ancient poets, contrary to the false opinion that now reigneth of them that suppose that in the works of poets is contained nothing but bawdry (such is their foul word of reproach) and unprofitable leasings.[2]

But first I will interpret some verses of Horace wherein he expresseth the office of poets. And after will I resort to a more plain demonstration of some wisdoms and counsels contained in some verses of poets. Horace, in his second book of Epistles*, saith in this wise, or much like:

> The poet fashioneth by some pleasant mean,
> The speech of children tender and unsure:
> Pulling their ears from words unclean.
> Giving to them precepts that are pure,

---

[1] *adminiculation*, aid.　　　　[2] *leasings*, falsehoods.

Rebuking envy and wrath if it dure,[1]
Things well done, he can by example commend.
The needy and sick he doth also his cure,
To recomfort, if aught he can amend.

But they which be ignorant in poets will, perchance, object, as is
their manner against these verses, saying that in Terence and others
that were writers of comedies—also, Ovid, Catullus, Martial, and all
that rout of lascivious poets that wrote epistles and ditties of love,
some called in Latin *elegiae* and some *epigrammata*—is nothing contained but incitation to lechery.

First, comedies which they suppose to be a doctrinal of ribaldry
they be undoubtedly a picture or, as it were, a mirror of man's life
wherein evil is not taught but discovered to the intent that men
beholding the promptness of youth unto vice; the snares of harlots
and bawds laid for young minds; the deceit of servants; the chances
of fortune contrary to men's expectation, they being thereof warned
may prepare themselves to resist or prevent occasion.

Semblably, remembering the wisdoms, advertisements, counsels,
dissuasion from vice, and other profitable sentences most eloquently
and familiarly showed in those comedies, undoubtedly there shall
be no little fruit out of them gathered. And if the vices in them expressed should be [the] cause that minds of the readers should be
corrupted, then by the same argument not only interludes in English
but also sermons wherein some vice is declared should be to the
beholders and hearers like occasion to increase sinners.

And that by comedies good counsel is ministered, it appeareth by the
sentence of Parmeno in the second comedy [*Eunuchus* v, 7] of Terence:

In this thing I triumph in mine own conceit,
That I have founden for all young men the way
How they of harlots shall know the deceit,
Their wits, their manners, that thereby they may
Them perpetually hate: for so much as they
Out of their own houses be fresh and delicate,
Feeding curiously; at home all the day
Living beggarly in most wretched estate.

There be many more words spoken which I purposely omit to
translate, notwithstanding the substance of the whole sentence is
herein comprised.

But now to come to other poets. What may be better said than is
written by Plautus in his first comedy [*Amphitryon* II, 2]:

Verily, virtue doth all things excel.
For if liberty, health, living, and substance,

[1] *dure*, exists.

Our country, our parents, and children do well,
It hapneth by virtue: she doth all advance.
Virtue hath all thing under governance,
And in whom of virtue is founden great plenty,
Anything that is good may never be dainty.

...

I could recite a great number of semblable good sentences out of
these and other wanton poets [Elyot quotes here from works of
Ovid and Martial] who in the Latin do express them incomparably
with more grace and delectation to the reader than our English
tongue may yet comprehend. Wherefore since good and wise
matter may be picked out of these poets, it were no reason for some
light matter that is in their verses to abandon therefore all their works,
no more than it were to forbear or prohibit a man to come into a
fair garden lest the redolent savours of sweet herbs and flowers shall
move him to wanton courage, or lest in gathering good and wholesome herbs he may happen to be stung with a nettle. No wise man
entereth into a garden but he soon espieth good herbs from nettles,
and treadeth the nettles under his feet while he gathereth good herbs
Whereby he taketh no damage, or if he be stung, he maketh light
of it and shortly forgetteth it. Semblably, if he do read wanton
matter mixed with wisdom, he putteth the worst under foot and
sorteth out the best: Or if his courage be stirred or provoked, he
remembereth the little pleasure and great detriment that should
ensue of it, and withdrawing his mind to some other study or
exercise, shortly forgetteth it.

And, therefore, among the Jews though it were prohibited to
children until they came to ripe years to read the books of *Genesis*,
of the *Judges*, *Canticum Canticorum* [*Canticle of Canticles*], and some
part of the book of Ezechiel, the Prophet, for that in them was contained some matter which might happen to incense the young mind
Wherein were sparks of carnal concupiscence, yet after certain years
of men's age, it was lawful for every man to read and diligently
study those works.

So although I do not approve the lesson of wanton poets to be
taught unto all children, yet think I convenient and necessary that
when the mind is become constant and courage is assuaged, or that
children of their natural disposition be shamefast and continent, none
ancient poet would be excluded from the lesson of such one as
desireth to come to the perfection of wisdom.

But in defending of orators and poets, I had almost forgotten
where I was. Verily, there may no man be an excellent poet nor
orator unless he have part of all other doctrine, specially of noble
philosophy. And to say truth, no man can apprehend the very

delectation that is in the lesson of noble poets unless he have read very much and in divers authors of divers learnings. Wherefore, as I late said, to the augmentation of understanding, called in Latin *intellectus et mens* [intellect and mind], is required to be much reading and vigilant study in every science, specially of that part of philosophy named moral which instructeth men in virtue and politic governance. Also, no noble author, specially of them that wrote in Greek or Latin before twelve hundred and fifty years passed, is not for any cause omitted.

For therein I am of Quintilian's opinion,* that there is few or none ancient work that yieldeth not some fruit or commodity to the diligent readers. And it is a very gross or obstinate wit that by reading much, is not somewhat amended. Concerning the election of other authors to be read, I have, as I trust, declared sufficiently my conceit and opinion in the tenth and eleventh chapters of this little treatise.

Finally, like as a delicate tree that cometh of a kernel which as soon as it burgeoneth out leaves, if it be plucked up, or it be sufficiently rooted and laid in a corner, it becometh dry or rotten and no fruit cometh of it; if it be removed and set in another air or earth, which is of contrary qualities where it was before, it either semblably dieth, or beareth no fruit, or else the fruit that cometh of it loseth his verdure and taste and, finally, his estimation. So the pure and excellent learning, whereof I have spoken, though it be sown in a child never so timely and springeth and burgeoneth never so pleasantly, if, before it take a deep root in the mind of the child, it be laid aside, either by too much solace or continual attendance in service, or else is translated to another study, which is of a more gross or unpleasant quality, before it be confirmed or established by often reading or diligent exercise, in conclusion, it vanisheth and cometh to nothing.

Wherefore let men reply as they list, but, in mine opinion, men be wonderfully deceived nowadays (I dare not say with the persuasion of avarice) that do put their children at the age of fourteen or fifteen years to the study of the laws of the realm of England. I will show to them reasonable causes why, if they will patiently hear me, informed partly by mine own experience.

TITLE-PAGE: *Londini in aedibus* Thos. Berthelet.... 1531.

STEPHEN GARDINER

c. 1483–1555

One of the most capable churchmen of his time, Stephen Gardiner, Bishop of Winchester, played an important role as theologian, humanist, and jurist in shaping the religious and social policies of the English Reformation and the Marian Reaction. Born at Bury St Edmunds, Gardiner was the son of John Gardiner, a wealthy clothmaker, and his wife Agnes. The earliest records concerning Gardiner's education show that he visited Paris, staying for a time with the Eden family. They most probably introduced him to Erasmus, then living in the French capital, whom Gardiner never ceased to admire.

Late in 1511 he entered Trinity Hall, Cambridge, spending most of his time studying Greek and Latin and becoming proficient in both languages. Gardiner's interest in law led him to take a bachelor's degree in civil law in 1518. Within the next four years he took a doctorate in both civil and canon law, lecturing at the university in 1521, after his ordination to the priesthood.

A protégé of Cardinal Wolsey, Gardiner became his personal secretary and filled the position until 1529. As a special ambassador for Henry VIII and Wolsey, he gained knowledge of the political and religious issues of the time. He sided with the king in his divorce proceedings against Katherine of Aragon, and in return for his allegiance the king appointed him principal secretary in the royal household and, in 1531, Bishop of Winchester. Until Wolsey's death in 1529, Gardiner, though in the service of Henry VIII, kept up an outward semblance of loyalty to his old master.

Even though Gardiner concurred in the king's divorce, he leaned strongly to the old faith and openly opposed Cranmer's efforts to avoid mention of the Eucharist in the Six Articles (1539) and the King's Book (1543). Gardiner succeeded Cromwell as Chancellor of Cambridge University in 1540, holding the office until he was ousted by the Duke of Somerset in 1547. He was reinstated in 1553 by Queen Mary.

During the reign of Edward VI Gardiner spent most of his time in prison writing treatises against Cranmer's Book of Homilies and refuting the attacks made against transubstantiation by Martin Bucer, the German theologian then teaching at Cambridge, and George Joye.

One of Queen Mary's first acts, in 1553, was to release Gardiner from the Tower and appoint him Lord Chancellor of England. Though opposed to the marriage of Mary and Philip II, Gardiner performed the ceremony in Winchester Cathedral. With Pole, he became one of the queen's trusted advisers. His close association with the Cardinal's plan to re-establish the Catholic religion in England caused him to be accused of cruelty to heretics. However, John Foxe clears him of the charge, commending him for his open protection of Protestant sympathizers, among whom were Roger Ascham and Sir Thomas Smith.

Gardiner died in 1555 after overtaxing his strength by delivering the opening speech in Parliament, hoping to bolster the queen's government against growing opposition.

Besides his letters, Gardiner wrote only a few treatises in English. Among these are A detection of the deuil's sophistrie (1546), a defence of the Eucharist; A declaration of such true articles as G Joye hath gone about to confute (1546); and An explication and assertion of the true catholique fayth, touchyng the moost blessed sacrament of the aulter (1551). The sermon which Gardiner preached on 29 June 1548 before Edward VI, defying Somerset's command to omit any mention of the Mass, is reprinted in John Foxe's Acts and Monuments. An English version of his widely read treatise opposing Papal Supremacy, De vera obedientia (1535), was printed in 1553.

Gardiner's extensive correspondence falls into two groups: letters, written mostly in Latin, to many prominent persons when he was secretary to Wolsey and those written to his colleagues at Cambridge; in the second group are letters sent from prison during the reign of Edward VI.

His Latin letter to Thomas Smith was written while he was Chancellor of Cambridge and concerned his edict, issued 15 May 1542, forbidding the use of a new pronunciation of Greek that had the support of Sir John Cheke, noted Greek scholar, and Smith, Greek lecturer and first Regius Professor of Civil Law at the University. The new pronunciation was believed by Cheke to be that used by the ancient Greeks. Gardiner's and Cheke's extensive Latin correspondence covering the debate was printed as Epistolae ad J. Checum de pronunciatione linguae Graecae (1555). Refusing to abide by Gardiner's edict, Smith upheld Cheke in a treatise, De recta et emendata linguae Graecae pronunciatione (1568). In his reply to Smith, Gardiner gives the substance of the entire controversy and his views on justice and certain phases of law.

A letter to Matthew Parker, Vice-Chancellor of Cambridge in 1545, shows Gardiner as an educationalist keenly interested in encouraging students to cherish a deep respect for Christian ideals. His anxiety over the Christ's College students' presentation of Pammachius (1538), an abusive anti-papal Latin morality play by the German priest Thomas Kirchmeyer, dedicated to Martin Luther, stems from memories of his own schooldays when with William Paget and Thomas Wriothesly, he acted in Miles Gloriosus. It was not his aim to crush initiative, for the students of Christ's continued to produce plays, the most famous being W.S.'s Gammer Gurton's Needle (c. 1556).

Letter to Thomas Smith

TRANSLATED BY JAMES A. MULLER

THE COURT [HAVERING]
18 September [*1542*]

In the midst of the most important engagements it has been my pleasure to read your treatise, Smith, from beginning to end. It was impossible for me, in the course of a brief conversation at a public gathering, to acquire a deep insight into your personality or to feel that I had explored beneath its surface. It was my purpose, therefore, by perusing this lengthy composition, with its uninterrupted flow of argument, to make myself better acquainted with you and to become possessed of a more accurate understanding of your nature. For the famous remark that a man's personality is reflected in his speech* is by no means untrue. I have not received information about you, moreover, from other people, whether friends or enemies of yours. If I feel any hesitation concerning you, it is now based on my own judgment, not on theirs.

I could only wish that everyone possessed self-knowledge. Now, that you may not seize upon this remark as in any way an insult, or regard me as a sarcastic person, let me say that I do not exempt even myself from the criticism implied; I do not claim immunity in the slightest degree from the limitations of human nature, as if I were some rare sort of creature.* But whatever kind of person I may be, it is not because of any distinction of my own, whether of character or ability or even of learning, but because of the privileges of my office, that I am in control over you, that I give orders to you and issue edicts—doing so, perhaps, in a more severe fashion than the matter at issue would require, were it not that the tendencies of the age, the lack of discipline and the uncontrolled licence to which people are prone, call for stringent correctives.

Now, your friendship for Cheke—one which recalls in some measure the famous friendship [of Damon and Pythias] so greatly admired by the tyrant Dionysius and which, indeed, exactly reproduces it to the extent that you are displaying eagerness to withdraw Cheke from the case and to take his place yourself—this friendship, I say, has led you to seize every opportunity which my words afford to tax me, now actually with some error, now with some slip, at another time with inexperience or ignorance. You do so, to be sure, guardedly and respectfully and gently and as though taking exception merely to an action; and all the while you employ complimentary terms of address, and by the use of rhetorical devices transfer the odium pertaining to my action to persons spoken of as slanderous and envious and as wishing ill to you and your friends, persons who are distressed at having had a choice bite suddenly snatched from their jaws* through your agency. But even if this account of the situation were conceivably correct, those people could in no wise browbeat me.

Any person, certainly, however careful and learned, is liable to make slips and errors and blunders when a question of taking action is involved. On the other hand, in an investigation pertaining to the world of letters, what more serious charge of ignorance could be brought against a person than to claim that he had reached a decision, not of his own accord but by reason of accusations laid by others, or as a result of the urging and the persuasive promptings of others, or in reliance on the opinions of others instead of on his own? Especially do I resent the imputation, since pressure of the opposite sort, derived from writings and from literary works, was so repeatedly brought to bear upon me to follow my own judgment, a judgment supported and approved indeed by many, and reinforced besides by weighty precedents, but one which I, applying my mind to deliberation and inquiry, had pondered over and reflected about and decided upon by myself and then finally made public in the form of an edict, which I promulgated with the approval of scholars. No outsider has led me astray, nor have I been led astray by any error of my own mind. Yet you and your friends fill page after page with that highly objectionable kind of argument, a kind of argument that is offensive to scholars, while you go on elaborating a point about which there is no controversy but which is freely conceded.

For who would deny that the character of the sounds indicated by the letters of the alphabet was different in antiquity from what it is today? How many times, indeed, have I conceded this very thing! Plato, in the *Cratylus*,* asserts that the word ἡμέρα, which had *eta* as its initial vowel in the period in which he lived, had been pronounced with an initial *iota* by men of an earlier age and with an initial *epsilon* by other people at some later period. What statement could have been made that would indicate more explicitly that the sounds of the letters were differentiated? Yet today, though we retain the later spelling with *eta*, the most ancient pronunciation of the word, which at that time was represented by the spelling with *iota*, seems to have been revived.

You maintain that this is done incorrectly. It is precisely there that the point at issue lies. My contention, indeed, is not that it is done because it is correct, but that because it is done, it is the correct thing to do. I quoted in this connexion a statement of Aristotle,* a passage in which he declared that certain expressions were conventional—and, what is more, I followed the commonly accepted rendering. Why you, who are so thoroughly acquainted with the field of law, should disapprove of this I fail to see. In that field the term 'convention' is certainly applied to an agreement; for whether you think of συνθήκη as an 'agreement' or a 'covenant' or a 'compact', all of these notions can be expressed with the greatest elegance by *placitum* ['convention'], a Latin word pure and simple, and most admirably adapted to expressing the idea. For 'convention' includes 'agreement' and 'covenant' and 'compact' as genus includes species. So there is no reason why that rendering should fail to meet with your approval, unless, as I am inclined to believe, you happen to feel that the preposition [in the phrase *ad placitum*] is not correctly employed. Yet we say in Latin that the word *ad* gives extended application, indicating thereby that a notion is extended in meaning to apply to a whole series of terms. So nothing prevents our using this preposition as a not inappropriate equivalent of the Greek κατά. As for your request that certain expansions of the phrase should be permitted, I shall not grant it, for the expansions would involve a sort of *petitio principii*....

[Gardiner uses a legal analogy to strengthen his refusal to grant Smith's request. As a professor of law, Smith should appreciate this. The latter's request for 'licence' in order to uphold academic freedom is reprimanded by Gardiner. 'But really, Smith,...it was highly disgraceful for you, who are a professor of law, holding a position of public responsibility among your students, to request of me what it was not lawful for me to grant.']

But it is a fine thing, you will say, to rebuild what has collapsed, to set up what has been torn down, to put together again what has been pulled apart, to restore to things their own proper splendour. We should be permitted, you will continue, while others snore away because of unwillingness or inability or lack of power to act, to take a bold step without arousing any ill will. Why are we prevented from putting something into effect which will bring glory to us and fame to our university without inconveniencing anybody, something that will be to the advantage of a great number of people? And what difference could it make to one side or the other in the controversy, pray, that untutored barbarians, lazy folk who tolerate no innovations, should have taken offence?

It was not to be supposed, however, you declare, that these people would have as their supporter such a man as I am, a bishop and a learned chancellor and all the rest. The passage that follows contains complimentary references to me, added in a fashion calculated to further your cause. For in the inscription at the head of your treatise I am referred to as 'most scholarly', though men like you who are entirely occupied with scholarly pursuits, are far more scholarly than I.

Yet when I was urging [John] Cheke to attempt a restoration of the sounds in every slightest detail, so to speak, he frankly acknowledged that he could not, in fact, accomplish this. And, to be sure, however closely you, following the verdict of your own ears, may judge the Greek αι to coincide with our 'ay', it cannot be found out with certainty whether the Greeks actually gave it this sound—if for no other reason, surely because of the distance in time and space that separates us from them. It is highly unlikely, therefore, that we received from the Greeks sounds which only within the space of a few years have we come to regard as so elegant, or that these sounds were conveyed from the Greeks to us.

But it is something, you will argue, to make any advance at all, even though we are not permitted to go on further. This is precisely true in regard to those activities which are of such a nature that it is necessarily advantageous to engage in them. In such matters, certainly, as Horace puts it,* 'moderate and passable achievement' is occasionally permissible. But, on the other hand, matters which involve no necessity of setting anything on foot and, because the feast might have gone on without them, are very properly hissed like an orchestra out of tune—such are the matters that you have in hand; and futile effort and unheeding wilfulness might properly arouse indignation rather than derision.

Consider the reply which Erasmus gave to Philip Melanchthon,* a young man addicted to introducing innovations, when Melanchthon was making a proposal to him by letter that [Duns] Scotus should be cast out and expelled, and his name erased from the list of approved writers, and the whole scholastic theology should to that extent be overthrown. The wise Erasmus replied that when he had determined upon a better theology to substitute for it, and not till then, would he consult about altering the scholastic theology....

It is inadvisable to dispute about pronunciation; it is in fact useless and absurd. I am filled with wonder at what your purpose can have been in wasting so much time on these trifles, a thing which you yourself acknowledged in my very presence that you had done. If it has been in order that you might find an opportunity of showing off your eloquence and recommending yourself to me, you are much mistaken in your expectation. For even though I take delight in literary studies and though I see that the luxuriance of your style provides a convincing testimonial to your powers of memory, I nevertheless do not regard erudition as a mere matter of words. It generally happens in the field of scholarship, as elsewhere, that to the extent to which increased opportunities for display are sought, there is likely to be a decrease in sound judgment.

The particular province of scholarship which you have taken over, that of expounding the law, calls for the exercise of all a man's powers; and in the man who undertakes it there must exist a sound and incorruptible judgment, which recognizes and distinguishes with unusual acuteness the classes to which things belong and the differences between them. The admirable talent in this direction which I discern in you, a talent which really promises great things, would be hampered by dealing with such trivialities as these.

At this point my duties call me away and demand that I bring my writing to an end. This is a very difficult thing for me to do when my pen is hurrying on with gathered momentum, though from all other points of view, inasmuch as the interest in the subject has been exhausted, I should with the greatest difficulty be induced to spend so much time over these trifles that have no profit in them. So farewell, and I trust that, attaining to a more mature judgment, you may make it your concern to lay to rest the matter of Greek pronunciation, which, as you yourself say, you were the first to stir up, so that I may appear to have issued my edict wisely and other men may appear to have obeyed it with profit.

AT COURT, *the 18th of September*

STEPH. WINTON, CHANCELLOR

Letter to Matthew Parker

LONDON

12 May 1545

Master Vice-Chancellor, after my hearty commendations:

I perceive by your letters, which I have received with the book of the tragedy [*Pammachius*],* that ye have assembled the sages of the University to know by their inquisition, severally, in their houses, what was uttered that might and ought to offend godly ears in the playing of the same at Christ's College. Wherein, as appeareth by your letters, report was made unto you that no man is offended. And yet perusing the book of the tragedy which ye sent me, I find much matter not stricken out, all which by the parties' own confession was uttered, very nought, and on the other part something not well omitted; where allowing and rejecting should proceed of judgment, and that to be taken for true which was uttered, and that for untrue which they note as untrue to be omitted and left unspoken.

So as this book declareth the parties to have double offended, both in denying that is true and also approving that is false; as in some part by their notes doth appear. And indeed in the tragedy untruth is so maliciously weaved with truth as, making the Bishop of Rome with certain his abuses the foundation of the matter, the author's reproach whereof is true, so many abominable and detestable lies be added and mingled with the other truth, as no Christian ears should patiently hear; and cannot, in the process of the matter, be, without a marvellous alteration other than was now used, dissevered asunder.

By mean whereof, where all other proof faileth, there the book maketh an undoubted proof of their lewdness to me here; and that which so many of the university, being present, heard and offended them not so deeply but it is now worn out and they be no longer offended, the same is by exhibition of the book so notified unto me and so grieveth me, being absent, as, how soon soever I forget the offense upon their reconciliation, I shall hardly of a great while forget the matter. And if open and notorious faults, which the offenders in pomp and triumph so utter as they would have men know them and mark them, shall from henceforth without all reformation be neglected and forgotten, or so by silence hidden as they shall not appear to be corrected, there is small hope of conservation of good order, and a marvellous boldness give to offenders, the means of reformation thus taken away.

Wise men have noted truly that it is *caput audaciae, impunitatis spes* [The hope of impunity is the fountain head of audacious deeds], which must needs grow where open faults be thus neglected and pretermitted; wherein they be chiefly to be blamed that forbear to make report of that they have heard when they be required. I would not be over curious, unless the crime were notable, to bring to light his fault that himself hath used means to hide from the world. But if the offender be so destitute of all fear and shame as these players were, why should any man forbear, when they walk in the street naked, to point them with his finger and say, 'There they go!'.

I hear many things to be very far out of order, both openly in the university and severally in the colleges, whereof I am sorry; and amongst other, in contempt of me, the determination of the pronunciation of certain Greek letters, agreed unto by the authority of the whole university, to be violate and broken without any correction therefor. The matter is low, and the contempt so much the more. I was chosen Chancellor to be so honoured (although above my deserts) of them, and I have given no cause to be despised. I will do that I can for the maintenance of virtue and good order there, and challenge again of duty, to be regarded after the proportion, not of my qualities, but mine office; requiring you, Master Vice-Chancellor, to communicate these my letters with the masters, presidents, and doctors, and on my behalf to desire them gravely to consider of what moment the good order of youth is, and to withstand the lewd lic[ence] of such as have neither shame nor fear of punish[ment] and correction. The lesson of obedience would be well taught and practised, and I will be more diligent to know how men profit in it than I have been.

I have showed the whole council the words spoken by Master Scot, from whom ye shall shortly receive answer in that matter. And as touching those that were chief players in the tragedy, I hear very evil matter, and I pray you call them unto you, and know whether they will acknowledge and confess their fault, or no, and to signify the same unto me. And so, fare ye well. At London, the twelfth of May.

Your loving friend

STE. WINTON

To my loving friend, Master Vice-Chancellor of Cambridge.

Stephen Gardiner, *Letters of Stephen Gardiner*, ed. James A. Muller (Cambridge, 1933).

TUDOR GRAMMARS

INTRODUCTION BY ELOISE L. PAFORT

MEDIEVAL HUMANISTS AND THE TUDOR GRAMMARIANS

The progress of the revival of the classics in English universities depended to a great extent on how zealously the schoolmasters in the grammar schools encouraged their students to learn Greek and Latin. Hence no study of English humanism is complete without recognizing the work of those scholars who spent their lives not only as teachers but as compilers of grammars, the most important of all textbooks in these schools.

At the beginning of the sixteenth century the study of grammar, retaining its medieval traditions, was as much concerned with literature as with accidence, syntax, and prosody. And the schoolmasters as Christian humanists were glad that chivalry had required a code of morals and manners and forced the grammarians of the era to preach as well as teach through the copious examples of sentence structure included in grammar texts.

Among the Latin scholars to whom the Tudor grammarians paid allegiance were Donatus, who taught in Rome in the fourth century A.D., and Priscian, who lived during the sixth century in Caesarea. Their works, the former's *Ars Minor* and *Ars Major*, and the latter's *Institutionum Grammaticarum*, in eighteen books, were revered and standard Renaissance texts. There were others—Alexander de Villa Dei, whose *Doctrinale* appeared in 1199, Everhard de Béthune, Lorenzo Valla, who in the first part of the fifteenth century urged an end of 'barbarisms' and a return to Cicero and Virgil, Nicolaus Perottus, and, finally, Joannes Sulpitius, the most influential of all Latin grammarians on the Continent and author of *Sulpitii Verulani opus insigne grammaticum*, first printed in England by Richard Pynson in 1494.

Deriving their belief in the importance of grammar from these old masters, the humanists of the early English Renaissance made grammar the core of the curriculum in grammar schools or, as they were variously called, Cathedral Church and Collegiate Church Schools, Chantry and Guild Schools, Chorister or Song Schools.

Though some of these schools dated from medieval times, most of them were founded in the middle of the fifteenth century when many boroughs, and even places with less than a hundred 'housling souls', had their own schools. The day's routine in each was practically the same. Studies began in the morning at seven and continued until the dinner recess. The afternoon session lasted until dark.

During this ten-hour school day attention was mostly given to grammar, and the time that remained to reading, writing, plain-chant, religious instruction or Bible study, and a lesson in 'curtesye' Good table manners were considered so important that each student was required to memorize verses from Joannes Sulpitius's *Stans puer ad mensam* (1515). Another frequently used text was Erasmus's *De civilitate morum puerilium* of which Robert Whittinton made an English version, *A lytell booke of good maners for chyldren* (1532) The Dutch scholar was well known in Tudor schools through his *Adagia* (1500), *Colloquia* (1518), and *Copia verborum* (1519).

Each school had its time-table or curriculum drawn up by the headmaster. Besides what was to be taught, he was careful to in-clude the names of the texts that were to be used in each form from the first to the seventh. The curriculum of the Winchester School, which was recognized as a model, shows the thoroughness of these early schoolmasters. In the third form the students

> hath for ther ruls Sulpices genders...and hath throwgh the weke, over nyght, a verbe set up to be examyned in the mornyng, and makith vulgars vpon yt. And afternone they have a theme to be made in laten, the which Latyne one of the said forme at the pleasure of the master makith openlie dyverse ways. And after that they write the Masteris owne latyne. For there constructyons, vponne Mondayes and Wednysdayes, Aesopes *Fabells*; Tuesdayes and Thursdays, Lucyans *Dialogs*; the Friday in the mornyng examynation of ther rules; at the afternone renderyng; Saterday in the mornyng, proper verses of meter of Lilies makyng, and after that repetytyon of there latens with the examynatyon of the same. The Sonday, a dialoge of Lucyane τ a fable of Esope to be seid withowt booke and construed.

THOMAS LINACRE AND LILY'S GRAMMAR

Most of the grammars which were prescribed in the Winchester curriculum for the first, second, and third forms were written by John Stanbridge: *Vocabula* [1496]; *Accidence* [1505?]; *Parvula* (1509); *Sum, es, fui* or *Gradus comparationum cum verbis anomalis, etc.* [1515?]. His main objective was to teach the student to speak and write Latin through the medium of English. Though the Stanbridge Grammars were generally popular, the works of other grammarians were used in several of the larger schools. John Holt's *Lac Puerorum* or *Mylke for Children* [1510?], 'a babys boke', was well liked. He conceived the idea of compiling in one grammar all the various exercises which his contemporaries, Stanbridge, Whittinton, and

Horman, used in individual tracts. And to aid the student to memorize cases and declensions, Holt worked out diagrams drawn in the shape of outstretched hands. The rules of the *Lac Puerorum* are in English and the Latin examples are in verse. Holt's little grammar so appealed to Sir Thomas More that he wrote an encomium in verse which was appended to later editions.

When Thomas Linacre resigned his teaching post at Oxford to tutor Princess Mary, the young daughter of Henry VIII and Queen Katherine, the need of a text for his royal pupil encouraged him to write his three grammars: the rare *Linacri progymnasmata grammatices, etc.* [1525]; a condensed version of the latter, *Rudimenta grammatices* [n.d.], dedicated to Princess Mary; and *De emendata structura Latini sermonis* (1524). These grammars are more concise in form and presentation than the usual Tudor texts. The *Emendata* is a series of rules for writing Latin, and each rule is illustrated by sentences from classical works, chosen principally from the writings of Cicero. There had been nothing like it in England, and it was widely praised. The greatest tribute came from Erasmus, Linacre's former student, who compliments him in *Praise of Folly*: 'I knew an old Sophister that was a Grecian, a Latinist, a mathematician, a philosopher, a physician, and all to the greatest perfection, who after three score years of experience in the world had spent the last twenty of them only in drudging to conquer the criticisms of grammar.' Eight editions of the *Emendata* were printed on the Continent, and one of them was edited by Melanchthon in 1531.

The most widely used of the Tudor texts was *Grammatices rudimenta*, compiled, in 1509, by John Colet, founder of St Paul's School, and his headmaster, William Lily. But the text was destined to become known simply as 'Lily's Grammar', though the many editions, printed even as late as the nineteenth century, have varying titles. Because of the widespread use of the Grammar and its great influence during the Renaissance, when all English schools were compelled by a royal decree to adopt it, so that it was probably studied by Shakespeare, it is important to note the contents of the book as it was planned by two early Tudor educationalists.

The Grammar consists of two parts, Colet's *Aeditio* and Lily's *Rudimenta*. In the former, written in English, Colet goes far afield from the usual elementary rules to emphasize 'manners and morals'. He includes two prayers, probably composed by himself, the *Sancta Maria Virgo et Mater Jesu*, and a short prayer to the Child Jesus, still said at St Paul's School. There is also a letter to his headmaster and a 'proheme'.

Lily's *Rudimenta* is a syntax that is in some measure more elementary than Colet's *Aeditio*. The former opens with the often repeated rule of the grammarians, 'When I have an englysshe to be tourned

into latin, I shall reherse it twyes or thries and loke out the verbe.'
His directions how to find the principal verb are plainly put, as are
the 'three concords of grammar', namely, rules for the agreement
of verb and noun, adjective and noun, and relative and antecedent.
The *Rudimenta* closes after thirteen pages (which is extremely short
compared to the forty-nine of the *Aeditio*) with the Greek alphabet,
Lily's *Carmen de moribus*, and three short Latin poems, praising his
work, by fellow-grammarians John Rightwise, Richard Vernamus,
and Richard Gunsonus.

It is obvious that the Grammar was planned to encourage the
student to learn the rudiments slowly and with more assurance; and
this was an improvement over previous methods that required the
schoolboy to read and repeat by rote.

The worth of 'Lily's Grammar' was recognized by Cardinal
Wolsey who reprinted it for use in his Ipswich School, founded in
1529, with some additions and a preface as *Rudimenta grammatices
et docendi methodus, non tam scholae Gypsuichianae per reuerendissimum
D. Thomam Cardinalem Eboracensem, feliciter institutae, quam omnibus
aliis totius Anglie scholis praescripta* (1529) [*Rudiments of grammar and
method of teaching, prescribed not only for the school at Ipswich, happily
founded by the most reverend lord Thomas Cardinal of York, but for all
other schools in England*]. For years Wolsey had been anxious to
introduce a uniform grammar in English schools, but he did not live
to see his plan carried out. The abrupt change in his political life
hastened his death, in 1531, and the Ipswich School was dissolved.

A UNIFORM TEXT ESTABLISHED BY THE KING

Within ten years however, Henry VIII, realizing that there was no
more effective way of asserting Royal Supremacy than by prescribing
the public and private use of authorized books, revived Wolsey's
plan, having long sanctioned the Cardinal's efforts, and ordered his
printer Thomas Berthelet to publish a grammar, based on Colet's
Aeditio and Lily's *Rudimenta*. Certain changes were made in the
catechism and prayers to agree with those introduced by the Reformers
in the English Church. The grammar was printed in two parts:
the first was *An Introduction of the Eyght Partes of speche and the construction of the same*, etc., an elementary manual for beginners and
compiled in English; the second part was a more complete treatise
in Latin, *Institutio Compendiaria totius grammaticae quam et eruditissimus
atque idem illustrissimus Rex noster hoc nomine evulgari jussit, ut non alia
quam haec una per totam Angliam pueris praelegeretur* (1542) [*A Short
Instruction in all the rules of grammar which our most learned and most
illustrious King has commanded to be published under this name in order
that none other than this text may be taught to youths throughout England*].

The preface to the first part confirms the mandatory use of the grammar:

> Henry the VIII. . . to all schoolemaisters and teachers of grammer within this his realm greetynge. . . to the intent that hereafter they [English children] may the more readily and easily attein the rudymentes of the latyne toung without *the* greate hynderaunce, which heretofore hath been, through the diuersitie of grammers and teachynges: we will and commaunde and streightly charge al you schoolemaisters and teachers of grammar within this our realme, and other our dominions, as ye intend to auoyde our displeasure *and* haue our fauour, to teache and learne your scholars this englysshe introduction here ensuing and the latyne grammer annexed to the same, and none other, which we haue caused for your ease and your scholars spedy preferment bryefely and playnely to be compyled and set forth. Fayle not to apply your scholars in lernynge and godly education.

In an address 'To the Reder', which follows the King's foreword and was most likely written by Berthelet, the fathers of families, schoolmasters, and students or the 'tender babes' of England are told of the importance of the new grammar. And the author of the address has unwittingly sketched its history, weaving in some of the scholastic problems of the times:

To the Reder

> . . . And as his maiesty purposeth to establyshe his people in one consent and harmony of pure and true relygion, so his tender goodnes toward the youth *and* chyldhode of his realme entendeth to haue it brought vp vnder one absolute and vniforme sorte of lernynge. For his maiestie, consideryng the great encombrance and confusion of the yong and tender wittes by reason of the diuersity of grammer rules and teachinges (for heretofore euery maister had his grammer and euery schole dyuers teachynges; and chaungyng of maisters and scholes dyd many tymes vtterly dull and vndo good wyttes) hath appoynted certein lerned men, mete for such a purpose, to compile one bryef, plaine, *and* vniforme grammer, which onely (al other set a part) for the more spedynesse and lesse trouble of yong wittes, his hyghnes hath commanded all scholemaysters and teachers of grammer, within this his realme, and other his dominions, to teache their scholers. . . . And somewhat to declare vnto you the condition *and* qualitie of this grammer, ye shall vnderstand that the VIII partes of spech and the Construction of the same be not here set forth in englysshe at large, but compendyously and briefely for the weake capacitie of yong and tender wyttes. And therefore if anythyng semeth here

to want in this englyshe Introduction, ye shall vnderstande, it was left out of purpose and shall be supplied in the latyn rules made for the same intent which chyldren shalbe apte to lerne, what tyme they shall haue competent vnderstandyng by these former rudimentes.

THE TUDOR STUDENT AND HIS FRENCH PRIMER

French was the only romance language formally taught in early Tudor England. To speak it fluently was a sign of elegance, and it was necessary for those who read law or travelled on the Continent.

When Alexander Barclay published his French primer, *The introductory to wryte and to pronounce Frenche* (1521), he was pioneering in the construction of a simplified grammar as well as in teaching phonetics. The pronunciation of French had retained the accent of the 'scole of Stratford atte Bowe', and to remedy it Barclay thought the best way to begin was to show 'how the letters A.B.C. are pnoūced, or sounded in frenche'. The accusation of plagiarism made against him by John Palsgrave stemmed most probably from jealousy. The latter's thousand-page *Lesclarcissement de la langue francoyse, etc.* (1530) was not as popular as Barclay's short, compact grammar. Patterned after the Greek grammar of Theodorus Gaza, it was the first effort to formulate rules for the French language. There is a lengthy section on pronunciation which Palsgrave thought important because the French take infinite care to be 'armonyous'.

WORD TREASURIES—VULGARIAS AND DICTIONARIES

The Vulgaria was the handmaid of the Tudor grammar. These treasuries of idiomatic English, containing a wealth of material on the manners, learning, and language of the early decades of the sixteenth century, were designed by the headmasters to encourage the student to speak and write the language with ease. The most widely used were those compiled by Stanbridge, Horman, and Whittinton. It was Stanbridge, however, who drafted the pattern for them in the *Vulgaria Stanbrigi* (1508), using sentences in contrast to the short paragraph form later adopted by William Horman.

Nicholas Udall was among the last of the headmasters to compile a vulgaria. His *Floures for Latine spekynge selected and gathered out of Terence and translated by N. Udall* (1533) includes a brief summary of the rules for 'the expedite knowlege in the latine tongue'. Never enamoured of the teaching profession, which Udall declares 'came about through a combination of circumstances and fortune', he determined nevertheless to do something creditable. And the *Floures* represents years spent in culling the best lines from three plays of Terence, *Andria*, *Eunuchus*, and *Heautontimorumenos*. Beside Udall belongs his fellow-schoolmaster John Palsgrave, who also used the drama to stimulate student interest in grammar.

With so much emphasis on Latin grammar, it was inevitable that the vocabulary lists, such as *Ortus Vocabulorum* (1500), would eventually evolve into a full-sized dictionary. Luis Vives first broached the idea for a Latin-English lexicon in *De tradendis disciplinis* (1531), deploring that there was no adequate 'dictionary' whereby 'one could translate from the vulgar tongue to Latin and vice versa'. Soon Sir Thomas Elyot set himself the task of compiling a 'perfyte' dictionary wherein no Latin word would be omitted. The worth of *The dictionary of Sir T. Elyot* (1538) was quickly recognized. It was reprinted and 'inriched' several times by Thomas Cooper who titled it *Bibliotheca Elyotae* (1545).

THE FIRST ENGLISH RHETORIC

Though the Tudor schoolmaster considered it a most important duty, if not really his principal one, to urge students to write and speak 'elegant' Latin, he was not wholly neglectful of English rhetoric. The first English treatise on the subject was written by Leonard Cox, headmaster of Reading School. In *The arte or crafte of rhethoryke* [1524], he gives the general rules, following closely those laid down by Plato, Aristotle, and Cicero. From the latter's *De oratore*, Cox condensed the rules for the 'whole activity' of an orator into 'four thynges': invention or imagination, judgment, order, and eloquence. The work had a maturing effect on students, and the value of the *Arte or crafte* and those rhetorics that followed, particularly, Sir Thomas Wilson's *The arte of rhetorique* (1553), is reflected in the quantity of great literature produced by Elizabethans.

As the mid-century approached, the foundations of modern English prose had been laid. This significant achievement of Christian humanism was largely due to the efforts of the quiet and scholarly headmasters and grammarians of Tudor schools.

JOHN STANBRIDGE
1463–1510

John Stanbridge, who succeeded John Anwykyll, the first headmaster of Magdalen School, was born in Northamptonshire in 1463. After finishing his studies at Wykeham's School at Winchester, he was appointed in 1481 a Fellow of New College, Oxford. When Stanbridge took a Master of Art. degree, he left the university, and was soon after ordained to the priesthood In 1487 he was appointed usher at Magdalen School, and seven years later was made headmaster. It was there that Stanbridge spent the greater portion of his teaching career, the while writing his famous grammars. According to Anthony à Wood in Athenae Oxonienses, *he was generally well liked. 'This John Stanbridge was a right worthy lover of his faculty and an indefatigable man in teaching and writing, as it may appear by those things that he hath published, very grateful to the Muses and public concerns. The last of which he consulted more than his own private interest and when in his old age,[1] he should have withdrawn himself from his profession (which is esteem'd by the generality a drudgery) and have lived upon what he had gotten in his younger years, he refused it, lived poor and bare to his last, yet with a juvenile and cheerful spirit.' By 1507, Stanbridge had resigned from Magdalen School and was appointed vicar of Winwick near Gainsborough. At the time of his death, in 1510, he was a canon of the Cathedral of Lincoln.*

Vulgaria Stanbrigiana

THE AUTHOR

All little children busily your style ye dress,
Unto this treatise with goodly advertance,
These Latin words in your heart to impress,
To the end that ye may with all intelligence,
Serve God, your Maker Holy, unto His reverence.
And if ye do not, the rod must not spare
You for to learn with his sharp moral sense.
Take now, good heed, and hearken your vulgar.

[1] Wood may have confused the grammarian with Thomas Stanbridge who died in 1522, at 57, a venerable age according to sixteenth-century reckoning.

VULGARIA QUEDAM CUM SUIS VERNACULIS COMPILATA IUXTA CONSUETUDINEM LUDI LITTERARII DIVI PAULI[1]

Good morning.	*Bonum tibi hujus diei sit primordium.*
Good night.	*Bona nox, tranquilla nox, optata requies.*
Good speed.	*Bona salus, salve, salvus sis, optata salus.*
How fare you?	*Qua valitudine praeditus es, ut vales?*
	Qua valitudine afficeris, ut te habes?
I fare well, thanked be God.	*Bene me habeo altithrono sit gratia.*
Whither goest thou?	*Quo tendis?*
I go to siege.[2]	*Ad foricam pergo.*
I shall bear thee company.	*Comitabor te: sociabo te.*
I shall quite thee.	*Referam tibi gratias: par pari referam.*
How doth my father?	*Ut pater se habet?*
He was at the point of death.	*Ferme moriens erat.*
God be here.	*Assit deus.*
Thou art welcome to me.	*Gratus est mihi tuus adventus....*

It is a great help for scholars to speak Latin.
Non nihil conducit discipulis loqui Latine.

I am sure thou lovest me not.
Constat mihi te me non amare.

I was set to school when I was seven years old.
Datus sum scholis cum septemnis eram.

From that day hiderwarde, I was never kept from school.
Ab eo tempore hucusque nunquam a studio detentus sum.

Scholars must live hardly[3] at Oxford.
Scholasticos Oxonii parce vivere oportet.

There is one at the door will speak with thee.
Quidam apud hostium te conventum expetit....

Thou pinchest me.	*Vellis me.*
Thou playest the fool.	*Ineptis.*

I have gotten his good will.
Suam benivolentiam na[c]tus sum.

Thou playest the mad man.	*Insanis.*

I am the worst of all my fellows.
Indoctissimus sum discipulorum.

I shall heal thy disease.	*Tuo morbo medificabor.*

---

[1] Conversational Latin phrases with English translations, suitably arranged according to the use at St Paul's School.
[2] *siege*, public privy.   [3] *hardly*, frugally.

My mind is not set to my book. *Animus a studio abhoret.*

My gown is the worst in all the school.
Toga mea in toto ludo deterrima est.

Wishers and woulders be small householders.
Affectantibus divitias modicam hospitalitatem observat.

I go my way.   *Abeo:* [or] *discedo: recedo.*

Will thou command me any service?
Nunquid mecum vis?

Nothing but God preserve you.
Nil praeterquam ut valeas.

Our Lord be with you.
Muniat: protegat: custodiat: tueatur te deus: dominus dux vel custos tibi sit.

Finis

COLOPHON. Imprinted at London in Fleet Street by Wynkyn
de Worde at the sign of the sun.... 1519.

JOHN COLET AND WILLIAM LILY

Though the famous Tudor textbook, Lily's Grammar *or the* J. Coleti
aeditio una cum quibusdam G. Lilii grammatices rudimentis[1] *was the
joint work of John Colet[2] and William Lily, the latter has remained a
shadowy figure of the early English Renaissance. Lily was born about 1466
in Hampshire. There is no record of his schooling until he entered Magdalen
College, Oxford, where he took a Bachelor of Arts degree in 1490. He soon
left England on pilgrimage to Jerusalem. Before he returned home, Lily
stayed in Rome for two years to study Greek under Demetrius Chalcondyles.
While in Italy he met William Grocyn and John Colet, who became his
lifelong friends.*

*When Lily returned to London, probably in 1504, he opened a private
boys' school where Greek was first publicly taught. The school closed in
1512 when Colet invited him to accept the position of headmaster of his new
St Paul's School. Though Lily's scholarliness appealed to him, Colet
found in him other qualifications for a headmaster. He wanted a married
man and one well known for his high moral principles. Lily's success as
headmaster is frequently referred to in the letters of Erasmus, Bishop John
Fisher, and Sir Thomas More, each of whom knew him personally.*

George Lily, the eldest of William Lily's fifteen children, was his father's

---

[1] Colet's accidence with certain Rudiments of Grammar by William Lily.
[2] For biographical sketch, see pp. 35-7.

first biographer. *His short sketch of the elder Lily was written at the request of the Italian historian Paulus Jovius for his biographical dictionary,* Elogia virorum *literis illustrium* (1551). *Only the principal facts concerning his father's stay on the Continent and in Jerusalem are given in the account, which closes with a description of the London plague of 1522 that took William Lily's life.*

Like his father, George Lily studied for a time in Italy, taking a degree at the University of Padua, where he was a protégé of Reginald Pole.

Besides collaborating with Colet on the Grammar, *William Lily wrote several epigrams and two poems,* Antibossicon (1521) *and* Carmen de moribus (1521). *The first work grew out of his feud with Whittinton; the second is a didactic poem, stressing good morals and manners for schoolboys.*

Lily's Grammar: Colet's Aeditio

ARTICLES OF ADMISSION TO ST PAUL'S SCHOOL

The master shall rehearse these articles to them that offer their children on this wise here following:

If your child can read and write Latin and English sufficiently, so that he be able to read and write his own lessons, then he shall be admitted into the School for a scholar.

If your child after reasonable season proved, be found here unapt and unable to learning, then ye, warned thereof, shall take him away that he occupy not here room in vain.

If he be apt to learn, he shall be content that he continue here till he have some competent literature.

If he be absent six days, and in that mean season ye show not cause reasonable (reasonable cause is only sickness), then his room to be void without he be admitted again and pay four pence.

Also, after cause showed, if he continue so absent till the week of admission in the next quarter, and then ye show not the continuance of his sickness, then his room to be void and he none of the school till he be admitted again and pay four pence for writing of his name.

Also, if he fall thrice into absence, he shall be admitted no more.

Your child shall on Childermass Day wait upon the Bishop at Paul's, and offer there.

Also, ye shall find him wax in winter.

Also, ye shall find him convenient books to his learning.

If the offerer be content with these articles, then let his child be admitted.

THE ARTICLES OF THE FAITH

Valet in Christo Jesu Fides quae per Dilectionem
operatur[1] (Gal. v. 6)   *Cathechyzon   Fides*

I believe in God the Father Almighty, Creator of heaven and earth;   I
And in His Son, Jesus Christ Our Lord.   II
Which was conceived by the Holy Ghost, and born of the clean
    Virgin Mary;   III
Which suffered under Pontius Pilate, and was crucified and died
    and was buried and descended to hell;   IV
Which rose again the third day from death to life;   V
Which ascended into heaven and sitteth at the right hand of the
    Father Almighty;   VI
Which shall come again and judge both quick and dead.   VII
And I believe in the Holy Ghost, the Holy Spirit of God.   VIII
I believe in the Holy Church of Christ, which is the clean con-
    gregation of faithful people in grace; and communion of saints
    only in Christ Jesus.   IX
I believe that in the Church of Christ is remission of sins, both
    by baptism and by penance.   X
I believe after this life, [the] resurrection of our dead bodies.   XI
I believe, at the last, everlasting life of body and soul. Amen.   XII

...

CHARITY
The Love of God

In this true belief I shall *first* love God the Father Almighty that
made me, and Our Lord Jesus Christ that redeemed me, and the
Holy Ghost that always inspireth me. This blessed Holy Trinity
I shall always love and honour and serve with all my heart, mind,
and strength; and fear God alone; and put my trust in Him alone.

The Love of Thine Own Self

Second: I shall love myself to Godward, and shall abstain from all
    sin, as much as I may, specially from the sins deadly.
I shall not be proud, nor envious, nor wrathful.
I shall not be gluttonous, nor lecherous, nor slothful.
I shall not be covetous, desiring superfluity of worldly things.
And evil company I shall eschew and flee as much as I may.
I shall give me to grace and virtue and cunning in God.
I shall pray often, specially on the holy days.
I shall live always temperately and sober of my mouth.
I shall fast the days commanded in Christ's Church.
I shall keep my mind from evil and foul thoughts.
I shall keep my mouth from swearing and lying and foul speaking.

---

[1] Faith which worketh through charity availeth in Christ Jesus.

I shall keep my hands from stealing and pykinge.
Things taken away, I shall restore again.
Things found, I shall render again.

The Love of Thy Neighbour

Third: I shall love my neighbour: that is, every man to Godward, as mine ownself: And shall help him in all his necessities, spiritually and bodily, as I would be helped mine ownself, specially my father and my mother that brought me into this world. The master that teacheth me, I shall honour and obey. My fellows that learn with me, I shall love....

PRECEPTS OF LIVING

Fear God.
Love God.

Believe and trust in Christ Jesus.
Worship Him and his Mother Mary.

Desire to be with Him.
Serve Him daily with some prayer.

Call often for Grace of the Holy Ghost.

Bridle the affections of thy mind.
Subdue thy sensual appetites.
Thrust down pride.
Refrain from wrath.
Forget trespasses.
Forgive gladly.

Be true in word and deed.
Reverence thy elders.
Obey thy superiors.
Stand in grace.
Falling down, despair not.
Ever take a fresh, new, good purpose.

Chastise thy body.
Be sober of thy mouth.
Be sober of meat and drink.
Be sober in talking.
Flee swearing.
Flee foul language.
Love cleanness and chastity.
Use honest company.
Beware of riot.
Dispend measurably.

Persevere constantly.
Use ofttime confession.
Wash clean.
Sorrow for thy sins.
Ask often mercy.
Be no sluggard.
Awake quickly.
Enrich thee with virtue.
Learn diligently.
Teach t[h]at thou hast learned lovingly.

Flee dishonesty.

Be fellow to thine equals.

By this way thou shalt be benign and loving to come to grace, to glory thine inferiors. Love all men in God. Amen.

...

A LITTLE PROLOGUE TO THE BOOK

Albeit many have written and have made certain introductions into Latin speech, called *Donates* and *Accidens*, in Latin tongue and in English, in such plenty that it should seem to suffice. Yet, nevertheless, for the love and the zeal that I have unto the new school of

Paul's and to the children of the same, somewhat I have also compiled
of the matter, and of the eight parts of grammar have made thi
little book: not thinking that I could say anything better than hath
been said before, but I took this business, having great pleasure to
show the testimony of my good mind unto the School. In which
little work, if any new things be of me, it is only that I have pu
t[h]ese parts in a more clear order, and have made them a little more
easy to young wits than, methinketh, they were before, judging that
nothing may be too soft nor too familiar for little children, specially
learning a tongue unto them all strange.

In which little book I have left many things out of purpose, considering the tenderness and small capacity of little minds: And that
I have spoken, also I have affirmed it none otherwise, but as it
happeth most commonly in Latin tongue. For many be the exceptions, and hard it is anything generally to assure in a speech so various

I pray God, all may be to His honour and to the erudition and
profit of children, my countrymen Londoners specially, whom
digesting this little work I had always before mine eyes, considering
more what was for them than to show any great cunning, [and]
willing to speak the things, often before spoken, in such manner as
gladly young beginners and tender wits might take and conceive.

Wherefore, I pray you, all little babies, all little children, learn
gladly this little treatise, and commend it diligently unto your
memories. Trusting of this beginning that ye shall proceed and grow
to perfect literature, and come at the last to be great clerks. And lift
up your little white hands for me which prayeth for you to God. To
whom be all honour and imperial majesty and glory. Amen.

Prologi finis

AN INTRODUCTION TO THE PARTS OF SPEAKING FOR
CHILDREN AND YOUNG BEGINNERS INTO LATIN SPEECH

In speech be these eight parts following:

Noun	Adverb
Four declinable ⎫ Pronoun	Conjunction
Four undeclinable ⎭	
Verb	Preposition
Participle	Interjection

The First Part Called a Noun

A *noun* is the name of a thing that is and may be seen, felt, heard,
or understood. As the name of my hand in Latin is *manus*: the
name of a house is *domus*: the name of goodness is *bonitas*.

The Division of Nouns

Nouns or the names of things: some be substantives, some be
adjectives.

A noun substantive is that [that] standeth by himself and looketh not for another word to be joined with him.

A noun adjective is that [that] cannot stand by himself, but looketh to be joined with another word, as *bonus*, *pulcher*: when I say in Latin *bonus*, good; or *pulcher*, fair. And therefore it must be joined with another word: as a good child, *bonus puer*; a fair woman, *pulchra femina*. And a noun adjective, either it hath three terminations, as *bonus*, *bona*, *bonum*, or else it is declined with three articles: *hic*, *haec*, *hoc*, as *hic*, *haec*, *et hoc felix* etc. [this happy, etc.]....

Of these eight parts of speech, in order well construed, be made reasons and sentences and long orations. But how and in what manner and with what construction of words and all the varieties and diversities and changes in Latin speech (which be innumerable) if any man will know and by that knowledge attain to understand Latin books and to speak and to write the clean Latin, let him above all busily learn and read good Latin authors of chosen poets and orators; and note wisely how th[e]y wrote and spoke, and study always to follow them; desiring none other rules but their examples. For in the beginning, men spoke not Latin because such rules were made, but contrariwise because men spoke such Latin. Upon that followed the rules [that] were made. That is to say, Latin speech was before the rules; not the rules before the Latin speech.

Wherefore, well-beloved masters and teachers of grammar, after the parts of speech [be] sufficiently known in your schools, read and expound plainly unto your scholars good authors, and show to them every word and in every sentence what they shall note and observe, warning them busily to follow and to do like, both in writing and speaking, and be to them your ownself, also speaking with them the pure Latin very present, and leave the rules. For reading of good books, diligent information of taught masters, studious advertance and taking heed of learners, hearing eloquent men speak, and, finally, easy imitation with tongue and pen more availeth shortly to get the true eloquent speech than all the traditions, rules, and precepts of masters.   *Explicuit Coleti aeditio*[1]

Lily's Grammar:
Guillelmi Lilj Angli Rudimenta[2]

TO MAKE LATIN

When I have an English to be turned into Latin, I shall rehearse it twice, or thrice, and look out the *verb*.

---

[1] Colet's book is completed.
[2] The Rudiments [of Grammar], by William Lily the Englishman.

THE VERB

I may know the verb by any of these words: do, did, have, had, will
shall, would, should, may, might, am, art, is, be, was, were, can, could,
let it or must, which stand either as signs before the verb, or else they
be verbs themselves. I call them verbs commonly when a noun or
pronoun followeth after them.

If there come none of these signs in the reason, the word that
answereth to this question, What do I? thou? or he? What did I?
thou? or he?, etc., shall be the verb.

The Principal Verb

If there be more verbs than one in the reason, the first is the
principal verb, so it be none infinitive mode nor verb, having before
him any relative, adverb, or conjunction that causeth the reason to
hang: as *qui*, the which; *cum*, when; *ut*, that....

The Nominative Case after the Verb

Sometimes the nominative case cometh after the verb or after the
sign of the verb, as in reasons, interrogatives, optatives, and in
reasons having 'it' or 'there', with such other, before the verb, as
thus: Cometh the king? or, Doth the king come? *Venitne rex?*;
Go we, or, Let us go. *Eamus*; There standeth a man at the door.
Stat quidam apud ostium; It is my brother. *Est frater meus*....

The Case of the Relative

When there cometh no nominative case between the relative and
the verb, then the relative shall be the nominative case to the verb.

When there cometh a nominative case between the relative and
the verb, then the relative shall be such case as the verb will have
after him of whom he is governed, as:

It is a man whom I love.	*Est vir quem diligo.*
Whom I desire to see.	*Quem cupio videre.*
Whom I pity.	*Cuius misereor.*
Whom I favour.	*Cui faveo.*
Whom I use familiarly.	*Quo utor familiariter.*
Whose wit I commend.	*Cuius ingenium laudo....*

Finis

COLOPHON: ...1527 [From the printed copy in the
Peterborough Cathedral Library.]

WILLIAM HORMAN

c. 1440–1535

William Horman, a prominent early Tudor schoolmaster and grammarian, was born in Salisbury about 1440. When he finished his studies at Wykeham's College at Winchester, he matriculated at New College, Oxford, where he was appointed a Fellow. In 1485, after taking his Master of Arts degree, Horman left the university to serve as headmaster at Eton. Though he also served in various offices at Winchester, his name is more closely associated with Eton because of the fame of the Vulgaria (1519), a compilation of exercises in Latin grammar given to his students.

The contract which Horman had with his printer Richard Pynson is among the earliest extant agreements of the kind. Since the Vulgaria was intended exclusively for his students, Horman specified that Pynson was to print only 800 copies 'hoole and perfytt'. Payment was to be made 'in the lawfull money of Inglonde' and at the rate of five shillings per printed ream.

Horman lived to be nearly a hundred years old. He died in 1535. According to John Bale, he wrote several treatises on philosophy and science, and also made several English translations of Greek classics. His only known works are the Vulgaria (1519) and Antibossicon G. Hormani ad G. Lilium (1521).

———————

Vulgaria Viri Doctissimi Guil. Hormani Caesarisburgensis[1]

DE ANIMI CULTU PER ERUDITIONEM ET DOCTRINAM: VBI DE SCHOLASTICIS INSTITUTIS ET EJUS SUPELLECTILI ET ARMIS[2]

I know nothing that I am more bound to thank God and my friends than that I was christened and sent to school.

Nihil habeo | quo nomine deo magis parentibusque gratulari oportet | quam quod christianismo sim initiatus liberalibusque studiis traditus.

[1] *Vulgaria*, by the most learned man William Horman of Salisbury.
[2] On the development of the mind through learning and teaching; in which [i.e. in this chap.] are discussed educational methods, tools and equipment (Chapter VIII).

There is no near way to come to cunning than to read good authors
and draw to learned men and be present when they be gathered in
communication.
*Nihil efficacius reddit eruditum | quam: ut quis probatos legat authores: et
in celebri doctorum hominum coitu versetur | et in circulis frequentioribus
inseratur.*

Eloquence is most allowed and made of among all other science of
the people.
Studia humanitatis | sunt alijs disciplinis magis popularia.

I rejoice in the increase of cunning that is nowadays.
Praesens studiorum successus cordi mihi est.

Latin speech that was almost lost is now after long absence recovered
and come again.
*Latinam linguam | quae ferme perierat | quasi quodam postliminio
recepimus.*

The gentle rehearsal of so many noble men courageth me and
quickeneth my spirits.
Iucunda nomenclatura tot virorum illustrium | animum tangit.

I am very glad that thou goest so lustily to thy book.
Voluptati | vel volupe est | quod tam aventer studeas.

By reading of substantial authors, thou shalt bring about or attain
to speak elegant and substantial Latin.
*Legendis clarissimis authoribus adipisceris gravitatem | candoremque
sermonis....*

Paper first was made of a certain stuff like the pith of a bulrush in
Egypt: and since, it is made of linen cloth soaked in water, stamped
or ground, pressed and smoothed.
*Chartae | seu papyri usus | olim ex Aegypto petebatur | fierique coepit
ex papiro frutice: aevo autem nostro ex macerato lino | vel cannabo e tritis
et pertusis panniculis.*

The principal commendation of paper is that it be thin, hard, white,
and smooth.
In chartis spectantur tenuitas | densitas | candor | et levor.

The greatest and highest of price is paper imperial:
Augustissimum papyrum imperiale | vel hieratum dicitur.

Paper royal is next.
Papyrum regium | vel regale | claudianum | vel macrocolum est ei secundum.

There is other fine and thin paper, serving for missive letters, but it
will not bear ink on both sides:
*Est papyri genus | quod dicunt augustum | caeteris tenuius | et epistolis
dicatum | quod tolerandis non sufficiat calamis | adhoc tramittens literas.*

There is other coarse paper that would serve for no writing but for merchants and pedlars to wrap their stuff in.

Emporetica charta scribendo inutilis est: at involucris curtharum segestrium-que in mercibus usum praebet.

Blotting paper serveth to dry wet writing lest there be made blotts or blurs.

Charta bibula atramentum sorbet / siccandae scripturae utilis / ne fiant liturae.

That stuff that we write upon: and is made of beast skins: is sometime called parchment; sometime, vellum; sometime, abortive; sometime, membrane. [It is called] parchment, of the city where it was first made; vellum, because it is made of a calf's skin; abortive, because the beast was scant perfect; membrane, because it was pulled off by hyldynge[1] from the beast's limbs.

Ea materia / quam ad scribendum pecudum pelles nobis suppeditant / interdum pergamentum dicitur / a Pergamo oppido: unde primum ejus usus / copiaque manavit: interdum vitulimum a vitulo. interdum abortivum / ab immaturitate partus: membranum / quod ex membris animalis detracta fieret. . . .

I go to Oxford for my learning.

Oxoniam peto ob animi cultum.

He hath told many shrewd tales upon me to the master.

Multis criminibus apud preceptorem me est insectatus. . . .

We have played a comedy of Greek.

Representavimus fabulam palliatam. . . .

Froben's print is called better than Aldus's, but yet Aldus is nevertheless thankworthy, for he began the finest way and left sample by which others were lightly provoked and taught to devise better.

Officina chalcographica Frobenij vulgo fertur Aldina praestantior: sed is / non inferiorem laudem meritus est: quando primus tam elegantem formulam posteris reliquit / unde facile possent argutiora commentari.

Let young children be well taken heed of that they learn no Latin but clean and fresh.

Pueris summopere sit cautum: ut nihil discant / quod non latinum sit et elegans.

Thou hast botched and counterfeit Latin.

Latinitate non nisi imaginariae / umbratilisque figurae uteris.

I am not well content with the cast and manner of thy style.

Subdisplicet mihi orationis / vel stili tui schema.

I intend to read you Tully; God speed us well.

Ego (quod mihi / vobisque feliciter vertat) paro Ciceronem enarrare.

---

[1] *hyldynge*, grasping.

He hath made a gay laud upon King Henry.
Edidit egregium epycedion in regem Henricum....

The school street in Oxford is full of schools to read and dispute in
every faculty or science to proceed in.
*Minervium Oxoniense numerosum est diatribis: in quibus profitentur e
disputant omnium scientiarum / et liberalium artium principes et candidati*

It is a shame that a young gentleman should lose time at the dice and
tables, cards and hasarde.[1]
*Dedecet ingenuum adolescentem tesseris / et alveolo / tabellis pictis / au
alea diem perdere.*

Let no day scape but thou learn somewhat.
Nullum diem intermittas / in quo non aliquid eruditioni tuae adjicias.

Many one set naught by losing of time; but wasteth it as it were o
no value, and at their own will when their own life is but borrowed
of God as long as pleaseth Him.
*Plerique temporis iacturam naucificantes / eo tanquam gratuito abutuntur
cum ipse spiritus / homini datus est praecario.*

I will be read after Duns' [Scotus] ways.
Volo praecepta mihi tradi / sed ad instituta Scoti.

Words of former years—so that they be not too old and out o
knowledge, nor studied for a purpose nor too oft brought forth—
make the language substantial and pleasant.
*Verba a vetustate repetita / modo non sint ab ultimis / et obliteratis adscit
temporibus / neque manifesta / neque crebra: orationi maiestatem afferun
non sine delectatione.*

COLOPHON: *Impressa Londini per Richardum Pynson / ...*[1519].

ROBERT WHITTINTON
1480?–1535?

*Robert Whittinton, the most prolific of the Tudor grammarians, was bor
in Lichfield in 1480. After studying in Magdalen Grammar School unde
John Stanbridge, Whittinton entered Magdalen College, Oxford. Hi
arrogant and quarrelsome nature, which later led to controversies wit
fellow-grammarians, showed in the* supplicat *made in 1513 for hi
Master of Arts degree. He pleaded that he had studied rhetoric fourtee
years and had taught it twelve, and in recognition for his work assume
the honour,* Protovates Angliae, *which he always used.*

---

[1] *hasarde,* game played with dice.

In 1515 Whittinton was appointed headmaster of Lichfield School, where he began writing his numerous grammars, complaining in the preface of each that his critics were harsh and unfair. His ill humour touched off a literary feud in 1521 when he nailed some caustic verses to the door of St Paul's Cathedral, denouncing William Lily's method of teaching Latin. Whittinton signed the verses with the pseudonym 'Bossus'. When Lily and William Horman replied, each titled his poem Antibossicon. In Praise of Folly, Erasmus ridiculed the 'bellum grammaticale' for the way 'they [grammarians] praise, admire, and claw one another'.

It was probably through Whittinton's patron Cardinal Wolsey that he was appointed in 1519 tutor to the pages at the court of Henry VIII. This position and the revision of his early grammars occupied his last years until his death in 1535.

Besides his numerous grammars, Whittinton translated several Latin classics. The MS. 'De difficultate justitiae servandae in reipublicae administratione' is dedicated to Wolsey, praising him as a cardinal and statesman.

Vulgaria: Principles of Grammar

THE SECOND PART:
CONCERNING THE CONSTRUCTION OF NOUNS

Praeceptum

A noun that betokeneth possession or a thing had in possession requireth a genitive case of the haver or owner, or else his possessive is joined with the haver in case, gender, and number. And sometimes instead of the genitive case, he will have a dative.

Brevitatis causa (deinceps) praecepta omitto: lectorem ad libellum nostrum De Concinnitate Grammatices recurrere volens: praeceptorum tamen hemistichia pro indice inservimus: eo ut exempla et vulgaria praeceptis applicet. [For the sake of brevity (from now on), I omit rules, but would ask the reader to refer to our little book, *De Concinnitate Grammatices*: however, we will use hemistichia or short sentences as illustrations so that he may compare instances and common expressions with the rules.]

Causae Efficientis [Efficient Cause] Exempla

King Henry the VII was a prince of most famous memory.
Rex Henricus septimus fuit princeps luculentissimae memoriae. vel luculentissima principis fuit memoria.

He was a Prince of great virtue.
Erat enim princeps magnae virtutis. vel: magna principis erat virtus.

Wherefore the laud and praise of that Prince flourisheth mos
singular.
*Quocirca praecipua principis laus viget. Vel: non mediocris laudis decan-
tatur princeps.*

Causae Formalis [Formal Cause] Exempla

He was a Prince both of famous victory; also, wondrous policy.
*Claruit enim princeps non minus corporis | quam ingenii virtute; vel sic.
Clara fuit in principe non modo corporis | sed etiam animi virtus.*

Besides that, he was a tall person of body and angel-like o
countenance.
*Ad hoc | erat vir prestantis formae | et divini vultus. vel sic: Praestans era.
viri forma et venustissimus quidem eiusdem vultus.*

Moreover the fortune of that Prince was most marvellous: for there
could no fraud so privily be conspired against his person but briefly
it came to light.
*Praeterea incredibilis erat principis fortuna. Vel sic: Incredibilis fortunae
fuit princeps: adeo ut in eum tam furtim coniurari posset nihil; quod nor
brevi | cito | facile|, vel, continuo adverteretur, rescisceretur, vel, in lucem
emergeret.*

Causae Materialis [Material Cause] Exempla

And I can not overpass the strong and mighty buildings of the
newest and goodliest cast which he made in his time.
*Neque silentio praeterire possum | miram structurarum (vel aedificiorum)
magnitudinem. Vel sic: Mirae magnitudinis structuras (et aedificia) et novis-
simae et pulcherrimae formae: daedaleaeque artis: suo viventis tempore
extructa.*

Also, the inestimable costs of banquets that he made to his great
honour and to all his realm at the coming of strangers and in especial
at the receiving of the King of Castile [Ferdinand V], spoken of
throughout all realms of Christendom.
*Tum innumeros sumptus: solemnium (vel regalium) epularum. Vel sic:
Saliares immensi sumptus cenas: quas ad summum cum sui | tum totius
regni honorem exhibuit in exterorum (et in primis Castelliae regis) occursu
ubivis christianorum decantatas.*

Causae Finalis [Final Cause] Exempla

Who is he but he may laud and praise the godly religion of that
Prince and the singular love of godly honour that appeareth in his
monuments.

Quis non extollat divinam principis religionem / et singularem divini cultus amorem: que in suis monumentis extant. Vel sic: Quis laudibus non efferat divine religionis principem? et singularem in eodem divini amoris cultum: ut sua declarant monumenta.

It cannot be thought the contrary but the merits of his good deeds be great.

Negare est nephas / merita suorum bonorum operum non fore immensa. Vel sic: Refragari est absurdum, meritorum suorum praemia non fore innumera.

What should I say of the goodly and sure ordinance of his godly intent and purpose that he hath established in Westminster and in the sanctuary founded of his cost?

Quid praedicem sancta suae religiosae providentiae statuta: tam in West- monasterio / quam in salvatoris hospitio suis sumptibus sancita. Vel sic: Quid commemorem religiosam suorum divorum statutorum constitutionem haud secus in Westmonasterio: / quam in salvatoris elemosinario suis impensis confirmatam?

I doubt not but he hath in fruition the reward of his true and faithful trust in God in eternal glory.

Prorsus non dubito: hunc frui suae verae in Christo fidei corona / in immortali gloria. Vel sic: Fidelissime spero christianam suae coronae fidem syderea immortalitate iamiam praemiatam.

Praeceptum

Post possessorem signans laudes, etc. [Signifying praiseworthy qualities, etc. the genitive case follows the possessor.] *Exempla:*

Thomas More is a man of angel's wit and singular learning.

Grammaticus loquendi modus: Morus est vir divini ingenii et singularis (vel egregie) eruditionis; Oratorius: Morus est vir mirando ingenio et praestantissima eruditione; Historicus: Morus est vir praeclarus ingenio et eruditione; Poeticus: Morus est vir praestans ingenii, etc.

He is a man of many excellent virtues (if I should say as it is), I know not his fellow.

Est enim vir claris virtutibus (ut facessat assentatio) qualem haud novi alterum.

For where is the man (in whom is so many goodly virtues) of that gentleness, lowliness, and affability.

Ubinam est vir (in quo tantae coruscant virtutes) ea benignitate, ea comitate, ea denique affabilitate.

And as time requireth, a man of marvellous mirth and pastimes, and sometimes of as sad gravity, as who should say, 'a man for all seasons'.

Tum (ut tempus postulat) vir lepidis salibus, facetis jocis. Rursus (aliquando) matura gravitate; vir (ut ita dicam) omnium horarum.

Praeceptum

Cum pretij nomen, etc. [Monetary value expressed by the genitive.]
Exempla:

Beef and mutton be so dear that a pennyworth of meat will scant suffice a boy at a meal.
Bovine et ovine carnes adeo sunt care | ut denarij obsonium vix puerum saturet | vel unica refectione.

When I was a scholar of Oxford, I lived competently with seven pence commons weekly.
Cum Oxonie studui: septenorum denariorum convictu singulis ebdomadis (sic satis) reficiebar.

My father hath two hundred pounds worth of stuff brought home today.
Pater habet ducentarum librarum merces domum comportatas hodie.

Fetch us a half-penny loaf, a pennyworth of eggs, and a half-penny-worth of ale.
Compares nobis oboli panem: denarij ova: et oboli cervisiam.

Praeceptum

Artificem signans, etc. [Genitive used in signifying a craftsman.]
Exempla:

We have in our ward bell founders, pewterers, plumbers, braziers.
Sunt in nostra vicinia fusores companarij | stannarii | plumbarij | erarij.

And a little beneath, there dwell tailors, shoemakers, hosiers, up-holsterers, glovers, sewsters,[1] cobblers.
Et paulo inferius habitant sutores vestiarij | calcearij | caligarij | lectarij | chirotecarij | sutrices lintearie | et sarctores calcearij.

In the street next above, be suesmiths,[2] scythesmiths, bladesmiths, cutlers, armourers, razormakers, carpenters, wheelwrights, cart-wrights, locksmiths, clocksmiths.
In vico autem superiori sunt fabri ferrarii | falcarii | secarii | cultellarii | arma-rarii | novacularii | lignarii | rotarii | plaustrarii | ferarii | horologiarii....

Praeceptum

Partem quod signat, etc. [Wherein the genitive signifies the whole of which a part is taken.]

Upon London bridge I saw three or four men's heads stand upon poles.
In londoniano ponte (non autem londoniae vel de londonia) vidi tria aut quattuor capita hominum vel humana perticis affixa.

---

[1] *sewsters*, seamstresses.   [2] *suesmiths*, blacksmiths.

Upon Ludgate, the fore-quarter of a man is set upon a pole.
In occidentali porta londoniensi exposit[us] est in pertica hominis vel humanus thorax partitus.

Upon the other side hangeth the haunch of a man with the leg.
E regione dependet hominis vel humana coxa cum crure.

It is a strange sight to see the hair of the heads fase[1] or moose[2] away, and the gristle of the nose consumed away.
Aspectu mirandum est | vel aspicere est mirum, pilos capitum (non dices capitales) decidere vel deciduos et cartilaginem nasorum tabefactam | vel tabidam.

The fingers of their hands withered and clung unto the bare bones.
Tum digiti manuum (non dices manuales) torrefacti et ossium tenus herentes....

THE THIRD PART:
CONCERNING THE CONSTRUCTION OF VERBS
Praeceptum

Effert; extollit; levat; etc. ['Translate'; 'raise up'; 'lift up'; etc.]
Exempla:

Linacre hath translated Galen out of [the] Greek tongue into Latin, and that in a clean style, lately.
Linachrus Galenum e graeca lingua in latinam (et stilo quidem cultissimo) extulit nuper.

Praeceptum

Defero prodo notans, etc.: [*Defero* meaning 'I bring' and 'I bring forth'.] *Exemplum:*

In the which translation he hath brought many things to light.
In qua editione multa in (vel ad) lucem detulit.

Praeceptum

Differo cum signat disto. [Use of *differo* when it implies 'a distance apart'.]

He [Linacre] is deeply expert in [the] Greek tongue so that divers men judge that there is small difference between Erasmus and him.
Graecae linguae peritia pollet | adeo ut nonnulli inter Erasmum et illum paululum differre contendant.

---

[1] *fase*, fade (?).   [2] *moose*, mould (?).

Pro disto. [*differo* used in the sense of 'to differ'.]

Their styles be so like that one differs little from the other.
Pari stilo ita conveniunt ut parum differat alter ab altero.

Pro divvulgo. [*differo* used in the sense of to 'spread abroad'.]

So that more and less publishe the praise of the man not only for learning but specially for his diligence.
Adeo ut primi nedum infimi hominis laudem amplissime differant cum ob eruditionem tum ob praecipuam industriam.

Pro dispono. [*differo* used in the sense of to 'arrange'.] *Exempla.*

He hath set and distinct that work into goodly order.
Hoc volumen miro ordine distulit.

Nor he did this in haste, but hath prorogued the edition many years full wisely.
Neque hanc editionem precipitavit, immo in multos annos non imprudenter distulit.

Praeceptum

Infert importo, concludo. [To 'bring in'; to 'import', to 'confine'.] *Exempla.*

Pro importo. [*Infert* used in sense of 'imported'.]

We be much bound to them that brought in the craft of printing.
Plurimum debemus hisce viris | qui imprimendi artem prius intulere.

Pro concludo. [*Infert* used in sense of 'confined'.]

It concludeth many things in shorter space than the written hand doth and more ornately showeth.
Multa contractiori spatio infert, quam litera scripta, et cultius pollet.

Pro contra facio vel eo. [*Infert* used to give the sense of 'hinder' or 'go against'.]

It hindereth not so much the scriveners, but profiteth much more poor scholars.
Non tantum bibliographis infert incommodum quantum egenis scholasticis commodum.

Iunctum cum me, te, se, nos, vos. [*Infert* used together with 'me', 'you', etc.]

It is not many years ago since it came first into England.
Non multi praeterfluxerunt anni postquam in Angliam se prius intulit....

THE FOURTH PART: CONCERNING THE CONSTRUCTION
OF IMPERSONAL VERBS

[A Dialogue on the duty and behaviour of students in class]

Preceptor. For as it belongeth unto a master to teach his scholars both manners and learning, I have contrived a brief process, as it came to mind, of manners for scholars.

Cum preceptoris est | haud secus moribus | ac disciplina suos instituere discipulos epitomen de scholasticis officiis extemporariam collegimus....

Praeceptum

His praesit patiens cum impersonalia fiant. [Be particularly careful when these verbs are used impersonally.]

Preceptor. To be brief: it becometh and rather it is necessary for a master before all things to use gravity in all things, and specially before his scholars.

Summatim ut agam | preceptorem (precipue) decet | immo oportet ubivis (et presertim) coram discipulis severitatem servare et prae se ferre.

Disciple. Yes, sir, but many masters turn that into austerity and cruelty, so that their scholars have no list to abide with them. I know it by experience.

At non pauci hanc in austeritatem | ac potius crudelitatem pervertunt, adeo, ut discipulos his adherere non iuvet vel delectet. Ut me expertum non latet....

Preceptor. Such inconvenientes[1] becometh not a master and ought not to be seen in a discreet teacher.

Haec errata haud decent praeceptorem, neque visa oportent in modesto saltem.

Disciple. The gentle exhortations of my master allured my mind marvellously. Aye, and made me more diligent than all his austerity could do.

Blande praeceptoris admonitiones animum mirifice mihi iuvabant; immo diligentiorem quam rigiditas extrema me effecerunt.

Praeceptum

Poenitet ac taedet miseretque. [To be 'vexed' and to be 'disgusted' with and to 'commiserate'.] *Exempla:*

Preceptor. It is requisite also in a master, besides learning and gravity, that he be not newfangled in the form of teaching; to teach this manner today, and tomorrow to be weary of the same.

---

[1] *inconvenientes,* mistaken ideas.

Ad hoc preceptori expedit (praeter eruditionem et gravitatem) ne in docen[
formula versipellis sit : nunc hoc ut doceat paulo post hunc tedeat ejusden[

Disciple. I know divers teachers so turn sick (of the which they ma[
be both sorry and ashamed) that their scholars profit little o[
nothing, so that a man would pity tender wits so to be wearied[
Nonnullos novi ita morosos praeceptores (cujus eos et poeniteat e[
pudeat) ut parum aut nihil proficiant discipuli, adeo ut misereat quemvi[
ingeniosorum defatigatorum.

Praeceptum   *Exempla :*

Desinit et debet, solet, incipit. [To 'end' and to be
'indebted', to be 'accustomed', to 'begin'.]

Preceptor. And summarily to conclude: a master should be circum
spect in word, gesture, and countenance, that he do nothing tha[
should appear to his scholars light, dissolute, or sounding anywise to dishonesty which he may or ought to be abashed o[
afterward.

Et in summa ut agam hunc circumspectum esse decet verbis gestu et vult[
ne quid agat effeminatum dissolutum quovis modo ne (denique) disci-
pulis quod videatur turpe, cuius postea hunc pudere possit aut debeat[

Disciple. Children commonly have a delight and will be glad t[
note their master of a fault which they may show to their friend[
at home, in especial when they wax weary of their master.

Pueros delectare solet et cupide volunt praeceptoris erratiunculam annotar[
quam parentibus domi referant, tum maxime ubi praeceptoris eos teder[
incipit. . . .

Praeceptum

Ecce petit rectum | en nunc rectum &c. ['Behold' (*ecce* or *en*)
takes the nominative.]

Exempla :

De ecce | en | heus | ah | vah | ohe | hem | proh | heu. [A list of Latir
interjections.]

Preceptor. Ah, see manners! Look upon rudeness! Hark, my child [
Thou mayst follow whether you will. Ah, cleanliness of virtue sc
little regarded! Phy,[1] vileness of vice so greatly used!

Ecce morum probitas! En turpitudo | vel hem! Heus mi puer! Utrum[
libet eligas. Ah, virtutis pudor sic parvipensae! Vah, flagitii squalo[
tantopere amplexi!

Disciple. Oh! good sir, such is the course of the world. Alas, for
misery! Worse was it never. Oh! merciful God, will it never
amend! Alas, for sin and wickedness!

Ohe, bone vir! sic sunt vel sic se habent res humanae! Hem, miseria[

[1] *phy,* fie.

vel miserie! Pessimum seculum! Proh, presentissime deus! vel proh deum clementissimum, redietne felicitas uspiam! Heu, impietas, vel heu, impietatem!

Praeceptum

Hei terno et recto vel soli jungito terno. [*Hei* may be followed by dative and nominative, or by the dative alone.]

Preceptor. Alack, this heavy world! Woe is my heart to remember the felicity and wealth that hath been! Poor men cry out of this scarcity of all things! O the felicity of old time! O this new misery! O good Lord, reform our manners that the old wealth may renew!

Hei calamitoso huic tempori! Hei antiquae felicitatis recordatio! Veh rerum penuriae! Calamitant pauperes! O prisca rerum opulentia! O novam miseriam! O bone deus! mores et vitam corrigas ut restituatur pristina felicitas!

COLOPHON: *Londini in aedibus Winandi de Worde....1520.*

ALEXANDER BARCLAY
1476?–1552

Alexander Barclay was one of the few early Tudor scholars interested in the study of Romance languages. Of Scottish origin, he was, according to tradition, born in Gloucestershire in 1476. It is possible that he attended both Oxford and Cambridge, but no record has been found that he took a degree at either. In his poems Barclay infers that he also studied at the University of Paris. A sojourn in France would account for his interest in the French language and his acquaintance with the French humanist Robert Gaguin.

After his return to England, Barclay entered holy orders, and spent the first years of his priesthood at the College of St Mary-at-Ottery in Devonshire. There he filled the dual office of capellanus and 'chaplen', his duties including those of choirmaster and librarian. While at Ottery Barclay translated Brant's Shyp of folys (1509). Two years later, when he left the college to enter the Benedictine monastery at Ely, the popularity of the Shyp had brought him a wide circle of friends. Among them were Thomas Howard, Duke of Norfolk, Richard, Duke of Kent, Sir Giles Alington, Sir Thomas More, John Colet, and Sir Nicholas Vaux.

It was through Vaux that Barclay was invited to Calais in 1520 to 'devise histories and convenient raisons to florisshe the buildings and banquet house withal' for the Field of Cloth of Gold to be held that year. There is no record that he accepted Vaux's offer.

Shortly after 1520 Barclay left the Benedictines to join the Observant Franciscans at Canterbury. His stay with them led to his association with William Tyndale, William Roy, and Jerome Barlow, who were secretly spreading the teachings of Luther in England. All four fled to Germany in 1528. After several years, Barclay renounced his heretical views and was reconciled with the Church through Cardinal Wolsey, whom he had bitterly denounced.

Barclay's open antagonism toward the English Reformation and his refusal on several occasions to preach against the old faith nearly cost him his life. With the aid of friends, particularly the Duke of Norfolk, he escaped a prison sentence. In spite of his hatred for the Reformers, Barclay was appointed successively vicar of churches in Essex and Somersetshire. At his death in 1552 he was rector of All Hallows Church in London.

Barclay's literary efforts were confined to translations, with the exception of his French grammar, The introductory to wryte and to pronounce Frenche (1521). The early success of the Shyp encouraged him to continue in the translator's field, and before 1524 he published five Eclogues, free renderings of Aeneas Sylvius's De curialium miseriis epistola (1473) and the Eclogues of Battista Mantua. He also translated Dominicus Mancinus's Myrrour of good maners (1523) and Sallust's Jugurthine War (1520).

The Introductory to Write and to Pronounce French

Here beginneth *The Introductory to Write and to Pronounce French:* compiled by Alexander Barclay compendiously at the commandment of the right high excellent and mighty Prince, Thomas Duke of Norfolk.

PROLOGUE OF THE AUTHOR

Many and divers lettered men expert in sundry sciences have done their devoir[1] to inclear[2] the dulness and wilful ignorance of their country's native.[3] And to bring this their enterprise to effect, some have written in solute[4] language maternal of our English tongue; some in the same language hath coaxed their style in metre and ballades of divers kind; some hath compiled; some translated; and some devised of divers matters to divers purposes; and some for temporal lucre or favour; some to be magnified and renowned; some to eschew idleness and to profit a commonweal. Among which sort myself have also often employed my barren diligence, but like

---

[1] *devoir*, best.   [2] *inclear*, make clear.
[3] *native*, origin.   [4] *solute*, free.

as the naked trees deprived of fruit and leaf stoppeth the birds' tune, and all that the winter depriveth, the summer restoreth again, right so, though divers causes have withdrawn my pen from my old diligence, the motion of certain noble gentlemen hath renewed and excited me again to attempt my accustomed business.

Wherefore at the commandment of the right noble, mighty, and excellent Prince, aforesaid, I purpose to compile a plain and a compendious *Introductory* to learn to write and to speak French. And though the said treatise hath been attempted of divers men before my day, yet I trust, with the aid of God, to make the same more clear, plain, and easy: partly, by reason that I have seen the drafts of others made before my time; and partly, for that I have been in my youth and hitherto accustomed and exercised in two languages of French and English. But who would understand the cause which hath moved my said honourable lord to have such treatise compiled? Briefly to answer: it is for the commonweal and pleasure of all Englishmen, as well gentlemen merchants as other common people, that are not expert in the said language.

And, furthermore, since it hath pleased Almighty God to reconcile the peace between the two realms of England and France and to confederate them in love and amity, my said lord hath thought it expedient that our people accompanying[1] with them of France should not be utterly ignorant in the French tongue: Which in times past hath been so much set by in England that who hath been ignorant in the same language hath not been reputed to be of gentle blood. Insomuch that (as the chronicles of England record) in all the grammar schools throughout England, small scholars expounded their constructions both in French and English.

And, moreover, that same tongue is not a little commended among the infidels, as Turks and Saracens, for the pleasant, compendious order and conveyance of the same, then how much more should it be pleasant to us which are joined with the same nation, as well by neighbourhood and confederation as by alliance. But whatever profit or pleasure that the reader may find in the same treatise, let him give laud and thanks to God and to my said most honourable lord by whose commandment, as said, this treatise is compiled. . . .

INTRODUCTORY OF ORTHOGRAPHY

Hereafter followeth a small treatise or *Introductory of Orthography*, or true writing, whereby the diligent reader may be informed truly and perfectly to write and pronounce the French tongue after the divers customs of many countries of France. For likewise as our English tongue is diversely spoken and varieth in certain counties

---

[1] *accompanying*, associating.

and shires of England, so in many counties of France, varieth their languages [as] by this treatise evidently shall appear to the reader.

First, how the letters of the A.B.C. are pronounced or sounded in French:

a	b	c	d	e	f	g	h	i	k	l	m
a	boy	coy	doy	e	af	goy	asshe	ii	ka	el	am

n	o	p	q	r	s	t	v	x	y	z
an	oo	poy	cu	aar	ses	toy	v	yeux	ygregois	zcdes.

Also, here is to be noted that many words be which sound near unto Latin and be used in both the language of French and English among eloquent men as terms indifferently belonging to both French and English. So that the same signification which is given to them in French is also given to them in English, as thus:

Amity. Advancement. Audacity. Bounty. Beauty. Brevity. Benevolence. Benignity. Curtesy. Curiousity. Conclusion. Conspiration. Conjuration. Compuction. Contrition. Confederation. Conjunction. Detestation. Detraction. Denomination. Devulgation. Divinity. Dignity. Disappearance. Exchange. Esperance. Evidence. Fable. Frailty. Fragility. Fragrant. Governance. Grace. Humility. Humanity. Intelligence. Intellection. Interpretation. Insurrection. Indenture. Laudable. Language. Murmuration. Mutability. Magnanimity. Patron. Patronage. Picture. Rage. Royal. Regal. Sovereign. Sustain. Traitor. Torment. Treachery. Treason....Variance. Variable. Vesture.

These words, with others like, betoken all one thing in English as in French. And who so desireth to know more of the said language must provide for more books made for the same intent, whereby they shall the sooner come to the perfect knowledge of the same.

COLOPHON: Imprinted at London in the Fleet Street at the sign of the Rose Garland by Robert Copeland....1521.

LEONARD COX
fl. 1550

Leonard Cox was the precursor of the Elizabethan rhetoricians, Roger Ascham, George Puttenham, and Sir Philip Sidney. His parents, Lawrence and Elizabeth Cox, were living in Monmouth in 1505, which is reckoned as the year of Cox's birth. Nothing is known of his early schooling. He took a Bachelor of Arts degree at Cambridge in 1526, and two years later was a candidate for the same degree at Oxford. Though he applied for a Master of Arts degree there, he left before taking it. Cox was ordained to the priesthood about 1530, and soon after was appointed headmaster of the grammar school at Reading Abbey by Abbot Hugh Farringdon.

In 1540 Cox left Reading to travel on the Continent, going as far east as Poland. His motive was probably to escape the unsettled conditions that followed the English Reformation. On his return to England during the reign of Edward VI, he opened a grammar school at Caerleon. It flourished until 1572, when John Hales founded the Coventry School and appointed Cox headmaster. How long he stayed at Coventry and the date of his death are not known.

Cox's only extant work is The arte or crafte of rhethoryke [1524]. *Among the works attributed to him are:* Commentaries upon William Lily's construction of the eight parts of speech [1549] *and a translation of Erasmus's* Paraphrase of Erasmus vpon yᵉ Epistle of Paule vnto Titus [1535?]. *None of Cox's letters have survived, but he is mentioned in the correspondence of Erasmus, Melanchthon, and John Frith. Cox defended the last when he was imprisoned as a 'vagabond' in Reading.*

The Art or Craft of Rhetoric

Whosoever desireth to be a good orator* or to dispute and commune of any manner thing, him [it] behoveth to have four things: the first is called *invention*, for he must first of all imagine or invent in his mind what he shall say; the second is named *judgment*, for he must have wit to discern and judge whether the things that he hath found in his mind be convenient to the purpose or not, for oftentimes if a man lack this property, he may as well tell that that is against him as with him, as experience doth daily show; the third is *disposition*, whereby he may know how to order and set every thing in his due place lest, though his invention and judgment be never so good, he may happen to be counted as the common proverb saith, 'To put the cart afore the horse'; the fourth, and in such things last, as he hath invented and by judgment known apt to his purpose, when they are set in their order so to *speak* them that it may be pleasant and delectable to the audience.

So that it may be said of him that histories make mention, that an old woman said once by[1] Demosthenes, and since hath been a common proverb among the Greeks, which is as much to say, 'This is he.' And this last property is called among learned men eloquence.

[1] *by*, about.

Of these four, the most *difficile* or hard is to invent what thou must say. Wherefore of this part the rhetoricians, which be masters of this art, have written very much and diligently.

Invention is comprehended in certain places, as the rhetoricians call them, out of whom he that knoweth the faculty may fetch easily such things as be meet for the matter that he shall speak of. Which matter, the orator calleth the theme, and in our vulgar tongue it is called improperly the anti-theme. The theme proposed, we must after the rules of rhetoric go to our places that shall anon show unto us what shall be to our purpose.

Example: In old time there was great envy between two noble-men of Rome of whom the one was called Milo and the other, Clodius. The which malice grew so far that Clodius laid wait for Milo on a season when he should ride out of the city, and in his journey set upon him; and there, as it chanced, Clodius was slain. Whereupon this Clodius's friends accused Milo to the Senate of murder. Tully which in those days was a great advocate in Rome should plead Milo's cause.

Now it was open that Milo had slain Clodius; but whether he had slain him lawfully, or not, was the doubt. So then the theme of Tully's oration or plea for Milo was this: that he had slain Clodius lawfully, and therefore he ought not to be punished. For the confirmation whereof, as doth appear in Tully's oration, he did bring out of places of rhetoric, arguments to prove his said theme or purpose. And likewise must we do when we have any matter to speak or commune of. As if I should make an oration to the laud and praise of the King's highness, I must for the *invention* of such things, as be for my purpose, go to places of rhetoric where I shall easily find, after I know the rules, that that I desire.

Here is to be noted that there is no *theme* but it is contained under one of the four causes or, for the more plainness, four kinds of orations. The first is called *logical*, which kind we call properly *disputation*; the second is called *demonstrative*; the third, *deliberative*; the fourth, *judicial*. And these three last, be properly called species or kinds of orations whose natures shall be declared separately hereafter with the craft that is required in every of them.

All themes that pertain to logic, either they be simple or compound. As if a man desire to know of me what justice is: this only thing 'justice' is my theme. Or if disputation be had in any company upon religion, and I would declare the very nature of religion, my theme should be this simple or one thing, 'religion'. But if it be doubted whether justice be a virtue, or not, and I would prove the part affirmative, my theme were now compound. That is to say, justice is a virtue, for it is made of two things knit or united together, justice and virtue.

Here must be noted that logic is a plain and a sure way to instruct man of the truth of everything. And that in it the natures, causes, parts, and effects of things are by certain rules discussed and searched out. So that nothing can be perfectly and properly known but by rules of logic, which is nothing but an observation or a diligent marking of nature, whereby in everything man's reason doth consider what is first, what last, what proper, what improper.

The places or instruments of a simple theme are: *the definition of the thing*; the *causes*; the *parts*; the *effects*. Example: If thou inquire what thing justice is, whereof it cometh, what parts it hath, and what is the office or effect of every part, then hast thou diligently searched out the whole nature of justice, and handled thy simple theme according to the precepts of logicians to whom our author leaveth such matters to be discussed of them.

Howbeit, somewhat the rhetoricians have to do with the simple theme. And as much as shall be for their intent, we will show hereafter. For many times the orator must use both definitions and divisions. But as they be in logic plain and compendious, so are they in rhetoric extended and painted with many figures and ornaments belonging to the science. Nevertheless to satisfy the reader's mind and to alleviate the tediousness of searching these places, I will open the manner and fashion of the handling of the theme aforesaid as plainly as I can after the precepts of logic.

First, to search out the perfect knowledge of justice, I go to my first place, *definition*, and fetch from Aristotle in his *Ethics* the definition of justice which is this: 'Justice is a moral virtue whereby men be the workers of rightful things'; that is to say, whereby they both love and also do such things as be just. This done, I search the *cause* of justice; that is to say, from whence it took the first beginning. And because that it is a moral virtue, and Plato in the end of his dialogue *Meno* concludeth that 'all virtue cometh of God', I am assured that God is the chief Cause of justice, declaring it to the world by His instrument, man's wit: which the same, Plato affirmeth in the beginning of his *Laws*.

The *definition* and *cause* had, I come to the third place called *parts*; to know whether there be but one kind of justice or else many. And for this purpose I find that Aristotle in the fifth [book] of his *Ethics* divideth justice in two species or kinds: one, that he calleth 'justice legitime' or legal; and another, which he called 'equity'. Justice legal is that that consisteth in the superiors which have power to make or statute[1] laws to the inferiors. And the office or end of this justice is to make such laws as be both good and according to right and conscience, and then to declare them. And when they are made and published, as they ought to be, to see that they be put in use. For

---

[1]   *statute,* establish.

what availeth it to make never so good laws if they be not observe
and kept. And, finally, that the maker of the law apply his whol
study and mind to the wealth of his subjects and to common prof
of them....

And this is the manner of handling of a simple *theme* dialecta
But yet, let not the reader deceive himself, and think that the ver
perfect knowledge is showed him here. What hath been shown now
is somewhat general and brief. More and sure exact knowledge
contained in logic to whom I will advise them that be studious t
resort and to fetch everything in his one proper faculty.

COLOPHON: Imprinted at London in Fleet Street by me
Robert Redman, dwelling at the sign of the George. [1524.]

GULIELMUS FULLONIUS
1493–1568

Acolastus, *one of the most important of the Continental Latin school play*
was written by William de Volder or Fullonius, as he is better known, wh
was born at the Hague in 1493. It is likely that this Dutch scholar receive
his early training in one of the schools conducted by the Brethren of th
Common Life, a community founded by Gerhard Groote, who were note
for their school plays.

After receiving a Bachelor of Arts degree from the University of Cologn
about 1516, Fullonius came under the influence of Luther and Melanchthor
Soon he began to attack monasticism and Catholic dogmas. Formal charge
were brought against him, and he was tried in a papal court and excom
municated. The Church banned Acolastus *because of its stress on justifica*
tion by faith alone. Fullonius immediately left Holland to accept a teachin
post in Prussia, where he taught theology for several years. Complain
were brought against him that he veered too close to Catholic philosophy
and he was tried in a Lutheran court and found guilty of heresy. Exile
from Prussia, he died in Emden in 1568.

Besides Acolastus, *which was widely translated and popular enough*
warrant sixty editions before 1585, Fullonius wrote three other school play
each of them in the classical tradition: Triumphus Eloquentiae (1523)
Morosophus (1541), *and* Hypocrisis (1544).

The first English version of Acolastus *was made by the Tudor schoo*
master, John Palsgrave, who changed its Lutheran slant and dedicated h
work to Henry VIII. It is likely that he was a member of the Norfol
family of Pagrave, and was born to Henry and Anne Pagrave about 148

he eldest son of twelve children. Nothing is known of Palsgrave's early
fe until 1504, when he took a Bachelor of Arts degree at Corpus Christi
College, Cambridge. Within the next few years he went to France and
udied theology at the University of Paris, where he was ordained to the
riesthood in 1512.

When Palsgrave returned to England in the same year, his efforts to
btain a teaching post in a grammar school were unsuccessful. In his
onstant struggle 'to trede vnder fote this horrible monster poverty', he did
rivate tutoring. Among his pupils were Princess Mary, sister of Henry VIII,
William Fitzroy, natural son of the king and Elizabeth Blount, and
Charles Blount, son of Lord Mountjoy.

Because of a violent quarrel with Cardinal Wolsey over his method of
eaching young Fitzroy, Palsgrave left England in 1515 to live at Louvain
where, through his friend and benefactor Sir Thomas More, he met
Erasmus. His visit to the Continent was short, but he returned to the
University of Louvain in 1527 to take a Bachelor of Divinity degree.
During the English Reformation Palsgrave took the Oath of Royal
Supremacy, and, in 1540, was appointed chaplain to Henry VIII. He was
member of the convocation that signed the declaration annulling the
marriage of the king to Anne of Cleves. Palsgrave lived in obscurity
throughout the reign of Edward VI, provided for by his former pupil,
Charles Blount. He died in 1554.

Many treatises have been attributed to Palsgrave, but his only known
works are a comprehensive French grammar, Lesclarcissement (1530) and
he translation of Acolastus (1540).

An educationalist at heart, Palsgrave's method of translating Acolastus
isplays an earnest endeavour to teach students something of the translator's
rt and to stimulate their interest in rhetoric. In marginal notes he points
ut the use that Fullonius made of the classics, especially the works of
Plautus, Terence, Virgil, and Seneca, also the influence of the proverbs of
Publilius Syrus and Erasmus's Adagia and Apophthegms. It was
Palsgrave's theory that the growth of a language depends on the enrichment
t receives from other languages. In his translation he borrowed from
Continental literature, and many of his English proverbs came from the
medieval poets and the prose of early Tudor writers. 'Before a man can say
reyace', is found in Gower's Confessio Amantis. Other vernacularisms
n his translation are from Heywood's Proverbs, Skelton's Magnificence,
nd the works of Sir Thomas More. To Elyot's Dictionary he was
ndebted for the meanings of many words, such as 'Emergo—to issue or
ome out of a place where a thing is drowned'. For a full discussion of these
eferences, the reader should consult the notes of P. L. Carver's excellent
dition of the play for the Early English Text Society. In his Introduc-
on Mr Carver points out that Palsgrave's free linguistic borrowings
repared the English language for the Elizabethans. When Acolastus
makes his 'moan' in the fifth act, scene two, wishing, 'it might be leful for

*me to break this light behated', Mr Carver asks: 'Do we not already hea
the tone of Hamlet's soliloquies?'*

*Equally important as Palsgrave's linguistic endeavours is the repor.
given in his preface, of the ills of the Tudor schools. His proposed correctiv
measures afford a forthright and enlightened discussion of the problems th
faced parents and teachers during the Renaissance.*

Ioannis Palsgraui Londoniensis, Ecphrasis Anglica in Comoediam Acolasti[1]

The comedy of *Acolastus* translated into our English tongue after such manner as children are taught in the grammar school: first, word for word as the Latin lieth, and afterward, according to the sense and meaning of the Latin sentences: by showing what they do value and countervail in our tongue; with admonitions set forth in the margin so often as any such phrase, that is to say, kind of speaking used of the Latins, which we use not in our tongue, but by other words, express the said Latin manner of speaking, and also adages, metaphors, sentences, or other figures poetical or rhetorical do require for the more perfect instructing of the learners and to lead them more easily to see how the exposition goeth. And afore the second scene of the first act is a brief introductory to some general knowledge of the divers sorts of metres used of our author in this comedy. And afore Acolastus's ballad is showed what kinds of metre his ballad is made of. And afore the sixth scene of the fourth act is a monition of the rhetorical composition used in that scene and certain other after it ensuing. Interpreted by John Palsgrave. *Anno* 1540.

PALSGRAVE'S PREFACE

To the most excellent Prince and our most redoubted sovereig
lord, Henry the VIII, by the grace of God, King of England and c
France, Defender of the Faith, Lord of Ireland, and Supreme Hea
in Earth immediately under Christ of the Church of England. H
most humble and most obedient chaplain, John Palsgrave, Bachelo
of Divinity, desireth perfect felicity and prosperous success in all h
noble affairs.

When I consider with myself, most high and most redoubte
Prince, and to me of all your humble subjects, most benign an
gracious sovereign lord, among others the great and weighty affai

[1] The English translation of the comedy *Acolastus* by John Palsgrave of London.

which lie under the moderation of your sceptre royal, how highly your grace doth tender the well bringing up of your youth in good letters—insomuch that whereas it is clearly perceived by your most prudent wisdom how great a damage it hath heretofore been, and yet is, unto the tender wits of this your noble realm to be hindered and confounded with so many divers and sundry sorts of precepts grammatical—you have for the redress thereof willed one self and uniform manner of teaching of all those grammatical ensignments[1] to be used throughout all your Highness' dominions, and [have] committed the disposing of that matter unto such singular personages, both of exact judgment and thereto of excellent literature, that I for my part do not a little hereof rejoice: and earnestly do I wish that I at these present days (which in that exercise have dispent no small time of my life) had observed but some vailable document to bring to this *gazophilacium*, something to help to the furtherance of this your noble grace's so goodly, and thereto so godly, and much fruitful a purpose.

Whereupon as it fortuneth among the loving and well-willing subjects when they hear of any gracious and beneficial purpose by their sovereign lord intended, whereby his commonwealth might receive so great a furtherance and advancement (especially tending to any such effect as they themselves have been most exercised withal), I hereupon took occasion thus to reason and to debate with myself. Now shall the great variety used aforetime in the teaching of the grammatical rules of the Latin tongue in this realm, whereby hitherto no small hinderance hath ensued, hereafter utterly cease and be put to silence. Whereby undoubtedly shall ensue a great commodity and furtherance, both to the masters and also to the young beginners which shall hereafter succeed.

For now is it intended that every school of your grace's realm should begin to wax one self school, as far as those said principles doth belong. But as yet unto my poor judgment (seeming to be a thing very much requisite) for the more effectual and speedy further-ance of your grace's said youth, I wish that unto this much expedient reformation of your schoolmasters' unstayed liberty, which hitherto have taught such grammars, and of the same so divers and sundry sorts as to every of them seemed best (and was to their fantasies most approved), might thereto also follow and succeed one steady and uniform manner of interpretation of the Latin authors into our tongue after that the Latin principles were by your grace's youth once surely conned and perceived. Upon the want and default whereof, besides the great and evident inconvenience (of which the effect is too much in every place espied), that is to say, the plainly apparent ignorance and want of a required sufficiency of many which in

---

[1] *ensignments*, instructions in.

private places take upon them to teach afore they be their craft'
masters; to whom the best grammatical rules that ever were or
could be devised cannot vailably be sufficient, I have by experience
learned that there be divers other occasions rising upon the schoolmasters' parts whereby your grace's youth is not a little hindered

For some instructors of your Highness' youth, for want of a perfect
judgment in this behalf, so much desire to seem affectedly curious
that having no due consideration to the tender wits which they take
under their charge to teach, in the stead of pure English words and
phrases, they declare to their children one Latin word by another,
and confound the phrases of the tongues: And thus not a little do
hinder their young scholars while they would seem for their own
parts to have a knowledge and erudition above the common sort
And some others again there be which having undoubtedly learning
enough, vailable and sufficient, yet while they by sundry ways and
manners of speaking used in our tongue, labour to express such Latin
authors' minds as they do take upon them for the time to interpret
and for to seem therein more diligent than the common sort,
dispend, in manner, whole forenoons and afternoons in the declaring
of a few lines of such Latin authors as they for the season have in
hand (as to confess the very truth, the schoolmasters' whole diligence
tendeth, in manner, chiefly to that effect and purpose).

They do by that means not only right little for the time further
their young audience, but also by that ways do oppress and overlay
the tender wits, the which they would so fain further, with their
multitude of sundry interpretations confusedly by them uttered.
So that finally their young scholars, to help their memory with, be
forced to fall a glossing, or rather a blotting, of their Latin books:
and as their childish judgment doth for the time serve them, of divers
English words in our tongue, being synonyms, or of divers manners
of interpretations used by their master, they choose most commonly
the very worst, and therewith scribble the books of their Latin
authors.

And some others, furthermore, there be which though they have
by their great study at your grace's universities, so much profited in
the Latin tongue that to show an evident trial of their learning they
can write an epistle right Latinlike, and thereto speak Latin, as the
time shall minister occasion, very well: Yea, and have also by their
diligence attained to a comely vein in making of verses: yet for all this,
partly because of the rude language used in their native countries
where they were born and first learned (as it happened) their
grammar rules, and partly because that coming straight from thence
unto some of your grace's universities, they have not had occasions
to be conversant in such places of your realm as the purest English
is spoken, they be not able to express their conceit in their vulgar

ongue, nor be not sufficient perfectly to open the diversities of phrases between our tongue and the Latin (which in my poor judgment is the very chief thing that the schoolmaster should travail in): insomuch that for want of this sufficient perfection in our own tongue, I have known divers of them which have still continued their study in some of your grace's universities, that after a substantial increase of good learning (by their great and industrious study obtained), yet when they have been called to do any service in your grace's commonwealth, either to preach in open audience or to have other administration requiring their assiduous conversanting with your subjects, they have then been forced to read over our English authors, [and] by that means to provide a remedy unto their evident imperfection in that behalf.

And when it hath fortuned any such for their good name and estimation to be called from your universities to instruct any of your Grace's noblemen's children, then evidently hath appeared their imperfection in that case to be notable, and that to no small detriment and hinderance of such as they have taken charge to instruct and bring forward....

I have chosen for my Latin author to be *ecphrastes* upon, the comedy entitled *Acolastus*, not only forbecause that I esteem that little volume to be a very curious and artificial compacted nosegay, gathered out of the much excellent and odoriferous sweet-smelling gardens of the most pure Latin authors, but also because that the maker thereof (as far as I can learn) is yet living, whereby I would be glad to move into the hearts of your grace's clerks, of which your noble realm was never better stored, some little grain of honesty and virtuous envy which on my part, to confess the very truth unto your grace, hath continually in all the time of these my poor labours taking, accompanied me and stirred me onwards to achieve this matter on this wise by me attempted. For thus have I thought to myself: Shall Fullonius, an Hollander born, thus many hundred years after the decay of the Latin tongue by the Goths, Vandals, and Lombards (three most barbarous nations utterly corrupted), through the diligent observation of the pure Latin authors be able to make so fine and so exact a piece of work, and I shall not be able at these years of mine age to do so much as to declare what he meaneth in my native tongue, seeing that he (regard had to his country) can challenge no more propretie[1] of the Latin tongue than I can, saving that through his great and industrious labour he hath mastered the Latinity, and forced it to serve him to set forth to all clerks his intent and purpose....

[Palsgrave hopes his own Latin labours will interest others in improving their knowledge of the language. This will eventually

---

[1] *propretie*, natural ownership of.

lead to 'a marriage between the two tongues'. To encourage good learning, he proposes 'six great and much vailable commodities'.

First, for if this kind of interpretation may take effect and be put in execution, not only the speech of your grace's subjects should by that means have a great advantage to wax uniform throughout all your grace's dominions, but also the English tongue, which under your grace's prosperous reign is come to the highest perfection that ever hitherto it was, should by this occasion remain more steady and permanent in his endurance. . . .

Second, for after this there should never be no utter ill school-masters within your grace's realm. For if such as would take upon them that office were not better than their English interpretations yet very shame would drive them that they should not be worse except they would stand in danger to be reproved of their own scholars, which if they were but young babes yet might their parents easily control them which might well enough perceive when they did notably amiss.

Thirdly, for then should the willing scholars which had already gotten their grammatical principles be so evidently encouraged to go forward that they should be great callers upon their fellows which by their negligence would drag: Besides that, the masters themselves should have no small provocation to use so their own parts [with] good diligence lest their scholars of their own mind should call for more of their author to be declared unto them than, perchance, they had prepared to read unto them before: whereas now the scholars, be they never so well willing to be furthered, they have no manner remedy but utterly and wholly to stay upon their master's mouth.

Fourthly, for then should all such as be already departed from the grammar schools, and afterward be taken with a repentance of their young time negligently by them overpassed, which aforetime were forced to despair, though their wills afterward waxed never so good, now by this means easily recover themselves again.

Fifthly, for then should young scholars with small pains engrosse[1] the whole arguments of the Latin authors in their memory; whereas heretofore after they have read the Latin authors in the school, they have not perceived what matter they entreated of: yea, and then their furtherance and speedy increase should be so notable that with pleasure, in manner, and with banishing of all servile rudeness out of grammar schools, they should sooner be able perfectly to go than they could aforetimes be able to creep.

Sixthly, for when the schoolmasters, and also the scholars, should by this means be eased, in manner, of three parts of their pains, then should the masters have both time and better occasion to open their further learning and to show unto their scholars the great artifice

[1] engrosse, implant.

ised of the authors in the composition of their works, which afore-
ime they had no such opportunity to do.

But what mean I, my most redoubted sovereign lord, which
knowing the inestimable clearness of your grace's judgment seem
here to be thus far abused as to be about to show light unto the bright
shining sun? I do therefore clearly and utterly submit me and these
my poor labours unto your noble grace's disposition and order,
availing them no more nor none otherwise but as by your noble
grace they shall be approved: only on this manner wise finishing my
simple epistle, that it is and shall be to my last day among the chieftest
of my desires and wishes of Almighty God that I may receive of
Him the grace and possibility to do the thing that may be acceptable
to your noble grace whose felicity and prosperous success in all your
noble affairs, I beseech Almighty God to maintain, increase, and with
increasings long to continue.

[To show Fullonius's 'great erudition', Palsgrave points out in
'Observation of the Rhetorical Composition', etc., that he has
followed the Latins, particularly Horace.]

First, therefore, we must consider that whereas Horace saith in
De Arte Poetica: Aliquando vocem comoedia tollit: that thing of all places
of any comedy is meetest to be done when the comedy is brought to
his *ecstasis*[1] and draweth shortly after towards his catastrophen: And
for this cause doth Fullonius in the setting forth of Acolastus's complaint use all such rhetorical precepts as should serve to make his
pronunciation figurated and most meet and convenient for a person
that in deliberating with himself falleth, in manner, into extreme
desperation. And therefore to move the audience unto commisera-
tion, the whole scene, in manner, is made of interrogations, sometimes by Acolastus left unanswered unto: partly because of great
difficulty to make any answer; and partly to move the audience to
compassion; and partly because they need none answer, they be so
evident; and sometimes by demanding of questions which he maketh
answer unto himself.

ACOLASTUS, ACT V, SCENE 2

Actus quinti, scena secunda

Trimetroi

Acolastus solus

Quis tam durae est mentis, quem non deiecerit
In luctum et lachrymas Fortunae acerbior
Casus? Argentum quod rebar dudum mihi
Fore immortale, Vah! quam puncto temporis

[1] *ecstasis*, climax.

Periit? Luxuria inopiae mater, quam mihi
Amicam habui unice charam, omnia abstulit,
Rem, nomen, amicos, gloriam, quid non?...

Of The Fifth Act, The Second Scene
Verses Iambic Trimeter
Acolastus Alone

Acola. Who is of so hard a mind? / Who is he that is so stiff stomached, or so hard hearted, whom a more bitter case of fortune / a passing grievous chance, or a great misfortune should not cast down into mourning, or bewailing and tears / should not drive him, or force him to mourn, or to bewail and weep the silver / the money, which I supposed, but lately to be hereafter immortal unto me / which I thought but late ago, would never have been spent? Out or propt,[1] how is it perished in a point of time! / How quite and clean is it gone, or ever a man could say treyace, excess of fleshly pleasures, the mother of neediness or poverty,* whom I have had a leman only dear unto me / whom I have kept or holden as my best beloved, hath taken away all things / hath taken away or bereaved me of all that ever I had, my thing / my goods or substance, my name / my good name and fame, my friends, my glory / my renown or estimation, what not?...

> *...Quid faciam igitur? Quid?*
> *In sordibus istis. Oportet sordescam magis*
> *Ac magis, unde emergendi spes mihi nulla sit?*
> *Utinam in matris nixu, occubuissem infantulus,*
> *Utinam invisam hanc lucem licuisset rumpere,*
> *Potius, quam vitam in tantis aerumnis traham.*
> *Neque, sciam, si meliora etiam instent mortuo.*
> *Ego mihi montis ardui casum imprecer,*
> *Qui me perdat, tam non suave est vivere,*

What must I in these filthies, or shall I be fain in these vilenesses to wax filthy more and more? From whence there is no hope to me to escape out again from drowning / from whence I have no manner hope to escape out of, or to be delivered of. Would to God I had died, being a young babe in my mother's travail / when my mother laboured with child of me. Would to God it might be leful[2] for me to break this light behated / to fordo myself, or to make an end of me, or to kill myself, rather than I should trail or linger my life in so many and so great infelicities / labours and travails of my mind and body, nor I wot not if better things be near at

---

[1] *propt*, alas.   [2] *leful*, lawful.

hand to me, being dead / nor I am not sure whether I shall be in better case when I am dead, than I am now in this life. I could find in my heart to beseech or to pray God, the fall of a high hill to me / that some steep upright hill might overwhelm me, which might lese[1] me / make an end of me, so much it is not sweet to live / so much my life is painful to me.

> *Mortis simulacrum qui volet videre, me*
> *Contempletur. Quid enim vivum in me advortitur?*
> *Quid sum praeter mutum pecus, et sine pectore*
> *Corpus? Veh luci, veh natalibus meis.*
> *Taedet coeli convexa contuerier amplius.*
> *Nam ut unda supervenit undam, ita alii fluctui*
> *Curarum insistit alius, aestuans mare*
> *Pectus meum dicas ex vero nomine.*
> *Num me deorum quisquam respicit?*
> *Quibus tam sum neglectui? haud equidem arbitror.*

He that would see an image or a picture of death, let him behold me. For why, what lively thing is considered in me? / What sign or token of life may a man perceive to be in me? What thing am I but a dumb beast and a body without a breast / without heart or courage? Out upon this light* (that shineth upon me)! Out upon mine offspring or the blood that I come of! It irketh me* or grieveth me, any more to behold these parts of the heaven that be next unto me / this hithermost part of the sky. For like as one wave (in the sea) overtaketh another, so unto me one surge of cares presseth in after another: thou mayst say my breast to be a rising sea of his own true name / thou mayst safely swear or maintain that my heart may be truly named or called a swelling sea, for the great storm I feel therein. Is there any of the gods that beholdeth me or looketh towards me / is there any of the gods that regardeth me, or hath any or taketh pity upon me? unto whom I am so much to despising / which do thus much despise me or set this little by me? Surely, I suppose it not / I suppose there be none.

William Fullonius, the maker of this present comedy, did set it forth before the burgesses of [The] Hague in Holland. *Anno*, 1529.

COLOPHON: *Impress. Lond. in aedibus Tho. Berthel....*1540.

[1] *lese*, lose.

SIR THOMAS ELYOT[1]

The Dictionary of Sir Thomas Elyot, Knight

PREFACE

To the most excellent Prince and our most redoubted sovereign lord King Henry the VIII, King of England and France, Defender of the Faith, Lord of Ireland, and Supreme Head in earth immediately under Christ of the Church of England, his humble and faithful servant, Thomas Elyot, Knight, desireth perfect felicity.

FOR about a year passed, I began a dictionary, declaring Latin by English, wherein I used little study, being then occupied about my necessary business which letted me from the exact labour and study requisite to the making of a perfect dictionary. But while it was in printing and uneth the half deal performed, your Highness being informed thereof by the reports of gentle Master Anthony Denny, for his wisdom and diligence worthily called by your Highness into your Privy Chamber, and of William Tildsley, keeper of your grace's library, and after most specially by the recommendation of the most honourable lord Cromwell, Lord Privy Seal, savourer of honesty and, next to your Highness, chief patron of virtue and cunning, conceived of my labours a good expectation.

And declaring your most noble and benevolent nature in favouring them that will be well occupied, your Highness, in the presence of divers [of] your noblemen, commending mine enterprise, affirmed that if I would earnestly travail therein, your Highness, as well with your excellent counsel as with such books as your grace had and I lacked, would aid therein me. With the which words, I confess, I received a new spirit, as meseemed, whereby I found forthwith an augmentation of mine understanding insomuch as I judged all that which I had written not worthy to come in your grace's presence without an addition. Wherefore, incontinent, I caused the printer to cease, and beginning at the letter M, where I left, I passed forth to the last letter with a more diligent study. And that done, eftesones[2] returned to the first letter, and with semblable diligence performed the remnant.

In the which my proceeding, I well perceived that although dictionaries had been gathered one of another, yet, nevertheless, in

---

[1] For biographical sketch, see p. 88–90. [2] *eftesones,* soon.

each of them are omitted some Latin words interpreted in the books which in order preceded. For Festus [in the epitome of M. V. Flaccus's *De Verborum Significatione* (*c.* A.D. 150)] hath many which are not in Varro's *Analogi* [*De Lingua Latina* (30 B.C.?) Bks v–x]. Nonius [in *De Lingua Latina* (*c.* A.D. 324)] hath some which Festus lacketh. Nestor [in his dictionary, *Onomasticon* (1483)] took not all that he found in them both. Tortellius is not so abundant [in *Commentariorum de Orthographia* (1471)] as he is diligent. Laurentius Valla wrote only of words which are called *Elegancies* [*Elegantiae* (1471)], wherein he is undoubtedly excellent. Perottus in *Cornu-copiae* [*Sive Linguae Latinae Commentariorum* (1489)] did omit almost none that before him were written; but in words compound, he is too compendius. Friar Calepino, but where he is augmented by others, nothing amended, but rather appaired [in his polyglot *Dictionarium* (1502)] that which Perottus had studiously gathered. Nebrisensis was both well learned and diligent, as it appeareth in some words which he declareth in Latin. But because in his dictionary [*Dictionarium Latinohispanicum* (1523)] words are expound in the Spanish tongue which I do not understand, I cannot of him show mine opinion.

Budé in the exact trial of the native sense of words [*Commentarii Linguae Graecae* (1529)], as well Greek as Latin, is assuredly right commendable; but he is most occupied in the conference of phrases of both the tongues which, in comparison, are but in a few works. Divers other men have written sundry annotations and commentaries on old Latin authors among whom also is discord in their expositions.

When I considered all this, I was attacked with a horrible fear, remembering my dangerous enterprise (I being of so small reputation in learning in comparison of them whom I have rehearsed) as well for the difficulty in the true expressing [of] the lively sense of the Latin words as also the importable[1] labours in searching, expending, and discussing the sentences of ancient writers. This premeditation abated my courage, and desperation was even at hand to rend all in pieces that I had written, had not the beams of your Royal Majesty entered into my heart by remembrance of the comfort which I of your grace had lately received. Wherewith my spirit was revived, and hath set up the sail of good courage. And under your grace's governance, your Highness being mine only master and steerer of the ship of all my good fortune, I am entered the gulf of disdainous envy, having finished for this time this simple *Dictionary* wherein, I dare affirm, may be found a thousand more Latin words than were together in any one dictionary published in this realm at the time when I first began to write this commentary, which is almost two years passed.

---

[1] *importable*, insupportable.

For besides the conference of phrases or forms of speaking Latin and English, I have also added proper terms belonging to law and physic; the names of divers herbs known among us; also a good number of fishes, found as well in our ocean as in our rivers; moreover sundry posies; coin and measures, sometime used among the ancient Romans, Greeks, and Hebrews, which knowledge to the readers not only of histories and orations of Tully but also of Holy Scripture and the books of ancient physicians shall be found pleasant and also commodious. Nor have I omitted proverbs, called *Adagia*, or other quick sentences which I thought necessary to be had in remembrance.

Albeit, forasmuch as partly by negligence at the beginning, partly by untrue information of them whom I trusted, also by too much trust in Calepino, some faults may be found by diligent reading. I therefore most humbly beseech your excellent Majesty that where your Highness shall happen to doubt of any one word in the first part of this work, or, perchance, do lack any word which your Majesty shall happen to read in any good author, that it may like your grace to repair incontinent unto the second part which is mine addition, seeking there for the same word in the letter wherewith he beginneth, trusting, verily, that your Highness there shall be satisfied. And forasmuch as by haste made in printing, some letters may happen to lack, some to be set in wrong places, or the orthography not be truly observed, I therefore have put all those faults in a table, following this preface, whereby they may be easily corrected.

And that done, I trust in God, no man shall find cause to reject this book, but rather thankfully to take my good will and labours, giving to your Majesty most hearty thanks as to the chief author thereof by whose gracious means men, being studious, may understand better the Latin tongue in six months than they might have done afore in three years without perfect instructors, which are not many and, such as be, are not easy to come by. The cause I need not to rehearse, since I once declared it in my book, called the *Governor*, which, about eight years passed, I did dedicate unto your Highness.

And, for my part, I render most humble thanks unto your Majesty for the good estimation that your grace retaineth of my poor learning and honesty, promising therefore to your Highness, that during my life natural I shall faithfully employ all the powers of my wit and body to serve truly your Majesty in everything whereto your most excellent judgment shall think my service convenient and necessary. In the meantime, and always as your bound servant, I shall heartily pray unto God to prosper your Highness in all your virtuous proceedings, granting also that your Majesty may long reign over us to the incomparable comfort and joy of all your natural and loving subjects. Amen.

THE DICTIONARY

A ante *B*

A. Signifieth of or from. *Ab* and *abs* be of the same signification; only *a* goeth before a word which beginneth with a consonant: *ab* and *abs* goeth before a word that doth begin with a vowel.

Abatis. Two words made of the preposition *a* and the ablative case plural of *batus* (which in English is a measure); signifieth an officer that hath the ordering of measures, as a clerk of the market.

Ab accidentibus. An officer unto whom it belongeth to write such things as do chance.

Abacti. Officers deposed or such as be constrained to resign their authorities.

Abactores. Thieves that steal cattle.

Abacus. A counting-table or cupboard.

Abaculus. Of Pliny is taken for 'accompt'.

Abalienatus. He whom a man putteth from him.

Abalieno, avi, are. To put or turn away.

Abana. A river in the country of Damascus under the hill called Libanus.

Abanec. A girdle that the priests of the Jews did wear.

THE ADDITION OF SIR THOMAS ELYOT, KNIGHT, UNTO HIS DICTIONARY

M ante *E*

Medica. An herb which I suppose to be clover-grass with purple, round flowers.

Melandria. The lean parts of the fish called tuna.

Melanurus. A kind of perches called ruffes.

Melita. An isle lying between Sicily and Africa, which is now called Malta, where at this time the company of the Knights Hospitallers do inhabit as they did at the Rhodes.

Merula. A fish called merling or whiting.

Minutum. *Idem quod* λεπτά [same as *lepta*, that is, fine or thin.]

Mygala. A field mouse with a long snout called a shrew.

Colophon. Thomas Berthelet *regius impressor excudebat.*....1538.

PART II

THE POLITICAL AND
SOCIAL ORDER

THE POLITICAL AND
SOCIAL ORDER

INTRODUCTION BY W. GORDON ZEEVELD

Englishmen in the sixteenth century, as in every century since, showed a unanimous respect for order. So widespread was the expression of this sentiment in Tudor thought, that it has been assumed to be a special characteristic of the English temperament. Earlier English history does not bear this out. Indeed, the first political order in almost a century was brought about with the defeat of Richard III on the field of Bosworth at the hands of the first Tudor, Henry VII. The general cry for order may be attributable less to temperament than to a desire for a strong government after generations of civil strife. It was a feeling that Henry himself must have felt when he addressed himself to what turned out to be the great task of his reign, the removal of stings from the mouths of adders, the poisonous serpents of rebellion. His title to the throne was far from clear, and he forced from Parliament what he could not claim by birth. Little wonder that he yearned for order and a stringent observance of law. A ruler by parliamentary dispensation had no alternative.

What father established, son continued. The rule of the Tudors was a constant resort to legalisms, the most conspicuous instance in the reign of Henry VIII being the vast legalism surrounding the divorce from Katherine of Aragon. Thomas More's fears for England 'if the lion knew his own strength' were doubtless sincere enough; but events hardly substantiated the implication that, for Henry, might would make right. Cautiously, painfully, Henry sought the legal sanctions for a step which was well within his power to take without recourse to law, and for which he had unquestioned popular support. At the same time, he was familiar enough with the popular mind to know that the lion's strength must be exerted within legal strictures. It is a strange misunderstanding of Tudor sentiments that the rejection of Falstaff has for so many years called forth the pity of critics. To abet the sowing of Prince Hal's wild oats was one thing, but to greet the news of the elevation to the throne of his former companion in riot with the boast, 'The laws of England are at my commandment', was no less than an abomination to the most cherished of English traditions.

THE TUDOR IDEAL OF GOVERNMENT

A strong governor, well supported by law, at the head of the state, each member of which contributes to its welfare, represented the Tudor ideal of government. Much of the political literature of the period was therefore directed toward defining the duties of prince and subjects so that the common weal could be served. More's *Utopia*, Erasmus's *Education of a Christian Prince*, Starkey's *Dialogue between Pole and Lupset*, and Elyot's *Governor*, all fall generally within this genre. Contemporaries recognized it as stemming from Plato' ideal commonwealth, but it owed much also to Aristotle's *Politic*. and to such characteristic medieval analogues of the commonwealth as the beehive or, more frequently, the body and its members, each with its individual function in the proper working of the whole When one adds to these formal treatises on government the flood of smaller literature adjuring obedience to the laws and to constituted authority, respect for that authority in the Tudor period seem almost formidably mandatory. 'There is no power but of God' said Tyndale in *The Obedience of a Christian Man*, but for the ordinary Englishman, the powers of God's representative, Henry VIII, must have seemed far more immediate and taxing. Tyndale made sure that there was no ambiguity: 'By *power* understand the authority of kings and princes.'

But laws were not an isolated phenomenon of this terrestrial ball. The laws of England fitted into the larger order of the universe from which even the mental dexterity of Falstaff could not hope to escape Beyond the reaches of man-made law, the law of nature still operated under which the whole of creation fitted into an all-inclusive juris-diction. And from the law of nature there could be no departure without violence, if not chaos, in the whole scheme of things. Once only, Richard Hooker dared to visualize such a cataclysm:

> Now if nature should intermit her course and leave altogether though it were but for a while, the observation of her own laws if those principal and mother elements of the world, whereof al things in this lower world are made, should lose the qualities which now they have; if the frame of that heavenly arch erected over our heads should loosen and dissolve itself; if celestial sphere should forget their wonted motions, and by irregular volubility turn themselves any way as it might happen; if the prince of the lights of heaven, which now as a giant doth run his unwearied course, should, as it were, through a languishing faintness begin to stand and to rest himself; if the moon should wander from her beaten way; the times and seasons of the year blend themselves by disordered and confused mixture; the winds breathe out their last

gasp; the clouds yield no rain; the earth be defeated of heavenly influence; the fruits of the earth pine away as children at the withered breasts of their mother no longer able to yield them relief: What would become of man himself, whom these things now do serve?

From this vision, Hooker rather illogically infers that 'obedience of creatures unto the law of nature is the stay of the whole world'. The hiatus in his logic, that conversely, man's disobedience to the law of nature is the cause of his fall, can be supplied from the classic description in Shakespeare's *Troilus and Cressida* of man's failure to observe degree:

> That everything includes itself in power,
> Power into will, will into appetite;
> And appetite, an universal wolf,
> So doubly seconded with will and power,
> Must make perforce an universal prey,
> And last eat up himself.

TRADITIONAL PRINCIPLE OF DEGREE

Ulysses' dire prophecy of the consequences of lawlessness involves ultimately the entire natural order, but it is noteworthy that 'the speciality of rule', that is, observance of degree, first shows disintegration on human levels. Social disorders breed political disorders; then the whole macrocosm is disrupted. The sun at the centre, like a king, maintains order only so long as the planets maintain it; but when they wander, all nature is violently shaken. Crowns and sceptres topple from their places; communities, degrees in schools, brotherhoods in cities, peaceful commerce, primogeniture, and respect for age no longer obtain. The son strikes his father dead. In a world where might and right have become synonymous, justice ceases to be.

This sense for order and abhorrence of disorder evidences itself in almost every aspect of society in the sixteenth century, and illustrations of it occur in every department of literature. It is present or implicit in John Rastell's prefaces, in Cuthbert Tunstall's *Letter to Cardinal Wolsey*, in William Tyndale's *Obedience of a Christian Man*, in John Colet's *A Right Fruitful Monition*, in Christopher Saint-German's *A Dialogue in English betwixt a Doctor of Divinity and a Student in the Laws of England*, and in John Cheke's *The Hurt of Sedition*, to glance over only the selections in the present anthology. Rastell, learned in the law, Tunstall, churchman and diplomat, Tyndale, the reformer, Colet, schoolmaster and scholar, Saint-German, legalist, Cheke, the scholar, represent a wide variety of training, background, and point of view; yet they are at one in their advocacy of a stable society.

> Take away order from all things [says Elyot in *The Governor*] what should then remain? Certes nothing finally, except some man would imagine eftsoons chaos. Also where there is any lack of order needs must be perpetual conflict. And in things subject to nature nothing of himself only may be nourished; but, when he hath destroyed that wherewith he doth participate by the order of his creation, he himself of necessity must then perish; whereof ensueth universal dissolution.... In everything is order, and without order may be nothing stable or permanent.

Such unanimity in praise of order suggests by implication the dangerous doctrines now besetting the inherited and customary scheme of things; and although the world did not seem to be in immediate expectancy of universal dissolution, a serious observer in the sixteenth century could hardly be unaware that from various points of the compass, the old political, social, and scientific landmarks were being modified, if not obliterated, by novel, even abhorrent doctrines. There were times when, everything including itself in power, power infecting will, and will in turn infecting appetite, civilization was confronted by the grim features of the universal wolf. The disturbing fact is that appetite in itself gave no hint of these qualities. 'Appetite is the Will's Solicitor', said Hooker, defining its normal and accustomed place of subordination. But, seconded by will and power, it might become a new and terrifying thing.

REALISM AND PLATONIC IDEALISM

The cancer of power, though evident in every phase of sixteenth-century life, was particularly virulent in statecraft. It is hard to hear Shakespeare's analysis of its effects without thinking of that master of politics, Machiavelli. Virtue, subtly transformed *virtù*, offered new possibilities in political conduct. *Policy* was no longer an innocent word. When Machiavelli rejected the ideal republics and principalities of the philosophers on the grounds that

> how we live is so far removed from how we ought to live, that he who abandons what is done for what ought to be done, will rather learn to bring about his own ruin than his preservation,

the shock to conservative opinion was profound. Reginald Pole listened with amazement to Thomas Cromwell's assertion that in conducting affairs of state he preferred the realism of Machiavelli to the idealism of Plato. But what Pole rejected, others around Cromwell found useful, and Machiavelli's consistent reference to pragmatic rather than utopian experience revolutionized both political theory and practical politics. In Machiavelli's scheme, the hierarchy of laws which bounded human activity was silently dropped, and fortune, that unstable goddess, ruled, or bore half the rule, as Machiavelli at one point grudgingly conceded. Man's destiny therefore depended chiefly on his ability to wrest power from the hands of fate. Regardless of the moralities involved, *virtù* in the individual must triumph in a world ordered solely by man-made law.

The evolution of government, as Machiavelli saw it, was not disposed by God but by chance. Men lived like beasts at the beginning of the world, and did not think of government until the increase in the human race made it necessary for them to defend themselves. Then they appointed one from their number, the strongest and most courageous, to rule over them, and instituted laws for the punishment of malefactors. But order thus established is never permanent. Monarchy degenerated into tyranny; aristocracy, set up as a cure by citizens with grandeur of soul, wealth, and courage, presently degenerated into oligarchy; and democracy, the cure for oligarchy, soon lapsed into anarchy, whence, to escape complete lawlessness, appeal was once more made to a prince to establish rule, and the cycle, if the state survived at all, began again.

By contrast, the history of government as Pole describes it in Starkey's *Dialogue*, was a steady progress upward. It was men 'of great wit and policy, with perfect eloquence and high philosophy', who, convinced of the excellent nature and dignity of man, and perceiving his potentialities, persuaded him to build cities and establish laws, 'whereby they might be induced to follow a life convenient to their nature and dignity'. Thus, 'by perfect eloquence and high philosophy', men were brought gradually to their present civilization. As for government, it made little difference whether they chose a monarchy, an aristocracy, or a democracy, so long as those in authority acted for the public good, the end of all government being 'to induce the multitude to virtuous living, according to the dignity and nature of man'.

Both theories of government were ultimately derived from Aristotle; their chief difference—and it was a fundamental difference —lay in the fact that for Machiavelli, man was basically evil.

SOCIAL EQUALITY

The dangers to order were as great in the social as in the political sphere. The traditional lines of society were clearly drawn, the levels plainly established, and social stability rested on the rigid observance of rank. But English society of the early sixteenth century had found these social levels increasingly anachronistic. The middle class which had established the first Tudor on the throne had increased in power under Henry VIII, in part because of the studied policy of depressing the old nobility, who constituted the likeliest threat to the throne, and aggrandizing the new men, often at the expense of the old. This process was greatly accelerated when Henry began the acquisition of church property. These new holdings proved to be an easy and cheap way to reward those who served the crown.

The laws of economics were meanwhile operating in the same direction. No one can read far into the history of the reign without becoming conscious of the widespread dislocation caused by the enclosing of formerly tilled land for sheep-rearing, an inevitable consequence of the growth of an industry which during the course of the sixteenth century was to absorb the energies of a greater part of the population. This major shift in economic activity put immense wealth in new and ambitious hands, and constituted the largest single factor in the shift of social power of the early sixteenth century.

This rise of new men in an expanding economy could not be accommodated within the traditional lines of social theory, particularly with regard to the medieval pattern of fixed social rank. In the oft-repeated analogy of the human body and its members, the agrarian society of the Middle Ages had been relatively comfortable, and St Paul's injunction that every man should labour in his vocation gave Scriptural warrant to the enforcement of stability within the existing pattern. But the ambition to rise had always run counter to this tradition, and under current conditions the elaborate structure of fixed rank showed indications of disintegration. Augustine's advice to the Carthaginian monks to 'labour with their hands for the common good, and submit to their superiors without murmur', frequently though it could be heard in the sixteenth century, no longer applied to a society in which

> commonly, poor men's sons natural born to labour for their living, after they be bound prentices to be merchants, all their labour, study, and policy is by buying and selling to get singular riches from the communalty, and never worketh to get their living neither by works of husbandry nor artificiality, but liveth by other men's works and of naught riseth to great riches, intending nothing else but only to get riches, which knoweth no common weal.

To the protest that Henry VII was surrounded by commoners whom he had raised to noble rank, and that the old nobility were being neglected, his defenders retorted, 'Let them have that they require, whom toucheth this so sore as themself, and all their posterity? What do they leave unto theirs, when they also take the possibility of better fortune?' It is a venal appeal to a rising, acquisitive generation, careless of the fact that it invited the destruction of the concept of fixed degree, the foundation of social order throughout the Middle Ages.

Such a breakdown involved inevitably the question of social equality. So long as the apologists for the King's policy were themselves beneficiaries, it remained a silent issue. When it did come up, it was in the Devonshire risings of 1549 in answer to a far graver demand for social levelling. In strikingly similar language to that used in 1536, John Cheke told the rebels, 'If there should be such equality then ye take away all hope from yours to come to any better estate than you now leave them.' In 1536 the rebels wanted to preserve the customary ranks; in 1549 Cheke believed that they intended to destroy them.

THE RISE OF SCIENCE

That same reassessment of generally accepted political and social ideas can be detected also in the field of science, particularly of medicine. The combination of astrology, magic, and plant lore which had for long associated itself with therapeutics would be outmoded during the sixteenth century by a new empirical approach, and though its greatest advances would not come until the end of the century, Englishmen of the early Tudor period were already coming in contact with its practitioners in Padua, whence the great new advances in science would emanate. And as in political and social thought, so in medicine, the direction of change would be from ideal to real. The distance travelled from Galen to Vesalius is not represented in this anthology, but the hints of direction are already evident.

It is a fact of some importance that Padua, the medical centre of Italy, should have been the most important and the most continuous resort of English scholars since its revival as a centre of learning in the early years of the sixteenth century. Thomas Linacre, whose medical knowledge was revered in England, had his training there, and he was followed by John Clement, son-in-law of Sir Thomas More, and Edward Wotton, later to become physician to Henry VIII and president of the Royal College of Physicians. Both Clement and Wotton helped Nicolo Leonico, Linacre's instructor in Greek, in editing the standard medical authority, Galen, in the Greek language. In the belief that the best physician is also a philosopher, Leonico had turned to Galen as 'the most skilful exponent of the teaching of Plato'. So rapid was the advance of scientific method at Padua that in less than a dozen years Vesalius had already begun there his work in experimental surgery. But it would be years before these studies had made an appreciable impression on the medical profession. In the meantime, the traditional compendiums continued to be printed, and experimental science and magical lore alike drew the attention of the best minds of the age.

If to a modern mind science moved deviously toward its destined aims, more like a stepchild to the occult arts than a legitimate enterprise, it held this in common with the new concepts of government and society, that each of those fields of knowledge was empirical in tendency. The impact of Machiavelli in politics and ethics and of Vesalius in medicine arose from the fact that both were interested in things, not as they might be, but as they are. In terms of the history of ideas, this break with tradition is one way to define the English Renaissance.

JOHN RASTELL
1475–1536

John Rastell, the most versatile member of the 'Thomas More Circle', was probably born in Coventry about 1475, and represented the third generation of a family prominent in English law. According to contemporaries, he was 'very properly learned', which probably referred to his education at the Coventry Guild School and the Middle Temple in London, where records show that a law student named Rastell was in attendance in 1501.

After his marriage, in 1503, to Elizabeth More, sister of Sir Thomas More, Rastell lived in Coventry and succeeded his father, Thomas Rastell, as Coroner. The position required him to participate in many chancery suits of which there are extant records. They show his interest in social reforms, particularly the dispute over the public grazing rights and the revolt of the citizens who wanted public instead of religious supervision of schools. On both issues, Rastell sided with the commoners.

In 1512 Rastell moved his wife and three children to London and entered the service of Sir Edward Belknap, a Privy Councillor to Henry VII and Henry VIII. As payment for his legal services during the war with France (1512–14) Belknap secured for Rastell a grant of all the properties of the wealthy draper Richard Hunne, who had been accused of heresy and mysteriously murdered in the Tower in 1514. Though the grant entailed a long series of lawsuits, the money enabled Rastell to make improvements in his printing shop and build a manor with elaborately landscaped grounds near the home of his father-in-law, Sir John More, at North Mimms. A large portion of the Hunne funds also helped him finance an unsuccessful expedition to the New World about 1517.

After this last venture, Rastell turned to designing sets for the elaborate pageants presented by Henry VIII. With his fees he purchased a new house in Finsbury, where he erected an outdoor stage for private productions. In some measure the venture was a forerunner of the Elizabethan theatre. The printing press which Rastell opened in London in Paul's Gate about 1524 was successful for some years, but the active management was left finally to his son William. The latter printed most of the works of his uncle, Sir Thomas More.

John Rastell became involved in lawsuits toward the end of his life and in desperation sought aid from Cromwell. He had sided with the heretical views of Tyndale and Frith and hoped on this account for court favour. When he was imprisoned in 1535 for opposing a royal proclamation which gave the clergy the right to collect tithes, it was ironical that the charges should be the same for which Hunne had been convicted twenty years before. After two years in prison Rastell wrote to Cromwell, begging to be released. He claimed that he was 'forsaken by his kinsmen', and had become 'the scorn of men and outcast of people'. The plea went unheeded, and he died in the Tower in 1536.

The earliest works of Rastell are his law books: Liber assissarum [1513], An abridgment of the statutes [1527]; and Exposiciones terminorum legum anglorum [1525?]. His plays are: A new commodye in englysh, adapted from Celestina [1525?]; A new interlude and a mery of the nature of the iiij. elements [1519?]; and Of gentylnes and nobylyte [1525?]. He also wrote a short history of England, The pastyme of people (1529), and a religious treatise, A new boke of Purgatory whiche is a dyaloge betwene Comyngo z Gyngemyn (1530). Besides these Rastell printed Terens in englysh (1520), his translation of Terence's 'furst comedye, called Andria'.

Though Rastell's prefaces to his law books lack grace and fluency of style, his is the first attempt in the Tudor era to arouse in the average citizen the necessity of knowing English common law that had held sway since Anglo-Saxon times and was looked on as springing directly from divine law and natural law. Having been a student at the Middle Temple, one of the four law schools that made up the Inns of Court, Rastell shows his training in the traditions that earlier had been taught by the common law enthusiasts, Thomas Littleton and Sir John Fortescue. Both men were admired by Rastell, and a comparison between his prefaces and Littleton's Tenures, of which he was the first to print an English translation (about 1525), and Fortescue's De laudibus legum Angliae (1546), to which he pays tribute, shows how closely he followed their legal and political theories, particularly Fortescue's belief in a monarchy limited by law and parliament, his hatred of tyranny, and the supreme importance that he attached to the law of God, expounded in Scripture and the ancient and medieval philosophers, especially St Thomas Aquinas.

Unlike Littleton and Fortescue, Rastell shows no interest in the long-standing controversy between the Inns of Court and the university law schools over the reception of the Continent's civil law, a complex body of laws, growing out of ecclesiastical decrees and the Justinian Code.

Regarding social reform and personal wealth, Rastell leaned more to the views of Plato than those of Aristotle. S. B. Chrimes, editor of Fortescue's De laudibus legum Angliae, believes that Rastell followed the elder lawyer in choosing passages from the quotation books Autoritates: Arestotilis, Senece, Boetij, Platonis, Apulei Affricani, Porphiry, Gilberti porritani, first printed by Gerard Leuu in Antwerp, in 1487, and revised and reprinted in over thirty editions until 1630. They were probably among the 'conning Laten bookys' which he regretted had not been translated into English so that 'all subtle science might be known'.

The Book of Assizes

PROLOGUE

Prologus Johannes Rastell: in laudem legum: quod respublica non consistit in divitiis, in potestate, nec honoribus, sed presertim in bonis legibus.[1]

Throughout all the world in every divers country, region, and coast, the thing that is ever among men most had in reputation and esteemed most digne and most universally desired is the public and commonweal of their country; and he that most endeavoureth himself for the augmenting of the same is ever among the people most magnified and lauded, best beloved and most honourable [and] renowned. To the increasing whereof, every man hath naturally a very love and zeal.

But yet wherein the commonweal standeth, and what thing it should be, is, and hath been, ever as well among philosophers, orators, poets, and other learned men great altercation, debate, and argument: of whom some affirmed the commonweal to consist in great abundance of riches, as them that multiply the riches of their whole country greatly to preserve their commonweal. Some hold that the commonweal of a country standeth not in riches, but that it is rather to multiply their power and strength. Of which opinion have been many great kings and princes which have all their lives studied and busied themselves to vanquish other realms to make themselves mighty and strong and so to increase their strength and power rather than to make themselves and their countries rich.

Some others there be of another opinion, that think to increase the commonweal of their country, [is] to cause it to shine in honour and glory and to be renowned, famed, and praised in the voice and speech of people. Also there be yet some others that esteem and judge that the commonweal resteth not in riches only, in power only, nor honour only, but in them all intermixed: for the Romans, that were the great conquerours, gathered not together their great abundance of riches only for the riches, but because they would thereby achieve to more honour, and with their riches so make themselves the more mighty and strong. They made not themselves puissant and strong for their strength and power only, but also because that by their might and power, they might the lightlier win great riches whereby they should the more be honoured and magnified.

---

[1] Prologue of John Rastell: in praise of Law: that the commonweal does not consist in riches, power, nor honours, but in good laws.

So evermore there hath been great altercation among men wherein the commonweal should stand, and what thing that the commonweal should be, that all men so much commend and praise. But as to my pretence what thing soever that the commonweal be, it must needs be the thing which of himself is a good thing and whereunto some goodness naturally is annexed, since that God, that is foundement[1] of all goodness, hath naturally given to every man a common and an universal love and zeal to the same, or else it were not digne nor worthy to be called a common good thing or a common *weal*, but rather a common *evil*. Wherefore of necessity it must needs be good of itself.

Then to proceed further: that thing that is good of itself, every man having free liberty may exercise and use it without doing of any evil to any other person; and also that thing that is merely good of itself, the contrary thereof must needs be evil. As by example: virtue which is good of itself, every man may use without doing evil to any other person. And the contrary to virtue is vice which of itself is evil and naught. So likewise the contrary to riches is poverty; the contrary to poverty is feebleness; and the contrary to honour is shame—which poverty, feebleness, and shame be ever esteemed evil things that all men eschew.

But great abundance of riches cannot lightly be gathered without causing of poverty; nor great puissance and strength without causing of feebleness; nor yet great honour nor glory without shame or reproof. For proof whereof, the great mighty people, the Romans, could never have won to themselves the great riches of the country of Persia and Carthage if they had not thereby the Persians and Carthaginians greatly impoverished. Nor the mighty, strong Greeks could never have augmented their power and strength so much as they did against the Trojans except that the Trojans by them had been vanquished and their city destroyed and so made more feeble and weak. Nor also the great, mighty, and famous Alexander could never attained by his conquest to so great honour and glory except he had subdued other great, mighty kings, as Darius of Persia and Porus of India, and so brought them to captivity which they esteemed shame and reproof.

Then since that a man cannot well exercise himself in increasing of his great riches, in augmenting his power, nor enhancing his honour without causing poverty, feebleness, or shame, which of themselves been evil things, it followeth well that riches, power, nor honour be not very perfect good things only of themselves, because, as I said, they cannot be attained without causing of evil things to other persons.

And then if that riches, power, or honour be not of themselves only good things, and the commonweal is that thing that is of itself

---

[1] *foundement*, foundation.

merely good, it must needs ensue that the commonweal can neither stand only in riches, power, nor honour. Then it is needful to search wherein that the commonweal should stand. Which now under correction, after mine opinion, the commonweal resteth neither in increasing of riches, power, nor honour, but in the increasing of good manners and conditions of men whereby they may be reduced to know God, to honour God, to love God, and to live in a continual love and tranquillity with their neighbours. For the which thing to be attained, it is to men most expedient to have ordinances and laws: for likewise as the bridle and the spur directeth and constraineth the horse swiftly and well to perform his journey, so doth good and reasonable ordinances and laws lead and direct men to use good manners and conditions, and thereby to honour, to dread, and to love God, and virtuously to live among their neighbours in continual peace and tranquillity, in firm concord and agreement, in a unity of will and mind, and in sincere and pure love and charity; which thing duly to perform is not given to mankind immediately and only by nature, as is given to all other creatures which be by nature constrained to do and to live after their kind.

For the which it followeth that man cannot attain these things but by a mean which is none other but good and reasonable ordinances and laws to instruct and direct men to the same: which reasonable ordinances and laws proceed and come principally of God, and to the which the providence and will of God is ever assistant and present. For likewise as nature, which is naught else but the final instrument of the Divine Providence, leadeth not itself, but is lead by that same Providence and aboundeth not in things superfluous nor lacketh not in things necessary, then doubtless the providence of God in all necessary things cannot be absent. And since that providence of God beholdeth, ordereth, and conserveth every singular kind of thing necessary to the use of man—as well elements, trees, herbs, fruits, fish, foul, and all other brute beasts—it followeth well that that same Providence more perfectly and diligently beholdeth and conserveth man himself in ordering reasonable laws which be to man's welfare most necessary and to the augmenting of the divine honour; and so from reasonable ordinances and laws, that Providence can in nowise be absent, but ever aiding and assistant. And so because the goodness of God causeth and maintaineth laws, it followeth necessarily that laws of themselves must needs be good.

Who may then in reason deny but that to constitute, to make, and to ordain laws is a thing of itself right good and honourable? And then to write laws is a thing right good and honest and not reprovable. To study and to learn and to teach laws is a life, good and virtuous. And, finally, to execute laws truly and justly is an act, right good and meritorious.

Wherefore I may conclude that because laws of themselves be good, and so great good cometh thereof, the commonweal by all reason must rather stand in augmenting and preferring of laws than either in riches, power, or honour. And so they that exercise and busy themselves in making laws, in ordering or writing of laws, in learning of laws, or teaching laws, or in just and true executing of laws, be those persons that greatly increase and multiply the commonweal.

Which premisses deliberately considered (because that the laws of this realm of England been ordained and made to the great commonweal and ease of the people of the same as much as the laws of any other realm, nation, or country as by the book that is compiled, *De Laudibus Legum Angliae* by the right honorable Master Fortescu, sometime Judge in this realm, more plainly is showed and by reason approbate, argued, and well declared) hath greatly exhorted and moved us at this time to take some pain and labour to order this present book which is called *The Book of Assises and Pleas of the Crown* as well in the new tables thereto devised as in the cotations[1] and numbering of the cases thereof and in the printing of the same; which [we] have not intended only to perform this work and to rest hereat, but we purpose further to put in print another book which, by God's grace, shall be better done and with much more diligence than this present *Book of Assises*, that is now done and finished in great haste; which other book shall be a great *Book of Abridgement*, of argued cases, ruled in many years of divers sundry kings, containing six or seven hundred leaves of great paper with divers great tables, belonging thereto, contained, ordered, and numbered with figures of algorisms[2] for the great expedition and furtherance of the studies of this law. And though that I myself, small of learning and discretion, have enterprised with the aid and help of divers other gentlemen and taken labours and also intend more labours to take, as well for the ordering of the calenders of the said great *Book of Abridgements* as in the numbering of the cotations and referments of the cases therein, yet the only praise of the making of the said great *Abridgement* ought to be given to Anthony Fitzherbert, sergeant at the law, which by his great and long study by many years continuing, hath compiled and gathered the same; exhorting and requiring all you honourable lords and masters, belonging to the law, that shall any of these said works see or read, that if anything therein be amiss, that ye by your discreet wisdom do it correct and amend, and that of your goodness ye hold us excused, considering it is no small labour to bring to a good, final conclusion so busy and so great a work: and if ye shall fortune to see or read anything therein that shall content you or do you pleasure, we be right glad thereof

---

[1] *cotations*, citations.   [2] *algorisms*, arabic numerical notations.

And for the more explanation of the tables of this present book, ye shall understand that the numbers ever upon your right hand showeth you in what year and of what number the case is in this *Book of Assises* which ye shall find argued there all at length. The numbers also upon your left hand showeth you in what title and in what number the same self case is abridged in the said *Book of the Great Abridgements* which (by God's grace, in as convenient time as can be) shall be imprinted. And though that every case in this *Book of Assises* be not referred to [in] the great *Book of Abridgements* nor therein abridged, ye may well perceive that it is not needful to abridge every case in this book nor to abridge every case in every other year.

And also I insure you that we have added divers other cases into this book which we have gathered out of other books of assises because this book should be the more complete of itself; which cases though they be not abridged, every man at his pleasure may them abridge and put them into this present calendar, for the which cause we have there left always some convenient space.

And furthermore because, peradventure, that every man to whom this book shall come cannot read well nor understand the numbers of algorism, here in the beginning of this book we have made a little table whereby a man without any other teacher may serve to read the numbers of algorism in the space of an hour.

COLOPHON: J. Rastell. [1513?]

An Abridgement of the Statutes

PROHEME

Because that the laws of this realm of England, as well the statutes as other judgments and decrees, be made and written most commonly in the French tongue, divers men thereof muse and have ofttimes communication and argument, considering that in reason every law whereto any people should be bounded ought and should be written in such manner and so openly published and declared that the people might soon [and] without great difficulty have the knowledge of the same laws.

But the very cause *why* the said laws of England were written in the French tongue should seem to be this: first, it is not unknown that when William Duke of Normandy came into this land and slew King Harold and conquered the whole realm, there was a great number of people, as well gentlemen as others, that came with him which understood not the vulgar tongue that was that time used in this realm, but only the French tongue: and also because the said King and other great wise men of his council perceived and supposed that the vulgar tongue, which was then used in this realm, was, in a manner, but homely and rude nor had not so great copy and abundance of words as the French tongue then [had]; nor that the vulgar tongue was not of itself sufficient to expound and to declare the matter of such laws and ordinances, as they had determined to be made for the good governance of the people, so effectually and so substantially as they could indite them in the French tongue. Therefore they ordered, wrote, and indited the said law that they made in the French tongue.

And, furthermore, long after the coming of King William [the Conqueror, because that the use of the French tongue in this realm began to minish and because that divers people then inhabited within this realm which could neither speak the vulgar tongue of this realm nor the French tongue, therefore the wise men of this realm caused to be ordered that the matters of law and actions between parties should be pleaded, showed and defended, answered, debated and judged in the English vulgar tongue; and, moreover, that written and entered of record in the rolls in the Latin tongue because that every man generally and indifferently might have the knowledge thereof, as appeareth by a statute made in the .xxxvi. year of [the reign of Edward III, chap. last. Wherefore, as I suppose, for these cause before rehearsed, the laws of this realm were indited and written in the French tongue, which was indited for a right good purpose.

But yet besides this, now of late days, the most noble Prince, our late sovereign lord, King Henry VII, worthy to be called the second Solomon (which excelled in politic wisdom all other princes that reigned in this realm before his time), considering and well perceiving that our vulgar English tongue was marvellously amended and augmented by reason that divers famous clerks and learned men had translated and made many noble works into our English tongue whereby there was much more plenty and abundance of English used than there was in times past; and by reason thereof our vulgar tongue so amplified and sufficient of itself to expound any laws or ordinances which were needful to be made for the order of this realm; and also the same wise Prince, considering that the universal people of this realm had great pleasure and gave themselves greatly to the reading of the vulgar English tongue, ordained and caused that all the statutes and ordinances which were made for the commonwealth of this realm in his days should be indited and written in the vulgar English tongue and to be published, declared, and imprinted so that then universally the people of the realm might soon have the knowledge of the said statutes and ordinances which they were bound to observe: and so by reason of that knowledge to avoid the danger and penalties of the same statutes and also the better to live in tranquillity and peace.

Which discreet, charitable, and reasonable order our most dread sovereign lord, that now is, King Henry VIII, hath continued and followed; and [he] caused all the statutes that have been made in his days to be also indited and written in our English tongue to the intent that all his liege people might have the knowledge thereof.

All which goodly purposes and intents, in my mind oftentimes revolved, hath caused me to take this little pain to translate out of French into English *The Abbreviation of the Statutes* [1481?] made before the first year of the reign of our late sovereign lord King Henry VII: and though that the statutes (made as well in the time of the said King Henry VII as in the time of our sovereign lord that now is) be sufficiently indited and written in our English tongue, yet to them that be desirous shortly to know the effect of them, they be now more tedious to read than though the matter and effect of them were compendiously abbreviated.

And wherefore now, as far as my simple wit and small learning will extend, I have here taken upon me to abridge the effect of them more shortly in this little book: beseeching all them to whom the sight thereof shall come, to accept it in gre;[1] and though they shall fortune to find anything misreported or omitted by my negligence or else by negligence of the printers, that it would like them to pardon me and to consider my good will, which have intended it for a commonwealth for the causes and confederations before rehearsed; and, also, if that it shall fortune them to be in doubt in any point thereof, yet, if it please them, they may resort to the whole statute whereof this book is but an abridgement and, in manner, but a calendar.

And, furthermore, I will advertise every man that shall fortune to have any matter in vre[2] to resort to some man that is learned in the laws of this realm to have his counsel in such points which he thinketh doubtful concerning the said statutes; by the knowledge whereof and by the diligent observing of the same, he may the better do his duty to his Prince and sovereign, and also live in tranquillity and peace with his neighbour according to the pleasure and commandment of Almighty God to whom be eternal laud and glory. Amen.

STATUTES

Good men and true which be no maintainers[3] in the country shall be assigned to keep the peace. (1 Edw. III, Stat. ii, chap. xvi.)

Two or three most worthy in every county shall be chosen to be

---

[1] *gre*, good will.   [2] *in vre*, pending.

[3] *maintainers*, those who intermeddle in a suit for the purpose of stirring up strife and continuing the litigation.

Justices of Peace; and they with other learned in the law shall determine felonies and trespass done against the peace. (18 Edw. III. Stat. ii, chap. ii.)

Justice of Peace shall inquire of them that sell iron at too high price, and shall punish them after the quantity of their trespass. (28 Edw. III, chap. v.)

Justice of Peace shall inquire of barrators[1] and wrong-doers, and shall punish them by their discretion, and also of all vagabonds; and shall imprison them that be suspect and not of good name, and take surety for their good abearing before they go out of prison; and that they may hear and determine all trespass and felonies done within the county; and shall inquire of measures and weights after the statutes thereof made. (23 Edw. III, chap. i.)

The commissions of the Justice of Peace shall make express mention that they shall hold their sessions four times in the year, sitting within the utas[2] of the Epiphany; the second week of Lent; between Whitsuntide and Saint John Baptist; and within the utas of Saint Michael. (36 Edw. III, chap. xii.)

COLOPHON: Printed in the Cheapside at the sign of the Mermaid next to Paul's gate; the 22nd day of December in the 19th year of the reign of our sovereign lord King Henry the VIII. *Per me*, Johannem Rastell. 1527.

Expositions of the Terms of English Laws

PROLOGUE

Likewise as the universal world can never have his continuance but only by the order and law of nature, which compelleth everything to do his kind, so there is no multitude of people in no realm that can continue in unity and peace without they be thereto compelled by some good order and law. Wherefore a good law observed, causeth ever good people: and a good, reasonable, common law maketh a good, common peace and a commonwealth among a great community of people. And one good governor which causeth one law to be observed among divers and much people bringeth divers and much people to one good unity. But divers rulers and governors, and divers orders and laws—one contrary to another—and when that every governor will have the law after his

---

[1] *barrators*, those who frequently excite and stir up quarrels and suits, either at law or otherwise.
[2] *utas*, octave of a saint's day or other festival.

mind, bringeth one multitude of people to variance and division. For as every man is variant from other in visage, so they be variable in mind and condition. Therefore, one law and one governor for one realm and for one people is most necessary.

And also lack of law causeth many wrongs to be committed willingly. And lack of knowledge of the law causeth divers wrongs to be done by negligence: therefore since law is necessary to be had and a virtuous and a good thing, *ergo* to have knowledge thereof is necessary and a virtuous and good thing: and that that is virtuous and good, is good for every man to use: *ergo* it followeth, it is a good thing for every man to have the knowledge of the law. And since that it is necessary for every realm to have a law reasonable and sufficient to govern the great multitude of the people, *ergo* it is necessary that the great multitude of the people have the knowledge of the same law to the which they be bound. *Ergo* it followeth that the law in every realm should be so published, declared, and written in such wise that the people so bound to the same might soon and shortly come to the knowledge thereof, or else such a law so kept secretly in the knowledge of a few persons and from the knowledge of the great multitude may rather be called a trap and a net to bring the people to vexation and trouble than a good order to bring them to peace and quietness.

And forasmuch as the law of this realm of England is ordained and devised for the augmentation of justice and for the quietness of the people and for the commonwealth of the same, *ergo* it is convenient that every one within this realm, bound to the same, may have the knowledge thereof: and [it is] not reasonable that any such ways should be had or used whereby the people should be ignorant of the law or should be exiled or restrained from the knowledge thereof.

I therefore, considering these foresaid causes, have taken upon me this little labour and study to declare and to expound certain obscure and dark terms concerning the laws of this realm and the nature of certain writs for the help and erudition of them that be young beginners which intend to be students of the law: for as the philosopher saith, *Ignoratis terminis, ignoratur et ars*. That is to say, 'He that is ignorant of the terms of any science must needs be ignorant of the science.' But yet I have not enterprised this for that that I think myself sufficient and able to expound them as substantially as other deep, learned men can do, but to [the] intent that some ease and furtherance of learning may come to young students by reading of this same.

And also I have compiled and indited this little work, first, in the French tongue, as is used in the books of our law; and after, translated this same compilation into our English tongue to the intent

that such young students may the sooner attain to the knowledge o
the French tongue, which knowledge so had shall be a great help and
furtherance unto them when they shall study other higher works o
the law of more difficulty, as be the Books of Years and Terms and
other books which be written in the French tongue, whereby they
shall come to the more knowledge of the law: which knowledge
of the law so had and the true execution of the same law shall be
greatly to the augmentation of the commonwealth of this realm
which the eternal God increase and preserve to His great honour and
glory. Amen.

COLOPHON: [J. Rastell, 1525?]

CUTHBERT TUNSTALL[1]

*Cuthbert Tunstall's views on the Lutheran heresy were the result o
personal observation. 'I was in Germany with Luther at the beginnings o
these opinions', he wrote, 'and I know how they began.' It is improbable
that Tunstall means that he actually met the German reformer while in
Flanders, in 1517, helping Erasmus prepare his second edition of the New
Testament. But Tunstall witnessed the uprisings that followed the posting
of Luther's theses at Wittenberg on 31 October 1517.*

*However, when Tunstall was again in Germany on a mission to the
court of Charles V, he passed through Worms soon after the Diet wa.
called in session in January 1521 by the emperor, to consider the charge.
brought against Luther. Tunstall's letter to Wolsey, the mutilated MS. o
which has been restored by Charles Sturge, shows the tense feeling in
Germany and his fears that Luther's 'opinions' if let come into England
would 'bring great trouble to the realm and Church'.*

Letter to Cardinal Wolsey

...furthermore the Chancellor showed me that many of the
temporal princes of the empire have declared to the emperor and
to his council, that the people of Allemand in every country be so
minded to Luther, whose opinions be condemned by the Pope
[Leo X], that rather than he should be by the Pope's authority
oppressed and not heard in his defense which he offereth, saying he

---

[1] For biographical sketch, see p. 48.

will be ready to revoke all that he cannot defend by Holy Scripture, the said people would spend a hundred thousand of their lives, and that they have informed the emperor that he is a [man of virtue and property] besides his learning.

The said Luther after [he perceived that he should] not be admitted to come to the Diet hither,* [for which he had authority] accorded and safe conduct therefore granted unto [him, though afterwards] at the instance of the Pope's orator was re[voked...], despairing to be heard in his defence did openly [in the town] of Wittenberg in Saxony gather the people and [the University], there being together, and burn the decretals and [...clementines]* as books erroneous, as he declared. [And the said] declaration he put in print* in the Dutch tongue, and sent [the same] about the country.

Which said declaration by some id[le person] hath been translated into Latin, which I send your grace [a copy],* enclosed to the intent you may see it and burn it when [you] have done; and also to the intent that your grace may call before you the printers and book-sellers and give them a straight charge that they bring none of his books into England, nor that they translate none of them into English lest thereby might ensue [as] great trouble to the realm and Church of England as is now here. All his books be in the Dutch tongue and in every man's hand that can read; and, as I under-stand, [they] be also in the Hungarian tongue.

It was thought before this Diet that at this time that matter should have been appeased, but now seeing the princes say they cannot appease it for the inclination of the people, whereto it may come, it is to be doubted.

The beginning of all this hath been because there is a great sum of money that yearly goeth to Rome for annates* which [the] country would be rid of; and the benefices be given by [the] Pope to such persons as do serve at Rome, [i.e. the] unlearned, [such] as cooks [and grooms, and not to] the virtuous and learned men of the country, as [they] say. So that the easiest [way] that I can think will be that the Pope shall lessen the said annates and collations of [bene]fices if he lose not the total obeisance of Allemand.

They say that there is a book since his condemnation printed wherein [he (Luther) uph]oldeth that four of the sacraments be alone *de jure posit*[*ivo*] [of the positive law] viz., Confirmation, Holy Orders, Extreme Unction, and Matrimony: Baptism, [the] Eucharist, and Penance be *de jure divino et evangelio* [of divine law and the gospel]: which book is entitled *De Babylonica Captivitate Ecclesiae* [*The Baby-lonian Captivity of the Church*]. They say there is much more strange opinions in it near to the opinions of Bohemia. I pray God, keep that book out of England. It is not brought hither because of the emperor's prohibition. They say it is in Dutch* as well as Latin, as all his works be: and that he hath made against the bull of his condemnation* a great treatise to justify his opinions* now late, which be not yet come forth.

They say also that many more than he, as well friars Augustine, of which Order he is, as also doctors seculars, do favour and hold his opinions save in certain points. At the exequies of the Cardinal [William] de Croy in the presence of the electors, the Emperor, the Pope's Ambassador, and the Cardinals, a friar preacher made a sermon, and in the beginning said the Pope was *Vicarius Christi in spiritualibus* [Vicar of Christ in the spiritual realm] and the Bishops were *apostoli* with a process thereupon [apostolic succession]. But how his tongue turned in his head, I cannot tell, but after, he concluded that the emperor, when they [bishops] do amiss, should reform their abuses *et usque ad depositionem* [even to the point of deposing them] as they report to him.

Whereupon the Pope's Nuncio [Hieronymus Alexander], having commissions against Luther, called him, laying the premisses to his charges. Which said Nuncio hath been openly threatened by many gentlemen not to meddle with him. [It is said that] he exhorted the emperor and all the princes to go [into Italy, which depends] on the empire, and to reform such abuses as shall be found there committed. I understand many and almost all the princes be inclined to it, that is to say, to the voyage to Italy because every man [thinketh to make] gain thereby. The said friar preacher is since ordained to preach [here during the whole season of] Lent, by whom I know not.

The Lord Chièvres showed [me that the] said Luther offereth if the emperor will go to Rome to reform the Church to bring him a hundred thousand men; whereunto the said emperor, as a virtuous prince, will not hearken, saying, nevertheless, that the said Luther hath many great clerks to hold with him [save] in some points, which the said Luther hath put forth more th[an he] can or will justify, to the entent that on the residue he might be heard and a council called for reformation of the abuses of the Church. Whereof the Pope will not hear, but standeth to his sentence of condemnation.

I have understood that the emperor hath determined to send out a commandment to execute the Pope's bull and to grant Ban Imperial* for the confiscation of the goods of those which shall maintain him or hold with his opinions. Which commandment is drawn and goeth forth now shortly....

WORMS

21 January 1521

Reprinted from the original MS. by Charles Sturge in *Cuthbert Tunstall* (London, 1938).

DESIDERIUS ERASMUS[1]

When Erasmus wrote Enchiridion militis Christiani *(1503), he was living at Louvain, devoting himself 'entirely to the study of Sacred Literature'. He addressed the work to a supposed friend, a military man, pointing out a way of life fitting for anyone in authority who must set an example for those under him. Erasmus's directives for 'the rule of a Christian prince' are contrary to the pragmatic counsel that Machiavelli gives rulers in* Il Principe *(1513), and which was to determine many of the political policies of Henry VIII.*

The spiritual fabric of the Enchiridion *is not unlike that found in the* Imitation of Christ. *Though the work of Thomas à Kempis is the more profoundly spiritual, both are the fruits of the religious training given those schooled by the Brethren of the Common Life.*

Until the anonymous English translation A book called in latyn Enchiridion and in englysshe the manuell of the christen knyght *was printed in 1533, the Latin edition was immensely popular in England. It was praised by Erasmus's friends Bishop John Fisher and Sir Thomas More. However, when it was rumoured that William Tyndale was the translator, the* Manuell *became unfortunately the centre of controversy, since the Reformer's works had been banned by ecclesiastical authority, and its appeal waned.*

Scholars have long accepted Tyndale as the translator of the Enchiridion *because of certain characteristics of style and vocabulary. In the* Manuell *he continued his penchant for coining phrases, and he introduced into Tudor prose such expressions, as 'jot and tittle', 'sackcloth and ashes', 'filthy lucre', and 'pick-quarrel'.*

Besides the six Latin editions of the Enchiridion *printed on the Continent before 1550, there were eight editions of the English version issued prior to the same year.*

Enchiridion

TRANSLATED BY WILLIAM TYNDALE

A book called in Latin, *Enchiridion Militis Christiani*, and in English, *The Manual of the Christian Knight*, replenished with most wholesome precepts made by the famous clerk Erasmus of Rotterdam, to the which is added a new and marvellous profitable preface.

HERE FOLLOW OPINIONS MEET FOR A CHRISTIAN MAN[2]

Let this excellent learning and paradoxes of the true Christian faith be sure and steadfast with thee, that no Christian man may think that

[1] For biographical sketch, see pp. 55-7.　　　[2] Chapter xv.

he is born for himself; neither ought [he] to have the mind to live
to himself: but whatsoever he hath, whatsoever he is, that altogether
let him ascribe not to himself, but unto God, the Author
thereof and of whom it came: all his goods let him think
to be common to all men.

A Christian man is not born for himself neither to follow his own pleasure

The charity of a Christian man knoweth no property:
let him love good men in Christ, evil men for Christ's
sake, which so loved us first when we were yet His
enemies that He bestowed Himself on us altogether for
our redemption: let him embrace the one because they
be good; the other, nevertheless, to make them good; he shall hate
no man at all, no more, verily, than a faithful physician hateth a
sick man: let him be an enemy only unto vices: the greater the
disease is, the greater cure will pure charity put thereto:

He must defy and abhor the vices, but not the man

he is an adulterer, he hath committed sacrilege, he is a
Turk: let a Christian man defy the adulterer, not the
man: let him despise the committer of sacrilege, not the
man: let him kill the Turk, not the man: let him find the
means that the evil man perish, such as he hath made himself to be,
but let the man be saved whom God made: let him will well, wish
well, and do well to all men unfeignedly: neither hurt them which
have deserved it, but do good to them which have not deserved it:
let him be glad of all men's commodities as well as of his own, and
also be sorry for all men's harms none otherwise than for his own.
For verily, this is that which the Apostle commandeth: To weep with
them that weep, to joy with them that joy[1], yea, let him rather take
another man's harm grievouser than his own: and of his brother's
wealth be gladder than of his own.

It is not a Christian man's part to think on this wise: 'What have
I to do with this fellow? I know not whether he be black or white;
he is unknown to me; he is a stranger to me; he never did aught for
me; he hath hurt me sometime; but did me never good.' Think
none of these things. Remember only for what deserving were given
those things which Christ hath done for thee, who would that His
kindness done to thee should be recompensed, not in Himself, but in
thy neighbour. Only see of what things he hath need, and what thou
art able to do for him. Think this thing only: he is my brother in our
Lord, co-heir in Christ, a member of the same body, redeemed with
one blood, a fellow in the common faith, called unto the very same
grace and felicity of the life to come, even as the Apostle said: One
body and one spirit as ye be called in one hope of your calling, one
Lord and one faith, one baptism, one God and Father of all which is
above all and everywhere, and in all us.[2]

How can he be a stranger to whom thou art coupled with so mani-

[1] Rom. xii. 15.   [2] Eph. iv. 4–6.

fold bonds of unity? Among the gentiles let those circumstances of rhetoricians be of no little value and weight, either unto benevolence or unto malevolence—he is a citizen of the same city, he is of alliance, he is my cousin, he is my familiar friend, he is my father's friend, he hath well deserved, he is kind, born of an honest stock, rich or otherwise. In Christ all these things either be nothing or, after the mind of Paul, be all one and the very selfsame thing: let this be ever present before thine eyes, and let this suffice thee: he is my flesh, he is my brother in Christ. Whatsoever is bestowed upon any member, reboundeth it not to all the body, and from thence into the head?

We all be members each one of another; members cleaving together make a body. The head of the body is Jesus Christ; the head of Christ is God. It is done to thee, it is done to everyone; it is done to Christ, it is done to God, whatsoever is done to any one member whichsoever it be, whether it be well done or evil. All these things are one: God, Christ, the body, and the members.[1] That saying hath no place conveniently among Christian men, 'Like with like', and the other saying, 'Diversity is mother of hate.' For unto what purpose pertain words of dissension where so great unity is: it savoureth not of Christian faith that commonly a courtier to a town dweller; one of the country to an inhabiter of the city; a man of high degree to another of low degree; an officer to him that is officeless; the rich to the poor; a man of honour to a vile person; the mighty to the weak; the Italian to the German; the Frenchman to the Englishman; the English to the Scotch; the grammarian to the divine; the logician to the grammarian; the physician to the man of law; the learned to the unlearned; the eloquent to him that is not fecund and lacketh utterance; the single to the married; the young to the old; the clerk to the layman; the priest to the monk; the Carmelites to the Jacobites; and that (lest I rehearse all diversities), in a very trifle, unlike to unlike is somewhat partial and unkind. Where is charity which loveth even his enemy when the surname [is] changed; when the colour of the vesture, a little altered; when the girdle or the shoe and like fantasies of men make me hated unto thee?

Charity is not in them which hate another man because his vesture or garment is a little altered or changed

Why rather leave we not these childish trifles, and accustom to have before our eyes that which pertaineth to the very thing whereof Paul warneth us in many places, that all we in Christ our Head be members of one body,[2] endued with life by one Spirit (if so be it, we live in Him) so that we should neither envy the happier members, and should gladly succour and aid the weak members: that we might perceive that we ourselves have received a good turn, when we have done any benefit to our neighbor: and that we ourselves be hurt,

[1] Cf. Eph. iv. 15–16.   [2] Cf. I Cor. xii. 12.

when hurt is done to our brother: and that we might understand
how no man ought to study privately for himself, but every man for

Let every
man bestow
in common
whatsoever
he received
of God

his own part should bestow in common that thing which
he hath received of God, that all things might redound
and rebound thither again, from whence they sprung,
that is to wit, from the Head....

The decree
of Christian
men

Let this, therefore, be a decree among Christian men:
to compare with all men in love, in meekness, and in
benefits or doing good; but in striving, hate or back-
biting, in rebukes and injury to give place even to them
that be of lowest degree, and that with good will. But

he is unworthy to whom a good turn should be done or an evil
forgiven, yet is it meet for thee to do it; and Christ is worthy for
whose sake it is done. 'I will neither', say they, 'hurt any man
neither suffer myself to be hurt.' Yet when thou art hurt, see thou
forgive the trespass with all thy heart, providing always that nothing
be which any man should remit or forgive unto thee.

Be as wary and diligent in avoiding that none offence or trespass
proceed from thee, as thou art easy and ready to remit another man's.

Offences
must be
forgiven

A gentleman

A cunning
man

A rich man

Poverty is
not enjoined
to monks
only

The greater man thou art, so much the more submit
thyself, that thou in charity apply thyself to all men. If
thou come of a noble stock, manners worthy of Christ
shall not dishonour, but honour the nobleness of thy
birth. If thou be cunning and well learned, so much the
more soberly suffer and amend the ignorance of the unlearned. The more is committed and lent to thee, the
more art thou bound to thy brother. Thou art rich?
Remember thou art the dispenser, not the lord: take
heed circumspectly how thou entreatest the common
good. Believest thou that property or impropriation
was prohibit, and voluntary poverty enjoined to monks
only? Thou art deceived: both pertain indifferently to

all Christian men. The law punisheth thee if thou take away anything of another man's: it punisheth not if thou withdraw thine own
from thy needy brother: but Christ will punish both. If thou be an
officer, let not the honour make thee more fierce, but let the charge
make thee more diligent and fuller of care. 'I bear not', sayest thou,
'no office of the church; I am not a shepherd or a bishop.' Let us
grant you that, but also art thou not a Christian man; consider thou
of whence thou art, if thou be not of the Church.

So greatly Christ is coming into contempt to the world, that they
think it a goodly and excellent thing to have nothing to do with
Him: and that so much the more every man should be despised, the
more coupled he were to Him. Hearest thou not daily of the lay
persons in their fury, the names of a clerk, of a priest, of a monk, to

be cast in our teeth, instead of a sharp and cruel rebuke, saying, 'Thou clerk, thou priest, thou monk, that thou art.' And it is done, utterly with none other mind, with none other voice or pronouncing, than if they should cast in our teeth incest or sacrilege.

Incest is to meddle with their own kin.

I verily marvel why they also cast not in our teeth baptism? Why also object they not against us with the Saracens, the name of Christ as an opprobrious thing? If they said, 'an evil clerk', 'an unworthy priest', or 'an unreligious monk', in that they might be suffered as men which note the manners of the persons, and not despise the profession of virtue. But whosoever counteth praise in themselves the deflowering of virgins, goods taken away in war, money either won or lost at dice or other chance, and have nothing to lay against another man more spiteful or opprobrious or more to be ashamed of than the names of a monk or a priest, certainly it is easy to conjecture what these, in name only Christian men, judge of Christ. There is not one Lord of the bishops and another of the temporal officers; but both be under One: and to the same, both must give accounts.

Sacrilege is to violate persons sacred to God or to rob churches

If thou look any other where save unto Him only, either when thou receivest the office or when thou ministerest it, it maketh no matter though the world call thee not a simoniac, He surely will punish thee as a simoniac. If thou labour and make means to obtain a common office, not to profit in common, but to provide for thine own wealth privately and to avenge thyself of them to whom thou owest a grudge, thy office is bribery or robbery afore God. Thou huntest after thieves, not that he should receive his own that is robbed, but lest it should not be with thee which is with the thieves. How much difference, I pray thee, is there between the thieves and thee, except, peradventure, that they be the robbers of merchants and thou, the robber of robbers.

A simoniac

A pretty note for shrieves and other officers

In conclusion, except thou bear thine office with this mind, that thou be ready and that with the loss I will not say of thy goods but of thy life to defend that which is right, Christ will not approve thy administration. I will add also another thing of the mind or judgment of Plato: No man is worthy of an office which is gladly in an office. If thou be a prince, beware lest these perilous witches, the voices of flatterers, do enchant or bewitch thee. Thou art a lord, over the laws thou art free; whatsoever thou dost is honest; to thee is lawful whatsoever thou list. Those things pertain not to thee which are preached daily of priests to the common people. Yea, but think thou rather, which is true, that

He is worthy to be an officer which is in office against his will

there is one master over all men, and He is Christ Jesus: to whom thou oughtest to be as like as is possible, to whom thou oughtest to conform thyself in all things as unto Him certainly whose authority or room thou bearest. No man ought to follow His doctrine more straitly than thou of whom He will ask accounts more straitly than of others.

Christ is Lord, both of laymen and also of priests

Think not straightway *that* to be right, that thou wilt; but only will thou which *is* right. Whatsoever may be filthy to any man in the world, see that thou think not that an honest thing to thee, but see thou in no wise permit to thyself anything which is used to be forgiven and pardoned among the common sort. That which in other men is but a small trespass, think in thyself to be a great outrage or excess. Let not thy riches greater than the common people bring unto thee honour, reverence and dignity, favour and authority, but let thy manners, better than the common people, utterly deserve them.

Desire but that which is right

Suffer not the common people to wonder at those things in thee wherewith are provoked and enticed the very same mischievous deeds which thou punishest daily.

The honesty of good manners

Take away this wondering and praise of riches, and where be thieves; where be oppressors of the commonwealth; where be committers of sacrilege; where be errant thieves and robbers or rievers? Take away wondering at voluptuousness, and where be ravishers of women, where be adulterers?

As often as thou wilt appear somewhat according after thy degree among thy friends and subjects, or them over whom thou bearest office, room, or authority, set not open thy riches and treasure to the eyes of foolish persons. When thou wilt seem somewhat wealthy, show not in boast the riotous example of expense and voluptuousness. First of all, let them learn in thee to despise such things; let them learn to honour virtue, to have measure in price, to rejoice in temperance, to give honour to sober lowliness or meekness. Let none of those things be seen in thy manners and conversation which thine authority punisheth in the manners and conversation of the people. Thou shalt banish evil deeds in the best wise, if men shall not see riches and voluptuousness, the matter and ground of evil deeds, to be magnified in thee. Thou shalt not despise, in comparison of thyself, any man: no, not the vilest of the lowest degree; for common and indifferent is the price wherewith ye both were redeemed.

Let not the noise of ambition, neither fierceness, neither weapons, nor men of the guard, defend thee from contempt, but pureness of living, gravity, manners uncorrupt and sound from all manner vices of the common people. Nothing forbiddeth (in bearing rule) to keep the chief room, and yet in charity to discern no room. Think, bearing of room or rule to be this: not to excel and go before other men in abundance of riches, but to profit all men as much as is possible. Turn not to thine own profit things which are common, but bestow those things which be thine own and thine own self altogether upon the commonwealth. The common people oweth very many things to thee, but thou owest all things to them. Though thine ears be compelled to suffer names of ambition, as most mighty, most christened, holiness, and majesty, yet let thy mind not be a-knowen of them, but refer all these things unto Christ to whom only they agree.

The rule of Christian princes

Let the crime of treason against thine own person (which others with great words make an heinous offence) be counted of thee a very trifle. He violateth the majesty of a prince indeed which in the prince's name doth anything cruelly, violently, mischievously, contrary to right. Let no man's injury move thee less than that which pertaineth to thee privately: remember thou art a public person, and that thou oughtest not to think but of common matters. If thou have any courage with thee and readiness of wit, consider with thyself not how great a man thou art, but how great a charge thou bearest on thy back: and the more in jeopardy thou art, so much the less favour thyself, fetching example of ministering thine office not of thy predecessors or else of flatterers, but of Christ. For what is more unreasonable than that a Christian prince should set before him for an example, Hannibal, Great Alexander, Caesar, or Pompey; in the which same persons when he cannot attain some certain virtues, he shall counterfeit those things most chiefly which only were to be refused and avoided.

The majesty of a prince

The manner and form of bearing rule must be set of Christ

Let it not, forthwithal, be taken for an example if Caesar have done anything lauded in histories, but if he have done anything which varyeth not from the doctrine of Our Lord Jesus Christ, or be such that though it be not worthy to be counterfeited, yet may it be applied to the study or exercise of virtue. Let not a whole empire be of so great value to thee that thou wouldst wittingly once bow from the right: put off that rather than thou shouldst put off Christ. Doubt not Christ hath to make thee amends for the empire refused, far better than the empire. Nothing is so comely, so excellent, so glorious unto kings as to draw as nigh as is possible unto the similitude of the highest King, Jesus, which as He was the greatest so was He also the best. But that He was the greatest that dissimuled,[1] yea, and hid secret here in earth; that He was the best; *that* He had liefer we should perceive and feel, because He had liefer we should counterfeit *that*. He denied His kingdom to be of this world when He was Lord of heaven and earth

What is comely for princes

Christ is the greatest, He is also the best

---

[1] *dissimuled*, disguised.

also.[1] But the princes of the gentiles use dominion upon them.[2] A Christian man exerciseth no power over his [dominion] but charity; and he which is the chiefest, thinketh himself to be minister unto all men, not master or lord....

In conclusion that which is in thy breast is not so greatly to be roared forth with cruel words, as to be declared and uttered with honest manners. And again thou oughtest not so to favour the infirmity of the common people that thou durst not at a time strongly defend the verity. With humanity men must be amended, and not deceived.

COLOPHON: Imprinted at London by Wynkyn de Worde, for John Byddell, otherwise Salisbury, the 15th day of November. And to be for to sell at the sign of our Lady of Pity next to Fleet bridge. 1533.

WILLIAM TYNDALE
1494?–1536

Through his English translation of the New Testament William Tyndale (or Hychyns as the family was known) became almost immediately the leader of the Reformation in England, though he lived and worked in exile in the Low Countries.

Tyndale was born in Gloucestershire about 1492, and according to John Foxe was 'brought up from a child' in Oxford, where he attended Magdalen College. Between 1512 and 1515 Tyndale took both a Bachelor and Master of Arts degree. While still at the university, he was ordained to the priesthood in the Hereford diocese. During the next three years, which were spent at Oxford, he probably kept on with his study of the Scripture, which Foxe says as a young student he especially enjoyed reading aloud and instructing those about him 'in knowledge and truth' of Holy Writ.

In 1519 Tyndale left Oxford and took up his residence at Cambridge. The change was probably to escape the 'war' that was going on at the former university over the teaching of the Greek and Latin classics. Bishop Fisher, Chancellor of Cambridge, had quietly introduced the study of classical literature, and the colleges had responded. While at the university, Tyndale had the opportunity to meet many of the men who were destined to work with him in the early days of the Reformation. Prominent among them were Miles Coverdale, John Frith, Hugh Latimer, Thomas Cranmer, Robert Barnes, and Stephen Gardiner.

[1] Cf. John xviii. 36.   [2] Matt. xx. 25.

At the invitation of Sir John Welsh to serve as tutor for his children, Tyndale left Cambridge in 1521. His life in the Welsh household seems to have been pleasant, and he enjoyed the discussions that he had with the prelates and scholars who came as guests. These talks revealed that Tyndale was beginning to question certain dogmas of the Church. He upheld Luther's doctrine of justification by faith and rejected the Church's teaching on sacramental grace and transubstantiation. It was at this time that he translated Erasmus's Enchiridion (1533) and dedicated it to Lady Welsh.

The most active period in Tyndale's life began in 1523 when he gave up teaching in the Welsh household and started work on his English translation of the New Testament. His controversy with Sir Thomas More also belongs to this period, as does the composition of several polemical treatises. One of the latter, Practyse of prelates (1530), angered Henry VIII because Tyndale denounced the king's proposed divorce from Katherine of Aragon. But Cromwell saw in the Reformer a capable Papal opponent, and he persuaded the king to overlook the incident and enlist Tyndale's aid in the royal cause against Rome.

The Crown's agent Stephen Vaughan was sent to Germany to induce Tyndale to become a pamphleteer in the king's service, but was unsuccessful. Fearing it was a ruse to get him back to London, the Reformer refused Vaughan's offers. Finally, losing patience, Henry VIII denounced him as having 'a malicious, perverse, uncharitable, and indurate mind', and rejoiced that the realm was rid of him. His arrest was ordered in 1534, but Tyndale successfully eluded the king's agents for several months until he was caught in Antwerp through a treacherous plot. In the late spring of 1535 he was tried and sentenced to death. For a year and a half Tyndale was kept in the state prison in Vilvorde, near Brussels. Tradition has it that he was brought to the place of execution the morning of 6 October 1536, and 'strangled first by the hangman, and afterwards with fire consumed'.

Besides Tyndale's English versions of the Old and New Testaments, his works consist of polemical and controversial treatises. Among the former are: The parable of the wycked mammon (1528); The obedience of a christen man (1528); and Practyse of prelates (1530). In the Parable, which Tyndale calls 'my book of Justifying Faith', he upholds Luther's doctrine of the justification by faith without good works. Besides his comments on the king's divorce in Practyse of Prelates, Tyndale vents a pent-up hatred for Cardinal Wolsey, who is made to typify all prelates.

Two years after publishing his New Testament, Tyndale wrote The obedience of a christen man, of which eight editions were printed before 1561. He is concerned in the treatise with two main points, namely, convincing the king of his God-given power to rule and discrediting the supreme authority of 'the comen knowen Catholic Church'.

The Obedience was praised by Henry VIII, who considered it a book *for himself and all kings to read. It proclaimed a freedom for rulers, amounting to tyranny, in which it directly opposed Erasmus's views in the* Manual of a Christian Knight, *or the* Enchiridion, *at one time so admired by Tyndale. But the 'litel' work suited the temper of the times, and once the tie with Rome was broken, it became a basic text for the king's pamphleteers.*

The Obedience of a Christian Man

The Obedience of a Christian Man: and how Christian rulers ought to govern, wherein also, if thou mark diligently, thou shalt find eyes to perceive the crafty conveyance of all jugglers.

THE OBEDIENCE OF SUBJECTS UNTO KINGS, PRINCES, AND RULERS

Let every soul submit himself unto the authority of the higher powers. There is no power but of God. The powers that be are ordained of God. Whosoever therefore resisteth the power, resisteth the ordinance of God. They that resist shall receive to themselves damnation. For rulers are not to be feared for good works, but for evil. Wilt thou be without fear of the power? Do well then, and so shalt thou be praised of the same, for he is the minister of God for thy wealth. But and if thou do evil, then fear, for he beareth not a sword for naught, for he is the minister of God to take vengeance on them that do evil. Wherefore ye must needs obey, not for fear of vengeance only but also because of conscience. Even for this cause, pay ye tribute: For they are God's ministers, serving for the same purpose.

Give to every man therefore his dues; tribute to whom tribute belongeth; custom to whom custom is due; fear to whom fear belongeth; honour to whom honour pertaineth. Owe nothing to any man, but to love one another: For he that loveth another, ful-filleth the law. For these [are] commandments: *Thou shalt not commit adultery; Thou shalt not kill; Thou shalt not steal; Thou shalt not bear false witness; Thou shalt not desire;* [1] and so forth. If there be any other commandment, all are comprehended in this saying: Love thine neighbour as thyself.[2] Love hurteth not his neighbour: there-fore is love the fulfilling of the law.

As a father over his children is both lord and judge, forbidding that one brother avenge himself on another, but if any cause of strife be between them will have it brought unto himself or his assigns to be judged and corrected, so God forbiddeth all men to avenge them-selves, and taketh the authority and office of avenging unto himself

[1] Exod. xx, 13–17.   [2] Matt. xxii, 39.

saying: Vengeance is mine and I will reward[1] (Deuter. xxxii. which text Paul allegeth Rom. xii). For it is impossible that a man should be a righteous, an equal, or an indifferent judge in his own cause: lusts and appetites so blind us. Moreover, when thou avengest thyself, thou makest not peace, but stirrest up more debate.

God therefore hath given laws unto all nations; and in all lands hath put kings, governors, and rulers in His own stead to rule the world through them. And hath commanded all causes to be brought before them, as thou readest [in] Exo. xxii: In all causes, saith He, of injury or wrong, whether it be ox, ass, sheep, or vesture, or any lost thing which another challengeth, let the cause of both parties be brought unto the gods: whom the gods condemn the same shall pay double unto his neighbour.[2] Mark that judges are called gods in the Scriptures because they are in God's room, and execute the commandments of God. And in another place of the said chapter, Moses chargeth saying: See that thou rail not on the gods; neither speak evil of the ruler of thy people.[3] Whosoever, therefore, resisteth them, resisteth God, for they are in the room of God: and they that resist, shall receive their damnation. *Judges are called gods*

Such obedience unto father and mother, master, husband, emperor, king, lords, and rulers, requireth God of all nations—yea, of the very Turks and infidels. The blessing and reward of them that keep them, is the life of this world, as thou readest [in] Leviticus xviii: Keep my ordinances and laws; which if a man keep he shall live therein.[4] Which text Paul rehearseth (Rom. x), proving thereby that the righteousness of the law is but worldly, and the reward thereof is the life of this world. And the curse of them that breaketh them, is the loss of this life, as thou seest by the punishment appointed for them.... *Blessing* *Curse*

God requireth the law to be kept of all men, let them keep it for whatsoever purpose they will. Will they not keep the law? So vouchsafeth He not, that they enjoy this temporal life. Now are there three natures of men: one altogether beastly which in no wise receive the law in their hearts, but rise against princes and rulers whensoever they are able to make their part good. These are signified by them that worshipped the golden calf. For Moses broke the Tables of the Law ere he came at them.[5] *Three natures*

The second are not so beastly, but receive the law. And unto them the law cometh: but they look not Moses in the face. For his countenance is too bright for them: that is, they understand not that

---

[1] Deut. xxxii. 35; also Rom. xii. 19.   [2] Exod. xxii. 9.
[3] Exod. xxii. 28.   Lev. xviii. 5; also Rom. x. 5.
[5] Exod. xxxii. 19.

the law is spiritual, and requireth the heart. They look on the
pleasure, profit, and promotion that followeth the keeping of the
law; and in respect of the reward, keep they the law outwardly with
works, but not in the heart. For if they might obtain like honour,
glory, promotion, and dignity, and also avoid all inconvenience if
they broke the law, so would they also break the law and follow
their lusts.

The third are spiritual, and look Moses in the open face and are
(as Paul saith, the second to the Romans), 'a law unto themselves
and have the law written in their hearts'[1] by the spirit of God. These
need neither king nor officers to drive them; neither that any
man proffer them any reward for to keep the law, for they do it
naturally....

That thou mayst perceive and feel the thing in thine heart, and
not be a vain sophister, disputing about words without perceiving,
mark this: The root of all evil, the greatest damnation and most
terrible wrath and vengeance of God that we are in, is natural
blindness. We are all out of the right way: every man *his* way. One
judgeth this best; another that to be best. Now is worldly

Worldly wit wit nothing else but craft and subtlety to obtain that
which we judge falsely to be best. As I err in my wit,
so err I in my will. When I judge that to be evil which indeed is
good, then hate I that which is good. And when I suppose that
good which is evil, indeed then love I evil. As if I be

The will is bound and led persuaded and borne in hand that my most friend is
mine enemy, then hate I my best friend: and if I be
brought in belief that my most enemy is my friend, then
love I my most enemy.

Now when we say, every man hath his free will to do what him
lusteth, I say verily that men do what they lust. Notwithstanding,
to follow lusts is not freedom, but captivity and bondage. If God

Freedom open any man's wits to make him feel in his heart that
lusts and appetites are damnable, and give him power to

All is sin that springeth not of the Spirit of God and all that is not done in the light of God's Word hate and resist them, then is he free even 'with the freedom wherewith Christ maketh free',[2] and hath power
to do the will of God.

Thou mayst hereby perceive that all that is done in
the world before the Spirit of God come and giveth us
light is damnable sin: and the more glorious, the more
damnable: so that that which the world counteth most

So do our spirituality in all their works glorious is more damnable in the sight of God than that
which the whore, the thief, and the murderer do. With
blind reasons of worldly wisdom mayst thou change the
minds of youth, and make them give themselves to what

[1] Rom. ii. 14.   [2] Gal. iv. 31.

thou wilt, either for fear, for praise, or for profit; and yet doth but change them from one vice to another, as the persuasions of her friends made Lucrece chaste. Lucrece believed if she were a good housewife and chaste that she should be most glorious, and that all the world would give her honour and praise her. She sought her own glory in her chastity, and not God's. When she had lost her chastity, then counted she herself most abominable in the sight of all men; and for very pain and thought which she had—not that she had displeased God, but that she had lost her honour—slew herself.

Look how great her pain and sorrow was for the loss of her chastity: so great was her glory and rejoicing therein, and so much despised she them that were otherwise, and pitied them not: Which pride God more abhorreth than the whoredom of any whore. Of like pride are all the moral virtues of Aristotle, Plato, and Socrates, and all the doctrine of the philosophers, the very gods of our schoolmen....

COLOPHON: At Marlborow in the lande of Hesse.... 1528, by me, H. Luft.

THOMAS STARKEY
1499–1538

Thomas Starkey, one of the most liberal-minded of the younger Tudor humanists, was born in Wrenbury in 1499, the son of Thomas and Maud Starkey, a middle-class couple to whom Henry VII granted an annuity. The elder Starkey, in spite of his slender means, gave his son a good education, a debt which he repaid by naming his father the principal beneficiary of his will.

During his stay at Magdalen College, Oxford, Starkey was a fellow-student of Reginald Pole, who became one of his closest friends. After taking a Master of Arts degree at the university in 1521, his ability as a classical scholar was recognized by Cardinal Wolsey, who gave him a proctorship in the college the following year.

In 1524 Starkey resigned to go to Padua, where he became a member of Pole's household, serving as his secretary for the next ten years. His duties left time for study, and Starkey completed his clerical course, and was ordained to the priesthood. Before he returned to England he received two degrees from the University of Padua, doctorates in civil and in canon law. For a short time he and Pole studied at Avignon under Giovanni Francesco Ripa, the celebrated authority on Justinian law.

Never a conservative, it was not surprising to Starkey's Paduan friends that he upheld the legality of the king's divorce in an unsolicited opinion sent to Henry VIII in 1533. A year later, ill and eager to return to London where he could use his legal talents to advantage, he left Italy. Pole secured a chaplaincy for him in the house of his mother, the Countess of Salisbury, where he thought the association with his brother Lord Montagu might dissuade Starkey from breaking with the Church.

Settled in London, Starkey wrote to Cromwell that he was willing to serve the king with his knowledge of civil and canon law; and he would gladly deliver a 'more stabyl and sure jugement of the polytyke ordur z customys vsyd amonge vs here in our countrey'. His offer accepted by the Chancellor, Starkey began to write. Among the treatises he completed was A dialogue between Reginald Pole and Thomas Lupset *which he dedicated to the king, who rewarded him with a royal chaplaincy in 1535. Believing in Starkey's influence, Henry VIII requested him to write to Reginald Pole, asking his support 'in such thyngys as hys gracys wysdome by court of parlyament therein had decreed'. He referred to the king's divorce and the Act of Royal Supremacy. Starkey was unsuccessful, and his career at court ended abruptly.*

Through Cromwell's aid he was appointed, in 1537, to the cure of a small parish in Chichester. Here he continued to correspond with his old friends, including Pole, with whom he did not wish 'to brek love z amyte'. He also contributed pamphlets to the propaganda literature that was circulated to nullify the effects of the Pilgrimage of Grace, sponsored by the Catholics in the north. Except for attendance at a council of bishops, Starkey lived quietly until his death in 1538. Most of his small estate was bequeathed to his father. His library was willed to his friend Sir Edward Wotton, with the request that he give some books to Magdalen College and to poor students.

Of the seven treatises written by Starkey only two have been printed: A Dialogue between Cardinal Pole and Thomas Lupset (1871), *first published by the Early English Text Society and* An exhortation to the people instructing them to unity and obedience [1540?]. *The extant MSS. of his works include the fragment, 'Conclusion of some discourse on the liberty of speaking and writing'; a Latin treatise, Primi fructus distribuendi pauperibus; 'What is pollycy after the sētēce of Arystotyl'; 'An inductyon to concord to the pepul of Englond'; and a collection of essays on preaching. Many of his letters to Henry VIII, Cromwell, Pole, and others have been published.*

The Dialogue, the longest of Starkey's works, gave his patron Henry VIII a realistic picture of the social conditions of the realm and remedies for them. Through the imaginary conversations of his friends Reginald Pole and Thomas Lupset, each an outstanding humanist, Starkey deplored the ills of the realm—widespread poverty, filth in the cities and towns, production of luxuries, importing of necessities, scarcity of money, and lack of education.

of the nobles. To remedy these things, Starkey proposed to revise the common law and canon law, and he urges the reception of the civil law of the Continent, retaining Fortescue's theory of a limited monarchy safeguarded from tyranny by a council elected by the people to prevent its dissolution by the king.

In amending canon law as it pertained to the education of the clergy, he would revise the curricula at Oxford and Cambridge, including more 'liberal science'. Houses of contemplative orders he would turn into schools for nobles. Lupset is made to encourage these latter changes, and throughout the Dialogue, *Pole advocates the reception in England of Roman law, the civil law of the Continent. But both men are rather creatures of Starkey's imagination than his Paduan friends, humanists and students of canon and civil law, with a penchant for innocent theorizing on statecraft and the social order.*

The Exhortation *is a discussion of the two laws, 'one cyuyle polytyke τ worldly; the other, heuēly, supernāl τ godly'. Using scripture, the classics, and the writings of the early Church Fathers, Starkey strives to prove that canon law is 'founded by mere pollycy', and can be amended by the ruler of a people.*

A Dialogue between
Reginald Pole and Thomas Lupset

IN WHAT DOES THE TRUE COMMONWEALTH CONSIST?[1]

[Lupset has questioned Pole regarding his views on man's chances of 'felicity' in this world. Pole bases his answer on Scripture, and the writings of Plato and Aristotle, especially the former's *Republic* and *Laws* and the latter's *Politics*. He declares that 'if we have regard not only of the life to come but also of the life present, then it is true that I say that felicity in the highest degree is not without worldly prosperity'.]

Lupset. Sir, therein, I think, you say truth: for divers consideration hath ever made divers opinion. And I am glad that both we say truth. But yet of one thing I somewhat marvel: that in the felicity of man you put divers degrees, to some attributing more and to some less. Meseemeth, felicity is the most perfect state which admitteth no degree, for nothing can be more perfect than that which is most. Wherefore I cannot see how they which to virtue have coupled also worldly prosperity should yet have higher felicity than they which without that have only virtue; the which if it be so, you then agree that virtue alone giveth man felicity.

[1] Chapter II.

Pole. You shall marvel nothing at this if you will remember what we have said before. If man be the soul only, then virtue only giveth to man high felicity; but if he be both together, the soul and the body, then you see it doth not so. But many other things are required thereto, by the reason whereof felicity admitteth degrees. And some have more weal, and some less; and he, as I said, hath most prosperous state and highest felicity which hath with virtue coupled all worldly prosperity—and this is without fail most convenient to the nature of man. So that now, I think, it is clear wherein standeth the felicity and weal of every particular man; by the which now, as a ground and foundation laid, we shall proceed to the rest of our communication.

Lupset. Sir, let us do so now, I pray you; for therein now I doubt no more.

Pole. First, this is certain: that like as in every man there is a body and also a soul in whose flourishing and prosperous state both together standeth the weal and felicity of man, so likewise there is in every commonalty, city, and country, as it were, a politic body and another thing, also, resembling the soul of man, in whose flourishing both together resteth also the true commonweal. This body is nothing else but the multitude of people, the number of citizens in every commonalty, city, or country. The thing which is resembled to the soul is civil order and politic law administered by officers and rulers. For like as the body in every man receiveth his life by the virtue of the soul, and is governed thereby, so doth the multitude of people in every country receive, as it were, civil life by laws well administered by good officers and wise rulers by whom they be governed and kept in politic order. Wherefore the one may, as meseemeth, right well be compared to the body and the other to the soul.

Lupset. This similitude liketh me well.

Pole. Then let us go forth with the same, and we shall find, by and by, that like as the weal of every man sunderly by himself riseth of the three principal things before declared, so the commonweal of every country, city, or town semblably riseth of other three things proportionable and like to the same, in the which all other particular things are comprehended.

And the first of them, shortly to say, standeth in health, strength, and beauty of this body politic and multitude of people, wherein resteth the ground and, as it were, the foundation of the commonweal. For if the country be never so rich, fertile, and plentiful of all things necessary and pleasant to man's life, yet if there be of people other[1] too few or too many, or if they be, as it were, eaten away, daily devoured and consumed by common sickness and disease, there

[1] *other,* either.

can be no image nor shadow of any commonweal; to the which first is required a convenient multitude and conveniently to be nourished there in the country. For whereas there be other too many people in the country, insomuch that the country by no diligence nor labour of man may be sufficient to nourish them and minister them food, there without doubt can be no commonweal, but ever miserable penury and wretched poverty. Like as if there be of people over few, insomuch that the country may not be well tilled and occupied nor crafts well and diligently exercised, there shall also spring thereof great penury and scarceness of all things necessary for man's life; and so then, civil life and true commonweal can in no case be there maintained. Wherefore a convenient multitude meet for the place, in every country and commonalty, as the matter and ground of the commonweal, is first to be required of necessity.

Further, also, though the number of people were never so meet to the place, city, or town, yet if they flourished not in bodily health but commonly were vexed with grievous sickness and contagious disease, by the reason whereof the people should be consumed, no man could say there to be any commonweal. But like as every particular man in bodily sickness (and in such specially whereof he himself is cause) lacketh the most prosperous state; so doth every country, city, and town likewise affected and disposed want much of his perfit commonweal. Therefore to this multitude of people and politic body, first, as ground and foundation of the rest of his weal, is required a certain health which also by strength must be maintained. For like as the body, if it be not strong, soon by outward occasions, as by intemperance of air, labour, and travail, is oppressed and overthrown and so loseth his health, so doth the multitude of people in every country, city, or town soon by wars and injury of enemies, without strength lose his wealth, and soon is oppressed and brought into misery and wretched captivity. Wherefore to this politic body, strength is also required; without the which his health long cannot be maintained, but shortly of necessity, it must decay.

This strength standeth in this point chiefly: so to keep and maintain every part of this body that they promptly and readily may do that thing which is required to the health of the whole. Like as we say, then every man's body to be strong, when every part can execute quickly and well his office determined by the order of nature, as the heart then is strong when he, as fountain of all natural powers, ministereth them with due order to all other; and they then be strong when they be apt to receive their power of the heart, and can use it according to the order of nature, as the eye to see, the ear to hear, the foot to go, and the hand to hold and reach; and so likewise of the rest. After such manner the strength of this politic body standeth in every part, being able to do his office and duty.

For this body hath his parts, which resemble also parts of the body of man, of which the most general to our purpose be these: the heart, head, hands, and feet. The heart thereof is the king, prince, and ruler of the state, whethersoever it be one or many, according to the governance of the commonalty and politic state. For some be governed by a prince alone, some by a council of certain wise men, and some by the whole people together, as hereafter, when occasion requireth, more plainly I will show.

But now to our purpose. He or they which have authority upon the whole state, right well may be resembled to the heart. For like as all wit, reason, and sense, feeling, life, and all other natural power springeth out of the heart, so from the princes and rulers of the state cometh all laws, order and policy, all justice, virtue and honesty, to the rest of this politic body. To the head, with the eyes, ears, and other senses therein, resembled may be right well the under-officers by princes appointed, forasmuch as they should ever observe and diligently wait for the weal of the rest of this body. To the hands are resembled both craftsmen and warriors which defend the rest of the body from injury of enemies outward, and work and make things necessary to the same. To the feet, ploughmen and tillers of the ground, because they by their labour sustain and support the rest of the body. These are the most general parts of this politic body which may justly be resembled, after the manner declared, to those chief parts in man's body. Now, as I said, the strength of these parts altogether is of necessity required, without the which the health of the whole cannot long be maintained.

And, furthermore, yet though this politic body be healthy and strong, yet if it be not beautiful, but foul deformed, it lacketh a part of his weal and prosperous state. This beauty also standeth in the due proportion of the same parts together, so that one part ever be agreeable to another in form and fashion, quantity, and number, as craftsmen and ploughmen in due number and proportion with other parts, according to the place, city, or town. For if there be other too many or too few of one or of the other, there is in the commonalty a great deformity. And so likewise of the other parts. Wherefore the due proportion of one part to another must be observed; and therein standeth the corporal beauty chiefly of this politic body. And so in these three things coupled together standeth, without fail, the weal and prosperous state of the multitude in every commonalty, which, as you now see, justly may be resembled to the body of every particular man.

And yet further to proceed in this similitude: Like as the weal of the body without riches and convenient abundance of things necessary cannot continue nor be maintained, so this multitude which we call the politic body without like abundance of all things necessary cannot flourish in most perfit state. Wherefore these exterior things—friends, riches, and abundance of necessaries—are justly in the second place to be required to the maintenance of this true commonweal which we now search.

For if a country be never so well replenished with people, healthy, strong, and beautiful, yet if there be lack of necessaries, it cannot long prosper; there will shortly grow in all kind of misery, for great poverty in any country hath ever coupled great misery. She is the mother of envy and malice, dissension and debate, and many other mischiefs ensuing the same. Wherefore without necessaries no country can flourish. Yea, and if there be no lack of necessaries for the sustenance of the people, but great abundance of riches and of all things necessary and pleasant for man's life, yet if the same country lack friendship of others joined thereto, and be environed and compassed about with enemies and foes lying ever in wait to spoil, rob, and destroy the same, I cannot see how that country can long flourish in prosperity. Wherefore the friendship of other countries is no less required than riches and abundance of other things necessary. And so in these things joined together resteth the second point required to the weal of every commonalty.

The third—which is chief and principal of all—is the good order and policy by good laws stablished and set, and by heads and rulers put in effect; by the which the whole body, as by reason, is governed and ruled to the intent that this multitude of people and whole commonalty, so healthy and so wealthy, having convenient abundance of all things necessary for the maintenance thereof, may with due honour, reverence, and love religiously worship God, as Fountain of all goodness, Maker and Governor of all this world, every one also doing his duty to the other with brotherly love, one loving one another as members and parts of one body. And that this is of the other points most chief and principal, it is evident and plain; for what availeth it in any country to have a multitude never so healthy, beautiful, and strong, which will follow no civil nor politic order, but every one, like wild beasts drawn by foolish fantasy, is led by the same without reason and rule? Or what availeth in any country to have never so great riches and abundance of all things both necessary and pleasant to man's life, whereas the people, rude [and] without polity, cannot use the same to their own commodity? Without fail, nothing.

But even like as every man having health, abundance of riches, friends, dignity, and authority, which lacketh reason and virtue to govern the same ever abuseth them to his own destruction, so every country, city, and town, though they be never so replenished with people, having all abundance of things necessary and pleasant to the maintenance of the same, yet if they lack good order and politic rule, they shall abuse all such commodities to their own destruction and ruin, and never shall attain to any commonweal, which without civil order and politic rule can never be brought to purpose nor effect.

Lupset. Sir, I pray you, here before you proceed any further in your communications (because it is, as meseemeth, much to our purpose, and much you speak thereof), declare somewhat at large what thing it is that you so oft name and call now 'policy', now 'civil order', and now 'politic rule', to the intent that I may the better understand the rest of your communication. . . .

[Pole complies, giving a short history of 'laws and ordinance at their first beginning'. He declares they were 'imperfect and somewhat rude'.]

Pole. Howbeit this ever is certain and sure among all sorts and nature of people, whether the state of the commonalty be governed by a prince, by certain wise men, or by the whole multitude, so long as they which have authority and rule of the state look not to their own singular profit nor to the private weal of any one part more than to the other, but refer all their counsel, acts, and deeds to the commonweal of the whole, so long, I say, the order is good and directed to good civility; and this is good policy. But when they which have rule, corrupt with ambition, envy or malice or any other like affect, look only to their own singular weal, pleasure, and profit, then this good order is turned into high tyranny; then is broken the rule of all good civility; there can be no politic rule nor civil order; the nature whereof now to perceive is, as I think, nothing hard at all. For it is a certain rule whereby the people and whole commonalty, whether they be governed by a prince or common council, is ever directed in virtue and honesty. So that the end of all politic rule is to induce the multitude to virtuous living according to the dignity of the nature of man.

And so thus you have heard what thing it is that I so oft speak of and call politic rule, civil order, and just policy. You have heard also how diverse it is, for it may be other under a prince, a common council of certain wise men, or under the whole multitude; and to dispute which of these rules is best and to be preferred above other, meseemeth superfluous, seeing that certain it is that all be good and to nature agreeable, and though the one be more convenient to the nature of some people than the other. Wherefore best it is, leaving this question, all men to be content with their state, so long as they be not oppressed with plain tyranny. . . .

And to see and plainly to judge when this commonweal most flourisheth, it is nothing hard but easy to perceive. For when all these parts thus coupled together exercise with diligence their office and duty, as the ploughmen and labourers of the ground diligently till the same for the getting of food and necessary sustenance to the rest of the body, and craftsmen work all things meet for maintenance of the same, yea, and the heads and rulers by just policy maintain the state stablished in the country, ever looking to the profit of the whole body, then that country must needs be in the most prosperous state. For there you shall see riches and convenient abundance of all things necessary; there you shall see cities and towns garnished with people that it shall be necessary in places desert to build more cities, castles, and towns for the minishing of such a multitude: which is a sure argument and certain token of the flourishing of this politic body.

So that of this you may be sure: wheresoever you see any country well garnished and set with cities and towns, well replenished with people, having all things necessary and pleasant to man, living together in civil life according to the excellent dignity of the nature of man, every part of his body agreeing to [the] other, doing his office and duty appointed thereto, *there*, I say, you may be sure is set a very and true commonweal; *there* it flourisheth as much as the nature of man will suffer.

And thus now, Master Lupset, shortly to conclude, after my mind you have heard rudely described what is the thing that I call the commonweal and just policy, wherein it standeth, and when it most flourisheth.

Thomas Starkey, *A Dialogue between Cardinal Pole and Thomas Lupset*, edited by J. W. Cowper, Early English Text Society, Ex. Ser. no. xii, 1871.

SIR ANTHONY FITZHERBERT
1470?–1538

Though there are several earlier English treatises on agriculture than The Boke of Husbandry *[1523?], none was so popular as this work dealing 'exhaustively with the best principles of arable farming of the time'. While paying this tribute, G. E. Fussell would claim authorship of the* Boke *for Sir Anthony Fitzherbert rather than his brother John to whom it has long been assigned, as has* The boke of surveying *[1523?]. Sir Anthony's knowledge of law prepared him to write on problems involving landed interests, and he could have acquired the 'forty years' experience in farming, the authority on which the writer of the* Boke *bases his advice, because the London court term was short and permitted him to spend a considerable portion of each year overseeing his lands. The lack of experience has been the principal reason for denying authorship to Sir Anthony.*

The brothers John and Anthony Fitzherbert were born between 1465 and 1470 in Norbury, where the family estates had been first acquired in 1125. There are no facts available of the life of Sir John. Except for Wood's statement that Anthony Fitzherbert 'laid a foundation for learning' at Oxford, nothing more is known about his education until he began his law studies at Gray's Inn. In 1508 he was appointed Recorder of Coventry, and later he held several political positions in London. Anthony Fitzherbert was knighted by Henry VIII, and made a Judge of the Court of Common Pleas.

In 1524 the king sent him to Ireland with Sir Ralph Egerton and Dr James Denton, and he was successful in drawing up a peace treaty with the Earls of Ormonde and Kildare. His fairness and impartiality throughout his long years in public life were acclaimed by his colleagues. Some of the most famous heresy cases of the Reformation were tried while Fitzherbert sat as one of the judges on the King's Bench. He heard the evidence against the Carthusians, Bishop John Fisher, and Sir Thomas More, who were tried for treason growing out of their refusal to take the Oath of Royal Supremacy. In these cases the commissioners had no choice, for, as Cresacre More states, 'they knew what the king would have done'.

Fitzherbert married twice, each time the daughter of well-to-do families. His first wife was Dorothy Willoughby, and the second Matilda Cotton, by whom he had three children. He died on 27 May 1538, and was buried at Norbury.

Books on English law—La Graunde Abbregement de le Ley [1516] and Loffice et auctoryte des Iustyces de peas (1538)—earned him the reputation of being the first to reduce English law into a systematic form. The Boke of Husbandry follows, to some extent, the pattern of the Norman French treatise, Le Dite de Hosebondrie [1175?], written by the Dominican friar Walter of Henley and translated into English by Grosseteste. Besides Fitzherbert's indebtedness to the latter work, printed by de Worde about 1510, he borrowed freely from Xenophon's Oeconomicus, the popular Tudor text, particularly in his detailed discussion of the relationship between husband and wife and the position and duties of each, points that are also stressed in Aristotle's Economics. But both Greek authors and Henley depict the wife as a noblewoman rather than the household drudge which Fitzherbert makes her.

The treatise on surveying which deals with the manorial rights of owner and tenant grew out of the statute, Extenta Manerii, passed in the time of Edward I, which Fitzherbert chose for reading at Gray's Inn. His commentary on it, The Reading on Statute Extenta Manerii, was printed posthumously in 1539.

The Book of Husbandry

Here beginneth a new tract or treatise most profitable for all husbandmen and very fruitful for all other persons to read: newly corrected and amended by the author with divers other things added thereunto.

THE AUTHOR'S PROLOGUE

Sit ista questio: This is the question: Whereunto is every man ordained? And as Job saith: *Homo nascitur ad laborem: sicut avis ad volandum.*[1] That is to say: A man is ordained and born to labour as a bird is ordained to fly. And the Apostle saith: *Qui non laborat; non manducet:*[2] *debet enim in obsequio Dei laborare qui de bonis ejus vult manducare.* That is to say: He that laboureth not, should not eat: and he ought to labour and do God's work that will eat of His goods or gifts. The which is a hard text after the literal sense. For by the letter the king, the queen, nor all other lords, spiritual and temporal, should not eat without they should labour: the which were uncomely and not convenient for such estates to labour.

But who that readeth in *The Book of the Moralities of the Chess** shall thereby perceive that every man from the highest degree to the lowest is set and ordained to have labour and occupation. And that book is divided in six degrees, that is to say, the king, the queen, the bishop, the knights, the judges, and the yeomen. In the which book is showed their degrees, their authorities, their works, and their occupations, and what they ought to do. And they so doing and executing their authorities, works, and occupations have a wondrous great study and labour: of the which authorities, occupations, and works were at this time too long to write, wherefore I remit that book as mine author thereof. The which book were necessary to be known of every degree that they might do and order themselves according to the same. And insomuch as the yeomen in the said *Moralities and Game of the Chess* be set before to labour, defend, and maintain all the other higher estates, the which yeomen represent the common people as husbands and labourers, therefore I purpose to speak first of husbandry.

HERE BEGINNETH THE BOOK OF HUSBANDRY: AND FIRST, WHEREBY HUSBANDMEN DO LIVE

The most general living that husbands can have is by ploughing and sowing of their corn and rearing or breeding of their cattle; and not

---

[1] Job v. 7.   [2] II Thess. iii. 10.

the one without the other. Then is the plough the most necessary instrument that a husband can occupy. Wherefore it is convenient to be known how a plough should be made.

DIVERS MANNERS OF PLOUGHS

There be ploughs of divers makings in divers countries, and likewise there be ploughs of iron of divers fashions. And that is because there be many manner of grounds and soil: some white clay, some red clay, some gravel, some chilturn,[1] some sand, some mean earth, some meddled with marle,[2] and, in many places, heath ground. And one plough will not serve in all places, wherefore it is necessary to have divers manner of ploughs.

In Somersetshire, about Gloucester, the sharebeam, that in many places is called the plough-head, is four or five feet long, and it is broad and thin, and that is because the land is very tough and would soak the plough into the earth if the sharebeam were not long, broad, and thin. In Kent they have other manner ploughs: Some go with wheels, as they do in many other places, and some will turn the sheld-brede[3] at every land's end and plough all one way. In Buckingham-shire are ploughs made of another manner and also other manner of plough irons, the which, meseemeth, generally good and likely to serve in many places, and specially if the plough beam and share-beam were four inches longer between the sheath and the plough-tail that the sheldbrede might come more aslope, for those ploughs give out too suddenly, and therefore they be the worse to draw, and for no cause else.

In Leicestershire, Lancastershire, Yorkshire, Lincoln, Norfolk, Cambridgeshire, and many other counties, the ploughs be of divers makings, the which were too long a process to declare how, etc. But howsoever they be made if they be well tempered and go well, they may be the better suffered.

A SHORT INFORMATION FOR A YOUNG GENTLEMAN THAT INTENDETH TO THRIVE

I advise him to get a copy of this present book and to read it from the beginning to the ending, whereby he may perceive the chapters and contents in the same: and by reason of oft reading, he may wax perfect [in] what should be done at all seasons. For I learned two verses at grammar school, and those be these: *Gutta cavat lapidem non vi sed saepe cadendo: sic homo sit sapiens non vi, sed saepe legendo.** A drop of water pierceth a stone not alone by his strength, but by his often falling. Right so a man shall be made wise not alone by himself, but

---

[1] *chilturn*, hilly ground found in Buckinghamshire.
[2] *marle*, clay.   [3] *sheldbrede*, shieldboard.

by his oft reading. And so may this young gentleman, according to the season of the year, read to his servants what chapter he will.

And also for any other manner of profit contained in the same, the which is necessary for a young husband that hath not the experience of husbandry nor other things contained in this present book to take a good remembrance and credence thereunto, for there is an old saying, but of what authority I cannot tell: *Quod melior est practica rusticorum quam scientia philosophorum*:* It is better the practice or knowledge of an husbandman well proved than the science or cunning of a philosopher not proved. For there is nothing touching husbandry and other profits contained in this present book but I have had the experience thereof and proved the same.

And over and beside all this book, I will advise him to rise betime in the morning, according to the verse of Scripture: *Sanat, sanctificat, et ditat surgere mane** [Early to bed, early to rise, etc.], and to go about his closes, pastures, fields, and specially by the hedges; and to have in his purse a pair of tables, and when he seeth anything that would be amended to write it in his tables, as and he find any horses, mares, beasts, sheep, swine, or geese in his pastures that be not his own—and, peradventure, though they be his own, he would not have them to go there—or find a gap or a sherd in his hedge, or any water standing in his pastures upon his grass, whereby he may take double hurt—both loss of his grass and rotting of his sheep and calves; and also [write in his tables] of standing water in his cornfields at the land's ends or sides; and how he would have his lands ploughed, dunged, stirred, or sown; and his corn weeded or shorn; or his cattle shifted out of one pasture into another; and look what ditching, quicksetting,[1] or plasshing[2] is necessary to be had; and to oversee his shepherd, how he handleth and ordereth his sheep; and his servants, how they plough and do their works; or if any gate be broken down or want any staves and go not lightly to open and tine[3] and that it do not trail and that the winds blow it not open; and with many more necessary things that are to be looked upon.

For a man always wandering or going about, somewhat findeth or seeth that is amiss and would be mended. And as soon as he seeth any such defaults, then let him take out his tables and write the defaults. And when he cometh home to dinner, supper, or at night, then let him call his baily or his head servant, and show him the defaults that they may be shortly amended. And when it is amended, then let him put it out of his tables.

For this used I to do ten or twelve years, and more. And thus let him use daily; and in short space he shall set much thing in good

---

[1] *quicksetting*, transplanting.
[2] *plasshing*, pleaching, strengthening a hedge by bending down the branches and interweaving them.   [3] *tine*, close.

order, but daily it will have mending. And if he cannot write, let him nick the defaults upon a stick, and to show his baily, as I said before.

Also take heed, both early and late and at all times, what manner people resort and come to thy house, and the cause of their coming, specially if they bring with them pitchers, cans, tankards, bottles, bags, wallets, or bushel-pokes. For if thy servants be not true, they do thee great hurt and themselves little advantage wherefore they would be well looked upon. And he that hath two true servants, a man-servant and another, a woman-servant, he hath a great treasure. For a true servant will do justly himself, and if he see his fellows do amiss, he will bid them do no more so: for and they do, he will show his master thereof. And if he do not this, he is not a true servant, etc.

WHAT WORKS A WIFE SHOULD DO IN GENERAL

First, in the morning when thou art waken and purpose to rise, lift up thy hand and bless thee and make a Sign of the Holy Cross, *In nomine patris et filii et spiritus sancti*. Amen: [In the Name of the Father, the Son, and the Holy Ghost]. And if thou say a *Pater Noster*, an *Ave*, and a *Credo*, and remember thy Maker, thou shall speed much better. And when thou art up and ready, then first sweep thy house, dress up thy dishboard, and set all things in good order within thy house. Milk thy kye,[1] suckle thy calves, sye[2] up thy milk, take up thy children and array them, and provide for thy husband's breakfast, dinner, supper, and for thy children's and servants'; and take thy part with them.

And ordain[3] corn and malt to the mill [in order] to bake and brew withal when need is: And mete it to the mill and from the mill, and see that thou have thy measure again beside the toll or else the miller dealeth not truly with thee or else thy corn is not dry as it should be. Thou must make butter and cheese when thou mayst. Serve thy swine both morning and evening, and give thy polayne[4] meat in the morning. And when time of the year cometh, thou must take heed how thy hens, ducks, and geese do lay; and gather up their eggs. And when they wax broody, set them so as no beasts, swine, nor other vermin hurt them. And thou must know that all whole-footed fowls will set a month and all cloven-footed fowls will set but three weeks except a peahen and such other great fowls, as cranes, bustards, and such others. And when they have brought forth their birds, see that they be well kept from the gleyd,[5] crows, martens, and other vermin.

And in the beginning of March, or a little afore, is time for a wife to make her garden and to get as many good seeds and herbs as she

[1] *kye*, cows, kine.   [2] *sye*, strain (?).   [3] *ordain*, set aside a portion.
[4] *polayne*, poultry.   [5] *gleyd*, kites.

can, and specially such as be good for the pot and to eat. And as oft as need shall require, it must be weeded, or else the weeds will overgrow the herbs. And also in March is time to sow flax and hemp, for I have heard old housewives say that better is March hurdes than April flax—the reason appeareth. But how it should be sowed, weeded, pulled, rippled, watered, washen, dried, beaten, braked, tawed, hackled, spun, wounden, wrapped, and woven, it needeth not for me to show, for they be wise enough. And thereof may they make sheets, boardcloths,[1] towels, shirts, smocks, and such other necessaries. And therefore let thy distaff be always ready for a pastime that thou be not idle.

And surely a woman cannot get her living honestly with spinning on the distaff; but it stoppeth a gap and must needs be had. The bolls of flax when they be rippled off must be riddled from the weeds and made dry with the sun to get out the seeds. Howbeit, one manner of linseed, called loken seed, will not open by the sun, and therefore when they be dry, they must be sore bruised and broken—the wives know how—and then winnowed and kept dry till [a] year's time come again. Thy female hemp must be pulled from the churl hemp, for that beareth no seed; and thou must do by it as thou didst by the flax. The churl hemp doth bear seed; and thou must beware that birds eat it not as it groweth. The hemp thereof is not so good as the female hemp, but yet it will do good service.

It may fortune sometime that thou shalt have so many things to do that thou shalt not well know where best to begin. Then take heed which thing should be the greatest loss if it were not done and in what space it would be done; and then think what is the greatest loss. There begin. . . .

It is convenient for a husband to have sheep of his own for many causes: and then may his wife have part of the wool to make her husband and herself some clothes. And, at the least way, she may have the locks of the sheep, either to make clothes or blankets and coverlets or both. And if she have no wool of her own, she may take wool to spin of cloth-makers; and by that means she may have a convenient living and many times to do other works.

It is a wife's occupation to winnow all manner of corns, to make malt, to wash and wring, to make hay, to shear corn, and in time of need to help her husband to fill the mucke-wayne or dung cart, to drive the plough, to load hay, corn, and such other. Also to go or ride to the market to sell butter, cheese, milk, eggs, chickens, capons, hens, pigs, geese, and all manner of corns. And also to buy all manner of necessary things belonging to the household and to make a true reckoning and account to her husband what she hath received and what she hath paid. And if the husband go to the market to buy or

[1] *boardcloths,* tablecloths.

sell (as they oft do), he [is] then to show his wife in like manner
For if one of them should use to deceive the other, he deceiveth him
self, and he is not like to thrive. And therefore they must be tru
either to other.

I could, peradventure, show the husband of divers points that th
wives deceive their husbands in; and, in like manner, how husband
deceive their wives, but if I should do so, I should show more subtl
points of deceit than either of them knew of before. And therefor
meseemeth best to hold my peace lest I should do as the Knight o
the Tower did, the which had many fair daughters. And of fatherl
love that he ought to them, he made a book to a good intent tha
they might eschew and flee from vices and follow virtues.

In the which book he showed that if they were wooed, moved, o
stirred by any man after such a manner as he there showed, that the
should withstand it. In the which book he showed so many way
how a man should attain to his purpose to bring a woman to vice
the which ways were so natural and the ways to come to their pur
pose were so subtly contrived and craftly showed, that hard it woul
be for any woman to resist or deny their desire: And by the sai
book hath made both the men and the women to know more vices
subtlety, and craft than ever they should have known if the bool
had not been made. In the which book he named himself, *Th
Knight of the Tower*.* And thus, I leave the wives to use their oc
cupations at their own discretion.

TO KEEP MEASURE IN SPENDING

Now thou husband and housewife, that have done your diligenc
and cure according to the first article of the philosopher, that is t
say, *Adhibe curam** [Take care]; and also hath well remembered th
saying of wise Solomon: *Quod otiosus non gaudebit cum electis i
caelo, sed lugebit in eternum cum reprobis in inferno:** [Therefore th
indifferent will not rejoice with the elect in heaven, but griev
eternally with the wicked in hell], then ye must remember, observe
and keep in mind the second article of the saying of the said philo
sopher, that is to say: *Tene mensuram,** that is to say in English, 'Hol
and keep measure'. And according to that saying, I learned two verse
at grammar school, and those be these:

> *Qui plus expendit quam rerum copia tendit,*
> *Non admiretur si paupertate gravetur.*
> He that doth more expend than his goods will extend,
> Marvel it shall not be though he be grieved with poverty.

And also according to that saying, speaketh Saint Paul, and saith
*Juxta facultates faciendi sunt sumptus ne longi temporis victum brevis hor
consumat.** That is to say, 'After thy faculty or thy honour make thin

expenses, lest thou spend in short space that thing that thou shouldst live by long'. This text toucheth every man from the highest degree to the lowest, wherefore it is necessary to every man and woman to remember and take good heed thereunto for to observe, keep, and follow the same: but because this text of Saint Paul is in Latin and husbands commonly can but little Latin, I fear lest they cannot understand it: and though it were declared once or twice to them, that they would forget it. Wherefore I shall show them a text in English, and that they may well understand, and that is this, 'Eat within thy tether'.*

COLOPHON: Thus endeth the *Book of Husbandry*. Imprinted at London in Southwark. . . . by Peter Treveris. [1525?]

SIMON FISH
d. 1531

Simon Fish belonged to the younger group of English Reformers. He attended Oxford, and studied law at Gray's Inn about 1525. But he seemed more interested in the new doctrines of Luther than in the practice of law. This zeal led to his friendship with William Tyndale whom he followed to the Low Countries. According to John Foxe's sketch of Fish, his departure from England followed participation in a play that ridiculed Cardinal Wolsey.

While in Antwerp Fish wrote his famous treatise, A supplicacyon for the beggars [1529?]. It was printed anonymously, and copies were quickly smuggled into England. Soon after its publication, he risked a visit to London, where his efforts to distribute Tyndale's English translation of the New Testament caused him to be charged with heresy.

Before he could be tried in an ecclesiastical court, Fish died of the plague in 1531. Sir Thomas More, who wrote an answer to Fish's Supplicacyon, declares that 'God gave him such grace' before he died 'that he repented and came into the Church again; and forsook and forswore all the whole bill of those heresies'.

Though Fish undoubtedly contributed pamphlets to aid the English Reformers, only two works have been associated with his name: A supplicacyon for the beggars [1529?] and A supplication of the poore Commons whereunto is added the Supplication of beggers (1546). Fish dedicated the Supplicacyon to Henry VIII, urging him to dissolve the monasteries and distribute their wealth to the poor. He condemned a belief in the doctrine of purgatory, claiming it was a device used by the clergy to exact money from the people on the pretext that prayers aid the souls of the dead and release them from suffering. Foxe writes that a copy of the treatise was given to Henry VIII by Anne Boleyn. Her 'brother, seeing [it] in her hand' one day, 'took and read, and gave it her again, willing her earnestly to give it to the King; which thing she did'. Fish's pamphlet may, or may not, have influenced Henry VIII, but it is perhaps more than coincidence that within the next seven years all monastic and church property in England was confiscated and annexed to the Crown.

A Supplication for the Beggars

To the King our Sovereign lord:

Most lamentably complaineth their woeful misery unto your Highness, your poor daily beadmen, the wretched hideous monsters (on whom scarcely for horror any eye dare look), the foul unhappy sort of lepers and other sore people—needy, impotent, blind, lame, and sick—that live only by alms: how that their number is daily so sore increased that all the alms of all the well-disposed people of this your realm is not half enough for to sustain them, but that for very constraint they die for hunger.

And this most pestilent mischief is come upon your said poor beadmen by the reason that there is in the times of your noble predecessors passed, craftily crept into this your realm another sort, not of impotent but of strong, puissant, counterfeit, holy, and idle beggars and vagabonds which since the time of their first entrance by all the craft and wiliness of Satan are now increased under your sight, not only into a great number but also into a kingdom.

These are (not the herds but the ravenous wolves, going in herds-clothing, devouring the flock) the bishops, abbots, priors, deacons, archdeacons, suffragans, priests, monks, canons, friars, pardoners, and summoners. And who is able to number this idle ravenous sort which (setting all labour aside) have begged so importunately that they have gotten into their hands more than the third part of all your realm. The goodliest lordships, manors, lands, and territories are theirs. Besides this they have the tenth part of all the corn, meadows, pasture, grass, wool, colts, calves, lambs, pigs, geese, and chickens; over and besides the tenth part of every servant's wages; the tenth part of the wool, milk, honey, wax, cheese, and butter.

Yea, and they look so narrowly upon their profits that the poor wives must be accountable to them of every tenth egg or else she getteth not her rites at Easter, and shall be taken as a heretic. Hereto have they their four offering days. What money pull they in by probates of testaments, privy tithes and by men's offerings to their

pilgrimages and at their first Masses? Every man and child that is
buried must pay somewhat for Masses and dirges to be sung for him,
or else they will accuse the dead's friends and executors of heresy.

What money get they by mortuaries,[1] by hearing of confessions
(and yet they will keep thereof no counsel), by hallowing of churches,
altars, super-altars, chapels, and bells, by cursing of men and ab-
solving them again for money? What a multitude of money gather
the pardoners in a year? How much money get the summoners by
extortions in a year by assiting[2] the people to the commissary's
court and afterward releasing the appearance for money?

Finally, the infinite number of begging friars, what get they in a
year? Here, if it please your Grace to mark, ye shall see a thing far
out of joint. There are within your realm of England 52,000 parish
churches. And this standing that there be but ten householders in
every parish, yet are there 520,000 households. And of every of
these households hath every of the five Orders* of friars a penny a
quarter for every Order; that is for all the five Orders five pence a
quarter for every house. That is for all the five Orders 20 d. a year for
every house. *Summa:* 520,000 quarters of angels.*

That is 260,000 half-angels; *summa.* 130,000 angels; *summa totalis*
43,333 l. 6s. 8d. sterling. Whereof not four hundred years passed,
they had not one penny. O grievous and painful exactions thus
yearly to be paid, from the which the people of your noble predecessors, the kings of the ancient Britons, ever stood free. And
this will they have, or else they will procure him that will not give
it them to be taken as a heretic. What tyrant ever oppressed the
people like this cruel and vengeable generation? What subjects shall
be able to help their Prince that be after this fashion yearly polled?
What good Christian people can be able to succour us poor lepers,
blind, sore, and lame, that be thus yearly oppressed?

Is it any marvel that your people so complain of poverty? Is it any
marvel that the taxes, fifteens,* and subsidies that your Grace, most
tenderly of great compassion, hath taken among your people to
defend them from the threatened ruin of their commonwealth have
been so slothfully, yea, painfully levied, seeing that almost the utmost
penny that might have been levied, hath been gathered before yearly
by this ravenous, cruel, and insatiable generation.

The Danes neither the Saxons, in the time of the ancient Britons,
should never have been able to have brought their armies from so
far hither into your land to have conquered it if they had had at that
time such a sort of idle gluttons to find at home. The noble King
Arthur had never been able to have carried his army to the foot of
the mountains to resist the coming down of Lucius, the Emperor,
if such yearly exaction had been taken of his people.

---

[1] *mortuaries*, burial fees.   [2] *assiting*, citing.

The Greeks had never been able to have so long continued at the siege of Troy if they had had at home such an idle sort of cormorants to find. The ancient Romans had never been able to have put all the whole world under their obeisance if their people had been thus yearly oppressed. The Turk now in your time should never be able to get so much ground of Christendom if he had in his empire such a sort of locusts to devour his substance.

Lay then these sums to the foresaid third part of the possessions of the realm that ye may see whether it draw nigh unto the half of the whole substance of the realm, or not. So shall ye find that it draweth far above.

Now let us then compare the number of this unkind idle sort unto the number of the lay people, and we shall see whether it be indifferently shifted, or not, that they should have half. Compare them to the number of men: so are they not the hundredth person. Compare them to men, women, and children: then are they not the four hundredth person in number. One part, therefore, in four-hundredth parts divided were too much for them except they did labour. What an unequal burden is it that they have half with the multitude, and are not the four hundredth person of their number? What tongue is able to tell that ever there was any commonwealth so sore oppressed since the world first began?

And what do all these greedy sort of sturdy, idle, holy thieves with these yearly exactions that they take of the people? Truly, nothing but exempt themselves from the obedience of your Grace: nothing but translate all rule, power, lordship, authority, obedience, and dignity from your Grace unto them: nothing but that all your subjects should fall into disobedience and rebellion against your Grace, and be under them as they did unto your noble predecessor King John, which for because that he would have punished certain traitors that had conspired with the French King to have deposed him from his crown and dignity (among the which a clerk called Stephen [Langton] whom afterward, against the King's will, the Pope made Bishop of Canterbury, was one), interdicted his land. For the which matter your most noble realm wrongfully, alas, for shame, hath stood tributary, not unto any kind temporal prince, but unto a cruel devilish bloodsupper[1], drunken in the blood of the saints and martyrs of Christ ever since. Here were an holy sort of prelates that thus cruelly could punish such a righteous King, all his realm, and succession for doing right. . . .

What remedy? Make laws against them. I am in doubt whether ye be able. Are they not stronger in your own Parliament House than yourself? What a number of bishops, abbots, and priors are lords of your Parliament? Are not all the learned men in your realm

---

[1] *bloodsupper,* bloodsucker.

n fee with them to speak in your Parliament House for them against your crown, dignity, and commonwealth of your realm—a few of your own learned council only excepted? What law can be made against them that may be available? Who is he, though he be grieved never so sore, for the murder of his ancestor, ravishment of his wife, of his daughter, robbery, trespass, mayhem, debt, or any other offence, dare lay it to their charge by any way of action: and if he do, then is he by and by by their wiliness accused of heresy.

Yea, they will so handle him or[1] he pass that except he will bear a faggot for their pleasure, he shall be excommunicated; and then be all his actions dashed. So captive are your laws unto them that no man that they list to excommunicate may be admitted to sue any action in any of your courts. If any man in your sessions dare be so hardy to indict a priest of any such crime, he hath, or the year go out, such a yoke of heresy laid [on] his neck that it maketh him wish that he had not done it. Your Grace may see what a work there is in London: how the Bishop rageth for indicting of certain curates of extortion and incontinency the last year in the warmoll quest.* Had not Richard Hunne commenced action of *premunire** against a priest, he had been yet alive and none heretic at all, but an honest man.

Did not divers of your noble progenitors, seeing their crown and dignity run into ruin and to be thus craftily translated into the hands of this mischievous generation, make divers statutes for the reformation thereof; among which the statute of mortmain was one to the intent that after that time they should have no more given unto them. But what availed it? Have they not gotten into their hands more lands since than any duke in England hath, the statute notwithstanding? Yea, have they not, for all that, translated into their hands from your Grace half your kingdom thoroughly? The whole name, as reason is, for the ancientie of your kingdom, which was before theirs and out of the which theirs is grown, only abiding with your Grace? and of one kingdom made twain: the spiritual kingdom, as they call it, for they will be named first, and your temporal kingdom. And which of these two kingdoms, suppose ye, is like to overgrow the other—yea, to put the other clear out of memory? Truly, the kingdom of the bloodsuppers, for to them is given daily out of your kingdom. And that that is once given them, cometh never from them again. Such laws have they, that none of them may neither give nor sell nothing.

What law can be made so strong against them that they, either with money or else with other policy, will not break and set at naught? What kingdom can endure that ever giveth thus from him and receiveth nothing again? O how all the substance of your realm, forthwith your sword, power, crown, dignity, and obedience of

_____
[1] *or*, ere.

your people, runneth headlong into the insatiable whirlpool of these greedy goulafres[1] to be swallowed and devoured.

Neither have they any other colour[2] to gather these yearly ex-actions into their hands but that, *they say*, they pray for us to God to deliver our souls out of the pains of purgatory, without whose prayer, *they say*, or at least without the Pope's pardon, we could never be delivered thence. Which if it be true, then is it good reason that we give them all these things—all, were it hundred times as much. But there be many men of great literature and judgment that for the love they have unto the truth and unto the commonwealth have not feared to put themselves into the greatest infamy that may be, in abjection of all the world, yea, in peril of death to declare their opinion in this matter, which is that there is no purgatory, but that it is a thing invented by the covetousness of the spirituality only to translate all kingdoms from other princes unto them, and that there is not one word spoken of it in all Holy Scripture.

They say also that if there were a purgatory and, also, if that the Pope with his pardons for money may deliver one soul thence, he may deliver him as well without money: if he may deliver one, he may deliver a thousand; if he may deliver a thousand, he may deliver them all, and so destroy purgatory. And then is he a cruel tyrant without all charity if he keep them in prison and in pain till men will give him money.

Likewise say they of all the whole sort of the spirituality, that if they will not pray for no man but for them that give them money, they are tyrants and lack charity and suffer those souls to be punished and pained uncharitably for lack of their prayers. These sort of folks, they call heretics; these they burn; these they rage against, put to open shame, and make them bear faggots. But whether they be heretics, or no, well I wot that this purgatory and the Pope's pardons is all the cause of the translation of your kingdom so fast into their hands. Wherefore it is manifest, it cannot be of Christ, for He gave more to the temporal kingdom: He Himself paid tribute to Caesar; He took nothing from him, but taught that high powers should be always obeyed. Yea, He Himself (although He were most free Lord of all and innocent) was obedient unto the high powers unto death.

This is the great scab, why they will not let the New Testament go abroad in your mother tongue, lest men should espy that they by their cloaked hypocrisy do translate thus fast your kingdom into their hands; that they are not obedient unto your high power; that they are cruel, unclean, unmerciful, and hypocrites; that they seek not the honour of Christ, but their own; that remission of sins is not given by the Pope's pardon, but by Christ, for the sure faith

[1] *goulafres*, ghouls.   [2] *colour*, excuse.

and trust that we have in Him. Here may your Grace well perceive that except ye suffer their hypocrisy to be disclosed, all is like to run into their hands. And as long as it is covered, so long shall it seem to every man to be a great impiety not to give [to] them.

For this I am sure your Grace thinketh (as the truth is), 'I am as good a man as my father: why may I not as well give them as much as my father did?' And of this mind, I am sure, are all the lords, knights, squires, gentlemen, and yeomen in England. Yea, and until it be disclosed, all your people will think that your statute of mortmain was never made with no good conscience, seeing that it taketh away the liberty of your people in that they may not as lawfully buy their souls out of purgatory by giving to the spirituality as their predecessors did in times passed.

Wherefore, if ye will eschew the ruin of your crown and dignity, let their hypocrisy be uttered: and that shall be more speedful in this matter than all the laws that may be made, be they never so strong. For to make a law for to punish any offender except it were more for to give other men an example to beware to commit such like offence, what should it avail? Did not Doctor Aleyn most presumptuously, now in your time, against all this allegiance [do] all that ever he could to pull from you the knowledge of such pleas as [be]long unto your high courts unto another court in derogation of your crown and dignity?

Did not also Doctor Horsey and his accomplices most heinously, as all the world knoweth, murder in prison that honest merchant Richard Hunne for that he sued your writ of premunire against a priest that wrongfully held him in plea in a spiritual court for a matter whereof the knowledge belonged unto your high courts. And what punishment was there done that any man may take example of to beware of like offence? Truly, none but that the one [Horsey] paid five hundred pounds,* as it is said, to the building of your Star Chamber; and when that payment was once passed, the captain of his kingdom (because he fought so manfully against your crown and dignity) have heaped to him benefice upon benefice, so that he is rewarded ten times as much. The other, as it is said, paid six hundred pounds for him and his accomplices which for because that he had likewise fought so manfully against your crown and dignity was immediately (as he had obtained your most gracious pardon) promoted by the captains of his kingdom with benefice upon benefice to the value of four times as much.

Who can take example of this punishment to beware of such like offence? Who is he of their kingdom that will not rather take courage to commit like offence, seeing the promotions that fell to these men for their so offending, so weak and blunt is your sword to strike at one of the offenders of this crooked and perverse generation.

And this is by the reason that the chief instrument of your law yea, the chief of your council, and he which hath your sword in hi hand, to whom also all the other instruments are obedient, is alway a spiritual man which hath ever such an inordinate love unto hi own kingdom that he will maintain that, though all the tempora kingdoms and commonwealths of the world should therefore utterly be undone.

Here leave we out the greatest matter of all lest that we, declaring such a horrible carrion of evil against the ministers of iniquity, should seem to declare the one only fault, or rather the ignorance, of ou best beloved minister of righteousness which is to be hid till he may be learned by these small enormities, that we have spoken of, to know it plainly himself.

But what remedy to relieve us, your poor, sick, lame, and sore beadmen? To make many hospitals for the relief of the poor people Nay, truly, the more the worse, for ever the fat of the whole founda tion hangeth on the priests' beards. Divers of your noble pre decessors, kings of this realm, have given lands to monasteries [so as to give a certain sum of money yearly to the poor people: Whereo from the ancientie of the time they give never one penny. They have likewise given to them to have a certain [number of] Masses saic daily for them, whereof they say never one. If the Abbot of West minster should sing every day as many Masses for his founders as he is bound to do by his foundation, a thousand monks were too few Wherefore, if your Grace will build a sure hospital, *that* never shal fail to relieve us, all your poor beadmen... [Fish urges the King to confiscate the property of the religious orders. The act will fill the royal treasury and promote a moral reformation in the kingdom.]

Then shall as well the number of our aforesaid monstrous sort, as o the bawds, whores, thieves, and idle people, decrease. Then shal these great yearly exactions cease. Then shall not your sword, power crown, dignity, and obedience of your people be translated from you. Then shall you have full obedience of your people. Then shal the idle people be set to work. Then shall matrimony be much better kept. Then shall the generation of your people be increased Then shall your commons increase in riches. Then shall the gospe be preached. Then shall none beg our alms from us. Then shall we have enough and more than shall suffice us, which shall be the bes hospital that ever was founded for us. Then shall we daily pray to God for your most noble estate long to endure.

Domine, salvum fac regem[1]

COLOPHON: London. [1529?]

[1] O Lord, protect the king.

ST THOMAS MORE[1]

The greater portion of Utopia *was written in 1515 while Sir Thomas More, then Under-Sheriff of London, was in Antwerp, representing the City Merchants as member of an embassy to the court of Archduke Charles, later Charles V. More finished the book the following year in London, and dedicated it to Peter Giles, a friend in Antwerp, where* Utopia *was first printed in 1517.*

Through Erasmus's letters of introduction to prominent people in the Low Countries, More met Peter Giles and Ralph Hythlodaye, the latter supposedly a mariner who had sailed to the New World with Amerigo Vespucci. His tales of adventure induced More to describe the imaginary commonwealth Utopia in a series of conversations.

The book is divided into two parts. The first part, which was written last, discusses the social conditions in England, comparing the life of Tudor Englishmen with that of Utopians, law-abiding pagans. In the second part More declares, as Erasmus puts it, 'the things that occasion mischiefs in commonwealths, having the English constitution especially in view, which he so thoroughly knows and understands'. When discussing the faults and excellence found in the government of the Utopians, particularly their attitude toward labour and war, Hythlodaye, the reformer and liberal, praises their laws regulating the common ownership of property. 'I cannot think', he states, 'that a nation can be governed justly or happily as long as there is any private property.' More contradicts him, declaring 'if people be pinched with want' and have no possessions to sell in order to help themselves, 'What can follow upon this but perpetual sedition and bloodshed, especially since reverence and authority due to magistrates fall to the ground?' Throughout the discussion, More makes a definite distinction between compulsory communism, urged by Hythlodaye, and voluntary communism, practised by the first Christians and down through the ages by the Orders of the Church.

As sources for Utopia, *More used Plato's* Republic, *Tacitus's* Germania, *St Augustine's* De Civitate Dei, *Erasmus's* Institutio Principis Christiani, *and Vespucci's* Quattuor Voyages. *Urged by friends to print an English version of* Utopia, *More refused on the grounds that the work would be easily accessible to many who would be incapable of interpreting it, and so misconstrue its meaning.*

The first English translation of Utopia *was made in 1551 by Ralph Robynson. Born in Lincolnshire in 1521, Robynson received his early education at Grantham and Stamford grammar schools, where he began a lifelong friendship with a classmate, William Cecil, later Lord Burghley. In 1539 Robynson entered Corpus Christi College, Oxford, and four*

---

[1] For biographical sketch, see pp. 64-6.

years later took a Bachelor of Arts degree. He was elected Fellow of the college in 1542, and after taking a Master of Arts degree left Oxford to accept a clerkship secured for him by Cecil. To show his gratitude, Robynson dedicated to him some Latin verses and the translation of Utopia. *There is no recorded date of Robynson's death. He lived beyond 1572, which date appears on the MS. of a poem appealing to Cecil for financial aid.*

While Robynson can be credited with encouraging English prose, and testing it with a variety of subtle expressions, his translation of Utopia *polished away much of More's charming fantasy, leaving a vigorous political debate.*

The first important English works of Sir Thomas More were written almost ten years after Utopia *and when he was filling the post of Lord Chancellor of England, to which he was appointed 25 October 1529. Though burdened with cares of state, he found the time to finish his* Dyaloge *against Tyndale and write* The supplycacyon of soulys; agaynst the supplycacyon of beggars [1529?], *an answer to the pamphlet written by Simon Fish. More divided his treatise into two books: the first discloses the motives of those who would make 'beggars' of the clergy; and the second gives the arguments of the 'sely soulys' for the existence of purgatory, based on reason and Scripture and their 'pyteouse' plea for the prayers of the living. The* Supplycacyon *affords an example of More's facility in discussing theological problems in terms readily understood by laymen.*

The Apologye of syr T. More, knyght, *written in 1533 after More had resigned from public office, was intended as an answer to those who believed that his Catholic orthodoxy interfered with his allegiance to the king. He also refuted the anonymous tract,* A treatise concernynge the diuision betwene the spirytualtie and temporaltie [1532?]. *The author of the latter, who refers to himself as a Catholic and a 'Pacifier', has been identified as Christopher Saint-German. He argues that the king and parliament should settle all differences between the clergy and laity. More believes such an act would endanger both the state and the individual. The legal aspects of heresy, which in Tudor times was considered a criminal offence and therefore punishable by the state, is explained by More, who as Chancellor was accused of burning heretics.*

Besides the Supplicacyon *and* Apologye, *More's last controversial works include* The debellacyon of Salem and Bizance (1533), *a reply to Saint-German's dialogue,* Salem and Bizance; *and* The answere to the fyrst parte of the poysened booke [by John Frith] wh. a namelesse heretyke [William Tyndale] hath named the souper of the lorde (1534). *More planned the latter work in two parts, intending it as a defence of the Eucharist, but he was put to death soon after the first part was completed.*

More's style, marked especially with a persuasive humour tinged with an occasional gleam of satire, is at its best in the Supplication *and* Apology. *Recognizing the former's popular appeal, John Frith referred to it as More's 'painted poetry'.*

Utopia

A fruitful pleasant and witty work of the best state of a public-weal and of the new isle called *Utopia*: written in Latin by the right worthy and famous Sir Thomas More, Knight, and translated into English by Ralph Robynson, sometime Fellow of Corpus Christi College in Oxford; and now by him at this second edition newly perused and corrected and also with divers notes in the margin augmented.

The second book of the communication of Raphael Hythlodaye concerning the best state of a commonwealth, containing the description of Utopia with a large declaration of the politic government and of all the good laws and orders of the same island.

OF SCIENCES, CRAFTS, AND OCCUPATIONS

Husbandry is a science common to them all in general, both men and women, wherein they be all expert and cunning. In this they be all instructed even from their youth; partly in their schools with traditions and precepts, and partly in the country nigh the city, brought up, as it were, in playing, not only beholding the use of it, but by occasion of exercising their bodies practising it also.

Besides husbandry which, as I said, is common to them all, every one of them learneth one or other several and particular science as his own proper craft. That is most commonly either clothworking in wool or flax, or masonry, or the smith's craft, or the carpenter's science; for there is none other occupation that any number to speak of doth use there. For their garments, which throughout all the island be of one fashion (saving that there is a difference between the man's garment and the woman's, between the married and the unmarried), and this one continueth forevermore unchanged, seemly and comely to the eye, no let to the moving and wielding of the body, also fit both for winter and summer: as for these garments, I say, every family maketh their own. But of the other foresaid crafts every man learneth one; and not only the men, but also the women. But the women, as the weaker sort, be put to the easier crafts, as to work wool and flax. The more laboursome sciences be committed to the men. For the most part every man is brought up in his father's craft, for most commonly they be naturally thereto bent and inclined: but if a man's mind stand to any other, he is by adoption put into a family of that occupation which he doth most fantasy,[1] whom not only his father, but also the magistrates do

---

[1] *fantasy*, fancy.

diligently look to, that he be put to a discreet and an honest house-holder. Yea, and if any person, when he hath learned one craft, be desirous to learn also another, he is likewise suffered and permitted. When he hath learned both, he occupieth whether he will, unless the city have more need of the one than of the other.

The chief and almost the only office of the syphogrants*
Idle persons is to see and take heed that no man sit idle, but that to be driven every one apply his own craft with earnest diligence; out of the weal public and yet for all that not to be wearied from early in the morning to late in the evening with continual work, like labouring and toiling beasts.

For this is worse than the miserable and wretched condition of bondmen; which nevertheless is almost everywhere the life of work-men and artificers, saving in Utopia. For they, dividing the day and the night into twenty-four just hours, appoint and assign only six of those hours to work, three before noon, upon the which they go straight to dinner: and after dinner, when they have rested two hours, then they work three: and upon that they go to supper. About eight of the clock in the evening, counting one of the clock at the first hour after noon, they go to bed. Eight hours they give to sleep. All the void time, that is between the hours of work, sleep, and meat, that they be suffered to bestow, every man as he liketh best himself; not to the intent that they should misspend this time in riot or sloth-fulness, but, being then licensed from the labour of their own occu-pations, to bestow the time well and thriftily upon some other good science as shall please them. For it is a solemn custom there to have lectures daily early in the morning, where to be present they only be constrained that be namely chosen and appointed to learning. How-beit a great multitude of every sort of people, both men and women, go to hear lectures: some one and some another, as every man's nature is inclined. Yet, this notwithstanding, if any man had rather bestow this time upon his own occupation, as it chanceth in many, whose minds rise not in the contemplation of any science liberal, he is not letted nor prohibited, but is also praised and commended as profitable to the commonwealth.

After supper they bestow one hour in play: in summer in their gardens; in winter in their common halls where they dine and sup. There they exercise themselves in music, or else in honest
Playing after and wholesome communication. Dice-play, and such supper other foolish and pernicious games, they know not; but they use two games not much unlike the chess. The one is the battle of numbers, wherein one number stealeth away another. The other is wherein vices fight with virtues, as it were, in battle array, or a set field: in the which game is very properly showed both the strife and discord that vices have among themselves, and again their unity

and concord against virtues; and also what vices be repugnant to what virtues; with what power and strength they assail them openly; by what wiles and subtlety they assault them secretly; with what help and aid the virtues resist and overcome the puissance of the vices; by what craft they frustrate their purposes; and, finally, by what sleight or means the one getteth the victory.

But here, lest you be deceived, one thing you must look more narrowly upon. For seeing they bestow but six hours in work, perchance you may think that the lack of some necessary things hereof may ensue. But this is nothing so; for that small time is not only enough but also too much for the store and abundance of all things that be requisite, either for the necessity or commodity of life; the which thing you also shall perceive if you weigh and consider with yourselves how great a part of the people in other countries liveth idle....

This commodity they have also above other, that in the most part of necessary occupations they need not so much work as other nations do. For first of all, the building or repairing of houses asketh everywhere so many men's continual labour, because that the unthrifty heir suffereth the houses that his father builded in continuance of time to fall in decay: so that which he might have upholden with little cost, his successor is constrained to build it again anew to his great charge. Yea, many times also the house that stood one man in much money, another is of so nice and so delicate a mind that he setteth nothing by it: and it being neglected, and therefore shortly falling into ruin, he buildeth up another in another place with no less cost and charge. But among the Utopians, where all things be set in a good order and the commonwealth in a good stay, it very seldom chanceth that they choose a new plot to build an house upon. And they do not only find speedy and quick remedies for present faults, but also prevent them that be like to fall. And by this means their houses continue and last very long with little labour and small reparations; insomuch that this kind of workmen sometimes have almost nothing to do: but that they be commanded to hew timber at home and to square and trim up stones, to the intent that if any work chance, it may the speedier rise.

How to avoid excessive cost in building

Now, sir, in their apparel, mark, I pray you, how few workmen they need. First of all, while they be at work, they be covered homely with leather or skins that will last seven years. When they go forth abroad, they cast upon them a cloak which hideth the other homely apparel. These cloaks throughout the whole island be all of one colour, and that is the natural colour of the wool. They therefore do not only spend much less woollen cloth than is spent in other countries, but also the same standeth them in much less cost. But linen cloth is made with less labour, and is therefore had more in use. But in linen cloth only whiteness, in woollen only cleanliness is regarded; as for the smallness or fineness of the thread, that is nothing passed for. And this is the cause wherefore in other places four or five cloth gowns of divers colours and as many silk coats be not enough for one man. Yea, and if he be of the delicate and nice sort, ten be too few; whereas their one garment will serve a man most commonly two years. For why should he desire more? seeing if he had them, he should not be the better happed or covered from cold, neither is his apparel any whit the comelier.

Wherefore, seeing they be all exercised in profitable occupations, and that few artificers in the same crafts be sufficient, this is the cause that, plenty of all things being among them, they do sometimes bring forth an innumerable company of people to amend the highways if any be broken. Many times also, when they have no such work to be occupied about, an open proclamation is made that they shall bestow fewer hours in work. For the magistrates do not exercise their citizens against their wills in unneedful labours. For why? in the institution of that weal public this end is only and chiefly pretended and minded, that what time may possibly be spared from the necessary occupations and affairs of the commonwealth, all that the citizens should withdraw from the bodily service to the free liberty of the mind and garnishing of the same. For herein they suppose the felicity of this life to consist.

OF WARFARE

War or battle, as a thing very beastly, and yet to no kind of beasts insomuch use as it is to man, they do detest and abhor; and contrary to the custom almost of all other nations, they count nothing so much against glory as glory gotten in war. And therefore, though they do daily practise and exercise themselves in the discipline of war, and that not only the men but also the women upon certain appointed days, lest they should be to seek in the feat of arms if need should require, yet they never go to battle but either in the defence of their own country or to drive out of their friends' land the enemies that be comen in, or by their power to deliver from the yoke and bondage of tyranny some people that be therewith oppressed with tyranny: which thing they do of mere pity and compassion.

Howbeit they send help to their friends: nor ever in their defence, but sometimes also to requite and revenge injuries before to them done. But this they do not unless their counsel and advice in the matter be asked while it is yet new and fresh. For if they find the cause probable and if the contrary part will not restore again such things as be of them justly demanded, then they be the chief authors and makers of the war. Which they do not only as oft as by inroads and invasions of soldiers prey and booty be driven away, but then also much more mortally when their friends' merchants in any land, either under the pretence of unjust laws or else by the wresting and wrong understanding of good laws, do sustain an unjust accusation under the colour of justice.

Neither the battle which the Utopians fought for the Nephelogetes* against the Alaopolitanes,* a little before our time, was made for any other cause but that the Nephelogete merchantmen, as the Utopians thought, suffered wrong of the Alaopolitanes under the pretence of right. But whether it were right or wrong, it was with so cruel and mortal war revenged, the countries round about joining their help and power to the puissance and malice of both parties, that most flourishing and wealthy peoples, being some of them shrewdly shaken and some of them sharply beaten, the mischiefs were not finished nor ended until the Alaopolitanes at the last were yielded up as bond-men into the jurisdiction of the Nephelogetes: for the Utopians fought not this war for themselves. And yet the Nephelogetes before the war, when the Alaopolitanes flourished in wealth, were nothing to be compared with them.

So eagerly the Utopians prosecute the injuries done to their friends, yea in money matters; and not their own likewise. For if they by covine[1] or guile be wiped[2] beside their goods, so that no violence be done to their bodies, they wreak their anger by abstaining from occupying with that nation until they have made satisfaction. Not for because they set less store by their own citizens than by their friends, but that they take the loss of their friends' money more heavily than the loss of their own; because that their friends' merchantmen, forasmuch as that they lose is their own private goods, sustain great damage by the loss; but their own citizens, lose nothing but of the common goods and of that which was at home plentiful and almost superfluous, else it had not been sent forth: therefore no man feeleth the loss.

And for this cause they think it too cruel an act to revenge that loss with the death of many; the incommodity of the which loss no man feeleth neither in his life, nor yet in his living. But if it chance that any of their men in any other country be maimed or killed, whether it be done by a common or a private counsel; knowing and trying out the truth of the matter by their ambassadors, unless the offenders be rendered unto them in recompense of the injury, they will not be appeased, but incontinent they proclaim war against them. The offenders yielded, they punish, either with death or with bondage.

They be not only sorry but also ashamed to achieve the victory

---

[1] *covine*, fraud.   [2] *wiped*, cheated.

with much bloodshed, counting it great folly to buy precious wares too dear. They rejoice and avaunt[1] themselves if they vanquish and oppress their enemies by craft and deceit; and for that act they make a general triumph; and as if the matter were manfully handled, they set up a pillar of stone in the place where they so vanquished their enemies in token of the victory. For then they glory, then they boast and crack that they have played the men indeed, when they have so overcome as no other living creature but only man could; that is to say, by the might and puissance of wit. For with bodily strength, say they, bears, lions, boars, wolves, dogs, and other wild beasts do fight; and as the most part of them do pass us in strength and fierce courage, so in wit and reason we be much stronger than they all.

Victory dear bought

Their chief and principal purpose in war is to obtain that thing which if they had before obtained, they would not have moved battle. But if that be not possible, they take so cruel vengeance of them which be in the fault, that ever after they be afeared to do the like. This is their chief and principal intent, which they immediately and first of all prosecute and set forward; but yet so, that they be more circumspect in avoiding and eschewing jeopardies than they be desirous of praise and renown....

Truce taken with their enemies for a short time they do so firmly and faithfully keep, that they will not break it; no, not though they be thereunto provoked. They do not waste nor destroy their enemies' land with foragings, nor they burn not up their corn. Yea, they save it as much as may be from being overrun and trodden down, either with men or horses, thinking that it groweth for their own use and profit. They hurt no man that is unarmed, unless he be an espiall.[2] All cities that be yielded unto them, they defend: and such as they win by force of assault, they neither despoil nor sack. But them that withstood and dissuaded the yielding up of the same, they put to death; the other soldiers they punish with bondage. All the weak multitude they leave untouched. If they know that any citizens counselled to yield and render up the city, to them they give part of the condemned men's goods. The residue they distribute and give freely among them whose help they had in the same war: for none of themselves taketh any portion of the prey.

Of truces

But when the battle is finished and ended, they put their friends to never a penny cost of all the charges that they were at, but lay it upon their necks that be conquered. Them they burden with the whole charge of their expenses; which they demand of them partly in money, to be kept for like use of battle, and partly in lands of great revenues to be paid unto them yearly forever. Such revenue

---

[1] *avaunt*, boast.   [2] *espiall*, spy.

hey have now in many countries; which by little and little rising of
livers and sundry causes, be increased above seven hundred thousand
ducats by the year. Thither they send forth some of their citizens as
lieutenants to live there sumptuously like men of honour and renown;
and yet, this notwithstanding, much money is saved, which cometh
to the common treasury, unless it so chance that they had rather
trust the country with the money; which many times they do so
long until they have need to occupy it. And it seldom happeneth
that they demand all. Of these lands they assign part unto them
which at their request and exhortation put themselves in such
jeopardies as I spake of before. If any prince stir up war against them,
intending to invade their land, they meet him incontinent out of
their own borders with great power and strength: for they never
lightly make war in their own country. Nor they be never brought
into so extreme necessity, as to take help out of foreign lands into
their own island.

COLOPHON: Imprinted at London in Paul's Churchyard, at
the sign of the Lamb, by Abraham Veale. 1551.

The Supplication of Souls

Made by Sir Thomas More, Knight, Councillor to our
sovereign lord the King and Chancellor of his Duchy of
Lancaster.

AGAINST 'THE SUPPLICATION OF BEGGARS'[1]

To All Good Christian People:

In most piteous wise continually calleth and crieth upon your
devout charity and most tender pity for help, comfort, and relief,
your late acquaintance, kindred, spouses, companions, playfellows,
and friends—and now your humble and unacquainted and half-
forgotten suppliants, poor prisoners of God, the sely[2] souls in
purgatory—here abiding and enduring the grievous pains and hot
cleansing fire that fretteth and burneth out the rusty and filthy spots
of our sin, till the mercy of Almighty God, the rather by your good
and charitable means, vouchsafe to deliver us hence.

From whence if ye marvel why we more now molest and trouble
you with our writing than ever we were wont before, it may like
you to wit and understand that hitherto though we have been with
many folk much forgotten of negligence, yet hath always good folk

---

[1] Book I.   [2] *sely*, pitiable.

remembered us; and we have been recommended unto God and eased, helped, and relieved both by the private prayers of good virtuous people, and specially by the daily Masses and other ghostly suffrages of priests, religious, and folk of Holy Church. But now since that of late there are sprungen up certain seditious persons which not only travail and labour to destroy them by whom we be much helped, but also to sow and set forth such a pestilent opinion against ourselves as, once received and believed among the people must needs take from us the relief and comfort that ever should come to us by the charitable alms, prayer, and good works of the world ye may take it for no wonder though we sely souls, that have long lain and cried so far from you that we seldom break your sleep, do now in this our great fear of our utter loss forever of your loving remembrance and relief, not yet importunately bereave you of your rest with crying at your ears at unseasonable time when ye would (as we do never) repose yourself and take ease, but only procure to be presented unto you this poor book, this humble supplication of ours Which it may please you parcelmeal[1] at your leisure to look over for all sely souls' sake, that it may be as an wholesome treacle at your heart against the deadly poison of their pestilent persuasion that would bring you in that error to ween there were no purgatory.

Of all which cruel persons so procuring, not the minishment of your mercy towards us, but the utter spoil and robbery of our whole help and comfort that should come from you, the very worst and, thereby, the most deadly deviser of our pains and heaviness (God forgive him!) is that despiteous and despiteful person which of late, under pretext of pity, made and put forth among you a book that he named *The Supplication for the Beggars*. A book, indeed, nothing less intending than the pity that it pretendeth; nothing minding the weal of any man but, as we shall hereafter show you, much harm and mischief to all men; and among other great sorrow, discomfort, and heaviness unto us, your even-Christians and nigh kin, your late neighbours and pleasant companions upon earth, and now poor prisoners here....

And first, to begin where he beginneth, when he saith that the number of such beggars as he pretendeth to speak for—that is, as himself calleth them, 'the wretched, hideous monsters on whom', he saith, 'scarcely any eye dare look, the foul, unhappy sort of lepers and other sore people, needly, impotent, blind, lame, and sick, living only of alms—have their number now so sore increased that all the alms of all the well-disposed people of the realm is not half enough to sustain them, but that for very constraint they die for hunger'. Unto all those words of his, were it not that though we well wist, ourself, [what] he said untrue, yet would we be loath so to lay

[1] *parcelmeal*, piecemeal.

as a lie to his charge anything whereof the untruth were not so plainly perceived, but that he might find some favourers which might say, he said true. Else would we, peradventure, not let to tell him that for a beginning, in these few words, he had written two lies at once.

If we should tell you what number there was of poor sick folk in days passed long before your time, ye were at liberty not to believe us. Howbeit he cannot yet on the other side, for his part neither, bring you forth a bead-roll* of their names. Wherefore we must for both our parts be fain to remit you to your own time, and yet not from your childhood (whereof many things men forget when they come to far greater age) but unto the days of your good remembrance. . . .

Now whereas he saith that 'the alms of all well-disposed people of this realm is not half enough to sustain them'—and the well-disposed people he calleth in this matter, all them that giveth them alms—and he speaketh not of one year or twain but of these many years now passed, for neither the number of the clergy nor their possessions nor the friars' alms, in which things he layeth the cause why the alms of good people is not half sufficient to keep and sustain the poor and sick beggars from famishing, any great thing increased in these ten or twelve or twenty years last passed; and therefore if that he said were true, then by all these ten years at the least, the alms of good people hath not been half able to sustain the poor and sick beggars from famishing. And surely if that were so that in four or five years in which was plenty of corn, the poor and sick beggars for lack of men's alms died so fast for hunger; though many should fall sick never so fast again, yet had they in the last two dear years died up of likelihood almost everyone. And whether this be true or not we purpose not to dispute; but to refer and report ourself to every man's eyes and ears, whether any man hear of so many dead or see so many the fewer.

When he hath laid these sure stones to begin the ground and foundation of his building with, that sore and sick beggars be so sore increased that the alms of all the good people of this realm is not half enough to sustain them, and that therefore by very constraint they daily die for hunger, upon them he layeth another stone—that the cause of all this evil is the great possessions of the spiritualty and the great alms given to the friars.

But herein first, he layeth that besides tithes and all such other profits as rise unto the Church by reason of the spiritual law or of men's devotion, that they have the third part of all the temporal lands of the realm. Which whoso can tell as much of the revenues of the realm as he can tell little that made the book, doth well know that though they have much, yet is the third part of all far another thing, and that he saith in this point untrue.

Then goeth he to the poor friars. And there, as we told you, he showeth that the alms given them of certain amounteth yearly unto 43,333 pounds, six shillings, eight pence sterling. Peradventure, men would ween the man were some apostate and that he never could be so privy to the friars' reckoning but if he had been long their limiter* and seen some general view of all their whole accounts. But surely since the man is bad enough besides, we would be loath, folk should reckon him for [an] apostate, for surely he was never friar for aught that we know, for we never wist that ever in his life he was half so well-disposed. And also when ye hear the ground of his reckoning, ye will yourself think that he neither knoweth much of their matters, and of all the realm besides make as though he knew many things for true which many men know for false.

For first, he putteth for the ground of his reckoning that there are in the realm two and fifty thousand parish churches, which is one plain lie to begin with. Then he putteth that every parish, one with another, hath ten households in it; meaning beside such poor houses as rather ask alms than give, for of such ye wot well the friars get no quarterage.* And that point albeit the ground be not sure, yet because it may to many men seem likely, therefore we let it pass. But then he showeth further for a sure truth a thing that all men know surely for a great lie: that is to say, that of every household in every parish, every [one] of the five Orders of friars hath every quarter a penny. For we know full well and so do many of you too, firstly, the common people speak but of four Orders—the white, the black, the Austin, and the grey—and which is the fifth, in many parts of the realm few folk can tell you. For if the question were asked about, there would be, peradventure, founden many more, the more pity it is, that could name you the green friars than the crowched.[1] Ye know right well also that in many a parish in England, of forty householders ye shall not find four [who] pay neither five pence a quarter nor four neither, and many a parish never a penny. And as for the five pence quarterly, we dare boldly say that ye shall find it in very few parishes through the realm, if ye find it paid in any. And yet this thing being such a stark lie, as many men already knoweth and every man shortly may find it, he putteth as a plain, well-known truth for a special post to bear up his reckoning.

For upon these grounds now maketh he a clear reckoning in this manner ensuing, which is good also to be known for folk that will learn to cast a count. There be fifty two thousand parishes; and in each of them ten households. So have ye the whole sum of them: households, five hundred and twenty thousand. Even just. Go now to the money then. Every order of the five Orders of friars hath of every of these households a penny a quarter. *Summa*, for every house

[1] *crowched*, crossed [friars].

among all the five Orders every quarter, five pence, and hereby may ye learn that five times one maketh five. Now this is, he showeth you, among the five Orders of every house for the whole year, twenty pence; and so learn ye that four times five maketh twenty. *Summa*, saith he, five hundred thousand and twenty thousand quarters of angels. Here we would not that because the realm hath no coin called the quarter angel, ye should therefore so far mistake the man as to ween that he meant so many quarter sacks of angels. For indeed (as we take him) by the naming and counting of so many quarters of angels, he meaneth nothing else but to teach you a point of reckoning and to make you perceive and know that twenty pence is the fourth part of six shillings, eight pence. For after that rate it seemeth that he valueth the angel noble. . . .

But he proveth you that the clergy must needs be the cause why there be so many poor men and beggars. For he saith that before the clergy came in there were but few poor people; and yet they begged not neither, but men, he saith, gave them enough unasked. But now where sat he when he saw the people give poor folk so fast their alms unasked that no man needed to beg before the clergy began. . . .

Now herein he showeth also a high point of wit, where he saith that the great living that the clergy hath, which he layeth and lieth to be more than half of the whole revenues and substance of the realm, is shifted among fewer than the four-hundredth part of the people. As though that of the clergy's part there had no lay people their living, no servant any wages, no artificer any money for working, no carpenter, no mason any money for building; but all the money that ever cometh in their hands, they put it by and by in their own bellies, and no layman hath any relief thereof. And therefore this point was wisely written, ye see as well as we.

Now for the truth thereof—if it were true that he saith, that the clergy compared to the residue of the men only, be not one to an hundred—then shall ye not need to fear the great Turk and he came tomorrow, except ye suffer among you to grow in great number these Lutherans that favour him. For we dare make you the warrantise that if his lie be true, there be more men, a great many in London and within four shires next adjoining, than the great Turk* bringeth into Hungary.

But in this ye must hold him excused, for he meddleth not much with augrim[1] to see to what sum the number of men ariseth that is multiplied by an hundred. All his practice in multiplication meddleth with nothing but lies; and therein match him with whom ye will, he will give you an hundred for one. . . .

[According to Fish, the subjection of the clergy will kindle a religious spirit in the realm.]

[1] *augrim*, counting device made of stones.

'Then shall the gospel be preached.' Yea, marry, that. There is the great matter that all this gaping is for. For undoubtedly all the gaping is for a new gospel. Men have been wont this many years to preach the gospel of Christ in such wise as Saint Matthew, Saint Mark, Saint Luke, and Saint John hath written it, and in such wise as the old holy Doctors, Saint Jerome, Saint Austin, Saint Ambrose, Saint Gregory, Saint Chrysostom, Saint Basil, Saint Cyprian, Saint Bernard, Saint Thomas, and all the old holy Fathers since Christ's days until your own days have understood it. This gospel hath been, as we say, always thus preached. Why, saith he, now that if the clergy were cast out for naught, that then the gospel should be preached? Who should then be these preachers? He meaneth not that the clergy shall, ye may see that well. Who then? Who but some lay Lutherans? And what gospel shall they preach? Not your old gospel of Christ, for that is it which was wont to be preached unto you. And he would, ye should now think, that the gospel shall begin to be preached, and yet not begin to be preached among you till the clergy be cast out. What gospel shall that be, then, that shall then be preached? What gospel but Luther's gospel and Tyndale's gospel? Telling you that only faith sufficeth you for salvation; and that there needeth no good works, but that it were sacrilege and abomination to go about to please God with any good works; and that there is no purgatory, nor that the sacraments be nothing worth, nor that no law can be made by man to bind you; but that by your only faith ye may do what ye will; and that if ye obey any law or governor, all is of your own courtesy and not of any duty at all, faith hath set you in such a lewd liberty.

This and many a mad frantic folly shall be the gospel that then shall be preached, whereof he boasteth now as of one of the most special commodities that shall succeed upon his goodly and godly devices. . . .

And therefore this beggars' proctor, or rather the proctor of hell, should have concluded his supplication not under the manner that he hath done, that after the clergy [are] cast out, then shall the gospel be preached, then shall beggars and bawds decrease, then shall idle folk and thieves be fewer, then shall the realm increase in riches, and so forth. But he should have said: After that the clergy is thus destroyed and cast out, then shall Luther's gospel come in, then shall Tyndale's Testament be taken up. Then shall false heresies be preached. Then shall the sacraments be set at naught. Then shall fasting and prayer be neglected. Then shall holy saints be blasphemed. Then shall Almighty God be displeased. Then shall He withdraw His grace and let all run to ruin. Then shall all virtue be had in derision. Then shall all vice reign and run forth unbridled. Then shall youth leave labour and all occupation. Then shall folk wax idle and fall to unthriftiness. Then shall whores and thieves, beggars and bawds increase. Then shall unthrifts flock together and swarm about, and each bear him bold of other. Then shall all laws be laughed to scorn. Then shall the servants set naught by their masters, and unruly people rebel against their rulers. Then will rise up rifling and robbery, murder and mischief and plain insurrection. Whereof what could be the end or when you should see it, only God knoweth.

All which mischief may yet be withstanden easily, and, with God's grace, so shall it if ye suffer no such bold beggars to seduce you with seditious bills. But well perceiving that their malicious purpose is to bring you to destruction, ye, like good Christian people, avoiding their false trains and grins, give none ear to their heinous heresies nor walk their seditious ways. But persevering in your old faith of Christ and observing His laws with good and godly works and obedience of your most gracious King and governor, go forth in goodness and virtue, whereby ye cannot fail to flower and prosper in riches and worldly substance. Which, well employed with help of God's grace about charitable deeds to the needy, and the rather in remembrance and relief of us whose need is relieved by your charity showed for our sake to your neighbour, be able to purchase you much pardon of the bitter pain of this painful place, and bring you to the joyful bliss to which God hath with His Blessed Blood bought you, and with His holy sacraments ensigned you.

And thus will we leave the man's malicious folly, tending to the destruction first of the clergy and after of yourself, wherein his mad reckoning hath constrained us to trouble you with many trifles, God wot, full unmeet for us. And now will we turn to the treating of that one point which, though it specially pertaineth to ourself, yet much more specially pertaineth it unto you; that is to wit, the impugnation of that uncharitable heresy wherewith he would make you, to our great harm and much more your own, believe that we need none help and that there were no purgatory.

The end of the first book.

ON PURGATORY[1]

For surely not only among Christian people and Jews, of whom the one hath, the other hath had, the perceiving and sight of faith, but also among the very miscreant and idolatrous Turks, Saracens, and paynims—except only such as have so far fallen from the nature of man into a brutish, beastly persuasion as to believe the soul and body die both at once—else hath always the remnant commonly thought and believed that after the bodies [were] dead and deceased, the

[1] Book II.

souls of such as were neither deadly damned [and] wretched forever, nor on the other side so good but that their offences done in this world hath deserved more punishment than they had suffered and sustained there, were punished and purged by pain after their death ere ever they were admitted unto their wealth and rest.

This faith hath always not only faithful people had, but also, as we say, very miscreants and idolaters have ever had a certain opinion and persuasion of the same. Whether that of the first light and revelation given of such things to our former fathers there hath always remained a glimmering that hath gone forth from man to man, from one generation to another, and so continued and kept among all people; or else that nature and reason have taught men everywhere to perceive it. For surely that they have such belief, not only by such as have been travelled in many countries among sundry sects, but also by the old and ancient writers that have been among them, we may well and evidently perceive.

And, in good faith, if never had there been revelation given thereof, nor other sight than reason, yet, presupposed the immortality of man's soul, which no reasonable man distrusted, and thereto agreed the righteousness of God and His goodness, which scant the devil himself denieth; purgatory must needs appear. For since that God of His righteousness will not leave sin unpunished, nor His goodness will perpetually punish the fault after the man's conversion, it followeth that the punishment shall be temporal. And now since the man often dieth before such punishment had, either of God's hand by some affliction sent him, or at his own by due penance done—which the most part of people wantonly doth forsloth—a very child almost may see the consequent, that the punishment at the death remaining due and undone is to be endured and sustained after. Which, since His Majesty is so excellent whom we have offended, cannot of right and justice be but heavy and sore.

Now if they would, peradventure, as in magnifying of God's high goodness, say that after a man's conversion once to God again, not only all his sin is forgiven but all the whole pain also; or that they will, under colour of enhancing the merit and goodness of Christ's Passion, tell us that His pain suffered for us standeth instead of all our pain and penance, so that neither purgatory can have place nor any penance need to be done by ourself for our own sin: these folk that so shall say, shall under pretext of magnifying His mercy not only sore minish His virtue of justice, but also much hinder the opinion and persuasion that men have of His goodness. For albeit that God of His great mercy may forthwith forgive some folk freely their sin and pain both, without prejudice of His righteousness—either of His liberal bounty, or for some respect had unto the fervent, sorrowful heart that fear and love with help of special grace have brought into the penitent at the time of his return to God, and also that the bitter Passion of Our Saviour besides the remission of the perpetuity of our pain do also lessen our purgatory and stand us here in marvellous high stead—yet if He should use this point for a general rule, that at every conversion from sin with purpose of amendment and recourse to confession, He shall forthwith fully forgive without the party's pain or any other recompense for the sins committed, save only Christ's Passion paid for them all: then should He give great occasion of lightness and bold courage to sin. . . .

If all this [More substantiates his arguments for the existence of purgatory by quotations from the Old and New Testaments] will not satisfy them, will ye see yet another clear place and such as none heretic can avoid. Doth not the blessed apostle Saint Peter, as appeareth in the second chapter of the Apostles' Acts, say of Our Saviour Christ in this wise: *Quem deus suscitavit solutis doloribus inferni*?[1] [Whom God hath raised up having loosed the pains of hell.] In these words he showeth that pains of hell were loosed. But these pains were neither pains of that hell in which the damned souls be pained, which neither were loosed then nor never be loosed, but be and shall be, as our Saviour saith Himself, everlasting. Nor these pains that were then loosed were not the pains in *limbo patrum* [Limbo of the Fathers] for there were none to be loosed, for the good souls were there, as Our Saviour showeth Himself, in quiet comfort and rest. And so appeareth it evidently that the pains of hell that were loosed were only the pains of purgatory, which is also called hell by occasion of the Latin word and the Greek word both.

For in these tongues (forasmuch as before the Resurrection of Our Saviour Christ there was never none that ascended up into heaven) there were no people that any otherwise spake of souls than that they were gone down beneath into the low place. And therefore in the words of the common Creed is it said of Our Saviour Christ after His Passion: *descendit ad inferna*, that is to say, He descended down beneath into the low places. Instead of which low places the English tongue hath ever used this word, *hell*. And certain is it, and very sure, that Christ descended not into all these low places, nor into every place of hell, but only into *limbus patrum* and purgatory. Which two places because they be parts of habitations of souls beneath (all which habitations beneath have in English been always called hell), therefore are these two places among other taken and comprehended under the name of hell. . . .

This much have we showed you of this word *hell* because we would not that the common talking thereof might bring you into any error. So that by this place ye see proved by the plain words of Saint Peter that Christ at His Resurrection did loose and unbind pains

[1] Acts ii. 24.

in hell, which, as we have showed you, could be nowhere there but in purgatory. For in the special hell of damned souls the pains were not loosed. And in *limbus patrum* was no pains to be loosed. And therefore, except they deny Saint Peter, they cannot deny purgatory.

COLOPHON. [W. Rastell...before 25 October 1529.]

The Apology of Sir Thomas More, Knight

Sir Thomas More, Knight, to the Christian Readers

THE FIRST CHAPTER

So well stand I not (I thank God), good reader, in mine own conceit, and thereby so much in mine own light, but that I can somewhat with equal judgment and an even eye behold and consider both myself and mine own. Nor I use not to follow the condition of Aesop's ape* that thought her own babes so beauteous and so far passing in all goodly feature and favour, nor the crow that accompted her own birds the fairest of all fowles that flew. But like as some (I see well) there are that can¹ somewhat less than I, that yet for all that put out their works in writing: so am I not so blind upon the other side but that I very well perceive very many so far in wit and erudition above me, that in such matter as I have anything written, if other men, as many would have taken it in hand as could have done it better, it might much better have becomen me to let the matter alone than by writing to presume anything to meddle therewith.

And therefore, good reader, since I so well know so many men so far excel and pass me in all such things as are required in him that might adventure to put his works abroad to stand and abide the judgment of all other men, I was never so far overseen as either to look or hope that such faults as in my writing should by mine oversight escape me could by the eyes of all other men pass forth unspied, but shortly should be both by good and well learned perceived, and among so many bad brethren as, I wist well, would be wroth with them should be both sought out and sifted to the uttermost flake of bran and largely thereupon controlled and reproved.

But yet against all this fear this one thing recomforted me, that since I was of one point very fast and sure, that such things as I write are consonant unto the common Catholic faith and determinations of Christ's Catholic Church and are clear confutations of false, blasphemous heresies by [William] Tyndale and Barons [Robert

¹ *can*, know.

Barnes] put forth unto the contrary; any great fault and intolerable should they none find of such manner, sort, and kind as the readers should in their souls perish and be destroyed by, of which poisoned faults mine adversaries' books be full.

Now then as for other faults of less weight and tolerable, I nothing doubted nor do, but that every good Christian reader will be so reasonable and indifferent as to pardon in me the thing that happeth in all other men; and that no such man will over me be so sore an auditor and over my books, such a sore controller as to charge me with any great loss by gathering together of many such things as are with very few men aught regarded: and to look for such exact circumspection and sure sight to be by me used in my writing, as except the Prophets of God and Christ and his Apostles, hath never, I ween, be founden in any man's else before: that is to wit, to be perfect in every point, clean from all manner of faults, but hath always been holden for a thing excusable, though the reader in a long work perceive that the writer have, as Horace saith of Homer,* here and there sometime fallen in a little slumber, in which places as the reader seeth that the writer slept, so useth he of courtesy if he cannot sleep, yet for company, at the leastwise, to nap and wink with him and leave his dream unchecked.

Which kind of courtesy if I should show how often I have used with Tyndale and Barons both, winking at their tolerable faults and such as I rather thought negligently escaped them of oversight or folly than diligently devised of wily falsehood or malice: If I would add all of those faults to their other, then should I double in length all my books in which the brethren find for the special fault that they be too long already.

But albeit that when I wrote, I was (as I have told you) bolded and encouraged by the common custom of all indifferent readers which would, I wist, well pardon and hold excused such tolerable oversight in my writing as men may find some in any man's almost that ever wrote before. Yet am I now much more glad and bold when I see that those folk which would fainest find my faults, cannot yet happen on them but after long seeking and searching for them; for all their business taken thereabout [they] are fain to put for faults in my writing such things as well considered shall appear their own faults for the finding.

For they find *first* for a great fault, that my writing is over-long, and therefore too tedious to read. For which cause they say they will never once vouchsafe to look thereon.

But then say they further, that such places of them as are looked on by those that are learned and can skill be soon perceived for naught and my reasons of little force. For they boast much that they hear sometime divers parts of my books answered and confuted fully in sundry of some men's sermons though my name be fore-borne, and then they wish me there, they say, for that it would do their hearts good to see my cheeks red for shame.

And over this they find a great fault that I handle Tyndale and Barons, their two new gospellers, with no fairer words nor in no more courteous manner.

And over this I write, they say, in such wise that I show myself suspect in the matter and partial toward the clergy.

And then they say that my works were worthy much more credence if I had written more indifferently and had declared and made open to the people the faults of the clergy.

And in this point they lay for a sample the goodly and godly, mild and gentle fashion used by him, whosoever he was, that now lately wrote the *Book of the Division between the Temporality and the Spirituality*; which charitable, mild, manner they say that if I had used, my works would have been read both of many more and with much better will.

And yet they say besides all this, that I do but pick out pieces at my pleasure, such as I may most easily seem to soil, and leave out what me list and such as would plainly prove the matter against me. And so they say that I use but craft and fraud against Tyndale. For as for Friar Barons, I perceive by sundry ways that the brotherhood speak much less of him,* either for that they find him in their own minds well and fully answered, or else that they take him in respect of Tyndale but for a man of a second sort. And that may, per-adventure, be because he leaveth out somewhat that Tyndale taketh in: that is to wit, the making of mocks and mows[1] against the Mass and the Blessed Sacrament of the Altar.

But, finally, they say further yet, that I have not fulfilled my promise. For I promised, they say, in my preface of my *Confutation*, that I would prove the Church; and that, they say, I have not done.

THE THIRTEENTH CHAPTER

But now good readers, if that it so were, that one found two men standing together and would come step in between them and bear them in hand [as] they were about to fight, and would with that word put the one prettily back with his hand and all to buffet the other about the face, and then go forth and say that he had parted a fray and pacified the parties, some men would say again (as I suppose) that he had as lief his enemy were let alone with him, and thereof abide the adventure, as have such a friend step in between to part them.

Howbeit, if this pacifier of this *Division* will say that this is nothing

---

[1] *mows*, grimaces.

like the present matter because he striketh neither party, but only telleth the one the other's faults, or else (as he will say) telleth them their faults both: if it so happened, good readers, he found a man that were angry with his wife (and happily not all without cause), if this maker of *The Book of Division* would take upon him to go and reconcile them again together and help to make them at one, and therein would use this way, that when he had them both before him and before all their neighbours, too, then saving for some change to make it meet for their persons, else he would begin holily with the same words, in effect, with which he beginneth his indifferent, mild *Book Of Division*.

And for an entry into his matter, first would say thus unto them: 'Who may remember the state that ye stand in without great heaviness and sorrow of heart? For whereas in times passed hath reigned between you charity, meekness, concord, and peace, there reigneth now anger and malice, debate, division and strife; which thing to see so misfortune between any two Christian folk is a thing much to be lamented, and then much more to be lamented when it mishappeth to fall between a man and his wife. And many good neighbours greatly marvel, I wiss, upon what causes this great grudge is grown. And therefore to the entent that ye may remove the causes and amend these matters, and, thereby, then, by the grace of God, agree, I will tell you what I hear men say that the causes be.'

And now after holy prologue made, go forth and tell them that some folk say, the wife hath this evil condition; and some other say that she hath that evil condition; and yet other some say that she hath another evil condition; and so with twenty divers *some says* of other men, say there himself by the poor woman all the mischief that any man could devise to say: and among those, some things, peradventure, true, which yet her husband had never heard of before. And some things false also, whereof because the Pacifier would be put unto no proof, he would not say them as of himself, but bring them forth under the fair figure of *some say*. And when he had all said, then yet at the last, say thus much of himself: 'As for these things here and there, I have heard some other say, whether they say true or no, the charge be theirs for me. But yet, in good faith, good sister, since ye know that the displeasure and grudge that your husband hath to you is grown upon these causes, I marvel much myself that you do use the same conditions still. I wiss till you meek yourself and amend them, this anger of your husband will never be well appeased.'

Lo, with such words he voideth the colour of his fair figure of *some say*, either by forgetfulness or else by the plain figure of folly. For when he saith of himself that she keepeth those evil conditions still and amendeth them not, he showeth that all his *some says* be of

his own saying, though he might happily in some of them hear some
other say so, too, beside.

But then if among all these faults so mildly rehearsed against her
he would, to show somewhat of his indifference, tell her husband
his *pars* verse, too, and say: 'But yet, forsooth, your wife hath not
given you so many causes of displeasure for naught. For I will be
plain with you and indifferent between you both: you have in some
things toward her not dealt very well nor like a good husband yourself. For this I know myself that ye have used to make her too homely¹
with you; and have suffered her to be too much idle; and suffered
her to be much conversant among her gossips; and you have given
her over-gay gear and too much money in her purse. And surely
till you mend all this gear for your part, I cannot much marvel
though she do you displeasure. And sometime evil words between
you causeth debate on both sides. For you call her (as I hear say,
"cursed queen" and "shrew". And *some say* that she behind your
back calleth you "knave" and "cuckold". And, I wiss, such words
were well done to be left on both sides, for surely they do no good.
And therefore if all these words were prohibited on both sides upon
great pains, I think it would do great good in this behalf.'

'Now get you hence, as wise as a calf', would, I ween, the good
wife say to this good ghostly Pacifier. For spake he never so mildly
and would seem never so indifferent, though he looked therewith
right simply and held up also both his hands holily, and would therewith swear to the woman full deeply that his intent were good, and
that he nothing meant but to bring her husband and her at one,
would she, think you, for all that, believe him? I suppose, verily
nay, nor her husband neither, if he were wise, although he saw some
part of his tale true, as none is so foolish to say all false that would
win him credence. But believe the husband as he list, I durst be bold
to swear for the wife that he should never make her such a fool as to
believe that he meant to mend the matter with rehearsing her faults
more than ever her husband had heard of, and some of them false
too, and colour all his tale with his proper invention of *some say*. But
she would for his *some say* shortly say to him: 'I pray you, good man
some say, get you shortly hence. For my husband and I shall agree
much the sooner if no such brother *some say* come within our door.'

Now, of very truth, this Pacifier, as *some say*, goeth yet worse to
work in his *Book of Division* than this *some say* that we put for a
sample between the man and his wife. For he gathered first, all the
causes of displeasures that he can find out or devise, and divers of
them, such as few lay people unlearned, yea, and few of the learned
too, had anything heard of before, as are divers of those which he
gathered out of John Gerson.*

¹ *homely*, remaining at home.

If he say that he meant, as [John] Gerson did, that he maketh mention of them because he would have the clergy mend them, surely whoso for such good will telleth a man his faults useth to tell it him secretly; and so did John Gerson himself when he wrote them in Latin and not in the vulgar tongue.

But this Pacifier, contrariwise, because he would have the lay people, both men and women, look on them, doth translate them into English, whereas John Gerson would not that a man should reproach and rebuke the prelates before the people.

Also this Pacifier aggrieveth (as much as in him lieth) the clergy of England for use of the laws, not made by themselves but by the common laws of all Christendom.

If he will say that he blameth but their abuses thereof, the truth appeareth in some place otherwise in his book. And yet since he proveth that point but by a *some say*, he might with the same figure lay like faults in the temporalty concerning the laws of this realm, and prove it, in likewise, with a great *some say*, too. And therein he showeth himself not indifferent when he bringeth in the one and leaveth the other out. And on the other side, if he bring in the other too, then shall he make two faults for one. For if he handle them as truly as he handleth these, then shall he make two lies for one.

And yet besides all the faults that he bringeth in under *some say* and *they say*, some that himself saith without any *some say* be such as *some say* that he can never prove; and some, they say, be plain and open false.

By all which manner of handling, it appeareth that if the man mean well himself (as by God's grace he doth), then hath some other subtle shrew that is of his counsel deceived him, not only in the misframing of his matter more toward division than unity, but also by causing him to plant in here and there some such word as might make his best friends to fear that he greatly forced not for the furtherance of the Catholic faith.

THE FORTIETH CHAPTER

And, verily albeit, as I said before, I purpose not to meddle with every part of his book that I think were well done for him to amend, yet in his seventh chapter and his eighth, which twain treat all of these matters of heresies, for the great weight of the matter I shall not forbear to show you some difference and diversity between his mind and mine:

Another occasion of the said *Division* hath been by reason of divers suits that have been taken in the spiritual courts of office, that is called in Latin *ex officio*; so that the parties have not known who hath accused them, and thereupon they have sometime been caused to abjure in causes of heresies; sometime to do penance or to pay great sums of money for redeeming thereof, which vexation and charges the parties have thought have come to them by the judges and the officers of the spiritual court, for they have known none other accusers, and that hath caused much people in divers parts of this realm to think great malice and partiality in spiritual judges. And if a man be *ex officio* brought before the ordinary[1] for heresy,* if he be notably suspected of heresy, he must purge himself after the will of the ordinary or be accursed, and, that is, by the law *extra. [extravagantes] de haereticis cap. ad abolendam.* And that is thought by many to be a very hard law, for a man may be suspected and not guilty, and so be driven to a purgation without proof or without offence in him, or be accursed.

I will in this point of conventing *ex officio* no further speak at this time than concerning the crime of heresy. For I am, in good faith, loath to meddle with this book of his at all. For loath am I anything to meddle against any other man's writing that is a Catholic man, saving that it seemeth me, verily, that be this man never so good, yet if his mind were followed in this matter, it would work this realm great harm and no good.

For surely if the conventing of heretics *ex officio* were left and changed into another order by which no man should be called, be he never so sore suspected, nor by never so many men detected but if some man make himself party against him as his accuser, the streets were likely to swarm full of heretics before that *right* few were accused, or, peradventure, any *one* either.

For whatsoever the cause be, it is not unknown, I am sure, that many will give unto a judge secret information of such things as though they be true, yet gladly he will not, or, peradventure, dare not, [let it] be openly known that the matter came out by him. And yet shall he sometime give the name of divers others which, being called by the judge and examined as witnesses against their wills, both know and will also depose the truth and he that first gave information also; and yet will never one of them willingly make himself an open accuser of the party, nor dare, peradventure, for his ears.

And this find we not only in heresy, but in many temporal matters among ourselves where I have had experience many a time and oft, both in the disclosing of felonies and sometime of much other oppression used by some one man or twain in a shire, whereby all their neighbours sore smarted, and yet not one durst openly complain. Howbeit, it cometh in heresies sometimes to much worse point. For I have wist where those that have been in the company at the time, being folk of good substance and such as were taken for

---

[1] *ordinary,* ecclesiastical judge.

worshipful, being called in for witnesses have first made many delays, and, afterward, being examined on their oaths, have sworn that they heard it not or remembered it not and took no heed to the matter at the time; whereas it well appeared by the dispositions of divers others, being with them at the time, that in every man's conscience, they lied. When would these folk become an heretic's accuser, against whom they would rather be forsworn than of the truth to bear witness?

And this thing maketh, that it may be sometime (albeit, very seldom it happeth) that in heresy upon other vehement suspicions without witnesses, a man may be put to his purgation and to penance also if he fail thereof: which thing why so many should now think so hard a law as this Pacifier saith they do, I cannot see; nor those wise men neither that made the law. And yet were they many wise men, and not only as wise but, peradventure, many more also in number than those that this Pacifier calleth 'many' now, that, as he saith, find now the fault. For though it be alleged in the *extravagant. de haereticis cap. ad abolendam*, yet was that law made in a general council.

And, verily, methinketh that he which cannot be proved guilty in heresy, and yet useth such manner of ways that all his honest neighbors ween he were one and therefore dare not swear that in their conscience they think him any other, is well worthy, methinketh, to do some penance for that manner of behaviour whereby he giveth all other folk occasion to take him for so naughty.

And by the common law of this realm, many times upon suspicion, the judges award a writ to inquire of what fame and behaviour the man is in his country, and himself lieth sometime still in prison till the return; and if he be returned good, that is to wit, if he be in a manner purged, then is he delivered, and yet he payeth his fees ere he go. And if he be returned naught, then use the judges to bind him for his good abearing and sometimes sureties with him, too, such as their discretion will allow.

And then to lie still till he find them, is sometimes as much penance to the one as the spiritual judge enjoineth to the other. For the one cometh to the bar as openly as the other to the consistory, and sometime his fetters weigh a good piece of a faggot, besides that they lie longer on the one man's legs than the faggot on the other's shoulder. And yet is there no remedy but both these must be done, both in the one court and in the other, or else instead of one harm (which to him that deserveth it not happeth seldom, and as seldom I am sure in heresy as in theft, and much more seldom, too), ye shall have ten times more harm happen daily to folk as innocent as they, and of *innocentes* many made *nocentes* to the destruction of themselves and others, too, both in goods, body, and soul.

And because this Pacifier taketh it for so sore a thing in the spiritual law, that a man shall be called *ex officio* for heresy, where he shall not know his accuser, if we should change the spiritual law for that cause, then had we need to change the temporal too in some such points; as change it when ye will, and ye shall change it into the worse, for aught that I can see, but if it be better to have more thieves than fewer.

For now if a man be indicted at a session, and none evidence given openly at the bar (as many be and many may well be, for the indicters may have evidence given them apart or have heard of the matter ere they came there, and of whom be they not bounden to tell, but be rather bound to keep it close, for they be sworn to keep the king's counsel and their own), shall then the party that is indicted be put unto no business about his acquittal? And who shall tell him there the names of his accusers to entitle him to his writ of conspiracy? This Pacifier will, peradventure, say that the same twelve men that are his indicters are his accusers, and therefore he may know them. But what helpeth that his undeserved vexation if he were faultless? For amends, the law giveth him none against any of them, nor it were not well done he should, but may when he is after by other twelve acquitted, go get him home and be merry that he hath had so fair a day, as a man getteth him to the fire and shaketh his hat after a shower of rain.

And now as it often happeth that a man cometh into a shower by his own oversight, though sometime of chance and of adventure, so surely though sometime it happeth that a man be accused or indicted of malice or of some likelihood which happed him of chance and not his fault therein, yet happeth it in comparison very seldom, but that the party by some demeanour of himself giveth occasion that folk have him so suspected.

Now if this Pacifier say that yet here is, at the leastwise, in a temporal judge an open cause appearing, whereupon men may see that the judge calleth him not but upon a matter brought unto him, whereas the spiritual judge may call a man upon his own pleasure if he bear the party displeasure, this is very well said as for the temporal judge. But what saith he now for the temporal twelve men? For, ye wot well, they may do the same if they were so disposed, and then had I as lief the judge might do it as they. For, in good faith, I never saw the day yet but that I durst as well trust the truth of one judge as of two juries. But the judges be so wise men that for the avoiding of obloquy, they will not be put in the trust.

And I dare say the ordinaries be not so foolish neither, but that they would as fain avoid it, too, if they might, saving that very necessity lest all should fall to naught, compelleth them to take this way which necessity sometime causeth, also, both the temporal judges and the king's council to put some folk to business or dishonesty sometimes without either jury or bringing of the accuser to the proof of the matter in the parties' presence.

For if the judge know by sure information that some one man is of such evil demeanour among his neighbours that they may not bear it, and yet that the man is besides so violent and so jeopardous that none of them dare to be a knowen to speak of it, will there no judges upon many secret complaints made unto them, without making the party privy who told him the tale, bind that busy, troublous man to good abearing? I suppose, yes: and have seen it so too: and wrong would it be sometime with good, poor, peaceable folk in the country but if it were so done among. And myself, when I was Chancellor,* upon such secret information have put some out of commission and office of justice of the peace, which else for much money I would not have done; and yet if I were in the one room still and they in the other again but if they be mended (whereof I neither then saw nor yet hear any likelihood), I would put them out again and never tell them who told me the tales that made me so to do.

But yet will, peradventure, this Pacifier say that sometime in some very special case he could be content that the spiritual judge should upon his discretion call one for suspicion of heresy *ex officio*, but he would not have men commonly called but either by accusation or presentment in their senes[1] or indictments at the common law. I had as lief for anything that I see, that this Pacifier should say thus: By this way that they be called, I would not have them called: but I would have them called after such an order as they might be sure that then should they never be called.

For as for accuse folk openly for heresy, every man hath experience enough that ye shall seldom find any man that will but if the judge should set an officer of the court thereto without any peril of expense, and then were this-way-and-that-way all of one effect. And as for presentments and indictments, what effect would come of them concerning heresy, ye see the proof, I trow, meetly well already.

For this is a thing well known unto every man, that in every sene, every session of peace, every session of gaol delivery, every let through the realm, the first thing that the jury have given them in charge is heresy. And for all this through the whole realm, how many presentments be there made in the whole year? I ween in some seven years, not one. And, I suppose, no man doubteth but that in the meantime some there be.

I will not be curious about the searching out of the cause, why it is either never or so very seldom presented—not five in fifteen years. But this I say, that since some will not, some cannot, and none doth,

---

[1] *senes*, sessions.

if he should put away the process *ex officio*, the thing should be left undone: and then should soon after with heretics increased and multiplied, the faith be undone: and after that through the stroke of God, revenging their malice and our negligence, should by sedition and trouble and dearth and death in this realm, many men, both good and bad, be undone. And, therefore, for conclusion of this piece, my poor advice and counsel shall be that for heresy, and specially now [at] this time, men shall suffer the processes *ex officio* stand, and for as many other sins, also, as are only reformable by the spiritual law, except there be any such sins of them as ye think were good to grow.

COLOPHON: Printed by W. Rastell in Fleet Street in Saint Bride's Churchyard. 1533.

CHRISTOPHER SAINT-GERMAN
1460–1540

Christopher Saint-German, prominent lawyer and controversialist, was born at Shilton in 1460. He was the son of Sir Henry and Lady Anne Saint-German, who belonged to a wealthy Warwickshire family. Early records show that Saint-German probably attended Exeter College, Oxford, but there is no record that he took a degree. In 1484 he entered the Inner Temple to study law. Though it has been proved by letters and records that Saint-German was a successful lawyer in London and that his services were sought at various times by Henry VIII and Cromwell, his desire for anonymity has blotted out much of his public career. Nothing is known of his private life. He inferred in a letter to Cromwell that he married twice. He died in London in 1540, leaving one of the finest private libraries of the time.

John Bale was the first to identify Saint-German's works, including in the list those works now generally attributed to him. Among these are: A dyaloge in Englysshe betwyxt a doctoure of dyuynyte and a student in the lawes of Englande (c. 1530) and Salem and Bizance (1533). It seems likely that he is also the author of The addicions of Salem and Bizance (c. 1534); A treatise concernynge the diuision betwene the spiritualtie and temporaltie (c. 1532); and A treatyse concerninge the power of the clergye, and the lawes of the realme (c. 1535?).

The Dyaloge in Englysshe, or the Doctor and student, as it is best known, is a translation, probably by Saint-German, of his Dialogus de fundamentis legum Anglie et de conscientia (1528), printed by John

Rastell, as was a second part, titled The secunde dyaloge (1530). Both were immediately popular as handbooks for law students and continued to be reprinted separately and also in one volume until 1638.

In presenting his arguments in the Doctor and student, Saint-German employed the methods used in the Inns of Court, those schools 'uncharted, unprivileged, unendowed, without remembered founders', as F. W. Maitland describes them, where 'in the course of time evolved a scheme of legal education; an academic scheme of the medieval sort, oral and disputatious'. Trained in one of these schools, strongholds of common law, Saint-German declares that common law as a system is consistent and reasonable; what seems to be contradictory to the rule of conscience to the canonist can be explained when presented in the proper way. In the Dyaloge, the Doctor is the canonist and the student the common lawyer.

Saint-German's study of comparative law follows the pattern of Littleton and Fortescue, whose works he used, and according to H. D. Hazeltine, his 'exposition of the canonists' theory of conscience became the foundation of the English system of equity'. In following the paths of his famed predecessors, Saint-German at the beginning of his career accepted the teachings of St Thomas Aquinas, as is shown in his fourfold division of law. For a definition of eternal law or jus divinum, Saint-German turned to St Augustine's De Libero Arbitrio and the Bible.

Though there is no anti-papal bias in the Doctor and Student, it is plain in the rest of the works attributed to Saint-German. Moreover, he is believed to have played a definite part in the production of anti-papal tracts which began to come from the press of the king's printer Thomas Berthelet in 1531. Ten years earlier Berthelet had printed the fourteenth-century treatise Defensor Pacis, by Marsilius of Padua, urging that 'religion should be wholly dependent on the state; that in the Church the prince should be supreme'. When Henry VIII determined to suppress the clergy regardless of the papal bull, Supernae dispositionis arbitrio, which declared that the laymen had no jurisdiction over the clergy by divine or human law, he moved to put the Marsiglian doctrine into practice, and five anonymous tracts, Saint-German's among them, came from Berthelet's press to aid the royal cause.

The first of these tracts was the medieval dialogue, variously attributed to William of Ockham and Pierre de Blois, Disputatio inter clericum et militem. It reported the bitter struggle over ecclesiastical power between Pope Boniface VIII and King Philip the Fair of France. Berthelet printed a Latin edition about 1530 and an English translation of the Disputatio, made in the fourteenth century by Trevisa. He titled it A dialogue betwene a knight and a clerk concernynge the power spiritual a. temporall (1531?). Within a short time, Redman printed an anonymous treatise, attributed to Saint-German, A treatise concernynge the diuision betwene the spiritualtie and temporaltie (c. 1532). It repeats the arguments of the knight and clerk, though claiming 'to pacify' each side. When

Sir Thomas More refuted the Pacifier's arguments in his Apologye, *it wa. Berthelet, the king's printer, who issued the rebuttal,* Salem and Bizance (1533), *also attributed to Saint-German. The latter work is a point-by-point reply to More's attack on the Pacifier's constant use of hearsay evidence and the former Chancellor's denial that the Church was to blame for the cruel treatment of heretics.*

With the printing of More's Debellacyon *of Salem and Bizance (1533) the pamphlet war continued. And in 1534, while Berthelet was printing Saint-German's* Addicions *of Salem and Bizance, the king's cause against 'the spirituality' was to be further strengthened by William Marshall's English version of Marsilius's* Defensor pacis *(1535).*

The simple and unembellished style of the Saint-German treatises i. characteristic of the propaganda literature that issued from the printing presses during the next two decades.

Doctor and Student

Hereafter followeth a dialogue in English betwixt a Doctor of Divinity and a student in the laws of England: of the grounds of the said laws and of conscience.

THE INTRODUCTION

A Doctor of Divinity that was of great acquaintance and familiarity with a student in the Laws of England said thus unto him: I have had great desire of long time to know whereupon the *Law of England* is grounded, but because much part of the *Law of England* is written in the French tongue, therefore I cannot through mine own study attain to the knowledge thereof, for in that tongue I am nothing expert. And because I have always found thee a faithful friend to me in all my business, therefore I am bold to come to thee before any other to know thy mind: what be the very grounds of the *Law of England*, as thou thinkest?

Student. That would ask a great leisure; and it is also above my cunning to do it. Nevertheless, that thou shalt not think that I would wilfully refuse to fulfill thy desire, I shall, with good will, do that in me to satisfy thy mind. But I pray thee that thou wilt first show me somewhat of other laws that pertain most to this matter and, that doctors treat of, how laws have begun. And then I will gladly show thee, as methinkest, what be the grounds of the *Law of England.*

Doctor. I will, with good will, do as thou sayst. Wherefore thou shalt understand that doctors treat of four laws, the which, as meseemeth, pertain most to this matter: The first is the *Law Eternal*;

the second is the *Law of Nature* of reasonable creature, the which, as I have heard say, is called by them that be learned in the *Law of England*, the *Law of Reason*; the third is the *Law of God*; the fourth is the *Law of Man*. And, therefore, I will first treat of the *Law Eternal*.

OF THE LAW ETERNAL[1]

Doctor. Like as there is in every artificer a reason of such things as are to be made by his craft, so likewise it behoveth that in every governor there be a reason and a foresight in the governor of such things as shall be ordered and done by him to them that he hath the governance of. And forasmuch as Almighty God is the Creator and Maker of all creatures, to the which He is compared as a Workman to His work, and is also the Governor of all deeds and movings that be found in any creature. Therefore as the reason of the wisdom of God in that creature created by Him hath the reason of all crafts and works that have been or shall be made, so the reason of the wisdom of God, moving all things, by Him made, to a due end, obtaineth the name and the reason of a law. And that is called the *Law Eternal*.

And this *Law Eternal* is called the first law: and it is well called the first, for it was before all other laws. And all other laws be derived of it. Whereupon Saint Augustine saith in his first book *Of arbitrament* [*De libero arbitrio*] that in temporal laws nothing is rightwise nor lawful but that the people have derived to them out of the *Law Eternal*. Wherefore every man hath the right and title to have that he hath rightwisely of the rightwise judgment of the first reason, which is the *Law Eternal*.

Student. But how may this *Law Eternal* be known, for as the Apostle writeth in the second chapter of his first epistle to the Corinthians: *Quae sunt Dei nemo scit nisi Spiritus Dei*:[2] That is to say: No man knoweth what is in God but the Spirit of God. Wherefore it seemeth that he looketh too high that attempteth to know it.

Doctor. This *Law Eternal* no man may know as it is in itself, but only blessed souls that see God face to face. But Almighty God of His goodness showeth of it as much to His creatures as is necessary for them. For else God should bind His creatures to a thing impossible, which may in no wise be thought in Him. Therefore it is to understand that [in] three manner of ways Almighty God maketh this *Law Eternal* known to His creatures reasonable: first, by the light of natural reason: second, by heavenly revelation; thirdly, by the order of a prince, or of any other secondary governor, that hath the power to bind his subjects to a law. And when the *Law Eternal* or the will of God, is known to His creatures reasonable by the light of natural

---

[1] Chapter I.　　　　[2] I Cor. ii. 11.

understanding or by the light of natural reason, then it is called the *Law of Reason*. And when it is showed by heavenly revelation, in such manner as hereafter shall appear, then it is called the *Law of God*.

And when it is showed unto him by the order of a prince, or of any other secondary governor, that hath power to set a law upon his subjects, then it is called the *Law of Man*, though originally it be made of God. For laws made by man that hath received thereto power of God, be made by God. Therefore the said three laws, that is to say, the *Law of Reason*, the *Law of God*, and the *Law of Man* (the which have several names after the manner as they be showed to man), be called in God, one *Law Eternal*. And this is the law of whom it is written [in the] *Proverbiorum octavo* where it is said; *Per me reges regnant et legum conditores iusta discernunt:*[1] [By Me, kings reign and lawgivers decree just things]. And this sufficeth for this time of the *Law Eternal*.

COLOPHON: Imprinted by me Robert Wyer, dwelling in Saint Martin's parish in the field beside Charing Cross in the Bishop of Norwich rents. [1530.]

Salem and Bizance

A Dialogue betwixt two Englishmen: whereof one was called Salem and the other Bizance.

THE INTRODUCTION

Sal. There is a book lately made by Sir Thomas More which he calleth *The Apology of Sir Thomas More, knight*, wherein among divers other things he layeth many objections against a book that he called *The book of division betwixt the spirituality and the temporality*. Hast thou, my friend Bizance, seen that *Book of division*?

Biz. I have seen a little book that in the beginning of the book hath this name set upon it, *A treatise concerning the division betwixt the spirituality and temporality*, and I suppose that it is the same book that thou meanest of. For, indeed, Sir Thomas More maketh many objections in the said *Apology* against the said *Treatise*, and reciteth in many places the very words of some part of the chapters of the said *Treatise*. Howbeit in some places he misrehearseth it; and in some places he turneth the sentence thereof

[1] Prov. viii. 15.

to another effect than can be reasonably taken to follow of it, as meseemeth.

Sal. Then I see well, it is the same book that I mean of. Howbeit, I perceive by thy words that Sir Thomas More somewhat varieth from the very true name of it. And, verily, if I were acquainted with the maker of the said *Treatise*, I would move him to make an answer to the said objections. For methinketh that in many places Sir Thomas More, as thou saith, doth mistake his sayings. And therefore, I pray thee, if thou canst, make me acquainted with him. For if he will not answer to it himself, I trow, I know a friend of mine that will.

Biz. To that purpose that thou speakest of, it shall not need that you be acquainted, for he hath made an answer to it himself already, although he hath not as yet set the name upon it. And I know his mind so well that I am sure he will be contented that I shall show it to whomsoever I will.

Sal. Then, I pray thee heartily, let me see it.

Biz. I shall cause it to be written hereafter in this *Dialogue* word for word as it is come to my hands, and then thou shalt with good will have it. And, I pray thee, let me then know thy further mind, what thou thinkest in it. And thou shalt understand that his answer beginneth at the beginning of this next chapter hereafter ensuing, and continueth unto the place where I shall show thee that it endeth. And he hath neither made as yet prologue, preface, nor introduction, but beginneth in this manner as followeth.

OF THE ANSWER TO THE 'APOLOGY' OF SIR THOMAS MORE, KNIGHT[1]

When I heard first that Sir Thomas More had made a book touching a little treatise that I had lately made *Concerning a division that is betwixt the spirituality and temporality*, I was right glad. For I thought verily that he had devised some more convenient way for a good reformation in that behalf than I had done or could do. For I knew right well that he could have done it if he would, and could yet do it if he list. But when his book came to my hands, I perceived well that he had not done so; but that rather to the contrary he had taken many exceptions and made many objections against it, whereof I marvelled greatly. And when I saw that he had named his book an *Apology*, then I marvelled more than I did before. For *apologia* in the Greek tongue is as much to say in Latin, *responsio* or *defensio*: that is to say, an 'answer' or 'defence'. Whereby it seemeth that he should mean that I had written something against his works or

---

[1] Chapter 1.

mistaken some of his works, that he had made in time past, which he therefore purposed to maintain and defend.

And, verily, I never wrote nor spake anything against him. For I never read his *Dialogue* [*Concerning Tyndale* (1528)]; his *Confutation* [*Of Tyndale's Answer* (1532–3)]; nor yet none other of his works. Howbeit that was not because I would not read his works, but because I have been let by other occasion, and could not. And so I cannot answer to his *Apology* as an apology against me that nothing have done against him.

But, nevertheless, that my silence should not make some other haply to think that such objections as he hath made in his said *Apology* against the said *Treatise* were good and reasonable, and also that he should not make the said *Treatise* appear to be made to another intent than it was made for indeed, I have made answer to some of his objections, whereby (as I suppose) it shall appear evidently that his objections proceeded of little charity; and that the said *Treatise* is good and reasonable; and that it was also made to a good intent, that is to say, to increase peace and quietness through all the realm.

Howbeit for the avoiding of tediousness to the readers, I intend not to make answer to all his objections, but to some of them. And though I do not make answer particularly to all, yet I suppose it shall appear by the answers and by certain considerations and some declarations that I shall make concerning the same that his objections are little to be pondered if the readers will diligently and advisedly search the grounds and circumstances of the said objections and of the said *Treatise* together. And I will not make answer to his *Apology* after the order of his chapters, but as I shall think shall serve best for opening of the truth of the matter as nigh as I can.

OF THIS TERM 'SOME SAY' AND OF THEM THAT BE JUDGES IN HERESY[1]

Master More in his *Apology* speaketh many times against a certain manner of speaking that I used in divers places of the said *Treatise* which is this: when I recited what opinions I have heard say there were among the people, I said that *some say* or *they say* this or that, or that many say so, and such other like sayings, without affirming that I knew it of mine own knowledge that it was so; for in some things I did not, indeed.

At this manner of speaking, Master More findeth a default in such a strange jesting manner that I marvel greatly at it. And I marvel the more because he useth the same terms himself in divers places of his *Apology*, as appeareth [on] folio 77 and folio 100. And I am well assured that in his jesting, he speaketh of the said terms of *some say*

[1] Chapter XVII.

and *they say*, or such other, many times more than I do in all the said *Treatise*. And surely, as he knoweth right well himself, a man may sometime say that some man say this or that, and say truly: where if he would say that he knew it himself, or that all men said so, he should say untruly. And then if the truth be so that some said, 'thus it is' in this matter or in that, and yet all men said not so, or if the truth were so, yet I knew it not. I wot not under what manner Master More would have had me speak of the matter but only under this manner as I have done, that *some say* so.

And then that he findeth a default at that manner of speaking where I could none otherwise have done it, is a marvel to many persons. And I have in divers places of the said *Treatise* said that *some say* this or that, where if I had said that a great part of all the lay people had said so, I had said but truly. And one of the *some says* that he findeth default at is this: I say in the eighth chapter of the said *Treatise* thus:

And here *some say* that because there is so great a desire in spiritual men to have men abjured or to be noted with heresy, and that some, as it were, of a policy do noise it that the realm is full of heretics more than it is; indeed, that it is very perilous that spiritual men should have authority to arrest a man for every light suspicion or complaint of heresy till that desire of punishment in spiritual men be ceased and gone: but that they should make process against them to bring them in upon pain of cursing; and then if they tarry forty days, the king's laws to bring them in by a writ of *excommunicato capiendo*,* and so to be brought forth out of the king's gaol to answer.

And it followeth in the said eighth chapter thus, but surely as it is somewhat touched before in the seventh chapter:

It seemeth that the [rulers of the] Church in time past have done what they could to bring about that they might punish heresy of themselves without calling for any help therein of the secular power. And therefore they have made laws that heretics might be arrested and put in prison and stocks, if need were, as appeareth in *clementinis* de haereticis cap. multorum quaerela*. And after, at the special calling on the spirituality, it was enacted by parliament that ordinaries might arrest men that preach, hold, teach, or inform others in heresy there prohibit, or that thereof hold any conventicles or schools. For some men think that the said *clementine* was not of effect in the king's laws to arrest any man for heresy. But if a man were openly and notably suspected of heresy, and there were sufficient record and witness against him, and there were also a doubt that he would flee and not appear whereby he might infect others, it seemeth convenient that he be arrested by the body, but not upon every light complaint that full lightly may be untrue. And that it will be right expedient that the King's Highness and his council look specially upon this matter, and not to cease till it be brought to more quietness than it is yet: and to see with great diligence that pride, covetousness, nor worldly love be not judges, nor innocents be punished, nor yet that wilful offenders go not without due correction.

And when Master More in his *Apology* hath recited the said words of the said *Treatise*, then he endeavoureth himself very much to make it appear that the motions that be made in the said *Treatise*, in the place before rehearsed, be unreasonable and cannot be brought about; or else that if they were brought about, they should do hurt and no good.

And to make his sayings the more acceptable, he layeth sometime default in my sayings, and saith that I thereby defame the judges spiritual where I defame them not, but say only that it is expedient that the King's Highness and his council see that pride, covetousness, nor worldly love be no judges. And whether those words amount to that effect that Master More saith they do, that is to say, that I defame all spiritual judges, it appeareth evidently they do not: nor yet they prove not that I would have all spiritual judges changed. For the spiritual judges that be now, may be judges still, and have all the properties before rehearsed as well as other, for anything that I have said.

And yet Master More taketh it otherwise, and saith I would have such judges as have no spice of any of the said points. And he sayth 'that till such judges may be found, heretics may make merry for a little season while men walk about and search for such judges': which he weeneth 'will not be done in a week's work'. And he saith that it will be the more hard to find such judges. For he saith that I have put that matter out of doubt, that whereas men would have wende[1] soonest to have found them, that there, I say, it will be marvellous hard to find any one of them, either prelates, secular priests, or religious persons. For he saith that I say plainly that have they never so many virtues besides, that yet I say, it will be hard to find any one spiritual man but that he is so infected with desire and affection to have the worldly honour of priests exalted that he is through such pride far from such indifference and equity as ought and must be in such judges, which, as he saith, I assign to be such that they must have no spice of pride, covetousness, nor love toward the world.

As to this last rehearsed sentence of Master More, this is the truth therein, I say in another place of the said *Treatise*, other than that that

---

[1] *wende*, thought.

Master More hath rehearsed here, that is to say, in the seventh chapter of the said *Treatise*, that 'though many spiritual men may be found that have many great virtues and great gifts of God, as chastity, liberality, patience, soberness, temperance, cunning, and such other, yet it will be hard to find any one spiritual man that is not infected with the said desire and affection to have the worldly honour of priests exalted'. And there my sentence endeth as to this purpose.

But then, as it appeareth before, Master More in his said *Apology* addeth immediately to those words of mine, words of his own putting in which be these: 'That he is through such pride far from such indifference and equity as ought and must be in those judges', which he saith, I assign....

Then saith Master More farther, that 'if *some say* be no sufficient proof, then is my tale all lost'. And to these words I will answer thus: I will agree that my saying that *some say* this or this, is no proof —neither to prove that *some say* so nor yet to prove that it *is* so. For in every proof must be two witnesses at least: but if two will say it is so, then is it a proof.

And surely if Master More will inquire for the truth in this matter, he shall find that there be many more than two that say so. And, verily, if many men say so, though the truth be not so, yet the tale is not all lost to say that some men say so. For then it shall put the bishops and rulers spiritual in mind that they are bound in conscience to help them that say so, all that they can from the danger that they run in by that saying. And if it be true, then may the spiritual rulers order the matter as they shall see cause, and reform it in such charitable manner that none shall say so hereafter but they will of malice do it and run into the slander of the Pharisees: and that would charitably be examined whether it be so or not.

Then saith Master More yet further: 'That which is a light suspicion and which is heavy, and which witness be sufficient and which not, must be weighed by the spiritual judges, and upon their weighing of the matter, for the light or heavy, to follow the arrest of the party or the leaving of the arrest.' Now, verily, in this point, methinketh that Master More maketh a right good motion; that is to say, that the matter should be examined before the arrest. For it hath been said in times past, that in such case the arrest hath many times gone before the examination....

And then Master More concludeth thus:

I little doubt (saith he), but that if the King's Highness do, as I doubt not but his Highness will do, maintain and assist the spirituality in executing the laws, even those that are already made against heresies, and command every temporal officer under him to do the same for his part, though there were never no new law made therefore, yet shall both innocents be saved harmless wel enough and offenders punished too.

Now, verily, to these words of Master More, I dare say thus: tha Master More or he had spoken those words had occasion by reason able conjecture to have doubted more at the matter than he hatl done: and to have thought it very like, that if the same laws shoulc stand as do now in every point concerning heresy, that many inno cents that be not guilty might upon suspicion of heresy be driver to purge themselves after the will of the ordinary, and yet be no guilty.

Yea, and over that, Master More might have reasonably doubted and, as I suppose, in conscience he ought to have doubted more tha he hath done, that sometimes innocents might happen upon the sui *ex officio* or upon light complaints by favour of officers or upon malicc or displeasure be arrested before examination: and yet Master Morc himself assenteth that the examination should be before the arrest And he might have doubted also that some innocents might by sucl perjured persons, as be above rehearsed in this chapter, be sometime condemned. And therefore the said words of Master More whereby he taketh upon him to say, as it were, in his own authority to per form it, that 'innocents' by the same laws as be already made fo heresy shall 'be saved harmless well enough' might happen to be o small effect to help an innocent man or woman that should happer to be wrongfully troubled in time to come against his words befor rehearsed.

COLOPHON: *Londini in aedibus Thomae Bertheleti.* 1533.

REGINALD POLE
1500–1558

The career of Reginald Pole, Cardinal and scholar, spanned the reigns o Henry VIII and Mary I. He was born in 1500 in Stanton Castle Staffordshire, the youngest son of Sir Richard and Lady Margaret Pole close relatives of Henry VII. After receiving his early education at th Charterhouse School at Sheen, Pole entered Magdalen College, Oxford and took a Bachelor of Arts degree in 1515. At the suggestion of Thoma Linacre and William Latimer, both of whom had directed his studies a Oxford, he went to Italy in 1519 to study under Nicola Leonicus at th University of Padua. His expenses while there were paid by his cousir Henry VIII, who 'loved him dearly'.

During Pole's several sojourns in Italy between 1519 and 1523, his house became the meeting-place for visiting English scholars and statesmen. Prominent among them were Thomas Lupset, Thomas Starkey, Richard Pace, ambassador to the Doge in Venice, Sir Richard Morison, John Clement, and Pole's protégés, George Lily, son of the grammarian, and William Shelley. Through Leonicus, Pole met many of the humanists of the Continent, particularly Erasmus, whom he admired.

In 1527 Pole returned to England, seeking seclusion in the Charterhouse at Sheen. At the insistence of Henry VIII he joined the small group that went to the University of Paris to seek the faculty's aid in the king's divorce proceedings against Katherine of Aragon. Though a favourable decision was given by the university, and Pole's letters indicate his interest in it, on his return from France he refused to support the divorce. After several stormy sessions with the king, who offered to recommend him for the bishopric either of York or Winchester if he would change his mind, Pole refused, insisting that he had not fully determined to enter the priesthood. Finally, with the king's consent, he left for Italy in 1532.

The following year, when Henry VIII became head of the English Church, he was eager to have Pole affirm the decision, believing that his scholarship and personal integrity would be valuable in swaying public opinion. When he refused to acknowledge the king's right to renounce Papal Supremacy in the name of the nation, Henry VIII wrote threatening letters and demanded his immediate return to England. Pole determined to remain in Italy but promised to send an opinion on the divorce and Royal Supremacy.

In the spring of 1536 he finished his letter to the king, Pro ecclesiasticae unitatis defensione, in which he denied the latter's authority to divorce Katherine of Aragon and to reject the Pope as head of the Church. Angered at Pole's presumption and the vigorous tone of the Pro ecclesiasticae, which had been sent to England by special courier, Henry VIII, abetted by Cromwell, who disliked the king's cousin intensely, beheaded Pole's widowed mother, who had been created Countess of Salisbury in 1513, and his brother Henry Pole, Lord Montague. As R. B. Merriman has said, 'The story of Pole's life between 1535 and 1540 is the thread which binds together the foreign, domestic, secular, and religious history of Cromwell's administration.'

Though not yet ordained to the priesthood, Pole was made a cardinal by Pope Paul III in 1536. The latter commissioned him, with two other cardinals, to open the Council of Trent. During its first session in 1545, Pole read a treatise on justification, refuting the Lutheran doctrine of justification by faith without good works. Owing to his sanctity and learning, he was very nearly elected pope in succession to Paul III.

Pole remained in Italy until 1554, a year after the death of Edward VI, when he was appointed Papal Legate to England. On his arrival there was given a public welcome by Mary I and her court. He at once assumed the role of counsellor to the queen, whom he had known since childhood, and he played an important part in her vain efforts to restore the nation to the Papal See. On 30 November 1554, in the presence of Mary and her husband, Philip II of Spain, Pole stood in Parliament and absolved the nation from schism. Since absolution from censures is a matter of jurisdiction only and does not require holy orders, the Pope could delegate Pole, a layman, to accept the submission of the English people to the Papal See, and absolve the censure imposed upon them by Pope Clement VII.

Of a deeply religious nature and, as mentioned by his secretary Ludovico Beccatelli, 'noted for the chastity of his life and conversation', Pole had for some reason deferred taking holy orders. In 1556 he was ordained to the priesthood and the same year consecrated Archbishop of Canterbury.

In the last year of his life, he was unfortunately drawn into a quarrel between Pope Paul IV and Philip II of Spain, over the Spanish occupation of Naples. Pole died on 17 November 1558 at Lambeth Palace, and was buried in Canterbury Cathedral near the tomb of Thomas à Becket.

Pole's principal works were written in Latin: Pro ecclesiasticae unitatis defensione (1551); Apologia (1554); and A Treatise on Justification, translated into English and printed in 1569. Most of his letters are in Latin, though a few are in English and Italian.

The Pro ecclesiasticae was edited by Pole and printed with an introductory epistle to Edward VI. It is perhaps the most learned sixteenth-century refutation of the newly revived political theory of the medieval Paduan Marsilius, whose treatise, Defensor pacis, maintains that the king or ruler of a nation must exercise supreme rule over his subjects in matters of religion as well as of state. Pole received a copy of the first English translation from Starkey in 1535. The Apologia, a letter to the Emperor Charles V, is an indirect attack on the Machiavellian theory of statecraft in Il Principe which Pole believed 'would poison all Christendom'.

The English letters of Pole show traces of his Latin style which at times robs them of a certain smoothness and facility of expression. But, considered apart from their literary worth, they provide critical evidence that is necessary in evaluating Pole as an apologist, Christian humanist, and statesman.

Letter to Henry VIII

[Pole's letter to Henry VIII concerning the former's book, Pro ecclesiasticae unitatis defensione.]

And now as touching the cause why your grace doth call me, which is for better information and understanding of those things written in my book, I cannot tell how much your grace hath read therein; but this I will say, which I think your grace's reading of the same shall find true, that for understanding of things written there, I have handled them with such plainness, clearness, and copiousness, that there needeth very small comment thereof, either of me, the author, or of any other, for the clear understanding—this being my chief purpose to make all things clear.

And so I doubt not but I have performed in such manner [that] whosoever understands anything therein [and] that hath the least practice of such matters, he shall understand the whole....My whole desire is, was, and ever shall be that your grace might reign long in honour, in wealth, in surety, in love and estimation of all men.

And this I do say again, remaining[1] those innovations your grace made of late in the Church, that the desire that I have—and all that love you—was, nor is, not a thing possible to take effect, but rather to be contrary [to that] that I desire, [since] with great loss of honour you stand in great peril divers ways, not only afore God, but in the face of the world, beginning here that same [dishonour] which hereafter should be more terrible. This any one of any small prudence might judge.

And this was in the mouth and judgment of all men that ever I could speak withal in such matters, [and] that were at any liberty to speak where they might show their mind. But these men did not only judge as of a thing to come, but of that they might see daily how your honour and estimation decreased in every man's opinion. Therewith your peril must needs increase. This I testify before God: I have not read [of] a prince spoken of universally with more dishonour, when your acts came abroad to be known, than I have heard with my ears in divers places and generally wheresoever I have come to....

Written in Venice, 15 July 1536.

[signed] RAYNOLD POLE

B.M. MS. Cotton, Cleopatra, E. vi, f. 328.

Letter to Cuthbert Tunstall

[Pole's letter to Bishop Cuthbert Tunstall in answer to the criticism of the *Pro ecclesiasticae unitatis* in England.]

...After this you come in more to the particularities of my book [*Pro ecclesiasticae unitatis*] to show how my whole book, as you write, runneth wide from the truth, the which you begin in this manner because you say, I presuppose this ground—the King to be

---

[1] *remaining,* regarding.

swarved from the unity of the Church. Now you say [the] very truth: I take that in my book for a ground; and that is the cause, as I wrote above, that I put no proof thereof as you rehearse I did.

But now, my lord, that this ground is not true, can you prove? I would you could, or that we both could, or that we prove the same. There was never a thing, I will put my hand unto gladlier. But I promise you, considering the King's innovation in the Church —taking upon him the name and office of him in his realm, the which in the whole Church doth keep as Head for the unity of the same—I am ashamed to say, he doth now separate himself from the unity of the Church.

And now what proof bring you this: how say first, that albeit 'the King be Supreme Head in the Church, yet he doth not take upon him the office of a priest, as to minister the sacraments and to preach and teach'. What proof this is to show that he doth not separate himself from the unity of the Church, I cannot tell, because he doth not utterly break all the whole order of the Church. Do you mean thereby he breaketh not the unity? You seem to call unity to agree in rites which, indeed, helpeth to unity, meaning by unity, concord and peace.

But this unity helpeth not except he agree in the Head of the Church that the rest of the Church doth follow, whereby *Ecclesia* is *una* [*the Church is one*]: and this, you granting, the King does not admit, how can you defend that he is not divided from the unity because you *write*, 'the King doth not take upon him to minister the sacraments nor to preach' which be the offices of priests, though he be *Supremum Caput Ecclesiae in Anglia* [Supreme Head of the Church in England]. How this agreeth together, I cannot see but after such manner as all those that be founded on a false ground, which neither agreeth with other truth nor yet with itself.

Good my lord, how is this possible that this name, Supreme Head of the Church in England, hath not annexed unto the same the Supreme office that is exercised in the same Church? How is it that an inferior member shall exercise a higher act in the Church than is granted to the highest? Is there any higher act in the Church than the administration of the sacraments? And this, you will the priests of whom you make the King Head, to exercise; and the Head himself, you will not to meddle with the same.

After this you go about to prove the King hath not separated himself from the Church because the purpose his grace hath[, is] 'to reduce his Church of England to the primitive estate'. As touching his grace's mind, it is not my part to judge but the best, nor otherwise I will not, but this I will pray, that God send him light of the truth and strength of mind withal to execute the same: which, in great part, the acts that be done in the realm, that be so strange that no realm in Christendom neither approveth nor followeth, the same giveth many men cause to think otherwise.

But I marvel much how you can deny [that] the King separateth himself from the unity of the Church, inasmuch as you cannot name him, as you would have him named, the Supreme Head of his Church in England; but withal you show that in taking the same upon him that the unity *is* broken. And where is this ever found in the primitive Church that kings were head of the Church? This, my lord, you that say, 'the King would reduce all things to the good order of the primitive Church', shall never find that it was at any time in the Church.

And bringing in so strange a thing in so great a matter, I marvel that ever you will speak of reducing things to the primitive Church's order except you call in this to be reduced to the primitive Church's order because at that time the best men were sorest persecuted; churches plucked down; [and] their goods taken from them. Here might be a similitude of the time of the primitive Church. For thus princes that were alienated from the name of Christ did order the Christian part; but Christian princes never....

Out of the love I bear to the King's Highness, my country, and friends, you do exhort me to leave the opinion that I have so much advanced in my book: and first of all, you allege unto me the estimation of my whole country; what they would think of me 'if they be delivered out of a great bondage'—meaning by that, the obedience to the Pope—and I should go about 'to reduce them into captivity again'. Here, my lord, I cannot tell what I may more lament, your words set under this manner or the mystery of the time in our country, giving place to your words which hath continued now some years in such that, meseemeth, the time of building the tower of Babylon is come again, when no man understood the other, for so it is now. This 'captivity', you speak of and this 'liberty', I understand not what you mean. But if sentence compound of words, having deeds conformable to the words, make all saying true, this I find indeed; in this I will not take record of one man or one city or one town but of one whole state of the realm, which is the spirituality,[1] which should have most ease by this renouncing of the Pope's power, the same extending most over them.

And now, my lord, you be one of them [the clergy], you may answer for all. But here needeth no answer. Your sweet 'liberty', now having got since you were delivered from the obedience papal, speaketh for itself: whereof the rest of the realm hath such part that you be without envy of other countries: that no nation wisheth the same to have such liberty granted them.

But thus I speak: we be brought to such case—worse than

[1] *spirituality*, clergy.

Babylon—that no man understandeth another in his own tongue: that one calleth 'captivity', another calleth 'liberty'; that one sayeth is 'against' the king, another calleth 'with' the king. And this began at such time as the practice of the unlucky marriage* was brought in—when the King would leave the noblest and best lady of the world and would needs couple himself with the vilest, as the cause of her death showed. Then came this confusion, for there being divers sentences: the one, that the King had lived twenty-two years together in an incestuous life—a life against nature and beastly, as they said, meaning the conjunction that he had with Queen Katherine so long time—therefore he must leave the same; another part, defending the contrary, which was also my sentence, that the King was a Prince of honour and married with greatest and highest counsel of two noble realms,* both England and Spain, whereunto agreed the consent of the Pope which took away all spot, if there were any, of illegitimate complying. And this might well be maintained by good learning. Every man, looking what the King would do, the conclusion was [that] he agreed to the former sentence that defamed his life, all the flower of his youth, and so agreed to it, they that were on the other part for good will, seeing their sentence, wherewith agreed all good learning, were first called adversaries to the King's cause, afterward, I trow, traitors. And none of those men's writings might go abroad that defended the honour of the King's marriage and his whole life. But those that most defamed him, that were thought most strongly to prove his unnatural, incestuous, and beastly life, these were had in most count.[1] Those were printed and read of every man. This, my lord, seemed monstrous unto me and to all the world beside, and ever doth and ever shall.

But to return to my purpose: How began the great confusion that no man could understand [the] other but what was afore-time called constancy of opinion in them, that would not let themselves be turned from an assured knowledge of the truth, this was [now] called obstinacy. Those men of whose virtue, learning, wisdom, fidelity, and love to the King and the realm were had such sure proof, that never of any born under the rule of a king could be had more, they were called first, ignorant and, afterward, condemned as traitors.

But to conclude, my lord, touching first my country, that you write would have so ill opinion of me if I follow that opinion that I am entered into, [that is], this confusion, if men cannot discern their friend from their foe, it shall not let me, my lord, but *per infamiam et bonam famam*[2] [by evil report and good report], as St Paul saith, I will do them good where I may have occasion. As touching the King, this will I say, if he be lese[3] and desolate of all counsel that maketh most to the wealth of his soul and of all other; if every other

---

[1] *count*, number.   [2] II Cor. vi. 8.   [3] *lese*, deprived of.

man for fear or some private respect, love not to meddle in such matters, surely I will never leave him. But wheresoever I have occasion, will show my mind grounded on the truth: and here is the bond you speak of toward him of my bringing up in virtue and learning which I will ever keep whatsoever peril or jeopardy to me privately depend thereof.

And that you write my lady, my mother [Margaret Pole, Countess of Salisbury], and other of my friends should take discomfort hereby, I know, my lord, they love the King too well, if they see the purpose of my mind to take any discomfort hereof. But all the discomfort I take myself is this, that this mind toward the King, which I do knowledge to proceed of the high benefit of God, taketh so little effect, knowing my cause so just, so profitable, so honorable, so sure for his grace.

You wish that you might be but one day with me to confer these matters. There is nothing, my lord, I would more desire if it might be. . . .

Written at a place in the country beside Padua where I lay this hot season. 1 August 1536.

[signed RAYNOLD POLE]

B.M. MS. Cotton, Cleopatra, E. VI, f. 337.

SIR JOHN CHEKE
1514–1557

Sir John Cheke, noted Greek scholar and political strategist at the courts of Henry VIII and Edward VI, was born in Cambridge in 1514. His parents, Peter and Agnes Cheke, belonged to the wealthy middle class, and young Cheke studied with private tutors until he entered St John's College, Cambridge, where he took a Bachelor of Arts degree in 1529. George Day, a Fellow and Master of St John's, is credited by Cheke with encouraging him to study Greek, in which he became so proficient that Henry VIII appointed him Regius Professor in 1542. Two years later he was named Public Orator of the university.

Offered a post in the royal household as tutor to Prince Edward and Princess Elizabeth, Cheke left Cambridge in 1544, and the loss to the university is described in Toxophilus *(1545) by his famous pupil, Roger Ascham.*

Cheke was related by marriage to several of the most powerful families in England. In 1547 his marriage to Mary Hill gave him a distant family tie with John Dudley, Duke of Northumberland. Cheke's sister Mary married his pupil William Cecil, later Lord Burghley. Using these connexions to advance himself at court, Cheke sought to aid the king and wrote pamphlets in 1549 against the Norfolk rebels, many of them tanners.

At the accession of Edward VI, Cheke was made Secretary of State, and became one of the most important advisers of the young king, who knighted him. His supposed connivance with Northumberland to gain the throne for Lady Jane Grey, whom he served as personal secretary during her brief reign, caused him to be imprisoned when Mary I came to the throne. He was soon released, and with his wife and children went to the Continent, living for some time at Strasbourg, where many of the English Reformers had settled. Anxious to visit Italy, he went to Padua; and, it is thought, lectured in Greek at the university, where English students had continued to study since 1500.

Through a ruse of Philip II, Cheke was brought back to England, in 1556, and imprisoned in the Tower. When he was condemned on charges of heresy and sentenced to be burnt at the stake, he sought an interview with Cardinal Pole, who urged him to recant. Reginald Pole was not, however, responsible for Cheke's submission to the Church. In a letter dated 15 December 1556, written by Pole's close friend Alvise Priuli to Archbishop Beccatelli, the Cardinal's secretary and biographer, Cheke's submission is credited to Abbot John de Feckenham, with whom he had in previous years publicly debated against the doctrine of the Eucharist. On his release from prison, Cheke lived in London until his death on 13 September 1557.

Cheke's only English work, The hurt of sedicion how greuous it is to a communewelth *(1549), was published anonymously. He uses Scripture to uphold his arguments for retaining the rigid system of degree, warning the Norfolk rebels against a class war which would endanger the welfare of the kingdom and bring down the wrath of God 'who intendeth to bestowe His gifts as He Himselfe listeth'.*

The most important of Cheke's Latin works (thirty-four have been attributed to him) is De pronuntiatione Graecae potissimum linguae, *printed in Basel in 1555. It climaxed a controversy, begun while he taught at Cambridge, over his attempt to revise the pronunciation of Greek in accordance with the method that Cheke believed was used by the ancient Greeks. A lengthy tribute to his efforts is given by Ascham in the* Scholemaster *(1570). John Strype in his biographical sketch of Cheke claims that his interest in English orthography and rhetoric encouraged him to begin a translation of the New Testament. It was left unfinished, and the extant fragment shows Cheke's preference for short sentences and an Anglo-Saxon vocabulary.*

The Hurt of Sedition: how Grievous it is to a Commonwealth

[Among so many and notable benefits wherewith God has already liberally and plentifully endowed us, there is nothing more beneficial than that we have by His grace kept us quiet from rebellion at this time. For we see such miseries hang over the whole state of the common-wealth through the great misorder of your sedition that it maketh us much to rejoice that we have been neither partners of your doings nor conspirers[1] of your counsels. For even as the Lacedemonians for the avoiding of drunkenness did cause their sons][2] to behold their servants when they were drunk, that…they might avoid the like vice, even so hath God like a merciful Father stayed us from your wicked-ness: that by beholding the filth of your fault, we might justly for offence abhor you like rebels whom else by nature we love like Englishmen.

And so for ourselves, we have great cause to thank God by whose religion and Holy Word, daily taught us, we learn not only to fear Him truly but also to obey our King faithfully and to serve in our own vocation like subjects, honestly. And as for you, we have surely just cause to lament you as brethren and yet juster cause to rise against you as enemies and most just cause to overthrow you as rebels. For what hurt could be done either to us privately or to the whole commonwealth generally that is now with mischief so brought in by you; that even as we see now the flame of your rage, so shall we necessarily be consumed hereafter with the misery of the same.

Wherefore consider yourselves with some light of understanding and mark this grievous and horrible fault which ye have thus vilely committed: how heinous it must needs appear to you if ye will reasonably consider that which, for my duty's sake and whole country's cause, I will at this present declare unto you.

Ye, which be bound by God's Word not to obey for fear like men-pleasers, but for conscience sake like Christians, have (con-trary to God's Holy Will, whose offense is everlasting death, and contrary to the godly order of quietness set out to us in the King's Majesty's laws, the breach whereof is not unknowen to you), taken-in-hand, uncalled of God, unsent by men, unfit by reason to cast away your bounden duties of obedience and to put on you, against the magistrates, God's office committed to the magistrates for the reformation of your pretended injuries.

In the which doing, ye have first, faulted grievously against God;

---

[1] *conspirers*, conspirators.
[2] This portion of the text is missing from the first edition.

next, offended unnaturally our sovereign lord; thirdly, troubled miserably the whole commonwealth, undone cruelly many an honest man, and brought in an utter misery both to us, the King's subjects, and to yourselves, being false rebels: and yet ye pretend that partly for God's cause and partly for the commonwealth's sake, ye do arise, when, as yourselves cannot deny, but ye that seek in word God's cause, do break, indeed, God's commandment: and ye that seek the commonwealth, have destroyed the commonwealth. And so ye mar that ye would make, and break that ye would amend, because ye neither seek anything rightly nor would amend anything orderly.

He that faulteth, faulteth against God's ordinance who hath forbidden all faults, and therefore ought again to be punished by God's ordinance who is the Reformer of faults. For He saith: Leave the punishment to Me, and I will revenge thee.[1] But the magistrate is the ordinance of God appointed by Him with the sword of punishment to look straitly to all evil doers: and therefore that that is done by the magistrate, is done by God whom the Scripture oftentimes doth call God because he hath the execution of God's office.

How then do you take in hand to reform? Be ye kings? By what authority or by what succession? Be ye the King's officers? By what commission? Be ye called of God? By what tokens declare ye that? God's Word teacheth us that no man should take in hand any office but he that is called of God like Aaron. What Moses, I pray you, called you? What God's minister bade you rise? Ye rise for religion: what religion taught you that? If ye were offered persecution for religion, ye ought to fly: So Christ teacheth you, and yet ye intend to fight. If ye would stand in the truth, ye ought to suffer like martyrs, and you would slay like tyrants.

Thus for religion, ye keep no religion: and neither will follow the counsel of Christ nor the constancy of martyrs. Why rise ye for religion? Have ye anything contrary to God's Book? Yea, have ye not all things agreeable to God's Word? But the new [Church] is different from the old, and therefore ye will have the old. If ye measure the old by truth, ye have the eldest; if ye measure the old by fancy, then it is hard because men's fancies changeth to give that is old. Ye will have the old, still? Will ye have any elder than that as Christ left and His apostles taught and the first Church after Christ did use? Ye will have that [that] the canons do establish. Why? That is a great deal younger than that ye have of later time and newlier invented, yet that is it that ye desire. Why then, ye desire not the oldest. And do you prefer the Bishop of Rome afore Christ; men's inventions afore God's law; the newer sort of worship before the elder? Ye seek no religion: ye be deceived; ye seek traditions.

They that teach you, blind you that so instruct you. If ye seek

[1] Deut. xxxii. 35.

what the old Doctors say, yet look what Christ, the oldest of all, saith. For He saith: 'Before Abraham was, I am.'[1] If ye seek the truest way, He is the very Truth; if ye seek the readiest way, He is the very Way; if ye seek everlasting life, He is the very Life.[2] What other religion would ye have now than His religion? Ye would have the Bibles in again. It is no marvel: your blind guides would lead you blind still. Why? Be ye houllates and backes[3] that ye cannot look on the light? Christ saith to every one: 'Search ye the Scriptures, for they bear witness of Christ':[4] you say, 'Pull in the Scriptures, for we will have no knowledge of Christ'.

The Apostles of Christ will us to be so ready that we may be able to give every man an account of our faith. Ye will us not once to read the Scriptures for fear of knowing of our faith. Saint Paul prayeth that every man may increase in knowledge;[5] ye desire that our knowledge might decay again. A true religion ye seek, belike and worthy to be fought for, for without the sword, indeed, nothing can help it; neither Christ nor truth nor age can maintain it.

But why should ye not like that which God's Word establisheth, the primitive Church hath authorized, the greatest learned men of this realm hath drawn [*The Great Bible* (1539)], the whole consent of the Parliament hath confirmed, the King's Majesty hath set forth? Is it not truly set out? Can ye devise any truer than Christ's Apostles used? Ye think it is not learnedly done. Dare ye, commons,[6] take upon you more learning than the chosen bishops and clerks of this realm have? Think ye folly in it? Ye were wont to judge your Parliament wisest, and now will ye suddenly excel them in wisdom? Or can ye think it lacketh authority which the King, the parliament, the learned, the wise have justly approved?

Learn, learn to know this one point of religion, that God will be worshipped as He hath prescribed, and not as we have devised; and that His Will is holy in His Scriptures which be full of God's Spirit and profitable to teach the truth, to reprove lies, to amend faults, to bring one up in righteousness that he that is a God's man may be perfect and ready to all good works. What can be more required to serve God withal? And thus much for religion-rebels.

The other rabble of Norfolk rebels, ye pretend a commonwealth. How amend ye it? By killing of gentlemen? By spoiling of gentlemen? By imprisoning of gentlemen? A marvellous 'tanned' commonwealth! Why should ye thus hate them—for their riches or for their rule? Rule, they never took so much in hand as ye do now. They never resisted the King; never withstood his council; they be faithful at this day when ye be faithless, not only to the King whose subjects ye be, but also to your lords whose tenants ye be.

---

[1] John viii. 58.   [2] Cf. John xiv, 6.   [3] *houllates and backes*, owls and bats.
[4] Cf. John v. 39.   [5] Cf. II Cor. viii. 7.   [6] *commons*, people.

Is this your true duty in sum of homage, in most of fealty, in all of allegiance, to leave your duties, go back from your promises, fall from your faith, and, contrary to law and truth, to make unlawful assemblies, ungodly companies, wicked and detestable camps, to disobey your betters, and to obey your tanners, to change your obedience from a King to a kett,[1] to submit yourselves to traitors, and break your faith to your true King and lords? They rule but by law: if otherwise, the law, the council, the King breaketh their rule.

Ye have orderly sought no redress, but ye have, in time, found it. In countries *some* must rule; *some* must obey: every man may not bear like stroke, for every man is not like wise. And they that have seen most and best able to bear it and of just dealing beside, be most fit to rule. It is another matter to understand a man's own grief and to know the commonwealth's sore:[2] and therefore not they that know their own case, as every man doth, but they that understand the commonwealth's state ought to have in countries the preferment of ruling.

If ye felt the pain that is joined with governance as ye see and like the honour, ye would not hurt others to rule them, but rather take great pain to be ruled of them. If ye had rule of the King's Majesty committed unto you, it were well done ye had ruled the gentlemen; but now ye have it not and cannot bear their rule, it is to think the King's Majesty foolish and unjust that hath given certain rule to them. And seeing by the Scripture, ye ought not to speak evil to any magistrate of the people,[3] why should ye not only speak evil of them whom the King's Majesty hath put in office, but also judge evil of the King himself, and thus seditiously in field stand with your swords drawn against him?

If riches offend you because ye would have the like, then think that to be *no* commonwealth, but *envy* to the commonwealth. Envy it is to appaire[4] another man's estate without the amendment of your own: and to have no gentlemen because ye be none yourselves, is to bring down an estate and to mend none. Would ye have all alike rich? That is the overthrow of labour and utter decay of work in this realm. For who will labour more if when he hath gotten more, the idle shall by lust [and] without right take what him list from him under pretence of equality with him. This is the bringing in of idleness which destroyeth the commonwealth, and not the amendment of labour that maintaineth the commonwealth.

If there should be such equality, then ye take all hope away from yours to come to any better estate than you now leave them. And as many mean[5] men's children cometh honestly up and are great succour

---

[1] *kett*, worthless fellow. [2] *sore*, disturbances. [3] Exod. xxii. 28.
[4] *appaire*, impair. [5] *mean*, middle-class.

o all their stock, so should none be hereafter holpen by you: but
because ye seek equality whereby all cannot be rich, ye would that
belike whereby every man should be poor: and think besides that
riches and inheritance be God's providence, and given to whom of
His wisdom He thinketh good: to the honest, for the increase of
their godliness; to the wicked, for the heaping up of their damnation;
to the simple, for a recompense of other lacks; to the wise, for the
greater setting out of God's goodness.

Why? Will your wisdom now stop God's wisdom and provide
by your laws that God shall not enrich them whom He hath by
prudence appointed as Him liketh. God hath made the poor, and
hath made them to be poor that He might show His might and set
them aloft when He listeth, for such cause as to Him seemeth, and
pluck down the rich to his state of poverty to show His power as He
disposeth to order them. Why do not we then being poor, bear it
wisely rather than by lust seek riches unjustly: And show ourselves
contented with God's ordinance which we must either willingly
obey, and then we be wise, or else we must unprofitably strive
withal, and then we be mad.

But what mean ye by this equality in the commonwealth? If one
be wiser than another, will ye banish him because ye intend an
equality of all things? If one be stronger than another, will ye slay
him because ye seek an equality of all things? If one be well favoured
than another, will ye punish him because ye look for an equality of
all things? If one have better utterance than another, will ye pull
out his tongue to save your equality? And if one be richer than
another, will ye spoil him to maintain an equality? If one be elder
than another, will ye kill him for this equality sake?

How injurious be ye to God Himself who intendeth to bestow
His gifts as He Himself listeth; and ye seek by wicked insurrections
to make Him give them commonly alike to all men as your vain
fancy liketh. Why would ye have an equality in riches, and in other
gifts of God there is no mean sought? Either by ambition ye seek
lordliness, much unfit for you, or by covetousness ye be unsatiable,
a thing likely enough in ye, or else by folly ye be not content with
your estate, a fancy to be plucked out of you.

But and we, being weary of poverty, would seek to enrich ourselves, we should go a far other way to work than this; and so should
we rightly come to our desire. Doth not Saint Peter teach us, afore
God, a right way to honour, to riches, to all necessary and profitable
things for us? He saith: Humble yourselves that God might exalt
you: and cast all your care on Him for He careth for you.[1] He
teacheth the way to all good things at God's hand is to be humble;
and you exalt yourselves. Ye seek things after such a sort as if the

[1] Cf. I Pet. v. 6–7.

servant should anger his master when he seeketh to have a good turn on him.

Ye would have riches, I think, at God's hand who giveth all riches, and yet ye take the way clean contrary to riches. Know ye not that he that exalteth himself, God will throw him down?[1] How can ye get it then by thus setting out yourselves? Ye should submit ye by humility one to another; and ye set up yourselves above the magistrates. See herein how much ye offend God! Remember ye not that 'if ye come nigh to God, He will come nigh unto you?'[2] If then ye go from God, He will go from you. Doth not the Psalm say: He is holy with the holy, and with the wicked man He is froward.[3] Even as He is ordered of men, He will order them again....

O noble peace, what wealth bringest you in! How doth all things flourish in field and in town! What forwardness of religion, what increase of learning, what gravity in council, what device of wit, what order of manners, what obedience of laws, what reverence of states, what safeguard of houses, what quietness of life, what honour of countries, what friendship of minds, what honesty of pleasure hast thou always maintained: whose happiness we knew not, while now we feel the lack: and shall learn by misery to understand plenty, and so to avoid mischief by the hurt that it bringeth: and learn to serve better where rebellion is once known, and so to live truly and keep the King's peace.

What good state were ye in afore ye began, not pricked with poverty, but stirred with mischief, to seek your destruction; having ways to redress all that was amiss; magistrates most ready to render all justice, and pitiful in hearing the poor men's causes, which sought to amend matters more than you can devise, and ready to redress them better than ye could imagine. And yet for a headiness, ye could not be contented, but in despite of God, who commandeth obedience, and contempt of the King, whose laws seeketh your wealth, and to overthrow the country, which naturally we should love, ye would proudly rise and do ye wot not what, and amend things by rebellion to your utter undoing.

What state leave ye us in now—besieged with enemies, divided at home, made poor with spoil and loss of our harvest, unordered and cast down with slaughter and hatred, hindered from amendments by your own devilish haste, endangered with sickness by reason of misorder, laid open to men's pleasures for breaking of the laws, and feebled to such faintness that seasely[4] it will be recovered.

Wherefore, for God's sake, have pity on yourselves and consider how miserably ye have spoiled and destroyed and wasted us all: and

---

[1] Matt. xxiii. 12.   [2] Cf. Ps. cxxxxiv. 18.
[3] Cf. Ps. xvii. 26–7.   [4] *seasely*, scarcely.

if for desperateness, ye care not for yourselves, yet remember your wives, your children, your country, and forsake this rebellion: with humble submission acknowledge your faults and tarry not the extremity of the King's sword; leave off with repentance and ruin to your duties; ask God's forgiveness; submit ye to your King; be contented for a commonwealth, one or two to die; and, ye captains, for the residue, sacrifice yourselves. Ye shall so best attain the King's gracious pardon, save the assembly and help the commonwealth: and declare your doings to proceed of no stubbornness, but all this mischief to grow out of ignorance, which seeing the misery would redress the fault and so recover best the blot of your disorder and stay the great miseries which be like to follow.

Thus if ye do not think truly with yourselves that God is angry with you for your rebellion; the King's sword drawn to defend his country; the cry of the poor to God against ye; the readiness of the honest in armour to vanquish ye; your death to be at hand which ye cannot escape, having God against ye, as He promiseth in word; the King's power to overthrow ye, gathered in the field; the commonwealth to beat ye down with stripes and with curses; the shame of your mischief to blemish ☞ ye forever. ✍

COLOPHON: Imprinted at London by J. Daye dwelling over Aldergate and W. Seres dwelling in Peter College.... 1549.

TRADITION AND EARLY TUDOR MEDICINE

INTRODUCTION BY GERTRUDE ANNAN

PICTORIAL ART AND EARLY MEDICAL PRACTICE

Europe's medieval medical schools that gave impetus to Tudor medicine traced their beginnings to the ancient civilizations of Asia and the Western world. Like the start of every human endeavour, medicine from the outset was closely affiliated with religious, philosophical, and social thought—an alliance that was destined to influence its progress through the ages. In the absence of early written records, the arts and crafts practised in antiquity record this alliance with such unswerving accuracy that the medical historian finds his prime sources in painting, sculpture, woodcuts, prints, ceramics, typography, architecture, numismatics, philately, and music.

In the late pagan and early Christian eras, when medicine came finally to be regarded as a science, pictorial art became a handmaid to the written word. It was indeed too great an educational as well as decorative device to be discarded. The herbalists especially found the 'picture' as essential in acquainting the reader with various plants as was a written description of their curative properties. A fifth-century manuscript cover shows Dioscorides, the greatest pharmacologist of antiquity, receiving a mandrake from Euresis, the goddess of discovery. In the foreground a dog is lying dead after having dug the magic plant.

When the illumination of manuscripts reached its greatest perfection in the twelfth and thirteenth centuries, letters of the alphabet became frames for charming miniatures in exquisite colours. In the initial letter of a medical treatise, one of the scenes frequently depicted is the apothecary shop with its attractive drug jars in the background. The apprentice works at the mortar and pestle, while the apothecary tends his customers. Within the small space of a letter, artists found ample room to show a physician demonstrating the anatomy of the thorax; or a clyster being used on a patient; or the latter being bled; or a physician holding high the urine glass. Miniatures painted in letters of a fourteenth-century manuscript on surgery by Roland of Parma record such scenes as an extraction of an arrow, treatment of fracture and of wounds of the neck and arm, bandaging and removal of a vesical calculus. In the fourteenth-century manuscripts of the English surgeon John of Arderne, the miniatures cover a wide variety of medical and surgical subjects, including anatomy, hygiene, and the series *foetus in utero* so often found in the early printed books on obstetrics.

The invention of printing in the fifteenth century had an important effect on medical illustration. Instead of a scattering of miniatures in valuable manuscripts, available only to a few, woodcuts, and later engravings, were made in quantity. Leonardo da Vinci's famous anatomical drawings were not, unfortunately, printed contemporaneously as were the crude figures of the late fifteenth- and early sixteenth-century editions of Johannes de Ketham's *Fasciculus Medicinae* (1491) and Berengario da Carpi's treatises on surgery, especially *Commentaria...super anatomia Mundini* (1521). These were climaxed by the magnificent cuts in Andreas Vesalius's *De humani corporis fabrica* (1543). Here for the first time were anatomical representations of accuracy and beauty. The muscle figures are alive and in motion, not static copies of specimens in the dissecting room. And the artist, following the physician's emphasis on man's social environment in relation to disease, was not content to display the figures alone, but provided a background of scenes of the countryside, rivers, houses, bridges, and unusual land formations; if placed in the proper sequence, these drawings form a charming frieze.

THE BEGINNINGS OF MEDICAL LITERATURE

In turning to the written traditions of early medicine, that is the medical literature, particularly of Europe, it is at once obvious that the religious, philosophical, and social aspects of the science that were so prominent in its pictorial history now influenced its fundamental concepts. The earliest extant treatises of Western medicine are those of Hippocrates and his school. The importance of Hippocrates's pioneering in medicine has been well stated by Francis Adams, first English translator of his *Complete Works* (1849), in his long preface wherein he remarks:

How strikingly the Hippocratic system differs from that of all other nations in their infantine state must be well known to every person who is well acquainted with the early history of medicine. His theory of medicine was further based on the physical philosophy of the ancients, more especially on the doctrines then held regarding the elements of things and the belief in the existence of a spiritual essence, diffused through the whole works of creation, which was regarded as the agent that presides over the acts of generation and which constantly strives to preserve all things in their natural state and to restore them when they are preternaturally deranged. This is the principle which he called Nature and which he held to be a *vis medicatrix*. 'Nature', says he, or, at least one of his immediate followers, 'is the physician of diseases.'

The theories and practices found in Hippocrates's treatises—*On Ancient Medicine*, *Prognostics*, *Aphorisms*, *Epidemics*, *The Physicians's Establishment*, or surgery—concerning the healing power of nature, the humoral theory, and the importance of recording the observations in the progress of disease for comparative study, became the tenets of the ancient medical centres in Pergamus and Alexandria and, later, of all the medical schools of Europe until the seventeenth century.

From the school in Alexandria in the second century A.D. came the first systematic study of anatomy, the work of its famous student Claudius Galen, one of the foremost men in the annals of European medicine. An ardent follower of Aristotle, Galen partly agreed with his peripatetic philosophy which made experience the basis of all scientific knowledge, insisting that the study of anatomy, displaying as it does the wisdom of God in creating a perfect balance and harmony in the workings of the human body, is a philosophical aim. This principle has been a factor in determining his genuine works from the five hundred attributed to him. Among the most important of his accepted works which served to carry on the Galenic tradition are: *On the Ideal Physician*; *On the Teachings of Hippocrates and Plato*; *On the Uses of the Parts of the Human Body* (seventeen books containing all of Galen's physiological doctrines); *On the Medical Art* (*Ars Parva*); *On Anatomical Preparations* (his principal anatomical work); and *On the Method of Treatment* (fourteen books).

THE GALENIC TRADITION

With the rise of Christianity Galen lost none of his prestige. As Major Greenwood has said of him in an essay *The Medical Dictator* (1936):

> The psychological line of succession from the Greeks passed not through physicians, but through theologians, through St Augustine of Hippo and the great scholastic writers culminating in St Thomas Aquinas. This culmination was from the purely intellectual point of view a wonderful thing. Galen might have envied the success of the medieval writer who had beaten him at his own game.

The only Christian personality of importance in the progress of medicine was Paul Aegina of the Alexandria School, whose seven-volume work *On Medicine* (*c.* 635) carried the Galenic tradition through the long interval from the ninth to the fourteenth century when Arabic medicine with its rigid philosophical approach all but stifled experiment. Its beginnings were coincident with the rise of the medieval medical schools, particularly Salerno, whose records date from the seventh century. The school's rule of health has been immortalized in *Regimen Sanitatis Salernitatis*, a poem which may have been written as early as the tenth century and was dedicated to a king of England whose identity has never been satisfactorily established, though frequently associated with William the Conqueror through a visit to Salerno by his son Robert, Duke of Normandy. In commenting on the work's value as a medical text, Arturo Castiglioni notes in his *History of Medicine* that it was memorized by thousands of physicians. It does not, he remarks, 'constitute a text of medical treatment' conformable to modern science, 'but the seductive quality of the verse had the virtue of spreading these useful, simple, and true maxims throughout the civilized world, popularizing with good common sense a sane criticism which evidences a Hippocratic quality that is the greatest glory of the school'.

Considering English medicine more closely, during the late Middle Ages it was linked with the Galenic tradition of the Continent through the exchange of medical students, those of Oxford and Cambridge attending the Universities of Paris and Montpellier. Perhaps even stronger links were the popular texts of the Milanese Guido Lanfranc, *The Science of Surgery* [*Cirurgia Magna*], one of the first works on surgery translated, about 1390, into English, and the *Chirurgia Magna* (1363) by Guy de Chauliac, French priest and papal surgeon, whom Douglas Guthrie calls 'the most famous surgeon of late medieval times'. The latter manual, which treats of the early removal of cancerous growths, treatment of fractures with slings and extension, and operation for hernia and cataract, was translated into English and printed by Robert Copland as the *Questyonary of Cyrurgyens*[1] (1542).

The immediate precursor of the early Tudor physician was John of Arderne, whom Sir D'Arcy Power credits with widening the horizons of the medical world. Arderne's contemporaries were in touch 'with the older beliefs in science whilst they were endowed with the knowledge which had been gained by Roger Bacon and Robert Grosseteste'. Like Bacon, Arderne was an independent thinker, as his rules for a surgeon show. His treatise *De Arte Phisicale et de Cirurgia*, translated into English in 1412, continued popular long after his death. It brought him fame for his daring treatment of fistula *in ano* by 'boldly incising and checking the bleeding by sponge pressure'.

---

[1] *cyrurgyens*, surgeons.

TWO GREAT MEDICAL FOUNDATIONS IN
TUDOR ENGLAND

The greatest single impetus to the progress of medical science in England was the act of 1511 prohibiting ignorant persons from practising medicine and surgery by requiring the candidate to pass an examination and receive the approval of the Bishop of London, or the Dean of St Paul's. This determined effort to place English medicine on a more scientific basis received the co-operation of three outstanding medical men—Thomas Linacre, Thomas Vicary, and John Caius. These men, trained on the Continent as physicians and surgeons, were intimately connected with the two great medical foundations in Tudor England, namely the Royal College of Physicians, established in 1518, and the Company of Barbers and Surgeons, incorporated by an act of 1540 which limited the field of the barbers to dentistry, a science not nearly so neglected as is sometimes thought.

This early recognition of dentistry is important, and it may have originated with Vicary, first Master of the Barbers and Surgeons. He had great respect for the traditions of Guy de Chauliac, whose *Chirurgia* urged the need for care of the teeth in relation to the individual's physical well-being. Guy's great manual, which was translated into English about this time, stresses the necessity of cleaning the teeth regularly and offers formulae for preparing powder and liquid dentifrices. He treats at length several methods of extracting teeth and healing abscesses; and he describes a way to replace lost teeth with either human teeth or artificial ones made from bone and held in place by fine metal wiring.

As was mentioned above, Linacre, Vicary, and Caius were closely associated with the progress of Tudor medicine. Of the three, Thomas Vicary deserves special notice for his efforts to advance the science of surgery. Appointed chief surgeon to the king in 1535, Vicary urged reforms in the practice of surgery, and he helped to bring about the act of 1540. The importance of the event is commemorated in Holbein's painting in which a large group of physicians and courtiers are shown kneeling around Henry VIII as he presents a scroll to Vicary, the first Master of the Company.

FIRST ENGLISH MEDICAL TEXTBOOKS

As Sir D'Arcy Power has noted in *The Education of a Surgeon under Thomas Vicary*, the need of medical textbooks in the vernacular was obvious to Vicary, and he wrote the first English treatise on anatomy, *A Treasure for Englishmen, containing the Anatomie of Mans Body*. There are no extant copies of the first edition, printed probably in

1548. The book had a curious fate that entangled it with a treatise of the Belgian Andreas Vesalius, who studied and taught anatomy in 1535 at the University of Padua where he did much of the work on his famous texts on anatomy, *Fabrica* and *Epitome*, printed at Basel in 1543, with the excellent illustrations of Jan Stephan van Calcar. Two years later a pirated edition, edited by the Fleming Thomas Geminus, was printed in England. The title was changed to *Compendiosa totius anatomie*, and the work was dedicated to Henry VIII. In the Latin preface, Geminus states, 'There is nothing more pleasing, at least to the natural man and a student of natural philosophy, nothing more desirable and essential in the preservation of health through medicine and surgery...than a thorough comprehension of the fabric of the human body.' Geminus declares that his purpose in publishing a 'compendium' of Vesalius's works was to acquaint the English public with the author, a great surgeon, and 'the most skilled man of our age in the art'.

Though Vesalius vigorously disapproved of Geminus's edition, the popularity of the *Compendiosa* was sufficient to warrant an English translation. In a short foreword to the English version, printed in 1553, Geminus explains why he employed the 'studious peines of Nicholas Udall and certaine other learned men whose exercise in translacions and penyng in this tounge hath ben (as I vnderstande) not without some fruite to the commonweal'.

Udall's translation of Geminus's *Compendiosa* has a twofold interest: first, the dramatist's connexion with it, and second, the substitution that he made in the text. Concerning the latter point, it has been established by Sanford V. Larkey in his article, *The Vesalian Compendium of Geminus and Nicholas Udall's Translation*, that Udall, without making any reference to the fact, substituted a treatise, *Of the Partes of Mannes Body*, in place of Vesalius's *Epitome*. This treatise, Larkey believes, is a part of Vicary's *Anatomie of Mans Body*. It was most likely expediency that dictated the use of Vicary's treatise. Contrary to Vesalius's method of dissection, which began with the head, Vicary, when dissecting a body while lecturing before the Company of Barbers and Surgeons, followed that of Guy de Chauliac, using first that portion endangered by putrefaction. The use of Van Calcar's woodcuts from the *Fabrica* increased the English *Compendiosa's* educational value, which is reflected in the history of English medicine.

Though the printing press during the early Tudor era was in its infancy, it became the greatest ally of medical science, turning out a quantity of literature, old and new, written on the Continent; herbals so necessary for *materia medica*; manuals for surgery and obstetrics; advice for personal hygiene and home treatment; and small tracts on syphilis and the plague, two of the most urgent problems of the time. English versions of these works could be had 'good chepe'.

HERBAL MEDICINE

Special note must be taken of herbals or books of medical recipes, based on plants and materials from the mineral and animal kingdom. Though burdened with superstition and magic, herbal medicine made a place for itself in the poor man's household, offering remedies to old and young—formulae that were simply prepared and easily obtained from the nearby fields or the town's apothecary shop. And the fact that Hippocrates and Galen recommended herbal medicine for certain diseases gave its use the necessary authority.

The long and fascinating history of the herbal is lost in antiquity and is proof that prehistoric man looked to nature for medicines to cure his ills. Many fragments of ancient herbals as well as entire works are extant, but the most important is conceded to be that of the Greek Dioscorides whose *De Universa Medicina*, written in the first century A.D., contains over five hundred names of plants and a careful description of each. Having become a standard text through the ages, its popularity warranted its printing by Aldus Manutius in 1490.

Illustrations were obviously a vital part of herbals, making identification of a particular herb less subject to error. As art in the Christian era developed, drawings in herbals of plants and animals, executed with great skill and detail, became delightful artistic creations which reached their height in the anonymous German herbal *Gart der Gesundheit* (1485), and finally that of the eminent Bremberg chemist Leonard Fuchs, *De Historia Stirpium* (1542).

While Germany took the lead in illustration, her herbals followed those of Dioscorides, as did the rest of the Continent and England. These manuscript herbals, generally in Latin and freely compiled without the supervision of medical men, gave place to printed versions that could be more easily checked by physicians for accuracy and fraud. Among the first English herbals were Richard Banckes's *Herball* (1525) and the anonymous *Great Herball* (1526), printed by Peter Treveris. Like *Macer's Herball* (*c.* 1530), a version of the popular Banckes's herbal, and not of the ancient physician Macer Floridus, they are translations of Continental works. But after the turn of the century, William Turner, preacher and herbalist, printed his *New Herball* (1551), and his exactness in giving botanical data and the perfection of his illustrations earned for him the title 'Father of British Botany'.

THE POPULAR HEALTH BOOKS

There remain to be mentioned the English health and diet books, sometimes compiled by educated men, who, lacking medical training, left themselves open to the attacks of Tudor physicians. A harsh rebuff was levelled at the scholarly Sir Thomas Elyot for his *Castel of Helth* (1530). In the work's second edition, printed in 1541, he answered his critics, claiming to have studied under Linacre and to have read the greatest medical books since Hippocrates. But the laymen appreciated Elyot's counsels on health; and written in English in quite plain fashion, *The Castel* went through seventeen editions, the last, 'newly perused' in 1610.

Another such work on health was undertaken by the lawyer and physician Thomas Phaer, who translated 'for the comfort of them that are diseased' *The Regiment of Life, whereunto is added a Treatise of the Pestilence, with the Booke of Children* (1544). In a racy and entertaining style, the 'merry' Andrew Borde, traveller, scholar, and medical student, wrote a *Dyetary* [1542] and a *Breviary of Healthe* (1552). Under a quaint title Thomas Moulton, a friar, compiled the *Glasse of Helth, a great Treasure for pore men, necessary and nedeful for every person to loke in that wyll kepe therye body from syknesses and dysseases. And it sheweth howe the planettes reygne every houre of the daye and the night* (c. 1539). Fifteen editions printed before 1580 made it vie in popularity with Elyot's *Castel*.

Moulton's remedies seem strange in the twentieth century, but the names of the complaints are all too familiar—colic, headache, toothache, stomach-ache, ague, itch, and fever. Simple cures for these would be considered today a 'Treasure for poor Men', for disease and pain are ever present in each generation. The story of medicine is an integral part of the story of man.

ANONYMOUS

———

The Great Herbal

The Great Herbal which giveth perfect knowledge and understanding of all manner of herbs and their gracious virtues which
God hath ordained for our prosperous welfare and health, for
they heal and cure all manner of diseases and sickness that fall
or misfortune to all manner of creatures of God, created and
practised by many expert and wise masters, as Avicenna and
others, etc. Also it giveth full and perfect understanding of the
book, lately printed by me Peter Treveris, named *The Noble
Experience of the Virtuous Handywork of Surgery*.

PREFACE

Consider the great goodness of Almighty God, Creator of heaven
and earth and all things therein comprehended, to whom be eternal
laud and praise, etc.: consider the course and nature of the four
elements and qualities whereto the nature of man is inclined, [and]
out of the which elements issueth divers qualities, infirmities, and
diseases in the corporate body of man; but God of His goodness, that
is Creator of all things, hath ordained [cures] for mankind (which He
hath created to His own likeness) for the great and tender love which
He hath unto him to whom all things earthly He hath ordained to
be obeisant for the sustentation and health of His loving creature
mankind, which is only made equally of the four elements and
qualities of the same.

And when any of these four abound or hath more domination
the one than the other, it constraineth the body of man to great
infirmities or diseases for the which the Eternal God hath given, of
His abundant grace, virtues in all manner of herbs to cure and heal
all manner of sickness or infirmities to him befalling through the
influent course of the four elements, before said, and of the corrup-
tions and the venemous airs contrary to the health of man, [and]
also of unwholesome meats or drinks, or wholesome meats and
drinks taken untemperately, which be called surfeits, that bringeth
a man soon to great diseases ,or sickness: which diseases been of
[a great] number and impossible to be rehearsed, and fortune as well
in villages, whereas neither surgeons nor physicians be dwelling nigh
by many a mile, as it doth in good towns where they be ready at
hand.

Wherefore brotherly love compelleth me to write, through the gifts of the Holy Ghost, showing and informing how man may be helped with green herbs of the garden and weeds of the fields as well as by costly receipts of the apothecaries prepared.

Also, it is to be understood that all manner of medicines that be contrary to sickness is for the great superfluity of the humours, or the diminution of them, or for to restrain the course where it is against the feebleness of the virtues, for the altercation or solution of continuities, or wounds, or other beginnings, etc.

It is also to be understood that we find medicines simple, laxative, appetisant,[1] and minishing the superabundance of humours; and also simple medicines current; and also medicines alterative* and consolidative,* etc.

This noble work is compiled, composed, and authorized by divers and many noble doctors and expert masters in medicines, as Avicenna, [the] *Pandectae*, Constantinus, William [of Salerno], [Johannes] Platearius, Rabbi Moses, Johannes Mesue, Haly Abbas, Albertus [Magnus], Bartholomeus [Anglicus], and others, etc.

DE LAPACIO[2]

Lapatium is an herb, called dock, and hath many names. Some call the seed *ematiphonos*. It is hot and dry; and is in three manners: for there is *lapatium* dock that hath rough leaves and is of most virtue; there is another that hath round leaves and is of less virtue; and there is another that is tame, that hath black speckled leaves: and that is best for medicines that is taken within. This herb hath power to spread humours and to open veins.

FOR DROPSY

Against dropsy, called *leucoflemance*, make confections of two ounces of the juice of docks with two drams of esula[3] and seethe them together with honey: and give it to the patient.

FOR THE BREATH[4]

Pancakes made of docks with meal or eggs is good for letting of the breath, called asthma. It is good if they be eaten: and this herb eaten raw or sodden is good against all scabs.

COLOPHON: Imprinted at London in Southwark by me Peter Treveris....1526.

[1] *appetisant*, appetizer. [2] Red dock (Chapter CCXXXVI).
[3] *esula*, species of spurge. [4] Asthma.

MACER FLORIDUS
(Aemilius Macer) d. 15 B.C.

Macer's Herbal Practised by Doctor Linacre

HEREAFTER FOLLOWETH THE VIRTUE OF THE OKEN TREE

In the oak be four things, besides the leaf, the which be right profitable to the health of a man: that is to wit, the acorn and the cup that it groweth in, the galls, and the lime. The kernel in powder be profitable against the feebleness or *vettiver*[1] of the *tetenuise*,[2] that is to say, against feebleness of the brain; and against the passion, called diabetes; and against the strangury;[3] and against the sickness, called dysentery; and against the stone in the raynes[4] and the bladder; and it is good for them that may not hold their water.

The cup of the acorn is good against vomits of colour and against nesing;[5] and it dryeth and consumeth phlegm in the mouth of the stomach. The gall, after the opinion of Albar, so that they be not greatly hollow, be good against the flux; and against sliding and slipperyness of guts; and against the flowers of women:* and that powder helpeth them of many infirmities, etc.

Also by experience of gardeners and planters, [it has been proved that if] the powder of the gall [is] mingled with honey [and] a hole pierced in a tree and put in therein, the fruit shall be black.

Now with the lime[6] of the oak, physicians and surgeons do many cures therewith: and of it is made an ointment for the palsy...and against an infirmity, called diabetes. Also, thereof is made syrup for the dropsy that cometh of cold called *hyposarco*,[7] and it consumeth watery humours. And, also, men be cured by the fruit of [the] axes,[8] quartan [fever],[9] tercian and quotidian. Also in the tree is a thing growing, which women know by experience it maketh them hastily to be delivered of child, which Dutchmen call archemsell,[10] [and] thereof is made beads.

The last conclusion of this oak [are the] leaves: of these leaves is distilled a water which healeth all the flux of women called dysentery, lavaria,[11] and diarrhœa. Also it is good for the flowers of women

---

[1] *vettiver*, Fr. *vetuste*, decay.
[2] *tetenuise*, Fr. *tête nuise*, head injury.
[3] *strangury*, painful urination.
[4] *raynes*, kidneys.
[5] *nesing*, nausea (?).
[6] *lime*, ash (?).
[7] *hyposarco*, obsolete word for œdema.
[8] *axes*, oak.
[9] *quartan*, a fever recurring every fourth day.
[10] *archemsell*, from Dutch *eikel*, acorn; also *akkermaalshout*, young oak.
[11] *lavaria*, leucorrhœa.

and for the hæmorrhoids. Also this leaf in powder put in the nose stauncheth the bleeding thereof and spitting of blood. Also this leaf is wholesome against the ache of the heart, against the epilacion[1] of the liver and of the spleen, and against the neysage,[2] and against the cough and the headache, and against the ache of the stomach, and the wind of the stomach, and against the colic and the ache of the womb and the flanks. And it breaketh the stone of the raynes and the bladder; and also women that be cold, it disposeth them to be able to conceive. It is wholesome to all manner of creatures, of all manner ages, and for all diseases, [and] to be taken at all times of the year.

Wherefore surgeons, knowing the truth, lieth oken leaves upon wounds, and that done they need none other ointment. It healeth all manner of wounds, the canker, the fistula, and Saint Anthony's fire.* A vein made in the water of the oak* healeth the dropsy and all leperousness. Also, whosoever once in the week eateth one of the leaves, he shall never have stinking breath nor the toothache nor putrefaction in his gums nor of his ears.

COLOPHON: Imprinted by me, Robert Wyer, dwelling in Saint Martin's parish at the sign of Saint John Evangelist beside Charing Cross. [1530.]

ACT OF PARLIAMENT

An Act for the Approbation of Physicians and Surgeons

IN THE THIRD YEAR OF THE REIGN OF HENRY VIII

The king our sovereign lord and to all the lords, spiritual and temporal, and commons in this present Parliament assembled: Forasmuch as the science and cunning of physic and surgery, to the perfect knowledge whereof be requisite both great learning and ripe experience, is daily within this realm exercised by a great multitude of ignorant persons of whom the great part have no manner of insight in the same, nor in any other kind of learning, some also can no letters on book so, farforth,[3] that common artificers, as smiths, weavers, and women, boldly and customarily take upon them great cures and things of great difficulty in the which they partly use sorcery and witchcraft, partly apply such medicines unto the disease

---

[1] *epilacion*, enlargement, from lat. *pila*, ball.   [2] *neysage*, nauseousness (?).
[3] *farforth*, to a great extent.

as be very noisome and nothing meetly, [and] therefore to the high displeasure of God, great infamy to the faculty, and the grievous hurt, damage, and destruction of many of the King's liege people, most specially of them that cannot discern the uncunning from cunning.

Be it therefore to the surety and comfort of all manner people by the authority of this present Parliament enacted: that no person within the city of London nor within seven miles of the same take upon him to exercise and occupy as a physician or surgeon except he be first examined, approved, and admitted by the Bishop of London, or by the Dean of Paul's, for the time being, calling to him or them four doctors of physic and for surgery other expert persons in that faculty: and for the first examination such as they shall think convenient, and afterwards always four of them that have been so approved. Upon the pain of forfeiture—for every month that they do occupy as physicians or surgeons not admitted nor examined after the tenor of this Act—of five pounds to be employed the one half thereof to the use of our sovereign lord the King and the other half thereof to any person that will sue for it by action of debt, in which no wager of law or protection shall be allowed.

And over this, that no person out of the said city and precinct of seven miles of the same except he have been, as is aforesaid, approved in the same, take upon him to exercise and occupy as a physician or surgeon in any diocese within this realm but if he be first examined and approved by the Bishop of the same diocese or, he being out of the diocese, by his vicar-general, either of them calling to them such expert persons in the said faculties as their discretion shall think convenient and giving their letters testimonials under their seal to him that they shall approve: upon like pain to them that occupy contrary to this Act, as is above said, to be levied and employed after the form before expressed:

Provided always that this Act nor anything therein contained be prejudicial to the Universities of Oxford and Cambridge or either of them or to any privileges granted to them.

COLOPHON: Printed at London in Fleet Street at the sign of the George by St Dunstan's Church. By me Richard Pynson, squire and printer unto the King's noble Grace. 1511.

JEROME OF BRUNSWICK
1450?–1500?

The anonymous English version of Jerome of Brunswick's The Noble
Experyence of the Vertuous Handy warke of Surgeri *(1525) is the
earliest extant treatise on surgery printed in England. Jerome was born
about 1450 in Strasbourg. Determined to enter the field of medicine, he was
apprenticed to a master surgeon. His success as a physician made his close
friend, the printer Johannes Grüninger, induce him to write a manual on
surgery in German so that it might be of service to the poorer classes unable
to read Latin. In his preface, Jerome reveals that he wrote especially for
those surgeons living in 'lonely villages and castles', who had to rely on
their own resources. In giving advice to physicians, he urges them to use
psychology in treating patients, particularly those who are incurable.*

The Handy warke *is a summary of seven treatises that deal in general
with wounds, fractures, and salves. Jerome gives the first detailed account
of the treatment of gunshot wounds in medical literature. The English
version, like the original German* Buch de Cirurgia *(1497) is profusely
illustrated. To forestall a pirated edition, Grüninger included a section on
anatomy in some of the first editions. It does not appear in the English
version printed by Peter Treveris.*

The Handywork of Surgery

The Noble Experience of the Virtuous Handywork of Surgery
practised and compiled by the most expert master Jerome of
Brunswick, born in Strasbourg in Almain, the which hath it first
proved and truly found by his own daily exercising. *Item.* Thereafter he hath authorized and done it to understand through the
true sentences of the old doctors and masters, very expert in the
science of surgery, as Galen, Hippocrates, Avicenna, Guido
[de Chauliac], Haly Abbas, Lancfranc of Milan, Jamerius, Roger
[of Parma], Albucasis, Placentinus, Brunus [Longo Burgensis],
William of Saliceto, and by many other masters, whose names
be written in this same book. Here also shall ye find for to cure
and heal all wounded members and other swellings. *Item.* If
ye find any names of herbs or of other things whereof ye have
no knowledge, that shall ye know plainly by the apothecaries.
Item. Here shall you find also for to make salves, plasters,
powders, oils, and drinks for wounds. *Item.* Whoso desireth

of this science the plain knowledge, let him oftentimes read this book, and then he shall get perfect understanding of the noble surgery.

THE PROLOGUE OF 'THE NOBLE HANDYWORK OF SURGERY'

To the laud of Our Saviour Christ Jesus and the honour of His Blessed Mother, Our Lady Saint Mary, and all the holy company of heaven and for the help of mankind, this book is translated out of Dutch[1] into English; and for the love and comfort of all them that intend to study the noble art of chyrurgia, the which is called *The Handywork of Surgery* [and] very useful and profitable to all that intend to occupy this noble science that herein is openly expressed and showed how it shall be practised and used. For many one is therein very ignorant that will meddle therewith, which never laboured nor never sapient of the beginning or ending thereof. Wherefore it is oftentimes seen and daily chanceth in small towns, boroughs, and villages that lie far from any good city or great town, that divers people hurt or diseased for lack of cunning men be taken in hand of them that be barbers or young masters to whom this science was never disclosed nor thinking on the words of the old learned men that say, 'It is not well possible to man that he should bring well to a good end that thing which he never or hath but little seen.'

Thus, you, young students, masters, and servants of barbers and surgeons, that intend this noble art and cunning, behold, oversee, and read with diligence this little book that I, Jerome von Braunschweig, born in Strasbourg, out of the line of Salerno, hath with great labour compiled, set, and gathered together to your behalf and great profit this little volume, thinking on many noble authors in divers books which plainly doth specify: 'Cursed be those that God hath with cunning endowed to the health, succour, and help of mankind, and will not occupy it; but blessed be they that among his even-Christians will liberally show and minister such gifts of grace as God hath endowed him with for the preservation of man.' Wherefore, my friends, think that you may now for a little money have great learning and cunning to your honour and profit, the which hereafter you might fortune not to get for ten times so much gold as it should cost you now.

O you, young beginning surgeons, unclose your ears with all your diligence and mark well the words of the great masters which command you when you be called or desired to any patient or diseased person that if the disease fall to your cunning too ponderous and that you be not fully perfect, then be not ashamed, but quickly

---

[1] *Dutch*, German.

get another discreet surgeon or twain, desiring them that they will help and counsel you in that business at your need. For your honesty lieth in that cure and also the great comfort of your patient so diseased.

First, you learn by chance that thing that you seldom or never have seen before. Secondly, if ought in your hands happen to misfortune, that the other may quickly then amend it. Thirdly, that the wounded person have the less grudge or mistrust in you. Fourthly, when the cure hath good speed, then be you partaker of all the honour thereof. And if that misfortune fall between your hands, then be they bound every man to bear the charge of your hinder and losses which were too much for you alone. Fifthly, for this wise deed you be praised of all them that be discreet or learned men that speak of you, which say, 'He desireth to learn, and will not that any man should be by him negligently spilt[1] or perished.' And thus may ye come to your purpose with honesty and pleasure which else might turn to your great shame and displeasure.

And also you may consider that two may better amend a fault than one. For no only workman can well perceive the fault of his own work alone until he hath very long wrought upon it or else nearhand[2] finished it; and then is it sometime evil and impossible to be mended, but principally in many operations belonging to surgery.

Therefore when you go two or more about the patient, take heed that you make no discord. In like wise, when any of you be present alone with your patient, blame not the other that is absent nor defame him not. But what you have to say with each other, let that be secret within yourself for growing[3] of your patient, for it might turn him to great pain and hindrance in his disease through your discomfort. The one shall follow the other's counsel; and you shall hide nothing from each other that you shall think profitable and behoveful for your patient or sick body, for that might turn you to shame and him to great pain.

Also, you ought not only to be expert in surgery, but also in astronomy or philosophy: wherefore you shall diligently study and often read such things as for you in this matter or science shall be utile and profitable, whereby you shall have perfect understanding and knowledge of your noble science that you do enterprise.

You shall for no gold nor silver take in hand that thing that you think is incurable or not likely to be cured, for saving of your good name. Also you shall not praise yourself nor blame none other. *Item.* You shall also comfort your patient howsoever it be with him; but to his good friends you shall show the truth and give them perfect knowledge of his disease.

Also you should know and understand perfectly your anatomy,

---

[1] *spilt*, destroyed.   [2] *nearhand*, almost.   [3] *growing*, frightening.

which is the gathering and also the dismembering of the limbs of the body, because you should preserve man from the jeopardy of death if it need require that you should cut him in any place without doing to him any scathe and to yourself an everlasting shame and great dishonesty.

THE ANATOMY OF THE BREAST AND HIS PARTS AND MEMBERS[1]

For to do the anatomy well of the limbs that be held, you must cut the breast towards the side and put away the first part for the mediastinum, and then may the inner part be seen; of the which the heart is the first in the midst of the breast, descending a little toward the left side for the place of the liver and to the intent that it should give room or place to the strings.[2] The form or shape of the heart is like a pineapple, for the point of the heart goeth toward the nether limbs or members of the body; and the breadth, of which is the root, goeth upwards.

The substance of the heart is hard, having on every side a ventricle or hollowness and in the midst a pit, as Galen saith, in which is consumed the gross feeding blood that cometh from the liver, and is made pure and is sent by the veins throughout all the parts of the body: first, to the brain; and there it conceiveth another nature and becometh *animalis* or understanding; and to the liver where it becometh natural and feeding; and to the stones or cods for generation; and so forth to all other members or limbs, and maketh them quick or giveth them life.

The heart is an instrument of all powers and might of the body and a full common bond or fastener of the soul. And in it be two orifices or mouths, and through the right orifice runneth a branch of the ascending veins bringing up the blood from the liver and descendeth from thence downward again to *vena* [vein] *arterial* [which] is for to feed the lungs.

Of the left orifice goeth the beating vein named *vena pulsatilis* whereof one part goeth to the lungs, and it is named *vena venalis*, bearing the vapours *capinoso** to the lungs and leading the air in for to cool the heart withal. Upon this orifice be three panicles of skin, opening and closing the passage of the blood. By this orifice be two little ears joined to the heart whereas the air or breath goeth out and in toward the lungs. Also there is a little gristle bone in it for to strengthen the heart with. The heart is covered with a strong panicle named pericardium, whereas the sinews come to and be bound with the lungs, fastened and supporting through the mediastinum.

---

[1] Chapter VI.
[2] *strings*, heartstrings, tendons supposed to brace the heart.

OF WOUNDS SHOT WITH A GUN WHEREAS THE VENOM OF THE POWDER ABIDETH IN[1]

Also, as anybody is shotten with a gun whereas the pellet is taken out of the wound, and in the wound abideth the venom of the powder, be it in the arm or leg, wheresoever it be so, thrust a little rope of hair through the wound [and] about all sides of the wound, and therewith shall you draw out the venom of the powder that is in the wound. And then will there no matter come out, then make a tent of bacon, and strike a little therewith of ear wax; and that shall draw out the venom of the wound and of the arrow, and bring the wound to matter. Then heal the wound with a good salve.

A salve

Take oil of roses two pounds; and turpentine a half ounce; and camphor, in powder, one dram: and the one with the other meddle: and thereof a little warmed and with weak tents, made of linen dipped therein, lay it in the wound, and then pull out the venom. And therewith shall you give him at all times treacle *electum* [choice] one dram, with white wine therewith sodden *castoreum*.* And were you in a broad field whereas you cannot have of the aforesaid salves or dryness, then take goat's milk or cow's milk and wash the wound therewith.

And if any man be shotten with a gun that the pellet be in the body, so must you make the wound wider with cutting or with tents, as far as it is possible, in likewise as I have declared before of the arrow. Then take a gun pellet tong, like as in the sixteenth chapter showeth the picture, therewith take the pellet out of the wound. If it be, also, that you cannot make the wound wider with cutting, then take the iron instrument, called balista, like as it showeth in the fifteenth chapter in the picture, and put that into the wound unto the pellet, and then thrust that instrument with your hand behind, and it will make the wound wider and to take the pellet the better out.

If it be, also, that you cannot find the pellet, you must do as Lord John of Duncanborough did to the King of Hungary; or else do as Hans Ulric of Baden did, which was called to one that was shot with a gun and the pellet was still in his body and nobody could find it. Wherefore the said Hans Ulric commanded that same man bend a cross bow with a girdle gird about his body: and as he began that to do that, what with pressing and straining of himself and so much straining his veins and sinews that he caused the pellet to come of the place unto the skin of his belly. Incontinent, the said Hans cut the skin and took out the pellet without tongs or instrument.

COLOPHON: Printed at London in Southwark by Peter Treveris....1525.

Chapter XVIII.

THOMAS GEMINUS
fl. 1545

A Compendious Rehearsal of all Anatomy
TRANSLATED BY NICHOLAS UDALL

NICHOLAS UDALL'S PREFACE

That which Galen in the sixth book entitled *De Sanitate Tuenda* saith, that he would have men for the diet and preservation of their bodies not to live like brute beasts, nothing regarding what is good or ill for them, but rather diligently to observe and mark what agreeth with them and what not: and what serveth for their health and what is hurtful. The same thing would I wish that all men should do in all other points, also, concerning the state and habit of their body to be known. Which if it so were, some persons, perchance, in a luxation or unknitting of their own limbs or of their children's arms and legs should less marvel at the case and be better able with less cost to help the same.

And not only for luxations and wrenches do I this say, but also for the reducing of the body, withinforth aggrieved, to a better temperature which might the more easily be done if every person, or, at the leastwise, such as were most apt, did know all the members and parts of the body, together with the placing, the natures, the properties, the use, and the operations of the same. For by knowing the office of every part and member, in case there should happen any impediment, they should easily be able to know and to judge where the impediment lay, how it grew, and how the same were to be removed.

And forsomuch as unto this purpose nothing is so effectual as the anatomy of man's body, that is to say, the cutting of every part and parcel severally, I cannot but commend the studious industry and labour of such as, either by description of the parts of man's body and woman's body with their pen or else by the lively setting forth of the same to the eye by apt figures and portraitures, have travailed to show unto all men where every member and limb and other part of our body lieth; where it taketh his beginning; where it endeth; what the nature of it is; and what operation; what virtue; what effect or property is annexed unto it. Neither can I well determine whether of both doth more effectually help toward the knowledge of the premises—he that by his high learning and profound science of natural things doth set it forth in writing, or else he that by plain figures and pictures doth proportion out everything to the eye of the unlearned.

For some have we known which being unlettered have been able to set in again any member that by any violent injury hath been broken or set out of joint: and very few there be which by the description of the learned have been able to espy how to do the same in men's joints or limbs, except such as after long practice and experience have by incision and cutting of dead men's bodies (which we call anatomy) gotten a perfect knowledge of the premises.

And not unto many nor but in few places, hath this knowledge or experience happened (whereas harms are common in all places and to a great number), but unto a very few, chiefly surgeons, which have for their better knowledge been fain to beg dead men's bodies and them to cut and some parts to view and the rest to let alone till another time because of the putrefaction soon coming in matter, so subject to corruption as man's flesh is. If, therefore, any person, through the help partly of books written by cunning men of experience and partly by practice of incision which they have been present at and partly by imitation of other expert artificers in this mystery, hath employed by industrious study and painful labour, not without great costs and charges, to teach every man that is disposed to search and mark it how he may know every bone, joint, vein, artery, sinew, tendon, or ligament of the body, where it lieth and how it standeth in the body, [he] is worthy of immortal thanks not only of surgeons for whose ease and profitable instruction this present work is set forth, but also of all others that may in time of need receive any benefit or commodity thereby.

Accept therefore in good part, gentle reader, this *Treatise of Anatomy* and thankfully take the use thereof, gently interpreting the labours of Thomas Geminus, the workman. And in case any shall by his cunning or experience see where it may be amended or better perfected, he that with his great charge, watch, and travail hath so lively set out this in figure and portraiture will, I doubt not, show himself most willing both to amend the same, his own workmanship, and also to honour and follow the party by whom he shall be admonished how this may be made more perfect.

Thus willing and wishing every one man thankfully to take and interpret another man's good studies and labours, I bid thee, O gentle reader, most heartily well-to-fare. At Windsor the 20th of July, 1552.

> The First Part of this *Treatise of Anatomy*
> wherein is contained a compendious or brief
> rehearsal of all and singular the parts of man's
> body; which shall hereafter be set forth to the eye
> in figures most lively, representing the same with
> their proportions, shape, and fashions, even all
> as by the practice cutting in anatomy, it is found.

A DIVISION OF THE BODY INTO
FOUR PRINCIPAL PARTS[1]

The body of man (in describing whereof we intend, by the grace of
God, to travail) is divided into four principal parts, that is to wit:
the head, the breast, the belly, and the other members, called
altogether in the Latin term, *artus*, in English, 'limbs', which are the
arms, the hands, the legs, and the feet, etc. The head, being called of
many men the uppermost ventricle, doth end where the neck
beginneth. And the head containeth the parts belonging to the soul.
The breast, which they also call the middle belly or ventricle, and
sometimes the upper belly, as in the eight and thirtieth aphorism*
of the seventh book, beginneth at the two canal bones and reacheth
to the midriff and is enclosed on either side with ribs and doth contain
the vital parts of the body. The nethermost belly, in which the natural
parts are contained, doth reach from the midriff to the bone above
the privy members. The fourth part of the division called *artus* is
the legs and hands, etc.

COLOPHON: Imprinted at London by Nicholas Hill, dwelling
in Saint John Street, for Thomas Geminus. 1553.

EUCHARIUS RÖESSLIN
d. 1526

The first treatise on childbirth that was translated into English, The Byrth
of Mankynde *(1540), was intended by its translator, Richard Jonas, to be
a source of information for the general reader as well as for Tudor midwives
and physicians. Little is known of Jonas's life except that he was a 'diligent
and studious clerk', interested in providing an illustrated modern text of
Eucharius Röesslin's* Der Swangern frawen und Hebammen
Roszgarten *(1513) which he believed would improve the crude practices
attending childbirth.*

*Röesslin was the City Physician of Worms, and his book, owing to its
simple style and well-drawn illustrations, the first woodcuts of the kind
ever printed, became popular throughout Europe. Soon after the first
printing in Strasbourg, it was translated into French, Dutch, Czech, and
Latin.*

It was from the Latin version De Partu Hominis *(1532) that Jonas
made his translation. Following Röesslin's plan, he divided the* Byrth

[1] Chapter I.

*into three parts: 1. Pre-natal period; 2. Birth; and 3. Care of the new-born
infant. The frequent quotations from the works of such traditional authorities
as Galen, Avicenna, Albertus Magnus, and Savonarola made the* Byrth
*readily accepted in England. To give his version prestige, Jonas dedicated
it to Queen Katherine Howard, wife of Henry VIII.*

In the second English edition the title was changed to The Byrth of
Mankynde, otherwyse named the womans booke *(1545). It was
'newly set furth' by T. Raynalde who came to be considered the author
rather than translator. However, Jonas's original manuscript, which is
extant, proves that he was the first translator. Twelve editions of the*
Byrth *were printed before 1634; and it was long recognized as the standard
English text in the field of obstetrics.*

The Birth of Mankind

TRANSLATED BY RICHARD JONAS

The Birth of Mankind, newly translated out of Latin into English:
In the which is entreated of all such things the which chance to
women in their labour, and all such infirmities which happen
unto the infants after they be delivered. And, also, at the latter
end, or in the third, or last book, is treated the conception of
mankind, and how many ways it may be letted or furthered:
with divers other fruitful things as doth appear in the table
before the book.

AN ADMONITION TO THE READER

Forasmuch as we have enterprised the interpretation of this present
book, offering and dedicating it unto our most gracious and virtuous
Queen Katherine [Howard], only by it minding and tendering the
utility and wealth of all women as touching the great peril and dangers
which most commonly oppresseth them in their painful labours,
I require all such men, in the name of God, which at any time shall
chance to have this book that they use it godly and only to the profit
of their neighbours, utterly eschewing all ribald and unseemly communication of any things contained in the same, as they will answer
before God, which, as witnesseth Christ, will require a count of idle
words and much more then of all ribald and uncharitable words.
'Everything', as saith Solomon, 'hath his time;[1] and, truly, that is far
out of time, yea, and far from all good honesty, that some use at the
common tables and without any difference before all companies
rudely and lewdly to talk of such things in the which they ought

[1] Eccles. iii. 1.

rather to know much and to say little, but only where it may do good, magnifying the mighty God of nature in all His works, compassionating and pitying our even-Christians, the women, which sustain and endure for the time as great dolour and pain for the birth of mankind and deliverance of the same into the world.

Praise God in all His works.

HOW THE INFANT, NEWLY BORN, MUST BE HANDLED, NOURISHED, AND LOOKED TO[1]

After that the infant is once born, by and by the navel must be cut three fingers breadth from the belly and so knit up: then, as Avicenna writeth, let be strewed on the head of that that remaineth the powder of bole armoniac,* *sanguis draconis** [dragon's blood], sarcocolla,* and myrrh: and common of each like and much beaten to powder, strew on the cut of that piece that remaineth. Then upon that, bind a piece of wool dipped in oil [of] olive that the powder fall not off. Some use first to knit the navel and after to cut it so much as is before rehearsed....

Now to return to our purpose. When that the navel is cut off and the rest knit up, anoint all the child's body with oil of acorns, for that is singularly good to confirm, steadfast, and to defend the body from noisome things which may chance from without, as smoke, cold, and such other things, which if the infant be grieved withal straight after the birth, being yet very tender, it should hurt it greatly.

After this anointing, wash the infant with warm water; and with your finger (the nail being pared) open the child's nostrils and purge them of the filthiness. *Item*. It shall be good to put a little oil into the eyes. And also that the mother, or nurse, handle so the child's sitting place that it may be provoked to purge the belly. And chiefly it must be defended from over much cold or over much heat....

Furthermore when the infant is swaddled and laid in the cradle, the nurse must give all diligence and heed that she bind every part right and in his due place and order, and that with all tenderness and gentle entreating and not crookedly and confusely; the which must be done oftentimes in the day, for it is in this as in young and tender imps, plants, and twigs, the which even as you bow them in their youth, so will they evermore remain unto age. And even so the infant if it be bound and swaddled, the members lying right and straight, then shall it grow straight and upright; if it be crookedly handled, it will grow likewise. And to the ill negligence of many nurses may be imputed the crookedness and deformity of many a

[1] Book I, Chapter x.

man and woman which otherwise might seem well-favoured as any other.

Item. Let the child's eyes be often times wiped and cleansed with a fine and clean linen cloth or with silk: and let the arms of the infant be very straight laid down by the sides that they may grow right. And sometime stroke the belly of the child before the vesica or bladder, to help to ease and provoke the child to the making of water. And when you lay it in the cradle to sleep, set the cradle in such a place that neither the beams of the sun by day nor the moon by night come on the infant, but rather set it in a dark and shadow place, laying also the head ever somewhat higher than the rest of the body.

And, further, let it be washed two or three times in the day and, that anon after sleep, in the winter with hot water [and] in the summer with lukewarm water. Never let it tarry long in the water, but unto such time as the body begins to wax red for heat. But take heed that none of the water come into the infant's ears, for that should greatly hurt his hearing another day.

Then to be short, when it is taken out of the bath, let it be wiped and handled with gentle and soft linen cloth warmed. Then lay it on the lap, the back upward the which with her hands let her tenderly stroke and rub; then lap it up and swaddle it; and when it is swaddled, to put a drop or two of water into the nostrils is very good for the eyesight. And so lay it to rest.

COLOPHON: Printed at London by T. R.....1540.

SIR THOMAS ELYOT[1]

The Castle of Health

THE PROHEME

Galen, the most excellent physician, feared that in writing a compendious doctrine for the curing of sickness,* he should lose all his labour: forasmuch as no man almost did endeavour himself to the finding of truth, but that all men did so much esteem riches, possessions, authority, and pleasures, that they supposed them which were studious in any part of sapience (which is in knowledge of things belonging as well to God as to man) to have no being.

Since this noble writer found that lack in his time, when there

---

[1] For biographical sketch, see pp. 88–90.

flourished in sundry countries a great multitude of men excellent in all kinds of learning, as it yet doth appear by some of their works, why should I be grieved with reproaches wherewith some of my country do recompense me for my labours taken without hope of temporal reward but only for the fervent affection which I have ever borne toward the public weal of my country? 'A worthy matter', saith one. 'Sir Thomas Elyot is become a physician and writeth physic which beseemeth not a knight. He might have been much better occupied.' Truly, if they will call him a physician which is studious about the weal of his country, I witsafe,[1] they so name me; for during my life, I will in that affection always continue.

And why, I pray you, should men have in disdain or small reputation the science of physic which, being well understood, truly experienced, and discreetly ordered, doth conserve health without the which all pleasures be painful; riches, unprofitable; company, annoyance; strength turned to feebleness; beauty to loathsomeness; senses, dispersed; eloquence, interrupted; remembrance, confounded.

The science of physic hath been considered of wise men, not only of the private estate but also of emperors, kings, and other great princes, who for the universal necessity and incomparable utility which they perceived to be in that science of physic, they did not only advance and honour it with special privileges, but also divers; and many of them were therein right studious insomuch as Juba, the King of Mauretania and Lybia, found out the virtuous qualities of the herb called *euphorbium;** Gentius, King of Illyria, found the virtues of gentian; the herb *lysimachia** took his name of King Lysimachus; Mithridates, the great King of Pontus, found first the virtues of scordium,* and also invented the famous medicine against poison, called mithridate; Artemisia, Queen of Caria, found the virtues of mother-wort, which in Latin beareth her name, whereby her noble renown hath longer continued than by the making of the famous monument over her dead husband, called Mausoleum, although it were reckoned among the wonderful works of the world, and yet her name with the said herb still abideth while the said monument, a thousand years passed, was utterly dissolved.

It seemeth that physic in this realm hath been well esteemed since the whole study of Salerno,* at the request of a King of England, was written and set forth [in] a compendious and profitable treatise called *The Governance of Helthe*—in Latin, *Regimen Sanitatis*. And I trust in Almighty God that our sovereign lord, the King's Majesty, who daily prepareth to establish among us true and uncorrupted doctrines, will shortly examine also this part of study in such wise as things apt for medicine, growing in this realm, by conference with most noble authors may be so known, [so] that we shall have less

---

[1] *witsafe*, vouchsafe.

need of things brought out of far countries [since] by the corruption whereof innumerable people have perished without blame to be given to the physicians, saving only that some of them [are] not diligent enough in beholding their drugs or ingredients at all times dispensed and tried.

Besides the said kings, whom I have rehearsed, other honourable personages have written in this excellent doctrine: and not only of the speculative part, but also of the practice thereof, whose works do yet remain unto their glory immortal, as Avicenna, Avenzoar, Rhazes, Cornelius Celsus, Soranus, and, which I should have first named, Machaon and Podalirius, noble dukes in Greece, which came to the siege of Troy and brought with them thirty great ships with men-of-war.

This well considered, I take it for no shame to study that science or to set forth any books of the same, being thereto provoked by the most noble and virtuous example of my noble master, King Henry the VIII, whose health I heartily pray God as long to preserve as God hath constituted man's life to continue. For his Highness hath not disdained to be the chief author and setter-forth of an Introduction into grammar* for the children of his loving subjects; whereby having good masters, they shall most easily and in short time apprehend the understanding and form of speaking of true and eloquent Latin....

But yet one thing much grieveth me, that notwithstanding I have ever honoured and specially favoured the reverend College of Approved Physicians, yet some of them, hearing me spoken of, have said in derision that although I were prettily seen in histories, yet being not learned in physic I have put in my book divers errors in presuming to write of herbs and medicines.

First, as concerning histories: as I have planted them in my works, being well understood they be not so light of importance as they do esteem them, but may more surely cure men's affections than divers physicians do cure maladies. Nor when I wrote first this book, I was not all ignorant in physic. For before that I was twenty years old a worshipful physician [Thomas Linacre], and one of the most renowned at that time in England, perceiving me by nature inclined to knowledge, read unto me the works of Galen: *Of Temperaments*, [and] *Natural Faculties*; the *Introduction* of Joannitius, and with some of the *Aphorisms* of Hippocrates. And afterward by mine own study, I read over in order the more part of the works of Hippocrates, Galen, Oribasius, Paulus Celius, Alexander of Tralles, [Aur. Cornelius] Celsus, Pliny, the one and the other, with Dioscorides. Nor did I omit to read the long *Canons* of Avicenna, the *Commentaries* of Averroes, the *Practises* of Isaac, Haly Abbas, Rhazes, Mesue, and also of the more part of them which were their aggregators and followers. And although I have never been at Montpellier, Padua, nor Salerno, yet have I found something in physic whereby I have taken no little profit concerning mine own health.

Moreover, I wote not why physicians should be angry with me since I wrote and did set forth *The Castle of Health* for their commodity [so] that the uncertain tokens of urines and excrements should not deceive them, but that by the true information of the sick man, by me instructed, they might be the more sure to prepare medicines convenient for the diseases: Also to the intent that men, observing a good order in diet and preventing the great cause of sickness, they should of those maladies the sooner be cured.

But if physicians be angry that I have written physic in English, let them remember that the Greeks wrote in Greek, the Romans in Latin, Avicenna, and the others, in Arabic, which were their own and proper and maternal tongues. And if they had been as much attached with envy and covetousness as some now seem to be, they would have devised some particular language with a strange cipher or form of letters wherein they would have written their science: which language or letters no man should have known that had not professed and practised physic. But those, although they were Paynims and Jews, in this part of charity they far surmounted us Christians [in] that they would not have so necessary a knowledge, as physic is, to be hid from them which would be studious about it.

Finally, God is my Judge, I write neither for glory, reward, nor promotion. Only I desire men to deem well mine intent, since I dare assure them that all that I have written in this book I have gathered of the most principal writers in physic: which, being thoroughly studied and well remembered, shall be profitable, I doubt not, unto the reader and nothing noyous to honest physicians that do measure their study with moderate living and Christian charity.

OF HONEY[1]

Honey, as well in meat as in drink, is of incomparable efficacy; for it not only cleanseth, altereth, and nourisheth, but, also, it long time preserveth uncorrupted which is put into it. Insomuch, as Pliny saith, such is the nature of honey* that it suffereth not the bodies to putrefy. And he affirmeth that he did see an hippo-centaur (which is a beast, half man and half horse) brought in honey to Claudius, the Emperor, out of Egypt to Rome. And he telleth also of one Pollio Romulus who was above a hundred years old [and] of whom Augustus, the Emperor, demanded by what means he lived so long and retained still the vigour or liveliness of body and mind. Pollio answered that he did it inwardly with mead (which is drink made

[1] Book II, Chapter XXII.

with honey and water) [and] outward with oil. Which saying agreeth with the sentence of Democritus, the great philosopher, who being demanded how a man might live long in health, he answered, 'If he wet him within with honey; without with oil.' The same philosopher when he was a hundred years old and nine prolonged his life certain days with the evaporation of honey, as Aristoxenus writeth.*

Of this excellent matter, most wonderfully wrought and gathered by the little bee, as well of the pure dew of heaven as of the most subtle humour of sweet and virtuous herbs and flowers, be made liquors commodious to mankind, as mead, metheglyn, and oximell.

Mead, which is made with one part of honey and four times so much of pure water, and boiled until no scum remain, is much commended of Galen [to be] drunk in summer for preserving of health. The same author always commendeth the using of honey either eaten with fine bread, somewhat leavened or sodden and received as drink. Also mead, perfectly made, cleanses the breast and lungs; causes a man to spit easily and to piss abundantly and purgeth the belly moderately.

Metheglyn (which is most used in Wales), by reason of hot herbs boiled with honey, is hotter than mead and more comforteth a cold stomach if it be perfectly made and is not new or very stale.

Oximell is where to one part of vinegar is put double so much of honey and four times as much of water, and that being boiled unto the third part and clean-skimmed with a feather. It is to be taken where in the stomach is much phlegm or matter undigested so that it be not red choler. Look the use thereof in Alexander of Tralles.

Many other good qualities of honey I omitted to write of until some other occasion shall happen to remember them, particularly where they shall seem profitable.

COLOPHON: *Londini in aedibus Thomae Bertheleti typis impress....1541.*

JOHN CAIUS
1510–1573

John Caius, eminent physician and third founder of Gonville and Caius College, Cambridge, was born in Norwich in 1510, the son of Robert and Alice Caius. After attending the local grammar school, Caius entered Gonville Hall, Cambridge, and in 1533 took a Bachelor of Arts degree. Six years later, he left to study medicine at the University of Padua, where he shared lodgings for almost a year with the brilliant Belgian student

Andreas Vesalius. In 1541 Caius received the degree of Doctor of Medicine and in the same year was appointed to lecture at the university, the first Englishman to receive the honour. His lectures on Plato and Aristotle were delivered in Greek, in which he was especially proficient. Before returning to England in 1544, Caius spent a short time in Pisa, where he wrote several treatises on the medical theories of Hippocrates and Galen, none of which is extant.

The medical profession in London was quick to recognize Caius's ability, and in 1546 he was appointed Reader of the Company of Barbers and Surgeons. Because of the fame of his dissections and lectures on anatomy, he was called 'a second Linacre'. Caius had a great respect for the renowned physician and humanist, and out of his own funds restored Linacre's tomb in St Paul's Cathedral.

Among the honours conferred on Caius was a Fellowship in the College of Physicians in 1547, six years before he was made President of the College, to which office he was re-elected nine times, the last in 1571. During these years Caius built up an extensive medical practice in London, including among his patients members of the royal family, the nobility, and high churchmen.

Caius spent his entire fortune renovating Gonville Hall. He endowed it and wrote new statutes, changing the name to Gonville and Caius College. On 25 March 1558 the college was reopened with solemn High Mass attended by the founder and the new Master, Thomas Bacon. A week later, Cambridge University conferred on Caius the degree of Doctor of Medicine honoris causa. In the following year, for a short time, after Bacon's death Caius became acting-Master of the College.

When Elizabeth I came to the throne, Caius was under constant surveillance because of his Catholic leanings. He was not molested until a few years before his death, when he was charged with being a recusant, and an investigation was ordered by Edwin Sandys, Bishop of London. Caius was found to own a chalice and Catholic vestments which were seized and publicly burned. The incident embittered his last years, and he retired from active life, spending his time writing a history of Cambridge University, left unfinished, and directing the affairs of the College of Physicians. He died in London, 29 July 1573.

According to Caius's own list of his works, they numbered seventy-two, of which fifty-six were translations from Greek and Latin. Of the four works that are extant, only one was written in English, A boke or coun-seill against...sweatyng sicknesse *(1552). It is important as the first English medical work, giving a detailed account of a specific disease. His widely used remedy for the disease was discovered during an epidemic while he laboured untiringly among those who were stricken until he contracted it himself.*

As a young physician, Caius may have assisted Thomas Geminus in preparing his Compendiosa *(1545), the pirated edition of Vesalius's*

Epitome. *The Belgian anatomist is thought most likely to have been accusing his former classmate when he complained of 'a certain Englishman', who aided in 'vitiating' his works.*

A Book against the Sweating Sickness

A Book or Counsel against the Disease commonly called the Sweat or Sweating Sickness.

Made by John Caius, Doctor in Physic.

Very necessary for every person and much requisite to be had in the hands of all sorts for their better instruction, preparation, and defence against the sudden coming and fearful assaulting of the same disease.

DEDICATORY EPISTLE

To the right honourable William Earl of Pembroke, Lord Herbert of Cardiff, Knight of the Honourable Order of the Garter and President of the King's Highness Council in the Marches of Wales, John Caius wisheth health and honour.

In the fearful time of the sweat (Right Honourable) many resorted unto me for counsel, among whom some being my friends and acquaintances, [and] desired me to write unto them some little counsel how to govern themselves therein: saying, also, that I should do a great pleasure to all my friends and countrymen if I would devise at my leisure something which, from time to time, might remain whereto men might in such cases have a recourse and present refuge at all needs, as then they had none.

At whose request, at that time, I wrote divers counsels, so shortly as I could for the present necessity, which they both used and did give abroad to many others; and further appointed in myself to fulfill (for so much as lay in me) the other part of their honest request for the time to come. The which the better to execute and bring to pass, I spared not to go to all those that sent for me, both poor and rich, day and night. And that not only to do them that ease that I could and to instruct them for their recovery, but to note also thoroughly, the cases and circumstances of the disease in divers persons and to understand the nature and causes of the same fully, for so much as might be.

Therefore, as I noted, so I wrote, as leisure then served, and finished one book in English, only for Englishmen not learned; one other, in Latin for men of learning more at large, and generally for the help of them which hereafter should have need, either in this or other countries, that they may learn by our harms. This I had thought to have set forth before Christmas and to have given to your lordship at New Year's tide but that divers other businesses letted me. Nevertheless that which then could not be done, cometh not now out of season, although it be never so simple, so it may do ease hereafter, which, as I trust, this shall.

So for good will I give and dedicate it unto your good lordship, trusting the same will take this with as good a mind as I give it to your honour, which Our Lord preserve and grant long to continue.

At London, the first of April, 1552.

A DESCRIPTION AGAINST THE SWEATING SICKNESS

In the year of Our Lord God, 1485, shortly after the seventh day of August, at which time King Henry the Seventh arrived at Milford in Wales, out of France, and in the first year of his reign, there chanced a disease among the people, lasting the rest of that month and all September, which for the sudden sharpness and unwont[ed] cruelness passed the pestilence. For this commonly giveth three or four, often seven, sometime nine (as that first at Athens which Thucydides describeth [in the *History* of the Peloponnesian War] in his second book), sometime eleven, and sometime fourteen days respectively, to whom it vexeth. But that [disease] immediately killed some in opening their windows; some in playing with children in their street doors; some in one hour, many in two, it destroyed; and, at the longest, to them that merrily dined, it gave a sorrowful supper.

As it found them, so it took them: some in sleep, some in wake, some in mirth, some in care, some fasting and some full, some busy and some idle; and in one house, sometime three, sometime five, sometime seven, sometime eight, sometime more, sometime all; of the which if the half in every town escaped, it was thought great favour. How or with what manner it took them, with what grief and accidents it held them, hereafter then I will declare when I shall come to show the signs thereof. . . .

This disease is not a sweat only (as it is thought and called) but a fever, as I said, in the spirits by putrefaction venomous with a fight, travail, and labour of nature against the infection received in the spirits; whereupon by chance followeth a sweat or issueth a humour compelled by nature, as also chanceth in other sicknesses which consist in humours when they be in their state* and at the worst in certain days judicial as well by vomits, bleedings, and fluxes, as by sweats.

That this is true, the self sweats do show. For as in utter businesses,[1] bodies that sore do labour, by travail of the same are forced to sweat, so in inner diseases the bodies travailed and laboured by them are moved to the like. In which labours if nature be strong and able to thrust out the poison by sweat (not otherwise letted), the person escapeth; if not, by it [he] dieth.

That it is a fever, thus I have partly declared and more will straight by the notes of the disease under one showing; also by the same notes, signs, and short tarriance of the same, that it consisteth in the spirits: first, by the pain in the back or shoulder, pain in the extreme parts, as arm, leg, [and] with a flushing or wind, as it seemeth to certain of the patients, flying in the same; secondly, by the grief in the liver and the nigh stomach; thirdly, by the pain in the head and madness[2] of the same; fourthly, by the passion[3] of the heart. For the flushing or wind, coming in the utter and extreme parts is nothing else but the spirits of those same gathered together at the first entering of the evil air against the infection thereof, and flying the same from place to place for their own safeguard.

But, at the last, infected, they [spirits] make a grief where they be forced, which commonly is the arm or leg (the furthest parts of their refuge) [and] the back or shoulder; trying there first a brunt, as good soldiers, before they will let their enemy come further into their dominion. The other griefs be, therefore, in the other parts, aforesaid, and sorer because the spirits be there most plenteous as in their fountains[4] whither always the infection desireth to go.

For from the liver, the nigh stomach, brain, and heart come all the three sorts and kinds of spirits,* the governors of our bodies, as first sprung there, but from the heart, [come] the livish[5] spirits, in putrefying whereof by the evil air in bodies fit for it, the heart is oppressed. Whereupon also followeth a marvellous heaviness (the fifth token of this disease) and a desire to sleep, never contented; the senses in all parts being, as they were, bound or closed up; [and] the parts, therefore, left heavy, unlivish, and dull.

Last, followeth the short abiding—a certain token of the disease to be in the spirits, as well may be proved by the *ephemera* that Galen writeth of, which because it consisteth in the spirits, lasteth but one natural day. For as fire in hardes[6] [*sic*] or straw is soon in flame and soon out, even so heat in the spirits, either by simple distemperature or by infection and putrefaction therein conceived, is soon in flame and soon out—and sooner for the vehemency or greatness of the same which without lingering consumeth soon the light matter, contrary to all other diseases resting in humours (wherein a

---

[1] *utter businesses*, outward illnesses.   [2] *madness*, delirium.
[3] *passion*, palpitation.   [4] *fountains*, sources.
[5] *livish*, living.   [6] *hardes*, boards (?).

fire once kindled is not so soon put out, no more than is the same in moist wood or fat sea coals) as well by the particular example of the pestilence (of all others most like unto this) may be declared, which by that it standeth in evil humours, tarrieth, as I said, sometimes from four, seven, nine and eleven until fourteen days, differently from this, by reason thereof, albeit by infection most like to this same.

COLOPHON: Imprinted at London by Richard Grafton, printer to the King's Majesty.... 1552.

PART III

SERMONS AND RELIGIOUS TREATISES

SERMONS AND RELIGIOUS TREATISES

INTRODUCTION BY W. E. CAMPBELL

MEDIEVAL TRADITIONS IN TUDOR SERMONS

In Tudor England religious conviction was the determining power not only of ecclesiastical but also of political events. This fact partially explains why sermons and religious treatises form the largest body of works printed in England before 1550.

Concerning the sermon literature, it must be noted that no simple homilies of the time are extant. This is in no small measure directly related to the neglect of preaching that began in the fifteenth century and continued well into the next. But whatever sermons the clergy may have preached were lost during Cromwell's systematic destruction of the records and papers of country parishes.

Before discussing the sermons that have survived—those preached on state occasions and those dealing with controversial subjects of a social or religious nature—it is well to glance at the late medieval English sermons which undoubtedly influenced alike the parish priest and the noted preacher of Tudor times. Fortunately these sermons were gathered into great manuscript collections when preaching had been popularized by the mendicant orders, and so escaped the fury of the Reformation.

Thumbing through the *Summa Praedicantium*, compiled by John Bromyard, Dominican prior and Chancellor of Cambridge University in 1360, one finds an inexhaustible collection of sermons, for the most part denouncing the low morals of both clergy and laity. Though Bromyard's satire is frequently vicious, he was deeply interested in the sanctification of the individual in every walk of life. Women bore the brunt of his scolding. Their vanity and love for fine clothes he likened to the 'devil's pack-horses' garlanded and ready for the market place; or again, clothes are 'masks':

> For two kinds of men use masks, to wit, those who play and those who rob. For players in the play which is commonly called a Miracle use masks beneath which the persons of the actors are concealed. Thus do the demons whose game is to destroy souls and lure them by sin: in which game they make use of masks, that is, the fashionably attired and those who dance, whose feet run to evil.

It is to be remembered that though Bromyard was anti-Wycliffe and strenuously opposed the Reformer's heretical views on papal authority and the Mass, he did not hesitate to criticize the clergy in extremely harsh terms. He might even seem to have had a single theme in his homilies—the complaint of the men of Jericho to Eleseus: '"Behold the situation of this city is very good; but the waters are bad", that is the clergy by whom others ought to be cleansed.' And this theme, which threads its way through the works of his contemporaries, Chaucer and Langland, who no doubt heard him preach, continued until it was caught up by the saintly John Fisher, Bishop of Rochester and John Colet, Dean of St Paul's.

Bromyard's satire in his Latin collection is only slightly less severe than that found in two English compilations, *Liber festialis* (1403) written by John Myrc, Prior of the Augustine Canons of Shropshire, and *Dives and the Pauper*, a later work wrongly attributed to the Carmelite, Henry Parker. Myrc may well have impressed the early Tudor preacher with the value of a proverb in pointing up the moral in a sermon. 'A maid should be seen but not heard', was 'an olde Englysche sawe', which he used to advantage in a homily on modest manners in women.

THE FIRST TUDOR PREACHERS

At the beginning of the sixteenth century the names of two scholars, John Alcock and William de Meltham, or Melton, are associated with treatises on preaching. Alcock, Bishop of Ely and founder of Jesus College, Cambridge, is the author of *Gallicantus ad praedicatores* [1498], a directive to the priests of his diocese, stressing the importance of the weekly sermon too frequently omitted. Equally earnest is Meltham's *Sermones hortatorii cancellari Eboracensis hiis qui ad sacros ordines petunt promoveri*. Though written about 1498, the *Sermones* were not printed until 1510, and carried John Colet's expressed declaration of approval. Meltham, once the Master of Michaelhouse, a small Cambridge college, and a tutor there of John Fisher, wrote as chancellor of York Minster, intending his instructions for aspirants to the priesthood. Candidates for holy orders, he declares, should have a thorough education and not just a 'fair knowledge of letters'. Nor will a smattering of Latin grammar suffice. Since a man's entry into the ministry should be for the whole motive of serving God, Meltham exhorts him 'after daily offering of Mass and Hours' to find 'delight and joy in constant study of Holy Scripture and the works of the early Church Fathers, the sacred reservoirs from which he should draw material for his sermons'. He will then be more original in the presentation of his ideas and depend less on the *exempla* and stock phrases of the books of sermons. As with Alcock and Meltham, reform of the clergy was one of the great labours of Colet and Fisher, as will be seen later in their sermons.

A practical way to improve and encourage preaching as a regular part of the Sunday services was begun by the indefatigable preacher, John Fisher, Bishop of Rochester. As Chancellor of Cambridge University, he persuaded the mother of Henry VII, the scholarly Lady Margaret Beaufort, to establish a preachership at the university in 1504. The recipient was required to preach six times a year, once at Paul's Cross and the other times in parish churches scattered throughout Fisher's diocese. But the Bishop went even further in his reforms. In 1504 he received permission from Pope Alexander VI to appoint twelve Doctors of Divinity, whose task was to travel through the countryside, preaching before gatherings of the clergy and at Sunday services in country parishes.

A few years later, when Fisher had persuaded Erasmus to teach Greek at Queens' College, Cambridge, he began encouraging him to write some directives on preaching which were, however, long delayed—*Ecclesiastes, sive concionator evangelicus* (1535) was not finished until a year before Erasmus's death. Because of the delay, the work is more mellow in tone than it might have been following hard on the *Enchiridion* and *Praise of Folly*. Indeed, Fisher's request seems a friendly nudge that would force the Dutch scholar into constructive criticism. And Mr Mullinger, the historian of Cambridge University, writes, 'In their views with respect to the necessity for a thorough reform in the prevailing style of preaching, they were so far at unison that Fisher, as we have already noted, could think of no one better qualified than Erasmus to prepare a manual of the preacher's art.'

A spirit of gentleness pervades Fisher's sermons, even those wherein he vehemently denounces heresy. This same virtuous quality courses through Erasmus's two sermons, *On the mercy of God* and *On the Child Jesus*, and recurs in *Ecclesiastes*. Gentleness and kindly persuasion becomes a preacher, he writes in his treatise on preaching, for it is in accord with the 'gentleness of the Gospel that the preacher should advise rather than reproach'. And again, the preacher's attitude should be 'I, a sinner admonish you who are sinners. Together we have erred; together we will mend our lives.'

Fisher's influence is surely evident in Erasmus's belated respect for the priesthood. To Fisher, sanctification of the laity depended on the clergy. 'All the fear of God, also the contempt of God', he frequently declared, 'come and is grounded in the clergy.' Even though there were good and bad among its members, he declared it to be a sacred calling, a point which Erasmus dwells on at length in *On the mercy of God* and states even more forcefully in *Ecclesiastes*. In the latter work he asks why so few strive 'for the office of preacher than which is nothing more pleasing to Christ'.

It would be wrong to represent Fisher as encouraging gentleness in the preacher at the expense of straightforwardness. When the Lutheran heresy began to creep into England, Fisher was quick to warn the prelates in England and Rome to reform the manners of their court 'and drive from it ambition, avarice, and luxury'. In no other way, he declared in *Lutheranae assertionis confutatio*, 'will they impose silence on revilers like you [Luther]'.

FAMOUS ENGLISH PULPITS AND NOTABLE SERMONS

Unfortunately the sermons delivered by Fisher's young Doctors of Divinity have not survived to show the fruits of his holy aims. Perhaps some idea of them can be had from his own sermons and those which Alcock and Colet preached on special occasions. The settings for these sermons were the cathedrals, monastery churches, university chapels, and London's famous outdoor pulpit, Paul's Cross. The opening of Parliament was frequently the occasion for an address that amounted to a sermon since it was delivered by the Lord Chancellor, who was generally a member of the hierarchy.

In the monastery church at Westminster Abbey, Fisher preached at the funeral services for Henry VII in 1509, and shortly afterwards for Lady Margaret Beaufort. In these eulogies, in which he was obliged and indeed anxious to commend his royal patrons, the young bishop was moderate in his compliments. The king had faults, but withal he was a man of 'perfect faith'. Of Lady Margaret he asked: 'What is it that this gentlewoman would not believe—she that ordained two continual readers in both the universities to teach the holy divinity of Jesus: she that ordained preachers perpetual to publish the doctrine and faith of Christ Jesu: she that builded a college royal to honour the name of Christ Jesu, and left to her executors another to be builded to maintain His faith and doctrine?'

But in no sense of the word could Fisher envisage the Tudors as rulers by divine right. In this stand, he was concurring with other eminent churchmen, John Alcock, John Morton, and William Warham, who, like himself, were close friends and advisers of the old king.

The greatest pulpit in London was that of St Paul's Cathedral where John Colet presided as Dean. How well he preached has been told by Erasmus in his sketch of Colet's life:

And now as Dean, feeling himself called to a great and serious work rather than to an empty honour, Colet restored the decayed discipline of the Cathedral body and began to preach himself at every great feast in his own pulpit—and that not merely on isolated texts, but he would begin some connected subject and go through with it to the end in succeeding sermons as, for instance, St Matthew's Gospel or the Creed or the Lord's Prayer. His preaching became very popular, attracting as listeners most of the prominent people both of the city and of the court.

During his lectures at Oxford in 1497 on the Epistles of St Paul, Colet had had a great deal to say on the high aims and ideals of the priesthood. By nature an ascetic, he had returned from Italy burning with the same zeal for reform that was the dominant theme of the sermons of Savonarola. And in writing a commentary on the *Ecclesiastical Hierarchy* by Dionysius, the so-called Areopagite, Colet took the opportunity to enlarge on his plea for a holy and clean priesthood, one 'scoured and polished inwardly' so that 'not a trace of sin may remain to prevent God from walking in the temple of our mind'.

Reform of the clergy was one of the great labours of Colet's life and the theme of his only extant sermon, which he preached at the Convocation of the clergy in St Paul's Cathedral in 1511. But it would not be fair to draw Colet as a radical fault-finder. As Mr Seebohm has well said, the impiety that Colet assailed in the clergy shows only his jealousy for 'the purity of the order to which he belonged'.

Unfortunately, we have only summaries of two other great sermons delivered by the Dean of St Paul's. One of them is the Good Friday sermon given in the Royal Chapel in 1513, advising the king against the futility and ungodliness of his war with France. Only 'wicked men' go to war; and out of hatred and ambition, 'kill one another'. The king would bring more glory on himself by imitating Christ than Caesar. Two years later Colet preached in Westminster Abbey at the investiture of Thomas Wolsey as Cardinal, warning him to minister to rich and poor alike. He reminded Wolsey that a Cardinal is clothed in red, a colour signifying nobility —not that found in haughty churchmen, but in martyrs.

There was scarcely a more important political event in England in 1518 than the betrothal of the young Princess Mary to the Dauphin Francis, son of Francis I, solemnized in the Royal Chapel at Greenwich. Wishful thinkers in both nations believed that the union heralded peace, instead of the long-threatened war with France. Cardinal Wolsey presided, and the able speaker Cuthbert Tunstall, Bishop of London, gave a Latin sermon *In laudem matrimonii*. It opens with a paean of praise for the universal rejoicings that marriage brings to all classes of men, rich and poor alike. Tunstall elaborated on the mystical quality and indissolubility of the marriage bond, placing himself on record as opposing divorce. But twenty years later he changed his mind when the king's divorce from Katherine of Aragon forced him to take a definite stand. And Chapuys, the Spanish Ambassador, attempting to account for the change, called Tunstall

> one of the most learned, prudent, and honest prelates in the whole kingdom, and has hitherto upheld the queen's cause by his word as well as his writings; but nowadays, not wishing to become a martyr and lose such ecclesiastical benefice as his, bringing him 15,000 ducats annually, he has been obliged to swear like the rest though with, it is said, certain reserves and restrictions.

It would seem, as his biographer, Charles Sturge, has said, that Tunstall, unlike his friends Fisher and More, was 'not quite the stuff of which martyrs are made'.

THE TWO JURISDICTIONS

The social problems which occasioned sermons in Tudor times generally concerned the question of the two jurisdictions, ecclesiastical and civil, handed down from the tragic days of St Thomas à Becket. In the succeeding centuries, there were clashes between these two authorities over the right of sanctuary for clerical malefactors. Abuses had crept into the general procedure, by which the civil authorities handed over any cleric accused of crime to his bishop to be tried in an ecclesiastical court. An attempt to solve the problem was made in 1490 by Prior Henry Selling of Canterbury, legate of Henry VII to Pope Innocent VIII, who issued a bull agreeing to certain changes.

One of the most important sermons dealing with the subject was preached in 1498 by Bishop Alcock on the text, 'He that hath ears to hear, let him hear.' Verily a legal brief, as it is so well documented with passages from Scripture, the early Church Fathers, and canon law, Alcock's sermon treats the subject fairly, recognizing that reforms were needed in the laws governing 'sanctuary' rights. But he is vehement in denying the absolute right of a 'temperall Iuge', to have 'ony jurisdiccon in a spirituall person'. And worried lest history repeat itself, he declared that it can be presumed 'brethren, that yf saynt Thomas of Canterbury wer now lyuyng, they whych directly now doo agaynst the lybertees of the chirche wolde put hym to dethe agayne'.

Henry VIII, thinking to settle the question, gave his ultimatum to Archbishop Warham after a sermon favouring the Church's stand preached by the Abbot of Winchombe, Richard Kidderminster, in 1514, and it never essentially changed:

We are by the sufferance of God, King of England; and the Kings of England in times past never had any superior but God. Know therefore that we will maintain the rights of the Crown in this matter like our progenitors; and as to your decrees, we are satisfied that you as the spirituality act expressly against the words of several of them, as has been well shown you by some of our spiritual council. You interpret your decrees at your pleasure; but as for me, I will never consent to your desires any more than my progenitors have done.

LUTHER AND THE ENGLISH REFORMERS

After Luther published his theses in Wittenberg in 1517, his doctrines gradually became widespread in England, and sermons refuting them increased, though comparatively few are extant. In spite of a strict censorship ordered by the King of all books and pamphlets, regardless of where they were printed, a quantity of Lutheran works and numerous copies of Tyndale's New Testament [1526] were smuggled into the country, many of them to be burned at Paul's Cross.

Luther's doctrines were slower coming from the pulpit than from the press, and for obvious reasons. The severe penalty of being burnt at the stake did not, however, deter some rugged preachers, particularly those at the universities. Fisher had a few teaching at Cambridge. Prominent among them were Hugh Latimer, Thomas Cranmer, Thomas Bilney, and Robert Barnes. The first strong echoes of the Lutheran heresy had come in 1525, when Barnes preached the Christmas Eve sermon in St Edward's Church at Cambridge. He denounced the celebration of Holy Days, veneration of statues, and devotion to the Virgin Mary.

Bishop Fisher and Stephen Gardiner, Wolsey's young secretary and one of Cambridge's most brilliant students of canon law, interceded with the cardinal for Barnes; and for the sake of the university he promised 'to be good to him'. On 11 February 1526, when Barnes recanted and carried his faggot to Paul's Cross, Bishop Fisher preached the sermon which is known as his *Quinquagesima Sunday Sermon*, 'concernyng certayne heretickes'. Considered the ablest theologian in the realm, Fisher's sermon was a veritable treatise on Papal Supremacy, and was so well liked by the king that he ordered his secretary Richard Pace to translate it into Latin.

Another 'burning of the books' took place at Paul's Cross in the following November, after Archbishop Warham had warned his bishops and clergy that 'the holy Gospel of God' was endangered 'by intermingling therewith of heretical glosses'. Bishop Tunstall preached the sermon, and it was probably the last great sermon for the Church's cause. Though no copy is extant, the tenor of it is conveyed in the *Monition against Tyndale's New Testament* (1526), issued that same day to his archdeacons, warning them against the 'naughtelie translated' New Testament:

> Many children of iniquity, maintainers of Luther's sect, blinded through extreme wickedness, wandering from the way of truth and the Catholic faith, have craftily translated the New Testament into our English tongue, intermeddling therewith many heretical articles and erroneous opinions, seducing the common people; attempting by their wicked and perverse interpretations to profane the majesty of Scripture which hitherto hath remained undefiled, and craftily to abuse the most Holy Word of God and the true sense of the same. Of this translation there are many books printed, some with glosses and some without, containing in the English tongue that pestiferous and pernicious poison dispersed in our diocese of London.

But, regardless of pulpit oratory, Tyndale's New Testament and Lutheran doctrines became a steadily greater disturbing influence in political as well as religious circles. While the Reformers were denied the pulpit, they hammered away in pamphlets, printed on the Continent, that transubstantiation, justification by both faith and good works, and free will were fables foisted upon the people by the medieval church, and were not the true teachings of Christ and his apostles.

The situation became intolerable for the Church, and it forced the English hierarchy to take a definite stand. Bishop Tunstall, encouraged by Archbishop Warham and Bishop Fisher and with the full approval of the king, placed the entire burden of rebuttal for the Catholic side on Sir Thomas More. His duty, Tunstall declared, 'was to make plain to simple and ignorant men the crafty malice of the heretics'.

For the time being, popular interest shifted from sermons to the printed word and ushered in the first great English vernacular controversy. It was carried on by men—More and Tyndale—of pre-eminent ability representing two groups: those who wished to remain Catholic in the pre-Reformation sense of the word, and those who would alter the old meaning of Catholic by doctrinal changes, in fact turn 'Catholic' into 'Protestant'.

THE KING AND THE CHURCH

An immense amount of scholarship has gone into the study of the English Reformation and its relation to Henry VIII. After the early years of his reign, he stood Janus-like supporting the Church and

the new doctrines. He let the Smithfield fires claim those found
guilty of spreading Lutheran doctrines; while at the same time he
permitted Hugh Latimer and Robert Barnes to preach openly against
Papal Supremacy on the pretext that they would mend their ways.

While neither of these preachers was a noted theologian, each had
a gift of oratory that the king found useful. Few preachers had
Latimer's ability to popularize his sermons with devices such as he
made use of in the *Sermon on the Card*, preached at Cambridge in
1528. He gave an elaborate exposition of the Ten Commandments,
using a card game called 'triumph' in which he made each card
symbolize a vice or virtue. But the future Bishop of Worcester
was to do his greatest work in the pulpit six years later.

In the meantime, preaching became more hazardous as the king's
divorce proceedings reached a climax in 1530. A preacher might be
equally guilty of heresy for preaching Papal Supremacy as for denying
the doctrine of transubstantiation. But with the 'Submission of the
Clergy' in 1532 to Henry's claim to be supreme head of the Church,
there came a change.

This is not the place to consider adequately the gradual rearing of
the national Church. It suffices to say that on 15 January 1535, the
Council proclaimed Henry VIII 'on earth Supreme Head of the
Church of England', and in six months he issued a proclamation to
the clergy, commanding on the pain of treason each bishop in his
'own proper person' to preach the doctrine of Royal Supremacy on
Sundays and solemn feast days. And, furthermore, he was so ordered
to instruct the clergy and schoolmasters in his diocese. In accordance
with the royal proclamation a sermon was delivered by John
Stokesly, Bishop of London, from the pulpit in St Paul's Cathedral.
It was devoted entirely to decrying the king's marriage to Katherine
of Aragon and denied Papal Supremacy. He condemned 'those
who favoured—even those who suffered death in its defence'. The
reference was most certainly to the Carthusian priors and Bishop
Fisher, who had suffered martyrdom only two weeks before, and
also to More, whose head two days previous had been 'pricked
upon a pole', and like the others was still to be seen 'high upon
London Bridge'.

To direct his preaching campaign, the king used a group of
young bishops—Thomas Cranmer, Stephen Gardiner, John Hilsey,
Provincial of the Black Friars, and Hugh Latimer, each of whom
replaced the late conservatives, Warham (Canterbury), Fox
(Winchester), Fisher (Rochester), and the Italian Bishop Girolamo
Ghinucci (Worcester). Of the old order only Cuthbert Tunstall,
Bishop of Durham, remained. But the king realized that no matter
how ardent the preacher might be, sermons would not validate the
doctrine of Royal Supremacy. The validity of the king's title of

'Supreme Head of the English Church' had yet to be proved. The task fell to the theologians Bishop Stephen Gardiner and Bishop Richard Sampson. They found support in the king's young lawyers Thomas Starkey and Richard Morrison, who, together with Thomas Cromwell, had discovered the most tenable grounds for the legitimacy of the king's title in the fourteenth-century treatise by Marsilius of Padua, *Defensor pacis*. Cromwell had subsidized the first English version made by William Marshall in 1535. Herein they found a modified doctrine of the divine right of kings. Working from the premiss, 'governors are ordained of God', recently declared by Tyndale, both Gardiner and Sampson wrote treatises that called on the Bible, the Greek and Latin classics, the Justinian Code, and the works of St Augustine and St Thomas Aquinas to witness the right of the king's claim.

Gardiner's *De vera obedientia* (1525), written in Latin so that the theologians of the Continent could read it, supported Royal Supremacy on the grounds that

> To obey truly is to obey truth. God is truth. Therefore true obedience is obedience to God and to those whom God appoints to represent him. . . . The Royal Supremacy is no new thing. The Kings of Israel exercised it; so did the Roman Emperors; so did the ancient Kings of England. To call the King, 'Supreme Head in earth of the Church of England', is merely expressing an existing right in plain words.

The book created a great stir in England, and a copy of it was sent to Reginald Pole, the king's scholarly kinsman, self-exiled in Italy. With it went a copy of Richard Sampson's *Oratio qua docet Anglos regiae dignitati ut obediant*, likewise a work intended to 'teach' the English people obedience to the king in spiritual as well as temporal matters. Both works, it was hoped, would induce Pole to support Royal Supremacy, but they only touched off a controversy that, had it been carried on in English, might have rivalled that of More and Tyndale. From the outset the controversy had in it the elements of tragedy: to Henry VIII, Pole was a traitor since, like Thomas à Becket, he had fled the kingdom; to Pole, Henry VIII was a king to whom as a citizen of the realm he owed loyalty, but not as a usurper of power.

Pole answered Gardiner and Sampson in *Pro ecclesiasticae unitatis defensione*, written as a letter to the king, whose role as a monarch he carefully defined:

> What is a king? A king exists for the sake of his people; he is an outcome from Nature in labour; an institution for the defence of material and temporal interests. But inasmuch as there are

interests beyond the temporal, so there is jurisdiction beyond the king's. The glory of a king is the welfare of his people; and if he knew himself and knew his office, he would lay his crown and kingdom at the feet of the priesthood as in a haven and quiet.... [In society Pole recognized] three grades: the people; the priesthood, head and husband of the people; and the king, who is the child, the creature, and minister of the other two.

The *Pro ecclesiasticae* angered Henry VIII more perhaps than the Pope's bull of excommunication which followed it. Left now to his own resources, the king set himself to defining doctrinal truths, and with the advice of the conservatives Gardiner and Tunstall, who leaned to many of the old doctrines, particularly transubstantiation and the Mass, several documents were compiled under the king's direction. The Ten Articles, or the *Articles to stablish Christian quietness*, were issued in 1536, and three years later were replaced by the Six Articles. Both documents were so close to the old religion that the Reformers said they made the king seem 'as it were a pope'.

Even more scrupulously orthodox, though it banned images, shrines, and many of the old ceremonies, was *The King's Book* or *A necessary doctrine and erudition for any Christen man, sette forth by the King's Majesty*. Henry VIII wrote the preface, and the *Book* was approved in 1543 by Parliament, which decreed at the same time that dissenters who preached or spoke against it were to be burnt at the stake or imprisoned for life.

EDWARDIAN POLICIES AND CRANMER

As mentioned in the beginning of this introduction, the turn of political events in those days depended greatly on religious conviction. In the strength of these convictions men were what they were, and did what they did. This was strikingly shown in the rise and fall of those ecclesiastics and laymen who fought for preference at the court of the young King Edward VI. In an effort to bring peace and order to the English Church, Archbishop Cranmer, hoping to clarify controversies over dogma, proposed to publish a book of homilies consisting of twelve sermons. One of the sermons was to be preached each Sunday in every church in the realm.

As Cranmer expected, the chief opposition came from Bishop Gardiner, who insisted that the sermons were not in accord with the teachings of Scripture, the early Church Fathers, or the established standards of the English Church. Cranmer believed the average person was interested in theology. To Gardiner, the 'rude' cared little for doctrinal debates. They like, he said, a good sermon, but they never could repeat what they heard. Cranmer believed a book of homilies would be comparable to the long-lived *Festialis* and

Legenda aurea. Admitting he had never read the *Festialis*, Gardiner called books of this sort 'foolish lying tales', and wished that Christ's religion could be rid of them.

The Bishop of Winchester lost the controversy, and the *Book of homilies* appeared in 1547, together with an English translation of Erasmus's *Paraphrase of the New Testament*, considerably altered. As Gardiner feared, the former revealed that every tie with the old religion as established by Henry VIII had vanished. As for the *New Testament*, issued for the instruction of the clergy, Gardiner called it an equal 'abomination' written when Erasmus's 'pen was wanton', and made worse by the 'arrogant ignorance of the translator'. His obstinate views brought him a short term in the Fleet.

During Edward's reign, Gardiner found himself in and out of prison because of his sermons, particularly on the doctrine of transubstantiation, or as he put it, 'the very presence of Christ's most precious body and blood in the Sacrament'. For him it was the centre of Christian worship. Well he knew it had been championed by his late majesty in the Six Articles and *The King's Book*. He knew well that Henry VIII had silenced Latimer and finally imprisoned him for preaching against the Mass, and had scolded the heretical Barnes, who out of deference to the king offered to yield to him as head of the Church. Gardiner relates the incident in a *Declaration* written in 1546 to refute the heretical views of George Joye:

'I am', quoth his Majesty, 'a mortal man.' And therewith rising and turning to the Sacrament and putting off his bonnet said, 'Yonder is the Master of us all, Author of truth: yield in truth to Him, and I shall', saith the King's Majesty, 'defend the truth. And otherwise, Barnes', quoth the King, 'yield not to me.'

Gardiner's persistent refusal to use the *Homilies* brought about one of the most colourful sermons of the time. He was released from prison on condition that he would abide by the king's injunction concerning the *Homilies*. But Gardiner's preaching was not satisfactory, and the Council demanded that he preach before the king, forbidding him to mention the Mass. In replying to the Protector Somerset, he wrote, 'I will not forbear to utter my faith and true belief therein [the Eucharist] which I think necessary for the King's Majesty to know; and therefore if I wist to be hanged when I come down, I would speak it.'

His sermon was delivered on St Peter's Day (29 June) 1548 in the King's garden at Whitehall in order to accommodate a large gathering. Gardiner chose for his text a verse from the gospel of the feast (Matt. xvi. 13–19), 'Thou art the Christ.' No copy of the sermon is extant. When Somerset asked for one beforehand, Gardiner claimed that he never wrote his sermons. From the notes taken down by

Nicholas Udall, whom the Bishop remembered in his will as 'my Schoolmaster' in the Winchester School, Gardiner after giving whole-hearted support to Royal Supremacy discussed the Mass and the Eucharist at great length, declaring his firm belief in both according to the old religion.

For his 'wilful disobedience', Gardiner remained in the Tower in almost solitary confinement until he was released by Mary I in 1553. During this time the Continental Calvinists whom Cranmer placed in Oxford and Cambridge began a controversy over transub-stantiation and Gardiner opposed them, writing four books in answer to the works of John Hooper and Cranmer and the Calvinists, Peter Martyr and Oecolampadius.

It was the second controversy between Cranmer and Gardiner. As soon as a copy of the Archbishop's *A defence of the true and catholike doctrine of the Sacrament* (1550) came into Gardiner's hands in the Tower, he set about refuting it in *An Explication and assertion of the true catholique fayth, touchyng the moost blessed sacrament of the aulter with confutacion of a booke written agaynst the same* [1551]. The following year he read the entire treatise at the thirteenth session of his trial before the King's Commissioners at Lambeth.

There can be little doubt that the controversy tempered the views of those who compiled the first Book of Common Prayer (1549). Cranmer was the principal author, and yet Gardiner could accept the Communion service. 'The holy mystery of the Sacrament', he wrote, 'is well termed and not distant from the Catholic faith in my judgment.'

When the Act of Uniformity, passed in 1549, seemed to have brought peace, social ills began to trouble the government. People complained that the new religion had not brought prosperity. There was rebellion in various parts of the realm and even bloodshed. To cope with the situation, Archbishop Cranmer began a preaching campaign, leaning for support on his staunch friends, Hugh Latimer, Nicholas Ridley, Miles Coverdale, Robert Crowley, and Thomas Becon. Their sermons had a single theme which Latimer had earlier voiced in his famous 'Sermon of the Plough' (1548), when he denounced the greed of the wealthy and the corruption in the courts. Indeed, these were crimes as great as any other before God.

To disobey the king was an equally heinous offence and was used by Thomas Becon in his dialogue, *The iewel of ioye* [1553] when the preacher Philemon declares, 'How grevously thei haue alwayes ben punished that were sedicious and walked without any godly feare towarde the civile magistrates, the historyes of Dathan and Abiron, of Zambry and Haasa, of Gagathan and Thares shewe magnificently.' And so a preacher could picture rebellion even against an evil ruler as crime. Only Crowley paused in his tirade against rebels to offer reward to those who would be loyal to the king. They would, he promised, be protected by God because 'the heart of a Kinge is in God's hand, and as he turneth rivers of water so turneth he it'.

THE MARIAN REUNION

During the reign of Mary I the preacher's role was more difficult than under any of her predecessors. In her first manifesto she gave them the trying task of leading rather than forcing men's consciences back to a belief in the old religion to which she herself belonged. Meanwhile it was her hope, she said, that her subjects would live together 'in quiet sort and Christian charity' and avoid the 'new-found devilish terms of papist and heretic'.

Her task for the preachers was a sizeable one, and at a time when her accession to the throne had been hindered by political intrigue born of treason and heresy. Repercussions were felt in the strife-weary religious groups throughout the nation. But impractical as the queen was in many of her dealings, it is to her credit that her first impulse was for peace, and at a time when dissension in the realm could easily have kindled a civil conflict.

To understand the young queen's determined efforts to restore the old religion at such desperate sacrifice of human life that accompanied it, it is well to recall the sketch of her written by the historian Gairdner:

The horrid epithet 'bloody' bestowed so unscrupulously alike on her and on Bonner and Gardiner and the bishops generally had at least a plausible justification in her case from the severities to which she gave her sanction; though it was really not just even to her. The spectacle of those cruel proceedings in public and the enduring recollection of them afterwards, blotted out from the public mind what even at first was but imperfectly known—the painful trials which she herself had so long endured at the hands of lawless persecutors who had deranged the whole system of Church government, and as queen she endeavoured to suppress them by means which, if severe, were strictly legal.

The word 'legal' had brought the most trouble to Mary's royal forbears in solving the realm's ecclesiastical problems. And she was confronted with a formidable body of doctrines, passed on by Parliament, which constituted the English Church. It was to the Reformers, who enacted these laws, as well as to the 'old' Catholics, now returned to power, that the queen's learned preachers must address their sermons, hoping to win them back and forge an amalgam of faith such as the nation had known in Bede's and Alfred's day.

One of these preachers was Dr Gilbert Bourne, a chaplain of Edmund Bonner, Bishop of London, whom the queen had just released from the Tower with Stephen Gardiner. Though never popular, Bonner was not the bloodthirsty 'cannibal' Foxe describes. Dr Maitland is more accurate when he calls Bonner a man of high character, one who had suffered keenly himself, and a 'judge who (even if we grant that he was dispensing bad laws badly) was obviously desirous to save the prisoner's life'. Bonner's most notable sermon was on the dignity of the priesthood. Several of his sermons were printed in 1555, under the title *A profitable and necessarye doctryne, with certayne homelies*.

Also among this group of special preachers was John Feckenham, Dean of St Paul's Cathedral and later Abbot of Westminster, who preached 'the godliest sermon that ever was heard' on the Eucharist at the request of Bishop Gardiner.

Following a custom begun by her great-grandmother, Lady Margaret Beaufort, the queen had a series of sermons preached during Lent of 1553 in the Royal Chapel at Whitehall. The brilliant young brothers, Nicholas and John Harpsfield, the former Arch-deacon of Canterbury Cathedral and the latter Archdeacon of St Paul's Cathedral, were both chosen as preachers. Two of the latter's sermons are extant: one, a Convocation sermon, was given in 1553, and the other was delivered on the first anniversary of the reunion of the English Church with Rome, *A notable sermon made upon Saint Andrewes daye*. Both were preached from Colet's old pulpit, and the text for the second sermon was taken from his beloved St Paul's Epistle to the Romans: 'With the heart we believe unto justice, but with the mouth confession is made unto salvation.'

Another preacher in the queen's Lenten series was James Brooks, Bishop of Gloucester and Master of Balliol College, Oxford, a fre-quent preacher at Paul's Cross. For his Lenten sermon Brooks took the words of Jairus to Christ, 'Lord, my daughter is even now dead', and he found them applicable to the English Church under the Reformers. Brooks is perhaps best known as the presiding official at the trial of Archbishop Cranmer at Oxford.

POLE—CARDINAL AND PAPAL LEGATE

The most eagerly awaited sermon in the early days of Mary's reign was that of Cardinal Pole, who returned to England as Papal Legate, having powers to absolve the nation from schism. But before Pole would approach Parliament, he encouraged Bishop Stephen Gardiner, whom the queen had made Lord Chancellor, to retract publicly his statements on Royal Supremacy made in *De vera obedientia*. Gardiner agreed. And on the first Sunday in Advent 1554, he entered the pulpit at Paul's Cross, and, as John Foxe relates, preached 'to such an audience as was never seen in that place'.

According to the only extant summary of the sermon in *Actes and Monumentes*, Gardiner chose his text from the Epistle of St Paul to the Romans from the Mass for the day: 'Brethren; Knowing that it is now the hour for us to arise from sleep: for now our salvation is nearer than when we believed.' It was a long sermon, and many must have been amazed to hear him say:

I am sure the king was determined to have given over the supremacy again to the pope, but the hour was not yet then come, and therefore it went not forward lest some would have said that he did it for fear.... But now *hora est*, not for the queen, nor the king, nor my lord cardinal, who have never fallen asleep—but for us! Us—I do not exclude myself forth from the number. I acknowledge my fault, and exhort all who have fallen into this sleep through me or with me, with me to awake!

Gardiner's public profession was well received. And Pole felt the time had at last come for him to speak. On 28 November in the presence of the queen and her husband, Philip II of Spain, Pole addressed both houses of Parliament on what Bishop Gardiner called 'one of the most weightiest causes that ever happened in this realm'.

Only a summary of the cardinal's address remains, but it shows the sincere resolve which marked his efforts to heal the breach between Rome and England. He began by expressing his gratitude for being invited back to his native land—'a man exiled and banished from the commonwealth', and asked for impartial consideration of his mission:

I am here deputed legate and ambassador, having full and ample commission from thence, and have the keys committed to my hands. I confess to you that I have the keys, not as mine own keys, but as the keys of him that sent me, and yet cannot open; not for want of power in me to give, but for certain impediments in you to receive which must be taken away before my commission can take effect. This I protest before you, my commission is not of prejudice to any person. I come not to destroy, but to build; I come to reconcile, not to condemn; I am not come to compel, but to call again; I am not come to call anything in question already done, but my commission is of grace and clemency to such as will receive it. For touching all matters that be past, they shall be as things cast into the sea of forgetfulness.

Two days later Pole's mission came to a successful climax when on the feast of St Andrew (30 November) he stood again in the House of Commons and received the submission of the queen, her husband, and both houses of Parliament to the see of Rome. Many issues, however, remained to be settled. And Pole went again to Parliament in

the hope of bringing a peaceful settlement to the question of the
Church properties given by Henry VIII to the nobles who supported
his policies. Though Pole's speech was long, according to report,
he made slight mention of the monastic lands except to say that any
settlement must 'not come in part of bargaining'. The nation's
return to Rome, he said, must 'be free and liberal'.

THE LONDON SYNOD

The question arises, what spiritual aims did the Marian theologians,
Pole, Gardiner, Harpsfield, Feckenham, and the rest, have for the
Church now reunited to Rome? Pole had very practical ideas of
reform that he had urged along during his stay in Italy and had put
forth at the Council of Trent. His first move as Archbishop of
Canterbury was to call a national synod which met in November
1555. Its work would follow closely Rome's well conceived plan
for reform, *Consilium de Emendata Ecclesia*, to which Pole had contributed. The changes in ecclesiastical policy proposed at the London
Synod show how urgently the ills of the Church needed remedying:
each pastor must reside in his parish; bishops, as well as priests, must
remain celibate and avoid extravagant living; and they must preach
regularly, exhorting and instructing their parishioners.

Though the Synod's *Reformatio Angliae* remained little more than
a blueprint owing to Pole's death in 1558 (he survived the queen
only five days), it etches the character of the cardinal better than
any other act of his life. As had Alcock, Colet, and Fisher, he placed
the burden of reform on the clergy who above all men, he said in his
opening address to the Synod, have the gravest charge since they are
responsible for men's souls 'to the highest Pastor of all'.

THE MARIAN PERSECUTIONS

Unfortunately, 1555 also marked the beginning of the Marian
persecutions for which Pole and Gardiner have been so bitterly
censured. From their letters and public statements, it is not possible
to prove that either of them condoned the brutality of the recently
revived heresy laws; but the fact remains that Pole, as William
Schenk, his recent biographer, points out (and it may be said of
Gardiner as well), 'avoided facing the issue and allowed inferior
officials to act in his name, not often inciting them to action, but not
often willing to hinder them either. His occasional haphazard
clemency can hardly be said to matter very much.'

To Foxe, 'Pole was a papist, but not a bloody one.' Of Gardiner,
who the Martyrologist intimates helped revive the old heresy
laws (believing that severe laws would curb the dissenters) Foxe
writes that after attending a 'burning' and seeing that 'his device'

did not frighten heretics, he from that day 'meddled no more in such kind of condemnations'.

The trial at Oxford of the Edwardian preachers, John Ridley, Hugh Latimer, and Thomas Cranmer, is familiar from the many accounts of historians. Each was well known as a prelate and a preacher, and though there was nothing illegal in their condemnation, and they had condemned others, Protestant and Catholic alike under the same laws, it was unfortunate that they should have been caught in the net spread by the heresy edict. The trial served to focus attention on the old wounds that the Church was hoping to heal. Torture could not intimidate such men. Only five months before Latimer's death, he wrote in his usual colourful style to 'all louers of Godds trewthe':

> Now the Devill and his ostelers and tapsters stand in every inn door in city and country of this world, crying vnto vs, 'Come in and lodge here, for here is Christe and there is Christe: therefore tarry with vs till the storme be ouerpast': not that they would not haue vs wet to the skinne, but that the time myght be ouerpast to our vtter destruction.

The same vigorous spirit animated Archbishop Cranmer, who after being tried at Oxford and condemned to the stake by a papal court had corresponded with Pole, leading him to believe he would recant. But in the end he refused to acknowledge Papal Supremacy and walked calmly to the pyre, praying that he might 'speak something' to the people 'whereby God may be glorified' and they 'edified' by his death.

DEATH OF MARY I

As the queen's health grew steadily worse in the fifth year of her reign, her life overflowed with the tragedy that she had complained of as a young princess when she wrote the devotional treatise, *Meditation on Adversity*. 'Sickness, weepings, sorrow, mourning, and all adversities', she declared, had ever been her lot, and instead of 'the dews of heaven' that Shakespeare's dying Katherine of Aragon wished might fall like 'blessings' on her daughter Mary, misfortunes, one after another, plagued her. A depleted treasury, an unpopular marriage, rebellion, and war connived against the one ambition of her life—to see the English Church so firmly reunited with Rome that another breach would be impossible.

But Mary's weakness lay in her friends Pole and Gardiner, whom she unhappily considered her greatest strength. Idealists, but not men of action, they lacked the statesmanship necessary to rule a kingdom that had known all the miseries of tyranny and rapine for twenty years.

At the queen's funeral, John White, Bishop of Winchester, who succeeded to the see at Stephen Gardiner's death, preached the sermon. Though he knew that he would be imprisoned for it, he praised her and declared 'the poorest creature in all this city feared not God more than she'. Her charity to the poor, her zeal for learning, and her political reforms were notable. In a word, he said, she had kept 'her promise to the realm'. Though history has shown her to be a woman of intellect and integrity, Mary, like all the Tudors, lacked the wisdom necessary for true greatness.

EARLY TUDOR DEVOTIONAL BOOKS

In spite of the great revival of preaching under the Tudors, it is well to note that the devotional treatise more than held its own in the affection of the public. The widespread popularity of the little religious books began in the previous century, and earlier, when preachers quoted short passages in their sermons from *Contemptu Mundi*, *Mirrour of the Blessed Life of Christ*, *Meditations of Saint Bernard*, *Imitation of Christ*, *Scale of Perfection*, the *Cloud of Unknowing*, and the *Contemplation of Sinners*. Besides these there were quotations from the numerous adaptations of the *Ars Moriendi* and the works of Richard Rolle.

Many reasons may be offered why the first half of the sixteenth century was comparatively barren of new authors of devotional works. It was due in some measure to the rising tide of materialism and the vigorous growth of religious controversy, neither being conducive to the practice of contemplation necessary for mystical experience. Furthermore, the symbolism so loved by the medieval writers and necessary for mystical expression, did not come readily to writers in those troubled years, whether living in the monastery or in the world busy with the cares of founding schools and colleges or translating the broadening aims of social thought into law and practice.

Whether consciously or not, the greatest single effort to encourage what we might loosely term 'mystical fervour' was made by John Colet. During the ten years following his return from Italy in 1496 he lectured at Oxford on the Epistles of St Paul, broadening the spiritual horizons of many scholars and students—among them Grocyn, Erasmus, More, Tyndale, and Tunstall. Those who expected him to discuss dogma were disappointed, for Colet was neither a theologian nor a philosopher; nor was he steeped in the works of Plato and Aristotle. What he knew of them, he learned from the writings of Dionysius, the so-called Areopagite, Mirandola, and Ficino.

Colet proposed to lecture on Holy Scripture so as to make men love the sacred writings. He felt that the perfect approach to them lay through the Epistles of St Paul who seemed 'to be a fathomless ocean of wisdom and piety', and with his accustomed vigour he declared, 'Here I stand amazed and exclaim those words of my Paul, "O the depth of the riches of the wisdom and knowledge of God".' He then paid tribute to 'beneficient Wisdom' that 'has chosen to teach us humanly that we may know divinely'.

When it was plain that Colet's lectures would be free from argument and debate, those who came to scoff at his simple way were strangely silent, and returned again and again to listen while he pointed out how all Scripture shows God's immeasurable love for man. Zealously, he urged man to reciprocate this love with his entire intellect and will.

TUDOR MYSTICISM

In making Colet a torch-bearer for mystical expression in his own day, it is essential to comment on the treatises written by Dionysius, the so-called Areopagite, which Colet translated, namely, the *Heavenly Hierarchy*, the *Ecclesiastical Hierarchy*, the *De Sacramentis Ecclesiae*, and a tract *On the Divine Names*. It is not of particular importance that he failed to recognize that the works of Dionysius dated from the fifth century, and consequently were not written by a disciple of St Paul, until Grocyn dramatically pointed it out, in 1497, in a course of lectures on his works at St Paul's Cathedral. If we can see Colet as a contemplative, 'a man of removed and secluded excellence', one who at the end of life wished for nothing more than to live close by the Carthusians where as an oblate he would be 'dead to the world', it becomes clear to us that he not only found the Dionysian treatises a medium for his own inner feelings concerning the soul's mystical union with God, but he would be justified in upholding their author whose work inspired *The Cloud of Unknowing*.

Though Colet did not always agree with the Schoolmen and St Thomas Aquinas, he was in accord with their veneration for the Dionysian treatise *On the Divine Names*, frequently mentioned in the *Summa*. And like the medievalists, he found in Dionysius's *Mystical Theology* a divine social order which could and did apply, he felt, to all mankind. In the *Commentaries* which Colet wrote on these treatises, particularly on the *Heavenly Hierarchy*, he elaborates on Dionysius's use of the word 'hierarchy', making it stand for God's law which regulates the rank and interdependence that exists among created beings—angels and men. He stresses the 'unity' that must prevail between each of these beings and the resultant 'fellowship' in the mystical body of Christ.

Within the next thirty years the meaning that Colet attached to these words had all but vanished. He had, however, so encouraged mystical thinking—or as Blessed William Exmewe happily expresses it in his transcription of *The Cloud of Unknowing*, a lifting up of 'the heart to God with a meek stirring of love'—that the most violent religious friction could not lessen people's affection for the little devotional books.

As we recall them to mind—*The Fruitful Sayings of David, Jesus Psalter, A Fruitful Monition, A Treatise to Receive the Blessed Body of Our Lord, The Song of the Magnificat*, and Savonarola's *In Te Speravi, Domine*—there is not one that does not show a 'desire of the spirit to Godward for that which she [the soul] lacketh'. These words of Tyndale echo the teachings of Colet but no more strongly than do those of the latter's spiritual protégé, Thomas More, when he pleads, 'Give me, good Lord, a full faith, a firm hope, and a fervent charity, a love to the good Lord incomparable above the love to myself; and that I love nothing to Thy displeasure, but everything in an order to Thee.'

This great body of religious literature—sermons, controversial and devotional treatises—of the early Renaissance is a real flowering of deep religious conviction. It is an uncommon flowering, nurtured at a time when men were ruled by the block and the stake; when opponents such as More and Tyndale fell victims of the same tyranny; when men spent a lifetime fitting humanism with its emphasis on reason and freedom into the framework of Christianity. And this literature, as R. W. Chambers profoundly declares, 'has for four hundred years exercised a supreme influence upon English prose'.

JOHN ALCOCK

1430–1500

John Alcock, Bishop of Ely, who opened the first Parliament when Henry Tudor came to the throne in 1485, took an active part in political and religious affairs, and in an age of shifting values was looked up to for his saintliness. According to a tradition that has grown out of Leland's Itinerary, *Alcock was born in Beverley, Yorkshire, in 1430, and like his illustrious fellow-townsman, John Fisher, attended the grammar school of the collegiate church of St John. He entered Cambridge University and took a Bachelor of Arts degree prior to 1461 when he was ordained to the priesthood. In 1465 he was a candidate for a doctor of laws degree, and his ability as a canonist as well as his knowledge of civil law is evident in his speeches and sermons. While still at Cambridge he debated publicly with the White Friars, and later cited one of them for heresy.*

During the difficult times when Henry VI and Edward IV were contending for the English throne, Alcock maintained a commendable neutrality. Among the honours which came to him from Edward IV was the post of ambassador to Scotland in 1470. Previously he had been made Dean of St Stephen's, Westminster. He held successively three bishoprics, Rochester (1472), Worcester (1476), and Ely (1486); the latter see was given him by Henry VII.

Alcock was outspoken in his zeal for social reform, which he made the burden of his address when as Chancellor he opened the first Tudor parliament. He deplored the spread of the vagabond life of the road resulting from the wretched working conditions of labourers. Twice during the reign of Henry VII Alcock served as Chancellor pro tem. and as a member of the Privy Council. The king appointed him Lord President of Wales, and he served three times as Keeper of the Great Seal. But one of the greatest works of Alcock's life was the founding of Jesus College, Cambridge, in 1496. His aim was to improve the education of the clergy, a thing he urged during his entire episcopate. He died in 1500. The last four years of his life were taken up with the cares of the new foundation at Cambridge and the reforms in ecclesiastical courts for which he had long contended.

Alcock's extant English works consist of sermons. The earliest of these is probably the Spousage of a virgin to cryste... *an exhortacyon made to relygyous systers; the sermon* Qui habet aures audiendi... audiat *[1496]; and* The hyll of perfeccōn *(1496). The boy-bishop sermon,* In die Innocencium *has been erroneously attributed to him. His only extant treatise is the Latin spiritual directive* Gallicantus in sinodo apud Bernwell *[1498], addressed to the synod at Barnwell, emphasizing the need for more thorough education of the clergy and the importance of preaching.*

The hyll of perfeccōn *furnishes an interesting illustration of adapting the rules for writing sermons set down by the medieval preacher Alanus de Insulis in* Summa de Arte Praedicatoria. *The procedure of the preacher, he believed, should be determined to a large extent by the nature of his congregation. Alcock was addressing Carthusian monks, in the Charterhouse of St Anne in Coventry, vowed to hermit-like solitude and silence, and his sermon, following Alanus, centres around contemplative life, its joys and temptations. But in spite of his cumbersome prose, Alcock shows originality in presenting his ideas, as in the striking parallel that he draws between Christ's transfiguration on Mount Tabor and the Carthusian ideal, namely, the mystical union with God which the monk strives for, aided by his vows of poverty, chastity, and obedience. Besides the frequent references to Scripture and the* Vitae Patrum, *he uses many exempla and a similitude from the* Ancren Riwle.

Mons Perfectionis: *Otherwise in English, The Hill of Perfection**

From the centre of the world and on a mountain,
He wrought our salvation.

Exhortacio facta Cartusiensibus et aliis religiosis per venerandum in Christo patrem et dominorum dominum, Johannem Alcok, Eliensis Episcopum [An exhortation made to the Carthusians and other religious by the venerable father in Christ and lord of lords, John Alcock, Bishop of Ely].

In monte te salvum fac[1] [Save thyself in the mountain]. These words were said unto Lot by an angel by the commandment of Almighty God when the cities of Sodom and Gomorrah, edified[2] in the vale, should be destroyed for their sin and demerits, that he should ascend and go up unto the mount, and there save himself from the wretchedness and the persecution of them that were in the vale. Experience showeth that a great abundance of water destroyeth all things that grow in the vale at many seasons. The contrary is in such things that be in the high mountains. The herbs and flowers there growing be of more virtue, by the reason that they be more cocte[3] and nourished by the sun than the herbs or flowers growing in the vale. For as John Chrysostom saith, 'The higher the hill be, the nearer it is heaven'; and so a place of more quietness, prayer, and perfection in token of Our Saviour, Christ Jesus: *In monte solus orabat*[4]

---

[1] Gen. xix. 17.   [2] *edified*, erected.
[3] *cocte*, cooked.   [4] Matt. xiv. 23.

[He went into a mountain alone to pray]. And, also, it is read that 'in monte' He made the great feast when He fed five thousand people, women, and children with five loaves and two fishes.

The secret of His Scriptures and of His love He taught His apostles and disciples *in monte*[1] [on the mount]: *et in monte operatus est salutem nostram in medio terre*[2] [He hath wrought salvation in the midst of the earth]. And *in monte* He made His *ultimum vale* [last farewell] and gave His elect and beloved disciples His blessing, there showing to them the way to heaven; and so ascended unto His Father.[3]

This mount is in figure, and signifyeth religion, which is, as David saith, *Mons pinguis, mons coagulatus, mons in quo beneplacitum est Deo*[4] [A curdled mountain, a fat mountain, a mountain in which God is well pleased to dwell]. And in the eighth chapter of Zachary: *Mons Domini exercituum, mons sanctificatus*[5] [The mountain of the Lord of Hosts, the sanctified mountain]. For a place of religion may be well called *mons pinguis*, for in it reigneth all perfection that should feed man's soul: '*Pinguis est panis Christi, praebens delicias regibus*[6] [The bread of Christ is fat, yielding dainties to kings]. And, also, religion is a place that my friends and oostes[7] shall fight in and have the victory of mine adversary and theirs, the devil. There be fair and delicate roses of charity, the beauteous lilies of chastity in body and soul, the odoriferous and sweet violets of all obedience and humility, with herbs and flowers sanatyf[8] to remedy all sicknesses, heaviness, and melancholy.

To receive all these noble gifts and refreshing of the body and soul in this world, the Exemie[9] prophet Isaias exhorteth all mankind, saying to them: *Venite, ascendamus ad montem Domini, et ad domum Dei Jacob*[10] [Come and let us go up to the mountain of the Lord, and to the house of the God of Jacob]. For religion may well be called *domus Dei*, as Saint Austin saith: *Si caelum sit in terra, est in claustro vel in studio* [If heaven be on earth, it is in the cloister or in the study]. And right as Almighty God, in the time of the innocency of mankind, ordained *paradisum terrestrem*, a place of all pleasure—nothing therein was omitted that might be to the consolation of man—and put our first progenitors, Adam and Eve, therein, and gave them lordship and to use [*sic*] all that noble fruits and things being in paradise, *cum libero arbitrio* [with free will] except the tree *scientiae boni et mali*[11] [of knowledge of good and evil] which He, as Maker of all, reserved to Himself as *Dominus universorum* [Lord of the Universe]....

The garment of Christ [during the Transfiguration on Mt Tabor] was all white *sicut nix quae descendit de caelo*[12] [as snow that falls

---

[1] Matt. v.   [2] Ps. lxxiii. 12.   [3] Acts i. 9–12.

[4] Cf. Ps. lxvii. 16–17. [5] Zach. viii. 3.   [6] Cf. Gen. xlix. 20.

[7] *oostes*, hosts.   [8] *sanatyf*, curative. [9] *Exemie, honorary title*.

[10] Isa. ii. 3.   [11] Gen. ii. 9.   [12] Cf. Mark ix. 2.

from heaven], showing by that garment of colour that all His servants should be clothed in white of chastity of body and soul, as it is read: *Ambulabunt mecum in albis; et lavaverunt stolas suas in sanguine agni et candidas eas fecerunt*[1] [They shall walk with me in white: and have washed their robes in the blood of the Lamb and have made them white]. For right as blood red, 'bis cocte'* [twice digested], is turned into milk, delicious and white of colour, right so the garments of your religion by the contemplation of remembrance of the Passion of Christ, that He suffered on Good Friday, shall be by your penance and abstinence turned into the heavenly colour of white, in the which colour He appeared on Easter day and [with] His angels in approving the [Carthusian] habit of your religion* of white which ye must only after your profession wear within your monastery.

To this glorious Transfiguration was called only of the apostles, Simon Peter, James the Greater, and John the Evangelist, *virgo electus* [virgin elect] which three, by interpretation, signifieth the three principal parts [poverty, chastity, and obedience] of your profession. And ye, keeping them accordingly, shall see no transfiguration of His Godhead and manhood, but see the Three Persons in fruition '*facie ad faciem*',[2] *secundum merita vestra, sine enigmate* ['face to face', according to your merits, without enigma].

Simon, by interpretation, signifieth the noble yoke of obedience which every subject ought to do to his superior. In token thereof, Christ Jesu, being equal to His Father in Godhead, taking our nature create, by the reason of it was obedient to His Father for the redemption of man *usque ad mortem autem crucis, propter quod datum est sibi nomen quod est super omne nomen, ut in nomine Jesu omne genu flectatur, caelestium, terrestrium, et infernorum*[3] [even to the death of the Cross, because that a name is given to him which is above all names, that in the Name of Jesus all knees should bend in heaven, on earth, and under the earth]. Obedience is the health of all faithful men, the mother of virtue, the finder of the kingdom of heaven. It openeth heaven; it elevateth a man from the earth [making him a] dweller with angels; and [is] the meet and comfort of all saints. Adam, being inobedient, was cast out of paradise, and by obedience was brought in again. Lucifer for his inobedience was cast out of heaven.

Obedience to teach all mankind, Christ came into the world, as it is writ: *Descendi de caelo non ut faciam voluntatem meam, sed voluntatem ejus qui misit me*[4]: And *Non sicut ego volo, sed sicut tu*[5]. [Because I came down from heaven, not to do my own will, but the will of Him that sent me]: And [Nevertheless not as I will, but as Thou wilt]. Saint Bernard saith: 'Who loses obedience, loseth Christ and everlasting life. Obedience is the image of the very heavenly man; and

---

[1] Apoc. iii. 4; vii. 14.   [2] I Cor. xiii. 12.   [3] Cf. Phil. ii. 8–10.
[4] John vi. 38.   [5] Matt. xxvi. 39.

inobedience, the image of a devilish man.'* Obedience maketh a man, brother to Christ, and, in manner, to be of kindred to Him on every part. Therefore saith Saint Ambrose: 'I, having so good a Lord and be obedient to my superior, I fear not to die'....*

It is read in *Vitis Patrum* that four religious men came before the holy Abbot Pambo, and each of them in the absence of [the] other showed the virtues of each other. One was a great faster; another would nothing have in possession; the third had great charity; the fourth was obedient by the space of twenty-four years to his superior. The Abbot Pambo said to them all four: 'The virtue of this obedient man is more than all the other, for each of you three with the virtue that ye have, have also your proper will, and this man hath left his own will and made himself a bondman.'* And all such men are the very confessors of Christ if they persevere therein. And therefore God Almighty speaketh unto His obedient lover: *Dilectus meus mihi et ego illi*[1] [My beloved to me, and I to him]....

The remedy to put away all such temptations and delusions is, as Saint John Chrysostom saith: 'Prayer and oft to be confessed.' The same John Chrysostom in a sermon which he maketh, he exhorteth all men that desire to see in this world a form or example to come to heaven, they should go and see a place where perfect religion is kept by devout servants of God. Their monastery in every corner thereof is all polite and clean, without anything that should offend the eye: no noise, no crying nor business of servants, no weeping of children, no clattering nor presence of women, but the servants of God being in their prayers and penance, *tanquam in cavernis et sepulcris terrae*[2] [as in dens and in caves of the earth]. And at first knoll of the bell they depart from their cells into the church with all devotion, where they love Almighty God *corde, ore et opere* [with the heart, with the mouth, and with work] singing psalms, hymns, and other devout prayers with the harmony and melody that exceedeth all manner of harmony instruments, or otherwise of music.

We desireth to see the angels of God, cherubim and seraphim, be *ardentes in caelo in amore Dei*[3] [burning in heaven in the love of God]: right so these servants of God, all their mind, soul, heart, and body, as 'burning' in the love of God, and none other thing in the earth desireth. If thou will see patriarchs, prophets, and the followers of Christ, and Saint John Baptist, which ate never flesh, drank no wine nor cider, clothed in a camel's skin, and in continual penance, right so this holy company, thus gathered, ate no flesh, drank no wine, clothed in skins of beasts, and be in continual penance.

I doubt not there is no man but gladly would speak and see the judges that shall sit upon him and deme with Christ, him and all the world, as Peter, James, and John, with other apostles and disciples,

---

[1] Cant. ii. 16.   [2] Cf. Heb. xi. 38.   [3] Cf. Ps. ciii. 4.

that hath that gift given unto them for relinquishing of their proper will and pleasures of the world. These religious men [Carthusians] for the love of God hath forsaken their fathers and mothers and all their carnal generation and their own proper will, and therefore after the promise of Christ Jesus, they shall sit with Him and deme [the] twelve *tribus Israel* [the twelve tribes of Israel]. And if you would see the brethren of Saint Stephen and [Saint] Lawrence, and *martyrum candidatum laudantium Deum exercitum*[1] [the white-robed army of martyrs who give praise to God], and them that suffereth longer martyrdom* than many of them, look on these religious men, clad all in white, that suffereth martyrdom, some by the space of thirty years, some forty, fifty, sixty, and more, and be in continual battle with the devil, the world, and the flesh, and excoriate and wound daily theirselves with sharp hair[2] and instruments made of penance that they use hourly, besides the infinite temptations that they suffer and overcome.

And if ye be desirous to see and behold the fellows of the confessors of the Church of God, as Saint Nicholas, that is named *honor sacerdotum** [honour of the priesthood]; and Saint Martin, *gemma sacerdotum* [jewel of the priesthood]; Saint Jerome, *exemplar paenitenciae* [example of penance]; *quorum 'lumbi sunt praecincti, et lucernae ardentes in manibus eorum'*,[3] *et semper fuerunt parati, vigilantes in orationibus et bonis operibus* [of whom, the 'loins be girt, and with lamps burning in their hands', and they were always prepared, vigilant in prayers and good works]: behold all these religious men, having all these virtues abundant in charity, their patience never broken, in humility most perfect, in prayer perseverant, in faith most stable, in hope not perishing, in abstinence continually being, in obedience most ready.

A custom is among them [Carthusians] that if one of them depart out of this world to call him not dead, but a departing from them to the presence of Christ. And so no weeping is among them for no sickness, but prayer to the pleasure of God. *Hic dissolvi et vivere cum Christo*[4] [Here to be dissolved and to live with Christ]: it is desirous to look and see a beauteous and fair fellowship of virgins and maidens assembled together, whose beauty the integrity of their souls and bodies together, not filed,[5] conserveth their pleasant beauty, and be likened to the rose rutilaunt[6] and the white lily, which flowers be preferred in sight and in odour [above] all other flowers. For neither Saint Katherine, Saint Margaret, nor the fair lady Cecilia were never more beauteous in colour of all parts of their bodies than these blessed virgins, men of religion and servants of God. They be not filed with no women, body nor soul; they be not ingorged with meat and

[1] Cf. Te Deum.   [2] *hair*, hair shirt.   [3] Cf. Luke xii. 35.
[4] Cf. Phil. i. 23.   [5] *filed*, defiled.   [6] *rutilaunt*, shining.

drink. Age in them appeareth not greatly; in many years, they conserved the beauty of the body by chastity, and as a special spouse, having night and day in their mind, and desireth nothing else but the presence of her spouse, singing: '*Amore langueo*',[1] *et* '*sicut cervus ad fontes aquarum, ita desiderat anima mea ad te, Deus*'[2] ['I languish with love', and 'as the hart panteth after the fountains of water, so my soul panteth after thee, O God'].

These holy religious men live in no dread of man, for if thieves or untrue men come to spoil them in their cells, they shall find there neither gold nor silver, precious garments, nor fair and soft bedding, but hard boards, calves and sheep skins that they been lapped in. For they have nothing but the body and soul; and if they [thieves] will spoil them or dissever their body and soul, they be ready, for the love of God, to suffer it.

Now, well beloved brethren, I trust that ye and everyone of you, truly and religiously observe your religion in every part, as it is above written, and remember your reward in your so doing, and that ye be not found among them whom Christ cursed, saying: *Vae vobis, scribae et pharisaei, ypocritae, qui similes estis sepulcris dealbatis, qui apparent aforis hominibus speciosa, intus vero sunt plena ossibus mortuorum et omni spurcitia*[3] [Woe to you scribes and Pharisees, hypocrites; because you are like to whited sepulchres, which outwardly appear to men beautiful, but within are full of dead men's bones and of all filthiness]. Among all others, principally that Christ cursed, were they that were double in their language, showing holiness outward, and in their inward conversation, do contrary. As Saint Jerome saith: 'All masters and religious men that teacheth one [thing] and do another, they be these that be cursed of Christ.' David the Prophet saith, and [it] is written, *Ego dixi, dii estis.*[4] *Hoc est dicere* [I have said, you are gods. This is to say]: Ye true and faithful religious men, living according to your religion; I say unto you: *Dii estis*. All others that live in hypocrisy, breaking their religion: *Vos autem sicut homines moriemini in peccatis vestris*[5] [You also, as men shall die in your sins]. For ye understand how ye should please God, and ye displease Him for the pleasure of man and yourself.

And therefore every man principally should take heed what precious thing is committed unto him; and what vow he hath made before God and all His angels, that ye would truly perform it, as the common opinion among the vulgar people is that ye of your religion [Carthusian Order] keepeth most perfectly your religion among all other.

And then, sure ye may be that the angels of heaven, patriarchs and prophets, apostles and martyrs, confessors and virgins, and all

---

[1] Cant. ii. 5.   [2] Ps. xli. 2.   [3] Matt. xxiii. 27.
[4] Ps. lxxxi. 6 and John x. 34.   [5] Cf. John viii. 21-4.

the whole company of heaven, whose life ye have followed here in earth, they will assist you with their power and present you to Almighty God, who will say to you: *Veni, anima mea, dilecta mea, a Libano; veni, acceptavi paenitentias tuas; veni coronaberis*[1] [Come my soul, my beloved, from Libanus; come, I have accepted thy repentance; come, thou shalt be crowned]. Amen.

COLOPHON: Imprinted at Westminster by Wynkyn de Word, the year of Our Lord, 1496...at the instance of the right reverend religious father, Thomas, Prior of the House of Saint Anne, the Order of the Charterhouse.

ST JOHN FISHER
1469?–1535

John Fisher, Bishop of Rochester, noted throughout his life for his saintliness and learning, while still a young man rose to great prominence as a churchman and educationalist. He was born in Beverley, Yorkshire, in 1469?, the son of Robert and Agnes Fisher. His father was a middle-class mercer and died when John, the youngest of his four children, was a year old. After attending the grammar school, attached to the collegiate church of St John in Beverley, Fisher entered Michaelhouse, Cambridge, where he came under the direction of William de Melton, theologian and preacher of Yorkshire, whom he greatly revered. In 1487 he took a Bachelor of Arts degree, and four years later, a Master of Arts.

Because of Fisher's prominence in opposing the divorce of Henry VIII, he is least known as a scholar and educationalist, yet his early manhood was spent at Cambridge, where he rose from a Fellow in his own college to become Master in 1497, and within four years was chosen Vice-Chancellor of the university. Prior to being named Chancellor in 1504, he was consecrated Bishop of Rochester, and he had been successful in his efforts to induce Henry VII and his mother, Lady Margaret Beaufort, to found Christ's College, which was completed in 1505. His interest in education, particularly of the clergy, is shown by his founding of St John's College, Cambridge, the expenses defrayed by gifts from Lady Margaret's will and from his own funds. Besides several endowments for readerships and preacherships, Fisher brought famous scholars, notably Erasmus, to Cambridge, to teach Latin and Greek. Though in 1514 he offered to resign the chancellorship in favour of Cardinal Wolsey, who refused to accept it, Fisher was unanimously elected Chancellor for life and retained the office until his death in 1535.

[1] Cf. Cant. iv. 8.

As a bishop, Fisher worked zealously for the good of his flock, going from town to town on horseback and stopping often to visit the poor and sick, whom he made his special care. As a theologian and preacher, he resembled John Colet, whom he knew and admired. Like him, Fisher preached against the vices of the times. Considered one of the ablest theologians in England, he was chosen to give the sermon on several occasions for 'the burning of the books' at Paul's Cross. These sermons are extant.

However, when the king's attitude toward the Church began to show a definite change, Fisher opposed the excessive authority he assumed in spiritual affairs. The bishop sealed his doom by supporting Katherine of Aragon in the divorce proceedings. For refusing to take the Oath of Royal Supremacy, he was brought to trial and pronounced a traitor 'for transgressing maliciously the statutes of the kingdom by which the king is head of the English Church'. Thinking to help Fisher's cause, Pope Paul III elevated him to the rank of cardinal, but the honour served only to antagonize Henry VIII. However, he commuted the barbarous execution usually suffered by traitors to decapitation, and Fisher was beheaded on Tower Hill on 22 June 1535. He was among the English martyrs canonized in 1935 during the pontificate of Pius XI.

His English works consist of sermons and devotional treatises. Four sermons preached on special occasions are extant: A mornynge remembraūce had at the moneth mynde of Margarete, countesse of Rychemond [1509]; The sermon... [over the body] of the moost famouse prynce Kynge Henry the VII (1509); The sermon of Johan the bysshop of Rochester [on John xv. 26] made agayn ỹ pnicyous doctryn of M. luuther [1521?]; A sermon had at Paulis, vpō quiquagesom sonday [11 Feb. 1525] cōcernynge certayne heretickes [1528]. Fisher's sermons on the Penitential Psalms were collected in one volume and printed as This treatise concernynge the fruytfull saynges of Dauyd (1508). While in the Tower, he wrote A spiritual consolation...to hys sister Elizabeth [1535].

His Latin works include Tractatus de orando Deum which was first printed in English, A godlie treatisse declaryng the benefites of prayer [1560]; De Unica Magdalena (1519), a discourse on the identity of Mary Magdalene; Lutheranae Assertionis Confutatio (1523), a defence of the king's book on the seven sacraments; Sacri sacerdotii defensio contra Lutherum (1525), an answer to Luther's attack on the priesthood; and a treatise on the Holy Eucharist, opposing the heresy of Œcolampadius, De veritate corporis et sanguinis Christi in Eucharistia (1527).

Fisher's sermons on the Penitential Psalms were preached during the first year of his episcopate before Lady Margaret Beaufort and the royal entourage, yet the quality of the audience did not lessen the stricture of their message. Besides their interest for anyone studying the characteristics of *the age, they are indicative of the revival of interest in preaching, for which Bishop Fisher was so much responsible.*

The sermons demonstrate an Augustinian approach to the verities of life, death, penance, and eternal reward. Each of the seven psalms is given an exegetical treatment of a simple kind, yet the results are far from simple. Imbued with the constant spiritual outlook of the preacher and enlivened by his stylistic traits, the sermons reveal an ability to derive useful lessons from every phrase of the Psalms.

After Wynkyn de Worde's first edition in 1508, the popularity of the Treatise warranted seven editions before 1555.

The Fruitful Sayings of David, the King and Prophet in the Seven Penitential Psalms

DOMINE, NE IN FURORE. (POSTERIOR. PRIMA PARS[1])

Marvel nothing although we begin not our sermon with the third Penitential Psalm in order. For or ever we took upon us to declare the two first Penitential Psalms, our promise was somewhat to speak of the nativity of Our Blessed Lady at the day, which purpose willing to keep, also desired of our friends to follow the order of the psalms though it seemed to be hard for us so to do. Notwithstanding, by the help of Our Blessed Lady, we have attempted the matter and made the first part of this psalm to agree with our first purpose.

QUAE EST ISTA QUAE PROGREDITUR QUASI AURORA CONSURGENS?[2]

After the offence of our first fathers Adam and Eve, all the world was confounded many years by darkness and the night of sin, of the which darkness and night a remembrance is made in Holy Scripture oftentimes. Notwithstanding, many that were the very servants and worshippers of Almighty God, to whom the said darkness and night of sin was very irksome and grevious, had monition that the very sun of rightwiseness should spring upon all the world and shine to their great and singular comfort and make a marvellous clear day. As the prophet Zachary said and prophesied of Christ: *Visitavit nos oriens ex alto illuminare his qui in tenebris et in umbra mortis sedent*:[3] Our Blessed Lord hath visited us from above to give light unto them which sit in darkness and in the shadow of death. Also, Christ in the

---

[1] O Lord, rebuke me not in thy indignation. (The latter [of two Penitential Psalms, vi and xxxvii, that begin, Domine, ne, etc.]. First Part.)

[2] Who is she that cometh forth as the morning rising? (Cant. vi. 9).

[3] Cf. Luke i. 78–9.

gospel of John saith: *Abraham vidit diem meum et gavisus est*:[1] Abraham saw my day, whereby he was made glad and joyful. The natural day which we behold should rather of congruence be called the day of the sun, of whom he has His beginning, than our day.

So this spiritual day wherein spiritually we live under the Christian faith which by the sun of rightwiseness hath brought forth Jesus Christ should be called more properly the day of Him than of us. Christ Our Saviour called it His day saying: *Vidit diem meum*: Abraham saw My day. Abraham saw not the present day of Christ as the apostles did; he had only the sight of it in his soul by true hope that it should come, notwithstanding he and many others desired greatly to see this spiritual Sun and the clear day of it. Our Saviour said to His apostles: *Multi reges et prophetae voluerunt videre que vos videtis; et non viderunt*:[2] Many kings and prophets would fain have seen the mystery of Mine incarnation which ye see, and yet they did not: and what marvel was it, if they that lay in darkness and in the blind night of sin, wherein no pleasure was to sleep and take rest, to desire fervently and abide the springing of the bright Sun, Our Saviour. Holy Fathers before the Incarnation, which marvellously irked and despised the works of darkness and the night of sin—every one of them daily and continually prayed that the very Sun of Rightwiseness might spring in their time. Nevertheless their good hope and trust of it was deferred many years: and, at the last, when time was hovable[3] and convenient in the sight of Almighty God, He caused this clear Sun to give light unto the world.

Notwithstanding, it was done in a just and due order. For of a truth, it had not been seeming and well ordered that after so great and horrible darkness of the night, the marvellous clearness of this Sun should have been showed immediately. It was according of very right that first a morning should come between which was not so dark as the night, neither so clear as the sun. This order agreeth both to nature, Scripture, and reason. First, by the order of nature we perceive that between the darkness of the night and the clear light of the day, a certain mean light cometh between which we call the morning; it is more light and clear than is the night, albeit, the sun is much more clear than it. Every man knoweth this thing well, for daily we have it in experience. Holy Scripture also teacheth that in the beginning of the world when heaven and earth should be create, all things were covered with darkness a long season, and or ever the sun in his very clearness gave light to the world, a certain mean light was made which had place between darkness and the very clear light of the sun. This is well showed by Moses in the beginning of Genesis. Reason also, which searcheth the knowledge of many causes, findeth when one thing is changed into his contrary, as from cold to heat, it

[1] John viii. 56.   [2] Matt. xiii. 17.   [3] *hovable*, appropriate.

is done first by certain means or by certain alterations coming between. Water which of his nature is very cold is not suddenly by the fire made hot to the uttermost, but first cometh between a little warmness, as we might say lukewarm, which is neither very hot nor very cold but in a mean between both. An apple, also, which first is green, waxeth not suddenly yellow, but first it is somewhat white, between green and yellow indifferent.

Thus we perceive by reason that it was not convenient [that] this great clearness of the Sun, our Saviour, should have been showed so soon and immediately after so fearful and the dark night of sin without rising of the morning which is a mean between both. Since it is so then that just and right order will it be so, and also it is according for a wise man so to order it, who will doubt but the wisdom of Our Lord God, unable to be showed, kept this due and reasonable order, namely, in His work whereby: *Salutem operatus est in medio terrae.*[1] He wrought health in the midst of the earth. Since also He kept the same in all His operations, as Saint Paul witnesseth saying: *Quaecumque ordinata sunt: a Deo sunt.*[2] All things well ordered, be by the ordinance of Almighty God.

Furthermore, because this matter should be expressed more openly, we shall endeavour ourself to show by the three reasons afore-rehearsed that this Blessed Lady, Mother to our Saviour, may well be called a morning, since before her, none was without sin. After her the most clear Sun, Christ Jesus, showed His light to the world, expulsing utterly by His innumerable clearness these darknesses wherein all the world was wrapped and covered before. We see by experience the morning riseth out of darkness as the wise man saith: *Deus qui dixit te tenebris splendescere.*[3] Almighty God commandeth light to shine out of darkness. The clerk Orpheus marvelleth* greatly of it saying, *O nox quae lucem emittis:* O dark night, I marvel sore that thou bringeth forth light. And, of a truth, it is marvellous to man's reason that light should spring out of darkness. So, in like manner, we may marvel of this Blessed Virgin; she, being clean without spot of any manner sin, notwithstanding should shine and originally come of sinners that were covered and wrapped in darkness and the night of sin. Also, after the morning, the sun ariseth, in manner, as it were, brought forth, and had his beginning of the morning, likewise our Saviour Christ Jesus was born and brought forth of this Blessed Virgin and spread His light over all the world. We also perceive like as the sun riseth of the morning and maketh it more clear by the effusion of his light, so Christ Jesus, born of this Virgin, defiled her not with any manner spot of sin, but endued and replete her with much more light and grace than she had before. Last, although it seemeth the morning to be cause of

---

[1] Ps. lxxiii. 12.   [2] Rom. xiii. 1.   [3] Cf. II Cor. iv. 6.

the sun, notwithstanding the sun without doubt is cause of it. And, in like wise, although this Blessed Virgin brought forth Our Saviour Jesus, yet He made her and was cause of her bringing into this world. Thus ye perceive by nature that this Blessed Virgin may well be likened to a morning.

The same shall be showed if we rehearse the order of Scripture. It is spoken in Genesis that first, Almighty God made heaven and earth. The earth was void and desolate; all was covered with darkness, and the Spirit of God was borne aloft. Then Almighty God commanded the first day, by His word only, that light should be made: and, anon, light was made: and after that the fourth day, the sun was create. This we read in the beginning of Genesis. But let us now show what it signifyeth for our purpose. First, heaven and earth may signify to us, man and woman, for the woman is subject to the man like as the earth is to heaven: woman is also barren and lacking fruit without the help of man. And the earth without the influence of heaven is barren and void of all fruit. Semblably, every generation of man from the creation of Adam was wrapped and covered with the darkness of sin, and though the Spirit of God was ever aloft ready to give grace, for all that, none was found able to receive it unto the time this Blessed Virgin was ordained by the Holy Trinity to spring and to be brought forth into the world, which, by the providence of Almighty God, was surely kept and defended from every spot and blemish of sin, so that we may well say unto her: *Tota pulcra es amica mea et macula non est in te*:[1] O Blessed Lady, thou art all fair and without spot or blemish of sin. The angel at her Salutation said: *Ave, plena gratiae*:[2] Hail, full of grace: this Blessed Virgin, full of the beams of grace, was ordained by God as a light of the morning, and afterward brought forth the bright shining Sun with His manifold beams, Our Saviour Christ; *Qui illuminat omnem hominem venientem in hunc mundum*:[3] Which giveth light to every creature coming to this world. Take heed how conveniently it agreeth with Holy Scripture, this Virgin to be called a morning.

Also, whereas reason of a congruence wills that between two contraries a mean must be had, maketh marvellously well that this Virgin may be called a morning, for like as the morning is a mean between the great clearness of the sun and the ugsome[4] darkness of the night, so this Blessed and Holy Virgin is the mean between this bright Sun, our Saviour, and wicked sinners and a partaker of both, for she is the Mother of God's Son and also the Mother of sinners. For when Our Saviour Christ hanged upon the Cross He commended and left to this Blessed Virgin, Saint John the Evangelist as her son, saying to her: *Mulier ecce filius tuus*:[5] Woman behold thy son. And

---

[1] Cant. iv. 7.   [2] Luke i. 28.   [3] Cf. II Cor. iv. 6.
[4] *ugsome*, ugly.   [5] John xix. 26.

unto Saint John He said: *Ecce mater tua*:[1] Behold thy mother. John, by interpretation is to say the grace of God, signifying that by God's grace, and not by their own merits, sinners be made the inheritors of the heavenly kingdom; sinners therefore be commended to this Virgin Mary as to a mother. She is Mother of sinners. Saint Augustine saith, it seemeth to be a noble kindred between this Blessed Virgin and sinners, for she received all her goodness for sinners; sin was cause why she was made the Mother of God.

Also, if we have taken any goodness, we have it all by her. Therefore of very right this Holy Virgin Mary is the Mother of sinners. All Christ's Church calleth her *mater miserorum*, the Mother of wretched sinners. She is also the Mother of Mercy, for Christ is very Mercy. The prophet, speaking of Him, saith thus: *Deus meus misericordia mea*:[2] My God and my Mercy. Christ is very Mercy; she is the Mother of Christ, therefore, the Mother of Mercy; for this cause, as we said before, she must needs be a mean between the mercy of God and the wretchedness of sin; between Christ, most innocent, and wretched sinners; between the shining light and black darkness: she is also the mean between the bright sun of the day and the dark cloud of the night. None was born before her without sin, either mortal, venial, or original. Many before were men of great virtue and holiness, as Jeremiah and Hely,[3] with others, but because they were not clean without every spot of sin, their virtue and holiness was hid, in manner, as under a cloud. And the holy angels, remembering this matter, beholding this light to show forth without any spot of darkness, after so long continuance of the dark night of sin, said each one to other with an admiration or marvelling: *Quae est ista quae progreditur quasi aurora consurgens*: What is she which goeth forth as a rising morning?

Therefore since this Blessed Lady Mary, as a morning, goeth between our night and the day of Christ, between our darkness and His brightness, and, last, between the misery of our sins and the mercy of God, what other help should rather be to wretched sinners whereby they might sooner be delivered from their wretchedness and come to mercy than by the help of this Blessed Virgin Mary, who may come or attain from one extremity unto another without a mean between both.

Let us, therefore, knowledge to her our wretchedness; ask her help; she cannot but hear us, for she is our Mother; she shall speak for us unto her merciful Son and ask His mercy, and, without doubt, He shall grant her petition, which is His Mother and the Mother of Mercy. Let us, therefore, call unto her saying: O most Holy Virgin, thou art the Mother of God, Mother of Mercy; the Mother of wretched sinners and their singular help [and] comfort to all

---

[1] John xix. 27.   [2] Ps. lviii, 18.   [3] *Hely*, Elijah.

sorrowful. Vouchsafe to hear our wretchedness and provide a convenient and behovable remedy for the same. But what miseries shall we most specially show unto her? Truly, the common wretchedness of all sinners which the Church hath taught us oft to have in remembrance, which also the Prophet David hath described in the third Penitential Psalm, whereof we shall now speak.

And as the woman of Canaan when she prayed to Our Lord was not heard anon, notwithstanding His disciples, having pity and compassion, spake to Christ, their Master, for her, so we now lest, peradventure, Our merciful Lord heard not Our prayers in the other psalms before, because of our grievous sins, let us turn our prayer to His most merciful Mother, beseeching her to show mercy and call to Almighty God for us as our advocate....

DE PROFUNDIS CLAMAVI AD TE, DOMINE: DOMINE, EXAUDI VOCEM MEAM

De profundis clamavi ad te, Domine: Domine exaudi vocem meam. Fiant aures tuae intendentes in vocem deprecationis meae[1] [Out of the depths I have cried to Thee, O Lord: Lord hear my voice. Let Thine ears be attentive to the voice of my supplication]. In the which words be expressed the three parts of penance. First, he prayeth for contrition, saying: *De profundis clamavi ad te, Domine.* For confession, he addeth: *Domine, exaudi vocem meam.* And third, for satisfaction: *Fiant aures tuae intendentes in vocem deprecationis meae.* First, contrition is a great inward sorrow, coming from the very deepness of the heart with meekness, by a profound consideration and remembrance of our sins. Truly, the deepness of sin is very great, as it was showed before. And for that cause we must make deep search in our conscience, remembering the greatness of every sin with great humility coming from the heart root.

Profundus est cor hominis:[2] The heart of man is deep: whosoever cryeth to Almighty God heartily, that is to say, from the deepness of his heart, must needs be heard. God may not expulse or forsake the heart that is so penitent and meek, for our Prophet saith in another place: *Cor contritum et humiliatum Deus non despicies*:[3] Blessed Lord, Thou shalt not despise a contrite heart. And how may the heart be more contrite and meek as when of very contrition, meekness, and profound consideration of our sins, we ask mercy and forgiveness of Almighty God. A little sorrow is not sufficient nor little penance, but we must have great sorrow and great penance which maketh a great noise before our most merciful Lord. And the person that cryeth to God on this wise, with great sorrow and

[1] Ps. cxxix. 1–2.   [2] Ps. lxiii. 7.   [3] Ps. l. 19.

penance, hath very contrition; he may well say: *De profundis clamavi ad te, Domine*: Lord, I have cried to Thee from my very heart root. But this cry must be soft, without noise of words; it must be in the secret places of the heart, no voice, no sound in any wise showed outwardly.

Contrition is none other but an inward sorrow of the mind set in the privy place of the heart, which needs must go before confession made by mouth, for truly confession without contrition had before, profiteth very little or nothing. Albeit contrition is secret within the privy place of the heart, notwithstanding, confession must be made by open words, manifest showing of the mind, expressing truly and openly every sin with the circumstance to a priest; all colouring, feigning, and hiding of our trespass set apart, which cannot be done in any condition but by speaking of words: therefore, every penitent in this second place is taught to ask of Almighty God that He vouchsafe mercifully to hear and accept his confession, saying: *Domine, exaudi vocem meam*: Lord, hear the voice of my confession.

We said satisfaction is the third part of penance, which is divided into other three parts—almsdeed, fasting, and prayer; among these, prayer is the chief and, in manner, all whole satisfaction. This may be showed for three reasons: first, because it includeth the other two, almsdeed and fasting; second, it is a sacrifice of a more noble thing than any other; And third, it is more common, more light, more easy for any person to do....

SI INIQUITATES OBSERVAVERIS, DOMINE: DOMINE, QUIS SUSTINEBIT[1]?

Lord, if Thou bear in mind our sins and will not forgive us, who may keep him from despair? By these words we may know that our sins cannot withstand the great mercy of God, if we be penitent. Now we shall show that the rightwiseness of God can be no obstacle against His mercy. It is required, both of right and equity, a recompense to be made for a trespass or unkindness showed to any person or ever the offence be utterly forgiven. And for that cause a certain solemn feast was institute in the old law by Moses, according to God's commandment, every year to be celebrate and kept, which they named the Feast of Making Clean and the Day of Mercy. In that solemn feast customably was offered up a certain general sacrifice for the sins of all the people. On that day when that the bishop of their Law had hallowed certain quick beasts in an outhouse of the temple, anon himself only, arrayed with solemn apparel, should enter in the temple and go forth to a place in the said temple called *Sancta Sanctorum*

[1] Ps. cxxix. 3.

[Holy of Holies], taking with him part of the beast's blood which seven times he should sprinkle before the Seat of God, which they called *Propitiatorium*, a Place of Mercy, wherewith Almighty God should be made more meek and the sooner exercise His mercy upon the people. So for this cause they named that solemn feast, the Day of Mercy.

All this sacrifice done by the bishop in the Old Law was only but a figure and, as Saint Paul wrote unto the Hebrews, 'a signification or token of the known truth to come'. Therefore, Christian people, since our time, now is the plenteous time of grace: we may not be in no worse condition than the Jews were. In their time, Almighty God was appeased by the means of their sacrifice. Now much more in our days whereas grace is superabundant, a sacrifice shall be made, the which is of much more strength, more virtue to purge and utterly do away our sins. Also it shall sooner move Almighty God to exercise His mercy upon us. Let us remember who is our bishop; what is our sacrifice; what manner blood it is; what is the inward part of the temple, and to what intent all these were ordained. The holy doctor Saint Paul showeth them at large in a marvellous epistle written to the Hebrews: *Christus, assistens pontifex futurorum bonorum, per amplius et perfectius tabernaculum non manu factum, id est, non huius creationis: neque per sanguinem hircorum, aut vitulorum, sed per proprium sanguinem, introivit semel in sancta, eterna redemptione inventa:*[1] Christ Jesus is our bishop; His most precious body is our sacrifice which He offered upon a Cross for the redemption of all the world. The blood shed for our redemption was not the blood of goats or calves, as in the Old Law, it was the very blood, most innocent, of our Saviour Jesus Christ. The temple wherein our bishop did sacrifice was not made by man's hand, but only by the power of God; He shed His precious blood for our redemption in the face of all the world, which is the temple, made only by the hand of God. This temple hath two divers parts: one is the earth whereon we be inhabit; the other is not yet known to us mortal creatures. First, He did sacrifice in the earth when He suffered His Passion. After, in a new clothing or garment, the vesture of immortality, and with His own precious blood, entered into *Sancta Sanctorum*, that is to say, into heaven where He showed His said most precious blood, before the throne of His Father, which He shed for all sinners seven times.

By this Holy Sacrifice [the Mass], Almighty God must needs have pity and execute His mercy to all true penitents: and this sacrifice shall ever continue, not only year by year, as the manner was of the Jews, but also it is daily offered for our comfort, and every hour and moment for our most strong succour: wherefore Saint Paul saith: *Eterna redemptione inventa*: By it we be redeemed forever. Every

[1] Cf. Heb. ix. 11–12.

contrite and true penitent person, not willing to fall again, but with a full purpose continue in virtuous living, is partaker of this Holy Sacrifice.

COLOPHON: Here endeth the exposition of the seven psalms. Imprinted at London in the Fleet Street at the Sign of the Sun by Wynkyn de Worde....1508.

DESIDERIUS ERASMUS[1]

Erasmus's interest in preaching has been gleaned almost wholly from his treatise Ecclesiastes sive Concionator Evangelicus (1535). *Very little has been written about his ability as a preacher or writer of sermons. Yet during his lifetime three of his sermons were translated into English, and he comments at the end of his* Catalogue of Lucubrations *that 'a great deal has perished which I should not care to have survived. But I should be glad to think that some of the sermons which I delivered when I was in the College of Montaigu [Paris] were still in existence.' These sermons were probably preached after 1494 in the Abbey Church of St Geneviève while Erasmus was living in France with the Augustinians.*

The earliest of his extant sermons that was translated into English is the Concio Puero Jesu, *written in 1509, but not printed until about 1540. English versions were also made of his* De Immensa Misericordia [1526?] *and a* Sermo [c. 1532] *on the marriage feast of Cana in praise of the Blessed Virgin Mary. Erasmus wrote the* Concio *at the request of John Colet for the formal opening of St Paul's School. Like the* Carmen de puero Jesu, *which he also wrote for the School, the* Concio, *a 'swete sermon' to be 'pronounced and preached of a chylde unto chyldren', has for its theme the life and attributes of the Boy Jesus. It differs from a Boy Bishop sermon in its limited appeal to children, neglecting entirely any discussion of religious and social problems such as marked those sermons delivered in St Paul's Cathedral on St Nicholas's Day. On the other hand, the tone of the* Concio *is devotional, and Erasmus limits himself to fostering a pattern of spiritual training for adolescents. He urges his listeners to follow the Boy Jesus as their Leader, the 'perfect Child among children'.*

Gentian Hervet has been mentioned as the English translator of the Concio, *but the style is inferior to his translation of Erasmus's* De Immensa. *The latter sermon was written by Erasmus in 1523 for his friend Christopher Utenheim, Bishop of Basel. It was delivered at the dedication of a chapel in Porrentruy, the temporary episcopal residence where the bishop had retired to avoid open dissension with the Swiss*

---

[1] For biographical sketch, see pp. 55–7.

Reformers. Though Erasmus visited Utenheim in Porrentruy in 1524, no record has been found that the Dutch scholar delivered the sermon.

Correspondence between Utenheim and Erasmus reveals that the bishop rejected the first draft of the sermon because it favoured some changes in church discipline that might be construed as sympathetic to Luther. Erasmus omitted the objectionable parts and emphasized free will and God's mercy to the repentant sinner—themes, especially the former, that he developed the same year in De Libero Arbitrio *(1524), a direct answer to Luther. The vigorous tone of the* De Immensa *and certain theological aspects of it are reflections of Erasmus's intense interest in the sermons and treatises of the early Church Fathers, Jerome, Athanasius, Basil, Cyprian, and John Chrysostom. Most of their works he had translated or edited between 1516 and 1524.*

Hervet's English version of the De Immensa *has particular interest because of his free use of idioms current in early Tudor speech. He includes a glossary of one hundred and fifty words, providing 'for them that shall rede this sermon and understand nat Latin and frenche termes used in englisshe'. Many of these terms have found a permanent place in the language, such as 'environ', 'fruition', and 'precept'. In the preface, Hervet gives one of the earliest biographical accounts of Erasmus, intimating contemporary opinion regarding his works, particularly the popular* Enchiridion. *This is among the earliest accounts of the scholar in English literature.*

Gentian Hervet (1499–1584), French humanist, was born near Orleans. As a young man of twenty he met Thomas Lupset in Paris and helped him proof Thomas Linacre's Latin translations of Galen's works. Accompanying Lupset to England, Hervet was employed as a tutor in the house of Margaret Pole, Countess of Salisbury, mother of Reginald Pole. The recompense he received enabled him to study for a time at Oxford. Out of gratitude to the Countess, Hervet dedicated to her his translation of Erasmus's sermon. Previously, at the request of her son Henry Pole, he Englished Xenophon's Treatise of householde *(1532), considered the first English translation made direct from Greek, and works of the early Greek Fathers of the Church.*

When Hervet's printer, Thomas Berthelet, unfortunately neglected to have the English version of the De Immensa *licensed, he violated the Monition issued in 1524 by Cuthbert Tunstall, Bishop of London, forbidding printers and booksellers to handle any works written by Germans. In spite of his English friends, Erasmus came under the ban, and the sale of the book was prohibited. It was reprinted in 1533 and in 1547. Besides the English editions, the sermon was translated during the sixteenth century into German, Dutch, Spanish, Italian, and Czech. A French version was printed in 1712.*

Sermon on the Child Jesus

A Sermon of the Child Jesus made by the most famous clerk, Doctor Erasmus of Rotterdam; to be pronounced and preached of a child unto children.

I, a child going about to speak before children of the ineffable Child Jesus will not wish the eloquence of Tully which might strike the ears with short and vain pleasure: for how much Christ's wisdom is in distance from the wisdom of the world (the distance is unmeasurable), so much ought the Christian eloquence differ from the eloquence of the world.

But this I would ye might, with brenning[1] vows, obtain with me of God, so good a Father of the good Child Jesus, from whom as a fountain springeth the Chief of all goodness; and which only with His plentiful Spirit maketh the tongues of infants copious and eloquent; which is also accustomed even 'out of the mouth of the sucking babes to draw out absolute and perfect praise',[2] that likewise as our whole life ought to express none other than the Spirit [of] Jesus Christ (of whom this day we do intend to speak), so likewise this our sermon may savour on Him, represent Him, breath Him, which is both the 'Word of the Father' and hath alone 'the words of life', whose lively and working speech 'is more piercing than any two-edged sword',[3] piercing to the very inward chambers of the heart. And that He 'from whose body floods of livish water do run',[4] will vouchsafe by the instrument of my voice, as it were, by the pipe of a conduit, to flow into the minds of all you with the plenteous moisture of the heavenly grace to water them.

This thing, so I trust, shall come to pass, most dearly beloved fellows, if we will join to the godly requests, ears which be purged and truly thirsting. That is to say, such ears as that Eternal Word, requiring in the gospel of Saint Matthew, the eleventh chapter saith: *Qui habet aures ad audiendum audiat*: That is to say: Who hath ears to the intent to hear, let him hear....[5]

Verily, I see that there be three things principally which be wont to kindle and inflame the hearts either of scholars or of soldiers to do valiantly and manly: the first, is to be brought into an admiration of their guide or captain; the second, to love him; the third, the reward. Wherefore to the intent we might with more fervent and cheerful courages obey our Master and Captain, Jesus, go we, too.

Let us consider severally, all these three things with a devout

---

[1] *brenning*, burning.   [2] Ps. viii. 3.   [3] Heb. iv. 12.
[4] John vii. 38.   [5] Matt. xi. 15.

curiosity in Him. First of all, how wonderful He is on every side and to be astonied at. After that, how greatly He is to be loved and for that cause also to be followed. And last of all, what high profit, fruit, and advantage shall arise unto us by this love.

Now it is the usage of rhetoricians in this kind of oration to show examples of noble princes to this purpose and intent, that by the comparison of him whom they praise with other, his nobleness and virtues might appear the greater. But our Captain so greatly and wonderfully surmounteth all the height of human dignity and highness that whomsoever a man showeth, be he never so worthy, excellent, and high, yet he shall seem to add darkness and not light. For whose progeny and nobleness shall not seem smoke if thou comparest him with Jesus, which by an unspeakable, nay, with an unthinkable reason, is born God of God, always without time, equal in all things to His eternal and most High Parent.

Howbeit, though we go no further than to His human nativity, I pray you, does it not easily enshadow and obscure the clearness of all other kings and princes in the world: as He which wonderfully above the course of nature, His Father of heaven, being the Worker and Author; the Holy Ghost, breathing; the angel, being the messenger; without man's industry was born of a Virgin, being pregnant and with child by the handiwork of the Heavenly Father; and was born a man and in time.

And, again, was so born a man that neither He left to be God, nor yet He drew none of our filthiness unto Him at all. Now, sir, what can be imagined more ample than He which being infounded through all, yet restrained in no place, abideth in Himself uncompassable and unmeasurable? What is more rich than He which is the very chief and principal Goodness from whom all good things do issue, and yet He is not thereby diminished? What is more renowned than He which is the renown of His Father's glory, and which only 'enlighteneth every man coming into this world'?[1] What is more mighty than He to whom the Father Almighty 'hath given all power in heaven and in earth?'[2] ... What is stronger and more victorious than He which alone death, which was to all others invincible, overcame with His own death, and which laid down and abated the tyranny of Satan by His heavenly prowess and virtue?

What is more triumphant than He which, breaking and spoiling hell,[3] accompanied with so many godly souls, like a valiant conqueror, ascended up to heaven and there sitteth at the right side of His Father? What is wiser than He which with so wonderful reason created all things, that even in the very little bees He hath left so many and so great miracles of His wisdom? And which with so

---

[1] John i. 9.   [2] Matt. xxviii. 18.   [3] *hell*, limbo.

wonderful order of things and harmony knitteth, containeth, administereth all which goeth round about all, and yet departeth not from Himself; moving all, being Himself unmoved; shaking all, Himself quiet.

Finally, that which is most foolish in Him passeth by long distance the whole wisdom of the wise men of the world whose authority ought so much the more be the greater unto us, that the Father Himself openly witnesseth of Him saying: Here is my well beloved Son in whom is My pleasaunce. Hearken to Him.[1] What is so reverent as He to whose eyes all things be open? What is so to be dread as He which with His only beck 'can send both soul and body into hell?[2] What is more beautiful than He whose countenance to behold is the high joy?

Finally, if many things be had precious for the antiquity, what is more ancient than He which neither had beginning nor shall have ending? But it were, perchance, more convenient that children should wonder at the Child. For here also He appeareth wonderful insomuch that the lowest of Him is more high than those things which be most high in men.

How great was He whom being but a Babe, crying, wrapped in clouts,[3] cast like an abject thing in the crib, yet the angels from heaven magnify with their song, the shepherds worship, yea, she that bore him worshippeth, the brute beasts acknowledge, the stars showeth, the wise astronomers reverence, King Herod feareth, all Jerusalem tremble at, holy Simeon embraceth, Anne prophesieth, the well-disposed people are brought into hope of salvation. O the low highness and high lowness!

If we wonder at new things, what like thing was ever either done or heard or thought? If we marvel at great things, what can be, by all manner of means, more ample than our Jesus, whom no creature can either express with the voice or conceive with thought: whose greatness who will compass with words, he doth much foolisher than if he went about to draw up the wide ocean sea with a little dish. His immensity is rather to be worshipped than expounded: at which we ought so much the more to wonder that we cannot attain it. And why should we not so do since that great pursuivant John Baptist pronounceth himself unworthy to 'unloose the latchet'[4] of His shoes?

Go ye, too, then, sweet children. Let us glory with an holy pride in this so noble a Child, Jesus, our Master, in this so worthy a Captain; let His highness encourage us to enterprise devoutly; in Him only let us please ourselves that [in] thinking all that is His to be common to us all, we may judge and count ourselves better than (being once

---

[1] Matt. xvii. 5.   [2] Matt. x. 28.
[3] *clouts*, swaddling clothes.   [4] John i. 27.

addict to such a Captain) to serve the world or vices, so vile and filthy masters . . . [End of the first part.]

Amen

Thus endeth the sweet *Sermon of the Child Jesus* made by the most famous clerk, Doctor Erasmus of Rotterdam.

COLOPHON: Imprinted at London in Fleet Street at the sign of the George by me Robert Redman. [1540.]

Sermon on the Mercy of God

TRANSLATED BY GENTIAN HERVET

A Sermon of the Exceeding Great Mercy of God made by the most famous Doctor Master Erasmus Rotterdamos. Translated out of Latin into English at the request of the most honorable and virtuous lady, the Lady Margaret, Countess of Salisbury.

GENTIAN HERVET'S PREFACE

To the most honorable lady, the Lady Countess of Salisbury, Gentian Hervet her humble servant greeting:

Seeing and understanding, most honourable lady, your great mind and deep affection both toward all manner of learning and, specially, toward that which either exciteth or teacheth virtue and goodness and concerneth the way of our salvation, I have translated out of Latin into English a sermon of Erasmus *Of the mercy of God*: the which translated for you and dedicated unto your ladyship, I thought it should be a good deed if for your ladyship's pleasure, it were printed and spread abroad. And whereas afore, learned men only did get out both pleasure and great fruit in reading this book, now every man, as well rude as learned, may have this sermon *Of the mercy of God* as common unto him as the mercy of God itself is.

And as touching the commendation either of the author or of the work, I know the tenderness of my wit, much more slender than that I can be able to bear the weight of such an enterprise, and I reckon [it] to be much better to hold my tongue utterly from the praising than of them to speak too little and, for fault of wit, to minish their excellence. Yet, nevertheless, it seemeth expedient unto me that by your ladyship, briefly, other folk may know how noble is the author of this work and how much we be bound to him for it.

The author of the book is Erasmus Rotterdamos whom my praises can no more ennoble than the sun with a candle may be made clearer. He is the man to whom in learning no living man may him-self compare: and not only passeth them that be alive, but also from the most part of old authors hath berafe[1] the prize—and not only paynims and gentiles but also Christian doctors. He is the man that when in his first days, truth was far hid in the deep veins of the ground, and, moreover, it was prohibited as a thing being worthy death that no man should for her inquire, he did not suffer the world to be con-founded with such a marvellous darkness, and either he hath digged up many lymmes[2] of truth or, at the least, he hath restored us free liberty to search [for] her.

He is the man that to Isaac may be compared, the which digged up the goodly springing wells that the Philistines destroyed and with dirt and dung overfilled.[3] The clear springs of the Holy Scripture* that the Philistines had so troubled, so marred, and so defiled, that no man could drink or have the true taste of the water, they be now by his labour and diligence to their old pureness and clearness so restored that no spot nor earthly filth in them remaineth. And though the Philistines did all that they could to disturb him from his holy purpose, and that among the people by the reason of them, he was greatly hated and envied, yet at the last, as it chanceth always unto them that with a bold stomach in their good deeds do continue, excellent virtue hath overcome envy when from this man there can come out nothing but both it is exceeding profitable and on every side all perfect.

Methinketh that this little treatise, being in every point as perfect as any other be in profit, not only giveth no place but also greatly passeth. For where afore, the works that he made were profitable, but specially to one kind of men—his *Proverbs* [*Adagia* (1500)], his *New Testament* [*Novum Instrumentum* (1516)], and many other treatises only to learned men—of the book of the *Instruction of Princes* (1516), the most profit redounded to princes: this book only, with the book called *The knife or weapon of a Christian soldier*, hath so far spread abroad his fruitful branches that there is no man but great fruit gather he may out of it except he that thinketh that it maketh no matter whether he be damned or saved. And as for *The knife of a Christian soldier*, which he named *Enchiridion* (1503), it bringeth a man out of the way of vices and leadeth him in the way of virtue and the path of salvation.

This little treatise *Of the mercy of God* teacheth a man to ascribe nothing to himself but all together to the mercy of God, seeing that the free will itself, that we be endued withal, is the free gift of Almighty God; and except it were by Him made clearer, it should be so dark with the rust of the original sin that the image of virtue in it should never be fast printed. And whosoever being entered

---

[1] *berafe*, taken.　　　[2] *lymmes*, limbs(?).　　　[3] Gen. xxvi. 15.

into the kingdom of God by baptism, doth ascribe anything to his own wisdom, to his merits, and to his deservings, and not acknowledgeth everywhere his own feebleness, trusting upon the free grace and mercy of Almighty God, it is to be dread lest for mercy, that is everywhere ready for him that calleth, he prove the sore and rigorous justice of God.

Now let us see whether it be more expedient for a man's salvation, either by justice to be feared from sin or by mercy to be enticed both to love and to virtue. Justice with her sore threatenings compelleth a man to flee vice and engendereth in him a certain bodily fear that it is an odious thing unto him to commit sin, not for the hate itself of sin but for fear of punishment. Mercy, contrary to it, putteth before a man's face the unspeakable love of God toward him, the which so loved him that He did not spare His only Son for his sake; the incredible benefits; the infinite desire of his salvation; the continual calling upon Him to bring him to the everlasting bliss.

Of the other side, she showeth him, as if it were in a glass, the weakness and feebleness of a man, the perils that he is compassed about with, the calamities, the misery, the wretchedness that on every side do utterly him wrap, and that in so many mischiefs there cometh no succour but from the mercy of God. Do not all these engender in him a certain childish love toward his Father, that he will perform His commandments not for fear of punishment nor for love of reward, but for because it pleaseth his most loving Father?...

But it is time, most honourable lady, to lay by my rude and uneloquent language that ye may hear Erasmus speak eloquently and in your own mother's tongue very plainly, the which so commendeth to the hearers the unmeasurable and infinite mercy of God that whosoever in his heart fast printeth it, he shall find out of it a marvellous great fruit, both to know his own misery and of God, the infinite bounty: the which two things be most effectuous to direct us to the everlasting felicity that is Christ Jesus, the which preserve your ladyship and all yours. Amen.

This endeth the preface.

A SERMON OF THE EXCEEDING GREAT MERCY OF GOD
MADE BY ERASMUS ROTTERDAMUS

Forasmuch as I purpose this day to speak of the greatness of the mercies of Our Lord, brethren and sistren, most well beloved in Christ, without whose help man's frailty and weakness can naught do, let us all together with a common prayer beseech the mercy of the common Lord of us all so to move the instrument of my tongue and so to stir and kindle your hearts that as we shall depart hence through the mercy of Our Lord more plenteously endued with heavenly grace, so every man to his neighbourward may more abundantly use the works of mercy. Some used here to greet the Virgin Mother: I deny not everywhere much honour ought to be given her, but, verily, to our purpose now, meseemeth more expedient if ye follow me thus going before you:

Jesus Christ, the Almighty Word of the everlasting Father, that promisest to be present wheresoever two or three were assembled in Thy name, Thou seest how many in Thy name be here gathered: Vouchsafe, therefore, according to Thy pro- *Invocation* mise to be among this company: that their hearts lighted through grace of the Holy Ghost may understand more fully the greatness of Thy mercy: whereby we all together may with a lustier mind both yield to Thee thanks for Thy mercy, that so oft hath been to us showed, and that more desirously in all our necessities, we may call thereon for help: And, lastly, that we humble servants may receive the mercy of Our Lord, that on us we have largely proved, to our power lovingly prosecute on our fellows, likewise servants.

If that every man, as the rhetoricians teach, is right diligent and attentive to hear those things that he understandeth should sharply touch him, then there ought none of you to nod or sleep in this sermontime, seeing that the salvation of us all *Attention* equally dependeth on the mercy of Our Lord: Nor there is none so young nor so old, of so low or so high birth, so poor nor so rich, so bond nor so free, so cunning nor so rude, so wicked nor so just but that he hath oftentimes both proved the mercy of Our Lord and needeth the mercy of Our Lord to all things that he righteously goeth about.

What matter more favourable may be treated, than that by the mercy of God, everlasting health is prepared for all folks. Of very right, therefore, in this sermontime, as many as be here present, he should not only take heed, but also be lusty and glad to hear it: for whosoever doth love and favour himself, will love and favour this sermon.

Among the manifold evils which draw mankind to everlasting damnation there be two chief and principal mischiefs of which they ought specially to beware that love virtue and goodness and desire to come to the fellowship of everlasting felicity. They be these: too much trust on one's own self and despair. The *Confidence* one cometh of a presumptuous mind against God that *Despair* the love of one's self hath blinded: the other is engendered one way by pondering of the great offences; another way by considering the righteous judgment of God without remembrance of His mercy.

Both these are so pestilent and cursed that many doubt which of them both is more to be abhorred. For what is greater madness nor more lamentable than man—that is earth and ashes, which whatsoever he is or may do, is for it all bound to the goodness of God—to rebel against Him of whom he was created, of whom he was redeemed, and of whom, by so many means, he is called to the company of everlasting life. Is it not a point of great unkindness to set naught by Him of whom thou hast received so many benefits? Is it not a point of great madness to will to rebel against Him that may destroy thee with a beck? Is it not a great point of wickedness not to knowledge thy Maker, not to honour thy Father, not to love thy Saviour?

Unhappy Lucifer was bold to do this first, which, ascribing to himself that [which] he freely received of Almighty God, said in his heart: 'I will get up above in heaven: I will sit upon the hill of testimony in the sides of the north wind: I will climb up above the height of the clouds: I will be like to Almighty God.'[1] But would to God that his unhappy fall might, at the least, fray[2] mortal creatures from following of his ungracious example if the wicked deed itself cannot fear them.

Truly, if God spared not proud presumptuous angels, but cast them heedling[3] down into hell and ordained them straitly bound in chains to be kept till the day of Doom,[4] what deserveth man, a silly worm, which (as now were crept out of the earth, must shortly return to earth again) is proud, presumptuous, and testy against God? The more low and vile the condition of man is, the more abominable is his presumption, desiring to be equal with God.

The ancient poets feigned there rose a strife,* on a time, among the gods, that constrained Jupiter himself to forsake heaven and flee into Egypt, and there in another shape to hide him: but a far more mischievous deed was that the giants went about, which, confederated together against Jupiter, did cast hills upon hills, that they might so conquer heaven and expel Jupiter thence. Ye may well laugh. These tales that ye hear be not gospel: but yet the erudite old time would signify somewhat under the covering of these fables that belongeth to the expressing of mortal folks manners....

I would to God there were none among Christians that followed the wickedness of Lucifer—I may not say, pass it. What? Look ye, that I should open somewhat of secret confessions? What need it, when in some countries in the market place, in the churches, at dinner, supper, in playing and sporting, we hear all about, they forswear themselves by the most honourable Name of God. This that I say is a light thing. We hear the name of God denied; the Holy Name of Christ with many vile words blamed; the forefinger

---

[1] Isa. xiv. 13.
[3] *heedling,* headlong.
[2] *fray,* frighten.
[4] II Pet. ii. 4.

bitten; God threatened; the thumb put between the foremost and middle finger: that is done against God, Fountain of all glory, that is wont to be done against an infamous person for reproach and shame.

Be there none among Christians, if they may be called Christians, which for riches, that they must shortly forego, or foul bodily pleasure or for transitory honours, forsake their own Prince and make a wicked composition with their foe Satan? The form of the oath taken, at once they foreswear whatsoever confederation was made with Christ and offer to hell part of their body as the first fruit to the prince whereof they vowed wholly their soul. These things spied out, we see punished daily by open execution. What thing like did Lucifer? For him, the Son of God died not; and yet he was not so hardy to blaspheme God: he only desired equal honour....

And, peradventure, we stand in our own conceit because among us the examples of crimes that I rehearsed now be seldom seen: but what matter maketh it if the tongue soundeth no blaspheming, when of many the whole life speaketh no other thing but blaspheming against God. The glutton for[1] God, worship their belly; who continually by right and wrong gape[2] to heap riches together; which by murder, treason, poisoning, and enchanting, stalk up to honours; which by tyranny oppress poor people; which to have a thing to their mind, kindle all the world to war; nor persevering in these great evils, have no shame nor repentance but with a shameless continuance, like a common woman, rejoice, yea, in things most mischievous, scorning and mocking the good livers. Do not the caitiffs by those deeds say: 'There is no God; God's behests been false; the threatenings of God be vain; the Word of God is a lie, yielding the joys of heaven to them that mourn here, that thirst and hunger justice, that be meek, that suffer persecution, that for justice been with vile words rebuked.'[3]

What can be more abominable than this blaspheming? And yet if anything can be worse than that which is most worse, despair is worse than the whole stinking multitude of other sins.

The wicked man, seeing [he] might do what thing he would unpunished, was proud of his prosperity, and said in his heart: 'There is no God, and there is no knowledge above. God careth not for mortal folks business.' And as He is less injurious against a man that believeth not He is than he that believeth Him to be cruel or false, to likewise they been less wicked that utterly say, there is no God shan they that believe He is unmerciful, taking away that virtue from Him without which kings be not kings but tyrants. But whosoever casteth hope of forgiveness aside and rolleth himself down into the hurlpit of despair, he doth not only believe that God is not almighty, supposing some sin so horrible that He cannot forgive,

[1] *for*, instead of.   [2] *gape*, yearn.   [3] Cf. Matt. v. 3–10.

but also he maketh Him a liar. He promiseth by the Prophet that He will incontinent clean forget all manner sins as soon as the sinner bewaileth them....[1]

If God overcome with the greatness of thy sin may not forgive thee, thou pluckest from Him His power almighty: if He will not do that He may, He is a liar and false that will not perform that He so many times promised by the prophets' mouths.

It is infinite whatsoever is in God. But three special things be in Him: most high power, most high wisdom, and most high goodness. And, albeit, that power is wont to be ascribed to the Father as His proper, wisdom to the Son, goodness to the Holy Ghost, yet there is none of these things but it is equally common to all Three Persons. His high power He showed when He created these marvellous works of the world only with a beck, of the which there is no part but it is full of miracle. Yea, the very pysmers[2] and spiders cry out, showing the great power of their Maker. Again when He divided the waves of the Red Sea;[3] when He restrained the stream of Jordan and made the river passable for a footman;[4] when while Josue fought, He made the sun and moon to stint their course;[5] when with touching, He healed lepers;[6] and with a word, raised dead men to life,[7] He showed Himself Lord of nature. And when He with equal wisdom conserveth and governeth those things which He by His power, that cannot be declared, hath made, He showeth Himself to be no less wise than almighty.

Albeit that His goodness everywhere shineth, as that same creation of angels, and this world was a point of high goodness when He to high felicity, that He hath of Himself, lacketh nothing that might be added, yet He made mankind properly to the intent that therein specially He might express the greatness of His goodness and mercy, for in that behalf God would not only be more loving to us, but also more marvellous....

They marvel, sometime, at a king's power and might that hate or have envy at him. But gentleness and liberality is loved, yea, of them that have no need, that is to say, through consideration of human chance whereby it may hap any [one], whatever he be, to have need. But there is no man, nor hath been nor shall be, but that he needeth the mercy of God....

But what saith the psalm .cxliiii: Our Lord is piteous and merciful, patient and much merciful: Our Lord is sweet to all, and His merciful pities pass all His works. *Ergo* something there is more marvellous than to have made the heavens with so many bright stars; to have created the earth with so many kinds of beasts, of trees,

---

[1] Ezech. xviii. 21–22.   [2] *pysmers*, ants.   [3] Cf. Exod. xiv. 21.
[4] Cf. Joshua iii. 16.   [5] Cf. Joshua x. 12.
[6] Cf. Matt. xi. 5; also Luke xvii. 11–17.   [7] Luke vii. 14–15.

and variableness of all things; to have created so many companies of
angelical minds.

Who durst be so bold to affirm it, except the Prophet showed
plainly, that the mercies of Our Lord pass the glory of all His other
works? And yet he shall not doubt it to be true, whosoever with a
religious curiosity will consider how much more marvellously He
redeemed than created man. Is it not more wonderful, God to be
made man than the angels to be created of God? Is it not more a
marvel that God wrapped in a babe's clothes should wail and cry
in the cratche or rack than to reign in the heavens that He made:
here, the angels, as thing of greatest wonder, sing glory to God in the
most high heavenly mansions. They see the lowliest humility and
know the most excellent highness.

All the counsel of redeeming mankind—Christ's life, Christ's
teaching, Christ's miracles, affliction, crucifying, resurrection,
appearing, ascension, the sending of the Holy Ghost, by a few silly,
poor, idiot men renewed the world—this counsel, I say, is it not on
every side full of miracles, yea, that the very angels cannot search
out. Wicked spirits see and understand the reason of the world's
creation, but the counsel of the world's restoring was hid from them.
And in this point, craft deceived craft: the craft of mercy beguiled
the craft of malice. The creation of the world was the work of
puissance: the world so restored, was the work of mercy. The ends of
the cross, saith Habacuc, '*are* in his hands: there is his strength hid'.[1]
What is more vile than the cross? What is weaker than the crucified?
Yet under that weakness, exceeding power of divine mercy lay hid
that brake, overcame, and clean destroyed all the tyranny of the
devil....

Neither in gifts of the soul, in which part man is more marvellous,
he hath ought that he may challenge as his own. He that made the
body, formed the soul: the body He made of slime and put in the
soul with inspiring of His mouth. And, therefore, of the other
beasts, the soul and body perish together: ours is alive after the body
till she receive it again in the resurrection promised.[2]

Now, how effectual a thing the soul is, the very death declareth;
which as soon as she departeth, there lieth the carcass unprofitable.
Where is the heat? Where is the colour? Where is the moving?
Where is the might of all the wits? And yet while the soul is held
fast, tied to this so unhappy, silly body, doing nothing but through
the bodily instruments, which [is] very oft let that she cannot put
forth her native power, how marvellous is the swiftness and profound understanding of man's mind! What an exceeding treasure
of remembrance! What is so hid in the secrets of nature or in the

---

[1] Hab. iii. 4.   [2] Cf. I Cor. xv. 51–3.

heavens or in earth that man's wit cannot mark, perceive, and discuss!...

I will speak nothing here of them that have learned so many sciences, so hard to know, and so many languages, and that that they learned, they retain still. Let him that will of you, think how many folk's faces and names he doth remember; how many shape of beasts, trees, herbs, places, and of other innumerable things, he knoweth and memorially cleapeth them by name. The common people call these 'gifts of nature', when indeed they be 'gifts of divine mercy' which are departed to each, not after our merits, but after His benignity.

All these things because the prodigal child abused the pleasure of human will, not only it is not withdrawn that was given, but by grace more abundant liberality of gifts is added. By law He instructed us; by His Son, whom whole He gave to us, He taught us the secrets of God; by His spirit He enriched our souls with divers gifts, passing man's power.

He giveth understanding of mystical Scriptures that give light and comfort to us in all ills; He giveth fore-knowledge of things to come; He giveth tongues to speak sundry languages, to condemn venom, to heal sicknesses, to raise the dead, to confound noyfull spirits; He giveth power to overcome hell's gates; He granteth us to be the members of Christ, children of God, partners of the kingdom celestial that never shall have end....

[Erasmus then emphasizes the necessity of giving alms to the poor if one expects mercy from God.]

If I be not deceived there is a sentence among the mimes [of] Publilius [Syrus] worthy for a Christian man: 'In giving, he received a benefit that gave [to] him that was worthy to have it.' Why stickest at it, thou froward ponderer, of another's dignity? He giveth to one worthy of it that giveth to the member of Christ; he giveth to one worthy that giveth to his brother. And so forth he giveth to one worthy whosoever for Jesus's love giveth to a poor creature. If thou seek winning, play the usurer with Him: if thou dread pain, thou hast whereby thou mayest redeem it. After sharp rebuke what saith Our Lord in the gospel? Yet give alms, saith He, and see all things be clean unto you....[1]

Alms deed knoweth not boasting, otherwise she loseth her name. They that give alms 'with a trumpet blowing before'; they give not alms but buy glory. For conclusion, alms before God is when 'thy left hand knoweth not what thy right hand doth'.[2] Put, saith He, thy treasure in the commandments of God, and it shall profit thee more than gold:[3] close thy alms in the poor man's heart, and it shall

---

[1] Luke xi. 41.   [2] Matt. vi. 2-3.   [3] Ecclus. xxix. 14.

deliver thee from all evil.[1] Thy treasure is never so sure buried or hid as in the poor man's heart. It is far better locked therein than in thy iron chests.

Forget that that thou hast given: let not the poor man know, if it may be, who is the author of the good deed. When thy need requireth an intercessor, thy alms shall not be dumb, but shall obtain of Our Lord that thou that did succour thy neighbour in any trouble shalt be delivered from all ill.

Will ye hear Alms Deed speaking: 'Come ye blessed children of My Father, for when I hungered, ye gave Me meat; when I thirsted, ye gave Me drink: when I was naked, ye clothed Me: when I wanted lodging, ye lodged Me: when I was sick, ye visited Me; when I was in prison, ye came to Me.' They remember not their benefits, and say: 'O Lord, when did we see Thee wanting those things, and succoured Thee?'

The other part rehearsed their virtues, and they hear: 'Go ye into everlasting fire.'[2] Shall not Alms Deed, then, be here a good spokeswoman that shall deliver us from hell, that is, from all mischief, and shall join us to Our Lord, Fountain of all goodness.

What resteth now, most dear brethren, but that we must beseech the mercy of Our Lord that we may be merciful to our neighbour, lest if we here set naught by His mercy, [we] shall afterwards require it in vain. But the more we be provoked by mercy here, the more sharp we shall find His judgment. Let mercy toward our brethren overcome in us worldly affection, that in God, mercy toward us may overcome judgment. So it shall come to pass that we with agreeable minds together shall sing the mercies of Our Lord forever, acknowledging His mercies above all His works: To whom be praise and glory through all coasts of the earth forevermore. Amen.

COLOPHON: Imprinted at London in Fleet Street by Thomas Berthelet, printer unto the King's most noble Grace, dwelling at the sign of Lucrece.... [1526.]

JOHN COLET[3]

Though John Colet, Dean of St Paul's, was one of the most famous preachers of his day, only one of his sermons is extant, namely, Oratio habita ad clerum in convocatione *(1511) or* The sermon of Doctor Colete made to the conuocation at Paulis. *The English version was printed about 1530. There are brief summaries of the sermon that Colet*

[1] Ecclus. xxix. 15.   [2] Matt. xxv. 34–46.
[3] For biographical sketch, see pp. 35–7.

preached before Henry VIII on Good Friday, 27 March 1513, in which he denounced war and the king's pending invasion of France, and also of the sermon that he preached in Westminster Abbey when Thomas Wolsey was elevated to the rank of cardinal in 1515.

In each of these sermons Colet seems to have spoken in the same forth-right manner which characterizes his Convocation Sermon, *given before the English hierarchy at the request of William Warham, Arch-bishop of Canterbury. The latter defended Colet when charges of heresy were brought against him by the clergy because of his stern rebukes. For his theme Colet chose a passage from his favourite Epistle of St Paul to the Romans: 'Be you not conformed to this world, but be you reformed.' Throughout the sermon he shows his familiarity with canon law and the rulings made by the great councils of the Church, particularly that of Nicaea (325). He urged the English bishops to adopt the recommendation made at Nicaea and later councils that twice a year diocesan synods and metropolitan or provincial councils should be held.*

It is likely that the sermon owes its English translation to Thomas Lupset, Colet's protégé at St Paul's School and Oxford. Professor John Gee credits Lupset with the preservation of the sermon and several of Colet's Oxford lectures. Whether the translator is Lupset or another of Colet's friends, he has caught the vigorous spirit and blunt tone of the Dean's remarks.

The Sermon of Doctor Colet made to the Convocation at Paul's

Ye are come together today, fathers and rightwise men, to enter council; in the which what ye will do and what matters ye will handle, yet we understand not. But we wish that once remembering your name and profession, ye would mind the reformation of the Church's matter. For it was never more in need; and the state of the Church did never desire more your endeavours. For the spouse of Christ, the Church, whom ye would should be without spot or wrinkle, is made foul and evil-favoured, as saith Isaias: The faithful city is made a harlot.[1] And saith Jeremias: She hath done lechery with many lovers, whereby she hath conceived many seeds of wickedness, and daily bringeth forth very foul fruit.[2]

Wherefore I came hither today, fathers, to warn you that in this your council, with all your mind, ye think upon the reformation of the Church. But, forsooth, I came not willingly, for I knew mine unworthiness. I saw besides, how hard it was to please the precise

[1] Isa. i. 21.   [2] Cf. Jer. iii. 1–2.

judgment of so many men. For I judged it utterly unworthy and unmeet, yea, and almost too malapert, that I, a servant, should counsel my lords: that I, a son, should teach you, my fathers. Truly, it had been meeter for some one of the fathers, that is to say, you prelates, might have done it with more grave authority and greater wisdom. But the commandment was to be obeyed of the most reverent father and lord [William Warham], the Archbishop, President of this council, which laid upon me this burden; truly too heavy for me.

We read that the Prophet Samuel said: Obedience is better than sacrifice.[1] Wherefore, fathers and right worthy men, I pray you and beseech you that this day ye would sustain my weakness with your goodness and patience; furthermore, to help me at the beginning with your prayers.

And before all things let us pray unto God the Father Almighty. First, remembering our most Holy Father, the Pope, and all spiritual pastors with all Christian people; furthermore, the most reverend father and lord, the Archbishop, President of this council, and all bishops and all the clergy and all the people of England. Remembering, finally, this your congregation, desiring God to inspire your minds so accordingly to agree to such profit and fruit of the Church that ye seem not after the Council [is] finished to have been gathered together in vain and without cause. Let us all say, *Pater Noster*.

To exhort you, reverend fathers, to the endeavour of reformation of the Church's estate, because that nothing hath so disfigured the face of the Church as hath the fashion of secular and worldly living in clerks and priests, I know not where more conveniently to take beginning of my tale[2] than of the Apostle Paul in whose temple ye are gathered together. For he, writing unto the Romans and under their name unto you, saith: Be you not conformed to this world: but be you reformed in the newness of your understanding that ye may prove what is the good will of God, well pleasing and perfect[3]....

In the which words the Apostle doth two things: first, he doth forbid that we be not conformable to the world and be made carnal. Furthermore, he doth command that we be reformed in the spirit of God, whereby we are spiritual.

I, intending to follow this order, will speak first of confirmation, then after of reformation.

'Be ye not', saith he, 'conformable to this world.'

The Apostle calleth the world, the ways and manner of secular living: the which chiefly doth rest in four evils of this world, that is to say, in devilish pride, in carnal concupiscence, in worldly covetousness, in secular business....

And, first, for to speak of pride of life: how much greediness and

[1] I Kings xv. 22.   [2] *tale*, account.   [3] Rom. xii. 2.

appetite of honour and dignity is nowadays in men of the Church?
How run they, yea, almost out of breath, from one benefice to
another; from the less to the more; from the lower to the higher.
Who seeth not this? Who seeing this, sorroweth not? Moreover
these that are in the same dignities, the most part of them doth go
with so stately a countenance and with so high looks that they seem
not to be put in the humble bishopric of Christ, but rather in the high
lordship and power of the world; not knowing nor advertising what
Christ, the Master of all meekness, said unto His disciples whom He
called to be bishops and priests: The princes of people, saith He,
have lordship of them: and those that be in authority have power,
but do ye not so: but he that is greater among you, let him be
minister. He that is highest in dignity, be he the servant of all men.
The Son of Man came not to be ministered unto, but to minister....[1]

The second secular evil is carnal concupiscence. Hath not this vice
so grown and waxen in the Church as a flood of their lust so that
there is nothing looked for more diligently in this most busy time of
the most part of priests than that that doth delight and please the
senses? They give themself to feasts and banqueting; they spend
themself in vain babbling; they give themself to sports and plays;
they apply themself to hunting and hawking; they drown themself
in the delights of this world....

Covetousness is the third secular evil: the which Saint John the
Apostle calleth concupiscence of the eyes; Saint Paul calleth it
idolatry. This abominable pestilence hath so entered in the mind
almost of all priests, and so hath blinded the eyes of the mind that we
are blind to all things but only unto those which seem to bring unto
us some gains. For what other thing seek we nowadays in the
Church than fat benefices and high promotions. Yea, and in the same
promotions, of what other thing do we pass upon than of our tithes
and rents. That we care not how many, how chargeful, how great
benefices we take, so that they be of great value....

To be short and to conclude at one word: All corruptness, all the
decay of the Church, all the offences of the world come of the
covetousness of priests. According to that [verse] of Saint Paul that
here I repeat again and beat into your ears: Covetousness is the root
of all evil.[2]

The fourth secular evil that spotteth and maketh ill-favoured the
face of the Church is the continual secular occupation wherein
priests and bishops nowadays doth busy themself—the servants
rather of men than of God; the warriors rather of this world than of
Christ.... Without doubt of this secularity and that clerks and
priests (leaving all spiritualness) do turmoil themself with earthly
occupations, many evils do follow:

[1] Matt. xx. 25–8.   [2] I Tim. vi. 10.

First, the dignity of the priesthood is dishonoured, the which is greater than either the king's or emperor's. It is equal with the dignity of angels. But the brightness of this great dignity is sore shadowed when priests are occupied in earthly things, whose conversation ought to be in heaven.

Secondarily, the priesthood is despised when there is no difference betwixt such priests and lay people. But according to the prophecy of Osee: As the people be, so are the priests.[1]

Thirdly, the beautiful order and holy dignity in the Church is confused when the highest in the Church do meddle with vile and earthly things; and in their stead vile and abject persons do exercise high and heavenly things.

Fourthly, the lay people have great occasion of evils and cause to fall when those men whose duty is to draw men from the affection of this world, by their continual conversation in this world teach men to love this world; and of the love of the world, cast them down heedling into hell.

Moreover in such priests that are so busied, there must needs follow hypocrisy. For when they be so mixed and confused with the lay people under the garment and habit of a priest, they live plainly after the lay fashion....

These be the four evils that I have spoken of, O fathers, O priests, by the which we are conformable to this world; by the which the face of the Church is made evil-favoured; by the which the state of it is destroyed, truly much more than it was in the beginning by the persecution of tyrants or afterward by the invasion that followed of heretics. For in the persecution of tyrants, the Church being vexed was made stronger and brighter: in the invasion of heretics, the Church being shaken was made wiser and more cunning in Holy Writ. But since this secularity was brought in, after that the secular manner of living crept in, in the men of the Church, the root of all spiritual life, that is to say, charity was extinct. The which taken away, there can neither a wise nor strong Church be in God....

THE SECOND PART OF REFORMATION

But be you reformed in the newness of your understanding: The second thing that Saint Paul commandeth is, that we be reformed into a new understanding: that we smell those things that be of God. Be we reformed unto those things that are contrary to those I spoke of even now, that is to say, to meekness, to soberness, to charity, to spiritual occupation. That as the said Paul writeth unto Titus: Reining all wickedness and worldly desires, we live in this world soberly, truly, and virtuously....[2]

[1] Hos. iv. 9.   [2] Tit. ii. 12.

The way whereby the Church may be reformed into better fashion is not for to make new laws, for there be laws many enough and out of number, as Solomon saith: Nothing is new under the sun.[1] For the evils there are now in the Church were before in times past: and there is no fault, but that [the] Fathers have provided very good remedies for it: there are no trespasses, but that there be laws against them in the body of canon law. Therefore it is no need that new laws and constitutions be made, but that those that are made already be kept. Wherefore in this your assembly, let those laws that are made be called before you and rehearsed. Those laws, I say, that restrain vice and those that further virtue.

First, let those laws be rehearsed that do warn you fathers, that ye put not over-soon your hands on every man or admit [him] unto Holy Orders. For there is the well of evils: that the broad gate of Holy Orders opened, every man that offereth himself, is all[2] where admitted without pulling back. Thereof springeth and cometh out the people that are in the Church, both of unlearned and evil priests. It is not enough for a priest, after my judgment, to construe a collette,[3] to put forth a question, or to answer to a sopheme; but much more a good, a pure, and a holy life, approved manners, meetly learning of Holy Scripture, some knowledge of the sacraments, chiefly, and above all things, the fear of God and love of the heavenly life.

Let the laws be rehearsed that command that benefices of the Church be given to those that are worthy. And that promotions be made in the Church by the right balance of virtue, not by carnal affection, not by acception[4] of persons whereby it happeneth nowadays that boys for old men, fools for wise men, evil for good, do reign and rule....

Let be rehearsed the laws and holy rules given of the Fathers of the life and honesty of clerks: that forbid that a clerk be no merchant; that he be no usurer; that he be no hunter; that he be no common player; that he bear no weapon; the laws that forbid clerks to haunt taverns; that forbid them to have suspect familiarity with women; the laws that command soberness and a measurableness in apparel and temperance in adorning of the body.

Let be rehearsed also to my lords, these monks, canons, and religious men, the laws that command them to go the straight way that leadeth unto heaven, leaving the broad way of the world....

Let the laws be rehearsed of the residence of bishops in their dioceses: that command that they look diligently and take heed to the health of souls: that they sow the Word of God: that they show themselves in their churches, at the least on great holy days: that they do sacrifice for their people: that they hear the causes and

---

[1] Eccles. i. 10.   [2] *all*, every.
[3] *collette*, proposition.   [4] *acception*, acceptance.

matters of poor men: that they sustain fatherless children and widows: that they exercise themself in works of virtue.

Let the laws be rehearsed of the good bestowing of the patrimony of Christ: the laws that command that the goods of the Church be spent not in costly building, not in sumptuous apparel and pomps, not in feasting and banqueting, not in excess and wantonness, not in enriching of kinsfolk, not in keeping of dogs, but in things profitable and necessary to the Church....

At the last, let be renewed those laws and constitutions of the fathers of the celebration of councils that command provincial councils to be oftener used for the reformation of the Church. For there never happeneth nothing more hurtful to the Church of Christ than the lack both of council, general and provincial....

Forsooth, if you keep the laws; and if you reform first your life to the rules of the canon laws, then shall ye give us light (in the which we may see what is to be done of our part), that is to say, the light of your good example. And we, seeing our fathers so keeping the laws, will gladly follow the steps of our fathers.

The clergy's and spiritual part once reformed in the Church, then may we with a just order proceed to the reformation of the lay part; the which, truly, will be very easy to do if we first be reformed. For the body followeth the soul. And such rulers as are in the city, like dwellers be in it. Wherefore, if priests that have the charge of souls be good, straight the people will be good. Our goodness shall teach them more clearly to be good than all other teachings and preachings. Our goodness shall compel them into the right way truly more effectuously than all your suspendings and cursings.

Wherefore, if we will have the lay people to live after your wish and will, first live you yourself after the will of God, and so, trust me, ye shall get in them whatsoever ye will.

Ye will be obeyed of them: and right it is. For in the epistle to the Hebrews these are the words of Saint Paul to the lay people: 'Obey', saith he, 'to your rulers; and be you under them.'[1] But if ye will have this obedience, first perform in you the reason and cause of obedience....

You will reap their carnal things and gather tithes and offerings without any striving: right it is. For Saint Paul writing unto the Romans saith: They are debtors and ought to minister unto you in carnal things....[2]

Ye will have the Church's liberty, and not to be drawn afore secular judges. And that also is right, for it is in the Psalms: Touch ye not mine anointed.[3] But if ye desire this liberty, first unloose yourself from the worldly bondage and from the services of men, and lift up yourself into the true liberty, the spiritual liberty of Christ....

[1] Heb. xiii. 17.   [2] Cf. Rom. xv. 27.   [3] Ps. civ. 15.

Ye would be out of business in rest and peace: and that is convenient. But if ye will have peace, come again to the God of peace and love. Come again to Christ in whom is the very true peace of the Holy Ghost, the which passeth all wit: come again to yourself and to your priestly living....

These are they, reverent fathers and right famous men, that I thought to be said for the reformation of the Church's estate. I trust, ye will take them of your gentleness to the best. And if, peradventure, it be thought that I have past my bounds in this sermon or have said anything out of temper, forgive it me: and ye shall forgive a man speaking of very zeal, a man sorrowing the decay of the Church. And consider the thing itself, not regarding any foolishness. Consider the miserable form and state of the Church, and endeavour yourselves with all your minds to reform it....

Go ye now in the Spirit that ye have called on: that by the help of It, ye may in this your council find out, discern, and ordain those things that may be profitable to the Church, praise unto you, and honour unto God unto whom be all honour and glory forevermore. Amen.

COLOPHON: Thomas Berthelet *regius impressor excudebat*....
[1530?]

HUGH LATIMER
1485–1555

Hugh Latimer was born in Leicestershire, the son of a yeoman, and rose to become one of the most influential bishops among the English Reformers. Even during his student days at Cambridge, Latimer was a vigorous dissenter. When he received his degree of Bachelor of Divinity, in 1510, he based his 'whole oration' on the errors of Luther and Melanchthon. At that time, he declared, 'I was as obstinate a papist as any in England.' His acquaintance with Thomas Bilney slowly weaned him away from his early orthodoxy; and he was accused of heresy and brought before Wolsey, who dismissed the charges and gave him licence to preach at any place in the kingdom.

Latimer's great opportunity for advancement came in 1529 when, among other Cambridge teachers, he was appointed to study the validity of the king's marriage to his brother's widow, Katherine of Aragon. Siding with those who favoured the divorce, Latimer curried favour with Henry VIII, and was soon appointed a royal chaplain.

Through the recommendation of his close friend Thomas Cranmer, Archbishop of Canterbury, Latimer was made Bishop of Worcester in

*1535. The next year he was appointed by the king to preach in St Paul's
before the Convocation of the English hierarchy. In his sermon, Latimer
made an earnest appeal to the Reformers to unite in the king's cause and
subdue those who clung to the tenets of the old faith. It was probably this
sermon that caused Cranmer to appoint Latimer to preach to the crowds
that gathered on such spectacular occasions as the burning of Catholic
dissenters, notably Friar John Forest, who refused to take the Oath of
Supremacy. Latimer claims, however, that he recoiled at such a difficult
task and only accepted in the hope that he might 'convert Forest'.*

*It was a disappointment to Latimer to find that so much of the old faith
had been retained in the Six Articles drawn up in 1539. His protests were
so outspoken that he was made to resign his bishopric.*

*The see was again offered to him when Edward VI came to the throne,
but Latimer refused it. Through Cranmer's urging, he accepted a place on
the royal commission that was appointed to reform ecclesiastical law. In
1549 he returned to preaching and gave his famous* Sermon on the plough
*in which he shows his keen disappointment in the failure of the Reforma-
tion to effect deep spiritual changes in the lives of the people. As a dutiful
clergyman, Latimer declared that he was obliged to castigate the rich, 'you
landlords, you rent-raisers, I may say, you step-lords, you have for your
possessions too much'. Such abuses 'pluck salvation from the people'. He
would have it remembered that it was chiefly the poor,'the yeomen's sons',
who had maintained 'the faith of Christ'. A practical Christian faith is
the keynote of Latimer's sermons in the reign of Edward VI, which brought
his active career as a preacher to an end.*

*When Mary I ascended the throne, in 1553, Latimer was soon charged
with heresy and tried several times before a committee of which Nicholas
Harpsfield was a member. Refusing to accept the doctrine of transubstantiation and the Mass, Latimer was found guilty of heresy and condemned to
the Tower to await execution. On 16 October 1555, with Nicholas Ridley,
Bishop of London, Latimer was burned at the stake outside Balliol College,
Oxford.*

*Latimer's writings consist wholly of sermons which were printed
separately and in collected editions. Some of the latter were reprinted as
late as 1635. In the* Sermon on the card *(1529), he made novel use of
a popular card game called, 'Triumph'. Latimer intended the sermon 'for
all men and women of the world'. He drew his text for it from the
Scriptural account of the baptism of Christ by St John the Baptist. His use
of the term 'Christmas cardes', though not in the modern sense, is the
earliest in the language.*

The Sermon on the Card

Tu quis es?[1] Which words are as much to say in English: Who art thou? These be the words of the Pharisees which were sent by the

Who art Thou? Jews unto Saint John Baptist in the wilderness to have knowledge of him whom he was: Which words they spoke unto him for an evil intent, thinking that he would have taken on him to be Christ; and so they would have had him done with their good wills because they knew that he was more carnal and given to their laws than Christ, [and,] indeed, should be,

Not the Christ as they perceived by their old prophecies; and also because they marvelled much of his great doctrine, preaching, and baptising, they were in doubt whether he was Christ, or not. Wherefore they said unto him: Who art thou? Then answered Saint John and confessed that he was not Christ.[2]

Now here is to be noted the great and prudent answer of Saint John Baptist unto the Pharisees, that when they required of him who he was, he would not directly answer of himself what he was himself, but he said, he was not Christ. By the which saying, he thought to put the Jews and Pharisees out of their false opinion and belief towards him in that they would have had him to exercise the office of Christ and so declared further unto them of Christ, saying: He is

Latchet of His shoe in the midst of you and amongst you whom ye know not, whose latchet of His shoe I am not worthy to unloose or undo.[3] By this you may perceive that Saint John spoke much in the laud and praise of Christ, his Master, professing himself to be in nowise like unto Him.

So likewise it shall be necessary unto all men and women of this world not to ascribe unto themself any goodness of themself, but all unto Our Lord God, as shall appear hereafter when this question aforesaid, Who are thou? shall be moved unto them—not as the Pharisees did unto Saint John of an evil purpose, but of a good and simple mind, as may appear hereafter.

Now then, according to the preacher's mind, let every man and woman of a good and simple mind, contrary to the Pharisees intent, ask this question, 'Who art thou?' This question must be moved to themself what they be of themself on this fashion: What art thou of thy only and natural generation between father and mother when thou camest into this world? What substance, what virtue, what goodness art thou of by thyself? Which question, if thou rehearse oftentimes unto thyself, thou shalt well perceive and understand how thou shalt make answer unto it, which must be made on this ways:

<hr>

[1] John i. 19. [2] John i. 20. [3] John i. 26–7.

I am of myself and by myself, coming from my natural father and mother, the child of the ire and indignation of God, the true inheritor of hell, a lump of sin, and working nothing of myself, but all towards hell except I have better help of another than I have of myself. . . .

Now then, seeing thou art a Christian man, what shall be thy answer of this question: Who art thou? The answer of this question is, when I ask it unto myself, I must say that I am a Christian man, a Christian woman, the child of everlasting joy through the merits of the bitter Passion of Christ. This is a joyful answer. Here we may see how much we be bound and in danger unto God that hath revived us from death to life, and saved us that were damned. Which great benefit we cannot well consider unless we do remember what we were of ourself before we meddled with Him or His laws. And the more we know our feeble nature and set less by it, the more we shall conceive and know in our hearts what God hath done for us; and the more that we know what God hath done for us, the less we shall set by ourself, [and] the more we shall love and please God. So that in no condition we shall either know ourself or God except we do utterly confess ourself to be mere vileness and corruption.

Well now it is come unto this point, that we be Christian men [and] Christian women. I pray you, what doth Christ require of a Christian man or a Christian woman? Christ requireth nothing else of a Christian man or a woman but that they will observe His rule. For likewise as he is a good Austin friar that keepeth well Saint Austin's rule, so is he a good Christian man that keepeth well Christ's rule.

Now then, what is Christ's rule? Christ's rule consisteth in many things, as in the commandments and the works of mercy, and so forth. And for because I cannot declare Christ's rule unto you at one time as it ought to be done, I will apply myself according to your custom this time of Christenmass: I will, as I said, declare unto Christ's rule but that shall be in Christ's cards. And where you are wont to celebrate Christenmass in playing at cards, I intend, with God's grace, to deal unto you Christ's cards wherein you shall perceive Christ's rule. Christmas-cards

The game that we will play at shall be called the Triumph* which, if it be well played at, he that dealeth shall win. The players shall likewise win, and the standers and lookers upon shall do the same, insomuch there is no man that is willing to play at this Triumph with these cards but they shall be all winners and no losers. Let, therefore, every Christian man and woman play at these cards that they may have and obtain the Triumph.

You must mark also that the Triumph must apply to fetch home unto him all the other cards whatsoever suit they be of. Now then, take ye this first card which must appear and be showed unto you as followeth: you have heard what was spoken to the men of the Old Law: Thou shalt not kill: whosoever shall kill shall be in danger of judgment. But I say unto you of the New Law, saith Christ, that whosoever is angry with his neighbor shall be in danger of judgment: and whosoever shall say unto his neighbor, Raca, that is to say, brainless, or any other like word of rebuking, shall be in danger of council: and whosoever shall say unto his neighbour, fool, shall be in danger of hell fire.[1] This card was made and spoken by Christ, as appeareth in the first [fifth] chapter of Saint Matthew.

Now it must be noted that whosoever shall play with this card must first, before they play with it, know the strength and virtue of the same. Wherefore you must well note and mark terms, how they be spoken and to what purpose. Let us, therefore, read it once or twice that we may be the better acquainted with it.

Now behold and see this card is divided into four parts: the first part is one of the commandments that was given unto Moses in the Old Law before the coming of Christ: Which commandment we of the New Law be bound to observe and keep, and [it] is one of our commandments. The other three parts spoken by Christ be nothing else but expositions unto the first part of this commandment, for, in very effect, all these four parts be but one commandment, that is to say: Thou shalt not kill. . . .[2]

[According to Christ's teaching, one may kill the soul as well as the body. In reference to the former, Latimer shows the several ways this commandment may be broken. He dwells especially on bad example and indifference or 'silence' to wrong-doing of young people by parents and those in authority.]

Wherefore, I exhort all true Christian men and women to give good example unto your children and servants, and suffer not them by silence to offend. 'Every man must be in his own house', according to Saint Austin's mind, 'a bishop': not all only giving good example, but teach according to it, rebuke and punish vice; not suffering your children and servants to forget the laws of God. You ought to see, they have their belief; to know the commandments of God, to keep their holy days, not to lose their time in idleness. If they do so, you shall all suffer pain for it if God be true of His saying, as there is no doubt thereof: and so you may perceive that there be many one that breaketh this card, Thou shalt not kill, and playeth therewith oftentimes at the blind trump, whereby they be no winners, but great losers.

But who be those nowadays that can clear themself of these manifest murders used to their children and servants? I think not the contrary, but that many hath these two ways slain their own children unto

[1] Matt. v. 21–2.   [2] Exod. xx. 13.

their damnation unless the great mercy of God were not ready to help them when they repent therefore.

Wherefore, considering that we be so prone and ready to continue in sin, let us cast down ourself with Mary Magdalen: and the more we bow down with her toward Christ's feet, the more we shall be afraid to rise again in sin: and the more we know and submit ourself, the more we shall be forgiven: and the less we know and submit ourself, the less we shall be forgiven, as appeareth by this example, following, of Christ:

When He was in this world amongst the Jews and Pharisees, there was a great Pharisee whose name was Simon. This Pharisee desired Christ on a time to dine with him, thinking in himself that he was able and worthy to give Christ a dinner. Christ refused not his dinner, but came unto him. In time of their dinner, it chanced there came into the house a great and a common sinner named Mary Magdalen. As soon as she perceived Christ, she cast herself down and called unto her remembrance what she was of herself, and how greatly she had offended God. Whereby she conceived in Christ great love, and so came near unto Him and washed His feet with bitter tears and shed upon His head precious ointment, thinking that by Him she should be delivered from her sins.

This great and proud Pharisee, seeing that Christ did accept her oblation, in the best part, had great indignation against this woman, and said to himself: If this Man Christ were a holy prophet, as He is taken for, He would not suffer this sinner to come so nigh Him. Christ, understanding the naughty mind of this Pharisee, said unto him: 'Simon, I have somewhat to say unto thee.' 'Say what you please', quod the Pharisee. 'Then', said Christ, 'I pray thee tell Me this—if there be a man to whom is owing twenty pounds by one and forty by another, this man to whom this money is owing perceiveth these two men be not able to pay him, and he forgiveth them both. Which of these two debtors ought to love this man most?' The Pharisee said, 'That man ought to love him best that had most forgiven him.' 'Likewise', said Christ, 'it is by this woman. She hath loved Me most, therefore most is forgiven her: she hath known her sins most, whereby she hath most loved Me: and thou hast least loved Me, because thou hast least known thy sins. Therefore because thou hast least known thine offences, thou art least forgiven.'[1] So this proud Pharisee had an answer to delay his pride.

And think you not but that there be amongst us a great number of these proud Pharisees which think themself worthy to bid Christ to dinner which will perk[2] and presume to sit by Christ in the church and have disdain of this poor woman Magdalen, their poor neighbour, with a high, disdainous, and solemn countenance. And being always

[1] Luke vii. 36–50.   [2] *perk*, act pertly.

desirous to climb highest in the church, reckoning theirself more worthy to sit there than another, I fear me, poor Magdalen under the board and in the belfry hath more forgiven of Christ than they have. For it is like, that those Pharisees do less know themself and their offences, whereby they less love God, and so they be less forgiven.

I would to God, we would follow this example and be like unto Magdalen. I doubt not but we be all Magdalens in falling into sin and in offending: but we be not again Magdalens in knowing ourself and in rising from sin. If we be the true Magdalens, we should be as willing to forsake our sin and rise from sin as we were willing to commit sin and to continue in it: And we then should know ourself best and make a more perfect answer than ever we did unto this question: Who art thou? To the which we might answer, that we be true Christian men and women. And then, I say, you should understand and know how you ought to play at this card, Thou shalt not kill, without any interruption of your deadly enemies, the Turks, [then menacing Europe, are used figuratively throughout the sermon to represent the evils that war against men's souls] and so triumph at the last, winning everlasting life in glory. Amen.

[From John Foxe's *Actes and Monuments*. The tenor and effect of certain *Sermons* made by Master Latimer in Cambridge about the year 1529. fol. John Day, 1563.]

JOHN DE FECKENHAM
c. 1518–1585

Westminster Abbey's last abbot, John de Feckenham, was one of the most noted scholars and preachers of early post-Reformation England. He was born about 1518 of poor parents in Feckenham Forest in Worcestershire. Facts in his life are few until 1539 when, as a young monk of the soon to be dissolved Evesham Abbey, he took a Bachelor of Divinity degree at Gloucester College, Oxford, a place of study for Benedictines, later closed by the king. Though the monks of Evesham were at first obstinate about taking the Oath of Supremacy, the majority did so, including Feckenham. First as chaplain to Bishop John Bell of Worcester and then to his lifelong friend, Edmund Bonner, Bishop of London, Feckenham, according to Thomas Stapleton, 'set forth [the Royal Supremacy] in his open sermons in King Henry's days'.

These early sermons have not survived nor those he preached at Paul's Cross in the king's last years when he argued that the young prince Edward, a minor, could not as king exercise the supremacy, and urged the nation to return to Rome. For his outspoken views, he was imprisoned during the entire reign of Edward VI. But Feckenham was revered by Catholics and Reformers alike for his kindness and impartiality, preferring debate to harsh tactics in religious dissension. These traits and his ability as a theologian were responsible for his being 'borrowed' from the Tower to take part in the famous doctrinal debates, particularly on the Eucharist, held at the houses of Sir William Cecil and Sir John Cheke, who through Feckenham recanted during Queen Mary's reign. One of his foremost opponents during these meetings was John Hooper, a brilliant scholar almost twice Feckenham's age, a former Cistercian monk at Gloucester, who was made Bishop of Worcester at the close of Edward's reign.

During the reign of Mary I, many honours came to Feckenham, but he had also to perform many difficult tasks. He was appointed royal chaplain and Dean of St Paul's Cathedral. His mission to 'console and convert' Lady Jane Grey was fruitless. But he was successful in persuading Mary to release her sister Elizabeth from the Tower, a good turn which the latter never forgot. The leniency and fairness that he urged at the trials of his friends Cranmer, Ridley, and Latimer won him the respect of the Reformers.

Feckenham's interest in education made him encourage the founding in 1555 of two colleges at Oxford, namely, Trinity College by Sir Thomas Pope and St John's College by Sir Thomas White. Both men were his close friends. In recognition of his efforts, the university conferred on him the degree of Doctor of Divinity.

The crowning event of Feckenham's life came when Mary I determined to restore Westminster Abbey to the Benedictine monks, and he was chosen abbot. A description of his installation as abbot is given in Machyn's Diary: 'On the 21st day of November, 1556, was Dr Feckenham, late Dean of St Paul's, put into the Abbey of Westminster as abbot there; and fourteen monks were shorn. And the morrow after, the Lord Abbot with his convent went a procession after the old fashion in their monk's weeds.... On the 29th day, at Westminster, was the Lord Abbot installed and did wear a mitre. The Lord Cardinal [Pole] was there and many bishops....The Lord Chancellor [Gardiner] sang Mass and the Abbot made the sermon.'

Feckenham's career came to an abrupt end with the queen's death. As Lord Abbot, he sat in Elizabeth's first parliament where prior to the passing of the Act of Uniformity, he made a long oration, giving three rules 'whereby your Honours shall be able to put difference between the true religion of God and the counterfeit; and therein never be deceived'. Feckenham's rules would have nullified the reforms made by Henry VIII and Edward VI. It was a fatal plea. In a final effort to win him over to her cause, the queen offered to make him Archbishop of Canterbury. When he refused, the Abbey was dissolved and Feckenham sent to the Tower, the beginning of twenty-four years of incarceration in various places in England.

According to a sketch of his life by Dom Hugh Aveling, Feckenham never lost his great sense of humour nor his genial way of trying to convert Reformers. In 1577 he was committed to the care of Richard Cox, Bishop of Ely, who was told by the queen, that Feckenham 'being a man of learning and temper', might be persuaded 'to acknowledge her supremacy and come to the Church'. But Cox, soon worn out with the abbot's fondness for debate, asked that he be moved. He was sent to Wisbech Castle prison, where he died in 1585.

Only two of his works were printed during Feckenham's lifetime: A notable sermon *(1555) and* Two homilies upon the crede *[1555?]. Though the sermon occasioned by the death of the Spanish Queen Joanna is long and rambling, it has some fine passages on preparation for death, using the ancient Christian motif, the 'Four Last Things'. Only a passing reference is made to the queen, due probably to the fact that she had been mentally ill most of her life and was only a nominal ruler of Spain under her son Charles V. The* Homilies *are extremely simple explanations of the first two articles of the Creed.* The oration of Dr Feckenham...made in Parliament House, 1559 *is printed in* a Collection of tracts on all subjects, *ed. J. Somers (London, 1748).*

A Notable Sermon

A Notable Sermon made within St Paul's church in London in the presence of certain of the king's and queen's most honourable privy council at the celebration of the exequies of the right excellent and famous princess, Lady Jane, Queen of Spain, Sicily, and Navarre, etc., the eighteenth of June, *anno.* 1555. By master John Feckenham, Dean of the said church of Paul's. Set forth at the request of some in authority whose request could not be denied. *Excusum Londini in aedibus Roberti Caly, typographi, mense Augusti, 1555. Cum privilegio.*

Gens absque consilio; et sine prudentia; utinam saperent et intelligerent ac novissima providerent;[1] People void of good counsel, void of wisdom and of all foresight of things to come: *utinam saperent et intelligerent:* would God, they would be wise and understand and provide for the last things. These are the words of the prophet Moses, written in the thirty-second chapter of Deuteronomy, which I have chosen as a theme or proposition, at this time, to stay upon forsomuch as you do so manifestly declare yourselves to be *gens absque consilio,* people clean void of all good consideration, know-

[1] Deut. xxxii. 29.

ledge, or counsel what to do, *et sine prudentia*, and without wisdom and foresight to know how things ought to be done. That by the declaration, made of the said theme, you might be brought into some more better consideration of yourselves and of your own most frail and brickel[1] estates; and thereby to learn, now at the length (after so oft callings upon and so many virtuous and most godly instructions), these three notable and chief lessons: whereof the first is *sapere*, to be wise; the second is *intelligere*, to understand; and the third is *novissima providere*, to make provision for the last things....

I shall entreat chiefly of these four last things, that is to say, of death, of the judgment of God, of the pains of hell, and of the joys of heaven. For the which four last things, I would have you in the short course of this present life to make provision: first, that we may here finish our life, and die well; second, that we may receive at the hands of God a comfortable and a merciful judgment; thirdly, we must here provide to avoid the horrible pains of hell; fourth, and last, we must provide so here to live that we may be partakers of the life everlasting and joys of heaven. And to avoid confusion herein, the manner of this our provision-making must be sundry and diverse, like as the vocations, degrees, and estates of men be sundry and diverse. As the bishops, priests, and prelates of Christ's Church, having the flock of Christ committed to their great cure and charge, they must make their provision for these four last things by a circumspect feeding of Christ's flock with good and wholesome doctrine, by a diligent search of their parts to be made for the lost sheep which have perished in the late plague of errors and heresies, by a wise bringing of them back again into the fold and unity of Christ's Church, by a merciful binding and knitting of the wounds of the sore cut and mangled sheep, by a charitable nourishing and comforting of the weak, sick, and feeble among them, having in their breasts toward their flocks the very zeal of a good pastor and shepherd: whose zeal is such (as Christ witnesseth) *qui animam suam dat pro ovibus suis*,[2] that he will not stick 'to give his life for his sheep', like as Our Saviour Christ hath given us example already and as Moses desired *deleri de libro vitae*:[3] to be blotted out of the Book of Life; and Saint Paul, *anathema esse a Christo pro fratribus*;[4] to be accursed from Christ for his brethren.

And their provision for these four last things being on this wise laid for and circumspectly made, God shall grant them all and send unto them a quiet and blessed death and a most comfortable and merciful judgment, delivering them from the horrible pains of hell and restoring them for the eternal bliss and joys of heaven.

All the rest of Christ's family and household which are **not**

---

[1] *brickel*, brittle. [2] John x. 11.
[3] Exod. xxxii. 32. [4] Rom. ix. 3.

shepherds but sheep of His fold and pasture, you must here begin and make your provision for these four last things. First, by a diligent giving ear and hearkening to the voices of your shepherds and by a circumspect and wise refusal of all counterfeit and strange voices: When the true sheep of Christ, *non sequuntur alienum sed fugiunt ab illo, quia non noverunt voces alienorum*,[1] do not follow a strange shepherd, but flee from him, for they know not the voices of strangers. Neither will they be deceived by the strange voices of the Arians in denying the deity of Our Saviour Christ; nor by the strange voices of the Nestorians and Eutychians in denying Christ's humanity; nor by the strange voices of Manicheans in their denial of the free choice of man; nor yet the strange voices of the Pelagians, attributing too much to the free will of man.

When the true sheep of Christ will not be deceived by the barren voice of Eunomius the Solifidiane; nor by the monstrous voice of Berengarius in his denial of Christ's very real and bodily presence in the most Blessed Sacrament of the Altar; nor yet by the evil skreaking[2] and most strange voices of Martin Luther, Martin Bucer, Peter Martyr, Corolastradius, Zwinglius, Oecolampadius, and others, the very pale-breakers of the unity of Christ's Church, the breeders of all schisms and contentions in the same, the blasphemers of Christ's sacraments, the subverters of all good orders and constitutions, the revivers of old cankered and rusty heresies, and now by them new furnished and set forth to the show, and therefore their books justly condemned here in this realm by a late proclamation* set forth by the King's and Queen's majesties. Whereunto I do exhort you to be obedient and to bring in your books of heresies according to the purpose thereof; forasmuch as the true sheep of Christ will give no ear unto their most monstrous and strange voices, when these and all other like voices which do dissuade from the antiquity, unity, and universality of Christ's Church, needs be most monstrous and strange voices.

Therefore, O ye Londoners and inhabitants of this city, cease your great folly, I beseech you, and be you no longer *sicut gens absque consilio, et sine prudentia*, as people without good counsel and all foresight what will ensue and follow hereafter; *utinam saperetis et intelligeretis ac novissima provideretis*, Would God, you would be wise, perceive and understand, and make provision for these four last things....

Ye gentlemen and noblemen, which in living here in this world be very politic and full of all manner of worldly provisions, *utinam saperetis et intelligeretis ac novissima provideretis*, Would God, you would be wise and understand, and make provision for these four last things that you may finish the race and course of this short life with a quiet death and, finally, to receive at the hands of God a merciful judgment

---

[1] John x. 5.   [2] *skreaking*, shrieking.

into joy and bliss, and not to sustain the torments of hell. The manner of this your provision-making must be by the maintenance of God's glory and honour, by your upright ministrations of justice, and by the authority committed unto you of God to defend the Catholic faith and religion of God, his Church and most blessed sacraments and all the ministers of the same, serving God in their bishoprics, cathedral churches, houses of religion, universities, colleges, or elsewhere. When otherwise, doubtless your provision made for these four last things shall be all too short and after a wrong sort....

[Feckenham admonishes parents, children, and servants to provide for their last end by attending to their particular duties in life.]

So that all kind of men for the time of their abode here in this world must make their provision for these four last things whether they be married, be unmarried, wife or single woman, parents or children, masters or servants, superiors or inferiors, magistrates, bearing rule, or subjects, being ruled; whether they be of the clergy or of the laity, every man must here provide by a circumspect and diligent walk in their vocations, for the love, favour, and friendship of God, by observation of His commandments, Christ Himself witnessing the same and saying, *Si praecepta mea servaveritis, manebetis in dilectione mea*:[1] If you will keep My precepts, you shall abide in My love and have My favour and friendship. Whose love and friendship at the last hour of death shall stand us in better stead than all the riches and lordships of the world. When at that hour though all thy friends, kinfolks, and acquaintances should come with millions of gold or yet by force of arms, they may not at that dreadful grisly and last hour, do thee any help or comfort. When other help, refuge, or succour at that time, thou shalt have none but only at the hands of God.

Let us, therefore, in all the mean space of this present life so dread and fear God, so embrace and love Him, and so honour and worship Him that we at the last hour may have His favour and friendship. *Et si deus pro nobis, quis contra nos?*[2] And if God be on our side, who can be against us? And then we shall be sure to have at the finishing and knitting up of this life, a very quiet and a joyful death; to receive at the hands of God a very merciful and most comfortable judgment, thereby to avoid and escape the torments of hell and to inherit the joys of heaven. To the which He will bring us all that hath so dearly bought it for us by the effusion of His most Precious Blood. To whom with God the Father and the Holy Ghost, be all praise, honour and glory for now and evermore. Amen.

COLOPHON: Imprinted at London by Robt. Caly...the xv day of August, M.D.L.V.

[1] John xv. 10.　　　　[2] Cf. Rom. viii. 31.

WILLIAM ATKINSON, 1457?–1504

AND

RICHARD WHYTFORD, 1476?–1542

The first English version of De imitatione Christi, *known as the 'old version', was made by an anonymous translator but was not printed until 1893. At the request of Lady Margaret Beaufort a second English translation was made by William Atkinson, a native of York. The scant records about his life show that he attended Cambridge University and was made a Fellow of Pembroke Hall in 1477. After taking a Bachelor of Divinity degree in 1485, Atkinson was ordained to the priesthood. In 1498 the university conferred on him the degree of Doctor of Divinity, and he was appointed a canon of Lincoln Cathedral. At the time of his death in 1504 he was a canon of Windsor, and was buried in St George's Chapel.*

Atkinson's only known work is the translation of the first three books of the Imitatio. *The fourth book was translated by Lady Beaufort from a French version. Seven editions were printed before 1585. Though not as distinguished as later versions because of its florid style, the popularity of the* Imitacyon *places it with those little books that did most to mould the thought and expression of the times.*

In 1530 Richard Whytford, a Welshman born near Holywell about 1476, made the third English translation of the Imitatio. *Little is known of his early life until he was appointed a Fellow of Queens' College, Cambridge. After leaving the university, Whytford was ordained to the priesthood and became a chaplain in the house of William Blount, fourth Lord Mountjoy. Some time prior to 1496, he went to Paris with Mountjoy's son to supervise the latter's studies and continue his own. Erasmus, who was then in the French capital, was engaged as the youth's tutor, and young Mountjoy and Whytford became lifelong friends of the Dutch scholar.*

While in France Whytford studied philosophy at the University of Paris and took a Master of Arts degree. When he returned to England in 1498, he was appointed chaplain to Bishop Richard Fox at Winchester Cathedral, and during this time a friendship sprang up with Sir Thomas More and Bishop Fisher. About 1505 Whytford followed in the footsteps of his uncle Richard Whytford and became a Brigittine monk in the famous Syon monastery in Middlesex. S. H. Sole in the preface to his edition of the Jesus Psalter *describes the monastery as 'a foundation of Henry V with a charter of the year 1414, its revenues being derived from the alien priories suppressed in his reign. It consisted of a double convent, the one for men, the other for women, wholly enclosed from the world and from each other, having one church with two floors of which the nuns occupied the upper and the monks the lower. The two communities made up together by the founder's design the number of the college of the apostles and the school of the disciples, that is, 13 apostles, counting St Paul, and 72 disciples. There were 60 nuns in one convent, and 13 priests, 4 deacons, and 8 lay brethren in the other; and of these the chief by name and office was the Father Confessor.'*

When Syon monastery *was suppressed by Cromwell in 1540, Whyt-ford with several other monks refused to take the Oath of Royal Supremacy and continued to preach against the new religion. But for the elder Mount-joy's influence, Henry VIII would have imprisoned Whytford. It was arranged for him to remain in the custody of the Mountjoys, who were then living in London. He took up his duties as family chaplain, and did not relinquish them until his death in 1542.*

Most of the fifteen works that have been attributed to Whytford were written before 1540. Among those that are definitely assigned to him are: A dayly exercyse and experyence of dethe (1537) *written at the request of Dame Elizabeth Gibbs, Abbess of Syon;* A werke of preparation unto cōmunion [1531], *later editions of which were augmented and the title changed to* A dialogue or cōmunicacion bytwene the curate and the parochiane for preparacion unto howselinge; The werke for householders; The boke called the Pype, or Tonne, of the lyfe of perfection (1532) *written in opposition to the Lutheran heresy; and* Here foloweth dyuers holy instrucyons necessarye for the helth of mannes soule (1541).

Whytford's translation of the Imitatio, *which he entitled* The folowynge of Cryste, *was made about 1510, but was not printed until about 1531. It was the first complete English version translated from the Latin. Atkinson, according to Whytford, had 'left oute moche parte of some of the chaptyres'. E. J. Klein, Whytford's first editor, commends his proficiency 'in rendering the concise phrasing characteristic of so much of the* Imitatio' *and his 'apt and telling use of English proverbs', many of which are original with him.*

Among the works attributed to Whytford is the Jesus Psalter, *but it is not likely that he did more than edit it, since several fifteenth-century manuscripts of it are extant. The earliest printed edition is 1529. The* Psalter *follows the pattern of medieval psalters in the repetition of the name Jesus, which is invoked ten times at the opening of each of the fifteen sections, thus equalling in number the one hundred and fifty psalms of David. In England the* Jesus Psalter *has remained to the present time one of the most popular forms of a peculiarly national devotion, namely, the cultus of the Holy Name.*

The Imitation of Christ

TRANSLATED BY
WILLIAM ATKINSON

A full devout and ghostly treatise of *The Imitation and Following the Blessed Life of Our Most Merciful Saviour Christ* compiled in Latin by the right worshipful Doctor Master John Gerson and translated into English the year of our Lord, 1502, by Master William Atkinson, Doctor of Divinity at the special request and commandment of the full excellent Princess Margaret, mother to our sovereign lord King Henry VII and Countess of Richmond and Derby.

THE FIFTH CHAPTER[1] IS OF
THE READING OF HOLY
SCRIPTURE

The principal thing that we shall inquire in Scripture is charity and not elegance in speech; and we should endeavour ourself to read the Scripture with as great fervour of spirit as it was received first. And wisdom would, we should follow those authors and books where we may have most sweet and profitable feeding for our soul. The fame of subtle philosophers, the knowledge of poets and rhetoric as a smoke or fume vanisheth away, but the truth of God abideth without end. And as Our Lord speaketh to us without exception of person most expediently to us, so we shall without any exception of faithful person or work, study and read those works that most we think should please God and to us most profitable.

If thou would draw the spiritual water of wisdom out of the well of Scripture, incline the vessel of thy soul by meekness and confidence

[1] Book I.

The Following of Christ

TRANSLATED BY
RICHARD WHYTFORD

A book newly translated out of Latin into English called *The following of Christ*.

ON THE READING OF HOLY
SCRIPTURE[1]

Charity is to be sought in Holy Scripture and not eloquence: and it should be read with the same spirit that it was first made. We ought also to seek in Holy Scripture ghostly profit rather than curiosity of style: and as gladly shall we read simple and devout books as books of high learning and cunning. Let not the authority of thine authors mislike thee, whether he were of great cunning or little, but that the love of the very pure truth stir thee to read. Ask not, "Who said this?", but take heed what is said. Men pass lightly away, but the truth of God abideth.

Almighty God speaketh to us in His Scripture in divers manners, without accepting[2] of persons, but our curiosity oft letteth us in reading of Scripture when we will reason and argue things that we should meekly and simply pass over. If thou wilt profit by reading of Scripture, read meekly, simply, and faithfully; and never desire to have thereby the name of cunning.

[1] Book I, Chapter v.
[2] *accepting*, favouring.

without desire of curiosity or name of excellence. Inquire diligently, and quietly receive the holy sentences of saints: let not the proverbs and holy, wise similitudes of blessed [early Church] Fathers displease thee, for they were not spoken without cause.

Ask gladly and hear meekly the saying of saints; and mislike thee not the parables of ancient Fathers, for they were not spoken without great cause.

COLOPHON: This book imprinted at London in Fleet Street at the sign of the George by Richard Pynson.... 1503.

COLOPHON: Imprinted by me Robert Wyer, dwelling in Saint Martin's parish beside Charing Cross in the Bishop of Norwich rents. [1531.]

RICHARD WHYTFORD[1]

A Work for Householders

A Work for Householders or for them that have the guiding or governance of any company. Gathered and set forth by a professed brother of Sion, Richard Whytford. And newly corrected and printed again with an addition of policy for householding, set forth also by the same brother.

Unto the devout readers: Richard Whytford a professed brother of Sion, due salutation in Our Lord God and most sweet Saviour Jesu:

THE PREFACE

Where I had sent forth this poor lesson unto a private person and special friend, the copy thereof came unto the sight of certain devout persons that were (as they said) well contented therewith and edified thereby. So that they instantly required me to put it newly forth in common,[2] supposing, in their devout mind, it should be unto other persons, as it seemed unto them, edificative and profitable. I beseech Our Lord, it may be so: And that you would not ascribe it unto any presumption in me, but rather unto their devotion and charity, and with like heart and mind to receive it. The end of the preface.

THE ARGUMENT

The matter is directed principally unto householders or unto them that have guiding and governance of any company, for an order to be kept both in themself and in them that they have in rule and charge.

[1] For biographical sketch, see pp. 376–7.   [2] *common*, general public.

ON THE SECOND COMMANDMENT

Wherefore I have set out here a pretty lesson which, I pray you, teach your children and every child that cometh into your company; you shall, I trust, do much good thereby:

> If I lie, backbite, or steal,
> If I curse, scorn, mock, or swear,
> If I chide, fight, strive, or threat,
> Then am I worthy to be beat,
> Good mother, or mistress mine.
> If any of these nine,
> I trespass to your knowing,
> With a new rod and a fine,
> Early naked before I dine,
> Amend me with a scourging.

And then, I pray you, fulfil and perform their petition and request, and think it not cruelly but mercifully done. For the wise man saith: Who spareth the rod, hateth the child.[1] And in another place: If thou have children, saith he, correct them betimes and hold them under while they been young.[2] Your daily practice doth show unto you that if you powder your flesh while it is new and sweet, it will continue good meat; but if it smell before it be powdered, all the salt you have shall never make it seasonable. Powder your children therefore betimes, and then you love them and shall have comfort of them.

I did appoint the correction before unto the mother or mistress, for commonly they done take the labour of that ministry and service. Notwithstanding there may be said, 'father' or 'master', and the staff or foot of the rhyme be all one. But whosoever do the correction, whether it be in lashes or in words, let it be done with the charity of Our Lord and with a mild and soft spirit that ever it be done for the reformation of the persons rather than for the revenging of the default. And therefore should you never do any manner of correction while you been vexed, chafed, troubled, wroth, or angry for any cause, but rather for that time defer the correction, and another time by good deliberation take the persons on part,[3] or if the trespass be openly known, then do it openly that all the lookers thereupon may be warned thereby: and give them a good lesson before the correction and tell them you do the correction against your mind, compelled thereunto by conscience, and require them to put you no more unto such labour and pain. 'For if you do', say you, 'you must suffer part of the pain with me, and therefore you

---

[1] Prov. xiii. 24.   [2] Ecclus. vii. 25.   [3] *on part*, aside.

shall now have the experience and proof what it is unto us both.'
And then pay truly: and afterward forthwith forgive them clearly
and gently so that they do no more so. . . .

ON THE THIRD COMMANDMENT

Now for the Third Commandment: I pray you, give good example
in your own self, and then teach all yours how they should keep duly
the holy day. That is to say, inasmuch as conveniently may be to be
void of all manner of worldly and bodily labours. I say inasmuch as
conveniently may be, for people must have meat and drink; the
houses must be apparelled; beasts must be cured and looked unto;
and very unfeigned necessity or need doth excuse in conscience.

The holy day is ordained of God and the Church only for the
service of God. The due place of that service is the church unto all
them that may conveniently come thereunto. And unto them that
may not, every honest place of good and lawful occupation is their
church. For God is there present where He is duly and devoutly
served. Take the pain, therefore, when you may, to go forth yourself and call your folks to follow. And when you been at the church,
do nothing else but that you came for. And look oft-times upon
them that been under your charge, that all they be occupied like, at
the least, unto devout Christians. For 'the church', as Our Saviour
saith, 'is a place of prayer';[1] not of clattering and talking.

And charge them also to keep their sight in the church, close upon
their books or beads. And while they been young, let them use ever
to kneel, stand, or sit; and never to walk in the church. And let them
hear the Mass quietly and devoutly, much part kneeling. But at the
gospel, at the preface, and at the *Pater Noster*, teach them to stand and
to make courtesy at this word *Jesus*, as the priest doth.

Thus in the forenoon let the time be spent all in the service of God.
And then in the afternoon must you appoint them their pastime
with great diligence and strait commandment. First, that in no wise
they use such vanities as commonly been used. That is to say, bear-
baiting and bull-baiting, football, tennis-playing, bowling, nor these
unlawful games of carding, dicing, closshing,[2] with such other unthrifty pastimes, or rather lost-times, wherein the holy day may rather
be broken than if they went to the plough or cart upon Easter Day,
so it were not done by contempt or despising of the Commandment
of the Law nor for unreasonable covetousness and love of worldly
goods.

For sin doth always more defoul and break the holy day than doth
any bodily work or occupation. Therefore let them beware of the
tavern and alehouse, for dread of drunkenness or of gluttony, and of

[1] Matt. xxi. 13.   [2] *closshing*, bowling.

suspect places, of wanton company, for fear of uncleanness or lechery which things been unto youth most perilous and of great danger and jeopardy of corruption. Assign you, therefore, and appoint you them the manner of their disports, honest ever and lawful, for a reasonable recreation. And as much as conveniently may be, let the sexes be departed in all their disports. That is to say, the kinds: men by themselves and the women by themselves. And also appoint the time or space that they [may] be not, for any disports, from the service of God. Appoint them also the place that you may call or send for them when case requireth. For if there be a sermon any time of the day, let them be there present all that been not occupied in needful and lawful business, all other laid on part; let them ever keep the preachings rather than the Mass* if, by case, they may not hear both.

To buy and sell or bargain upon the holy day is unlawful except it be for very need. Charity unto the poor and needy neighbours doth lawfully excuse bodily or worldly labours upon the holy day. Look well, you neither do nor say wilfully and by deliberation upon the holy day anything that you know in conscience should be contrary unto the honour of God: and then done, you justly keep your holy day.

A very good, sure pastime upon the holy day is to read or hear this book, or such other good English books, and gather thereunto as many persons as you can. For I tell you, there should be no time lost nor misspent upon the holy day. Let this poor lesson now, content you, for these three Commandments of the first Table which, as I said, done appertain and belong unto Almighty God Himself.

Of your charity, pray for the same old wretch of Sion,
Richard Whytford.

COLOPHON: Imprinted at London in Fleet Street at the sign of the Sun by me Wynkyn de Worde. The year of Our Lord God, 1530, the 20th day of December.

The Jesus Psalter

An Invocation Glorious: named the *Psalter Of Jesus*

It is to be understood that there be three manners of psalters: the first is called *David's Psalter* which containeth thrice fifty psalms; the second is called the *Psalter Of Our Lady*, containing thrice fifty *aves*; the third is called the *Psalter of Jesus* or the Invocation of Jesus, containing fifteen principal petitions which ten times repeated make also thrice fifty. In the which *Psalter* and invocation is the glorious name of Our Saviour Jesus called 5280 times. Who so useth to say it, trust they verily, they shall find thereby special help to resist temptation and have increase of grace and virtue by the singular help of Jesus.

Of this blessed Name, Saint Peter in the Acts of the Apostles saith: There is none other Name under heaven given to men in the which it behooveth us to be saved.[1] And Our Saviour saith in the gospel of Saint John that we should make our petitions in His Name[2] which is the Mediator of our salvation, whose glorious vision and most amorous fruition in the celestial glory shall be our perpetual joy and incomprehensible consolation.

Dominus noster, Jesus Christus, humiliavit semetipsum pro nobis factus obediens usque ad mortem, mortem autem crucis.[3] [Our Lord Jesus humbled Himself for us, becoming obedient unto death, even unto the death of the Cross.] Jesus, Jesus, Jesus, mercy! (Say this foresaid line ten times and at the beginning of every petition following of this *Psalter*.)

PETITION SIX

Jesus, Jesus, Jesus, light me! (Ten times.)

1. Jesus, light me with ghostly wisdom for to know Thy goodness and those things which are most acceptable to Thee.
2. Grace to give good example to souls profitable, that none be hurt by me.
3. To help those with good counsel which have offended Thee.
4. Make me proceed from virtue to virtue until such time that I shall clearly see Thee in Thy majesty.
5. Let me not turn to those sins which I have sorrowed for and by confession have accused me.
6. The horrible sentence of endless death, the terrible judgment of damnation, Thy wrath, ire, and indignation, merciful Lord, let never fall upon me.
7. Thy mercy and Thy merits, my Saviour, ever be between them and me.
8. Have mercy on the souls in purgatory for Thy bitter Passion, I beseech Thee, and for Thy glorious Name Jesus.
9. The Holy Trinity, one very God, Have mercy on me!

Pater Noster: Ave Maria

COLOPHON: Printed at London in Fleet Street at the sign of the Rose Garland by Robert Copland....1529.

---

[1] Acts iv. 12.   [2] John xiv. 13–14.   [3] Phil. ii. 8.

JACOBUS DE GRUYTROEDE

c. 1400–1475

*Among the devotional books by the Flemish mystical writers of the
fourteenth and fifteenth centuries, none was more popular on the Continent
and in England during the early Renaissance than the* Speculum aureum
animae peccatricis *or* The mirroure of golde for the synfull soule,
*which Lady Margaret Beaufort translated into English. Since the sixteenth
century, bibliographers have listed the* Speculum *as the work of the
Carthusian monk Jacobus de Gruytroede, prior of the Liége Charterhouse
from 1440 to 1475, yet the English version is always attributed to his
friend Denis de Leuwis or Dionysius the Carthusian, as he is better known.
The question of authorship may be satisfactorily settled as the result of
recent research by an English Carthusian scholar in the library of the
Certosa in Farneta. He noted that the editors of Dionysius's* Opera
omnia *(Tournai, 1913) explain how the error in authorship began. In
volume xlii they point out that, owing to the Carthusian tradition of
anonymity during a monk's lifetime, the* Speculum *was printed anonymously until 1495, in which year the Nuremberg printer Paul Wagner
first issued it as a work by Dionysius. He found the manuscript of the*
Speculum *in the library at Ruremond, where Dionysius was prior until
his death in 1471, and supposed it was written by him, as were the other
works he intended to print. The two priors were close friends, and dedicated
several of their works to each other. Some of the two hundred or more
manuscripts left by Dionysius are addressed to* 'carissimo Jacobo'.

Wagner's mistake regarding the authorship of the Speculum *was
corrected by sixteenth-century Carthusian historians and also by the
Belgian bibliographers, Petreio, Morotio, Foppens, the Jesuit Fisen, and in
the more recent listings by Hain and Copinger.*

*Available facts in De Gruytroede's early life are few. He was born
about 1400. Records show that he was prior of the Liége Charterhouse of
the HolyApostles from 1440 until his death in 1475, except for an interval
of two years. A brief sketch of him as a scholar and author was written by
Richard Brathwait, the seventeenth-century English essayist, novelist,
and poet, who included in* A spiritual spicerie *(1633), a translation of
De Gruytroede's* Dialoge *between Christ and a sinner. Brathwait
describes the Liége prior as* 'a German, a man singularly versed in divine
and humane learning, and opposite in constancy of opinion and conformacie
of doctrine to those surreptitious Errours of the Time; who as he had
commendably passed his youth in the liberall sciences, so he consecrated and
happily bestowed the residue of his time to the honour of God in a devout
privacie, having his pen ever versed in works of devotion and piety; never
in arguments of division or controversy. He lived in the year 1472.'*

De Gruytroede is the author of thirty-three Latin works which include, besides several dialogues, De quattuor novissimis; De preparatione ante missam; De definitione nominis monachi; De nomine Jesu et Mariae; De vita Domini Jesu; *and the* Specula omnis status humanae vitae *[A mirror for each state of human life]. The last work is in five sections, each of which is entitled* Speculum *or* Mirror *and is respectively addressed to prelates, ecclesiastical subordinates, priests, the laity, and the aged. The fourth section,* The Mirroure of Golde, *is addressed to the laity or those of the 'secular world'.*

The French edition of the Speculum, *namely* Le Mirouer dor de lame pecheresse, *printed anonymously in Paris, in 1484, was the one used by Margaret Beaufort for her English translation. When de Worde printed it, in 1522, and again in 1526, fourteen years after the death of his royal patroness, he issued it as an anonymous work, referring to it as 'This present book', and he reprinted from the French text that 'it had been seen and corrected at length of many clarkis, Doctours and maisters in diuinite'. De Worde also included a portion of De Gruytroede's preface in which the prior states that according to St Gregory 'there is noon more acceptable sacrifice to god then is good zeal, that is to say, an hernest desyre to the weale of soules. For which cause I have willede to make and accomplysshe this present tretyse, gederinge and assembling many divine auctorites of holy doctours of the church to the entent that the pore synfull soule troubled by the fraude of enmye and overcome, may by holy monicions and auctorites be addressed to the light of justice and truth and so led by the mean of the Holy goost that ye shepe that were perysshed may be reduced and led again to theyr green paster.' The author divided this section of the book into seven chapters in order that on every day of the week the sinful man may have 'a newe mirroure wherein he may beholde and consider the face of his soul'.*

De Gruytroede's theme throughout the Mirroure of Golde *is the saying of Ecclesiastes, 'Vanity of vanities, and all is vanity.' Though he writes in the mystical tradition of the followers of Jan van Ruysbroeck, the* Mirroure *lacks an intimate or personal appeal despite the penitential mood that is encouraged by the vigorous style of Margaret Beaufort's translation.*

The Mirror of Gold for the Sinful Soul

TRANSLATED BY LADY MARGARET BEAUFORT

OF THE VAIN JOY, MIGHT, DIGNITY, HONOURS, AND RICHES OF THE WORLD[1]

If thou would know what is the joy, might, dignity, honours, and riches of the world, understand and hearken the Prophet Baruch in his third chapter, the which demandeth in this manner: Where be

[1] Chapter v.

the princes of the people that had seigniories and domination of the beasts of the earth, and that played and disported with the birds of heaven? Where be the men that gathereth gold and silver and assay them in their treasury, never satisfied with getting? I wis they be all passed and dead and descended into hell, and others be come in their places which now joy and use of their goods, they left.

And where be the great clerks and the creators; or where be the great divers in excess and superabundance of meats; or they that have put their pleasaunce to nourish horses, palfreys, and such other? And where be the emperors, kings, dukes, princes, marquis, earls, barons, noble bourgeoise, merchants, labourers, and folks of all estates?* They be all in powder and rottenness: and of the most great there is no more but a little memory upon their sepulcher in letters contained. But go see in their sepulchers and tombs, and look if thou canst well know and truly judge which is the master and which is the varlet; which bones be of the poor and which be of the rich. Divide, if thou may, the labourer from the king; the feeble from the strong; the fair from the foul and deformed.

Now certainly it is well to be understood that this worldly joy, what that ever may come of it, is to be fled: first, for it is right vile of conditions; secondly, for it is right false of promise; thirdly, for it is right frail and vain in enduring; fourthly, for the retribution is right cursed and damnable....

Therefore, saith Saint Augustine,* 'He is well blessed and happy that putteth his only desire in the heavenly joy and rejoiceth not himself in prosperity of this world; neither in adversity is ashamed or abashed. He that thinketh that nothing in this world is to be loved, feareth little to lose and forsake the goods and prosperities of this world for God's sake.'

The joy of this world is none other but as a blast of wind passing by the ears of man. Wherefore, miserable sinner, behold how thou art blinded if thou desire this worldly joy. For as saith Saint Anselm,* 'Thou mayst not be in worldly honour without pain and labour.' Thou mayst not be in prelatry without envy and trouble, nor in honour and high dignity without vain glory: and therefore if thou wilt withstand the danger and peril to the which thou runnest in desiring temporal honour and joy of the world, without doubt it is necessary to thee to leave, flee, and renounce the miserable vanities of the same.

COLOPHON: Imprinted at London in Fleet Street at the Sign of the Sun by Wynkyn de Worde.... 1522.

RICHARD DE METHLEY
1450?–1528

The English devotional writings of Richard de Methley, a Carthusian monk of the Mount Grace Charterhouse in Yorkshire, follow the pattern of Hilton's Scala Perfectionis *and the works of Richard Rolle. Methley, whose surname was Furth, was born about 1450 in Methley, a village in the West Riding of Yorkshire. From his knowledge of theology and Latin, it is supposed that he attended either Oxford or Cambridge. In 1476 Methley was professed in the Carthusian order. At the time of his death in 1528 he held the office of vicar in the Yorkshire Charterhouse.*

Methley's only extant English work is the fragment A pystl of solytary lyfe, *now printed for the first time. He is the author of two Latin works.* Experimentum veritatis *and a short untitled discourse on the daily routine of life in the Charterhouse. The* Experimentum *is a study of contemplative life and its proximity to the spirit world. Of the original twenty-seven chapters only fourteen are extant. Both works are still in manuscript.*

The Pystl *was written for a novice, probably in the Charterhouse, reminding him that temptations will beset him during his hermit-like life, and his one means of overcoming them is constant recourse to the prayer of the psalmist,* Eripe me. . . . *In reward for his spiritual travail Methley promises after a while he 'shalt lyfe lyke a throstel cok or a nyghtyng gale for ioy'.*

As an author of Latin and English works, Methley takes his place among such learned men of his order as Theobald English, John Olney, John Blacman (whose History of Henry VI *has been translated into English by M. R. James), Nicholas Love, translator of the popular work attributed to St Bonaventure,* Mirrour of the lyfe of Jesu Chryste *(which was printed by Caxton in 1486(?) and again by De Worde and Pynson), John Percivall, Thomas Spenser, John Batmanson, William Exmewe, and Maurice Chauncey. The latter's* Passio XVIII Carthusianorum in regno Angliae *was printed on the Continent in 1550 and reprinted several times, together with his short histories* De captivitate et martyrio D. Joannis Fisheri *and* De D. Thomae Mori captivitate. *Chauncey also transcribed the* Cloud of Unknowing *and the* Epistle of Privy Counsell.

Though the greater portion of the works written by the English Carthusians in the sixteenth century was destroyed during the dissolution of the monasteries, those that are extant are singularly spiritual, summoning the individual to a life of faith and active and meditative prayer. In this 'silent' preaching the Carthusians were carrying out the command of their great twelfth-century Prior of the Grande Chartreuse, Guigo I, who

*urged that 'books should be most industriously written'. Since their vow
of silence forbids preaching the word of God with their mouths, 'we must',
he wrote, 'do so with our hands'.*

An Epistle of Solitary Life

Here beginneth a Pystyl[1] of Solitary Life nowadays

To Hugh, hermit:

CHAPTER I

God Almighty, all witty, all lovely, in Whom is all goodness, the
well of mercy and grace, the glorious Trinity, one God and Persons
Three, that is for to say, the Father and the Son and the Holy Ghost,
[may] He bless us with His gracious goodness and bring us unto His
bliss in heaven !

Dear brother in Christ Jesu: Thy desire is good and holy that thou
would be informed after thy state, that is a hermit: how thou
shouldst please God to His worship and perfect to thyself. God for
His mickle[2] mercy, meekness, and grace, give us both grace: me, to
say well, and thee, to do thereafter to His worship and our meed.
Amen.

CHAPTER II

*Eripe me de inimicis meis, domine: ad te confugi: doce me facere voluntatem
tuam quia deus meus es tu,*[3] that is to say in English thus: Lord, deliver
me from mine enemies: to Thee I have fled. Teach me for to do Thy
will, for Thou art my God. These words are pertaining to all
Christian people that ask to be delivered from their enemies, bodily
and ghostly, the which do flee from the love of the world, but
specially they pertain to thee that has fled to God in the wilderness
from man's fellowship that thou may the better learn to do His will,
for He is thy God, and thou art to love Him specially. Therefore
how thou shalt ask Him to be delivered from thine enemies, I shall,
by His grace, tell thee.

CHAPTER III

Thou hast principally three enemies: the world, thy flesh, and the
evil spirit. Thou mayst flee from the world to God. But thy flesh
and thy enemy will go with thee into the wilderness. Thou hast
marvel why I say 'into the wilderness' when thou dwellest in a fair
chapel of Our Lady, blessed, worshipped, and thanked must she be.
Ask no more fellowship for to talk withal but her, I pray thee; and

---

[1] *pystyl*, epistle.   [2] *mickle*, great.   [3] Ps. cxlii. 9.

then I say that thou dwellest *well* in the wilderness, and since it is so
that thou hast fled from all women. If thou may not flee from thine
own flesh, have no woman in thy mind so ofte as her; and then, well
I wot, thou shalt overcome thy three enemies by these three virtues:*
that is to say, against thine enemy, ghostly obedience; against thy
flesh, clean chastity; against the world, that thou turn not to it again,
but deep poverty with a good will. And thou may then well say
to God Almighty: Lord, deliver me from mine enemies, for I have
fled to Thee. Teach me to do Thy will, for Thou art my God. *Eripe
me de inimicis meis, domine: ad te confugi: doce me facere voluntatem tuam
quia deus meus es tu.*

CHAPTER IV

But how shalt thou keep well obedience, chastity, and poverty? Be
obedient to God Almighty after His law, and as thou promised before
the bishop when thou took thee to a hermit life, and also now be
obedient to thy curate, that is, thy ghostly father after God and [who]
hath charge of thy soul. Remember thee, then, every morning and
evening, what thou art bounden to, and thank God that hath called
thee thereto; and ask Him mercy of all that thou hast not well kept,
and say to Him thus: *Eripe me de inimicis meis, domine: ad te confugi:
doce me facere voluntatem tuam quia deus meus es tu.* And ask Him grace
for to do better in time for to come.

CHAPTER V

Also clean chastity must thou needs keep. I know none other in thee
but thou dost keep it. But yet I shall tell as, I trow, will do thee good,
by God's grace. And thou keep clean chastity, by God's grace, in
body and in soul, truly to please God and our Lady withal, there is
no virtue that so soon shall bring thee to the true feeling of the love
of God in earth. But how shalt thou keep it by grace perfectly?
Flee all women's fellowship, and also the thought of them put out
of thy mind as soon as it cometh: and rise up in thy thought, in thy
heart, and in thy word to God in heaven, and say thus: Jesu, Jesu,
Jesu! *Eripe me de inimicis meis, domine: ad te confugi: doce me facere
voluntatem tuam quia deus meus es tu.*

CHAPTER VI

And I let thee wit[1] there is no manner of way that is lawful to thee
to have the lust of thy flesh. And think on well that I say, 'no manner
of way', neither lykyl[2] nor mickle, neither one way, neither other.
And therefore a remedy I shall now tell thee, and I pray thee keep
it well. Thy thought may not be clean always, but if it be in heaven

---

[1] *wit*, know.   [2] *lykyl*, little.

with God and Our Lady or with some other good saint or angel, and
thy thought be there with love, dread, and reverence and meekness;
then dwellest thou there, as Saint Paul saith: *Nostra conversatio in
caelis est*:[1] Our living is in heaven. And, I pray thee, love well Our
Blessed Lady, and let her be thy leman sweet. And say to her thus:
Tota pulchra es amica mea et macula non est in te:[2] All fair thou art,
O leman mine, and there is not one spot in thee! And to her pray
and by her send thy prayers to God, and say thus: *Eripe me de
inimicis meis, domine: ad te confugi, doce me, etc.*

CHAPTER VII

Against riches of the world is willful poverty a good remedy. And
it is called *willful* poverty, for it must be with a good will. And it
would be full of a good will if thou keep it perfectly. But how shalt
thou come to this good will? By the love of God. For Scripture
saith thus: *Si dederit homo omnem substantiam domus suae pro dilectione
quasi non despiciet eam.*[3] If a man should have given all the riches of
his house for the love of God, as it were naught he shall despise it.
And I say, and thou felt once in thy heart the love of God, thou
wouldst despise all the world: not despising the creatures of God
but thinking in comparison of the love of God, all the world is but
vanity. And therefore when thou art tempted to have gods of the
world at the first beginning of thy thought, tarry no longer, but say
to God thus in English or in Latin, as thou hast most devotion: *Eripe
me de inimicis meis, domine, etc.* And I shall teach thee to understand
well this verse: *O domine*, O Lord; *eripe me*, deliver thou me; *de
inimicis meis*, of mine enemies; *confugi*, I have fled altogether; *ad te*,
to Thee; *doce me*, teach me; *facere voluntatem tuam*, to do thy will;
quia deus meus es tu, for why Thou art my God.

CHAPTER VIII

Other three things there is needful for thee to keep well: one is thy
sight; another, thy cell; third is thy silence. That is as to say, hold
thy tongue well. Thy sight must be needs kept well from vanities;
and then think to come to heaven's bliss. For the Prophet Jeremiah
saith thus: *Oculus meus depraedatus est animam meam.*[4] Mine eye hath
deprayed[5] my soul. That is for to say, mine eye hath wrest my soul
[from] prayer as thieves do the which lie in the wayside to rob men
and wait their prey when any come by. So when thou shouldst so
think on goodness, that is for to say, on God and heavenly or healthful
things for thy soul, thine eye will ravish thy mind here and there but[6]
if thou keep it well; and then as oft as thou sinnest thereby, so oft

[1] Phil. iii. 20.	[2] Cant. iv. 7.	[3] Cant. viii. 7.
[4] Lam. iii. 51.	[5] *deprayed*, robbed.	[6] *but*, except.

robbest thou thy soul as a robber in the way. And as great as the sin is, so great a virtue takest thou from thy soul, and so great a stroke givest thou thy soul. And, wete thou well, that there is no sin little but in comparison of a greater; it is nò little thing to offend God Almighty. And have no doubt, thou shalt have great strife with thyself or thou canst overcome thy sight, but ask God [for] mercy, health, and grace, and say to Him thus: *Eripe me de inimicis meis, etc.*

CHAPTER IX

Thy cell is the second thing that I said. And what call I thy cell, trowest thou, but the place or the chapel of Our Blessed Lady where thou dwellest. And wote thou well, thou hast great cause to keep it well, for thou dare not run here and there to seek thy living. God hath provided for thee; and therefore keep thy cell, and it will keep thee from sin. Be no home-runner for to see marvels; no gazelle from town to town; no land leaper, waving in the wind like a laverook.[1] But keep thy cell, and it will keep thee. But now thou saith, peradventure, thou mayst not keep it, for thou art sent for to gentlemen in the country whom thou dare not displease. I answer and say thus: Tell them that thou hast forsaken the world, and therefore but in the time of very great need, as in the time of death or such other great need, thou mayst not let[2] thy devotion. And when thou shalt help them, look thou do it truly for the love of God and take nothing but for thy cost. And when thou sittest by thy own[3] in the wilderness and art weak or weary, say this to Our Lady, as Saint Godric said,* that holy hermit: *Sancta Maria, virgo mater Jesu Christi Nazareni, protege et adjuva tuum Hugonem; suscipe et adduc cito tecum et in tuum regnum vel in dei regnum.* He said, *adjuva tuum Godricum,* but thou may say, *tuum Hugonem,* for thy name is Hugh. This is thus to say in English: Saint Mary, Maiden and Mother of Jesu Christ of Nazareth, hold and help thy Hugh; take and lead safe with thee into thy kingdom (or say) into the kingdom of God— both is good.

And I counsel thee, love well Saint Hugh of our Order of the Charter monks. But now thou saith, I trow, thou must come forth to hear Mass. That is full well, sinning but[4] if thou had Masses sung within thy chapel. But when thou hast heard Mass, then flee home but if thou have a full good cause, and thou saith in this wise, *Ad te confugi;* to Thee, Lord, I have fled wholly, both body and soul, as Thou [space in MS.] all. For and thou flee with thy body and not with thy heart from the world, thou art then a false hypocrite, as Scripture saith: *Simulatores callidi provocant iram dei.*[5] That is thus in

---

[1] *laverook,* lark.   [2] *let,* hinder.   [3] *own,* self.
[4] *but,* only.   [5] Job xxxvi. 13.

English: False, wily dissemblers provoke the ire of God. Therefore in thy need against such temptations, say this verse: *Eripe me de inimicis meis, etc.*

CHAPTER X

The third thing is thy silence. And, wete thou well, it will do thee great good; and then think thus in thy heart, making no vows but if thou list: 'Good Lord, by Thy grace, I think this day to keep well my tongue to Thy worship and my weal.' And specially on fasting days, I counsel thee, keep thy silence and speak with no creature, and[1] thou mayst eschew it. I have known some holy persons that would so keep their silence as on Friday, on Wednesday, or a great Saint's eve. And the Prophet David saith thus: *Obmutui et humiliatus sum et silui a bonis*:[2] I have held my tongue; and I have been meeked; and I have kept me still from good speech. Note well that he saith from *good thing* or from *good speech*, 'I have kept me still'. And why? For fear that among good speech, happen some ill. For, wote thou well, thou canst not speak mickle good speech but some will be void or ill. And on the Day of Doom any[3] man must give a count of every idle word that he speaketh. And therefore eschew speech. And when thou feelest thee tempted to speak, say this verse: *Eripe me domine, etc.*

CHAPTER XI

Now thou mayst ask me, how thou shalt be occupied day and night. I say: with thy duty that thou art bounden to, and then with more that thou puttest to it by grace and thy devotion. Five things there be according for thee, that is to say: good prayer, meditation, that is called holy thinking; reading of holy English books; contemplation, that thou mayst come to by grace and great devotion, that is for to say, to forget all manner of things but God and for great love of Him be rapt into contemplation; and good deeds with thy hand. And, I pray thee, do thine own chores thyself, and thou may; and when thou art tempted to have workmen where no myster[4] is, say the said verse: *Eripe me, etc.*

CHAPTER XII

What I say now, I pray thee, give good heed. Scripture saith thus: *Non enim habent amaritudinem conversationes illius nec tedium quietus illius sed laetitiam et gaudium.*[5] Understand it thus: The conversation, that is to say, the holy living of a good man with God, hath no bitterness in heart nor irksomeness to live with God, but gladness and joy. So if thou wilt live always in joy, keep thy thoughts always on God with love and dread and other virtues. And in the morning

[1] *and, if.*   [2] Ps. xxxviii. 3.   [3] *any, every.*
[4] *myster, need.*   [5] Wisd. of Sol. viii. 16.

and evening use long prayers or other spiritual exercises, as is meditation, as I said before, and other like; and between morn and even
many prayers or spiritual exercises, but shortly and oft, and work
betwixt them. In the time of thy work, let not thy mind go from
God. And in the beginning, thou shalt feel some penance or pain,
but ever after, thou shalt live like a throstel-cock or nightingale for
joy. And thank God and pray for me; and as ofte as thou hast
myster, say the said verse, *Eripe me, etc. Deo gratias.* Amen.

Per Richard de Methley of Mount Grace, Order of Carthusians,
to Frater Hugh, devout hermit.

[P.R.O. MS. 716.]

JOHN COLET[1]

A ryght frutefull monicion *is John Colet's single extant devotional
treatise written in English. In the sixteenth century it vied in popularity
with such favourites as the* Imytacyon of Christ, *Whytford's* The werke
for householders, *and Fisher's sermons on the Penitential Psalms. Written
probably in 1515, the first extant edition of the* Monicion, *printed in
1534, was bound with Fisher's* Fruytfull Saynges.

The Monicion *urges a Christian way of life. Colet's sincerity and
simple style, which led him to paraphrase passages from the Book of
Proverbs, made the little treatise widely loved, and before 1577 twenty
editions were printed.*

A Right Fruitful Monition

A Right Fruitful Monition concerning the order of a good
Christian man's life very profitable for all manner of estates and
others to behold and look upon. Made by the famous Doctor
Colet sometime Dean of Paul's.

Remember first of all, virtuous reader, that it is high wisdom and
great perfection thyself to know and then thyself to despise as to
know thou hast nothing that good is of thyself but of God. For the
gifts of nature and all other temporal gifts of this world which been
lawfully and truly obtained, well considered, been comen to thee
by the infinite goodness and grace of God and not of thyself. And

[1] For biographical sketch, see pp. 35–7.

most in especial it is necessary for thee to know how that God, of His great grace, hath made thee His image, having regard to thy memory, understanding, and free will; and to know how God is thy Maker, and thou His wretched creature; and to know how thou art redeemed of God by the Passion of Christ Jesus; and to know how God is thy Helper, thy Refuge, and thy Deliverer of all evil; and to consider and to know the goodly order which God, of his infinite wisdom, hath ordained thee to be ordered by, as to have these temporal goods for the necessity of the body; the body and sensual appetites to be ordered by thy soul; thy soul to be ordered by reason and grace; by reason and grace to know thy duty to God and to thy neighbour.

And by all common reason if thou keep this convenient order to God and His creatures, they shall keep their order to thee. But if thou break thine order to them, of likelihood they shall break their order to thee. For how should thy wife, children, servants, and other creatures, with which thou hast doings, do their duty and keep their order to thee if thou dost not so to God and to them.

And also think thou of a surety that if thy sensual appetite be not ordered by reason and grace, thou art worse ordered than a beast. For then thou livest out of order, and so doth not a beast, which is a great shame and rebuke to thee, a reasonable creature; and without the great mercy of God, it shall be to thine eternal damnation.

And therefore think and thank God and utterly despise thyself: and think thyself a great wretch in that God hath done so much for thee, and thou hast so oft offended His Highness and also done Him so little service. Surely it is also great wisdom to think that if it had pleased God for to have given to all other men (as well beggars as others) like grace as He hath given to thee that they would have served His goodness better than thyself hast done. Wherefore, think thyself a wretch of all wretches except [for] the mercy of God. And therefore by His infinite mercy and grace call unto thy remembrance the degree or dignity the which Almighty God, of His goodness, hath called thee unto, and according thereunto yield thy debt and do thy duty.

First, and principally: Honour God as thy Maker. Love Him as thy Redeemer; Fear Him as thy Judge.

Secondarily: Thy neighbour, which is thy superior, obey. Have concord and peace with them which been even with thee in degree; and have mercy and pity on thine inferiors.[1]

Thirdly: Provide thee to have a clean heart and a good custody of thy tongue. Pray and take labour by grace to have wisdom and cunning to do thy duty to God and to thy neighbour. And in all thy words and deeds have ever in mind that God and His angels

[1] Cf. Matt. xxii. 37–9.

heareth and seeth everything, and that nothing is so privily done but it shall be made open.[1]

And, in especial, have in mind that thou shalt die shortly, and how Christ died for thee; and the subtlety and falseness of this temporal world; the joys of heaven; and the pains of hell. And every morning among other thy meditations and prayers, pray unto thy Lord God that the day following, thou (according to the degree the which He, of His infinite goodness and mercy, hath called thee unto) mayst use this temporal wretched world in thy thoughts, words, and deeds; that by them and the merits of Christ's Passion thou mayst eschew the pains of hell and come to the joy everlasting.

And in executing thereof, keep truth in words and deeds. Defend no man nor no matter against the truth. In all things think and trust in God, and He shall direct thy ways. Trust not to thine own wit, but fear God, and He will keep thee from evil. If thou trust more in thine own wit than in the grace of God, thy policy shall be soon subverted. Be content to hear good counsel though it be contrary to thy will, for he is a very fool that will hear nothing gladly but that is according to his mind.

Do thou no man harm lest thou sufferest the same. As thou willest be done unto thee, so do thou unto another.[2] Be such to others as thou desirest they should be to thee.

If thou be religious, remember that the due execution of true religion is not in wearing of the habit, but with a clean mind in very deed to execute the rules and ordinances of religion. For so it is, that to wear the habit and not to execute the rule and order of religion is rather to be deemed hyprocrisy or apostasy than otherwise.

If thou be lay and unmarried, keep thee clean unto the time thou be married. And remember the sore and terrible punishment of Noah's flood and the terrible fire and brimstone and sore punishment of Sodom and Gomorrha done to man for misusing of the flesh. And, in especial, call to remembrance the marvellous and horrible punishment of the abominable great pocks* daily appearing to our sight, growing in and upon man's flesh; the which sore punishment (everything well remembered) cannot be thought but principally for the inordinate misuse of the flesh.

And if thou intend to marry, or be married and hast a good wife, thank Our Lord therefore, for she is of His sending. And remember that three things in especial been pleasant to the spirit of God, that is to say: concord between brethren, love and charity between neighbours, and a man and his wife well agreeing. And if thou have an evil wife, take patience and thank God, for all is for the best well taken. Howbeit, thou art bound to do and pray for her amendment lest she go to the devil from whom she came. And have in

---

[1] Cf. Luke xii. 2.   [2] Cf. Matt. vii. 12.

remembrance that the intent of marriage is not in the beastly appetite or pleasure in the thing, but the intent thereof is to eschew the sin of the flesh or else to have children.

And if thou have children, as much as thou mayst, bring them forth in virtue to be the servants of God. For it is better for thee and them not to be born than otherwise.

In thine authority busy thee rather to be beloved of thine inferiors than to be dread. Let thy subjects and servants rather serve and obey thee for love than for dread or need. With such a sovereign goodness govern thy subjects that they may be glad to serve thee both in punishing and in cherishing.

Keep a mannerly mean: be not too strait. Forgive not too soon. Keep a convenient measure in all thy works.

Go not to meat as a beast, but as a reasonable man. Say thy grace, and then remember that more sicken and die by superfluities of meats than otherwise. Wherefore eat with measure to live in health. At thy meal have none other but honest communication and such as is according to thy cunning.

Backbite no man. Be merry in honesty, for sorrow and care hath killed many, and there is no profit therein. In no wise swear without compulsion of the law; for whereas is great swearing, from thence is never the plague of God.

In no wise brawl nor chide without an urgent cause. For Solomon saith: Better is a little with joy than a house full of vitals with brawling.[1] Also he saith: An evil person is ever chiding, and therefore the angel of God shall be sent against him.[2]

Be content at thy dinner and also at other times, to give part of that which God hath sent thee, for he that will not hear the cry of a poor man, he shall cry to God and not be heard.

After thy meat, thank God of that He hath sent thee, or else thou dost not as a reasonable man, but like a beast which in eating remembereth nothing but his meat.

With good providence and discretion see the time where, when, how, why, or wherefore thou speakest, doth, or biddest anything to be done.

When thou deemest or judgest anyone, be he poor or rich, behold and consider the cause and not the person. Be as meek in other men's causes and offences as in thine own. Sit never in doom and judgment without pity or mercy: for while thou hast pity and art merciful to other men's offences, thou hast mercy on thyself. For in what measure thou measureth, it shall be measured to thee.[3] Yet thou must execute judgment; but it must be with pity or mercy. For of a surety to do mercy and justice is more pleasant to God than to pray or do sacrifice unto Him. Deem no man by light suspections. First

[1] Prov. xvii. 1.   [2] Prov. xvii. 11.   [3] Matt. vii. 2.

prove, and then deem. In doubts reserve the sentence to God's might. That thou knowest not, commit it to God.

Have little or none affection and perfect love to these earthly and temporal things. For blessed be the rich man that trusteth not in his money and treasure. And remember, as a man loveth, so he is: for the lover is in the thing loved more properly than in himself. Wherefore, if a man love earthly things, he may be called an earthly man: and if he love principally heavenly things or God, he may be called an heavenly or a godly man; and therefore love God and heavenly things. For undoubtedly that is best and most assured love, for they be and ever shall be permanent: and all earthly things been soon vanished and ended, and so the love of them is in vain.

Also, it is wisdom to fear God, for as He saith Himself: Fear not Him that may kill the body and cannot hurt the soul. But fear him that can kill the body and also the soul and commit them to everlasting pain.[1] Wherefore every evening ere thou go to bed, call to remembrance (as much as thou canst) thy thoughts, words, and deeds said and done that day: and if any have been to thine own profit and to the pleasure of God, heartily thank Him, for by His grace it was done. And if any have been contrary to His pleasure, ask heartily mercy and reconcile thyself shortly by repentance to eschew the everlasting and terrible pains of hell.

For as Saint Austin saith, 'There is not a greater madness than for a little temporal delectation (which is soon done) to lose the eternal joy and to be bound to everlasting pain.' From the which the Almighty Father of Heaven by His infinite power and mercy, and the bitter Passion and infinite wisdom of Jesus Christ, and by the infinite goodness and charity of the Holy Ghost keep us. Amen.

Deo Gratias

Use well temporal things.   Desire eternal things.

Finis

COLOPHON: At London by Robert Copland for John Byddell, otherwise Salisbury, the 7th day of January. And be for to sell at the sign of Our Lady of Pity next to Fleet Bridge. 1534.

[1] Matt. x. 28.

ST JOHN FISHER[1]

Written in Latin about 1520, A godlie treatisse *remained unpublished for forty years. Manuscript copies were made in Latin and English for circulation among Fisher's friends. It is from one such Latin copy that the current version is derived. Richard Hall, the biographer of Bishop Fisher, translated it into English for the London publication by John Cawood in 1560. This edition was reissued without change by Cawood's son Gabriel in 1577 despite Elizabethan proscription of Catholic 'propaganda'. The first Latin printing was made in Rome about 1565, and another was made, in 1597, in Wurzburg, where the* Opera Omnia *of Bishop Fisher was printed (though all of his works, despite the title, were not included).*

Internal evidence reveals that the copy used by Hall, in 1560, was the basic text of a Latin edition of the Treatise *printed in Paris in 1631. This edition in turn became the source for a new and more simple translation by a Benedictine monk, Anthony Batt, an Englishman residing in exile in the Lowlands. His version was printed in Paris in 1640.*

The outstanding feature of the Treatise *is its clear-cut dependence on the* Summa Theologica *of the Angelic Doctor, Thomas Aquinas. Because of this it is one of the first Thomistic works printed in England, and it represents a milestone on the road of interest in Aquinas, whose works had lost some of their popularity in England since their proscription at Oxford in the thirteenth century. The* Pars Secunda Secundae *(Q. 83) on Prayer and Fisher's* Treatise *have a kindred treatment; each uses scriptural quotations and appeals to patristic authorities.*

The portion printed below is a modern version made from the 1631 Latin text, with the retention here and there of typical Fisher rhetoric found in his English sermons and treatises.

A Treatise upon these Words of Our Saviour Christ: Oportet semper orare

TRANSLATED BY THOMAS W. CUNNINGHAM

Inasmuch as the saying of Our Saviour Christ: *Oportet semper orare*:[2] A man must always pray, written in the gospel of Saint Luke, pertains generally unto all Christian men, who does not see how profitable and necessary it is for every man to apply himself diligently and effectually to prayer. Since it is so expedient and beneficial a

---

[1] For biographical sketch, see pp. 333–5.   [2] Luke xviii. 1.

thing, it is in no way to be neglected on account of vain and hurtful delectations and pleasures.

Wherefore to the end that our prayer may wax sweet and pleasant unto us, first of all, it shall be very commodious and profitable to have at hand and in remembrance certain reasons with which, in a most apt and convenient way, we may stir up our minds and our hearts to prayer whenever we notice ourselves waxing cold in devotion and become, as it were, oppressed with a slothful unreadiness to serve God.

Moreover, it shall marvellously profit and exceedingly further us if we are not ignorant of the singular fruits and commodities that very many people have obtained by prayer. For by the knowledge thereof, we shall the more easily invite and prepare ourselves to pray.

Finally, it shall be very necessary for us to understand the very true manner which is especially required of every man to be observed in the time of prayer. Inasmuch as in every difficult work which a man undertakes, the acquired knowledge of how a thing must be done assists in the proper execution and perfect completion of the same, I have therefore intended, with the help of God, to treat in order these three things: the necessity of prayer, the fruits of prayer, and the true use and manner of prayer.

Because the words of Our Saviour, quoted above, cast some scruples and doubts upon many men's minds, it shall not be out of place, but rather make for a better understanding, if we first explain and declare how these words are to be understood.

To begin: this saying of Our Saviour, *Oportet semper orare*, is most assuredly true. Prayer is necessary for us every day, every hour, every minute. And yet, Almighty God does not demand too severe an accounting from us. That is to say, He does not bind us to incessant prayer with our mouth—a thing which no man has ever done or ever could observe. However, because there is no instant of passing time in which we do not have great need of the help and assistance of Almighty God, we are therefore of necessity constrained to practice continual prayer; to ask and beg humbly for His divine help and succour. Who is he who does not perceive, if he puts his mind diligently to it, the fact that we will return back to dust and ashes whenever God withdraws and withholds His help from us?

There is no man powerful enough to exist for a single moment of time without Him. As Job declares: In His hand is the life of every living creature.[1] Each one of us is now no better off than if he were hanging in a basket over a great, deep pit, suspended by a cord held by another. In such a case, the man so situated needs the diligent help of the one who holds the rope because if the latter should let go, the other must plunge headlong into the bottom of the pit. In like

[1] Job xii. 10.

manner something would befall us if God did not constantly sustain us with His hand and power. It is He who holds the rope lest we by a grievous fall be bruised and crushed to pieces and therein consumed. I shall say nothing about many other dangerous perils and precipices with which we are surrounded.

To return: who is the man so gross in wit and blind in understanding, who cannot realize that there is no time, not even a moment of time, in which we do not have very great need to call earnestly upon God in order to beg His aid, defense, and succour. For which reason we must pray incessantly. However, because there is no man who does satisfy and fulfil the words of Our Saviour by actual prayer, as we call it, that is by devoting every moment to prayer, we have the necessity of searching out some other sense and meaning thereof.

This saying of our Christ might indeed be understood in another sense. For example, a certain monk, one of the old fathers, upon being asked how he obeyed that saying or commandment of Christ, *Oportet semper orare*, made this answer: 'When I have finished saying my prayers each day, I make use of the time which remains by labouring with my hands as far as the ability and strength of my body permits. It thereby happens that each day I earn something with which I assist not only myself but other poor people. They, in turn, pray for me at such times as I through disturbance and trouble of body cannot pray for myself.' In this way he believed that he satisfied the commandment.

Indeed, Holy Scripture is consonant with this opinion, for it says: Hide thy alms in the bosom of the poor, and that shall pray for thee.[1] See how Holy Scripture proves that our alms pray for us. Therefore, if a man makes up his mind to show mercy and pity to his neighbours, if he seeks to defend the orphans and fatherless children, if he labours to comfort the widows who are destitute of all consolation, if he takes care to preserve from injury and wrong those who are oppressed by violence, if he shows himself ready to help with his own power any one in want of succour and relief, and if, besides all this, he does not neglect the ordinary appointed times of prayer set by the Church of God, he may be judged to have fulfilled the words of Christ. For that man does pray *always*, either by himself or by his alms and charitable deeds which make up for the deficiency appearing in his own prayer.

This is the way in which the aforesaid words of Christ may be understood, wherein He teaches us to continue always in prayer—which is the same as saying, 'to live well and to do well always', a thing that men may do even when they sleep. For whether we sleep or wake, walk or sit, eat or drink, are vexed or undisturbed, what-

[1] Ecclus. xxix. 15.

ever we do, if all these deeds be referred with true faith to the honour and glory of God, they will lend aid, without a doubt, to the increase of a good and perfect life. If this were not so, Saint Paul would not have directed the Corinthians to the effect that whatsoever they did, they should do for the glory of God: Whether you eat or drink or do anything else, do all to the honour of God.[1] Surely if God be moved by our prayers and our supplications to become gracious unto us, He will be much more stirred by our good works and well-doing. Therefore the favour of God is turned toward us by our good works which we do purposely in order to please His Divine Majesty, because these express the vehemency of prayer in a mighty fashion, even more than the prayers themselves. Whosoever dedicates all that he does and suffers to the glory of God, surely prays continuously, and so at all times he satisfies the aforesaid precept of God. We may justly say that a man does continue in prayer who always directs his works and deeds to the honour and glory of God.

Now albeit that this saying may be understood in this sense, nevertheless, because Christ has deliberately appointed a difference between praying and working and has declared a diversity between alms, prayer, and fasting, we shall now add unto these two meanings a third conception of these words.

Saint Paul admonishes the people of Thessalonica that they should pray incessantly, saying: *Sine intermissione orare*:[2] [to pray without ceasing]. In several places in his epistles he declares that he did continually remember many people in his prayers. Moreover in the Acts of the Apostles, it is written that while Peter was detained in prison the Church of God offered continual prayer and intercession for him.[3] It is manifest and apparent from these words that every true Christian man prays in each action and work which he does, yea, even though he be asleep.

Such a thing would not be true unless we understand that prayer is the continual desire of the heart which is strong and has its continual movement in man's mind. For just as a man, bound with weighty iron fetters in prison is compelled by the tedious weariness of those miseries and afflictions which he endures, to desire and seek vehemently and earnestly after liberty, if he once conceives any sort of hope for his deliverance, then he incessantly longs, wishes, and craves to be loosed from the painful bonds: likewise, is it true that every Christian man who is not ignorant of the fact that he is daily invaded and assaulted by the flesh, the world, and the devil, and that he suffers divers and manifold miseries and calamities in this vale of wretchedness, and that his life is subjected to great and daily dangers, is forced every moment to desire the aid and help of God's grace; by which

---

[1] I Cor. x. 31.   [2] I Thess. v. 17.   [3] Acts xii. 5.

means he, being delivered at last from those calamities and great evils, may ascend into the beautiful sight and vision of God Himself and the most happy fruition of everlasting felicity.

This eager desire is understood in the Sacred Scriptures as a loud cry in the ears of God when the Prophet says: God hath heard the vehement desire of the poor.[1] Doubtless the earnest desire of those who are vexed and punished in mind and soul speedily breaks in and makes a ready way to the presence of God Himself, and it raises a wonderful outcry and noise in His ears.

Because such a desire never ceases to be in the hearts of good men, it continually occupies and moves them with grace so that they always desire and long for the succour and aid of God's might and power, whether they sleep, wake, eat, drink, or whatever else they do. For an explanation whereof Saint Augustine saith* thus, 'To pray without ceasing, what else is it than to desire incessantly from God to lead a good and honest life? Let us always crave and beg this grace from God, and then we do always pray.'

Without this hearty desire, no noise or sound of words, be they ever so long, can stir up the ears of Almighty God. But if that be fervent, although there be no sound of any word heard, it does most easily penetrate and obtain without delay a thorough and gracious audience at the hand of God, as shall afterwards be more largely and plainly shown.

Therefore whosoever, in this wise, understands the aforesaid words of Our Saviour, shall, in my judgment, think most rightly. And, in another sense, a man cannot easily conceive how he may be able to pray continuously without ceasing. But by the fervency of this desire, which is never quenched in the hearts of good men, prayer is always and incessantly made before God; and we do continually knock at the gates of God's mercy, begging His grace and divine assistance. It is therefore very true, that which Christ did say: *Oportet semper orare*. We must always pray, and never give over. And yet it is not necessary that we recite any certain prayer, conceived and made in any form of words; but no minute of time must pass in which we do not desire the succour of His grace and the felicity that is to come.

But inasmuch as occasion serves to speak somewhat more about this matter later, it shall be good in the meantime to show certain ways by which, if we are diligent, we may quicken ourselves when we are dull, and raise up our minds when we will.

Joan. Fisheri,...*de Orando Deum*... (Paris, 1631).

[1] Job xxxiv. 28.

KING HENRY VIII

1491–1547

Few writings, if any, can be proved to be by Henry VIII. It seems likely, however, that he wrote, or at least closely supervised, two works opposing the Lutheran heresy. The religious feud between Luther and the English king began in 1520 when the German reformer published his De captivitate Babylonica ecclesiae, railing at the papacy and urging all peoples to accept what he called a 'new' Christianity. Scarcely a year passed before Henry VIII defended the Church in his treatise Assertio septem sacramentorum adversus M. Lutherum (1521), and in recognition of his work he received from Pope Leo X the title, 'Defender of the Faith'. The Assertio was immediately translated into German under the title, Ob der Künig usz engelland ein lügner sey oder der Luther (1522) by Thomas Mürner, the Franciscan friar and friend of Henry VIII. As a consequence it was widely read by German Catholics. Luther immediately replied to the English king in the tract Contra Henricum Regem Angliae Martinius Luther [1522], referring to Henry VIII in such terms as 'rex infelix', 'asinus', 'porcus', 'rex mendacii', 'damnabilis putredo', 'faeces latrinae', and 'scurra levissimus'.

This abuse heaped on the king brought both the clergy and laity to his defence. Several of the former, particularly Bishop John Fisher, preached against Luther in support of Henry VIII. Fisher's sermon on a text from the gospel of St John (xv, 26) 'made agayn ye pnicyous doctryn of M. Luther' was printed about 1521 and widely circulated. Though the king was anxious to answer Luther, his counsellors advised against it, and it is commonly accepted that Sir Thomas More was chosen to prepare the king's reply. A vigorous and harshly phrased treatise, Eruditissimi viri G. Rossei opus quo refellit Lutheri calumnias quibus Angliae regem Henricum octavum insectatur (1523) was soon printed, and the author's pseudonym, William Ross, has always been identified as More's, even by his earliest biographers.

The controversy gathered momentum when Ross's book appeared, and Luther promptly wrote a letter, a so-called apology, to Henry VIII, expressing doubt that the king was the author of the Assertio. He insisted that it was the work of Cardinal Wolsey and Sir Thomas More.

Henry VIII himself is believed to have written The answer of King Henry the VIII...unto the letter of Martin Luther [1525]. The king's letter, as does the Assertio, reveals an adequate knowledge of theology. The explanations which he gives of Catholic dogma are of special interest in evaluating the religious policy during the latter part of his reign, when he reversed his stand on such issues as Papal Supremacy and divorce.

Letter to Martin Luther

A copy of the letters wherein the most redoubted and mighty
Prince, our sovereign lord King Henry the Eighth, King of
England and of France, Defender of the Faith, and Lord of
Ireland, made answer unto a certain letter of Martin Luther,
sent unto him by the same; and also the copy of the foresaid
Luther's letter in such order as here followeth:

THE LETTER OF MARTIN LUTHER

Unto the most mighty and noble Prince, lord Henry the VIII,
King of England and of France, his most benign lord:

Grace and peace in Christ Jesu, Our Lord and Saviour. Amen.
Notwithstanding, most noble King and excellent Prince, that
I ought of reason to be afraid to attempt your Highness with letters,
which am well knowing unto myself that your Highness is most
grieviously displeased with my book which I, not of mine own
courage, but by the instigation of them that did not well favour your
Highness, foolishly and hastily set forth. Nevertheless, I have good
comfort and stomach to write not only because of that your kingly
clemency—which is daily so much told of unto me, both by words
and writing of very many men, that, seeing you be yourself mortal,
I cannot think you will bear enmity immortal—but also forasmuch
as I have by credible persons been informed that the book [*Assertio
septem sacramentorum*] made out against me in the name of your
Highness is not the King's of England, as crafty sophisters would it
should seem: which when they abused the name of your Highness,
considered not in what peril they put themselves by the slandering of
a King, and, especially above other, that monster and common hate
of God and men, the Cardinal of York, [Thomas Wolsey] that
pestilence of your realm.

Wherefore I am now so sore ashamed that it irketh and abasheth
me to lift up mine eyen afore your Highness which have suffered
myself to be with such lightness moved against such and so great a
King by those works of wickedness, namely, being myself but dregs
and a worm which had ought only by contempt to have been either
overcome or let alone.

Also, another thing is which seriously caused me, being never so
vile, yet for to write because your Highness beginneth to favour the
gospel and wax not a little wary of that sort of ungratious folks.
Verily, that was gospel, indeed, that is to say, glad tidings unto my
heart. Wherefore I prostrate myself with these letters unto the feet

of your Highness, as humbly as I can devise, and beseech for the Cross and honour of Christ that your Highness would vouchsafe to incline something and pardon me in whatsoever I have offended your Highness, like as Christ prayed and commanded us also one to forgive another his debt.

Moreover, if your Highness think it not to be refused that I make out another book and therein unsay my former writing and now on the contrary side honour the name of your Highness, please it your Majesty to give me some mild token; and there shall be no tarrying in me, but I shall do it most gladly: for though I be a man of no reputation in comparison of your Highness, yet might we trust that no small fruit should grow unto the gospel and the glory of God hereby if I might have liberty to write in the cause of the gospel unto the King of England.

In the mean season, Our Lord increase your Highness, as He hath begun, that you may with full spirit, both obey and favour the gospel: and He suffer not your regal ears and mind to be holden with the mischievous voices of those mermaids that can nothing but cry that 'Luther is a heretic.' And it may like your Highness to consider, what harm can I teach that teacheth none other thing but that we must be saved by the faith of Jesus Christ, Son of God, which for us suffered and was raised again, as witness the gospel and the epistles of the Apostles: for this is the head and so foundation of my doctrine upon which afterward I build and teach charity toward our neighbour, obedience unto the heads and rulers of countries, and, finally, to crucify the body of sin like as the doctrine of Christ commandeth.

What ill is in these chapters of doctrine? Yet let the matter be looked upon; let it have hearing and judgment first. Why am I condemned; neither heard nor convicted? Furthermore, where I rebuke the abusion of Popes which teach other than these foresaid chapters, and not only other but also clean contrary and, in the meantime, leaning themself upon pope[1], money, their bellies, yea, and kingdoms, principalities, [and] every man's riches, doth not the very common people perceive this and damn it: and their ownselves be constrained to confess it. Why do they not amend themselves and teach well if they will be without hate and blame? Also, your noble Majesty seeth how great princes in Almayne favoureth my party, and, thanked be God, would I should not be condemned: unto whose company and number, I pray Christ, He add and adjoin your Highness and separate you from those tyrants of souls.

Now what wonder is it though Caesar and certain princes be sore against me? Doth not nations murmur against Our Lord and His Christ? As the second psalm saith: People study; kings of the earth

---

[1] *pope,* papal power.

conspire; and princes come together: insomuch that it is more to be marvelled at if any prince or king favour the gospel: and I desire with all my heart inwardly that I may once have cause to rejoice and make congratulation of this miracle in your Highness.

And I pray God, by whose favour and assistance I write this letter, that He so work with my word that the King of England may be made shortly the perfect disciple of Christ and professor of the gospel, and, finally, a most benign lord unto Luther. Amen.

Some answer, if it may like your Highness, I look after, mild and benign. At Wittenberg, the first day of September, the year of Our Lord, 1525.

Most humble subject unto your regal Majesty. Martin Luther, his own hand.

HENRY VIII TO LUTHER

The answer of the most mighty and noble Prince King Henry the VIII, King of England and of France, Defender of the Faith, and Lord of Ireland unto the Letter of Martin Luther.

Your letter, written the first day of September, we have received the 20th day of March: In which ye write yourself to be sorry and ashamed that ye follily and hastily, not of your own mind, but by the instigation of others, such as little favoured me, did put out your book against me [and] with which ye know yourself that ye have sore offended me, and therefore have cause to be in dread and shame to write unto me.

Notwithstanding, ye say that ye be the more bold now to write unto me, not only because ye perceive my benignity such that considering myself a man mortal I will not bear immortal enmity but also forasmuch as ye, by credible information, understand that the book put forth in my name for the assertion of the sacraments was not mine own but fraudulently devised by false sophisters to mine ignominy and rebuke, and specially by the Cardinal of York whom ye call 'a monster, odious to God and man', and the 'pestilence' of my realm. And therefore ye say that ye be now ashamed to lift up your eyen to me that have of lightness so suffered yourself to be moved against such a King, which, notwithstanding, ye write that ye be forced and compelled earnestly to write unto me because that I have now begun to bear favour to the gospel which is (as ye say) joyful tidings to your heart: wherein ye beseech God to increase me that I may with whole heart obey and favour the gospel. And that He suffer not mine ears to be occupied with the pestilent voices of those sirens which can nothing else do but cry out that 'Luther is a heretic.'

Ye write also that ye would I should consider that there can be no harm in your doctrine since ye teach (as ye say) nothing else but only

that man must needs 'be saved in the faith of Jesus Christ'. And
that upon this foundation, ye build 'charity' to your neighbours and
'obedience' to your governors, with the crucifying of 'the body of
sin'. And in these ye desire to be heard, much marvelling that ye be
condemned unheard and unconvicted.

Then after your accustomed manner, ye rail upon the Church of
Rome, boasting that many princes of Almayne take your part.…
These be, Luther, all things which were in your letter contained:
in which as we right well perceive your covert fraudulent purpose,
so shall we on the other side, after our accustomed plainness (lest
your crafty ways might abuse good simple folk), to every point give
you true and open answer.…

And whereas your pestilent tongue is so lewd to rail upon the most
reverend father in God, the lord Legate, Cardinal of York, our chief
counsellor and Chancellor, it grieveth him little (I wot well) to be
railed upon with the blasphemous tongue that raileth and rageth
against Christ's whole Church, His saints, His apostles, His Holy
Mother, and Himself, as it evidently (as well by many parts of your
pestilent books as by the furious act of your faction) appeareth. And
his fatherhood now is, and shall be, so much in more cordial favour
with me in how much I perceive him to be the deeper in the hatred
of you, or other such as ye be: whom where ye call the 'pestilence'
of my realm, I purpose to give you no reckoning what manifold
good fruit my realm and I receive by his faithful diligence, labour,
travail, and wisdom.

Howbeit, all other things set apart, it well appeareth that his
fatherhood is in this one point to my realm very good and wholesome in that he, conformable to my mind and according to my
commandment, studiously purgeth my realm from the pestilent
contagion of your factious heresies; with which among there
entereth some into my realm right sick out of such place as your unwholesome breath hath infected: who, as they have been found, we
have by the wholesome and good diligence of the said most reverend
father not only kept off from the infecting of our own people but
have also, with right charitable handling, helped and cured them.

For as for our own subjects, we trust in God's help, have and shall
have little faith in your erroneous opinions whatsoever hope ye be
put in, either by other ways or by one or two friars, apostates, run
out of our realm, reigning in riot and unthrifty liberty with you, of
whom we reckon our realm so well rid that if there were any more
such here (as we trust there be not many), we would, ye had them,
too.

It is a 'glad tidings' to your heart, ye say, that I now have begun
to bear favour to the gospel, as though I had never favoured the
gospel before. Howbeit that, I have not so late (as ye make for)

begun to love and reverently read the gospel, though ye list to dissimulate it: Yet ye right well perceive by that I have already by the plain gospel disproved evidently some of your pernicious heresies; whereby ye will find that this is not the first time that I have intermeddled me with the said gospels. Wherefore, wete ye well, the gospel long hath been and ever shall be my chief study as the doctrine most wholesome to every man that will in the study thereof use a way contrary to that that ye do: Which in the interpretation thereof use to follow your own fantastical invention against all the world, besides contrary to the counsel of the wise man that saith: Son, lean not unto thine own wit, nor take not thyself for a wise man.[1]

But as for me, I well know and acknowledge that I am unable of myself to [come to] the understanding thereof, and, therefore, calling for God's help, most humbly submit myself to the determination of Christ's Church and interpretations of the old holy Fathers whom His goodness plenteously enlightened with learning, illumined with grace, furnished with faith, garnished with good works, and, finally, with many miracles, declared their faith and living to like[2] Him. Where ye on the contrary side, setting all these old saints at nought and villanously blaspheming their memories, procuring the detraction of their honour, lest the reverence and estimation of their holy lives should stand in your light, admit no man's wit but your own (which only you admit in all things): and defending a manifest folly for wisdom, an open false heresy for a truth, [you] have nothing else to stand by, but only cry out that the Scripture is evident for your part, and all that ever took it otherwise were but fools—were they never so many, never so wise, never so well learned, never so holy.

And when ye have thus well and worshipfully quit yourself in words, then instigate and set out rude rebellious people under pretext of evangelical liberty to run out and fight for your faction.

If any man had so little wit to doubt which of these two ways were the better—yours now new begun, or the faith of the old Fathers—Our Saviour putteth us out of doubt when He saith: By their fruits ye shall know them.[3] For of them no man doubteth but they were good men and of holy living, serving God in fasting, prayer, and chastity, and all their writings full of charity; and of you, men doubt as little when they see that all your doing began of envy and presumption, proceedeth with rancour and malice, blown forth with pride and vain glory, and endeth in lechery.

And, therefore, cloak ye never so much your doctrine under the pretext of evangelical liberty: notwithstanding that I know how slender mine own learning is, yet [it] is not so slender that ye can make me believe that ye mean well when ye speak fast of the spirit

[1] Cf. Prov. iii. 5–7.   [2] *like*, resemble.   [3] Matt. vii. 20.

and fall all to the flesh; when ye make as [if] ye would exhort all the world to live after the gospel, and then exhort me from chastity, to which the gospel effectually counseleth, and forsake yourself your vowed chastity, promised and dedicated to God, to the keeping and observance whereof all Holy Scripture bindeth you. . . .

Would God, Luther, that these words of yours were as true as I know them for contrary. For what charity build you upon faith, when ye teach that faith alone without good works sufficeth? For albeit that in your book, made against me, waxing for shame [and] half wary to hear thereof, ye laid to my charge that I did therein misreport you, yet did ye not only make none earthly answer to your own words which I laid to your charge, openly proving in you that detestable heresy, but also said the same again in the self book [*Contra Henricum Regem*] in which ye pretend yourself to have been wrongfully charged therewith before, saying that sacrilege it is and wickedness to have any will to please God by good works and not by only faith. Which words be as open as those ye wrote before in *Babylonica* where ye write this sentence:*

> Thus thou seest (say ye) how rich is a Christian man, or he that is baptized, which though he would, cannot lose his salvation by any sins, be they never so great, but[1] if he will not believe: for no sin can damn him but only lack of belief: for as for all other sins, if there stand still or come again faith and credence in God's promise that God made to His sacrament of baptism, they be supped up in a moment by the same faith.

These words of yours show so manifestly what ye mean that there neither needeth nor boteth[2] any gloss. It can receive no colour but that contrary to Christ's words: The way is strait and narrow that leadeth to heaven.[3] Ye, with your evangelical liberty, make a broad and easy way thither to win you favour of the people, teaching that it shall be enough to believe God's promise without any labour of good works, which is far from the mind of Saint Paul which teacheth us a 'faith that worketh by love'[4] and also by faith. . . .

I would have given you a short answer without any touch of your heresies in speciality had ye not been so shameless to write that ye teach nothing else but that men must be saved in the faith of Christ with charity builded thereupon, and obedience, and crucifying of the body of sin, which your shameful and shameless lieing hath driven me so to show and specify one or two of your open heresies that every man may perceive how far they be of another kind than the faith of our salvation or charity or obedience or crucifying of the body of sin, which ye say be the only things that ye teach: and yet

---

[1] *but*, except.   [2] *boteth*, is demanded.
[3] Matt. vii. 14.   [4] Gal. v. 6.

have I nothing touched the great high heap of all your other heinous heresies which yet more plainly declare and prove your shameless untruth in writing that ye teach nothing else but the faith of our salvation, charity, obedience, and crucifying of the body of sin.

For when ye so plainly write against the sacraments of Christ's Church; when ye damn chastity of priests; deny all Holy Orders; join bread with the Body of Christ; take from all men the benefit of the Mass; rail against the holy canon of the same; when ye make women, confessors and ministers of all sacraments; and make them consecrate the Body of Christ; when ye teach so little difference between Our Blessed Lady and your lewd leman; when ye blaspheme Christ's holy Cross; when ye teach that there is no purgatory, but that all souls shall sleep till the Day of Doom; that sinners may be bold for so long with a thousand shamefull heresies besides; are ye not now ashamed to say that ye teach nothing else but man must be saved by the faith of Jesu Christ when ye go about, indeed, to destroy the faith of Jesus Christ, who if He had come to teach such ways as ye teach, He had not come to call the world from bad to good nor had been a teacher of virtue, as He was, indeed, but a very patron of sin: Whereof on the contrary He did well show in suffering the punishment of the Cross for the only redemption and remission of our sins. . . .

Howbeit, if the lack of grace and the infirmity of your flesh cannot sustain that whereby ye dare not for dread of death revoke your errors presently among them where ye have sown them, yet disdain not to follow Saint Peter himself, though ye condemn his successors; wherefore if ye dare not confess the truth, but deny and forswear Christ within, get you out, at the least-ways, from them whom yourself have corrupted, unlike Saint Peter in that point, and bitterly weep for your sin, withdrawing yourself somewhere far off into some religious place, and there take recourse to the Fountain of Grace and Remission, Our Saviour Christ.

And there do penance for your sin, where ye may revoke and in writing call again your old errors and heresies for the health and safeguard of your soul without any peril of your body. There with revoking and lamenting your former errors and evil lieing, with the meek and humble hope of God's great mercy, with the gesture, words, and heart of the Publican, labour to procure by the good continuance of fruitful penance remission and forgiveness of your fore passed offences, of which your amendment and other by your means, I would be as glad to hear as I have been sorry to see you [and] by you so many more piteously spilt and lost.

COLOPHON: Imprinted at London in Fleet Street by Richard Pynson, printer to the King's most noble Grace. . . . [1526?]

THE BIBLE

When the printing press increased the demand for a personally owned Bible, Europe was flooded, in the late fifteenth and early sixteenth centuries, with vernacular versions in Spanish, Italian, French, Dutch, German, and Bohemian, each a more or less careful rendering of St Jerome's Vulgate. Though there existed no complete English version of the Bible, preachers and writers of every type of literature quoted the Bible in the English vernacular, and in this way the greater portion of the Old and New Testaments became familiar to a broad segment of the people.

Though a complete English version of the Bible was for many years delayed, England, in a manner, helped to foster the first critical or scientific edition of the New Testament that had been made in any tongue, ancient or modern. It was the work of the Dutch scholar Erasmus, who finished the major portion while teaching Greek at Queens' College, Cambridge, where he had gone in 1511, at the request of the university's Chancellor, Bishop John Fisher. On Erasmus's return to Basel three years later, he took the nearly completed manuscript with him, delivering it shortly to John Froben, the German printer, who published the work under the title Novum Instrumentum (1516), a thousand-page folio containing the Latin Vulgate, Erasmus's own Greek version of the New Testament, and annotations. The Novum Instrumentum was dedicated to Pope Leo X and praised by him and scholars on the Continent. In England Colet wrote to Erasmus that 'it was bought with avidity and read everywhere here'. Seventy editions were printed before Erasmus's death in 1536.

At almost this same time, the Spanish Cardinal Francisco Ximenes started Greek and Jewish scholars to work on the 'Complutensian Polyglot Bible' (1520), the texts of which, printed in parallel, included the Hebrew Bible, the Septuagint, the Latin Vulgate, and a Syriac paraphrase of the Pentateuch. Though Erasmus and Ximenes worked independently, each realized the necessity of presenting well edited early texts of the Scripture, besides the Vulgate, to which future translators could turn.

One of the first to appreciate their labours was Martin Luther, who used both the Novum Instrumentum and the 'Polyglot Bible' in preparing his German version of the New Testament, printed in 1522. They also served Tyndale, whose New Testament was printed in Worms, in 1526, a year after a fragment of it (a portion of St Mark's gospel) had been printed in Cologne, where government authorities forced the printers to stop work. Then, with the aid of his friend William Roy, a Franciscan friar, Tyndale engaged printers in Worms, and without any difficulty six thousand copies were printed and shipped to England. As they began filtering through the London book trade, Henry VIII ordered the seizure of all copies, and they were destroyed in a spectacular 'burning of the books' at Paul's Cross in 1527. At the same time Cuthbert Tunstall, Bishop of London, issued an injunction to his archdeacons, declaring 'the holy gospel of God is endangered' because of the heretical glosses that 'are inserted' throughout. However, several years later, when Henry VIII had broken with Rome, he lifted the ban for a time on Tyndale's New Testament, but the ban was re-imposed in 1543.

The More-Tyndale controversy, which rose out of the latter's version of the New Testament, made it obvious to the king and the English hierarchy that a Bible in English was sorely needed. Still friendly to the papacy in 1530, Henry VIII appointed a commission that year to inquire into the need of having 'in the English tongue both the New Testament and the Old'. Though the committee favoured an English version, the growing tension between Church and State over the king's divorce postponed any definite action.

A tacit royal approval was extended for the time to all versions made by private persons, such as Coverdale's Biblia (1535), translated 'oute of Douche and Latyn' and based partly on Tyndale's translation, and the 'Matthew's Bible' (1537), a revision of the former made by John Rogers, a London rector. Archbishop Cranmer recommended Rogers's version until such time as 'we bishops put forth a better translation', adding that this would likely be the 'day after Doomsday'. But the English hierarchy's eagerness for an acceptable text finally won the king's permission to invite Coverdale to undertake a new translation. Thomas Cromwell, the Chancellor, persuaded the reformer to return to England late in 1537 to begin the work.

According to Cromwell's plan, the new text would be carefully collated with Tyndale's New Testament and the 'Matthew's Bible'. As the work progressed, it became obvious that the manuscript was too large for the presses in England to handle, and Coverdale and the printer, Richard Grafton, took it to Paris. Before it was half printed, the French government threatened to seize the type, and Coverdale and Grafton hurried back to London where the 'Great Bible', as it was called, was finished by Grafton in 1539. The title-page of the folio shows Henry VIII giving the 'Word of God' to Cromwell and Archbishop Cranmer, who distribute it to the clergy and laity gathered about them. It was a triumph for the Chancellor, and was known as 'Cromwell's Bible'. To insure its use throughout the realm, the king, early in 1543, banned all other versions, including Coverdale's Biblia, and it enjoyed the sanction of the bishops of the English Church until the 'King James' or Authorized Version of 1611.

No formal decision on vernacular Bibles had as yet been made by Rome. The Church's ruling on the matter became the task of the bishops who met, in 1543, in oecumenical council at Trent. During an early session, they ruled that every translation of the Bible that did not use the Vulgate as a basic text was to be banned in every country. Admitting the pressing need of an English translation of the Bible, they hoped one would be made shortly, if not in England, then on the Continent by the Catholic refugees *who were steadily arriving in France and the Netherlands. But no English version was printed until the Douai version of the New Testament, supervised by the exiled English Cardinal William Allen, in 1582, the two-hundredth anniversary of the Wycliffe Bible.*

New Testament	*New Testament*
TRANSLATED BY	TRANSLATED BY
WILLIAM TYNDALE	MILES COVERDALE

THE GOSPEL OF SAINT MATTHEW: THE .XV. CHAPTER	MATTHEW'S: THE .XV. CHAPTER

Then came to Jesus scribes and Pharisees from Jerusalem saying:[1] Why do Thy disciples transgress the traditions of the seniors? For they wash not their hands when they eat bread. He answered and said unto them: Why do ye also transgress the commandment of God through your traditions? For God commanded, saying: Honour thy father and mother: and he that speaketh evil against his father or mother shall suffer death. But ye say: Every man shall say to his father or mother, Whatsoever thing I offer that same doth profit thee; and so shall he not honour his father and mother. And thus have ye made that the commandment of God is without effect through your traditions. Hypocrites, well prophesied of you Isaias, saying: This people draweth nigh unto Me with their mouths and honoureth Me with their lips, yet their heart is far from Me: but in vain they worship Me, teaching doctrine which is nothing but men's precepts. And He called the people unto Him, and said to them: Hear and understand: that which goeth into the mouth defileth not a man; but that which cometh out of the mouth defileth the man.

Then came unto Him from Jerusalem the scribes and Pharisees, saying: Why do Thy disciples transgress the traditions of the *elders*? For they wash not their hands when they eat bread. But He answering, said unto them: Why do ye also transgress the commandment of God for your own traditions sake? For God hath said: Honour, thou, father and mother. And whosoever curseth father or mother, let him die by death. But ye say: Whosoever shall say to father or mother: What gift soever is of me, it shall profit thee: and he shall not honour his father or his mother. And the commandment of God, have ye made of none effect for your own traditions sake? Ye hypocrites, well hath Isaias prophesied of you saying: This people honoureth Me with lips, but their heart is far from Me. In vain do they serve Me, teaching the doctrines and precepts of men. And when the people were called together unto Him, He said unto them: Hear and understand: that which entereth into the mouth defileth not a man, but that which proceedeth out of the mouth, that defileth a man. Then His disciples coming nigh, said unto Him:

[1] *Side note reads*: Profit. Mar. viii. Mark the leaven of the Pharisees. God would that the son should honour his father and mother with his temporal goods, and the Pharisees, for their temporal lucre, interpreted it, saying: God is thy father and thy mother: offer to Him. Levi. .xxix. So were the Pharisees dishes full with robbery and extortion, and the poor fathers and mothers perish for hunger and need.

Then came His disciples and said unto Him: Perceivest Thou how that the Pharisees are offended, hearing Thy sayings? He answered and said: All plants which My Heavenly Father hath not planted shall be plucked up by the roots. Let them alone: they be blind leaders of the blind. If the blind lead the blind, both shall fall into the ditch.

Then answered Peter, and said to Him: Declare unto us this parable.[1] Then said Jesus: Are ye yet without understanding? Perceive ye not, that whatsoever goeth in at the mouth descendeth down into the belly and is cast out into the draught? But those things which proceed out of the mouth come from the heart, and they defile a man. For out of the heart come evil thoughts, murder, breaking of wedlock, whoredom, theft, false-witness-bearing, [and] blasphemy. These are the things which defile a man. But to eat with unwashen hands, defileth not a man.

And Jesus went thence and departed into the coasts of Tyre and Sidon. And behold a woman which was a Canaanite came out of the same coasts and cried unto Him, saying: Have mercy on me, Lord, the Son of David, my daughter is piteously vexed with a devil. And He gave her never a word to answer. Then came to Him His disciples and besought Him, saying: Send her away, for she followeth us crying. He answered and said: I am not sent but unto the lost sheep of the house of Israel. Then she came and worshipped Him, saying: Master, sucker me. He answered and said: It is not good to take the children's bread and to cast it to whelps. And she answered and said: It is truth; nevertheless, the whelps eat of the crumbs which fall from their master's table. Then Jesus answered and said unto her: O woman, great is thy faith. Be it to thee even as thou desirest. And her

Knowest Thou that the Pharisees when they heard this saying were offended. And He answering, said: Every plant that My heavenly Father hath not planted shall be rooted out. Let them alone: they are blind and the leaders of the blind. If the blind lead the blind, they fall both into the ditch. Peter answering, said unto Him: Expound unto us this parable. And He said unto them: Be you also yet without understanding? Do ye not understand that everything which entereth into the mouth goeth into the belly and is cast out into the draught? But those things which proceed out of the mouth go out from the heart, and they defile a man: For out from the heart go evil thoughts, manslaughters, adultries, fornications, thefts, false witnesses, and blasphemies. These are they that defile a man. But to eat with unwashen hands, defileth not man.

And Jesus being departed thence went forth into the coasts of Tyre and Sidon. And behold a woman of Canaan, being come forth out of those coasts, cried, saying unto Him: Have mercy on me, O Lord, Thou son of David. My daughter is evil vexed of a devil. Which answered her not a word. And His disciples approaching nigh besought Him, saying: Send her away, for she crieth after us. But He answering, said: I am not sent but unto the sheep of the house of Israel which are perished. And she came and worshipped Him, saying: O Lord, help me. Which answering, said: It is not good to take the children's bread and to cast it unto dogs. And she said: Yea, Lord, for the whelps also eat of the crumbs that fall from their lord's table. Then Jesus answering, said unto her: O woman, great is thy faith: Be it unto thee even as thou wilt. And her daughter was healed from that hour. And when Jesus was departed thence, He came by the seaside of Galilee; and He

---

[1] *Side note reads*: Traditions of men must fail at the last: God's Word bideth ever.

daughter was made whole even at that same time.

Then Jesus went away from thence and came nigh unto the sea of Galilee, and went up into a mountain and sat down there. And much people came unto Him, having with them halt, blind, dumb, maimed, and other many: and cast them down at Jesus' feet. And He healed them insomuch that the people wondered to see the dumb speak, the maimed whole, and the halt to go, the blind to see, and glorified the God of Israel.

Jesus called His disciples to Him and said: I have compassion on the people because they have continued with Me now three days, and have nothing to eat: and I will not let them depart fasting lest they perish in the way. And His disciples said unto Him: Whence should we get so much bread in the wilderness as should suffice so great a multitude? And Jesus said unto them: How many loaves have ye? And they said: Seven and a few fishes. And He commanded the people to sit down on the ground, and took the seven loaves and the fishes and gave thanks and break them and gave to His disciples, and His disciples gave them to the people. And they all ate and were sufficed; and they took up of the broken meat that was left seven baskets full. They that ate were four thousand men, besides women and children. And He sent away the people, and took ship and came into the parts of Magdala.

going up into a mountain sat there. And there came unto Him much people having with them dumb, blind, lame, feeble, and many other, and those they laid at His feet, and He healed them so that the people marvelled, seeing the dumb speaking, the lame walking, the blind seeing; and they magnified the God of Israel. Jesus when His disciples were called together said: I have pity on the people, for they continue with Me now three days and have not that they may eat: And I will not let them go away fasting lest they miscarry in the way. And the disciples say unto Him: Whence shall we get us, then, so much bread in the wilderness that we may satisfy so great a multitude? And Jesus said unto them: How many loaves have ye? And they said: Seven and a few little fishes. And He commanded the people that they should sit down upon the ground. And taking the seven loaves and the fishes, He, giving thanks, break and gave to His disciples, and the disciples gave unto the people. And they all did eat and were satisfied. And that which remained of the broken meats, took they away seven baskets full. They that did eat were four thousand of men, besides children and women. And when the multitude was sent away, He went up into a little ship and came into the coasts of Magedan.

[Reprinted from the fragment of the uncompleted Cologne edition of 1525, ed. A. W. Pollard (Oxford, 1926).]

TITLE-PAGE: *Anno* 1538. Printed... in Southwark by James Nicholson.

WILLIAM TYNDALE[1]

Imbued with the idea of the need of an English vernacular Bible, Tyndale, in 1523, gave up his teaching post in the Welsh family in England and went to work in earnest on a translation of the New Testament. Since 1408, when the Church banned Wycliffe's Bible, it was forbidden to make an English version without episcopal licence. Tyndale probably sought such permission when he applied for living quarters in the house of Cuthbert Tunstall, Bishop of London. All that is known of the incident is that Tunstall refused him lodging, insisting that his 'house was full'. Bitter over the rejection, Tyndale remained in London for a year and continued to preach and write. With the help of friends, he left for Germany in the spring of 1524, going at once to Wittenberg, where he matriculated at the university.

Within the next year Tyndale completed his English translation of the New Testament, aided by Luther and Erasmus's Latin text. Though his version, printed in Worms in 1526, was banned in England, Tyndale was undaunted in his determination to publish a complete English Bible, and he spent the next six years in Germany and the Netherlands, translating portions of the Old Testament, having prepared himself for the task by learning Hebrew.

The Beginning of the New Testament translated by William Tyndale

THE PROLOGUE

I have here translated, brethren and sisters, most dear and tenderly beloved in Christ, the New Testament for your spiritual edifying, consolation, and solace. Exhorting instantly and beseeching those that are better seen in the tongues than I, and that have higher gifts of grace to interpret the sense of the Scripture and meaning of the spirit than I, to consider and ponder my labour, and that with the spirit of meekness.

And if they perceive in any place that I have not attained the very sense of the tongue or meaning of the Scripture or have not given the right English word, that they put to their hands to amend it, remembering that so is their duty to do. For we have not received the gifts of God for ourselves only or for to hide them, but for to bestow them unto the honouring of God and Christ and edifying of the congregation which is the body of Christ.

[1] For biographical sketch, see pp. 188–90.

The causes that moved me to translate, I thought better that others should imagine than that I should rehearse them. Moreover I supposed it superfluous; for who is so blind to ask why light should be showed to them that walk in darkness where they cannot but stumble, and where to stumble is the danger of eternal damnation, either so despiteful that he would envy any man (I speak not [of] his brother) so necessary a thing or so bedlam mad to affirm that good is the natural cause of evil, and darkness to proceed out of light, and lying should be grounded in truth and verity, and not rather clean contrary, that light destroyeth darkness, and verity reproveth all manner of lying.

After it had pleased God to put in my mind and also to give me grace to translate this afore-rehearsed New Testament into our English tongue, howsoever we have done it, I supposed it very necessary to put you in remembrance of certain points which are that ye well understand what these words mean—the old Testament, the New Testament, the law, the gospel, Moses, Christ, nature, grace working and believing, deeds and faith—lest we ascribe to the one that which belongeth to the other, and make of Christ, Moses; of the gospel, the law; despise grace and rob faith; and fall from meek learning into idle despiteous brawling and scolding about words.

The Old Testament is a book wherein is written the law and commandments of God and the deeds of them which fulfil them and of them also which fulfil them not.
The Old Testament

The New Testament is a book wherein are contained the promises of God and the deeds of them which believeth or believe them not.
The New Testament
The Gospel or *evangelion*

Evangelion (that we call the gospel) is a Greek word and signifieth good, merry, glad, and joyful tidings that maketh a man's heart glad and maketh him sing, dance, and leap for joy. As when David had felled Goliath, the giant, came glad tidings unto the Jews that their fearful and cruel enemy was slain and they delivered out of all danger. For gladness whereof, they sang, danced, and were joyful.

In like manner is the *evangelion* of God (which we call gospel and the New Testament), joyful tidings and, as some say, a 'good hearing', published by the apostles throughout all the world of Christ, the Right David, how that He hath fought with sin, with death and the devil, and overcame them. Whereby all men that were in bondage to sin, wounded with death, overcome of the devil, are without their own merits or deservings loosed, instified,[1] restored to life, and saved; brought to liberty and reconciled unto the favour

---

[1] *Instified*, enlivened.

of God, and set at one with Him again, which tidings as many as believe, laud, praise, and thank God are glad, sing, and dance for joy.

The law (saith the gospel of John in the first chapter) was given by Moses, but grace and verity by Jesus Christ.[1] The Law (whose minister is Moses) was given to bring us unto the knowledge of ourselves that we might thereby feel and perceive what we are of nature. The law condemneth us and all our deeds and is called of Paul (in the third chapter of the second Epistle unto the Corinthians) 'the ministration of death'.[2] For it filleth our consciences and driveth us to desperation, inasmuch as it requireth of us that which is impossible for us to do.

It requireth of us the deeds of a whole man. It requireth perfect love from the low bottom and ground of the heart, as well in all things which we suffer as in the things which we do. But saith John (in the same place): Grace and verity is given us in Christ. So that when the law hath passed upon us and condemned us to death (which is his nature to do) then have we in Christ, grace, that is to say, favour, promises of life, of mercy, of pardon freely by the merits of Christ; and in Christ have we 'verity and truth' in that God fulfilleth all his promises to them that believe.

Therefore is the gospel the ministration of life. Paul calleth it in the afore-rehearsed place, of the second [third] chapter to the Cor., 'the ministration of the spirit' and of righteousness. In the gospel when we believe the promises, we receive the spirit of life and are justified in the blood of Christ from all things whereof the Law condemned us. Of Christ it is written in the afore-rehearsed first chapter of John: This is He 'of whose abundance, or fullness, all we have received, grace for grace', or favour for favour. That is to say, for the favour that God hath to his Son Christ, He giveth unto us His favour and good will as a father to his sons. As affirmeth Paul saying: Which loved us in His Beloved before the creation of the world.[3] For the love that God hath to Christ, He loveth us, and not for our own self. Christ is made Lord over all and is called in Scripture, God's 'mercy stool':[4] whosoever flyeth to Christ can neither hear nor receive of God any other thing save mercy....

Here shall ye see compendiously and plainly set out the order and practice of everything afore-rehearsed.

The fall of Adam hath made us heirs of the vengeance and wrath of God and heirs of eternal damnation, and hath brought us into captivity and bondage under the devil. And the devil is our lord and our ruler, our head, our governor, our prince, yea, and our god. And our will is locked and knit faster unto the will of the devil than

[1] John i. 17. [2] II Cor. iii. 7.
[3] Eph. i. 3–4. [4] Ps. lxxxxviii. 5.

could a hundred thousand chains bind a man unto a post. Unto the devil's will, consent we with all our hearts, with all our minds, with all our might, power, strength, will, and lust.

With what poisoned, deadly, and venomous hate, hateth a man his enemy? With how great malice of mind inwardly, do we slay and murder? With what violence and rage, yea, and with how fervent lust, commit we adultery, fornication, and such like uncleanness? With what pleasure and delectation inwardly, serveth a glutton his belly? With what diligence, deceive we? How busily seek we the things of this world? Whatsoever we do, think, or imagine, is abominable in the sight of God.

And we are, as it were, asleep in so deep blindness that we can neither see nor feel in what misery, thraldom, and wretchedness we are in till Moses came and wake us and published the Law. When we hear the Law truly preached: how that we ought 'to love and honour God with all our strength and might from the low bottom of the heart, and our neighbours (yea, our enemies) as ourselves', inwardly from the ground of the heart, and to do whatsoever God biddeth and abstain from whatsoever God forbiddeth with all love and meekness, with a fervent and a burning lust; from the centre of the heart, then beginneth the conscience to rage against the Law and against God.

No sea, be it never so great a tempest, is so unquiet. It is not possible for a natural man to consent to the law that it should be good or that God should be righteous which maketh the law. Man's wit, reason, and will are so fast glued, yea, nailed and chained unto the will of the devil. Neither can any creature loose the bonds save the blood of Christ....

Here, see ye the nature of the law and the nature of the *evangelion*. How the law bindeth and damneth all men, To bind and loose and the *evangelion* looseth them again. The law goeth before, and the *evangelion* followeth.

When a preacher preacheth the law, he bindeth all consciences; and when he preacheth the gospel, he looseth them again. These two salves (I mean, the law and the gospel) useth God and His preacher to heal and cure sinners withal. The law driveth out the disease and maketh it appear, and is a sharp salve and a fretting corsey,[1] and killeth the dead flesh, and looseth and draweth the sores out by the roots and all corruption. It pulleth from a man the trust and confidence that he hath in himself and in his own works, merits, deservings, and ceremonies. It killeth him, sendeth him down to hell, and bringeth him to utter desperation, and 'prepareth the way of the Lord,[2] as it is written of John the Baptist.

For it is not possible that Christ should come to a man as long as

---

[1] *corsey*, corrosive.   [2] John i. 23.

he trusteth in himself or in any worldly thing. Then cometh the
evangelion, a more gentle plaster, which sowpleth[1] and swageth the
wonder of the conscience and bringeth health. It bringeth the Spirit
of God, which looseth the bonds of Satan and coupleth
us to God and His will through strong faith and fervent
love with bonds too strong for the devil, the world, or
any creature to loose them. And the poor and wretched
sinner feeleth so great mercy, love, and kindness in God,
that he is sure in himself how that it is not possible that
God should forsake him or withdraw His mercy and love
from him. And [he] boldly cryeth out with Paul, saying:
Who shall separate us from the love that God loveth us
withal? That is to say, what shall make me believe that
God loveth me not? Shall tribulation? Anguish? Persecution? Shall hunger? Nakedness? Shall a sword? Nay,
I am sure that neither death nor life, neither angel, neither rule nor
power, neither present things nor things to come, neither high nor
low, neither any creature is able to separate us from the love of God
which is in Christ Jesus Our Lord.[2]

A Christian man feeleth the workings of the Holy Ghost in his soul. And in all tribulations and adversities feeleth God a merciful Father and a loving.

In all such tribulations, a Christian man perceiveth that God is his
Father, and loveth him even as He loved Christ when He shed His
blood on the Cross. Finally, as before when I was bound to the
devil and his will, I wrought all manner evil and wickedness; not
for hell's sake, which is the reward of sin, but because I was heir of
hell by birth and bondage to the devil, did I evil. For I could none
otherwise do: to do sin was my nature. Even so, now since I am
coupled to God by Christ's blood, do I well, not for heaven's sake,
but because I am heir of heaven by grace and Christ's purchasing
and have the Spirit of God; I do good freely, for so is my nature, as
a good tree bringeth forth good fruit, and an evil tree, evil fruit:
By the fruits shall ye know what the tree is.[3] A man's deeds declare
what he is within, but make him neither good nor bad, etc.

We must be first evil ere we do evil, as a serpent is first poisoned
ere he poison. We must be, also, good ere we do good, as the fire
must be first hot ere it warm anything. Take example: As those blind
which are cured in the *evangelion* could not see till Christ had given
them sight; and [those] deaf could not hear till Christ had given them
hearing; and those sick could not do the deeds of a whole man till
Christ had given them health; so can no man do good in his soul till
Christ have loosed him out of the bonds of Satan and have given
him wherewith to do good. Yea, and first have poured into him
that self good thing which he sheddeth forth afterward on others.

Whatsoever is our own, is sin. Whatsoever is above, that is
Christ's gift, purchase, doing, and working. He bought it of His

---

[1] *sowpleth*, soothes.   [2] Rom. viii. 35–9.   [3] Matt. vii. 17–20.

Father dearly with His blood, yea, with His most bitter death, and gave His life for it. Whatsoever good thing is in us, that is given us freely without our deserving or merits for Christ's blood's sake. That we desire to follow the will of God, it is the gift of Christ's blood. That we now hate the devil's will (whereunto we were so fast-locked and could not but love it) is also the gift of Christ's blood unto whom belongeth the praise and honour of our good deeds, and not unto us.

[Facsimile of the unique fragment of the uncompleted Cologne edition of 1525, ed. A. W. Pollard (Oxford, 1926).]

MILES COVERDALE
1488?–1568

Miles Coverdale's determined efforts to translate the Bible into English places him next in importance to his friend William Tyndale as a leader in the English Reformation. Coverdale's youth is obscure until about 1506, when he began his studies for the priesthood at the Austin Friary at Cambridge. He was ordained at Norwich in 1514. It was in this or the next year that Tyndale was ordained, but their friendship probably did not begin until Tyndale arrived at Cambridge in 1519.

Coverdale's first move away from the Church came in 1526 when he successfully assisted Richard Barnes, his prior, to escape sentence from charges of heresy brought against him in London. Back at Cambridge, Coverdale continued his studies at the university, and in 1531 took a Bachelor's degree in canon law. Probably at the suggestion of his patron Thomas Cromwell, he soon left England to join other English Reformers in the Low Countries. He spent the first years there aiding Tyndale with his translation of the New Testament and working on his own version, to be published in Zürich in 1535.

At Cromwell's urging, Henry VIII invited Coverdale back to England in 1538 to work with scholars on the 'Great Bible'. Personal difficulties developed in 1541 when he defied the ruling of the Six Articles in regard to the celibacy of the clergy, and he left England to live in Germany, where he married Elizabeth Macheson. During the second year of the reign of Edward VI, Coverdale returned to England, and, at the request of Archbishop Cranmer, began to work on The Book of Common Prayer, serving also with Hugh Latimer on a commission appointed to study ecclesiastical reforms. In 1551 Coverdale was made Bishop of Exeter and continued to distinguish himself as a preacher during Edward's reign by vigorously opposing the Calvinists, Anabaptists, and Catholics for their criticism of the Prayer Book.

When Mary I came to the throne, Coverdale was permitted to go to Denmark. Returning in 1558 at Elizabeth's I accession, he was offered his old bishopric, but declined it and served as a canon in the parish of St Magnus in London. His refusal to wear vestments and adhere strictly to the Act of Uniformity brought about his resignation from the parish in 1566. Until his death two years later, Coverdale busied himself with translating works of the German Reformers.

His principal work is the translation of the Old and New Testaments, the Biblia *(1535), the first complete English version of the Bible. Besides this he wrote* An Exposicion vpon the Songe…called Magnificat *(1538). Other religious treatises have been attributed to Coverdale though most are translations from German. Among the most important of these are* The defense of a certayne poore christen man *(1545) and* An exhortacion to the careinge of Chrystes crosse *[1550?].*

As a translator of the Bible, Coverdale's style is direct and simple, but on the whole his version is not scholarly, due principally to his failure to translate from Greek and Hebrew texts. The Songe *was dedicated to the son of a German count, and in his dedicatory epistle Coverdale warns against the misuse of princely power, a warning directed possibly at Henry VIII, who had just put Tyndale to death. Coverdale's translation of the* Magnificat *has a charming rhythm, and his phrasing was retained in a great measure by the translators of the Douai New Testament and the Authorized Version.*

The New Testament

The New Testament: Both in Latin and English, each correspondent to the other after the Vulgate text, commonly called, [of] Saint Jerome. Faithfully translated by John Hollybushe [Miles Coverdale].

TO THE READER

I must needs advertise thee, most gentle reader, that this present text in Latin, which thou seest set here with the English, is the same that customably is read in the church, and commonly is called Saint Jerome's translation. Wherein though in some places I use the honest and just liberty of a grammarian (as needful is for thy better understanding), yet because I am loath to swerve from the text, I so temper my pen that, if thou wilt, thou mayst make plain construction of it by the English that standeth on the other side.

This is done now for thee that art not exactly learned in the Latin tongue and wouldst fain understand it. As for those that be learned in the Latin already, this our small labour is not taken for them save only to move and exhort them that they, likewise knowing of whom they have received their talent of learning, will be no less grieved in their calling to serve their brethren therewith than we are ashamed herewith this our small ministration to do them good. I beseech thee, therefore, take it in good worth: for so well done as it should and might be, it is not. But as it is, thou hast it with a good will.

Whereas by the authority of the text I sometime make it clear for thy more understanding, there shalt thou find this mark [ ] which we have set for thy warning, the text, nevertheless, [is] neither wrested nor perverted. The cause whereof is partly the figure called *eclipsis*, divers times used in the Scriptures, the which though she do garnish the sentence in Latin, yet will not so be admitted in other tongues. Wherefore of necessity we are constrained to enclose such words in this mark: Partly because that sundry, and sometimes too rash, writers out of books have not given so great diligence as is due in the Holy Scripture and have left out and sometime altered some word or words; and another using the same book for a copy hath committed like fault.

Let not, therefore, this our diligence seem more temerious unto thee, gentle reader, than was the diligence of Saint Jerome and Origen unto learned men of their time, which using sundry marks in their books showed their judgment what were to be abated or added unto the books of Scripture that so they might be restored to the pure and very original text. Thy knowledge and understanding in the Word of God shall judge the same of us, also, if it be joined with love to the truth. And though I seem to be all too scrupulous, calling it in one place 'penance' that in another I call 'repentance', and 'gelded' that another calleth 'chaste', this, methink, ought not to offend thee, seeing that the Holy Ghost, I trust, is the Author of both our doings.

If I of mine own head had put into the New Testament these words: *nisi paenitueritis; paenitemini; Sunt enim eunuchi; paenitentiam agite* ['unless you shall do penance' (Luke xiii. 3); 'be penitent' (Acts iii. 19); 'For there are eunuchs' (Matt. xix. 12); 'do penance' (Acts ii. 38)]; etc., then as I were worthy to be reproved, so should it be right necessary to redress the same. But it is the Holy Ghost that hath put them in, and therefore I heartily require thee, think no more harm in me for calling it in one place 'penance' that in another I call 'repentance' than I think harm in him that calleth it 'chaste' which I by the nature of this word *eunuchus* call 'gelded'.

Let every man be glad to submit his understanding to the Holy Ghost in them that be learned; and no doubt we shall think the best, one by another, and find no less occasion to praise God in another man than in ourselves. As the Holy Ghost then is One, working in thee and in me as He will, so let us not swerve from that unity, but be one in Him. And for my part, I insure thee, I am indifferent to call it as well with the one term as with the other, so long as I know that it is no prejudice nor injury to the meaning of the Holy Ghost: Nevertheless, I am very scrupulous to go from the vocable of the text.

And, of truth, so had we all need be. For the world is captious, and many there be that had rather find twenty faults than to amend one. And ofttimes the more labour a man taketh for their commodity, the less thank he hath. But if they that be learned and have wherewith to maintain the charges did their duty, they themselves should perform these things and not only to look for it at other men's hands. At the least, if they would neither take the pain of translating themselves nor to bear the expenses thereof nor of the printing, they should yet have a good tongue and help one way that they cannot do another.

God grant this world once to spy their unthankfulness! This do not I say for any lucre or vantage that I look for at your hands, ye rich and wealthy bellies of the world! For He that never failed me at my need hath taught me to be content with such provision as He hath and will make for me. Of you, therefore, that be servants to your own riches, require I nothing at all save only that which Saint James saith unto you in the beginning of his fifth chapter, namely, that 'ye weep and howl on your wretchedness that shall come upon you'. For certainly ye have great cause so to do: neither is it unlike but great misery shall come upon you, considering the gorgeous fare and apparel that ye have every day for the proud pomp and appetite of your stinking carcasses, and ye be not ashamed to suffer your own flesh and blood to die at your doors for lack of your help.

O sinful belly gods! O unthankful wretches! O uncharitable idolators! With what conscience dare ye put one morsel of meat into your mouths? O abominable hell-hounds, what shall be worth of you? I speak to you, ye rich niggards of the world, which as ye have no favour to God's Holy Word, so love ye to do nothing that it commandeth. Our Lord send you worthy repentance.

But now will I turn my pen unto you that be lords and rulers of your riches: For of you whom God hath made stewards of these worldly goods: Of you whom God hath made plenteous as well in His knowledge as in other riches: Of you, I say, would I fain require and beg (even for His sake, that is the Giver of all good things) that, at the last, ye would do but your duty, and help as well with your good counsel as with your temporal substance that a perfect provision may be made for the poor and for the virtuous bringing up of youth.

That as we now already have cause plentiful to give God thanks for His Word and for sending us a Prince [Henry VIII] (with thousands of other benefits), even so we, seeing the poor, aged, lame, sore, and sick provided for and our youth brought up as well in

God's knowledge as in other virtuous occupations, may have like-wise occasion sufficient to praise God for the same.

Our Lord grant that this our long begging and most needful request may once be heard. In the meantime, till God bring it to pass by His ministers, let not thy counsel nor help be behind, most gentle reader, for the furtherance of the same. And for that thou hast received at the merciful hand of God already, be thankful always unto Him; loving and obedient unto thy Prince; and live so con-tinually in helping and edifying of thy neighbour that it may re-dound to the praise and glory of God forever. Amen.

TITLE-PAGE: *Anno.* 1538.... Printed in Southwark by James Nicholson.

Exposition on the Magnificat

An Exposition upon the song of the Blessed Virgin Mary called Magnificat. Translated out of Latin into English by John Hollybushe [Miles Coverdale].

DEDICATORY EPISTLE

To the renowned and most noble prince and lord, John Frederick, Duke of Saxony, Count of Düren and Marquis[1] of Meissen, my gracious lord and defender:

I have, most doughty Prince, received your Grace's letters at the last, the which, according to my duty, I have humbly taken in my hands, and cheerfully and with entire consideration thought upon their argument and meaning. But seeing I have long since promised unto your Highness the declaration of the Virgin's song of praise called *Magnificat* (from the which purpose of mine, the wicked enterprises of many of mine adversaries have oft withdrawn me), I have thought now at the last to answer your Highness's letters with this treatise (fearing lest the further delay thereof might be to my reproof and that further excusation should be of no value) that your Highness's noble young courage were steered to the love of Scripture and, by further exercise in the same, might be more ferventer and established; to which thing I pray God to send His grace and to help; for it is greatly necessary, seeing that in the person of so great a Prince, the which, being withdrawn from himself, is governed by God's grace, the salvation of many one consisteth: and, again, the perdition and damnation of many one if he, being permitted to him-self, is guided without grace.

[1] *marquis*, margrave.

For though it be said of all men's hearts 'that the king's heart is in the hand of God which can wend it where it pleaseth Him',[1] yet is it not for naught said of kings and princes: Whereby God will beat His fear in the superiors that so they may learn and be sure that they cannot once think ought in their mind without God do give it severally in their minds. The deeds of other men doth either hurt or profit only them or a few besides, but princes and superiors only be set in that room that they either profit or hinder so many more as their dominion doth reach further.

For the which cause doth Scripture call the godly and fearing-God, princes, angels of God, yea, gods, also, as in the seventh chap. [ver. 1] of Exo.: I have made thee a god over Pharaoh. And in the twenty second [ver. 28] chapter: Thou shalt not speak evil of the gods. And again: The wicked and ungodly princes, she calleth lions, dragons, and furious beasts, whom God also calleth one of his four plagues when he rehearseth them, namely, pestilence, dearth, war, and furious beasts.[2] Because then that the heart of man, being natural flesh and blood, doth presume everything lightly and coveteth thereby dominion, riches, and honour, he is steered out of reason by such occasion to a rash tranquillity and rest, so that he forgetteth God and careth nothing for his subjects, and using the bridle to his pleasure in sinning, he becometh a wodde[3] and furious beast.

It chanceth also that a prince, taking his pleasure only and using his affections by name, he is a lord: but in deed he is a beast, so that it was well said of Bias,* one of the seven sages of Greece: *Magistratus virum ostendit*, that is, authority or rule of a community declareth what a man is. For dominion doth utter a man what he is, seeing also that the common people dare not withstand for fear of punishment the commandments of their heads, though they were wicked and ungodly.

For this cause ought the superiors greatly to dread God, seeing they need to fear men so little and to know Him and His works perfectly and with great care and diligence to walk and exercise himself therein, as Paul doth exhort in the twelfth chapter [ver. 8] to the Romans, saying: Let him that ruleth be diligent.

Moreover there is nothing in all the Scripture that doth so greatly concern the superiority as this most holy Song of the Blessed Virgin and Mother of God, the which ought to be well learned and exercised of all them that will rule well and be good governors. For the Mother of God singeth here most pleasantly of the fear of God; what Lord our God be; and what His works be in high and low estates. Let others give ear to their paramours, singing some wanton worldly song, but unto this so-mannered Virgin becometh a prince and lord to give ear: the which singeth a spiritual, chaste, and wholesome Song.

[1] Prov. xxi. 1.   [2] Cf. Rev. vi. 8.   [3] *wodde*, wild.

Neither is it a custom reprovable that in all churches this Song is daily sung at evensong, and that with a sundry and honest tune (if the understanding thereof were also so earnestly declared). Now would God, the spirit of the same beautiful Mother of God were given me, which may pithfully and profitably declare her Song that your princely grace and all we may suck thereout a healthful understanding, a laudable life, and after this life to sing the everlasting *Magnificat* in the life to come. Amen.

THE SONG OF MARY CALLED 'MAGNIFICAT'

My soul magnifieth the Lord.

And my spirit rejoiceth in God my Saviour.

For he hath looked upon the low degree of his handmaiden;

Behold from henceforth shall all generations call me blessed.

For He that is mighty, hath done great things unto me; and Holy is His name.

And His mercy endureth throughout all generations upon them that fear Him.

He showeth strength with His arm; and scattereth them that be proud in the imagination of their heart.

He putteth down the mighty from the seat, and exalteth them of low degree.

He filleth the hungry with good things, and letteth the rich go empty.

He remembereth mercy, and helpeth up His servant Israel:

Even as He promised unto our fathers, Abraham, and to his seed forever.[1]

MY SOUL MAGNIFIETH THE LORD

That word brusteth[2] out of a vehement heat and overflowing joy wherewith her mind and conversation heave itself wholly in spirit inwardly. Wherefore she saith not: I do 'magnify the Lord', but 'my soul', as if she would say, 'My life and all my thoughts drive, compel, and overflow in the love and praise of God and exceeding gladness, so that I (even besides myself) am rather heaved than do heave to praise God'—even as it chanceth also unto them that be endued with godly sweetness and spirit, so that they feel more than they can utter and express with words.

For is not man's work to give thanks unto God with joy? It is rather a joyful mind and the only work of God; the which is not perceived by utterance, but by experience, as saith David in the thirty-third psalm [ver. 9]: Taste and see how good the Lord is. Happy is the man that trusteth in Him. He saith first 'taste' and then 'see', because He cannot be known without a man's own experience,

---

[1] Luke i. 46-55. [2] *brusteth*, bursteth.

whereunto, nevertheless, no man cometh without he do wholly and fully trust in God when he is into the depth and anguish. And for this cause doth he add continently, and saith: Happy is the man that trusteth in Him. For such one shall perceive the work of God in himself: and by this way he shall come to the perceivable sweetness, and thereby come to all understanding and knowledge.

COLOPHON: Imprinted at Southwark by J. Nicholson, 1538.

DESIDERIUS ERASMUS[1]

Erasmus's friendship with Justus Ludovicus Decius, an Alsatian, who had amassed a great fortune in Poland and settled in Cracow, becoming a liberal patron of the arts, led to the Dutch scholar's writing a treatise on the Pater Noster *or* Precatio Dominica in septem portiones distributa (1523). *It was written at Decius's request after his first meeting with Erasmus at Cracow in 1522. Soon after the latter returned to Basel, he completed the* Precatio, *referring to it in the dedicatory epistle to Decius as* 'opus recens ac modo natum et mox excusum' [a recent work but lately born and hurried through the press]. *The theme was chosen to accent the pressing need to spread the doctrines of Christianity among the pagans, and also the Turks, who were a continual threat to the Church.*

The Precatio *was well received in Cracow, and in the same year of its publication John Haller, a Polish printer, published the correspondence between Erasmus and Decius,* De conscribendis epistolis, *and dedicated it to Decius. Translations of the* Precatio *were soon made in German, French, Bohemian, Polish, Spanish; and a Dutch version was printed in 1593.*

Margaret Roper, daughter of Sir Thomas More, made the first English translation, A devout treatise upon the Pater Noster [1526?]. *She is the famous 'Meg' in the letters of her father and was among the first to urge the widespread education of women. Born in London in 1505, Margaret was the eldest child of More and his first wife Jane Colt. According to Thomas Stapleton, who knew the family, she resembled her father 'as well in stature, appearance, and voice as in mind and in general character'. With her sisters Elizabeth and Cicely, a brother John, and a foster-sister Margaret Gigs, she attended the 'school' in More's house in London where Fellows from Oxford and Cambridge, Nicholas Kratzer, William Gunnell, Richard Hyrd, and John Clement, served at various times as tutors. Each of More's children was proficient in Greek and Latin, and he encouraged them to write to him in Latin, rewarding them for their efforts.*

[1] For biographical sketch, see pp. 55–7.

Even after Margaret's marriage to William Roper, in 1521, she kept up her studies. Her husband, who wrote the first biography of Thomas More, was the son of a wealthy landowner in Canterbury and probably attended one of the universities before he began his law studies at Lincoln's Inn in 1518. Nicholas Harpsfield comments that Roper 'was a mervailous zealous Protestant' when he married Margaret, and More brought him around to Catholicism 'by prayer', for he could neither 'argue nor dispute with him'.

Margaret's interest in medicine may have been aroused by John Clement, a medical student at the University of Padua and the husband of Margaret Gigs. She and Margaret Roper took personal charge of the aged and sick poor for whom More rented a hospice, entrusting the management of it to the two young matrons.

During the year and a half that her father remained in the Tower before his execution, Margaret's letters and visits were his greatest comfort. She made faint efforts to induce him to take the Oath of Royal Supremacy which she had taken 'as far as it would stand with the law of God'. This last clause nullified it for her, but More knew he would not be permitted to take such an oath. William Roper has described how his wife ran to her father after he was sentenced to death in Westminster Hall; breaking through the crowds and the guards around him, she 'there openly in the sight of them all, embraced him and took him about the neck and kissed him'.

After More was beheaded on 6 July 1535, Margaret and her sisters with their maid Dorothy Colly claimed his body and buried it in the chapel of St Peter in Chains in London Tower. She was permitted to take his head from atop a pole on London Bridge, and the king allowed her to keep it with her father's letters 'for her solace'. Though she was not molested by the government, her husband and brother were both imprisoned for several years. In 1538 they all fled to Belgium, where Margaret remained until her death in 1544, devoting herself to the care of her five children. Mary, the youngest of her three daughters, married James Basset and was lady-in-waiting to Mary I. Like her mother, Mary Basset was proficient in Latin and Greek. She translated the Latin portion of Sir Thomas More's Treatise on the Passion *and a Latin version of Eusebius's* Ecclesiastical History.

Among the contemporary scholars who knew Margaret Roper and praised her were Reginald Pole, Juan Luis Vives, and Cuthbert Tunstall. Erasmus called her 'the flower of all the learned matrones in Inglond', and his Commentary on the Christmas Hymn of Prudentius *(1523) was written in honour of the birth of her first child, Thomas Roper. Henry VIII invited her and her two married sisters to hold a debate at court in 1524.*

The chief extant writings of Margaret Roper are her translation of Erasmus's Treatise upon the Pater Noster *[1526?] and her letters to her father. The simplicity and apt phrasing of her version of the* Treatise *resulted in part from collaborating with More on his treatise* The Four

Last Things. *He regarded her work as* 'in no way inferior' *to his.* *Richard Hyrd, a tutor for More's children, wrote the preface for the* Treatise, *urging the importance of the education of women.* *Margaret Roper's letters are written in clear and fluent prose, and, studied together with those of her father and his last works, which she smuggled out of the Tower, display her subtlety in drawing opinions from him on the involved religious issues of the times.*

Though no other writings of Margaret Roper are extant, Stapleton mentions that 'she wrote very eloquently prose and verse, both in Greek and Latin' *and emended several Greek texts.*

A Treatise upon the Pater Noster

TRANSLATED BY MARGARET MORE ROPER

A Devout Treatise Upon the Pater Noster made first in Latin by the most famous Doctor, Master Erasmus Rotterdamus, and turned into English by a young virtuous and well-learned gentlewoman of nineteen years of age.

Hereafter follow the seven petitions of the *Pater Noster*, translated out of Latin into English.

THE FIRST PETITION

Pater noster, qui est in caelis: sanctificetur nomen tuum[1] [Our Father, who art in Heaven, hallowed be Thy Name]. Hear, O Father in Heaven, the petition of Thy children which though they be as yet bodily in earth, notwithstanding, in mind ever they desire and long to come to the country celestial and their Father's house where they well know and understand that the treasure of everlasting wealth and felicity, that is to say, the inheritance of life immortal, is ordained for them.

We acknowledge Thine excellency, O Maker, Saviour, and Governor of all things contained in heaven and in earth. And, again, we acknowledge and confess our own vileness; and in no wise we durst be so bold to call Thee, Father, which are far unworthy to be Thy bondmen, nor take upon us the most honourable name of Thy children, which unneth[2] Thou vouchsafest Thine angels, except Thy mere goodness had by adoption received us into the great honour of this name.

The time was when we were servants to wickedness and sin by the miserable generation of Adam. We were also children of the

[1] Matt. vi. 9. [2] *unneth*, only.

Fiend by whose instinction and spirit we were driven and compelled to every kind of mischief and offence. But that Thou, of Thine infinite mercy by Thine only begotten Son Jesus made us free from the thraldom of sin and deliverest us from the devil, our father, and by violence riddest us from the inheritance of eternal fire, and, at the last, Thou vouchsafest to adopt us by faith and baptism as members in the most holy body of Thy Son, not only into the fellowship of Thy name but also of Thine inheritance. And because we should nothing mistrust in Thy love toward us, as a sure token thereof Thou sendest from heaven down into our hearts the most Holy Spirit of Thy Son which, all servantly fears shaken off, boldly crieth out in our hearts without ceasing, '*Abba, Pater!*'[1] Which in English is as much to say as, 'O Father, Father!'

And this Thy Son taught us, by whom, as Minister, Thou givest us all things, that when we were, as it were, born again by Thy Spirit and at the fontstone in baptism [had] renounced and forsaken our father, the devil, and had begun to have no father in earth, then we should acknowledge only our Father Celestial by whose marvellous power we were made somewhat of right naught; by whose goodness we were restored when we were lost; by whose wisdom incomparable, evermore we are governed and kept that we fall not again into destruction.

Thus, Thy Son gave us full trust to call upon Thee. He assigned us also a way of praying to Thee. Acknowledge, therefore, the desire and prayer of Thy Son; acknowledge the Spirit of Thy Son which prayeth to Thy Majesty for us by us. Do Thou not disdain to be called Father of those whom Thy Son, most likest Thy Image, vouchsafe to call His brethren. And yet we ought not hereupon to take liking in ourself, but to give glory to Thee and Thy Son for that great gentleness, since no man can here of himself ought deserve but that thing, whatsoever good it be, cometh of Thy only and free liberality.

Thou delightest rather in names loving and charitable than terrible and fearful; Thou desirest rather to be called a father than a lord or master; Thou wouldest we should rather love Thee as Thy children than fear Thee as Thy servants and bondmen. Thou first loved us, and of Thy goodness also it cometh, and Thy reward that we do love Thee again. Give ear, O Father of Spirits, to Thy children spiritual which in spirit pray to Thee. For Thy Son told us that in those that so prayed, Thy delight was, whom therefore, Thou sendest into the world that He should teach us all verity and truth.[2]

Hear, now, the desires of unity and concord, for it is not fitting nor agreeable that brethren whom Thy goodness hath put in equal honour should disagree or vary among themselves by ambitious

[1] Gal. iv. 6.　　　　　[2] Cf. John xvi. 13.

desire of worldly promotion, by contentious debate, hatred, or envy. All we hang of one Father: we all one thing pray for and desire: no man asketh ought for himself specially or apart, but as members of one body, quickened and relieved with one soul. We require and pray in common for that which indifferently shall be expedient and necessary for us all. And, indeed, we dare none other thing desire of Thee than what Thy Son commanded us, nor otherwise ask than as He appointed us; for in so asking, His goodness promised we should obtain whatsoever we prayed for in His name.[1]

And forasmuch as when Thy Son was here in earth, He nothing more fervently desired than that Thy most Holy Name should appear and shine not only in Judea but also through all the world; besides we also, both by His encouraging and example, this one thing above all desire, that the glory of Thy most Holy Name may replenish and fulfil both heaven and earth, so that no creature be which dreadeth not Thy high power and majesty; which do not worship and reverence also Thy wisdom and eternal and marvellous goodness: for Thy glory, as it is great, so neither having beginning nor ending but ever in itself flourishing, can neither increase nor decrease, but it skilleth yet mankind not a little that every man it know and magnify for to know and confess Thee only very God. And Jesus Christ whom Thou sendest into the world is as much to us as life eternal. Let the clear shining of Thy Name shadow and quench in us all worldly glory....

Therefore, good Lord, we pray Thee, let Thy goodness work in us and Thy clear light shine in us as in all things that Thou hast created doth shine Thy eternal and endless power; Thy wisdom unable to be expressed; and Thy wonderful goodness which most specially yet Thou vouchsafest to show to mankind.

Now then whithersoever we look, all things glorify Thy Name: the earthly spirits, both day and night, never lynne[2] praying their Lord and King; the wonderful, also, and heavenly engine that we behold; the disagreeing concord, moreover, of the elements; the flowing and ebbing of the sea; the bubblishing of rivers; the enduring courses of waters; so many divers kinds of things; so many kinds of trees and of herbs; so many of creatures: and to everything, the proper appointed and set nature, as in the adamant stone to draw iron; the herbs to cure and heal diseases and sickness: All these things, I say, what other thing do they show to us than the glory of Thy Name and that Thou art only very God, only immortal, only of all power and might, only wise, only good, only merciful, only just, only true, only marvellous, only to be loved and had in reverence.

Then, Father, we may well see that he doth wrong to Thy glorious Name whosoever takes upon himself to be called by any of

---

[1] John xvi. 23. [2] lynne, cease.

these names. For though there be in us any of these rehearsed virtues, yet all that cometh to us from Thy liberal goodness.

Grant now, therefore, Father, that Thy Name on every side be glorified; and that the light and glory of Thy Name may no less appear and shine in our manners and living than it shineth in Thy angels and in all things that Thou hast created and made: that, in likewise, as they which behold and look upon this world of Thy wonderful and marvellous workmanship do guess the excellency of the Maker thereof, so they that know Thee not, and stirred by our example, may both confess their own misery and wretchedness and marvel Thy liberal goodness and, by these means turned and converted, may together with us glorify the most Holy Name of Thee, of Thy Son, and of the Holy Ghost to whom indifferently all honour and glory is due forever. Amen.

COLOPHON: Thus endeth the exposition of the *Pater Noster*. Imprinted at London in Fleet Street in the house of Thomas Berthelet near to the Conduit at the sign of Lucrece.... [1526?]

ST THOMAS MORE[1]

In 1529, the same year Sir Thomas More was named Chancellor of England, he first published A dyaloge against Luther and Tyndale. *This work which is divided into four books, and with a preface contains approximately 175,000 words, touched off the first great religious controversy carried on in English. The* Dyaloge *was written at the request of Cuthbert Tunstall, Bishop of London, to refute the heresies in the Lutheran works that had slipped through the tight censorship on the London book trade and also to take issue with Tyndale's unauthorized English version of the New Testament.*

By presenting his arguments in the form of a dialogue, which as a medium for controversy had retained its popularity from medieval times, More could answer directly his friend's messenger who sought advice on certain matters of faith 'which some people were beginning to question'. The inquisitiveness of the messenger is used by More as an opportunity to clarify the Church's stand on doctrines such as celibacy of the clergy, justification by faith only, and Papal Supremacy.

Though the Dyaloge *is spiced throughout with 'merry wit', the issues are clean cut: More takes the side of the Church whose teaching on all doctrines, he professes, are supreme and final for the individual. The messenger poses his questions so as to advance the stand of the Reformers,*

[1] For biographical sketch, see pp. 64–6.

namely, the individual alone has the right to pass judgment on matters of faith. Of particular interest is the chapter on 'Why the New Testament of Tyndale's was burned.' Besides expressing his belief in the pressing need of an authorized English Bible, More presents in a forthright manner points of doctrine which the Reformers were soon formally to repudiate.

After William Tyndale published An answere vnto Sir Thomas Mores dialoge [1530], in which he offers a full explanation of the terminology used in his New Testament, More, having resigned as Chancellor, began the third round of the controversy, giving his entire energy to writing The cõfutacyon of Tyndales answere (1532). Because of its great bulk, some 500,000 words, it was not so widely read as Tyndale's Answere. Issues that More brushed over in the Dyaloge, he delves into thoroughly; and the work remains unparalleled in Catholic apologetic literature. More's other controversial works are discussed in Part II of this volume.

In the spring of 1534, when More was imprisoned in the Tower for refusing to take the Oath of Royal Supremacy, he continued to write, but the works that he produced during the fifteen months prior to his death concerned only those things that loom large at the time of great personal distress. A dyalogue of comfort agaynste tribulacyon, written particularly for the solace of his own family while he was separated from them, is a series of conversations, some quite 'merrie', between Anthony, an old Hungarian nobleman, and his nephew Vincent, both of whom fear the Turkish domination of Europe—a situation which More parallels with those suffering under the tyranny of Henry VIII. The work has been called 'the nearest approach to an autobiography that More ever wrote'. As a theme, he chose the ninetieth Psalm, summing it up, 'Whensoever a man falleth into tribulation for the maintenance of justice or defense of God's cause...if he stand and persevere still in his confession of his faith, all his whole pain shall turn into glory.' The chapter 'On Imprisonment and Comfort there Against' has a psychological as well as a deeply spiritual interest.

As the time of More's execution grew imminent, he turned for strength and courage to the Passion of Christ and the Eucharist. The treatise upon the Passion of Christe, which was begun in English and continued in Latin, was not finished because his writing materials were taken from him. His granddaughter Mary Basset translated the Latin portion for its first printing in William Rastell's edition of More's English Works (1557).

In the treatise To receaue the Blessed Body of Our Lorde, More urges the reception of the Eucharist, 'this margarite, this pure perle, the blessed bodi of our saviour, himself'. Of all More's writings, the Tower works are the most subjective and possess the devout simplicity found in the writings of à Kempis, Hilton, Fisher, Methley, and the author of The Cloud of Unknowing.

Dialogue against Luther and Tyndale

A Dialogue of Sir Thomas More, Knight, one of the Council of our sovereign lord, the King, and Chancellor of His Duchy of Lancaster: wherein be treated divers matters, as of veneration and worship of images and relics, praying to saints, and going on pilgrimage: with many other things touching the pestilent sect of Luther and Tyndale, by the one begun in Saxony and by the other laboured to be brought into England. Newly overseen by the said Sir Thomas More, Chancellor of England. (1530.)

THE INTRODUCTION[1]

It is an old said saw that one business begetteth and bringeth forth another. Which proverb, as it happeth, I find very true by myself, which have been fain by occasion, first of one business, after to take the second, and upon the second now to *One business* take the third. For whereas a right worshipful friend of *begetteth* mine sent once unto me a secret sure friend of his with *another* certain credence to be declared unto me touching many such matters, as being indeed very certain and out of doubt, [which] be nevertheless of late by lewd people put in question, the specialities whereof do so ferforth[2] in the first chapter of this book appear that we shall here need no rehearsal thereof. I thought it, first, enough to tell the messenger my mind by mouth, accounting that after our communication ended I should never need further business therein.

But after that the messenger was departed, and I felt my stomach well eased in that I reckoned all my labour done, bethinking myself a little while thereon, my business that I took for finished, I found very far from that point and little more than begun. For when I considered what the matters were, and how many great things had been treated between the messenger and me, and in what manner fashion, albeit I mistrusted not his good will and very well trusted his wit (his learning well serving him to the perceiving and reporting of our communication), yet finding our treaty so diverse and so long, and sometimes suchwise intricate that myself could not without labour call it orderly to mind, methought I had not well done, without writing, to trust his only memory, namely, since some parts of the matter be such of themselves as rather need to be attentively read and advised than lightly heard and passed over....

And therefore after that such [i.e. theologians] had read it and

---

[1] Book I.   [2] *ferforth*, in a certain degree.

severally said their advice, I found, as it often happeth, that something which one wise and well learned man would have out, twain of like wisdom and learning specially would have in, neither side lacking good and probable reasons for their part. Wherefore, since it became not me to be judge over the judgment of them whom I took and chose for my judges, being such of themself as hard it were for any man to say which of them before the other he could in erudition, wit, or prudence anything prefer, I could no further go

Lean to the more part but lean to the more part; which I so ferforth have followed, that likewise as I divers things put out or changed by their good advice and counsel, so let I nothing stand in this book but such as twain advised me specially to let stand, against any one that any doubt moved me to the contrary.

And thus much have I thought necessary for my declaration and excuse to advertise you all that shall happen to read this rude, simple work, praying you of patience and pardon, whom God of His especial grace grant as much profit in the reading as my poor heart hath meant you and intended in the making.

WHY TYNDALE'S NEW TESTAMENT WAS BURNED[1]

The author showeth why the New Testament of Tyndale's translation was burned. And showeth for a sample, certain words evil and of evil purpose changed.

¶ But now, I pray you, let me know your mind concerning the burning of the *New Testament in English* which Tyndale lately translated, and, as men say, right well; which maketh men much marvel of the burning.

¶ It is, quod I, to me great marvel that any good Christian man, having any drop of wit in his head, would anything marvel or complain of the burning of that book if he know the matter. Which who so calleth the New Testament calleth it by a wrong name, except they will call it 'Tyndale's Testament' or 'Luther's Testament'. For so had Tyndale, after Luther's counsel, corrupted and changed it from the good and wholesome doctrine of Christ to the devilish heresies of their own, that it was clean a contrary thing.

¶ That were marvel, quod your friend, that it should be so clean contrary. For to some that read it, it seemed very like. ¶ It is, quod I, nevertheless contrary; and yet the more perilous. For like as to a true silver groat as a false copper groat is, it is nevertheless contrary though it be quicksilvered all over; but so much the more false in how much it is counterfeited the more like to the truth; so was the translation so much the more contrary, in how much it was craftily

[1] Book III, Chapter VIII.

devised like; and so much the more perilous, in how much it was to folk unlearned more hard to be discerned.

❡ Why, quod your friend, what faults were there in it? ❡ To tell you all that, quod I, were in a manner to rehearse you all the whole book wherein there were founden and noted wrong and falsely translated above a thousand texts by tale. ❡ I would, quod he, fain hear some one.

❡ He that should, quod I, study for that, should study where to find water in the sea. But I will show you for example two or three such, as every one of the three is more than thrice three in one.

❡ That were, quod he, very strange except ye mean more in weight, for one can be but one in number. ❡ Surely, quod I, as weighty be they as any lightly can be. But I mean that every one of them is more than thrice three in number. ❡ That were, quod he, somewhat like a riddle.

❡ This riddle, quod I, will soon be read. For he hath mistranslated three words of great weight, and every one of them is, as I suppose, more than thrice three times repeated and rehearsed in the book.

❡ Ah, that may well be, quod he, but that was not well done. But, I pray you, what words be they? ❡ The one is, quod I, this word *priests*. The other, the *church*. The third, *charity*. For priests, wheresoever he speaketh of the priests of Christ's Church, he never calleth them *priests* but always *seniors*. The *church* he calleth always the *congregation*, and *charity* he calleth *love*. Now do these names in our English tongue neither express the things that be meant by them, and also there appeareth (the circumstances well considered) that he had a mischievous mind in the change.

For first, as for priests and priesthood, though that of old they used commonly to choose well elderly men to be priests, and therefore in the Greek tongue priests were called *presbiteri*, as we might say, elder men, yet neither were all priests chosen old, as appeareth by Saint Paul writing to Timotheus: *Nemo juventutem tuam contemnat*.[1] Let no man contemn thy youth, nor every elder man is not a priest. And in our English tongue this word *senior* signifieth nothing at all, but is a French word used in English more than half in mockage, when one will call another 'my lord' in scorn. And if he mean to take the Latin word *senior*, that word in the Latin tongue never signified a priest, but only an elder man. By which name of elder men if he would call the priests Englishly, then should he rather signify their age than their office. And yet the name doth in English plainly signify the aldermen of the cities and nothing the priests of the church. And thus may we perceive that rather than he would call a priest by

[1] I Tim. iv. 12.

the name of a priest, he would seek a new word—he neither wist nor cared what.

Now where he calleth the *church* always the *congregation*, what reason had he therein? For every man well seeth that though the church be indeed a congregation, yet is not every congregation the church but a congregation of Christian people, which congregation of Christian people hath been in England always called and known by the name of the *church*: which name what good cause or colour could he find to turn into the name of *congregation*, which word is common to a company of Christian men or a company of Turks?

Like wisdom was there in the change of this word *charity* into *love*. For though *charity* be always *love*, yet is not, ye wot well, *love* always *charity*.

¶ The more pity, by my faith, quod your friend, that ever love was sin. And yet it would not be so much so taken if the world were no more suspicious than they say that good Saint Francis was, which, when he saw a young man kiss a girl once in way of good company, kneeled down and held up his hands unto heaven, highly thanking God that *charity* was not yet gone out of this wretched world.

¶ He had, quod I, a good mind and did like a good man that deemed all thing to the best. ¶ So say I, too, quod he, but how far be folk fallen from the good mind now? Men nowadays waxen so full of mistrust, that some man would, in faith, ween his wife were nought if he should but find her in bed with a poor friar.

¶ Forsooth, ye be a wanton, quod I. But yet in earnest, how like you the change of these words? ¶ Surely, quod he, very nought. And that it was not well nor wisely done, there will, I trow, no good wise man deny. But yet whether Hychens [Tyndale] had in the translation thereof any malicious purpose or not therein, will I (till I see further) play Saint Francis's part, and judge the man no worse than the matter requireth.

¶ First, quod I, would ye that the book should go forth and be read still in that fashion?

¶ Nay, in good faith, quod he, that would I not if he use it so very often.

¶ With that word, quod I, ye hit the nail on the head. For surely, if he changed the common known word into the better, I would well allow it. If he changed it into as good, I would suffer it. If somewhat into worse, so he did it seldom, I would wink at it. But now when he changeth the known usual names of so great things into so far the worse, and that not repeateth seldom, but so often and so continually inculketh[1] that almost in the whole book his lewd change he never changeth. In this manner could no man deem other, but that the man meant mischievously—scant[2] such a good silly soul as

---

[1] *inculketh*, reiterates.   [2] *scant*, except.

would ween all were well when he found his wife where ye said right
now. If he called *charity* sometimes by the bare name of *love*, I would
not stick thereat. But now whereas *charity* signifieth in
Englishmen's ears not every common *love*, but a good,   Charity
virtuous and well-ordered *love*, he that will studiously flee from that
name of good *love*, and always speak of 'love', and always leave
out 'good', I would surely say that he meaneth nought.

¶ In good faith, quod he, so is it not unlikely.

¶ Then, quod I, when ye see more, ye shall say it is much more
than likely. For now it is to be considered that at the time of this
translation, Hychens was with Luther in Wittenberg, and set certain
glosses in the margin, framed for the setting forth of the ungracious
sect.

¶ By Saint John, quod your friend, if that be true that Hychens
were at that time with Luther, it is a plain token that he wrought
somewhat after his counsel, and was willing to help his matters forward here. But whether Luther's matters be so mad as they be made
for, that shall we see hereafter.

¶ Very true, quod I, but as touching the confederacy between
Luther and him, is a thing well known and plainly confessed by such
as have been taken and convicted here of heresy, coming from thence,
and some of them sent hither to sow that seed about here, and to
send word thither from time to time how it sprang.

But now the cause why he changed the name of *charity*, and of
the *church*, and of *priesthood*, is no very great difficulty to perceive.
For since Luther and his fellows among other their damn-
able heresies have one, [namely,] that all our salvation   Luther's
standeth in faith alone, and toward our salvation nothing   heresies
force of good works, therefore it seemeth that he laboureth of purpose to minish the reverent mind that men bear to *charity*, and
therefore he changeth the name of holy virtuous affection into the
bare name of *love*, common to the virtuous love that man beareth to
God and to the lewd love that is between Flecke and his make.[1]
And for because that Luther utterly denieth the very Catholic
Church in earth and saith that the Church of Christ is but an unknown congregation of some folk—here two and there three, no
man wot where—having the right faith which he calleth only his
own new forged faith, therefore Hychens in the New Testament
cannot abide the name of the *church*; but turneth it into the name
of *congregation*, willing that it should seem to Englishmen, either that
Christ in the gospel had never spoken of the Church, or else that the
Church were but such a congregation as they might have occasion to
say, that a congregation of such some heretics were the church that
God spake of.

[1] *Flecke and his make*, a dog and his mate.

Now as touching the cause why he changed the name of *priest* into *senior*: ye must understand that Luther and his adherents hold this heresy, that all Holy Orders is nothing. And that a priest is nothing else but a man chosen among the people to preach; and that by that choice to that office, he is priest by and by without any more ado, and no priest again whensoever the people choose another in his place; and that a priest's office is nothing but to preach. For as for saying Mass and hearing of confession and absolution thereupon to be given, all this, he saith that every man, woman, and child may do as well as any priest.

Now doth Hychens, therefore, to set forth this opinion withal after his master's heresy, put away the name of *priest* in his translation, as though priesthood were nothing. Wheresoever the Scripture speaketh of the priests that were among the Jews, there doth he in his translation call them still by the name of priests. But wheresoever the Scripture speaketh of the priests of Christ's Church, there doth he put away the name of *priest* in his translation, because he would make it seem that the Scripture did never speak of any priests different from laymen among Christian people. And he saith plainly in his book of *Obedience* [*of a Christian Man*] that priesthood and all Holy Orders among Christian people be but feigned inventions, and that priests be nothing but officers chosen to preach, and that all the consecration whereby they be consecrate is nothing worth. And for this cause in all his translation wheresoever he speaketh
A priest of them, the name of *priest* which to us in our own tongue hath always signified an anointed person and with Holy Orders consecrated unto God, he hath changed into the name of *senior*, no word of our language, but either used half in mockage when we speak French in sport, '*Dieu vous garde, senior*', or at the furthest, nothing betokening but *elder*. So that it is easy to see what he meant in the turning of these names.

❡ In good faith, quod your friend, it seemeth verily that he meant not well.

❡ Surely, quod I, ye would well say so if ye saw all the places which I shall cause you to see when ye will; and ye shall soon judge them yourself. For it were too long to rehearse them all now. Nor these have I not rehearsed you as for the chief, but for that they came first to mind. For else I might shortly rehearse you many things more as far out of tune as these be.

For he changeth commonly the name *grace* into this word *favour*; whereas every favour is not grace in English for in some favour is there little grace. *Confession* he translateth into *knowledge*. *Penance* into *repentance*. *A contrite heart* he changeth into *a troubled heart*. And many more things like; and many texts untruly translated for the maintenance of heresy, as I shall show you some when we look in the book. Which things we shall not now reason upon, for they be not worthy to be brought in question. But I tell you this much only, for this cause, that ye may perceive that he hath thus used himself in his translation to the intent that he would set forth Luther's heresies and his own thereby. For, first, he would make the people believe that we should believe nothing but plain Scripture, in which point he teacheth a plain pestilent heresy. And then would he with his false translation make the people ween further that such articles of our faith as he laboureth to destroy and which be well proved by Holy Scripture, were in Holy Scripture nothing spoken of, but that the preachers have all this fifteen hundred years misreported the gospel and Englished the Scripture wrong to lead the people purposely out of the right way.

THE SCRIPTURE IN ENGLISH[1]

The messenger rehearseth some causes which he hath heard laid by some of the clergy wherefore the scripture should not be suffered in English. And the author sheweth his mind that it were convenient to have the Bible in English. And therewith endeth the Third Book.

¶ Sir, quod your friend, yet for all this can I see no cause why the clergy should keep the Bible out of laymen's hands that can no more but their mother tongue.

¶ I had wente, quod I, that I had proved you plainly that they keep it not from them. For I have shewed you that they keep none from them but such translation as be either not yet approved for good or such as be already reproved for nought, as Wyclif's was, and Tyndale's. For as for other old ones, that were before Wyclif's days, remain lawful and be in some folk's hands had and read.

> What manner of English Bibles are kept from men

¶ Ye say well, quod he. But yet, as women say somewhat, it was always that the cat winked when her eye was out. Surely, so is it not for nought that the English Bible is in so few men's hands when so many would so fain have it....

¶ And therefore, as I say, forsooth, I can in no wise agree with you that it were meet for men unlearned to be busy with the chamming[2] of Holy Scripture, but to have it chammed unto them. For that is the preacher's part, and theirs that after long study are admitted to read and expound it. And to this intent weigh all the words, as far as I perceive, of all holy doctors that anything have written in this matter. But never meant they, as I suppose, the forbidding of the Bible to be read in any vulgar tongue. Nor I never yet heard any reason laid why it were not convenient to have the

[1] Book III, Chapter XVI.   [2] *chamming*, breaking into bits.

Bible translated into the English tongue; but all those reasons, seemed they never so gay and glorious at the first sight, yet when

There can be
no reason
why the
Bible should
not be trans-
lated into
English
they were well examined they might in effect, for aught that I can see, as well be laid against the holy writers that wrote the Scripture in the Hebrew tongue, and against the blessed Evangelists that wrote the Scripture in Greek, and against all those, in like wise, that trans- lated it out of every of those tongues into Latin as to their charge that would well and faithfully translate it

out of Latin into our English tongue. For as for that our tongue is called barbarous, is but a fantasy; for so is, as every learned man knoweth, every strange language to other. And if they would call it barren of words, there is no doubt but it is plenteous enough to express our minds in anything whereof one man hath used to speak with another.

Now as touching the difficulty which a translator findeth in ex- pressing well and lively the sentence of his author (which is hard always to do so, surely, but that he shall sometime minish either of the sentence or of the grace that it beareth in the former tongue), that point hath lain in their light that have translated the Scripture already, either out of Greek into Latin or out of Hebrew into any of them both, as by many translations which we read already, to them that be learned, appeareth.

Now as touching the harm that may grow by such blind bayardes[1] as will when they read the Bible in English be more busy than will become them, they that touch that point harp upon the right string and touch truly the great harm that were likely to grow to some folk, howbeit, not by the occasion yet of the English translation, but by the occasion of their own lewdness and folly, which yet were not in my mind a sufficient cause to exclude the translation and to put other folk from the benefit thereof, but rather to make provision against such abuse and let a good thing go forth....

Wherefore there is, as methinketh, no remedy but if any good thing shall go forward, somewhat must needs be adventured. And some folk will not fail to be nought. Against which things, provision must be made that as much good may grow and as little harm come as can be devised; and not to keep the whole commodity from any whole people because of harm that by their own folly and fault may come to some part—as though a lewd surgeon would cut off the leg by the knee to keep the toe from the gout; or cut off a man's head by the shoulders to keep him from the toothache.

There is no treatise of Scripture so hard but that a good virtuous man, or woman either, shall somewhat find therein that shall delight and increase their devotion. Besides this, that every preaching shall

[1] *bayardes*, old horses.

be the more pleasant and fruitful unto them when they have in their mind the place of Scripture that they shall there hear expounded.

For though it be, as it is indeed, great wisdom for a preacher to use discretion in his preaching and to have a respect unto the qualities and capacities of his audience, yet letteth that nothing but that the whole audience may without harm have read and have ready the Scripture A preacher in his preaching must use discretion

in mind that he shall in his preaching declare and expound. For no doubt is there but that God and His Holy Spirit hath so prudently tempered their speech through the whole corps of Scripture that every man may take good thereby and no man harm but he that will in the study thereof lean proudly to the folly of his own wit.

For albeit that Christ did speak to the people in parables and expounded them secretly to his especial disciples and sometimes forbare to tell some things to them also, because they were not as yet able to bear them: and the apostles in likewise did sometime spare to speak to some people the things that they did not let plainly to speak to some others, yet letteth all this nothing the translation of the Scripture into our own tongue no more than in the Latin. Nor it is no cause to keep the corps of Scripture out of the hands of any Christian people, so many years fastly confirmed in faith, because Christ and His apostles used such provision in their utterance of so strange and unheard mysteries, either unto Jews, Paynims, or newly Christened folk, except we would say that all the expositions which Christ made Himself upon His own parables unto His secret servants and disciples withdrawn from the people, should now, at this day, be kept in likewise from the commons,[1] and no man suffered to read or hear them but those that in His Church represent the state and office of His apostles, which there will, I wote well, no wise man say, considering that those things which were then commonly most kept from the people be now most necessary for the people to know.

As it well appeareth by all such things, in effect, as Our Saviour at the time taught His apostles apart. Whereof I would not for my mind withhold the profit that one good, devout, unlearned layman might take by the reading, not for the harm that a hundred heretics would fall in by their own wilful abusion, no more than Our Saviour letted for the weal of such as would be with His grace of his little chosen flock to come into this world and be *lapis offensionis et petra scandali*,[2] the stone of stumbling and the stone of falling, and ruin to all the wilful wretches in the world beside.

Finally, methinketh, that the constitution provincial of which we spake right now, hath determined this question already. For when the clergy therein agreed that the English Bibles should remain which were translated afore Wyclif's days, they consequently did agree

<hr>

[1] *commons*, people.   [2] Isa. viii. 14.

that to have the Bible in English was none hurt. And in that they forbade any new translation to be read till it were approved by the bishops, it appeareth well thereby that their intent was that the bishop should approve it if he found it faultless and also of reason amend it where it was faulty but if the man were an heretic that made it or the faults such and so many as it were more easy to make it all new than mend it, as it happed for both points in the translation of Tyndale.

Now if it so be that it would haply be thought not a thing meetly to be adventured to set all on a flush at once, and dash rashly out the Holy Scripture in every lewd fellow's teeth, yet, thinketh me, there might such a moderation be taken therein as neither good virtuous lay folk should lack it nor rude and rash brains abuse it. For it might be with diligence well and truly translated by some good Catholic and well learned man, or by divers, dividing the labour among them, and after, conferring their several parts together each with other. And after that might the work be allowed and approved by the ordinaries, and by their authorities so put into print, as all the copies should come whole unto the bishop's hand. Which he may after his discretion and wisdom deliver to such as he perceiveth honest, sad, and

Good counsel

virtuous, with a good monition and fatherly counsel to use it reverently with humble heart and lowly mind, rather seeking therein occasion of devotion than of despition. And providing, as much as may be, that the book be after the decease of the party brought again and reverently restored unto the ordinary. So that as near as may be devised, no man have it but of the ordinary's hand, and by him thought and reputed for such as shall be likely to use it to God's honour and the merit of his own soul. Among whom, if any be proved after to have abused it, then the use thereof to be forboden him, either forever, or till he be waxen wiser.

¶ By Our Lady, quod your friend, this way misliketh not me. But who should set the price of the book?

¶ Forsooth, quod I, that reckon I a thing of little force. For neither were it a great matter for any man, in manner, to give a groat or twain above the mean price for a book of so great profit, nor for the bishop to give them all free, wherein he might serve his diocese with the cost of ten pounds, I think, or twenty marks. Which sum, I dare say, there is no bishop but he would be glad to bestow about a thing that might do his whole diocese so especial a pleasure with such a spiritual profit.

¶ By my troth, quod he, yet wene I that the people would grudge to have it on this wise delivered them at the bishop's hand, and had liefer pay for it to the printer than have it of the bishop free.

¶ It might so happen with some, quod I. But yet in mine opinion there were in that manner more wilfulness than wisdom or any good

mind in such as would not be content so to receive them. And therefore I would think, in good faith, that it would so fortune in few.
But afore God, the more doubt would be lest they would grudge and
hold themself sore grieved that would require it and were haply
denied it: which I suppose would not often happen unto any honest
householder to be by his discretion reverently read in
his house. But though it were not taken to every lewd   A 'pot-
lad in his own hands to read a little rudely when he list,   parliament'
and then cast the book at his heels, or among other such as himself
to keep a *quodlibet*[1] and a 'pot-parliament' upon, I trow there will
no wise man find a fault therein.

Ye spake right now of the Jews among whom the whole people
have, ye say, the Scripture in their hands. And ye thought it no
reason that we should reckon Christian men less worthy thereto
than them. Wherein I am, as ye see, of your opinion. But yet would
God, we had the like reverence to the Scripture of God that they
have! For I assure you, I have heard very worshipful   How
folk say, which have been in their houses, that a man   reverently
could not hire a Jew to sit down upon his Bible of the   the Jew doth
Old Testament, but he taketh it with great reverence   use the
in hand when he will read, and reverently layeth it up   Scripture
again when he hath done. Whereas we, God forgive us, take a little
regard to sit down on our Bible—with the Old Testament and
the New, too. Which homely handling, as it proceedeth of little
reverence, so doth it more and more engender in the mind a negligence
and contempt of God's Holy Words.

COLOPHON: William Rastell.... 1530.

Dialogue of Comfort against Tribulation

A Dialogue of Comfort against Tribulation made in the year of
Our Lord, 1534, by Sir Thomas More, Knight, while he was
prisoner in the Tower of London: which he entitled thus as
followeth: *A Dialogue of Comfort against Tribulation made by
an Hungarian in Latin, and translated out of Latin into French
and out of French into English.*

OF IMPRISONMENT AND COMFORT THERE AGAINST[2]

Anthony. That shall I, cousin, with good will [i.e. discuss imprisonment and its effects on the prisoner]. And first, if we could
consider what thing imprisonment is of his own nature, we should

[1] *quodlibet*, inquiry.　　　　[2] Book III, Chapter XIX.

not, methinketh, have so great horror thereof. For of itself it is, parde, but a restraint of liberty which letteth a man from going whither he would.

Vincent. Yes, by Saint Mary, uncle, methinketh, it is much more sorrow than so. For besides the let and restraint of liberty, it hath many more displeasures and very sore griefs knit and adjoined thereto.

Anthony. That is, cousin, very true indeed. And those pains, among many sorer than those, thought I not after to forget. Howbeit, I purpose now to consider first, imprisonment, but as imprisonment only, without any other incommodity besides. For a man may be, parde, imprisoned, and yet not set in the stocks nor collared fast by the neck: and a man may be let walk at large where he will, and yet a pair of fetters fast riveted on his legs. For in this country [Hungary], ye wot well, and in Seville and Portugal, too, so go there all the slaves.*

Howbeit, because that for such things men's hearts hath such horror thereof, albeit that I am not so mad as to go about to prove that bodily pain were no pain, yet since that because of these manner of pains we so especially abhor the state and condition of prisoners, we should, methinketh, well perceive that a great part of our horror groweth of our own fantasy, if we would call to mind and consider the state and condition of many other folk in whose state and condition we would wish ourself to stand, taking them for no prisoners at all that stand, yet for all that, in much part of the selfsame points that we abhor imprisonment for. Let us therefore consider these things in order.

Horror

And first, as I thought to begin, because those other kinds of griefs that come with imprisonment are but accidents thereunto—and yet neither such kinds of accidents as either be proper thereunto but that they may almost all fall unto a man without it, nor are not such accidents thereunto as are unseparable therefrom but that imprisonment may fall to a man and none of all them therewith—we will, I say, therefore begin with considering what manner pain or incommodity we should reckon imprisonment to be of himself and of his own nature alone. And then in the course of our communication you shall, as you list, increase and aggrieve the cause of your horror with the terror of those painful accidents.

Imprisonment

Vincent. I am sorry that I did interrupt your tale. For you were about, I see well, to take an orderly way therein. And as yourself have devised, so I beseech you proceed. For though I reckon imprisonment much the sorer thing by sore and hard handling therein, yet reckon I not the imprisonment of itself any less than a thing very tedious, all were it used in the most favourable manner that it possibly might. For, uncle, if it were a great prince that were taken prisoner upon the field and in the hand of a Christian king, which use in such case (for the consideration of their former estate and mutable chance of the war) to show much humanity to them and in very favourable wise entreat them (for these infidel emperors handle oftentimes the princes that *A prince in prison* they take more villainously than they do the poorest men, as the great Tamberlane kept the great Turk, when he had taken him, to tread on his back always while he lept on horseback) but, as I began to say, by the sample of a prince taken prisoner were the imprisonment never so favourable, yet were it in my mind no little grief in itself for a man to be penned up though not in a narrow chamber, but although his walk were right large and right fair gardens, too, therein, it could not but grieve his heart to be restrained by another man within certain limits and bounds and lose the liberty to be where him list.

Anthony. This is, cousin, well considered of you. For in this you perceive well that imprisonment is of himself and his own very nature alone nothing else but the retaining of a man's person within the circuit of a certain space, narrower or larger as shall be limited to him, restraining his liberty from the further going into any other place....

Anthony. In good faith, cousin, methinketh you say very true. But then one thing must I yet desire you, cousin, to tell me a little farther. If there were another laid in prison for a fray, and through the jailer's displeasure were bolted and fettered and laid in a low dungeon in the stocks where he might hap to lie, peradventure, for a while, and abide in the mean season some pain, but no danger of death at all, but that out again he should come well enough, which of these two prisoners stood in worse case: he that hath all this favour or he that is thus hardly handled? *Of two sorts of prisoners which is in worst case*

Vincent. By Our Lady, uncle, I ween that most part of men, if they should needs choose, had liefer be such prisoners in every point as he that so sorely lieth in the stocks than in every point such as he that at such liberty walketh about the park.

Anthony. Consider then, cousin, whether this thing seem any sophistry to you that I shall show you now. For it shall be such as seemeth in good faith substantial true to me. And if it so happen that you think otherwise, I will be very glad to perceive which of us both is beguiled.

For it seemeth to me, cousin, first, that every man coming into this world here upon earth, as he is created by God so cometh he hither by the providence of God. Is this any sophistry first, or not?

Vincent. Nay, verily, this is very substantial truth.

Anthony. Now take I this also for very truth in my mind, that

there cometh no man nor woman hither into the earth but that ere
ever they come quick into the world out of the mother's womb,
God condemneth them unto death by His own sentence
and judgment for the original sin that they bring with
them, contracted in the corrupted stock of our forefather
Adam. Is this, think you, cousin, verily thus, or not?

*Every man
condemned
to death by
God*

Vincent. This is, uncle, very true, indeed.

*None can
escape death*

Anthony. Then seemeth this true farther unto me, that
God hath put every man here upon the earth under so
sure and under so safe keeping, that of all the whole people living
in this wide world there is neither man, woman, nor child, would
they never so far wander about and seek it, that possibly can find
any way whereby they may escape from death. Is this, cousin, a fond
imagined fantasy, or is it very truth indeed?

Vincent. Nay, this is none imagination, uncle, but a thing so
clearly proved true that no man is so mad to say, nay.

Anthony. Then need I no more, cousin.... And is not then, cousin,
by your own granting before, every man a very prisoner when he
is put in a place to be kept, to be brought forth when he would not,
and himself wot not whither?

Vincent. Yes, in good faith, uncle, I cannot but well perceive this
to be so.

Anthony. This were, you wot well, true, although a man should
be but taken by the arm and in fair manner led out of this world
unto his judgment. But now while we well know that there is no
king so great but that all the while he walketh here, walk he never
so loose, ride he never so strong an army for his defence, yet himself
is very sure, though he seek in the mean season some other pastime
to put it out of his mind—yet is he very sure, I say, that escape can
he not; and very well he knoweth that he hath already sentence given
upon him to die, and that verily die he shall, and that himself though
he hope upon long respite of his execution, yet can he not tell how
soon. And, therefore, but if he be a fool, he can never be without
fear that either on the morrow or on the selfsame day the grisly,
cruel hangman Death, which from his first coming in hath ever
hoved aloof and looked toward him and ever lain in wait on him,
shall amidmong[1] all his royalty and all his main strength neither
kneel before him nor make him any reverence nor with any good
manner desire him to come forth, but rigorously and fiercely grip
him by the very breast and make all his bones rattle and so by long
and divers sore torments strike him stark dead in this prison and then
cause his body to be cast into the ground in a foul pit within some
corner of the same there to rot and be eaten with the wretched worms
of the earth, sending yet his soul out farther unto a more fearful

[1] *amidmong*, in the midst of.

judgment, whereof at his temporal death his success is uncertain and therefore though by God's grace not out of good hope, yet for all that in the meanwhile in very sore dread and fear and, peradventure, in peril inevitable of eternal fire, too.

Methinketh, therefore, cousin, that, as I told you, this keeping of every man in this wretched world for execution of death is a very plain imprisonment indeed, and that, as I say, such that the greatest king is in this prison in much worse case in all his wealth than many a man is by the other imprisonment that is therein sore and hardly handled. For where some of those lie not there attainted nor condemned to death, the greatest man of this world and the most wealthy in this universal prison is laid in to be kept undoubtedly for death.

A prince in worse case than a prisoner

Vincent. But yet, uncle, in that case is the other prisoner, too, for he is as sure that he shall die, parde.

Anthony. This is very true, cousin, indeed, and well objected too. But then you must consider that he is not in danger of death by reason of that prison into which he is put, peradventure, but for a light fray, but his danger of death is by the other imprisonment by which he is prisoner in the great prison of this whole earth in which prison all the princes thereof be prisoners as well as he.

Treatise on the Blessed Body

A Treatise to receive the Blessed Body of Our Lord, sacramentally and virtually both, made in the year of Our Lord, 1534 by Sir Thomas More, Knight, while he was prisoner in the Tower of London, which he entitled thus as followeth: To receive the Blessed Body of Our Lord, sacramentally and virtually both.

They receive the Blessed Body of Our Lord both sacramentally and virtually, which in due manner and worthily receive the Blessed Sacrament. When I say, worthily, I mean not that any man is so good, or can be so good, that his goodness could make him, of very right and reason, worthy to receive into his vile earthly body that holy, blessed, glorious Flesh and Blood of Almighty God Himself with His celestial soul therein and with the majesty of His eternal Godhead, but that he may prepare himself, working with the grace of God, to stand in such a state as the incomparable goodness of God will, of His liberal bounty, vouchsafe to take and accept for worthy to receive His own inestimable precious Body into the body of so simple a servant.

Such is the wonderful bounty of Almighty God that He not only doth vouchsafe, but also doth delight, to be with men, if they prepare to receive Him with honest and clean souls, whereof He saith, *Deliciae meae esse cum filiis hominum*:[1] My delight and pleasures are to be with the sons of men.

And how can we doubt that God delighteth to be with the sons of men, when the Son of God, and very Almighty God Himself, liked not only to become the Son of Man, that is to wit, the son of Adam, the first man, but over that in His innocent Manhood to suffer His painful Passion for the redemption and restitution of man. . . .

In this proving and examination of ourself, which St Paul speaketh of [For I am not conscious to myself of anything, yet am I not hereby justified: but He that judgeth me, is the Lord],[2] one very special point must be to prove and examine ourself and see that we be in the right faith and belief concerning the holy Blessed Sacrament Itself. That is to wit, that we verily believe that It is, as indeed It is, under the form and likeness of bread, the very Blessed Body, Flesh, and Blood of Our holy Saviour Christ Himself, the very selfsame Body and the very selfsame Blood that died and was shed upon the Cross for our sin, and the third day gloriously did arise again to life and with the souls of holy saints fetched out of hell, ascended and stied[3] up wonderfully into heaven and there sitteth on the right hand of the Father and shall visibly descend in great glory to judge the quick and the dead and reward all men after their works.

We must, I say, see that we firmly believe that this Blessed Sacrament is not a bare sign or a figure or a token of that holy Body of Christ, but that It is, in perpetual remembrance of His bitter Passion that He suffered for us, the selfsame precious Body of Christ that suffered it [and] by His own almighty power and unspeakable goodness consecrated and given to us.

And this point of belief is in the receiving of this Blessed Sacrament of such necessity and such weight with them that have years and discretion that without it they receive It plainly to their damnation. And that point, believed very full and fastly, must needs be a great occasion to move any man in all other points to receive It well. For note well the words of St Paul therein, *Qui manducat de hoc pane et bibit de calice indigne, judicium sibi manducat et bibit, non dijudicans corpus domini*:[4] He that eateth of this bread and drinketh of this cup unworthily, eateth and drinketh judgment upon himself in that he discerneth not the body of our Lord.

Lo! Here this blessed Apostle well declareth that he which in anywise unworthily receiveth this most excellent Sacrament receiveth

---

[1] Prov. viii. 31.   [2] I Cor. iv. 4.
[3] *stied*, soared.   [4] I Cor. xi. 27.

It unto his own damnation, in that he well declareth by his evil demeanour towards It in his unworthy receiving of It, that he discerneth It not nor judgeth It nor taketh It for the very Body of Our Lord, as indeed It is....

But now having the full faith of this point fastly grounded in our heart, that the Thing which we receive is the very Blessed Body of Christ, I trust there shall not greatly need any great information farther to teach us or any great exhortation farther to stir and excite us with all humble manner and reverent behaviour to receive Him.

For if we will but consider, if there were a great worldly prince which for special favour that he bare us would come visit us in our own house, what a business we would then make, and what a work it would be for us to see that our house were trimmed up in every point to the best of our possible power, and everything so provided and ordered that he should by his honourable receiving perceive what affection we bear him and in what high estimation we have him, we should soon by the comparing of that worldly prince and this heavenly Prince together (between which twain is far less comparison than is between a man and a mouse) inform and teach ourself with how lowly mind, how tender, loving heart, how reverent, humble manner we should endeavour ourself to receive this glorious heavenly King, the King of all Kings, Almighty God Himself, that so lovingly doth vouchsafe to enter not only into our house (to which the noble man, [the] Centurio[n], acknowledged himself unworthy), but His precious Body into our vile wretched carcass and His Holy Spirit into our poor simple soul.

What diligence can here suffice us? What solicitude can we think here enough against the coming of this Almighty King, coming for so special [and] gracious favour, not to put us to cost, not to spend of ours, but to enrich us of His, and that after so manifold deadly displeasures done Him so unkindly by us against so many of His incomparable benefits before done unto us! How would we now labour and foresee that the house of our soul (which God were coming to rest in) should neither have any poisoned spider or cobweb of deadly sin hanging in the roof nor so much as a straw or a feather of any light lewd thought that we might spy in the floor, but we would sweep it away!

But forasmuch, good Christian reader, as we neither can attain this great point of faith nor any other virtue but by the special grace of God, of whose high goodness every good thing cometh (for as St James saith, *Omne datum optimum et omne donum perfectum desursum est, descendens a patre luminum*:[1] Every good gift and every perfect gift is from above, descending from the Father of Lights), let us, therefore, pray for His gracious help in the attaining of His faith and

[1] James i. 17.

for His help in the cleaning of our soul against His coming, that He may make us worthy to receive Him worthily. And ever let us of our own part fear our unworthiness, and on His part trust boldly upon His goodness if we forslow[1] not to work with Him for our own part. For if we willingly upon the trust and comfort of His goodness leave our own endeavour undone, then is our hope no hope, but a very foul presumption.

Then when we come unto His Holy Board, into the presence of His Blessed Body, let us consider His high glorious Majesty which His high goodness there hideth from us and the proper form of His Holy Flesh covereth under the form of bread, both to keep us from abashment, such as we could not, peradventure, abide if we (such as we yet be) should see and receive Him in His own form such as He is, and also for the increase of the merit of our faith in the obedient belief of that Thing at His commandment whereof our eyes and our reason seem to show us the contrary.

And yet forasmuch as although we believe It, yet is there in many of us that believe very faint and far from the point of such vigour and strength, as would God it had, let us say unto Him with the father that had the dumb son, *Credo, domine, adjuva incredulitatem meam*:[2] I believe, Lord, but help thou my lack of belief: and with His blessed apostles, *Domine, adauge nobis fidem*:[3] Lord, increase faith in us. Let us also with the poor Publican, in knowledge of our own unworthiness, say with all meekness of heart, *Deus, propitius esto mihi, peccatori*:[4] Lord God, be merciful to me, sinner that I am. And with the Centurio[n], *Domine, non sum dignus ut intres sub tectum meum*:[5] Lord, I am not worthy that thou shouldst come into my house.

And yet with all this remembrance of our own unworthiness and therefore the great reverence, fear, and dread for our own part, let us not forget on the other side to consider His inestimable goodness, which disdaineth not, for all our unworthiness, to come unto us and to be received of us.

But likewise as at the sight or receiving of this excellent Memorial of His death (for in the remembrance thereof doth He thus consecrate and give His own Blessed Flesh and Blood unto us), we must with tender compassion remember and call to mind the bitter pains of His most painful Passion. And yet therewithal rejoice and be glad in the consideration of His incomparable kindness which in His so suffering for us to our inestimable benefit, He showed and declared towards us. So must we be both sore afeared of our own unworthiness, and yet therewith be right glad and in great hope at the consideration of His unmeasurable goodness.

---

[1] *forslow*, neglect. [2] Mark ix. 23. [3] Luke xvii. 5.
[4] Luke xviii. 13. [5] Matt. viii. 8.

St Elizabeth at the visitation and salutation of Our Blessed Lady, having by revelation the sure inward knowledge that Our Lady was conceived with Our Lord[1]—albeit that she was herself such as else for the diversity between their ages she well might and would have thought it but convenient and meetly that her young cousin should come visit her, yet now because she was mother to Our Lord she was sore amarvelled of her visitation and thought herself far unworthy thereto and, therefore, said unto her, *Unde hoc, ut veniat mater Domini mei ad me?* [2] Whereof is this, that the Mother of Our Lord should come to me? But yet for all the abashment of her own unworthiness, she conceived thoroughly such a glad blessed comfort that her holy child St John the Baptist leapt in her womb for joy; whereof she said, *Ut facta est vox salutationis tuae in auribus meis, exultavit gaudio infans in utero meo:*[3] As soon as the voice of thy salutation was in mine ears, the infant in my womb leapt for joy.

Now like as St Elizabeth by the Spirit of God had those holy affections, both of reverent considering her own unworthiness in the visitation of the Mother of God, and yet for all that so great inward gladness therewith, let us at this great high visitation in which not the Mother of God, as came to St Elizabeth, but One incomparably more excelling the Mother of God than the Mother of God passed St Elizabeth, doth so vouchsafe to come and visit each of us with His most Blessed Presence, that He cometh not into our house but into ourself, let us, I say, call for the help of the same Holy Spirit that then inspired her and pray Him at this high and holy visitation so to inspire us, that we may both be abashed with the reverent dread of our own unworthiness and yet therewith conceive a joyful consolation and comfort in the consideration of God's inestimable goodness....

Now when we have received Our Lord and have Him in our body, let us not then let Him alone and get us forth about other things and look no more unto Him (for little good could be, that so would serve any guest), but let all our business be about Him. Let us by devout prayer talk *to* Him; by devout meditation talk *with* Him. Let us say with the Prophet, *Audiam quid loquatur in me Dominus:*[4] I will hear what Our Lord will speak within me.

For surely if we set aside all other things and attend unto Him, He will not fail with good inspirations to speak such things to us within us as shall serve to the great spiritual comfort and profit of our soul. And therefore let us with Martha provide that all our outward business may be pertaining to Him in making cheer to Him and to His company for His sake, that is to wit, to poor folk of which He taketh every one, not only for His disciple, but also as for Himself.

[1] Luke i. 24. [2] Luke i. 43.
[3] Luke i. 44. [4] Ps. lxxxiv. 9.

For Himself saith, *Quamdiu fecistis uni de his fratribus meis minimis, mihi fecistis:*[1] That that you have done to one of the least of these My brethren, you have done it to Myself.

And let us with Mary, also, sit in devout meditation and hearken well what Our Saviour, being now our Guest, will inwardly say unto us. Now have we a special time of prayer while He that hath made us; He that hath bought us; He whom we have offended; He that shall judge us; He that shall either damn us or save us is of His great goodness become our Guest and is personally present within us, and that for no other purpose but to be sued unto for pardon and so thereby to save us.

Let us not lose this time: therefore, suffer not this occasion to slip, which we can little tell whether ever we shall get it again or never. Let us endeavour ourself to keep Him still, and let us say with His two disciples that were going to the castle of Emmaus, *Mane nobiscum, Domine:*[2] Tarry with us, good Lord; and then shall we be sure that He will not go from us but if we unkindly put Him from us. . . .

With such alacrity, with such quickness of spirit, with such gladness, and such spiritual rejoicing as this man ['the good Publican Zaccheus'] received Our Lord into his house, Our Lord give us the grace to receive His Blessed Body and Blood, His Holy Soul, and His Almighty Godhead, both into our bodies and into our souls, that the fruit of our good works may bear witness unto our conscience; that we receive Him worthily and in such a full faith, and such a stable purpose of good living as we be bounden to do. And then shall God give a gracious sentence and say upon our soul, as He said upon Zaccheus, *Hodie salus facta est huic domui:*[3] This day is health and salvation come unto this house: which that holy, Blessed Person of Christ, which we verily in the Blessed Sacrament receive, through the merit of His bitter Passion (whereof He hath ordained His only Blessed Body in that Blessed Sacrament to be the Memorial) vouchsafe, good Christian readers, to grant unto us all.

COLOPHON: Thus endeth this book. Imprinted at London in Fleetstreet at the sign of the hand and star, at the cost and charge of John Cawod, John Waly and Richard Tottell. . . . 1557.

---

[1] Matt. xxv. 40.　　　　[2] Luke xxiv. 29.　　　　[3] Luke xix. 9.

WILLIAM TYNDALE[1]

When Tyndale made a point-by-point reply to More's Dyaloge, he defended particularly the use of certain terms in his version of the New Testament. Also, he accused the Chancellor of seeking 'honour, promotion, dignity, and money by help of our mitred monsters'. But his arguments against the Church veered too close to Luther's to please Henry VIII, who had not yet broken with Rome. He sent word through Cromwell to Stephen Vaughan, then in Antwerp tracking down Tyndale for the king, that 'his Highness liked nothing in the book, being filled with seditions, slanderous lies, and fantastical opinions'.

It was the least popular of the Reformer's treatises, and the only edition is that of 1530, probably printed in Antwerp. The style is succinct and direct, and Tyndale's share in this first great controversy carried on in English helped to stabilize Tudor prose.

An Answer to More's Dialogue

An Answer unto Sir Thomas More's Dialogue made by William Tyndale

WHY HE USETH THIS WORD 'ELDER'
AND NOT 'PRIEST'

Another thing which he [More] rebuketh is, that I interpret this Greek word *presbiteros* by this word *senior*. Of a truth, *senior* is no very good English, though senior and junior be used in the universities: but there came no better in my mind at that time. Howbeit I spied my fault since, and long ere M. More told it me, and have mended it in all the works which I since made, and call it an *elder*.

M. More condemneth the Latin text

And in that he maketh heresy of it to call *presbiteros* an *elder*, he condemneth their own old Latin text of heresy also, which they use yet daily in the Church, and have used, I suppose, this fourteen hundred years. For that text doth call it an *elder*, likewise. In the fifth chapter of the first Epistle of Peter thus standeth it in the Latin text: *Seniores qui in vobis sunt obsecro ego consenior pascite qui in vobis est gregem Christi:*[2] The *elders* that are among you, I beseech, which am an *elder* also, that ye feed the flock of Christ which is among you. There is *presbiteros* called an *elder*. And in that he saith 'feed' Christ's flock, he meaneth even the ministers that were chosen to teach the people and to inform them in God's Word, and no lay person's.

---

[1] For biographical sketch, see pp. 188-90. [2] I Pet. v. 1-2.

And in the second Epistle of John, saith the text: *Senior Electae dominae et filiis ejus*:[1] The *elder* unto the Electa, lady, and to her children. And in the third Epistle of John: *Senior Gaio dilecto*:[2] The *elder* unto the beloved Gaius. In these two Epistles *presbiteros* is called an *elder*. And in the twentieth [chap.] of the Acts, the text saith: Paul sent for *majores natu ecclesiae*, the *elders* in birth of the congregation or Church, and said unto them: Take heed unto yourselves and unto the whole flock over which the Holy Ghost hath made you *episcopos ad regendam ecclesiam dei*:[3] Bishops or overseers to govern the Church of God. There is *presbiteros* called an *elder* in birth, which same is immediately called a bishop or overseer to declare what persons are meant.

Hereof, ye see, that I have no more erred than their own text which they have used since the Scripture was first in the Latin tongue; and that their own text understandeth by *presbiteros*, nothing save an *elder*. And they were called *elders* because of their age, gravity, and sadness, as thou mayst see by the text, and bishops or overseers by the reason of their offices. And all that were called *elders* (or *priests*, if they so will) were called bishops also, though they have divided the names now. Which thing thou mayst evidently see by the first chapter of Titus, and the twentieth of the Acts and other places more....

WHY HE USETH 'LOVE' RATHER THAN 'CHARITY'

He [More] rebuketh also that I translate this Greek word *agape* into *love* and not rather into *charity*, so holy and so known a term. Verily, *charity* is no known English in the sense which *agape* requireth. For when we say, 'Give your alms in the worship of God and sweet saint *charity*', and when the father teacheth his son to say, '*Blessing*, Father, for saint *charity*', what mean they? In good faith, they wot not.

Moreover, when we say, 'God help you, I have done my *charity* for this day', do we not take it for alms? And the man [that] is ever chiding and out of charity, and I beshrew him saving my *charity*, there we take it for patience. And when I say a 'charitable' man, it is taken for 'merciful'. And though mercifulness be a good love, or rather spring of a good love, yet is not every good love, mercifulness. As when a woman loveth her husband godly, or a man, his wife or his friend that is in none adversity, it is not always mercifulness.

Also we say not this man hath a great *charity* to God, but a great *love*. Wherefore I must have used this general term *love* in spite of mine heart oftentimes. And *agape* and *caritas* were words used among the heathen ere Christ came, and signified, therefore, more than a godly *love*: And we may say, well enough, and have heard it spoken

[1] II John i. 1.   [2] III John i. 1.   [3] Acts xx. 17–28.

that the Turks be charitable one to another among themselves and some of them unto the Christian, too. Besides all this, *agape* is common unto all *loves*.

And when Master More saith, every *love* is not *charity*, no more is every apostle, Christ's Apostle; nor every angel, God's angel; nor every hope, Christ's hope; nor every faith or belief, Christ's belief, and so by an hundred-thousand words. So that if I should always use but a word that were no more general than the word I interpret, I should interpret nothing at all. But the matter itself and the circumstances do declare what *love*, what *hope*, and what *faith* is spoken of.

And, finally, I say not *charity* God or *charity* your neighbour, but *love* God and *love* your neighbour. Yea, and though we say a man ought to *love* his neighbour's wife and his daughter, a Christian man doth not understand that he is commanded to defile his neighbour's wife or his daughter.

WHY 'FAVOUR' AND NOT 'GRACE'

And with like reasons rageth he [More] because I turn *caris* into *favour* and not into *grace*, saying that 'every *favour* is not *grace*'; and that 'in some *favour* there is but little *grace*'. I can say, also, in some *grace* there is little goodness. And when we say, 'He standeth well in my lady's *grace*', we understand no great godly favour. And in universities many ungracious *graces* are gotten....

AN ANSWER UNTO MASTER MORE'S THIRD BOOK, CHAPTER XVI

The messenger asketh him if there be an old lawful translation of the Bible before Wyclif, how happeneth it that it is in so few men's hands, seeing so many desire it? He answereth [that] the printer dare not print it and then hang on a doubtful trial whether it were translated since or before. For if it were translated since, it must be first approved.

Old translation

What may not Master More say by authority of his poetry! There is a lawful translation that no man knoweth—which is as much as no lawful translation. Why might not the bishops show which were that lawful translation, and let it be printed? Nay, if that might have been obtained of them with large money, it had be printed, ye may be sure, long ere this.

But, sir, answer me hereunto: How happeneth that ye defenders translate not one yourselves to cease the murmurs of the people and put to your own glosses to prevent heretics? Ye would, no doubt, have done it long since if ye could have made your glosses agree with the text in every place. And what can you say to this: How that besides they have done their best to disannul all translating by Parliament, they have disputed before the King's Grace that [it is] perilous and not meet, and so concluded that it shall not be under a pretence of deferring it of certain years: where Master More was their special orator to feign lies for their purpose.

More. Nothing discourageth the clergy so much as that they of the worst sort most calleth after it.

Tyndale. It might well be: Pharisees full of holiness long not after it, but Publicans that hunger after mercy might sore desire it. Howbeit, it is, in very deed, a suspect thing and a great sign of a heretic to require it.

Then he [More] juggleth with allegories. Sir More's delivered them all that he had received of God, and that in the mother tongue, in which all that had the heart thereto studied, and not the priests only, as thou mayst see in the Scripture. And the Apostles kept nothing behind, as Paul testified, Acts. xx, how he had showed them all the counsel of God, and had kept naught back. Should the lay people less hearken unto the expositions of the prelates in doubtful places if the text were in their hands when they preached.

More. The Jews gave great reverence unto the Bible, and we sit on it.

Tyndale. The pope putteth it under his feet and treadeth on it in token that he is lord over it; that it should serve him, and he not it.

More. God hath ordained the ordinaries for chief physicians.

Tyndale. They be lawyers ordained of the pope, and can no more skill of the Scripture than they that never saw it: yea, and have professed a contrary doctrine. They be right hangmen to murder whosoever desireth for the doctrine that God hath given to be the ordinary of our faith and living.

And when he [More] maketh so great difficulty and hardness in Paul's Epistles, I say, it is impossible to understand either Peter or Paul or ought at all in the Scripture for him that denieth the justifying of faith in Christ's blood. And again, it is impossible to understand in the Scripture more than a Turk for who[m]soever hath not the law of God written in his heart to fulfil it. Of which point, and of true faith, too, I fear me that you are void and empty with all your spirituality, whose defender ye have taken upon you to be, for to mock out the truth for lucre and advantage.

COLOPHON: Antwerp. [1530.]

JOHN FRITH
1503-1533

John Frith, a close friend and disciple of William Tyndale, was one of the most industrious writers among the Reformers. He was born about 1503 in Kent, the son of an innkeeper. From his earliest years Frith showed an aptitude for learning, and was sent to Eton. In 1525 he took a degree at King's College, Cambridge, where Stephen Gardiner, later Bishop of Winchester, was his tutor. Frith's proficiency in Greek and Latin brought him to the attention of Wolsey, who made him a Junior Canon in his own college, Christ Church, Oxford.

Because of his outspoken views against Catholic doctrine, Frith was tried on charges of heresy in 1528, and imprisoned. After his release, probably in 1529, he fled to Germany and settled down at the University of Marburg. During his stay there he came under the influence of Tyndale, whom he had met in England, and a fast friendship developed between them. While on the Continent, and probably with Tyndale's aid, Frith wrote a treatise against the doctrine of purgatory, addressing it to Bishop John Fisher, Sir Thomas More, and John Rastell.

The Lutheran bias in Frith's works stirred up considerable ire in England, and in 1531 Cromwell wrote to Stephen Vaughan, the king's agent, who was busy tracking down Tyndale in Flanders, requesting him to interview Frith, since Henry VIII heartily wished that the young Oxford scholar would give up his 'venemous and pestiferous work'. According to Vaughan's reply, Frith was obstinate. A year later, he ventured across the Channel to Reading on a business trip. While there he was charged with vagrancy, but the charges were dismissed with the aid of Leonard Cox, headmaster of the Reading Abbey school.

Frith was fearless in his efforts to spread Lutheran reforms, and was soon arrested by London agents. He was imprisoned, and during a year's stay in the Tower spent his time writing treatises against the Church. Indifferent to his fate, he wrote a 'lytle treatise', in which he disputed the doctrine of the Eucharist, and gave it to a casual acquaintance. The work came to the attention of Sir Thomas More who answered it in the Souper of the Lord (1533). This again focused attention on Frith, and he was brought to trial on charges of heresy on 20 June 1533. His case is unusual in that his judges, mindful of his youth and great scholarship, urged him to recant. Tyndale wrote him two letters, urging him to be more cautious and to keep his unorthodox views to himself. But Frith was only more vehement and outspoken in his beliefs. He was sentenced to death, and burnt at the stake at Smithfield on 4 July 1533.

Frith's principal works are: A pistle to the christen reader: the reuelation of antichrist (*1529*); A disputacion of purgatorye deuided into thre bokes [*1533*]; A boke made by J. Frith answering vnto M. Mores lettur (*1533*); A mirrour or glasse to know thyselfe [*1533*]; *and* A myrrour or lokynge glasse wherein you may beholde the Sacramente of baptisme described (*1533*).

In the Disputacion, *Frith's arguments against a belief in purgatory were so persuasive that he converted Rastell, one of the three to whom the book was addressed. But, as in all his works, Frith was more of an idealist than a theologian. The* Mirrour *contains some of his most colourful and spirited prose.*

A Mirror to know Thyself

A Mirror to know Thyself: that all Goodness cometh from God and all Evil from Ourselves

THE FIRST CHAPTER

The philosophers to whom God had inspired certain sparkles of truth acknowledged that the chiefest point of wisdom and direction of a man's life was to know himself, which sentence the Scripture[1] establisheth so clearly that no man may dissent from the truth of the same. For Solomon saith that, The Fear of the Lord is the beginning of wisdom.[2] Now who can fear the Lord but only he that knoweth himself,[3] as the Scripture teacheth him? For if I perceive not the imperfection of my nature, which is subject unto corruption and void of all stableness; if I perceive not the unstableness of my flesh, being prone to all sin and rebellious to rightwellness, and that there dwelleth no goodness in me;[4] if I perceive not the poison of the old serpent and hell and sin, which lieth hid within me unto which are prepared pains intolerable,[5] I shall have none occasion to fear God, but rather to advance myself equal with God, as Lucifer,[6] Nebuchadnezzar,[7] Herod,[8] and such others have done, which after were sore chastened for their folly.

What hast thou, vain man, whereof thou mayst rejoice?[9] For the Scripture testifieth: That every good and perfect gift cometh from above from the Father of Lights with whom is no transmutation.[10] So that whether they be outward gifts or inward, pertaining either to the body or soul,[11] if they be good, they come 'from above from the Father of Lights'. For if thou behold the proportion of thy bony stature or beauty, thou shalt easily perceive that it cometh of God,

---

[1] Cf. Rom. i. 19.   [2] Prov. i. 7.   [3] Cf. Rom. viii.
[4] Cf. Rom. vii.   [5] Cf. Matt. xxiii. 33.   [6] Cf. Isa. xiv. 13.
[7] Cf. Dan. iv.   [8] Cf. Acts xii. 22.   [9] Cf. Rom. iii. 27.
[10] James i. 17.   [11] Cf. Matt. vi.

even by the words of Christ which exhorteth us not to be careful. For there is none of us, although we be never so careful, that 'can add one stature',[1] either 'make one white hair or black'.[2]

And as touching our wisdom, eloquence, long life, victory, glory, and such other, the Scripture testifieth that they come of God and not of ourselves. For St James saith: If any man lack wisdom, let him ask it of God which giveth it abundantly,[3] as it is evident by Solomon which of God desired wisdom to judge between good and evil. And the Lord made him answer that because he asked that thing and not long life, nor riches, nor the destruction of his enemies, but rather wisdom to discern in judgment: Behold I have given unto thee a heart full of wisdom and understanding in so much that none before thee hath been like unto thee, neither yet after thee shall any be like unto thee. And besides that, I have given thee riches and glory.[4]

Furthermore, the most glorious gifts concerning our souls come from God, even of His mercy and favour which He showeth us in Christ and for Christ, as predestination, election, vocation, and justification. And, albeit, M. More with his painted poetry and crafty conveyance do cast a mist before your eyes that you might wander out of the right way, endeavouring himself to instruct you, that God doth predestinate and [hath] chosen us before the beginning of the world because He knew before that we should do good works, yet will I set you upon a candle which shall shine so bright, and so clearly dispel his mist and vain poetry that you shall plainly perceive him dancing naked in a net, which, notwithstanding, thinketh himself to go invisible.

More's mist

M. More dancing in a net, thinketh himself invisible

And although there be Scriptures enough, both Tit. iii and Rom. xi, to prove the same true, yet will I let that pass and allege for me St Austin, which is the candle that I speak of, which shall disclose his [More's] juggling and utter his ignorance. For St Austin saith:* Some men will affirm that God did choose us because He saw before that we should do good works; but Christ saith not so which saith: Ye have not chosen Me, but I have chosen you.[5] For, saith he [St Augustine], if He had chosen us because He saw before that we should do good works, then should He also have seen before, that we should first have chosen Him, which is contrary to the words of Christ and mind of the Evangelist. Here may you see how evidently St Austin confuteth Master More's poetry and openeth his serpentine deceit.

Finally, St Paul saith (Eph. ii) that we are 'saved through grace, and that it cometh not of ourselves. It is the gift of God, and cometh not of works lest any man should boast himself': Which words

---

[1] Matt. vi. 27. [2] Matt. v. 36. [3] James i. 5.
[4] III Re. iii. 12–13. [5] John xv. 16.

M. More might be ashamed to hear, if he were not another Lucian,*
neither regarding God nor man. But St Austin addeth* thus much
more unto it: *Non erit gratia ullo modo nisi fuerit gratuita omni modo*:
That is to say, that it can nowise be grace or favour except it be
always free. And, therefore, I may conclude that it is neither of the
works going before nor the works coming after, but only of the free
favour of God.

And this are we sure of, that whomsoever He chooseth, them He
saveth of His mercy: and whom He repelleth, them of His secret
and unsearchable judgment, He condemneth. 'But why He chooseth
the one and repelleth the other, inquire not',* saith St Austin, 'if thou
wilt not err.' Insomuch that St Paul could not attain to the knowledge thereof, but cried out: O the depth of the riches and wisdom
of the knowledge of God. How unsearchable are His judgments and
how incomprehensible are his ways![1] But M. More had liefer loved
to lie and [go] far to err than to let God alone with His secrets or to
acknowledge his ignorance in anything.

And to be short, St Paul saith: What hast thou, that thou hast not
received? If thou hast received it, why dost thou advance thyself as
though thou hast not received it?[2] So we may conclude that all
goodness cometh of God, and all sin or mischief of our own poisoned
nature. Insomuch that we may say with the Prophet Daniel: *Tibi,
Domine, gloria, nobis autem confusio faciei*:[3] O Lord, all glory be unto
Thee, and unto us shame and confusion, so that he that rejoiceth,
may rejoice in the Lord.

[n.p. 1533?]

THE BOOK OF COMMON PRAYER

*The greatest single document connected with the establishment of the
Church of England is* The Boke of Comon Praier *(1549). It followed
logically the Act of Supremacy (1534) which made the king supreme head
of the English Church, severing it completely from the Papal See. Though
the Prayer Book was preceded by directives issued by Henry VIII and his
council—the Ten Articles of 1536,* The godly and pious Injunction of
a Christian man *(1537) or the 'Bishops' Book', the Injunctions of 1538,
and the Six Articles of 1539—each of which was intended to strengthen the
foundation of the national Church, it was the firm belief of Thomas
Cranmer, Archbishop of Canterbury, that a creed bearing no resemblance to*

[1] Rom. xi. 33.   [2] I Cor. iv. 7.   [3] Dan. ix. 7.

the ancient Roman creed with its Mass and liturgy must be established to
ensure the growth of the English Church.

With the sanction of Henry VIII, Cranmer began to formulate The Boke
of Comon Praier *in 1541. According to John Foxe, he had the aid of*
only a few of the king's council. After Henry's death in 1547, Cranmer
had a freer hand in omitting doctrines that he considered essentially
Catholic, especially transubstantiation, which he had opposed from the
beginning of the Reformation. From the old service books, Cranmer and
his assistants compiled a new ritual to be followed in each church ceremony,
and all prayers were to be said in English. But in basing the new ordinal
on the Sarum-use breviaries and primers, most of them from early medieval
times, the service in the first edition of the Prayer Book is frequently close
to the Catholic liturgy.

The preface, most likely the work of Archbishop Cranmer, is written in
clear and simple prose, declaring a return to what is called 'the godly and
decent order of the ancient Fathers'. Eleven editions of it were printed in
1549, but the Prayer Book was not destined to remain unchanged. Within
three years a revised version appeared. There were further doctrinal
changes, but more important was the fiat *of the bishops, inaugurating a*
religious policy that encouraged 'critical re-examination of belief and
practice where the measure of orthodoxy' need not be 'the authority of the
teaching church, but their own scriptural and patristic learning'. It was a
policy that was to be enlarged and continued far beyond the Tudor era, and
influenced the social and political as well as the religious thought of
succeeding centuries.

Preface to the Book of Common Prayer

The Book of Common Prayer and Administration of the Sacraments, and Other Rites and Ceremonies of the Church after
the Use of the Church of England.

PREFACE

There was never anything by the wit of man so well devised or so
surely established, which, in continuance of time, hath not been
corrupted, as, among other things, it may plainly appear by the
common prayers in the Church, commonly called divine service:
the first original and ground whereof, if a man would search out by
the ancient Fathers, he shall find that the same was not ordained but
of a good purpose and for a great advancement of godliness: For
they so ordered the matter, that all the whole Bible, or the greatest
part thereof, should be read over once in the year, intending thereby
that the clergy, and specially such as were ministers of the congrega-

tion, should by often reading and meditation of God's Word be stirred up to godliness themselves, and be more able also to exhort others by wholesome doctrine, and to confute them that were adversaries to the truth. And, further, that the people by daily hearing of Holy Scripture read in the church should continually profit more and more in the knowledge of God, and be the more inflamed with the love of His true religion.

But these many years passed, this godly and decent order of the ancient Fathers hath been altered, broken, and neglected by planting in uncertain stories, legends, responses, verses, vain repetitions, commemorations, and synodals that commonly when any book of the Bible was begun, before the third or fourth chapters were read out, all the rest were unread. And in this sort, the *Book of Isaias* was begun in Advent, and the *Book of Genesis* in Septuagesima: but they were only begun, and never read through. After a like sort were other books of Holy Scripture used. And, moreover, whereas St Paul would have such language spoken to the people in the church as they might understand and have profit by hearing the same, the service in this Church of England these many years hath been read in Latin to the people, which they understood not, so that they have heard with their ears only: and their hearts, spirit, and mind have not been edified thereby.

And, furthermore, notwithstanding that the ancient Fathers had divided the psalms into seven portions, whereof every one was called a nocturne, now of late time a few of them have been daily said and often repeated, and the rest utterly omitted. Moreover, the number and hardness of the rules, called the pie,[1] and the manifold changings of the service was the cause that to turn the book only was so hard and intricate a matter that many times there was more business to find out what should be read than to read it when it was found out.

These inconveniences therefore considered, here is set forth such an order, whereby the same shall be redressed. And for a readiness in this matter, here is drawn out a calendar for that purpose, which is plain and easy to be understood, wherein, so much as may be, the reading of Holy Scripture is so set forth that all things shall be done in order. without breaking one piece thereof from another. For this cause be cut off anthems, responses, invitatories,* and such like things, as did break the continual course of the reading of the Scripture.

Yet because there is no remedy but that of necessity, there must be some rules: therefore certain rules are here set forth, which as they be few in number so they be plain and easy to be understood. So that here you have an order for prayer, as touching the reading of Holy Scripture, much agreeable to the mind and purpose of the old

[1] *pie*, a calendar of religious services.

Fathers and a great deal more profitable and commodious than that which of late was used. It is more profitable because here are left out many things, whereof some be untrue, some uncertain, some vain and superstitious: and is ordained nothing to be read but the very pure Word of God, the Holy Scriptures, or that which is evidently grounded upon the same: and that in such a language and order as is most easy and plain for the understanding, both of the readers and hearers. It is also more commodious, both for the shortness thereof, and for the plainness of the order, and for that the rules be few and easy. Furthermore by this order, the curates shall need none other books for their public service but this book and the Bible: by the means whereof, the people shall not be at so great charge for books as in time past they have been.

And where heretofore there hath been great diversity in saying and singing in churches within this realm—some following Salisbury-use,* some Hereford-use, some the use of Bangor, some of York, and some of Lincoln—now from henceforth, all the whole realm shall have but one use. And if any would judge this way more painful because that all things must be read upon the book, whereas before by the reason of so often repetition they could say many things by heart, if those men will weigh their labour with the profit in knowledge which daily they shall obtain by reading upon the book, they will not refuse the pain in consideration of the great profit that shall ensue thereof.

And forsomuch as nothing can almost be so plainly set forth but doubts may rise in the use and practising of the same, to appease all such diversity, if any arise, and for the resolution of all doubts concerning the manner how to understand, do, and execute the things contained in this book, the parties that so doubt or diversely take anything shall always resort to the bishop of the diocese, who by his discretion shall take order for the quieting and appeasing of the same, so that the same order be not contrary to anything contained in this book.

Though it be appointed in the afore-written preface, that all things shall be read and sung in the church in the English tongue, to the end that the congregation may be thereby edified: yet it is not meant, but when men say matins and evensong[1] privately, they may say the same in any language that they themselves understand; neither that any man shall be bound to the saying of them but such as from time to time in cathedral and collegiate churches, parish churches, and chapels to the same annexed, shall serve the congregation.

[1] *evensong*, vespers.

The Form of Solemnization of Matrimony

First, the banns must be asked three several Sundays or holy days in the service time; the people being present, after the accustomed manner.

And if the persons that would be married dwell in divers parishes, the banns must be asked in both parishes, and the curate of the one parish shall not solemnize matrimony between them without a certificate of the banns being thrice asked from the curate of the other parish.

At the day appointed for the solemnization of matrimony, the persons to be married shall come into the body of the church with their friends and neighbours.

And there the priest shall thus say:

Dearly beloved friends: we are gathered together here in the sight of God and in the face of His congregation to join together this man and this woman in holy matrimony which is an honourable estate instituted of God in paradise in the time of man's innocence, signifying unto us the mystical union that is betwixt Christ and His Church: which holy estate Christ adorned and beautified with His presence, and the first miracle that He wrought in Cana of Galilee,[1] and is commended of Saint Paul to be 'honourable among all men';[2] and therefore is not to be enterprised nor taken in hand unadvisedly, lightly, or wantonly, to satisfy mens' carnal lusts and appetites, like brute beasts that have no understanding, but reverently, discreetly, advisedly, soberly, and in the fear of God. Duly considering the causes for the which matrimony was ordained: one cause was the procreation of children, to be brought up in the fear and nurture of the Lord and praise of God. Secondly, it was ordained for a remedy against sin and to avoid fornication, that such persons as be married might live chastely in matrimony and keep themselves undefiled members of Christ's body. Thirdly, for the mutual society, help, and comfort, that the one ought to have of another, both in prosperity and adversity. Into the which holy estate these two persons present, come now to be joined. Therefore, if any man can show any just cause why they may not lawfully be joined so together, let him now speak, or else hereafter forever hold his peace.

[1] John ii. 1–11. [2] Cf. Heb. xiii. 4.

And also speaking to the persons that shall be married,
he shall say:

I require and charge you, as you will answer at the dreadful day of judgment when the secrets of all hearts shall be disclosed, that if either of you do know any impediment why ye may not be lawfully joined together in matrimony, that ye confess it. For be ye well assured, that so many as be coupled together otherways than God's Word doth allow, are not joined of God; neither is their matrimony lawful.

At which day of marriage if any man do allege any impediment why they may not be coupled together in matrimony, and will be bound, and sureties with him, to the parties, or else put in a caution to the full value of such charges as the persons to be married do sustain to prove his allegation, then the solemnization must be deferred unto such time as the truth be tried.

If no impediment be alleged, then shall the curate
say unto the man:

N. Wilt thou have this woman to thy wedded wife to live together after God's ordinance in the holy estate of matrimony? Wilt thou love her, comfort her, honour, and keep her in sickness and in health? And forsaking all other, keep thee only to her so long as you both shall live?

The man shall answer,

I will.

Then shall the priest say to the woman:

N. Wilt thou have this man to thy wedded husband to live together after God's ordinance in the holy estate of matrimony? Wilt thou obey him, and serve him, love, honour, and keep him in sickness and in health? And forsaking all other, keep thee only to him so long as you both shall live?

The woman shall answer,

I will.

Then shall be said after the gospel a sermon, wherein ordinarily (so oft as there is any marriage) the office of man and wife shall be declared according to Holy Scripture. Or if there be no sermon, the minister shall read this that followeth:

All ye which be married, or which intend to take the holy estate of matrimony upon you, hear what Holy Scripture doth say as touching the duty of husbands toward their wives and wives toward their husbands.

Saint Paul in his Epistle to the Ephesians, the fifth chapter, doth give this commandment to all married men:

Ye husbands, love your wives even as Christ loved the Church, and hath given Himself for it to sanctify it, purging it in the fountain of water through the Word, that He might make it unto Himself a glorious congregation, not having spot or wrinkle or any such thing; but that it should be holy and blameless. So men are bound to love their own wives as their own bodies: he that loveth his own wife, loveth himself. For never did any man hate his own flesh, but nourisheth and cherisheth it, even as the Lord doth the congregation, for we are members of His body, of His flesh and of His bones. For this cause shall a man leave father and mother, and shall be joined unto his wife, and they shall be one flesh. This mystery is great: but I speak of Christ and of the congregation. Nevertheless, let every one of you so love his own wife, even as himself.[1]

Likewise the same Saint Paul, writing to the Colossians, speaketh thus to all men that be married: Ye men, love your wives, and be not bitter unto them.[2] Hear also what Saint Peter, the apostle of Christ, which was himself a married man, saith unto all men that are married: Ye husbands, dwell with your wives according to knowledge: giving honour unto the wife, as unto the weaker vessel, and as heirs together of the grace of life, so that your prayers be not hindered.[3]

Hitherto ye have heard the duty of the husband toward the wife.

Now likewise, ye wives, hear and learn your duty toward your husbands, even as it is plainly set forth in Holy Scripture. Saint Paul, in the forenamed Epistle to the Ephesians, teacheth you thus: Ye women, submit yourselves unto your own husbands as unto the Lord: for the husband is the wife's head, even as Christ is the Head of the Church: And He also is the Saviour of the whole body. Therefore, as the Church, or congregation, is subject unto Christ so likewise let the wives also be in subjection unto their own husbands in all things.[4] And again he saith: Let the wife reverence her husband.[5] And in his Epistle to the Colossians, Saint Paul giveth you this short lesson: Ye wives, submit yourselves unto your own husbands, as it is convenient in the Lord.[6]

Saint Peter also doth instruct you very godly, thus saying: Let wives be subject to their own husbands, so that if any obey not the Word, they may be won without the Word, by the conversation of the wives. While they behold your chaste conversation, coupled with fear: whose apparel let it not be outward with braided hair and trimming about with gold, neither in putting on of gorgeous apparel: But let the hidden man, which is in the heart, be without all

---

[1] Eph. v. 25–33. [2] Col. iii. 19. [3] I Pet. iii. 7.
[4] Eph. v. 22–4. [5] Tit. ii. 4. [6] Col. iii. 18.

corruption, so that the spirit be mild and quiet, which is a precious thing in the sight of God. For after this manner in the old time did the holy women, which trusted in God, apparel themselves, being subject to their own husbands: as Sara obeyed Abraham, calling him lord; whose daughters ye are made, doing well, and being not dismayed with any fear.[1]

The new married persons (the same day of their marriage) must receive the holy communion.

COLOPHON: Imprinted at London in Fleet Street, at the Sign of the Sun over against the conduit, by Edward Whitchurch.... 1549.

[1] I Pet. iii. 1–6.

PART IV

CHRONICLES AND HISTORIES

TUDOR CHRONICLES AND HISTORIES

INTRODUCTION BY F. S. BOAS

THE MEDIEVALISTS AND THE TUDOR CHRONICLE

The prose of English chronicles and histories reaches back to well-nigh the beginnings of our literature. *The Old English Chronicle*, of which the first version is usually credited to the influence of King Alfred, is continued in its various recensions till in the Peterborough version it is carried down to the year 1154. Composed at very different times and by a number of hands, it exhibits much of the variety of style and treatment which, as will be seen, was to characterize this literary type when it revived in English dress in a later age.

In the twelfth and thirteenth centuries English as the medium of historical record gave place to Latin in the hands of a remarkable succession of chroniclers who, as has been truly said, though using a foreign tongue, wrote from a national English standpoint. Yet here again there is a striking diversity of outlook and technique, ranging from the scholarly and judicious labours of William of Malmesbury and Matthew Paris to the brilliant romancing of Geoffrey of Monmouth.

Ralph Higden's *Polychronicon*, an encyclopaedic record from the Creation to his own day, is a fourteenth-century offshoot from this Latin school of history. But by 1350 English was beginning again to come into its own as evidenced in John Trevisa's translation of the *Polychronicon*, completed in 1387. For in the dialogue between a Lord and a Clerk (Lord Berkeley and Trevisa), prefixed to the translation, the case is argued for writing histories in English and in prose, instead of in Latin or in the French and English verse of Wace and Layamon; they would thus be understood by the common man.

This was all the more imperative in the light of the statement inserted by Trevisa in Higden's Chapter LIX that since the Black Death schoolmasters 'leue all Frensshe in scoles and vse all construccyon in Englysshe'. So in his prefatory epistle to Lord Berkeley, Trevisa declares that at his patron's behest he will undertake the task of translating Higden's work, and adds, in his at times over-alliterative style, 'For blame of bakbyters wyll I not blynne / for enuye of enemyes / for euyll spytyng ʒ speche of euyl spekers wyll I not leue to do this dede / for trauyll wyll I not spare.' A more favourable example of his style is his reading of the passage in Higden's first chapter extolling history as the great remembrancer: 'Dedes yᵗ wolde flee out of mynde: Storye calleth agayne. Dedes yᵗ wolde dye: Storye kepeth them for euermore.'

Trevisa's racy and vigorous prose ensured the success of his translation from which later chroniclers long continued to borrow after it had been printed successively by Caxton in 1482, Wynkyn de Worde about 1495, and Peter Treveris in 1527. Thus, Robert Fabyan, who is the first link in the chain of Tudor chroniclers, in his account here reproduced of Alfred and the Danes more than once says, 'as affermeth *Policronica*'. But in his description of the king's visit to the Danish camp, he introduces what is a distinctively Tudor, not a medieval touch. 'With his Instrument of musyke he entred the Tentes ⁊ Pauylyons of the Danys / ⁊ in shewynge there his Enterludes ⁊ Songes / he espyed all theyr slouthe and Idelnesse.' Interludes are not entertainments appropriate to the age of Alfred, or even that of William I, of whom Fabyan gives a critical sketch, but to the court of Henry VII, with a panegyric on whom he ends his volume. As he leant on Trevisa and others, so he provided material for successors like Hall, Stow, and Holinshed. Shakespeare may well have read him as well as them; and he appears to have furnished Marlowe with the 'jig' sung by the 'fleering Scots' about Bannockburn quoted in *Edward II*, Act II, sc. ii.

THE MORAL CONCEPT OF TUDOR HISTORIANS

With the translation of Froissart by John Bourchier, Lord Berners, 'Chronicle' gains a different significance from that which it bore for Higden, Trevisa, and Fabyan. They had taken, according to their lights, the whole of history from the beginnings for their province. Froissart's survey was limited to a period covering the reigns of Edward III and Richard II, of which he had a good deal of first-hand knowledge. But in the 'Preface' to his translation, Berners discourses on the value of history in general:

> The most profytable thyng in this worlde / for the instytucion of the humayne lyfe / is hystorie. Ones the contynuall redyng therof / maketh yonge men equall in prudence to olde men: and to olde fathers stryken in age / it mynystreth experyence of thynges. More / it yeldeth priuate persons worthy of dignyte / rule / and gouernaunce. It compelleth themperours hygh rulers and gouernours to do noble dedes to thende they may optayne immortall glory.

Berners thus does homage to history not like Higden and Trevisa, primarily as a recorder of past events, but as a stimulant to high achievement. Unfortunately, he thought it necessary here to improve the occasion by adopting an ornate, overloaded style of which such repetitions as 'dignyte / rule / and gouernaunce' and 'themperours hygh rulers and gouernours' are specimens. And it is in something of the same exotic vein that he should instance 'the strōg and ferse Hercules' and the 'noble duke Theseus' as having sought historic immortality.

On the other hand, in his translation of Froissart's work, Berners reproduced much of the simplicity and grace of the original, and could fairly claim that if 'I haue nat followed myne authour worde by worde: yet I trust I haue ensewed the true reporte of the sentence of the mater'. Froissart, as he himself states, had been in his youth 'clerke and seruaūt' to Edward III and his queen, and later was in the court of Richard II more than three months and had there 'good chere'. He had therefore a special interest in the train of events which led to Richard's abdication and death, of which he could give a detailed account.

As Froissart gives a semi-dramatic setting to the relations between Richard and Henry of Lancaster before his accession, so the author of *The First English Life of Henry V* gives a similar setting to the relations between Henry IV, when he had become king, and his eldest son. This *Life* is mainly a version of the Latin *Vita Henrici Quinti*, written about 1438 by the Italian Tito Livio da Forti, who was for a time in the service of Humphrey, Duke of Gloucester. The anonymous translator, however, supplemented Livio's narrative from other sources, especially from oral information given him by his 'lord and master', James Butler, the fourth Earl of Ormonde, to whose 'credible reports' he several times refers. To these reports we owe the accounts of the momentous interviews between Henry IV and Prince Henry, of the Prince in disguise despoiling for a time 'his owne receauers' of the money they had collected, and of his change 'into a newe man' when he came to the throne.

The *Life*, written between 1513 and 1514, remained in manuscript till the twentieth century but its contents were known to Stow and Holinshed, and through them the 'credible reports' about Prince Henry passed to Shakespeare, who adapted and immortalized them in the familiar scenes in *King Henry IV*. And in the 'translator's' description of the battle of Agincourt, his allusions to the French playing for the English at dice, to King Henry's cry, 'I woulde not that my companie were increased of one person more than nowe it is', and to his 'thanks and laude to God' for the victory, have their close Shakespearian parallels.

With John Rastell's *The Pastyme of People* we revert to the large-scale chronicle, though in his 'Prologue' Rastell shows himself sceptical of the traditional accounts of how Britain first became inhabited. Yet even 'a feined story' has often in his eyes a moral value which makes it worth repeating. Here belongs the tale of Lear and his daughters in its early form, in which Lear returns from France with Cordelia and is restored to his throne. In contrast with such legendary figures stand Joan of Arc and Jack Cade in Rastell's account of the earlier years of Henry VI.

Rastell among his manifold activities refers in his *Interlude of the Four Elements* to a voyage in which he took part in 1516–17, intended to reach the new-found western lands, but which was frustrated by mutiny on board. The earliest account in English of these lands, containing the name 'Armenica' [America], comes strangely enough about 1511 from the printing house of Jan Van Dvesborch in Antwerp. Though purporting to relate to the voyages of Portuguese mariners, it 'reflects the legends of the Middle Ages rather than any real knowledge of more recent explorations'.

Very different is Richard Eden's translation, published in 1555, of the *Decades* written in Latin by Peter Martyr d'Anghiera, describing the voyages of Columbus, Amerigo Vespucci, and Sebastian Cabot. The impassioned 'Preface to the Reader' shows Eden exhorting his countrymen, as Rastell had done in his *Interlude*, to take their due share in the enterprise of exploration, both for religious and commercial ends.

Whether the *History of Richard III* was from the pen of Sir Thomas More, as the collector of his *English Works* in 1557 believed, or whether, as Sir George Buc and the author of *A defense of Richard III* asserted, it was primarily the work of Cardinal John Morton and was only revised by More, it has a special place in this section of early Tudor prose. As the English *Life of Henry V* is a sustained panegyric on that monarch so the *History of Richard III* is a no less sustained study in vilification. And it is a work of far more conscious art which lifts it from the level of a chronicle to that of an analytical character sketch. Touch is added to touch till the picture is completed of a dissembling, hypocritical, remorseless villain 'who spared no man's deathe whose life withstode his purpose'. It has been truly said that the narrative has in it an element of Greek tragedy. Nemesis dogs the evil-doers, of whom Richard is chief. 'Through all the time of his reygne, neuer ceased there cruel death and slaughter, till his owne destruccion ended it. But as he finished his time with ye beste death, and ye most righteous, y^t is to wyt his own: so began he with the most piteous and wicked, I meane the lamentable murther of his innocent nephewes.' There follows the affecting account of this piteous outrage and of Richard's haunted life thereafter till its miserable close on Bosworth Field. And by Shakespeare this conception of the last of the Lancastrians, whether or not historically justified, has been indelibly impressed on the popular imagination.

REFLECTION OF THE VARIED PAGEANTRY OF THE
TIMES ON TUDOR BIOGRAPHY

It is a relief to turn from these sombre scenes to the glowing pages of Edward Hall. If he had little sense of the deeper political and economic movements of his age, we may be thankful that he had an eye for its brilliance and colour. With him as guide, we can watch the court festivities of the first Tudor reigns, as in the account, here reproduced, of the revels at Christmas, New Year, and Epiphany, 1512–13. On the Epiphany night, 'the kyng with a eleven other were disguised, after the maner of Italie, called a maske, a thyng not seen afore in Englande'. What exactly the innovation was is not clear but from this time forward 'mask' begins to displace the older terms of 'mumming' or 'disguising'.

Another festivity on a grander scale was the magnificent series of pageants arranged by the citizens of London, in which also the clergy and the resident aliens, Easterlings, and Italians took part, to welcome the Emperor Charles V when, accompanied by Henry VIII, he made his entry into the capital on 6 June 1522. Hall recalls every detail of the ceremonial with infectious gusto.

There is something of the same rich colouring in the pages of George Cavendish's *Life of Wolsey*, when he describes the state with which the cardinal as Chancellor made his way to Westminster Hall: 'Then was attending him, when he was mounted, his two Crosse-bearers, his two Pillow-bearers, all upon great horses, all in fine Scarlet, then he marched on with a traine of Gentrie, having foure Foot-men about him, bearing every one a Pole-axe in his hand.' Yet Cavendish, as gentleman-usher to Wolsey, was only too well aware that 'advancement and authoritie are not permanent, but many times slide and vanish suddenly away'. This was evidenced not only in the downfall of his master but in the divorce proceedings against Queen Katherine, of which he gives a first-hand account.

It was true, also, after another manner, of Sir Thomas More, the last of the great figures who passes in procession through this section. The selection from Hall's *The Union of the two noble and illustre famelies of Lancastre and York* describes the meeting of Parliament in April 1523, when Bishop Tunstall discoursed on the true office of a king, and when Sir Thomas More was chosen Speaker by the Commons and Henry welcomed him knowing 'his witte, learnyng and discrecion'. A companion picture of More is provided by the Carthusian Dan John Bouge in a letter to Dame Katherine Mann in which he calls him 'a gentleman of great learning both in law, art, and divinity'.

Then comes the 'heauy change' to Nicholas Harpsfield's narrative of More's last days in the Tower, his trial and execution. This excerpt from Harpsfield's *Life and Death of S^r. Thomas More* (printed in full in 1932) has been used because it combines with Roper's account the fuller and more authentic details recorded (as Dr Elsie Hitchcock points out) in the *Newsletter* sent to Paris shortly after More's death. But through the darkness of the tragic scene glows a spiritual light from Sir Thomas's lofty bearing and his serene confidence of a 'merry' reunion with his friends in heaven.

This deeply moving narrative forms a fitting close to this series of extracts from early Tudor chronicles and histories which illustrate their variety of prose styles from 'plain to coloured', and of their conception of the historian's scope from simple record of events to conscious moral edification, or propagandist aim, or character-analysis. And not only have they furnished materials to Shakespeare and his fellow-playwrights but they contain within themselves elements of dialogue and action which anticipate, and help to explain, the rich dramatic harvest of the later Tudor years.

ROBERT FABYAN

c. 1450–1513

When Richard Pynson printed The newe cronycles of England and of Fraunce *in 1516, he omitted the name of the compiler. But William Rastell, who reprinted it in 1533, changed the title to* Fabyans cronycle newly prynted, *ascribing it to Robert Fabyan, a wealthy landowner and member of the Drapers' Company in London, where he was born about 1450, the son of John and Agnes Fabyan.*

Little is known of Fabyan's youth until 1476, when he became an apprentice of William Holme in the Drapers' Company. Within the next ten years, Fabyan began an active political career. His first appointment was to the office of City Auditor in 1486. He was elected sheriff in 1493, and alderman in the following year.

Through his marriage to Elizabeth Pake, daughter of John Pake, a wealthy draper, Fabyan acquired large estates in Essex. His will, dated 11 July 1511, shows that he had amassed a considerable fortune, most of which he left to his family with a portion to be spent for pious and charitable purposes. He died in 1513, survived by his wife and six of their sixteen children.

Whether Fabyan actually compiled the Newe cronycles, *or collaborated with others, there are several records that show he had a general interest in chronicles. The earliest of these records mentions the 'grete boke of* Croniques of Fraunce *wreton in Frensh', a Guildhall manuscript which had been a 'long tyme in the kepyng of the sayd M. Fabyan'. It was returned to the Guildhall by his widow shortly after his death. There are frequent references to the* Croniques *in the* Newe cronycles. *Another record states that in 1534 the council of Aldermen ordered the chamberlain to 'provyde a book of Mr fabyans cronycles, the same to remayne always yn thys courte'. Fabyan is referred to as the author of the* Newe cronycles *by John Stowe, John Foxe, and Richard Hakluyt, all of whom used his work extensively.*

Fabyan divided the Newe cronycles *into two volumes and seven sections, piously dedicating each section to one of the seven joys of 'that most blessid vyrgyn ouir lady Seynt Mary'. The first volume begins with the English* Brut *and continues until 1223; the second ends in 1485, the close of the reign of Richard III. Some time after 1504, when Fabyan completed the last section, he wrote a panegyric on Henry VII which Pynson printed in the 1516 edition.*

Another chronicle, called The Great Chronicle of London, *has been attributed to Fabyan. It was printed for the first time in 1938 from an early sixteenth-century manuscript belonging to the Guildhall Library in London.*

The New Chronicles of England and of France

THE SIXTH PART: ALFRED[1]

Aluredus [Alfred], the fourth son of Adolfus [Aethelwulf] and brother to Ethelredus, the last king, began his reign over the West

England

Saxons and other provinces of England, in the year of Our Lord, 872 and the twenty-first year of Charles [the Bald], forenamed, then King of France. This Alured, or after some writers, Alfred, was twelve years of age or he were sent to school. But for all that, he sped so well his time that he passed his brother and others that were long sent forth before him. And by counsel of Neot or Notus,* he ordained the first grammar school at Oxford and other free schools, and franchised that town with many great liberties; and [he] translated many laws, as Mercian law and others,* out of British speech unto Saxon tongue. He was also a subtle master in building and devising thereof and excellent cunning in all hunting; fair he was of stature and most beloved of his father of all his children. . . .

[Alfred was in poor health from 'the xx yere of his age till the xlv yere of his said age'.]

But that notwithstanding he wedded a noble woman, named Ethelwyda, of the which he received two sons, Edward, surnamed

History

the elder, and Egelwarde; and three daughters, Elphleda, that after was Lady of Mercia, Ethelgota, a menchon or nun, and the third, was named Elfrida: the which he caused all, as well daughters as others, to study the art or science of grammar, and to be nourished with all virtue.

And when this Alured was admitted to be King, he well considered the great danger that his land was in. Wherefore he gathered to him his lords and such as he might not win without strife, and he won with great justice and fair hestes.[2] So that he shortly assembled a strong host, and in the second month that he was made king, he met with the Danes beside Wilton, and yielded to them battle, but not without great loss of men on both parties. Then he removed his people, and in sundry places fought with the Danes in that first year six times: by means whereof his people were so sore minished and weakened that he was forced to take peace with his enemies upon covenant that they should avoid the countries and provinces that he had dominion of. Upon which agreement firmly concluded, the

---

[1] Chapters CLXXI–CLXXIII.
[2] *hestes*, behests.

Danes for a time avoided those countries and drew toward London and rested them about that coast the more part of the year following....

About the fifth year of the reign of Alured, the Danes, as affirmeth [the] *Polychronicon*, sailed from Warham toward Exeter, in the which journey they lost six score of their small ships by a tempest in the sea: But some of them occupied the town of Chippenham and the country thereunto adjoining, and chased the Angles or made them as subjects to the Danes. And so sore the power of them augmented, that the Angles lost daily and they increased: And the more by reason of the landing of a prince of the Danes, named Gutteron or Gowthram, which is named King of Denmark.

Alured, being thus overset in multitude of enemies, as affirmeth [the] *Polychronicon* and others, led an uncertain life and uneasy, with few folks about him in the wood country of Somerset- shire; and [he] had right scant to live with but such as he The poverty and his people might purchase by hunting and fishing. of the King In which misery he thus, by a certain time continuing, was by a vision to him showed of Saint Cuthbert comforted, as followeth: Upon a time when his company was from him departed and busied in purchasing of victuals, and he for a pastime was reading on a book, a pilgrim came to him and required him alms in God's name. The King lifted up his hands toward heaven, and said: 'I thank God that of His grace He visiteth His poor man this day by another poor man, and that He will witsafe to ask of me that He hath given to me.' Then the King anon called his servant that had but one loaf and a little whatte¹ of wine, and bade him give the half thereof unto the poor man. The which received it thankfully and suddenly vanished from his sight so that no step of him was seen in the nesche² fen or moor that he passed through. And also all that was given to him was left thereby in suchwise as it was to him given. Shortly after, his company returned to their master and brought with them great plenty of fish that they had then taken.

The night following when the King was at his rest, one appeared to him in bishop's weed, and charging him that he should love God and keep justice and be merciful to the poor men and worship priests. And said, moreover, 'Alured, Christ A vision knoweth thy conscience and thy will, and now will put an end of thy sorrow and care; for tomorrow strong helpers shall come to thee; by whose help thou shalt subdue thine enemies.' 'Who art thou?' said the King. 'I am Cuthbert', said he, 'the pilgrim that yesterday was here with thee, to whom thou gavest both bread and wine; I am busy for thee and thine; wherefore, have thou mind hereof when it is well with thee.' But how he had his Pilgrim in

¹ *whatte,* a certain quantity. ² *nesshe,* marshy.

mind after, by the freedom that he gave with the possessions unto Durham church,* it is well and evidently seen.

Then Alured, after this vision, was well comforted, and showed him more at large, so that daily resorted to him men of Wiltshire, Somersetshire, and Hampshire till that he was strongly companied. Then the King put him in a great jeopardy, as saith William [of Malmesbury in] *De Gestis Regum Anglorum*, for he did[1] on him the habit of a minstrel, and with his instrument of music he entered the tents and pavilions of the Danes; and in showing there his interludes and songs, he espied all their sloth and idleness and heard much of their counsel; and after, returned unto his company and told to them all the manner of the Danes.

Then the King with a chosen company fell upon the Danes by night and distressed and slew of them a great multitude and chased them from that coast. And when the King had thus chased the Danes, by counsel of his knights he builded there a tower and named it, Edelynge, which is to mean in our speech, a tower of noble men....

Thus King Alured, daily pursuing his enemies by help of God and his subjects, which hearing of his victories and manful deeds, drew to him daily out of all coasts, by whose powers and assistance he held the Danes so short that he won from them Winchester and many other good towns, and forced them lastly to search for peace. The which was concluded upon certain covenants, whereof the one and principal was, that their King named, as before is said, Guthrum or Gowthram or, after the *English* [*Anglo-Saxon*] *Chronicle*, Gurmund, should be christened and a certain of his dukes with him. And for[2] the King would have the Danes banished out of the west part of England, he granted to him East Anglia to abide and dwell in. Then this Prince of the Danes, according to the covenants, was christened at Winchester and twenty of the greatest of his dukes. And to this said Danish prince, Alured was godfather at the font-stone, and named him Athelstane.

Conditions of peace

[Some of the Danes refused to accept Christianity and 'sailed into France'. They returned to England in the twenty-first year of Alfred's reign. After desperate fighting, he drove them into Wales.]

It is told of him [Alfred] that he divided the day and night in three parts, if he were not let by war or other great business. Whereof eight hours he spent in study and learning of science; and other eight, he spent in prayer and alms deeds with other charitable deeds; and other eight hours he spent in his natural rest, sustenance of his body, and the needs of the realm. The which order he kept duly by waxen tapers kept by certain persons.

Virtues of Alfred

Thus this martial knight, continuing in all prowess and virtue

[1] *did*, put. [2] *for*, because.

lastly died when he had reigned over the more part of this land by the term of twenty-eight years full. And was first buried at Wilton, and after certain years removed and carried unto Winchester; leaving after him a son named Edward, surnamed the Elder, for the other brother called Egelwarde died before his father.

THE SEVENTH PART: WILLIAM THE CONQUEROR[1]

And when he felt him thus grieved, he called his sons before him, and exhorted them in his best manner that they should charitably love and favour every of them the other, and hold together as loving brethren: and after, [The death of William the Conqueror.] made his testament; and therein ordained William Rufus, or William the Red, to be King of England; and Normandy he beset unto Robert Curthose; and to Henry, his youngest son, he bequeathed his treasure and movable goods. And that done, he informed his two eldest sons of the disposition of both peoples, and warned William to be loving and liberal to his subjects, and Robert to be stern and surdy[2] unto his. Then he was moved with mildness and delivered from prison his own brother [Odo], the Bishop of Bayeux; Marcharus, Earl of Northumberland; Wilnotus, the son of Harold, or after some, the son of Godwin, that was sent to William by Edward the Confessor to remain for a pledge for his said father, Godwin; and shortly after these things, with others done, he died in Normandy and was buried in the city of Caen, when he had reigned as King of England twenty-one years and upon ten months in the month of July, and the year of his duchy, the fifty-second year.

When William was dead, men spoke of him, as they do of other princes, and said that he was wise and guileful; rich and covetous; and loved well to be magnified and praised; a fair speaker and a great dissimulator; a man of skilful stature, but somedeal fat in the belly; stern of face and strong in arms and therewith bold and had therewith great pleasure in hunting and in making of great feasts; but he passed all others in levying of taxes which condition his subjects construed three manner of ways: and said it was to the intent, that he would excel all other in richness, or else for to withstand and defend his enemies, or else to staunch the appetite of his covetous mind.

He builded two abbeys in England, one at Battle in Sussex, where he won the field against Harold, and is at this day called the Abbey of Battle, and that other, he set beside London upon the southside of Thames, and named it Barmoundesaye: and in Normandy he builded other two. Also this man made the New Forest in the country of Southampton. The which to bring about he cast down divers

---

[1] Chapter CCXXIII.   [2] surdy, sturdy.

churches by the space of thirty miles, and replenished it with wild beasts and made hard and sharp laws for the increasing of them, as losing of eyen, and other. And he held Englishmen so low, that in his day was almost no Englishman that bare any office of honour or rule: but yet somedeal he favoured the city of London and granted to the citizens the first charter that ever they had,* the which is written in Saxon tongue and sealed with green wax and expressed in eight or nine lines.

OF KING HENRY THE SEVENTH[1]

Henry VII of that name, son unto the Earl of Richmond, began his dominion over the realm of England the twenty-second day of August, in the year of Our Lord God 1485 and the second year of the [reign of] Charles VIII, then King of France. And the thirtieth day of October following, with great solemnity the said Henry was crowned at Westminster. [This year [1509] upon the Saturday next before Saint George's day, in the night, which Saturday was the twenty-first of April, died the King our sovereign lord at his manor Richmond...].[2] This magnificent and excellent prince, Henry the Seventh, thus paid to death his debt of nature, as before is said, of whom sufficient laud and praise cannot be put in writing, considering the continual peace and tranquillity which he kept this his land and commons in, with also this subduing of his outward enemies of the realms of France and Scotland by his great policy and wisdom more than by shedding of Christians' blood or cruel war, and over ruled so mightily his subjects and ministered to them such justice that not only they loved and dreaded him, but all Christian princes, hearing of his glorious fame were desirous to have with him amity and alliance.

And for that he in all temporal policies and provisions exceeded all princes, by his time reigning: divers popes, as Alexander the Sixth, Pius the Third, and Julius the Second (now being Pope), by their times, either of them sunderly with authority and consent of their spiritual and divine counsellors, elected and chose this excellent Prince and admitted him for chief defender of Christ's Church before all other Christian princes. And for a confirmation of the same sent unto this invincible Prince, by three sondry, famous ambassadors, three swords with three caps of maintenance.

What might I write of the steadfast continency, great justice, and merciful dealing of this Prince! What might I report of his excellent wisdom and most sugared eloquence; or of his immovable patience and wonderful discretion; or what should I tell of his most beautiful buildings; or exceeding charges of manifest reparations, and over all this, of his exceeding treasure and riches innumerable! But, as who

[1] After the *Tabula*, Second Book.
[2] The passage in [ ] is from the 'corrected' edition, printed by W. Bonham in 1542.

would say, to consider in order all his notable acts, which would ask a long tract of time, with also the liberal and sumptuous endowment of the monastery of Westminster, and other, to write, I might conclude that his acts passed all the noble acts of his noble progenitors since the Conquest, and may most congruly[1] above all earthly princes be likened unto Solomon, King of Israel, and be called the second Solomon for his great sapience and acts by him done [and in] his lifetime executed: upon whose soul and all Christians, Jesus have mercy. AMEN.

And so, [as] foresaid, this noble Prince reigned twenty-three years and seven months and one day thereof lacking.

COLOPHON: Thus endeth *The New Chronicles of England and of France*; imprinted by Richard Pynson.... 1516.

JOHN BOURCHIER
c. 1467–1533

John Bourchier, Lord Berners, translator of the Valenciennes chronicler, Froissart, was born in Hertfordshire about 1467, and belonged to a courtly Tudor group who were little affected by the revival of classicism. Berners left Balliol College, probably without taking a degree, to seek a military career. At sixteen he joined the Lancastrian forces in a premature attempt to seize the throne. Finally, when Henry VII was crowned king, Berners rose rapidly in royal favour, signing a contract in 1492 to serve 'the king in his warres beyond the sea' for one year. His military tactics in crushing the Cornish rebellion at Blackheath in 1497 gave him the reputation of a 'martial man, well seen in all military discipline'.

Berners continued to receive royal patronage under Henry VIII, and his career shifted from active military duty to positions at court. After serving on special missions to France, Berners was appointed Chancellor of the Exchequer in 1513, for a short time, and Holbein made a portrait of him in his official robes. On relinquishing the post, the king sent him on several diplomatic missions, particularly to Spain to negotiate a peace with Charles V. He was a member of the retinue of Henry VIII at the Field of the Cloth of Gold in 1519. A year later he was made deputy of the port of Calais.

Life at the port, he complained, was dull, and to avoid idleness, 'the moder of al vices', Berners says that he began the English translations of French and Spanish romances that have brought him lasting fame. At his death in 1533, Berners was hopelessly in debt, and his property was

---

[1] *congruly*, fitly.

confiscated by the Crown. Extant records show that his entertainments at Calais had been lavish. He left considerable personal property. One 'item' concerning the disposal of his library reads, 'in the stody iiij xx books', most of them in Latin and French, and 'iiij pictours'.

Berners's translations include The Cronycle of Froyssart, *in two parts (1523–5)*; Huon of Bordeaux *(1534)*; Antonio de Guevara's *The* Golden boke of Marcus Aurelius *(1535)*; Diego de San Pedro's *Castell of Love [1540]; and* Arthur of lytell Brytayne *[1555].*

It was at the king's 'highe commaundemant', that Berners translated the popular fourteenth-century Chronicle *of Jean Froissart, the troubadour-historian and cleric. Apart from the value of the* Chronicle, *which provided material for Hall, Fabyan, and Holinshed, Berners's translations and prefaces afford some of the most vivid and charming prose of the time. Because of his frequent use of the balanced sentence, his name has been associated with the rise of Euphuism.*

The Chronicle of Froissart

Here beginneth the First Volume of Sir John Froissart of *The Chronicles Of England, France, Spain, Portugal, Scotland, Brittany, Flanders, and other Places adjoining.* Translated out of French into our maternal English tongue by Sir John Bourchier, Knight, Lord Berners, at the commandment of our most high redoubted sovereign lord King Henry the VIII, King of England and of France, and high Defender of the Christian Faith, etc.

THE PREFACE OF JOHN BOURCHIER, KNIGHT, LORD BERNERS, TRANSLATOR OF THIS PRESENT CHRONICLE

What condign graces and thanks ought men to give to the writers of histories, who with their great labours have done so much profit to the human liae? They show, open, manifest, and declare to the reader by example of old antiquity, what we should inquire, desire, and follow; and also, what we should eschew, avoid, and utterly flee: for when we (being unexpert of chances) see, behold, and read the ancient acts, gestes, and deeds, how and with what labours, dangers, and perils they were gested and done, they right greatly admonest,[1] ensign, and teach us how we may lead forth our lives. And farther, he that hath the perfect knowledge of others joy, wealth, and high prosperity, and also trouble, sorrow, and great adversity hath the expert doctrine of all perils. And albeit that mortal folk are marvellously separated, both by land and water, and right wonderously situated, yet are they and their acts (done, peradventure,

[1] *admonest,* admonish.

by the space of a thousand years) compact together by the historio-grapher, as [if] it were the deeds of one self city and in one man's life.

Wherefore I say that history may well be called a divine provi-dence; for as the celestial bodies above complecte[1] all and at every time, the universal world, the creatures therein contained and all their deeds, semblably, so doth history. Is it not a right noble thing for us by the faults and errors of others to amend and erect our life into better? We should not seek and acquire that others did; but what thing was most best, most laudable, and worthily done, we should put before our eyes to follow. Be not the sage counsels of two or three old fathers in a city, town, or country, whom long age hath made wise, discreet, and prudent, far more praised, lauded, and dearly loved than of the young men? How much more then ought histories to be commended, praised, and loved in whom is included so many sage counsels, great reasons, and high wisdoms of so in-numerable persons, of sundry nations, and of every age, and that in so long space as four or five hundred years.

The most profitable thing in this world for the institution of the human life is history. Once,[2] the continual reading thereof maketh young men equal in prudence to old men, and to old fathers stricken in age it ministereth experience of things. More, it yieldeth private persons worthy of dignity, rule, and governance; it compelleth the emperors, high rulers, and governors to do noble deeds to the end they may obtain immortal glory; it exciteth, moveth, and stirreth the strong hardy warriors, for the great laud that they have after they been dead, promptly to go in hand with great and hard perils in defence of their country; and it prohibiteth reprovable persons to do mischievous deeds for fear of infamy and shame.

So thus through the monuments of writing, which is the testimony unto virtue, many men have been moved—some to build cities, some to devise and establish laws right profitable, necessary, and behoveful for the human life, some other to find new arts, crafts, and sciences very requisite to the use of mankind. But above all things, whereby man's wealth riseth, special laud and praise ought to be given to history: it is the keeper of such things as have been virtuously done and the witness of evil deeds; and by the benefit of history all noble, high, and virtuous acts be immortal. What moved the strong and fierce Hercules to enterprise in his life so many great incomparable labours and perils? Certainly, nought else but that for his merit immortality might be given to him of all folk. In semblable ways did his imitator, noble duke Theseus, and many other innumerable worthy princes and famous men, whose virtues been redeemed from oblivion and shine by history. And whereas

----

[1] *complecte*, weave or knit together.   [2] *once*, first.

other monuments in process of time by variable chances are confused and lost, the virtue of history diffused and spread through the universal world hath to her custos[1] and keeper it, that is to say, time, which consumeth the other writings.

And albeit that those men are right worthy of great laud and praise, who by their writings show and lead us the way to virtue, yet, nevertheless, the poems, laws, and other acts that they found, devised, and writ been mixed with some damage, and sometime, for the truth, they ensign a man to lie. But only history, truly, with words representing the acts, gestes, and deeds done, complecteth all profit: it moveth, stirreth, and compelleth to honesty; detesteth, erketh, and abhorreth vices; it extolleth, enhanceth, and lifteth up such as been noble and virtuous; depresseth, poistereth,[2] and thrusteth down such as been wicked, evil, and reprovable. What knowledge should we have of ancient things past, and history were not? which is the testimony thereof, the light of truth, the mistress of the life human, the president of remembrance, and the messenger of antiquity. Why moved and stirred Phalerius, the King Ptolemy, oft and diligently to read books? Forsooth, for none other cause but that those things are found written in books that the friends dare not show to the prince.

Much more I would fain write of the incomparable profit of history, but I fear me that I should too sore torment the reader of this my preface; and also I doubt not but that the great utility thereof is better known than I could declare; wherefore, I shall briefly come to a point. Thus, when I advertised and remembered the manifold commodities of history, how beneficial it is to mortal folk, and eke how laudable and meritorious a deed it is to write histories, I fixed my mind to do some thing therein; and ever when this imagination came to me, I volved, turned, and read many volumes and books containing famous histories. And among all other, I read diligently the four volumes or books of Sir John Froissart of the country of Hainault, written in the French tongue, which I judged commodious, necessary, and profitable to be had in English, since they treat of the famous acts done in our parts, that is to say, in England, France, Spain, Portugal, Scotland, Brittany, Flanders, and other places adjoining; and specially they redound to the honour of Englishmen.

What pleasure shall it be to the noble gentlemen of England to see, behold, and read the high enterprises, famous acts, and glorious deeds done and achieved by their valiant ancestors! Forsooth, and God this hath moved me at the high commandment of my most redoubted sovereign lord King Henry the Eighth, King of England and of France, and High Defender of the Christian Faith, etc., under his gracious supportation to do my devoir to translate out of French

---

[1] *custos*, guardian,   [2] *poistereth*, presses down.

into our maternal English tongue the said volumes of Sir John Froissart: which Chronicle beginneth at the reign of the most noble and valiant King Edward the Third, the year of Our Lord, a thousand three hundred and twenty-six, and continueth to the beginning of the reign of King Henry the Fourth, the year of Our Lord God, a thousand and four hundred: the space between is threescore and fourteen years: requiring all the readers and hearers thereof to take this my rude translation in gre.

And in that I have not followed mine author word by word, yet, I trust, I have ensued the true report of the sentence of the matter; and as for the true naming of all manner of personages, countries, cities, towns, rivers, or fields, whereas I could not name them properly nor aptly in English, I have written them according as I found them in French; and though I have not given every lord, knight, or squire his true addition, yet, I trust, I have not swerved from the true sentence of the matter. And there as I have named the distance between places by miles and leagues, they must be understood according to the custom of the countries whereas they be named, for in some place they be longer than in some other; in England a league or mile is well known; in France, a league is two miles, and in some places, three; and in other countries, is more or less; every nation hath sundry customs.

And if any fault be in this my rude translation, I remit the correction thereof to them that discreetly shall find any reasonable default; and [in] their so doing, I shall pray God to send them the blessings of heaven. Amen.

COLOPHON: Imprinted at London in Fleet Street by Richard Pynson....1523.

'THE TRANSLATOR'
fl. 1513

The first English biography of King Henry V was written about 1513, by a Tudor scholar who refers to himself as 'The Translator'. In the 'proem' he states that his sources were mainly two works which he had translated, 'the one of Titus Livius [Forojuliensis] out of fecund Latin; the other of Enguerrant de Monstrelet out of the common language of France'. These were prime sources for a life of the popular hero-King. Livio's Vita Henrici Quinti *was the official biography written at the request of Humphrey, Duke of Gloucester, brother of Henry V and Protector for the young Henry VI. The Duke brought the Italian humanist to England, in*

*1430, and placed all the official records and documents at his command. The
importance of Monstrelet's* Chronique *lies in his vivid descriptions of the
French campaigns of Henry V.*

*To supplement these authors the Translator took such material as he
needed from Higden's* Polychronicon *and 'divers sayings of the English
chronicles', giving special credence to the now lost report of James Butler,
Earl of Ormonde, a contemporary of Henry V, whom he knew personally;
this may have been the Jacques de Ormond whom the king knighted on
the way to the battle of Agincourt. Ormonde's scholarly tastes are shown
in his commissioning John Yonge in 1423 to translate Aristotle's* Secreta
Secretorum.

*Aware of the inadequacy of the Tudor English vocabulary, the Translator
complained that from 'all practique and famous inditinge, it is farr exiled',
so that he was forced to coin words from Latin and French, many of which
have remained in the language.*

*As a biographer, the Translator's ability is evident in the incidents he
added to round out Livio's account, particularly the stories taken from
Ormonde's report. These include the king's duel with the Sire de Barbazan in
the mines at Melun and the sermon preached before Henry V by St Vincent
Ferrer, the Dominican friar. The authenticity of these incidents is not so
vital in evaluating the historical and literary importance of the Translator's*
Life *as is his use of them to stress the* de casibus *theme which Lydgate had
brought into English in the* Fall *of Princes, and, like Livio's* Vita, *was
also written at the request of Humphrey, Duke of Gloucester. There is no
belittling of the vices or over-praise for the virtues of Hal as prince and
king, the model Christian ruler. His life would serve as an example for all
princes, especially the young Henry VIII.*

The earliest mention of the Translator's Life *was made by Nicholas
Harpsfield in* Historia Anglicana Ecclesiastica *in which he states that
Livio's work had been translated into English 'by one who added some
things of his own, taken, as he says, from the Earl of Ormonde'. Extensive
use of the* Life *was made by Stow, who states he owned a copy of the
Translator's MS. and loaned it to Holinshed, who quotes freely from it in
his* Chronicles. *Though he does not always give the Translator credit,
Holinshed, as Mr Kingsford, the first modern editor of the* Life, *states,
must have 'derived some colouring of opinion', which is evident in his*
Chronicles, *and in turn was caught up by the author of* The famous
victories *of Henry V and by Shakespeare.*

The first English Life of Henry V

[HENRY, SON OF THE BANISHED BOLINGBROKE,
AT THE COURT OF KING RICHARD II]

The Welshmen [were] in esperance by reason of their prophesies that amongst them should be born a prince that should govern the universal realm of England, whose prophecy was accomplished in this most victorious prince, King Henry the Fifth, born at Monmouth in Wales amongst them. This Prince in the exile and time of his father, the Duke of Hereford, was nourished in the King's court right honorably in all things that was convenient for his estate by King Richard the Second, that time King of England.

This Prince Henry in the virtuous passing of his noble youth obtained the favour and love of the King, of all the princes, and also of all other men of every degree of whom he had acquaintance. Of this Prince, the King [Richard II] right often in open audience of the court used to say these words: 'Of the greatest of my house shall be born a child whose name shall be Henry, which for his knightly acts and resplendishing virtues shall be renowned throughout the world.' And of whom he thus prophesied, he verily trusted to be the same Henry. After this when the Irishmen rebelled against the King, this young Henry went in this journey with the King against them, both to learn and exercise the feats of arms.

[KING HENRY IV AND THE SCOTTISH REBELLION]

Whose father when he was returned from exile, after the death of King Richard, as was his right, was preferred to the crown of the realm. And when he after went with armed power to oppress the Scots, which rebelled against him, he left the great substance of his riches and goods in the guard and tuition of this young Prince, his son, whose virtues were marvellously excellent and great.

After this was a great insurrection in the North parts of England made against the King: for the reformation whereof and to subdue those conspiracies unto his obeisance, the King in his person and this young Henry, the Prince, with a great power of armed men went against them to Shrewsbury, where they encountered and met with a great armed power of those seditious people against whom both the King, the father, and the Prince had a right cruel and long battle; wherein the courage and strength of the young Prince Henry appeared marvellously excellent. For in the same battle, as he with a fervent mind fought (peradventure, unwarily) amongst the rebels, he was wounded in the face with an arrow, so sore that they that were there present with him were in despair of his life, wherefore they pained them[1] to withdraw him from the battle. But that noble Prince perceiving their intent gave to them this answer: 'With what stomach', said he, 'shall our people fight, when they see their Prince and King's son withdraw myself, and recoil for fear. Bring me, therefore, wounded as I am, amongst the first and the foremost of our party, that not only by words but also by deeds I may enforce the courage of our men, as it becometh a prince for to do.' That when he was thus brought into the front of the battle, he made upon his enemies a greater assault than before.

They fought long on both parts with great occision[2] of men and with the effusion of much blood. But, at last, our lord Sovereign had the right; Sir Henry Percy, the Earl of Northumberland's son, was slain; Sir Thomas Percy, his uncle, Earl of Worcester, was taken prisoner: Which two lords were the principal captains of those rebellions; after whose death and discomfiture, their conflicts discouraged and in despair of victory left the field and fled. And so the victory of the field remained with honour to the King and his son. ....

[THE YOUTHFUL CAREER AND CHARACTER OF PRINCE HENRY]

For these and many other valiauntises,[3] noble feats, and victories, which God of His infinite goodness daily gave unto him, the Prince was honoured and renowned not only in his realm but also in other realms and quarters. He was also taken of the King, his father, as the first and principal of his country's council; and, as nature appeareth, he was right dear and well beloved of the King until such time as his fame appeared by the sinister report of some evil disposed people which laboured to make dissension between the King and the Prince, his son. By reason whereof and by the acts of youth, which he exercised more than meanly, and for the great recourse of people unto him—of whom his court was at all times more abundant than the King, his father's—the King suspected that he would usurp the crown, he being alive: which suspicious jealousy was occasion that he in part withdrew his affection and singular love from the Prince.

But when this noble Prince was advertised of his father's jealousy and mistrust by some of his secret friends of the King's council, he disguised himself in a gown of blue satin or damask, made full of eyelets or holes, and in every eyelet the needle* wherewith it was made, hanging there by the thread of silk; and about his arm he wore a dog's collar set full of S's[4] of gold and the teretts[5] of the same also

---

[1] *pained them*, took the trouble.   [2] *occision*, slaughter.
[3] *valiauntises*, acts of bravery.
[4] *S's*, the letter S, standing for sorrow(?).   [5] *teretts*, rings or links.

of fine gold. And thus apparelled [and] with [a] great company of lords, he came to the King, his father, who at that time lay at Westminster; where at his coming by his own commandment not one of his company durst advance himself farther than the fire in the hall, notwithstanding, they were greatly and often desired to the contrary by the lords and great estates of the King's court. And that the Prince had commanded so as to give the less occasion of mistrust to the King, his father; but he himself, accompanied of the King's house, only passed forth to the King, his father, to whom, after due salutations, he desired to show the intent of his mind in secret manner. Then the King caused himself to be borne in his chair (because he was diseased and might not go) into his secret chamber; where in the presence of three or four persons in whom the King had his most confidence, he commanded the Prince to show the effect of his mind.

Then the Prince, kneeling down before his father, said to him these words: 'Most redoubted lord and father, I am this time come as your liegeman and as your son natural, in all things to obey your Grace as my sovereign lord and father. And whereas I understand that you have me in suspect of my behaviour against your Grace, and that you fear I would usurp your crown against the pleasure of your Highness. Of my conversation your Grace knoweth that if you were in fear of any man within your realm, of what estate soever he were, my duty were to endanger my life to punish that person, thereby to erase that sore from your heart. And then how much rather ought I to suffer death to bring your Grace, that hath been, and yet be, the most hardy and renowned King of the world, from that fear that ye have of me that am your natural son and liegeman. And to that intent I have this day by confession and by receiving my Maker, prepared myself. And, therefore, most redoubted lord and father, I desire you in your honour of God for the easing of your heart, here before your knees, to slay me with this dagger.' And at that word, with all reverence, he delivered to the King his dagger, saying, 'My lord and father, my life is not so desirous to me that I would live one day that I should be to your displeasure; nor I covet not so much my life as I do your pleasure and welfare. And in your thus doing, here in the presence of those lords and before God and the Day of Judgment, I clearly forgive you my death.'

At these words of the Prince, the King, taken with compassion of heart, cast from him the dagger and embraced the Prince and kissed him, and with effusion of tears said unto him: 'My right dear and heartily beloved son, it is of truth that I partly had you in suspect, and as I now perceive, undeserved on your part; but seeing this your humility and faithfulness, I shall neither slay you nor from henceforth any more have you in mistrust for no report that shall be made unto me. And therefore I assure you upon mine honour.' And thus by his great wisdom was the wrongful imagination of his father's heart utterly avoided, and himself restored to the King's former grace and favour.

[KING HENRY IV ADVISES HIS SON]

I remember also to have heard of the credible report of my said lord and master, the Earl of Ormonde, that this Prince had of his father, the King, divers notable doctrines and insignments,[1] that not only of him but of every prince are to be holden and followed for the prosperity of himself and of his realm and country; which though they be known to every prince that hath governance of lands, yet I trust the hearing and reading of part of them shall not be tedious to any person that hath in such manner charge, but rather profitable, and renew the remembrance of them. Among which eruditions one is this:

The King, lying grievously diseased, called before him the Prince, his son, and said unto him: 'My son, I fear me sore after my departure from this life, some discord shall sourd[2] and arise betwixt thee and Thomas, thy brother, the Duke of Clarence, whereby the realm may be brought to destruction and misery, for I know you both to be of so great stomach and courage; wherefore I fear that he through his high mind will make some enterprise against thee, intending to usurp upon thee, which I know thy stomach may not abide easily. And for dread hereof, as oft as it is in my remembrance, I sore repent me that ever I charged myself with the crown of this realm!'

To these words of the King, the Prince answered thus: 'Right redoubted lord and father, to the pleasure of God, your Grace shall long continue with us and rule us, both. But if God have so provided that ever I shall succeed you in this realm, I shall honour and love my brothers above all men, as long as they be to me true, faithful, and obedient, as to their sovereign lord. But if any of them fortune to conspire or rebel against me, I assure you I shall as soon execute justice upon any one of them as I shall upon the worst and most simplest person within your realm.'

The King, hearing this answer, was therewith marvellously rejoiced in his mind. 'My dear and well-beloved son, with this answer thou hast delivered me of a great and ponderous agony. And I beseech thee and, upon my blessing, charge thee, that like as thou hast said, so thou minister justice equally, and in nowise suffer them not to be oppressed long that call upon thee for justice; but redress oppressions, and indifferently and without delay, for no persuasions of flatteries, or of them that be partial, or such as use to have their hands replenished with gifts; defer not justice until tomorrow, if that

---

[1] *insignments*, directions.   [2] *sourd*, grow.

thou mayst do justice today, lest, peradventure, God do justice on thee in the meantime and take from thee thine authority. Remember, the wealth of thy body and soul, and thy realm resteth in the execution of justice; and do not thy justice so that thou be called a tyrant, but use thyself meanly betwixt justice and mercy in those things that belong unto thee. And betwixt parties do justice duly and extremely [1] to the consolation of thy poor subjects that suffereth injuries and to the punition of them that be extortioners and doers of oppression, that others thereby may take example. And in thus doing, thou shalt obtain the favour of God and the love and fear of thy subjects; and therefore, also, shalt thou have this realm in tranquility and rest, which shall be occasion of great prosperity within this realm, which Englishmen naturally desire; for so long as they have wealth and riches, so long shalt thou have obeisance; and when they be poor, then they be ready at every motion to make insurrections and to rebel against their sovereign lord, for the nature of them is rather to fear the losing of their goods and worldly substance than the jeopardizing of their lives. And if thou keep them thus in subjection, mixed with love and fear, thou shalt have the most peaceful and fertile country and the most loving, faithful, and manly people of the world, which shall be cause of no small fear of thine adversaries.

'My son, when it shall please God to call me to the way decreed to every worldly creature, to thee (as to my son and heir) I must leave my crown and my realm, which I advise thee not to take vainly and as a man elate in pride and rejoiced in worldly honour. But think that thou art more oppressed with charge to purvey for every person within thy realm than exalted in vain honour of the world. Thou shalt be exalted to the crown of the wealth and conversation of thy realm, and not for thy singular commodity and avail. My son, thou shalt be minister to thy realm to keep it in tranquillity and defend it: like as the heart in the midst of the body is principal and chief thing in the body, and serveth to covet and desire that thing that is most necessary to every of thy members, so, my son, thou shalt be amongst thy people, as chief and principal of them to minister, imagine, and acquire those things that may be most beneficial for them; and then thy people shall be obedient to thee, to aid and succour thee, and in all things to accomplish thy commandments; like as thy members labour, every [one] of them in their office to acquire and get that thing that the heart desireth, and as thy heart is of no force and impotent without the aid of thy members, so without thy people, thy reign is nothing.

'My son, thou shalt fear and dread God above all things; and thou shalt love, honour, and worship Him with all thy heart. Thou shalt attribute and ascribe to Him all things wherein thou seest thyself to

[1] *extremely*, fully.

be well fortunate, be it victory of thine enemies, love of thy friends, obedience of thy subjects, strength and activeness of thy body, honour, riches, or fruitful generations, or any other thing whatsoever it be that chanceth to thy pleasure. Thou shalt not imagine that any such thing may fortune to thee by thine act nor by thy desire; but thou shalt think that it cometh only of the goodness of Our Lord. Thus thou shalt with all thine heart praise, honour, and thank God of all His benefits that He giveth unto thee. And in thyself to eschew all vainglory and elation of heart, following the wholesome counsel of the Psalmist, which saith *Non nobis, domine, non nobis, sed nomini tuo da gloriam*:[1] which is this to say: Not to us Lord, not to us, but to thy Holy Name be given laud, joy, and praising.'

These and many other goodly notable demonstrances, admonishments, and doctrines, this victorious King showed unto this noble Prince and son, who with effect ensued and followed them after the death of his father, whereby he obtained grace of Our Lord to obtain great victories; and to many glorious and incredible conquests through the help and succour of Our Lord, whereof he was never destitute. And this sufficeth as to that purpose.

[PERSONAL APPEARANCE AND ACCOMPLISHMENTS OF PRINCE HENRY]

Then to turn to our former purpose and matter. This Prince Henry exceeded the mean stature of men; he was beauteous of visage, his neck was long, his body slender and lean, his bones small.

Titus Livius

Nevertheless he was of marvellous great strength: he was passing swift in running, insomuch that he with two other of his lords by force of running, without any manner of hounds or greyhounds, or without bow or other engine, would take a wild buck or doe at large in a park. He delighted in song and musical instruments.

He exercised meanly[2] the feasts of Venus and of Mars, and other pastimes of youth for so long as the King, his father, lived; by[3] whose life (as I have learned of the credence before rehearsed,

Translator

and also as the common fame is)* accompanied with some of his young lords and gentlemen would await in disguised array for his own receivers, and distress[4] them of their money. And sometimes at such enterprises both he and his company were surely beaten; and when his receivers made to him their complaints, how they were distressed and robbed in their coming unto him, he would give them discharges of so much money as they had lost,

---

[1] Ps. cxiii. 1.
[2] *meanly*, moderately.
[3] *by*, during.
[4] *distress*, rob.

and besides that they should not depart from him without great rewards for their trouble and vexations. And he that best and most manly had resisted him and his company in their enterprise, and of whom he had received the greatest and most strokes, should be sure to receive of him the greatest and most bounteous rewards.

[THE PRINCE SUCCEEDS HIS FATHER AS
KING HENRY V]

His father drawing to his end (and in whom nature had accomplished her course) after the Mass by him devoutly heard, and after due thanks and supplication given to God, gave his bene- diction to the Prince, his son, and so he yielded to God his spirit. After whose death the Prince, as he that should succeed his father in his reign, called to him a virtuous monk of holy conversation to whom he confessed himself of all his offences, tres- passes, and insolences of times past. And in all things, at that time, he reformed and amended his life and his manners. So after the decease of his father was never no youth nor wildness that might have any place in him, but all his acts were suddenly changed into gravity and discretion. _{Titus Livius}

And in that he had grace of Our Lord to accomplish in him that thing that is written of the Archbishop of Canterbury* of whom it is said, *Subito mutatus est in virum alium*, which is to say: He was suddenly changed into a new man.... _{Translator}

The year of Our Lord God one thousand four hundred and thirteen, and of the age of this prince the twenty-sixth year, the ninth day of April was this noble prince King Henry the Fifth crowned and anointed King with all solemnity and pomp, used in the realm of England. And that done im- mediately after Easter, and after that he had catholicly received the Blessed Sacrament of the Altar, and that fealty of all the estates of his realm was given unto him in time convenient, amongst the first acts of his coronation called unto him all those young lords and gentlemen that were the followers of his young acts and had before been most familiar with him to every of whom severally he gave right rich and bounteous gifts, whereby they were all right greatly enhanced in substance. _{1413. Titus Livius}

And then he commanded them that would change their life and conversation in like manner as he intended to do, should abide with him and continue in his court. And to all them that would persevere in their former light conversation he gave express commandment upon pain of their heads never after that day to come to his presence....

And when this noble prince had thus avoided those young and

suspicious company from his presence, he then intended[1] to ghostly and worldly business. And, at first, he commandeth to edify his royal manor* that then was called Shene, and now Richmond, which as yet is known to many men that have seen the same. He also founded two monasteries* upon the Thames, not far from his said manor royal. The one of the religion of the Carthusians, and that he named Bethlehem....

Titus Livius

Polychronicon

And also in the said first year of his reign, he caused the corpse of King Richard the Second to be taken from the earth, whom King Henry the Fourth had intimulate[2] in the Friars of Langley,* and with due observance to be from thence transported into the Abbey of Westminster, where after solemn obsequies for him done, was buried in Saint Peter's Church in the said Abbey on the south side of Saint Edward's shrine by Queen Anne, his wife, as he himself by his life had desired.

[KING HENRY V AT THE BATTLE OF AGINCOURT]

Howbeit all other authors that I have read, recite that he [King Henry V] was lodged that night at Agincourt, but whereso he was lodged, it was not greatly material, inasmuch as all mine authors accord in this point, that the field was fought in a plain adjoining to Agincourt, and for that reason the field beareth the name of the Town.

Translator

The Frenchmen with all their great lords and captains fixed their banners and standards with great joy and mirth with the banner royal, whereof the constable had the conduct and charge, in the field by them devised and chosen, which was in the county of St Paul in the ground of Agincourt, by which, the day following, the Englishmen should pass to go to Calais.

Enguerunt

And that night the Frenchmen made great fires, every man under his banner; and that night the Frenchmen, fishing before the net, played the Englishmen at dice, as if they had been assured of the victory, where, by the purveyance of God, they were disappointed....

Polychronicon

The twenty-fifth day of October, after matins, Masses, prayers, and supplications of the King's priests said and done with all devotion, that most Christian King of England in the morning very early sent forth his host in array. He commanded that his horses and all other carriages and impediments should be left in that village, where he had lodged that night, under the guard and keeping of a few persons; and with him, he took nothing but men's bodies, harness, and weapons. The order of his field was [that]

Titus Livius

---

[1] *intended*, attended.   [2] *intimulate*, entombed.

his own battle[1] was not distant far from another. The middle battle, whereof the King was conductor and wherein he intended to fight, was set in the middle of the field directly against the middle battle of their adversaries. On the right hand or side was the first battle and therewith the right wing. And on the left side, the last battle and the left wing.

And these battles joined nigh together, and, by the purveyance of God, was proved unto the King, which had his special confidence in God and in justice, a defensible place for his host. For the village, wherein he was lodged that night before, defended his host from all hostile invasions on the back; and the field, wherein he was, was defended on both sides with two small rivers.

This noble King was armed with sure and beauteous shining armour, and upon his head was a bright helmet whereupon was set a crown of gold replete with pearls and precious stones, marvellous rich; and in his shield he bare the arms of England and of France. And thus armed, as he that feared not not to be known of his adversaries, he was mounted upon a great and goodly horse, and after him were led certain noble horses with their bridles and trappers[2] of goldsmith's work, marvellously rich, as the manner of kings is. And upon them, also, in the same work were beaten the arms of England and of France.

Thus this most victorious King, prepared and disposed to battle, encouraged his people to the field that approached at hand. And to one great estate of his company, which desired, to the pleasure of God, that every man of war within England were there with them presently, ready apparelled for battle, the King made this answer: 'Truly, I would not that my company were increased of one person more than now it is. We be, as to the regards of our enemies, but a very small number. But if God, in His infinite goodness, favour our causes and right, as we surely trust, there is none of us that may attribute this so great a victory to our own power but only to the hand of God; and by that we shall the rather be provoked to give Him due thanks therefor: and if, peradventure, for our sins we shall be given into the hands of our enemies and to the sword, which God forbid, then the less our company be, the less damage and dishonour shall be to the realm of England; or else if we were in great number and should then have victory of our enemies, then our minds should be prone and ready to pride. And then, peradventure, we should ascribe our victory rather to our own strength than to the hand of God, and thereby we should purchase to ourselves His indignation. But be ye of good courage, and fight with all your might, and God and our right shall defend us and deliver into our hands all this great

---

[1] *battle*, battalion.   [2] *trappers*, trappings.

multitude of our proud enemies that ye see, or at the least the most part of them.'

The night before this cruel battle, by the advice and counsel, as it is said, of the Duke of York, the King had given commandment through his host that every man should provide him a stake, sharp at both ends, which the Englishmen fixed in the ground before them in the field to defend them from the oppression of the horsemen. The Frenchmen had so much their confidence in the great multitude of their people, in their shining armour and beauteous, and in their great and mighty horses, that many of their great princes and lords, leaving behind them their servants and soldiers and, namely, leaving behind them their standards and banners and other ensigns, came towards the Englishmen in right great haste, as if they had been assured of victory. Amongst whom the Duke of Brabant, which for haste had left behind him his banners, took from a trumpeter his banner of arms, and commanded it to be borne before him upon a spear instead of his banner....

The Frenchmen abode in their array without moving until nine or ten o'clock of the day, being ascertained[1], that the Englishmen should not escape their hands, seeing how they exceed[ed] the English host in number. And when they had stood long thus—the one against the other, without doing anything saving that the horsemen of the French host ran divers courses upon the Englishmen, by whose archers they were at all times driven to their host, and that a great part of the short day was thus passed—the King counselled with his wise men what was to be done thereupon. Amongst whom it was considered that long abiding in the realm of his adversaries, where they had no comfort, was unto them perilous and should turn to their great danger, and, namely, because they had scarcity of victuals, and that the Frenchmen being in their own country where they had no enemies, and also they should daily increase in number and in strength.

Wherefore it was concluded by them to go to their enemies, inasmuch as they came not to them. But before the King removed his host, upon surety safely to return, came unto the King three men of France, among whom was the Lord Helley, which before time had been taken of the English soldiers, and was brought as a prisoner into England, from whence, by breaking of prison, he secretly escaped and returned into France.

This lord spake unto the King in this manner: 'Noble King, it hath often been showed unto me, and also to others of our realm, that I should flee from you shamefully and otherwise than a knight should do, which report I am here ready to prove untrue. And if there be any man of your host hardy to reproach me thereof, let him

---

[1] *ascertain*, confident.

prepare him to a single battle. And I shall prove it upon him before thy Majesty, that wrongfully that report hath been imagined and furnished of me.'

To whom the King made this answer: 'No battle shall be here fought at this time for this cause; another time shall be thereto more convenient than this. Therefore return you, and call forth your company to the field before the night approach. And, we trust in God, that like as you, having no regard to the order or honour of knighthood, escaped from us, so this [day] ye shall either be taken and brought to us again, or else by the sword you shall finish your life.'

'Noble King,' said the lord, 'for you I shall not warn my company, nor they shall in nothing attempt your commandment. Both we and you with your host be within the hand of the most Christian King of France, Charles [VI] to whose commandment we shall obey, and not to yours. And we that be his lieges shall come to battle at our own pleasure, and not at yours.'

'Depart you from hence', said the King, 'to your host; and we believe you shall not return with so full speed, but we shall be shortly after you.'

Then these lords departed. And the King forthwith advanced his banners and standards to the French host. And he in his person, with his battle in the same order wherein they stood, following, exhorted and encouraged every man to battle, notwithstanding he went to invade his enemies; yet [he] kept his accustomed order: that is, that the first battle went before; the second battle followed; and the third came immediately after.

He commanded his priests and chaplains to abide in prayers and divine supplications; and his heralds, bearing their coat armours to attain to their offices. Then every Englishman fell prostrate to the ground, and committing themselves to God, every one of them took in his mouth a little piece of earth in remembrance of that they were mortal and earth, or else in remembrance of the Holy Communion. Thus all the carriages and baggages left behind, only charged with their harness, weapons, and staves, they marched toward their enemies with great bruit and noise. Then they began to sound their trumpets and their tabors, which greatly encouraged the heart of every man.

Their enemies, seeing them approach, advanced themselves also, and met with them in the field, betwixt whom was begun a marvellous fierce and cruel battle. The battles of the Englishmen were as long as the field, wherein they fought, would suffer; which was greatly to their advantage, for by that their enemies were letted to come upon them at the sides and back of the host. The Frenchmen had ordained their battles with two sharp fronts like unto two horns, which always backward was broader; and these sharp battles set upon the King's middleward in intent to run through the King's field.

The order and array of the English had been sore troubled of the horsemen of France, if they had not been slain, beaten, and wounded by the bows of England and by the help of the stakes that the Englishmen had fixed before them in the ground, whereby the horsemen were constrained to return, or else they must run upon the stakes, where many of them were overthrown and wounded, and many, both men and horses, slain.

The battle and fight increased marvellously; every man enforced him to be a victor by the space of three hours, by which time without delay or respite endured this mortal battle; no man approached the place of the battle but either he must slay or else he was slain. There no man intended to prowess, but to victory; no man was taken prisoner, but an innumerable company were slain. And when it came to the middle of the field, the Englishmen were more encouraged to slay their enemies than before, as to whom was no trust of life but only in victory. They slew them that came first unto them, upon whose dead bodies [an] innumerable company were [thrown and] slain; and the victory surely remained to the Englishmen.

Thus after a long and cruel battle by the demerits of their great pride there approached no man [of the French] to battle, but only to death: of whom, after that an innumerable company were slain, and that the victory surely remained to the Englishmen, they spared to slay, and took prisoners of the Frenchmen, both princes, lords, and gentlemen [in great number]. In this mortal battle the noble King never spared his body from labour, from perils, nor from fighting; nor he never failed his men for no danger of death, nor for no pain; but he fought with his adversaries with an ardent heart as a famished lion for his prey; in his helmet and in the residue of his armour he received many strokes....

Then the King, assured of this great victory, gave the greatest thanks and laud to God that might be. And because that day the Church solemnized the commemoration of St Crispin and St Crispian (by whose suffrages it seemed him that this great victory was given him of God) and he ordained during his life the commemoration of them to be said daily in the Mass he heard.

The First English Life of Henry V, ed. C. L. Kingsford (Oxford, 1911).

JOHN RASTELL[1]

John Rastell's flair for punning no doubt prompted the title Pastyme of people *(1529), for his brief compilation of world history. The* Pastyme *opens with a prologue that gives the legendary history of England. Though it is inadequate as a chronicle, often sacrificing orderly arrangement of facts for brevity, Rastell included events omitted by other chroniclers, such as the granting of Magna Charta, the deaths of Edward II and Humphrey, Duke of Gloucester, Protector for the boy king Henry VI. Tyrants are denounced with the accustomed vigour of the times.*

True to his trade, Rastell praised the rapid growth of the 'crafte of printynge books'. He foresaw the power of the press, believing it would bring 'great changes, and is lyke to be the cause of many strange things hereafter to come'.

An important feature of the Pastyme *is the boldly drawn woodcuts of each English king from William I to Richard III, whose death closes the chronicle.*

The Pastime of People

The chronicles of divers realms, and most specially of the realm of England, briefly compiled and imprinted in Cheapside at the sign of the Mermaid next to Paul's Gate.

PROLOGUE

It is well affirmed by divers and many historians that after the destruction of Troy, Æneas with his son Ascanius, begotten of his wife, Crusa, daughter to Priam, King of Troy, came into Italy and there married Lavina, daughter to King Latinus, and after the death of Latinus was there king and reigned three years. After whom succeeded his son Ascanius which built the city of Alba in Italy and reigned there twenty eight years. And after Ascanius, reigned Silvius which was born in the woods, and for that cause he was called Silvius, which Silvius was a common name to all the kings that reigned after in Alba. He was, also, by some writers called *Postumus* because that he was born after the death of his father. Of this Silvius there be divers opinions: For some say he was son to Ascanius, and some hold that he was son to Æneas by his wife Lavina, and also some writers hold that Lavina had by Æneas a son called Ascanius. But whether that Ascanius, son to Æneas and Lavina, or Ascanius, son to Æneas and Crusa, was the King of the Latins,

[1] For biographical sketch, see pp. 167–8.

there be divers opinions. But all writers agree that Ascanius was King of the Latins, next after Æneas, and that Silvius reigned next after Ascanius and was the third King of the Latins after King Latinus, of whom Romulus descended, that first builded the city of Rome, and of him took the name of Rome first, as hereafter shall appear in the process of this work.

And, also, of the beginning of the inhabitation of this realm of England, sometime called Britain and before that Albion, there be divers opinions. We read in the English Chronicle that one Diocletian, King of the Syrians, had thirty-two daughters which were married upon one day to thirty-two kings: which women all waxed stubborn and disobedient, so that their husbands complained to their father thereof, which father called them all together and therefore foul rebuked them. But all they, being incorrigible, waxed more froward and by one assent the same night after for anger slew all their husbands and cut their throats. Wherefore the said Diocletian was so sore moved that he intended to put them all to death, but yet by the advice of his council refrained that, and put them all in a ship in the sea, and no other person with them: which women after, by adventure, arrived here in this realm, which then was all wilderness and desolate of people, and called the land Albion, after the name of the eldest sister, called Albion. And after that, the devil taking bodies of the air and man's nature, in other countries shed by pollution, came and lay by those women here and begat of them horrible giants which there continued till the coming of Brutus. But this story seemeth more marvellous than true: and though it hath continued here in England and [is] taken for a truth among us Englishmen, yet other people do therefore laugh us to scorn, and so, meseemeth, they may right well.

And I marvel in my mind that men having any good natural reason will to such a thing give credence; for no man can tell who is the author of this story nor of whom it should come; nor of any writer of name in this land that ever wrote thereof; nor also we read in no histories of any other country of any such King in Syria nor of any such story; which story if it were true, would have been put in writing by some historier in the same country or in some other country, considering that in every country they write of many other things of much less wonder....

But, furthermore, how this land, after that, took the name of Britain, there be divers opinions. Howbeit the common opinion is that Brute, son to Silvius, son to Ascanius, son to Æneas, which came from Troy, was the first that inhabited this land when there was no people here but only giants; which saying we have only of one Galfridus Monemutensis which wrote that story [*Historia Regum Britanniae* (c. 1135)] in the time of King Henry the Second, about the year of Christ 1170, and as it appeareth by his prologue, he directed his book to Robert, Earl of Gloucester, which was uncle to the said King Henry, affirming in the same prologue that one Walter, Archdeacon of Oxford, brought him an old book, written in the Britain speech, which he translated into Latin, comprehending the said story of Brute; albeit, he writeth not the name of the book nor who was the author thereof. But the oldest writing that we read of any author is the book of the *Commentaries* of Julius Caesar which indited the work himself at the time when he conquered this land and made it subject to the Romans, which was forty-eight years before the birth of Christ. In the which he took great diligence to describe the realm, insomuch that he showeth plainly and truly first, the form and fashion of this land and the quantity thereof, how many miles it containeth every way, how the great rivers run, and also he describeth the manner of the use of the people. Howbeit he speaketh nothing of Brute; nor for all the search that he made, he could never come to the knowledge how this land was first inhabited.

Also, Gildas that wrote *De Gestis Britonum*, about the year after the birth of Christ, 600, and, also, holy Bede that wrote *Historia Ecclesiastica Gentis Anglorum*, about the year of Christ, 730, speak nothing that this Brute should be the first inhabitor of this land, sometime called Great Britain, yet Bede writeth precisely in his said book that the first inhabitors of this land that caused it to be called Britain were the Britains that came from little Britain, then called Armorica; and also that the Picts that came from Scythia were the first that inhabited the land of Scotland. Also we cannot find in the chronicles of the Italians nor of the Romans that ever there was any King called Silvius that had any such son called Brutus which should slay his father, as Galfridus writeth. Which thing men think if it had been true, they would have put that in their chronicles as well as they did other things of less marvel, considering that they touch and speak both of Ascanius and of Silvius and of all their children and what became of them and how they ended that succeeded them as kings....

But that, notwithstanding, I will not deny that story of Galfridus nor I will not precisely affirm it; for although that many men suppose it to be but a feigned story, yet I will not let here in this little work to rehearse it somewhat after Galfridus, seeing not only for this cause that I would have every man precisely to believe it, but because that in the same story reading, a man may see many notable examples of divers noble princes that wisely and virtuously governed their people, which may be an example to princes now living to use the same: and also a man reading in the same shall see how that the stroke of God fell ever upon the people, either by battle, dearth, or death, for their vice and misliving: and also how divers princes and great men, exalted in pride and ambition, using tyranny and cruelty or else being negligent in governing of their people or giving themselves to vicious living, were ever by the stroke of God punished for the same. Therefore, according to my promise, I shall briefly rehearse the said story, as hereafter in this process doth appear.

LEAR

Lear, son to Bladud, reigned next. He made the town of Leicester after his name. He had three daughters; and because the eldest daughter Genoril said she loved him better than her life, and the second called Rogane, said she loved him passing all creatures, and the third daughter, called Cordell, said that she loved him as she ought to love her father, he therefore married his eldest daughter to the King of Scotland, and the second, to the Earl of Cornwall, nothing regarding his youngest daughter. And [he] gave his whole realm and land in his life to his two eldest daughters.

But the King of France, called Agampe, heard speak of the beauty and goodness of Cordell, and took her to wife though the father had nothing to give her. After this, Lear sojourned with his eldest daughter awhile, with forty knights and squires waiting on him, so long till that she was weary of him: wherefore he departed thence and went to his other daughter into Cornwall, and there sojourned so long till that she was also weary of him: wherefore he departed privily into France to his youngest daughter which there received him lovingly. And when King Agampe knew how unkindly his two daughters served him, he sent him over again with his daughter and a great people with him, which in strong battle had the victory. And so Lear had his land again, and lived after that three years, and in all reigned forty years.

HENRY THE SIXTH

Henry the Sixth of that name and son to Henry the Fifth, being of the age nine months, was proclaimed King of England, the first day of September, the year of Christ, 1422. Also, in the month of October next, Charles [VI], the French King, died. And soon after that, the corpse of his father King Henry the V was brought over into England and in the sixth day of November with great solemnity buried at Westminster. And then anon after, a parliament was held at Westminster where as well the governing of this young King as of both the realms was provided for. And then the Duke of Gloucester, the King's uncle, was made Protector of England, and the Duke of Bedford, the King's other uncle, was made Regent of France....

King Henry crowned at Westminster

Also, in the eighth year of King Henry, he was crowned at Westminster; and then after that, he passed over the sea into France.

Also, about this time a maiden called Jane, a poor man's daughter in France, came to Charles, the Dolphin of France, whom the Frenchmen called King Charles the VII, and said she was sent to him by God to help to relieve the misery of France. Whereupon they got her armour and accompanied her with knights and soldiers, which went forth and gave many conflicts to the Englishmen and won from them many great towns and holds;[1] and, as some writers say, she, by her providence, caused the said Charles to be crowned King of France at Rheims. But other writers say, he was never crowned till after the death of the Duke of Bedford.

This said maid, called by the Frenchmen, Le Pusell de Dieu or the Maid of God, put the Englishmen ofttimes to the worse. But yet, at the last, she with her company at a place called Compiègne came to remove a siege laid thereunto by the King of Burgundy and the Englishmen, and gave them battle; in the which fight the Frenchmen were discomfit.[2] And there the said maid was taken by a Burgundian knight, and after brought to Rouen where she was by the Englishmen judged to death and burnt.

Le Pusell de Dieu, the Maid of God

Also, in the tenth year [1431] of King Henry, he was crowned in Paris; and after that, he returned into England, leaving the Duke of Bedford, as regent of France, behind him. And about this time was a great blazing star seen in England....

King Henry crowned at Paris

Also, in this twentieth year, ambassadors were sent into Guienne to conclude a marriage between King Henry and the Earl's daughter of Armagnac; which conclusion was put back by means of the Earl of Suffolk, which kindled a great grudge between the lord Protector, Duke of Gloucester, and the said Earl; for the said Earl, the next year after, went over the sea into France and there concluded a marriage between the King and Lady Margaret, the King's daughter of Sicily, for the which marriage there was promised to the King of Sicily, the Duchy of Anjou and the Earldom of Maine.

The King's marriage concluded

Also, about this time the steeple of Paul's church in London was set on fire by lightning....

Also, about this time [1448, twenty-eighth year of the reign of Henry VI] the commons rebelled in divers places of England, and named the captains Bluebeard and other names, and intended to have gathered more company; but, anon, the King's council hearing thereof, caused them to be taken and put to death. But yet, anon after, the commons of Kent arose and made them a captain called Jack Cade; which in a great number came to Blackheath and made a proclamation that they came to reform the injuries of the people done by means of the King's evil councillors. And the King gathered a great people and came toward them

Jack Cade

---

[1] *holds*, forts.　　　　[2] *discomfit*, routed.

to give them battle; whereof hearing, the Captain Jack Cade drew back with his people. And the King went to Greenwich and left part of his host lying upon Blackheath, and sent Sir Humphrey Stafford and his brother with many other gentlemen with a great number of people to follow them. And then nigh Senoke, Jack Cade with his people turned again, and gave them a great battle and had the victory, where the said Sir Humphrey Stafford and his brother were both slain and much other people of his party, and the residue fled.

When tidings came to the King and his council of this, and heard tell that part of his host would take part with Jack Cade, the King removed to Kenilworth; wherefore Jack Cade with his people drew near to London and came in[to] Southwark, and, after, entered over the bridge into the city, and there made proclamation in the King's name, and that on pain of death none of his people should take no victual nor other thing but they paid for it; but Jack Cade himself was the first that broke it.

Also this Jack Cade took the said Lord Saye, that then was prisoner in the Tower, and smote off his head at the standard in Cheape, whereby he got favour of the people of the city; and so continued four or five days in the city, and in the night lay in Southwark; and in that while put to death other persons which favoured the Lord Saye. But at the last, Jack Cade himself went into an alderman's house, called Philip Malpas, and robbed and spoiled his house, and, after, went to another man's house, called Gyser, and dined in his house, and after dinner robbed and spoiled his house of all that ever he had; for which two robberies the citizens of London grudged marvellous sore against him. Wherefore the Mayor and the citizens sent to the Lord Scales and one Matthew Gough, having the rule of the Tower, praying them to have their assistance to resist the Captain; which granted to them their good minds and help.

And the next day when the Captain Jack Cade and his people would have come over the bridge, the Mayor and citizens with the said Matthew Gough kept the bridge; but the Captain and the Kentishmen set so fiercely upon them that they drove them back to the drawbridge, where between them was a cruel fight, and many men of London drowned and slain, for this skirmish continued all night long till the morrow at nine of the clock; and, at the last, the Kentishmen burnt the bridge. And after this, the Chancellor of England sent to the Captain a pardon general for him and all his meany;[1] and then they departed and went every man to his own.

And after that there were proclamations made, that whosoever could take the said Jack Cade alive or dead should have [a] thousand marks for his labour. Whereupon one Alexander Eden, a gentleman

The skirmish upon London Bridge

[1] *meany*, household.

of Kent, took him in a garden; in which taking, the said Jack Cade was slain. And after that, the King came into Kent and caused his justices to sit upon this riot, where many of them, as well in Kent as in Sussex, were therefore put to death. And also in the same year the commons in the west country arose and slew the bishop of Salisbury* [William Aiscough], wherefore the King went thither and punished those doers.

Jack Cade slain

COLOPHON: *Cum privilegio regali.* fol. J. Rastell, 1529.

JAN VAN DVESBORCH
1508–1540?

The strong literary relations between Germany and England in the sixteenth century were due in no small measure to the industrious Flemish printer Jan van Dvesborch or, as he called himself, John of Doesborowe or Doesborch. He was one of the most successful of the Continental printers to enter the English book trade. Other than that Dvesborch was born in Flanders in the town from which he took his name, nothing else is known of his private life. It is thought that he died after 1540, since his press was still busy at that date.

A wide variety of books came from Dvesborch's press, most of them anonymous works by German and Flemish authors—grammars, romances, devotional tracts, medical treatises, humorous tales, and chronicles. Many of them were translated into English, but unfortunately Dvesborch's translators were not well acquainted with the language, and they turned out only crude versions.[1]

Among the few extant English titles from Dvesborch's press, the best known are Mary of Nimeguen *[1518];* Tyll Howleglas *[1510?];* Parson Kalenborowe *[1521]; and* Of the newe lāds *[1520]. Only a fragment of the last tract is extant. It is an anonymous account of a voyage to the New World. Edw. Arber in* The First Three Books on America *states that it is 'perfectly clear that* Of the New Lands *is mainly a compilation from two early Dutch tracts and that most of the woodcuts of the English text had already appeared in its Dutch originals'.*

[1] The description of the three-dimensional positions in the last paragraph, pp. 510–11 is, according to Professor E. G. R. Taylor, a muddled attempt to deal with space relations of people on a globe. If we try to show the relative positions on a meridian circle, they are roughly triangular: the Lisbon people looking over the equinoctial see the 'Armenicans' 'south cornerwise', while if you imagine the Lisbon man upright, the Himalayas can be said to 'hang upon our head' and the 'Armenican's ribs' are towards him. The absence of winds from the north in the 'south lands' is explained by Professor Taylor as an 'assumption that north winds could not cross the equinoctial line'.

Of the New Lands

Of the New Lands: and of the people found by the messengers
of the King of Portugal named Emanuel.

Here, aforetimes, in the year of Our Lord God, 1496, and so be, we
with ships of Lisbon sailed out of Portugal through the commandment of the King Emanuel. So have we had our voyage. For by
Fortunate Islands over the great sea, with great charge and danger,
so have we at the last found one lordship, where we sailed well nine
hundred miles by the coast of Zeland. There we at the last went
a land; but that land is not now known, for there have no masters
written thereof nor it know. And it is named Armenica* [America].

There we saw many wonders of beasts and fowls that we have
never seen before. The people of this land have no king nor lord nor
their God. But all things is common. This people goeth all naked.
But the men and women have on their head, neck, arms, knees, and
feet, all with feathers bound for their beautiness and fairness.

These folk live like beasts without any reasonableness. And the
women be also as common. And the men hath conversation with
the women whosoever that they be or who they first meet, is she
his sister, his mother, his daughter, or any other kindred. And the
women be very hot and disposed to lechery. And they eat also one
another. The man eateth his wife [and] his children, as we also have
seen. And they hang also the bodies or persons' flesh in the smoke,
as men do with us swine's flesh.

And that land is right full of folk, for they live commonly three
hundred years and more, as with sickness they die not. They take
much fish, for they can go under the water and fetch so the fish out
of the water. And they war also upon another. For the old men bring
the young men thereto, that they gather a great company thereto of
two parties and cometh the one against the other to the field or battle,
and slay one the other with great heaps; and now holdeth the field,
they take the other prisoners. And they bring them to death and
eat them. And as the dead is eaten, then slay they the rest, and they
been then eaten also. Or otherwise live they longer times and many
years more than other people, for they have costly spices and roots
where they themself recover with and heal them as they be sick....

We have in this voyage sailed about the fourth part of the world,
for to reckon from Lisbon which is far [from the] equinoctial line
39 grades[1] and one-half, so have we sailed over the line equinoctial
50 grades; that maketh 90 grades. Therefore they of Lisbon is under
that foresaid line 39 grades and one-half. In the high head of the

[1] *grades*, degrees.

Himalayas is the breadth[1] of the west; so is them of Lisbon to these folk [American] to see the 50 grades is over the self[2] line south cornerwise, 5 grades in perpendicular line, which line as we stand right of that point, the Himalayas hang upon our head and these folk in their sides or ribs and were set in the manner of a triangle, or tricantich-cornered. Therefore it must needs be that the south lands be tempered with sweet earth, for the north winds cannot there blow.

COLOPHON: Imprinted by me John of Doesborowe. [1520.]

PETER MARTYR D'ANGHIERA
1459–1526

The most comprehensive work on the discoveries and explorations in the New World was written by Peter Martyr d'Anghiera, historian and geographer, who was born in 1459 in Arona, Italy. Martyr's career began in his native land where he served as secretary to prominent men, including Cardinal Ascanio Sforza. An enticing offer from the Count of Tendilla, a Spanish diplomat, lured Martyr in 1487 to Spain, where he did his greatest work as a military man, diplomat, priest, and author.

Martyr rose from a humble position at the Spanish court to become the trusted adviser of Ferdinand and Isabella; this gave him an opportunity of learning about Columbus's voyages to the New World, and also those of Vasco da Gama, Vespucci, Fernando Cortes, and Magellan. His letters to friends show that Martyr knew some of these men personally, particularly Columbus, to whom he refers as 'Ligurian', which affords proof of the explorer's Italian origin.

In 1518 Martyr was named a member of the Council of the Indies; and because of his own extensive travels to Constantinople and the East, together with his knowledge of the New World through personal contact with explorers, he was later made Councillor and retained the post until his death in 1526. The tablet marking his tomb in the Cathedral of Granada bears the epitaph: 'Rerum aetate nostra gestarum et novi orbis ignoti hactenus illustratori.'

Though Martyr began to write his great chronicle, De Orbe Novo Decades Octo *in 1505, and finished the first three 'Decades' in 1515, sending a copy to Pope Leo X who praised his work and authorized publication, it was not until shortly before his death that the entire eight 'Decades' were*

---

[1] *breadth*, farthest point from the west(?).   [2] *self*, same.

completed. De Orbe Novo Decades Octo *was printed posthumously in Alcala in 1530.*

Richard Eden, who, in 1555, made the first English translation of the Decades, was born in Hertfordshire about 1521, of a well-to-do family. Nothing is known of his early schooling beyond his comment 'when I was a yonge scoler I have read in the poet Hesiodus'. Eden began his studies at Queens' College, Cambridge, in 1535, and it is believed remained there for ten years, coming under the direction of Sir Thomas Smith in 1542. The scientist, Eden wrote, was then 'the floure of the University'. There is no record that he took a degree. He did acquire a lifelong interest in science, most probably encouraged by Smith, a close friend of the Cambridge humanist Sir John Cheke.

Between 1547 and 1552 Eden held several minor positions at court, and in the latter year, possibly through the influence of Cheke, was appointed secretary to William Cecil, later Lord Burghley, retaining the post until the accession of Mary I in 1553. Impressed by the pageantry that followed the marriage of Philip II and Mary, Eden was prompted to commemorate the event 'for all time', and he began his great compilation of travel literature that included Martyr's Decades. This work occupied his time until 1555. During this interim he married, but there are no particulars about it beyond that he raised a large family. Alban Eden, a son, survived him.

Eden's ability as a translator and editor (he edited and revised Thomas Geminus's Compendiosa totius anatomie delineatio, 1559) made him well known in court circles, where he was befriended by Sir William Cecil, who gave him small political commissions that enabled him to continue his translating, especially of Italian works. In 1562 he left England to travel on the Continent. His wife had died, and he entered the service of the French diplomat Jean de Ferrière, remaining with him until 1569, when he returned to London. Eden failed to receive recognition for his work from Elizabeth I or to draw a pension as a Poor Knight of Windsor, and he lived in poverty until his death in 1576.

The first translation made by Eden was Sebastian Münster's Treatise of the new India (1553). It was followed by Martyr's The Decades of the newe worlde or West India (1555), in which volume he included translations of the Italian metallurgist V. Biringuczius's Pyrotechnia and Martin Cortes's The arte of navigation, which contains the earliest outline map of the New World printed in England and woodcuts of various mathematical instruments. Published posthumously were his translations of Ludovico Barthema's Travels in the East (the original printed in 1503), and John Taisnier's The nature of magnets, intended as a complement to a new edition of Cortes's Arte of navigation. An account of the death of Sebastian Cabot is given by Eden in the latter work, and is the only one recorded.

Martyr's Decades embrace thirty-four years of discovery and exploration, beginning with Columbus's first voyage. Eden's translation added to

*the versions already made in the principal languages of Europe; but more
important, it gave impetus to the development of nautical science in
England. And his own views so vigorously and fluently expressed in the
address 'To the Reader' on the necessity of planting Christian colonies in
the New World did much to overcome the nation's timidity and general
apathy toward maritime discovery. Eden's work was carried on by Richard
Hakluyt, who was especially indebted to him for unpublished notes giving
descriptions of Muscovy and the Tartars that form an important section of
the* Principal Navigations *(1598).*

The Decades of the New World

TRANSLATED BY RICHARD EDEN

The Decades of the new world or West India, containing the
navigations and conquests of the Spaniards, with the particular
description of the most rich and large lands and islands, lately
found in the West Ocean, pertaining to the inheritance of the
King of Spain. In the which the diligent reader may not only
consider what commodity may hereby chance to the whole
Christian world in time to come, but also learn many secrets
touching the land, the sea, and the stars, very necessary to be
known to all such as shall attempt any navigations or otherwise
have delight to behold the strange and wonderful works of God
and Nature.

Written in the Latin tongue by Peter Martyr of Anghiera and
translated into English by Richard Eden. *Londini. In aedibus
Guilhelmi Powell. Anno.* 1555.

The Third English Book on America

PREFACE

...But whereas now by the power of Neptune (I wote nere[1] with
what wind) I have been driven thus far from my navigations, I have
thought good to turn my sails and to follow the ordinary
course which I began, and by the example of this worthy *The naviga-*
captain King Ferdinand encourage all others to their *tions of the
Spaniards*
power to attempt the like voyages. As touching the
which, in few words to declare my opinion, if any man should ask
me what I think these things will grow to in time, I will answer as

---

[1] *nere,* not.

doth the author of this book, that when I consider how far our posterity shall see the Christian religion enlarged, I am not able with tongue or pen to express what I conceive hereof in my mind.

Yet one thing I see which enforceth me to speak and lament, that 'the harvest is so great and the workmen so few'. The Spaniards have showed a good example to all Christian nations to follow. But as God is great and wonderful in all His works, so besides the portion of land pertaining to the Spaniards (being eight times bigger than

Italy is 1020 miles in length and 126 in breadth Italy, as you may read in the last book of the second *Decade*) and besides that which pertaineth to the Portuguese, there yet remaineth another portion of that mainland, reaching toward the northeast, thought to be as large as the other, and not yet known but only by the sea-coasts, neither inhabited by any Christian men, whereas, nevertheless, (as writeth Gemma Frisius)* 'in this land there are many fair

The land called Terra Florida and Regio Baccalearum and fruitful regions, high mountains, and fair rivers with abundance of gold and divers kinds of beasts, also cities and towers so well builded and people of such civility that this part of the world seemeth little inferior to our Europe, if the inhabitants had received our religion.

Look the last Book, third Decade They are witty people, and refuse not bartering with strangers.' These regions are called *Terra Florida* and *Regio Baccalearum* or *Bacchallaos*, of the which you may read somewhat in this book in the voyage of the worthy old man, yet living, Sebastian Cabot, in the sixth book of the third *Decade*. But Cabot touched only in the north corner and most barbarous part hereof, from whence he was repulsed with ice in the month of July.

Nevertheless, the west and south parts of these regions have since been better searched by others and found to be as we have said before.

This region is now called Nova Hispania. Some think this city is Quinsai of Marco Polo The chief city in the south-west parts of these regions is called Temixetan or Mexico, in manner, under the circle called *Tropicus Cancri* and strongly defended by the nature of the place. For it standeth in a very great lake, having about it innumerable bridges and buildings to be compared to the works of Daedalus. The inhabitants also can write and read. Some writers connect this land to the firm land of Asia. But the truth hereof is not yet known. And although the Spaniards have certain colonies in that part of this land, that is now called *Nova Hispania*, yet are the people for the most part idolaters.

How much, therefore, is it to be lamented, and how greatly doth it sound to the reproach of all Christendom, and especially to such as dwell nearest to these lands (as we do), being much nearer unto the same than are the Spaniards (as within twenty-five days' sailing

and less), how much, I say, shall this sound unto our reproach and
inexcusable slothfulness and negligence, both before God and the
world, that so large dominions of such tractable people   Look the last
and pure gentiles, not being hitherto corrupted with any   Book of the
other false religion (and therefore the easier to be allured third *Decade*
to embrace ours) are now known unto us, and that we   and the
have no respect neither for God's cause nor for our own   beginning of
                                                             the Book,
commodity to attempt some voyages into these coasts   *Of The*
to do for our parts as the Spaniards have done for theirs,   *Lands Lately*
                                                             Found
and not ever like sheep to haunt one trade and to do
nothing worthy memory among men or thanks before God, who
may herein worthily accuse us for the slackness of our duty toward
Him. . . .

Furthermore, Damian a Goes writeth* in his book *De Deploratione
Lappianae Gentis* [On the lament of the people of Lapland] that
he was the first that moved Erasmus to speak somewhat
hereof: And that he (Erasmus, I mean) was deter-   Damianus
mined to write a just volume of this matter if he had   a Goes
not been prevented by death. 'Albeit', saith Damianus, 'in his
book entitled *Ecclesiastes*, he did not keep silence of so wicked an
ungodliness, which surely is such that it may, in manner, make all
Christian men (and especially such unto whom God
hath given power and knowledge) guilty of so heinous   To the
a crime that He may take vengeance of them in the day   Christian
                                                         princes
of judgment before the just Judge, Christ. Now, therefore (saith he) let the Christian monarchs take heed what accompt
they shall make before the tribunal of Christ at the last day, when
neither favour nor pardon nor flattery can take place to be any
excuse for the loss of so many souls.' And these be the very words
of the worshipful and learned man Damianus a Goes, written to the
Bishop of Rome, Paul the Third* of that name, whom he further
chargeth to look diligently hereunto, as a thing most chiefly pertaining to the office of Christian prelates.

Methink, verily, that the sheep of Europe should by this time be
so well fed that they should, by good reason, be so strong and mighty
in Christ's religion (except they be infected with the
disease which the physicians called cachexia, being an   The sheep
                                                          of Europe
evil disposition of the body whereby the more they are
fed, the worse they like) that many shepherds might well be spared
to be sent to other sheep which ought to be of the same fold. For
this purpose the doctor of divinity, when he commenceth, hath his
scapular cast over his head in token that he hath forsaken
the world for Christ's sake, and his boots on his legs in   The doctor
                                                            of divinity
token that he shall ever be in a readiness to go forward
in preaching the gospel; as, I doubt not, there be many in England

would gladly do, even among these new gentiles if they were thereto
maintained by the aid of the secular power, as in this case it shall be
requisite for the furniture of necessaries hereunto appertaining.

I must now, therefore, appeal unto you, you rich men and rulers
of the world, to whom God hath given goods as things neither good

An admoni-
tion to rich
men nor bad of themselves, but only as they are used well or
evil. If you use them well, they are the gifts of God
wherewith you may do many things acceptable both to

God and men. And if you use them otherwise, you
possess not them, but they possess you, and their canker and rust (as
saith the Apostle) shall be a testimony against you in the Day of the
Great Audit.[1]

Think not, therefore, that this thing pertaineth not unto you if
you pertain unto Christ and look to have any part with Him.

The
merchant Consider with yourselves, if it were only to get worldly
riches, how ready and greedy you would be to venture
a great deal to get a third part without casting of any

peril by land or by sea, as the witty poet Horace hath in few words
described the merchant's desire and adventures to obtain riches:

> *Impiger extremos currit mercator ad Indos,*
> *Per mare pauperiem fugiens, per saxa, per ignes.*[*]

The which verses are thus, to say in effect:

> The merchant in hope great riches to find,
> By fire and by water passeth to Inde,
> By the burnt line or equinoctial,
> To fly from poverty and hazard all.

As the poet hath in these verses, by the merchant declared the desire
that covetous men have to obtain slippery riches, the like affection

The desire
of worldly
fame to obtain worldly fame and honour may we see in valiant
and noble captains in the wars where they contend to
put themselves forward to the most dangerous adventure

as to have the forward of the battle, a token surely of
much nobility and manly courage. But O immortal God! Is it not
to be lamented that men can be so valiant, stout, and, in manner,
desperate in their own private matters, pertaining only to their

Men are
slothful in
God's cause bodies, and yet so cold, negligent, and fearful in God's
cause and things touching the health of their souls! If
there were neither devil nor law to accuse men before

God in this case, shall not their own conscience be a law
of condemnation against them in that they have not showed that
love to mankind, which the very law of nature moveth brute beasts

[1] James v. 1–3.

to show one to another in their generations. But what hope is there (except God would, in manner, by miracle convert the hearts of such men), what hope is there, I say, that they will depart with any of their goods, much less adventure their bodies to the furtherance of Christ's religion in these regions, being so far from them, whereas many show little love, charity, or liberality (if not rather cruelty, tyranny, and oppression) to their poor neighbours and brethren dwelling even at home at their own elbows.

But as this covetousness is to be reproved, so is the liberality of such to be commended as have been at great cost and charges in setting forward such voyages: wherein not only the merchants of London, but also divers noblemen and gentlemen, as well of the council as others, which both with their money and furtherance otherwise have furnished and sent forth certain ships for the discovering of such lands and regions as were heretofore unknown, have herein deserved immortal fame, forasmuch as in such attempts and dangerous voyages, they have showed no small liberality upon uncertain hope of gain: wherein they have deserved so much the greater praise as their intent seemed to be rather to further honest enterprises than for respect of vantage. *Voyages from England*

And here certainly in the mention of these voyages I might seem ungrateful if I should omit to give due commendation to the two chief captains of the same, as the worthy knight Sir Hugh Willoughby and the excellent pilot Richard Chancellor who have therein adventured their lives for the commodity of their country—men doubtless worthy for their noble attempts to be made Knights of the Ocean or otherwise preferred, if ever God send them home again although they fail of their purpose. For as such [men] have obtained absolute glory that have brought great things to pass, so have they deserved immortal fame which have only attempted the same: forasmuch as fortune (who sometimes favoreth the unworthiest) is not in the power of man.... *Sir Hugh Willoughby and Richard Chancellor* *Glory and fame*

And, surely, if ever since the beginning of the world any enterprise have deserved great praise as a thing achieved by men of heroical virtue, doubtless there was never any more worthy commendation and admiration than is that which our nation have attempted by the north seas to discover the mighty and rich empire of Cathay, by which voyage not only gold, silver, precious stones, and spices may be brought hither by a safer and shorter way, but also much greater matters may hereof ensue in time if it shall please God to give unto Christian men such passage into those regions, whereby such familiarity may further grow between the Christian princes of Europe and the great *The voyage to Cathay by the north seas* *Society between the Tartars and the Christians. The Turk. The Sophie* emperor of Cathay that, as writeth Hayton* [in] 'De Societate Christianorum et Tartarorum', there can nothing be imagined more effectual for the confusion of the Turk if the Great Khan of Cathay and the Sophie[1] of Persia on the one side and the Christian princes on the other side should with one consent invade his dominions.

[Imprint is on the title-page.]

ST THOMAS MORE[2]

Sir Thomas More possibly wrote The Historie of Kyng Rycharde the Third *about 1513. It is only a fragment, written partly in Latin and English, of a proposed history of the early Tudor period, ending with the death of Henry VII. The delineation of the character of the 'ill-featured' King as an arch-tyrant has a factual basis, but it shows as well the humanist influence of Grocyn and Colet, obliging More to point a moral and warn the state, less subtly than in* Utopia, *of the evils that spring from misgovernment.*

In More's portrait of Richard III there are reflections of Lucian's Dialogi, *the* Contemptu Mundi *of Innocent III, Boccaccio's* De Casibus Virorum Illustrium, *and Erasmus's* Moriae Encomium.

The History of King Richard the Third

The History of King Richard the Third [Unfinished] Written by Master Thomas More, then one of the Under-sheriffs of London, about the year of Our Lord 1513. Which work hath been before this time printed, in Hardyng's *Chronicle* and in Hall's *Chronicle*, but very much corrupt in many places, sometimes having less, and sometimes having more, and altered in words and whole sentences: much varying from the copy of his own hand by which this is printed.

THE DESCRIPTION OF RICHARD THE THIRD

Richard, the third son, of whom we now entreat, was in wit and courage equal with either of them [his brothers Edward IV and George, Duke of Clarence]; in body and prowess far under them both, little of stature, ill-featured of limbs, crook-backed, his left

---

[1] *Sophie*, a former title of the supreme ruler of Persia; the shah.
[2] For biographical sketch, see pp. 64–6.

shoulder much higher than his right, hard-favoured of visage, and such as in states[1] called warlike, in other men otherwise; he was malicious, wrathful, envious, and from afore his birth ever froward.

It is for truth reported that the Duchess, his mother, had so much ado in her travail that she could not be delivered of him uncut; and that he came into the world with the feet forward, as men be born outward, and (as the fame runneth) also not untoothed—[but it is a question] whether men of hatred report above the truth, or else that nature changed her course in his beginning, which in the course of his life many things unnaturally committed.

None evil captain was he in the war, as to which his disposition was more meetly than for peace. Sundry victories had he, and sometimes overthrows, but never in default as for his own person, either of hardiness or politic order. Free was he called of dispense and somewhat, above his power, liberal—with large gifts he got him united fast friendship, for which he was fain to pill[2] and spoil in other places and get him steadfast hatred.

He was close and secret, a deep dissimulator, lowly of countenance, arrogant of heart, outwardly compinable[3] where he inwardly hated, not letting to kiss whom he thought to kill; despiteous and cruel, not for evil will always, but ofter for ambition, and either for the surety or increase of his estate. Friend and foe was muchwhat indifferent; where his advantage grew, he spared no man's death whose life withstood his purpose. He slew with his own hands King Henry the Sixth, being prisoner in the Tower, as men constantly say, and that without commandment or knowledge of the King [Edward IV], which would, undoubtedly, if he had intended that thing, have appointed that butcherly office to some other than his own born brother.

Some wise men also ween that his drift,[4] covertly conveyed, lacked not in helping forth his brother Clarence to his death: which he resisted openly, howbeit somewhat (as men deemed) more faintly than he that were heartily minded to his wealth.[5] And they that thus deem, think that he, [for a] long time in King Edward's life, forethought to be king in case that the King, his brother, (whose life he looked that evil diet should shorten) should happen to decease (as indeed he did) while his children were young. And they deem that for this intent he was glad of his brother's death, the Duke of Clarence, whose life must needs have hindered him so intending, whether the same Duke of Clarence had kept him true to his nephew, the young King, or enterprised to be king himself. But of all this point is there no certainty, and whoso divineth upon conjectures may as well shoot too far as too short.

---

[1] *in states*, among lords. [2] *pill*, pillage. [3] *compinable*, sociable.
[4] *drift*, scheme. [5] *wealth*, well-being.

THE PROTECTOR TAKETH UPON HIM TO BE KING

But when he [Richard III] saw there was none other way but that either he must take it [the crown] or else he and his both go from it, he said unto the lords and commons: 'Since we perceive well that all the realm is so set, whereof we be very sorry that they will not suffer in anywise King Edward's line to govern them, whom no man earthly can govern against their wills, and we well also perceive that no man is there to whom the crown can by so just title appertain as to ourself as very right heir—lawfully begotten of the body of our most dear father, Richard, late Duke of York, to which title is now joined your election, the nobles and commons of this realm, which we, of all titles possible, take for most effectual—we be content and agree favourably to incline to your petition and request; and, according to the same, here we take upon us the royal estate, pre-eminence, and kingdom of the two noble realms, England and France: the one, from this day forward by us and our heirs to rule, govern, and defend; the other, by God's grace and your good help, to get again and subdue and establish forever in due obedience unto this realm of England, the advancement whereof we never ask of God longer to live than we intend to procure.'

With this there was a great shout, crying, 'King Richard! King Richard!' And then the lords went up to the king (for so was he from that time called), and the people departed, talking diversely of the matter, every man as his fantasy gave him....

‡ The next day the Protector, with a great train, went to Westminster Hall, and there when he had placed himself in the Court of the King's Bench, declared to the audience that he would take upon him the crown in that place there, where the king himself sitteth and ministreth the law, because he considered that it was the chiefest duty of a king to minister the laws. Then with as pleasant an oration as he could, he went about to win unto him the nobles, the merchants, the artificers, and, in conclusion, all kind of men, but especially the lawyers of this realm.

This that is here, between this mark‡ and this mark★ was not written by Master More in this *History* written by him in English, but is translated out of this *History* which he wrote in Latin

And, finally, to the intent that no man should hate him for fear, and that his deceitful clemency might get him the good will of the people, when he had declared the discommodity of discord and the commodities of concord and unity, he made an open proclamation that he did put out of his mind all enmities, and that he there did openly pardon all offences committed against him. And to the intent that he might show a proof thereof, he commanded that one Fogg, whom he had long deadly hated, should be brought then before him; who being brought out of the sanctuary [near] by (for thither had he fled, for fear of him) in the sight of the people, he took him by the hand. Which thing the common people rejoiced at and praised, but wise men took it for vanity. In his return homeward, whomsoever he met, he saluted. For a mind that knoweth itself guilty, is, in a manner, dejected to a servile flattery.

When he had begun his reign, the [26th] day of June [1483], after this mockish election, then he was crowned the [6th] day of the same month [actually July]. And that solemnity was furnished for the most part with the selfsame provision that was appointed for the coronation of his nephew.*

Now fell there mischiefs thick. And as the thing evil gotten, is never well kept, through all the time of his reign never ceased there cruel death and slaughter, till his own destruction ended it. But as he finished his time with the best death and the most righteous, that is to wit his own, so began he with the most piteous and wicked, I mean the lamentable murder of his innocent nephews, the young King and his tender brother, whose death and final infortune hath nonetheless so far come in question that some remain yet in doubt whether they were in his days destroyed or no: [and] not for that only that Perkin Warbeck, by many folks' malice and more folks' folly, so long space abusing the world, was, as well with princes as the poorer people, reputed and taken for the younger of those two, but for that also that all things were, in late days, so covertly demeaned, one thing pretended and another meant, that there was nothing so plain and openly proved, but that yet, for the common custom of close and covert dealing, men had it ever inwardly suspect, as many well counterfeited jewels make the true mistrusted.

Perkin Warbeck

Close dealing is ever suspected

Howbeit, concerning that opinion, with the occasions moving either party, we shall have place more at large to entreat if we hereafter happen to write the time of the late noble prince of famous memory, King Henry the Seventh, or, percase, that history of Perkin in any compendious process by itself. But, in the meantime, for this present matter, I shall rehearse you the dolorous end of those babes, not after every way that I have heard, but after that way that I have so heard by such men and such means as methinketh it were heard, but it should be true.

THE YOUNG KING AND HIS BROTHER MURDERED

King Richard after his coronation, taking his way to Gloucester to visit in his new honour the town of which he bare the name of his old, devised as he rode to fulfil that thing which he before had intended. And forasmuch as his mind gave[1] him, that his nephews living, men would not reckon that he could have right to the realm, he thought therefore without delay to rid them, as though the killing of his kinsmen could amend his cause and make him a kindly king. Whereupon he sent one John Green, whom he specially trusted, unto Sir Robert Brackenbury, constable of the Tower, with a letter and credence also, that the same Sir Robert should in any wise put the two children to death.

This John Green did his errand unto Brackenbury, kneeling before Our Lady in the Tower; who plainly answered that he would never put them to death, to die therefor: with which answer John Green, returning, recounted the same to King Richard at Warwick, yet in his way.

Wherewith he took such displeasure and thought that the same night he said unto a secret page of his: 'Ah, whom shall a man trust? Those that I have brought up myself, those that I had weened would more surely serve me, even those fail me and at my commandment will do nothing for me.'

'Sir,' quoth his page, 'there lieth one on your pallet without, that, I dare well say, to do your grace pleasure, the thing were right hard that he would refuse'—meaning by this, Sir James Tyrell, which was a man of right goodly personage and for nature's gifts worthy to have served a much better Prince, if he had well served God and by grace obtained as much truth and good will as he had strength and wit. The man had an high heart and sore longed upward, not rising yet so fast as he had hoped, being hindered and kept under by the means of Sir Richard Ratcliff and Sir William Catesby, which longing for no more partners of the Prince's favour, and, namely, not for him whose pride they wist would bear no peer, kept him by secret drifts out of all secret trust. Which thing this page well had marked and known.

Authority loveth no partners

Wherefore, [as] this occasion offered, of very special friendship he took his time to put him forward and by such wise do him good that all the enemies he had, except the devil, could never have done him so much hurt. For upon this page's words King Richard arose (for this communication had he sitting at the draught,[2] a convenient carpet for such a counsel) and came out into the pallet chamber, on which he found in bed Sir James and Sir Thomas Tyrell, of person like and brethren of blood, but nothing of kin in conditions. Then said the King merely to them: 'What, Sirs, be ye in bed so soon!' and calling up Sir James, broke to him secretly his mind in this mischievous matter; in which he found him nothing strange. Wherefore, on the morrow, he sent him to Brackenbury with a letter, by which he was commanded to deliver Sir James all the keys of the Tower for

---

[1] *gave*, suggested. [2] *draught*, privy.

one night, to the end he might there accomplish the King's pleasure in such thing as he had given him commandment.

After which letter delivered and the keys received, Sir James appointed the night next ensuing to destroy them, devising before and preparing the means. The Prince, as soon as the Protector left that name and took himself as King, had it showed unto him that he should not reign, but his uncle should have the crown. At which word the Prince, sore abashed, began to sigh, and said: 'Alas, I would my uncle would let me have my life, yet, though I lose my kingdom.' Then he that told him the tale, used him with good words and put him in the best comfort he could. But forthwith was the Prince and his brother both shut up; and all others removed from them; only one, called Black Will or William Slaughter except, set to serve them and see them sure.

After which time the Prince never tied his points[1] nor aught wrought of himself, but with that young babe his brother lingered in thought and heaviness till this traitorous death delivered them of that wretchedness. For Sir James Tyrell devised that they should be murdered in their beds. To the execution whereof, he appointed Miles Forest, one of the four that kept them, a fellow fleshed[2] in murder beforetime. To him he joined one John Dighton, his own horsekeeper, a big, broad, square, strong knave. Then all the others being removed from them, this Miles Forest and John Dighton about midnight (the sely[3] children lying in their beds) came into the chamber and suddenly lapped them up among the clothes, and so bewrapped them and entangled them, keeping down by force the feather-bed and pillows hard unto their mouths that within a while, smothered and stifled, their breath failing, they gave up to God their innocent souls into the joys of heaven, leaving to the tormentors their bodies dead in the bed. Which after that the wretches perceived, first by the struggling with the pains of death, and after long lying still, to be thoroughly dead: they laid their bodies naked out upon the bed, and fetched Sir James to see them. Which upon the sight of them, caused those murderers to bury them at the stair foot, meetly deep in the ground under a heap of stones.

Then rode Sir James in great haste to King Richard, and showed him all the manner of the murder, who gave him great thanks, and, as some say, there made him knight. But he allowed not, as I have heard, the burying in so vile a corner, saying that he would have them buried in a better place because they were a King's sons. Lo, the honourable courage of a King!...

---

[1] *points*, laces with tags for tying up hose.   [2] *fleshed*, initiated.
[3] *sely*, innocent.

THE OUT AND INWARD TROUBLES OF TYRANTS

King Richard himself, as ye shall hereafter hear, [was] slain in the field, hacked and hewn of his enemies' hands, harried on horseback dead, his hair in despite torn and tugged like a cur dog. And the mischief that he took within less than three years of the mischief that he did, and yet all the meantime spent in much pain and trouble outward, much fear, anguish, and sorrow within. For I have heard by credible report of such as were secret with his chamberers, that after this abominable deed done, he never had quiet in his mind, he never thought himself sure. Where he went abroad, his eyes whirled about, his body privily fenced, his hand ever on his dagger, his countenance and manner like one always ready to strike again; he took ill rest at night, lay long, waking and musing, sore wearied with care and watch, rather slumbered than slept, troubled with fearful dreams, suddenly sometime start up, leap out of his bed and run about the chamber: so was his rest less heart continually tossed and tumbled with the tedious impression and stormy remembrance of his abominable deed.

COLOPHON: Imprinted at London in Fleetstreet at the sign of the hand and star, at the cost and charge of John Cawod, John Malley, and Richard Tottle....1557.

EDWARD HALL
1498?–1547

The foremost chronicler of the beginnings of the Tudor dynasty, namely, the houses of Lancaster and York, was Edward Hall, born about 1498, the son of a distinguished Shropshire couple, John and Catherine Hall. He received his early training at Eton, and went on to King's College, Cambridge, where in 1518 he took a Bachelor of Arts degree.

After completing his law studies at Gray's Inn, Hall entered politics; in 1532 he was made common serjeant of London and soon after a judge in the Sheriff's court. His strong sympathies with the Reformers won Hall the position of London Commissioner for the suppression of heresy, and for his loyalty to Henry VIII he received a grant of abbey lands. At the time of his death in 1547 he was a member of Parliament for Bridgenorth.

Hall's only known work is his chronicle, The union of the two noble and illustrious families Lancaster and York, *which he left unfinished. The first edition was printed, in 1542, by Thomas Berthelet, but only a fragment remains. A second edition was printed by Richard Grafton in 1546, and was followed by two more in 1550 and 1552(?). Latin verses for the pageant were composed by William Lily. An*

anonymous English version of them was printed by Pynson, Of the
tryumphe, and the verses that themperour & the kyng of England
were saluted with, etc. [*1522?*].

*The extreme bias which Hall shows at times for the policies of Henry VIII,
so that he has been called the king's panegyrist, has lessened the chronicle's
historical value, but does not detract from his competence as a narrator. One
of his earliest critics was Roger Ascham, who disliked Hall's 'indenture
English'. But he was praised by others as having a 'masculine style'.
Grafton, Stow, and Holinshed made free use of Hall's chronicle.*

The Union of Lancaster and York

*The Union of the two Noble and Illustrious Families Lancaster
and York,* being long in continual dissension for the crown
of this noble realm, with all the acts done in both the times
of the Princes—both of the one lineage and of the other—
beginning at the time of King Henry the Fourth, the first author
of this dissension, and so successively proceeding to the reign of
the high and prudent prince King Henry the Eighth, the in-
dubitable flower and very heir of both the said lineages.

THE THIRD YEAR OF KING HENRY THE VIII[1]

The King this year kept the feast of Christmas at Greenwich, where
was such abundance of viands served to all comers of any honest
behaviour as hath been few times seen. And against New Year's
night was made in the hall a castle, gates, towers, and dungeon,
garnished with artillery and weapon after the most warlike fashion:
and on the front of the castle was written *Le Fortresse Dangerus;* and
within the castle were six ladies, clothed in russet satin, laid all over
with leaves of gold, and every owde[2] knit with laces of blue silk and
gold, [and] on their heads, coifs and caps all of gold.

After this castle had been carried about the hall, and the Queen
had beheld it, in came the King with five others, apparelled in coats,
the one half of russet satin, spangled with spangles of fine gold; the
other half, rich cloth of gold, [and] on their heads caps of russet
satin, embroidered with works of fine gold bullion. These six
assaulted the castle; the ladies seeing them so lusty and courageous
were content to solace with them, and upon farther communication
to yield the castle; and so they came down and danced a long space.
And, after, the ladies led the knights into the castle, and then the
castle suddenly vanished out of their sights.

On the day of the Epiphany, at night, the King with eleven others

[1] 1511-12.   [2] *owde*, seam(?).

were disguised after the manner of Italy, called a mask, a thing not seen afore in England; they were apparelled in garments long and broad, wrought all with gold, with visors and caps of gold: and after the banquet done, these maskers came in with six gentlemen, disguised in silk, bearing staff torches, and desired the ladies to dance; some were content, and some that knew the fashion of it refused, because it was not a thing commonly seen. And after they danced and commoned together, as the fashion of the masks is, they took their leave and departed; and so did the Queen and all the ladies.

THE FOURTEENTH YEAR OF KING HENRY THE VIII[1]

The King had perfect knowledge that Charles [V] the Emperor would be at the King's town at Calais, the twenty-third day of May, to pass through England into Spain, wherefore the King sent the Marquis Dorset, accompanied with divers knights and gentlemen, to receive him at Calais, which in all haste sped him thither. Likewise the Cardinal [Wolsey] took his journey toward Dover, the twentieth day of May, and rode through London, accompanied with two earls, thirty-six knights, and a hundred gentlemen, eight bishops, ten abbots, thirty chaplains, all in velvet and satin, and yeomen seven hundred; and so by journeying he came to Dover, the 26th day being Monday.

In the mean season, tidings were brought to the King, that the French King [Francis I] had sent a great army toward Calais, and the men of war lay at Abbeville, Montreuil, Boulogne, and about, near the English pale. Wherefore the King, like a Prince that foresaw all and intending not to be desceived, wrote to his nobles and cities and towns to prepare certain men of war in a readiness, which was shortly done, and they were sent to the navy, so that they might shortly be at Calais if need required. . . .

On Friday, the sixth day of June, the King and the Emperor with all their companies marched toward London, where, in the way, a mile from Saint George's Bar, was set a rich tent of cloth of gold; in which tent were two lodgings, one, for the Emperor and another, for the King, where these two Princes shifted them. And when the heralds had appointed every man their room, then every man set forward in order, richly apparelled in cloth of gold, tissue, silver, tinsel, and velvet of all colours.

There lacked no massive chains, nor curious collars: an Englishman and a stranger rode ever together, matched according to their degrees: before the Emperor and the King were borne two swords naked, then the two Princes followed in coats of cloth of gold, embroidered with silver, both of one suit: after them followed the

[1] 1522-3.

King's henchmen in coats of purple velvet, piled and panned[1] with rich cloth of silver, and with them were matched the Emperor's henchmen, in equal number, in coats of crimson velvet with two guards, the one, gold and the other, silver: then followed the captains of the guards, then the Emperor's guard on the right hand, and the English guard on the left hand, and so in this order they went forward; and, in the way, the Mayor, John Milborne, and his brethren, in fine scarlet and well horsed, met with the Emperor and the King, where one Sir Thomas More, Knight, and well learned, made to them an eloquent oration in the praise of the two Princes, and of the peace and love between them, and what comfort it was to their subjects to see them in such amity, and how that the Mayor and citizens offered any pleasure of service that in them lay, next their sovereign lord.

When this was done, they came into Southwark where the clergy received them in copes, with crosses and censers, and so kept the one side of the street all the city through. When they came by the Marshalsea at the King's Bench, the Emperor desired pardon of the King for the prisoners; and he at the Emperor's request pardoned a great number of them. When they were almost at the bridge foot, there was a stay: the King demanded the cause, and it was told him that the heralds had appointed two gentlemen to ride together, one was the ambassador from the Marquis of Mantua to the Emperor, and the other, from the city of Siena to the Emperor, also; and the city and the Marquis were not friends. The Emperor, incontinent, sent his lord chamberlain to them saying, that if they would that day do him honour, he would thank them; and if they would not ride as they were appointed, he prayed them to depart. When the lord chamberlain had told this message, they rode forth and made no more courtesy.

When they were come to the drawbridge, there were set targets of the arms of the Emperor and his dominions richly painted, and on the other side stood one great giant representing Hercules with a mighty club in his hand, and on the other side stood another giant representing Sampson with the jaw bone of an ass in his hand. These two giants held a great table in the which was written in golden letters all the Emperor's stile.[2] From the drawbridge these two princes passed to the middle of the bridge, where was raised a fair edifice with towers embattled and gates all like masonry of white and black—like touche[3] and white marble; above this building was a fair pageant in the which stood Jason all in harness, having before him a golden Fleece, and on the one side of him stood a fiery dragon, and on the other side stood two bulls which beasts cast out fire continually; and in a tower, on the one side, stood a fair maid,

---

[1] *panned*, embossed.   [2] *stile*, title.   [3] *touche*, black granite.

representing the lady Medea which was very strangely and richly apparelled, and above this pageant were written these verses:

> *Laetitiae quantum Minyis praebebat, Iason*
> *Aurea Phrixeae vellera nactus ovis*
> *Laetitiae quantum tulerat Pompeius, et urbi,*
> *Hoste triumphato, Scipio Romulidum*
> *Tantum tu nobis, Caesar mitissime Princeps,*
> *Intrans Henrici principis hospitium.*

> [What great joy was it to the people of Minyis,
> What time the high renowed knight Jason
> Had conquered in Colchis the golden fleece!
> What joy, eke, was the triumph of Scipion!
> And of him, Pompey to the Romans each one!
> Like joy to us, Charles, Prince of clemency,
> Is at thy coming with puissant King Henry.]

When they had beheld this pageant, they came to the conduit at Gracious street where was made a Bastille with two great gates, one on the side of the way and the other on the other side, and over these gates and between these gates were made three great towers embattled and vaulted with loops and lacunars, like masonry, curiously wrought; and in the middle tower was a cloth of estate under which sat one, representing the Emperor, and in the third tower, representing the King. And Charlemagne, having two swords, gave to the Emperor the sword of Justice, and to the King the sword of triumphant Victory, and before him sat the Pope to whom he gave the Crown of Thorns and Three Nails. About this pageant were set all the arms of the Electors of the Empire and these verses in a table:

> *Carole Christigenum decus et quem scripta loquuntur*
> *A magno ductum Carolo habere genus,*
> *Tuque Henrice pia virtutis laude refulgens,*
> *Doctrina ingenio religione fide....*

> [Charles, clear lamp of Christian nation,
> Of thee it is spoken plainly in writing,
> Of great Charles to have generation.
> And, eke, thou, Henry, our sovereign lord and king,
> Thy great laud of sweet virtue so bright shining.
> High doctrine, wisdom, faith and religion
> Doth excel the fortune of kings each one....]

This pageant was made by the Easterlings.

From Gracious street where the Easterlings stood in good order, the two Princes came to Leden Hall where overthwart the great street that leadeth to Bishop's gate was erected a goodly pageant, wonderfull [and] curiously wrought; it was thirty-eight feet broad and eighty of length. At the foot of the pageant sat John, Duke of Lancaster, called John of Gaunt, son to King Edward the Third. This duke sat in a root, and out of the root sprang many branches curiously wrought with leaves which by policy dropped sweet water; and on every branch sat a king and a queen, or some other noble personage, descended of the said duke, to the number of fifty-five images, and on the top stood the Emperor, the King of England and the Queen, as three in the sixth degree from the said Duke. This pageant was made at the cost of the Italians, and was much praised.

From thence they passed to the conduit in Cornhill where the street was enclosed from side to side with two gates to open and shut, and over the gates were arches with towers embattled, set with vanes[1] and scutcheons of the arms of the Emperor and the King, and over the arches were two towers, the one, full of trumpets and the other, full of shalmes and shagbuttes[2] which played continually: Between these two towers was a place; [here] under a rich cloth of estate sat King Arthur at a round table and was served with ten kings, dukes, and earls, all bearing targets of their arms; and when the Emperor and the King were coming thither, a poet said:

> *Laudat magnanimos urbs inclita Roma Catones,*
> *Cantant Hannibalem punica regna suum,*
> *Gentis erat Solimae rex ingens gloria David,*
> *Gentis Alexander gloria prima suae.*
> *Illustrat fortes Arcthuri fama Britannos,*
> *Illustras gentem Caesar et ipse tuam....*

[The noble city of Rome highly doth commend
The worthy Catons; and Carthage, Hannibal.
Of Solime, the glory, David did descend:
Alexander, his country enchanced over all,
The fame of worthy Arthur shall never apall
Among the strong Bretons whose like be not found
Of fierce hardiness throughout all the world round.
So thou, Charles; thou, Caesar, omnipotent
Shalt cause thy fame and honour for to blow
Over all the world from East to Occident,
That all folks thy worthiness shall know....]

When this was said, they came to the stocks where was a quandrant stage whereon was an arbour full of roses, lilies, and all other flowers curiously wrought, and birds, beasts, and all other things of pleasure. And about the arbour was made the water full of fish, and about it

---

[1] *vanes*, flags.   [2] *shalmes and shagbuttes*, oboes and trombones.

was the elements, the planets and stars in their places, and every thing moved; and on a tip in the top was made the Trinity with the angels singing, and the Trinity blessed the King and the Emperor, and under his feet was written, 'Behold the Lover of Peace and Concord'. And so they passed through the poultry[1] to the great conduit in Cheapside, where was made on the right hand of the said conduit, as they passed, in manner of a quandrant with four towers, at every corner one with goodly tip; between every tower was a gallery, which galleries were hanged with cloth of gold and silver within, and so covered over. The forefronts of every gallery were hanged with white and green sarcenet, wreathed and with great knots of gold let down in manner of a valence before the gallery; and under the said galleries were targets and scutcheons of the Emperor's and King's arms and devices. In the four towers were four fair ladies for the Cardinal Virtues, so richly beseen that it was great pleasure to behold, every virtue having a sign and token of her property. In the galleries sat children, mixed with men and women, singing and playing on instruments melodiously; of the which sort one child said these verses following:

> *Quanto amplexetur populus te, Caesar, amore,*
> *Testantur variis gaudia mixta sonis,*
> *Aera, tubae, litui, cantus, citharae, calamisque*
> *Consona te resonant organa disparibus....*

[With what joy, Charles, the people thee amplect,
Their right great joys done plainly testify,
Mixed with sweet sounds of many a sect,
Some sounding trumpets and clarions wonders high,
Some other singing most melodiously,
Some upon lutes, some upon harps play,
Thee to rejoice in all that ever they may.
Some with pipes maken sweet harmony....]

When they came to the standard there was made a mighty building of timber with towers set in gables and forced with arches buttand[2] and all habiliments embossed and the lintels enhanced with pillars quadrant and the vaultes in orbes with crobbes[3] depending and monsters bearing up the pillars: and in the roof was a lower swelling, in the top whereof was a banner of the arms of Spain and England and all the pageant full of scutcheons of arms of the two Princes. At the foot of this pageant sat Alphonso, King of Spain, richly apparelled; and out of his breast a branch, of which sprang many kings, queens, and princes which sat and were lively persons richly apparelled, every one with a scutcheon of arms showing their marriages; and

---

[1] *poultry*, the poulterers' market.   [2] *buttand*, abutted.   [3] *crobbes*, crabs(?).

in the highest branch sat the Emperor [and] the King, and just five and seven degrees from the said King of Spain, to whom the said King Alphonso said these verses:

> Carole qui fulges sceptro et diademate sacro,
> Tuque Henrice simul stemmata iuncta gerens,
> Alter germanis, lux alter clara Britannis,
> Miscens Hispano sanguine uterque genus
> Vivite felices, quot vixit secula Nestor,
> Vivite Cumanae tempora fatidicae!

[O Charles, shining with sceptre and diadem,
And likewise, Henry, of kings, the great glory:
The one, of Germany; the other, clear light of Britain's realm,
Together knit by Spanish genealogy,
God grant you both to live as long joyfully
As Nestor and Cumana. God grant my request,
For then shall reign among us peace and rest.]

After this pageant seen and the verses said, they came to the little conduit in Cheapside where was builded a place like heaven curiously painted with clouds, orbs, stars, and the hierarchies of angels; in the top of this pageant was a great tip, and out of this tip suddenly issued out of a cloud a fair lady richly apparelled; and then all the minstrels which were in the pageant played and the angels sang, and suddenly again she was assumpted into the cloud, which was very curiously done; and about this pageant stood the Apostles, whereof one said these verses:

> Ob quorum adventum toties gens ipsa Britanna,
> Supplex diis superis vota precesque dedit.
> Quos aetas omnis, pueri, iuvenesque senesque,
> Optarunt oculis saepe videre suis,
> Venistis tandem auspicio Christi Mariaeque,
> Pacis coniuncti foedere perpetuo.
> Heroes salvete pii! salvete beati!...

[O how oft, Princes, the people of Britain
For your coming have made supplication
Unto God! All ages prayen with heart glad and fain,
Children, young folk, and old with devotion
Desiring entirely with great affection
Your noble persons for to behold and see,
Until that time contented they cannot be.
At last ye come, conducted by Christ and Mary,
Knit together with perpetual bond of peace.
Hail! most puissant princes, full of clemency!...]

Yet you must not forget for all the pageants, how the citizens, well apparelled, stood within rails set on the left side of the streets and the clergy on the right side in rich copes, which censed the princes as they passed: and all the streets were richly hanged with cloths of gold, silver, velvet, and arras, and in every house, almost, minstrelsy; and in every street were these two verses written in letters of gold:

> *Carolus, Henricus, vivant defensor uterque:*
> *Henricus fidei, Carolus Ecclesiae.*

[Charles and Henry, may you both have long life!
Henry, Defender of the Faith; Charles, of the Church!]

Which verses were also written in other tables in golden letters as ensueth:

> Long prosperity
> To Charles and Henry,   Princes most puissant
> The one, of faith
> The other, of the Church,   Chosen defendant.

When they were past the little conduit, they came to the west end of Paul's Church, and there they alighted; and there was a canopy ready under which the two stood and were received by the Archbishop of Canterbury [William Warham] and twenty-one prelates in pontificals; and so they offered at the high altar and returned to horseback and came to the Black Friars where the Emperor was lodged in great royalty. All his nobles were lodged in his new palace of Bridewell, out of the which was made a gallery to the Emperor's lodging, which gallery was very long, and that gallery and all other galleries there were hanged with arras. The King's palace was so richly adorned of all things that my wit is too dull to describe them or the riches of the hangings or the sumptuous building and gilting of the chambers....

The fifteenth day of April [1523] began a Parliament at the Black Friars in London; and that day the Mass of the Holy Ghost was sung, all the lords being present in their Parliament robes. And when Mass was finished, the King came into the Parliament chamber,

The oration of Doctor Tunstall, Bishop of London and there sat down in the seat royal or throne, and at his feet on the right side sat the Cardinal of York [Thomas Wolsey] and the Archbishop of Canterbury. And at the rail behind stood Doctor [Cuthbert] Tunstall, Bishop of London, which made to the whole Parliament an eloquent oration, declaring to the people the office of a King:

'First, he must be a man of judgment according to the saying of the Prophet David: *Deus judicium tuum regi da,*[1] etc. [Give to the

---

[1] Ps. lxxi. 1.

king Thy judgment, O God]. Also, he must be a man of great learning according to the saying of the Prophet: *Erudimini qui judicatis terram*[1] "[Receive instruction, you that judge the earth]." According to the which sayings he said that 'God had sent us a Prince of great judgment, of great learning, and great experience, which according to his princely duty forgot not to study to set forward all things which might be profitable to his people and realm, lest might be laid to his charge the saying of Seneca: *Es rex et non habes tempus esse rex?*: Art thou a king and hast no time to be a king? Which is as much to say as, Art thou a king, and dost nothing profitable to thy people? Art thou a king, and seest the people have an insufficient law? Art thou a king, and wilt not provide remedy for the mischief of thy people? These things have moved the King's Highness to call this, his high court of Parliament, both for the remedy of mischiefs which be in the common law, as recoveries, foreign vouchers, and corrupt trials. And for making and ordering of new statutes which may be to the high advancement of the commonwealth, wherefore he willeth the Commons to repair to the Common House, and thereto elect them a Speaker or their common mouth and to certify the Lord Chancellor of the same, which should thereof make report to the King's most noble Grace, which should declare his pleasure when he would have him presented before his person.'

This was the cause of the Parliament, he said. But surely of these things no word was spoken in the whole Parliament, and, in effect, no good act made, except the grant of a great subsidy were one.

But according to this instruction the Commons departed to the Common House, and chose for their Speaker Sir Thomas More, knight, and presented him the Saturday after in the Parliament chamber, where he, according to the old *The Oration* usage, disabled[2] himself both in wit, learning, and dis- *of Sir* cretion to speak before the King, and brought in for *Thomas* his purpose, how one Phormio desired Hannibal to *More* come to his reading, which thereto assented. And when Hannibal was come, he began to read *de re militari*, that is of chivalry. When Hannibal perceived him, he called him an arrogant fool because he would presume to teach him which was master of chivalry in the feats of war. So the speaker said, if he should speak before the King of learning and ordering of a commonwealth, and such other like, the King, being so well learned and of such prudence and experience, might say to him as Hannibal said to Phormio. Wherefore he desired his Grace that the Commons might choose another Speaker. The Cardinal answered, that the King knew his wit, learning, and discretion by long experience; wherefore he thought that the Commons had chosen him as the most meetest of all, and so he did admit him.

[1] Ps. ii. 10.   [2] *disabled*, distinguished.

Then Sir Thomas More gave to the King his most humble thanks, and desired of him two petitions: the one, if he should be sent from the Commons to the King on a message and mistake their intent, that he might, with the King's pleasure, resort again to the Commons for the knowledge of their true meaning; the other was, if in communication and reasoning any man in the Common House should speak more largely than of duty he ought to do, that all such offences should be pardoned, and that to be entered of record. Which two petitions were granted; and so thus began the Parliament and continued, as you shall hear.

COLOPHON: London *in officina* Richard Grafton *Typis Impress*....1548.

GEORGE CAVENDISH
1500–c. 1562

George Cavendish, secretary or gentleman usher to Cardinal Wolsey, ranks, with Sir Thomas More and Nicholas Harpsfield, as an eminent Tudor biographer. He was born in Glemsford, Suffolk, in 1500, the eldest son of Thomas Cavendish, a clerk in the Exchequer. Nothing is known of his early life or schooling, which, however, was evidently ample to qualify him for the post he filled in Wolsey's household.

In 1524 Cavendish married Margery Kempe, niece of Jane Colt, first wife of Sir Thomas More. Two years later he took up his secretarial duties, and, according to Wolsey, abandoned for four years 'his own country, wife, children, his house and family, his rest and quietness only to serve me'. How well he served the cardinal is obvious from the intimate knowledge of his affairs that is revealed in the Life. *After Henry VIII removed Wolsey from the office of Chancellor, in 1529, Cavendish stayed with him until his death one year later in Leicester Abbey. This last fateful year is vividly described, as is the cardinal's death and funeral.*

From the few autobiographical details given at the end of the Life, *it appears that Cavendish was sent for by Henry VIII to give a full report of the cardinal's death. Satisfied with the information that he gave, the king offered him a position in the royal household. Cavendish accepted and remained in London for a few months to relieve his impoverished state, having collected no salary for over a year. In 1531 he returned to his ancestral home, Cavendish Overall, in Suffolk, where he lived in seclusion and poverty. He remained a staunch member of the old faith until his death about 1562.*

Cavendish's works, The Life of Thomas Wolsey *and thirty short poems, were published posthumously. The* Life *was first printed in 1641, from a very imperfect manuscript. In 1825 S. W. Singer published a text which he believed to be the author's own manuscript (now in the British Museum, MS. Egerton 2402), and this Life is the basic text for all modern editions.*

Cavendish probably wrote the greater portion of Wolsey's biography during the reign of Mary I, when he could openly 'rehearse all these things' in order to refute the 'innumerable lies' about his 'lord and master'. The many copies of the manuscript that were in circulation at the time show that it must have been popular. John Stow was among the later Tudor chroniclers who owned a copy which he loaned to Holinshed. In the latter's Chronicles *the description of the court scene during the divorce proceedings of Henry VIII and Katherine of Aragon are taken almost verbatim from Cavendish's Life. This is particularly true of the long speeches by the king and queen. In Shakespeare's free use of the* Chronicles, *he turned these speeches into blank verse in* Henry VIII, *and his characterization of the tragic figure of Wolsey follows closely Cavendish's honest and sympathetic portrayal.*

The thirty short poems or elegies which Singer has titled Metrical Visions *are biographical sketches of prominent Tudor nobles, including Anne Boleyn, Thomas Cromwell, Henry Howard, Earl of Surrey, Lady Jane Grey, Sir Thomas Arundel, and the Countess of Salisbury, mother of Reginald Pole. Each laments how cruelly 'fykell Fortune' turns her wheel. Though written in mediocre verse, the* Visions *are interesting for the information they give about people whom Cavendish knew personally.*

Life of Thomas Wolsey

Thomas Wolsey, late Cardinal, entitled of St Cecilia Trans Tiberim, Presbyter, and Lord Chancellor of England, his Life and Death: Compiled by George Cavendish, his gentleman usher.

THE PROLOGUE

Meseems it were no wisdom to credit every light tale, blasted abroad by the blasphemous mouth of the rude commonalty. For we daily hear, how, with their blasphemous trump[et], they spread abroad innumerable lies, without either shame or honesty, which *prima facie* showeth forth a visage of truth, as though it were a perfect verity and matter indeed, whereas there is nothing more untrue. And amongst the wise sort so it is esteemed with whom those babblings be of small force and effect.

Forsooth, I have read the exclamations of divers worthy and notable authors made against such false rumours and fond opinions of the fantastical commonalty, who delighteth in nothing more than to hear strange things and to see new alterations of authorities, rejoicing sometimes in such new fantasies which afterwards give them more occasion of repentance than of joyfulness. Thus may all men of wisdom and discretion understand the temerous[1] madness of the rude commonalty, and not give to them too hasty credit of every sudden rumour until the truth be perfectly known by the report of some approved and credible person that ought to have thereof true intelligence. I have heard and also seen set forth in divers printed books some untrue imaginations after the death of divers persons, which in their life were of great estimation, that were invented rather to bring their honest names into infamy and perpetual slander of the common multitude than otherwise.

The occasion therefore that maketh me to rehearse all these things is this: forasmuch as I intend, God willing, to write here some part of the proceedings of Legate and Cardinal Wolsey, Archbishop of York, and of his ascending and descending from honourous estate, whereof some part shall be of mine own knowledge, and some, of other person's information.

Forsooth, this Cardinal was my lord and master whom in his life I served, and so remained with him after his fall, continually during the term of all his trouble until he died, as well in the south as in the north parts, and noted all his demeanour and usage in all that time, as also in his wealthy triumph and glorious estate. And since his death I have heard diverse sundry surmises and imagined tales made of his proceedings and doings, which I myself have perfectly known to be most untrue; unto the which I could have sufficiently answered according to truth, but, as meseemeth, then it was much better for me to suffer and dissemble the matter and the same to remain still as lies than to reply against their untruth, of whom I might, for my boldness, sooner have kindled a great flame of displeasure than to quench one spark of their malicious untruth.

Therefore I commit the truth to Him who knoweth all things. For whatsoever any man hath conceived in him when he lived, or since his death, thus much I dare be bold to say without displeasure to any person, or of affection, that in my judgment I never saw this realm in better order, quietness, and obedience than it was in the time of his authority and rule, nor justice better ministered with indifference, as I could evidently prove if I should not be accused of too much affection, or else that I set forth more than truth. I will therefore here desist to speak any more commendation, and proceed farther to his original beginning [and] ascending by fortune's favour to high honours, dignities, promotions, and riches.

Finis quod G.C.

[1] *temerous*, rash.

[EARLY LIFE AND EDUCATION]

Truth it is, Cardinal Wolsey, sometime Archbishop of York, was an honest poor man's son, born in Ipswich within the county of Suffolk; and being but a child was very apt to learning; by means whereof his parents, or his good friends and masters, conveyed him to the University of Oxford where he prospered so in learning that, as he told me [in] his own person, he was called the boy-bachelor, forasmuch as he was made Bachelor of Arts at fifteen years of age, which was a rare thing and seldom seen.

Thus prospering and increasing in learning, [he] was made a Fellow of Magdalen College, and after, appointed for his learning to be schoolmaster there; at which time the Lord Marquis Dorset had three of his sons there at school with him, committing as well unto him their virtuous education as their instruction and learning. It pleased the said Marquis against a Christmas season to send as well for the schoolmaster as for his children, home to his house for their recreation in that pleasant and honourable feast. They being then there, my lord, their father, perceived them to be right well employed in learning for their time; which contented him so well that he having a benefice in his gift, being at that time void, gave the same to the schoolmaster in reward for his diligence at his departing after Christmas upon his return to the university.

And having the presentation thereof, [he] repaired to the ordinary[1] for his institution and induction: then being fully furnished of all necessary instruments at the ordinary's hands for his preferment, he made speed without any further delay to the said benefice to take thereof possession. And being there for that intent, one Sir Amyas Pawlet, knight, dwelling in the country thereabout, took an occasion of displeasure against him, upon what ground I know not: but, sir, by your leave, he was so bold [as] to set the schoolmaster by the feet during his pleasure, the which was afterward neither forgotten nor forgiven. For when the schoolmaster mounted the dignity to be Chancellor of England, he was not oblivious of the old displeasure ministered unto him by Master Pawlet, but sent for him; and after many sharp and heinous words, enjoined him to attend upon the council until he were by them dismissed, and not to depart without licence upon an urgent pain and forfeiture. So that he continued within the Middle Temple the space of five or six years or more; whose lodging there was in the gate-house next the street which he re-edified very sumptuously, garnishing the same on the outside thereof with cardinals' hats and arms, badges and cognizances of the Cardinal, [and] with divers other devices in so glorious a sort that he thought thereby to have appeased his old unkind displeasure....

[1] *ordinary*, bishop.

[CARDINAL AND CHANCELLOR OF ENGLAND]

Now will I declare unto you his order in going to Westminster Hall daily in the term season. First, before his coming out of his privy chamber, he heard most commonly every day two Masses in his privy closet; and there then said his daily service with his chaplain: and, as I heard his chaplain say, being a man of credence and of excellent learning, that the Cardinal, what business or weighty matters soever he had in the day, never went to his bed with any part of his divine service unsaid, yea, not so much as one collect: Wherein, I doubt not, he deceived the opinion of divers persons.

And after Mass he would return in his privy chamber again, and being advertised of the furniture of his chambers without, with noblemen, gentlemen, and other persons, would issue out into them apparelled all in red in the habit of a cardinal, which was either of fine scarlet, or else of crimson satin, taffeta, damask, or caffa,[1] the best that he could get for money; and upon his head a round pillion[2] with a noble[3] of black velvet set to the same in the inner side. He had also a tippet of fine sables about his neck; holding in his hand a very fair orange whereof the meat or substance within was taken out and filled up again with the part of a sponge wherein was vinegar and other confections against pestilent airs; the which he most commonly smelt unto passing among the press[4] or else when he was pestered with many suitors. There was also borne before him first, the great Seal of England, and, then, his cardinal's hat by a nobleman, or some worthy gentleman, right solemnly bareheaded.

As soon as he was entered into his chamber of presence, where there was attending his coming to await upon him to Westminster Hall as well noblemen and other worthy gentlemen as noblemen and gentlemen of his own family, thus passing forth with two great crosses of silver borne before him and also with two great pillars[5] of silver and his pursuivant at arms with a great mace of silver gilt. Then his gentlemen ushers cried, and said: 'On, my lords and masters, on before! Make way for my lord's Grace!' Thus passed he down from his chamber through the hall: and when he came to the hall door, there was attendant[6] for him his mule, trapped altogether in crimson velvet and gilt stirrups. When he was mounted, with his cross bearers and pillar bearers also upon great horses trapped with scarlet, then marched he forward with his train and furniture, in manner as I have declared, having about him four footmen with gilt pole-axes in their hands.

---

[1] *caffa*, a material on which designs were painted. It came from India.
[2] *pillion*, clerical head-dress.   [3] *noble*, ornament.   [4] *press*, crowd.
[5] *pillars*, emblems implying that the dignitary before whom they were carried was a 'pillar of the Church'.   [6] *attendant*, waiting.

Thus he went until he came to Westminster Hall door. And there alighted and went after this manner up through the hall into the chancery. Howbeit, he would most commonly stay awhile at a bar, made for him a little beneath the chancery, and there commune sometime with the judges and sometime with other persons. And that done he would repair into the chancery, sitting there till eleven of the clock, hearing suitors and determining of divers matters. And from thence he would divers times go into the Star Chamber, as occasion did serve, where he spared neither high nor low, but judged every estate according to their merits and deserts.

[WOLSEY PRESIDES AT THE COURT PROCEEDINGS OF THE KING'S DIVORCE]

Ye shall understand, as I said before, that there was a court erected in the Blackfriars* in London where these two Cardinals [Wolsey and Lorenzo Campeggio] sat for judges. Now will I set you out the manner and order of the court there. First, there was a court placed with tables, benches, and bars, like a consistory, a place judicial for the judges to sit on. There was also a cloth of estate under the which sat the King; and the Queen sat some distance beneath the King: under the judges' feet sat the officers of the court. The chief scribe there was Dr Stephen [Gardiner], who was after Bishop of Winchester; the apparitor[1] was one Cooke, most commonly called Cooke of Winchester. Then sat there within the said court, directly before the King and the judges, the Archbishop of Canterbury, Doctor [William] Warham, and all the other bishops. Then at both the ends, with a bar made for them, the counsellors on both sides. The doctors for the King were Doctor [Richard] Sampson, that was after Bishop of Chichester, and Doctor [John] Bell, who after was Bishop of Worcester, with divers others. The proctors on the King's part were Doctor Peter, who was after made the King's chief secretary, and Doctor [John] Tregonwell, and divers other.

Now on the other side stood the counsel for the Queen, Doctor [John] Fisher, Bishop of Rochester, and Doctor [Henry] Standish, sometime a Grey Friar, and the Bishop of St Asaph in Wales, two notable clerks in divinity, and in especial the Bishop of Rochester, a very godly man and a devout person who after suffered death at Tower Hill, the which was greatly lamented through all the foreign universities of Christendom. There was also another ancient doctor, called, as I remember, Doctor [Nicholas] Ridley, a very small person in stature, but surely a great and an excellent clerk in divinity.

The court being thus furnished and ordered, the judges commanded the crier to proclaim silence. Then was the judges' commission,

---

[1] *apparitor*, a petty officer in a civil or ecclesiastical court.

which they had of the Pope [Clement VII], published and read openly
before all the audience there assembled. That done, the crier called
the King by the name of 'King Henry of England, come into the
court, etc.' With that the King answered, and said, 'Here, my lords!'
Then he called also the Queen by the name of 'Katherine Queen of
England, come into the court, etc.' Who made no answer to the
same but rose up incontinent out of her chair whereas she sat, and
because she could not come directly to the King for the distance
which severed them, she took pain to go about unto the King,
kneeling down at his feet in the sight of all the court and assembly to
whom she said, in effect, in broken English as followeth:

'Sir,' quoth she, 'I beseech you for all the love that hath been
between us and for the love of God, let me have justice and right;
take of me some pity and compassion, for I am a poor woman and
a stranger born out of your dominion; I have here no assured friend
and much less indifferent counsel: I flee to you as to the head of
justice within this realm. Alas, Sir, wherein have I offended you?
Or what occasion of displeasure have I designed against your will
and pleasure, intending (as I perceive) to put me from you? I take
God and all the world to witness that I have been to you a true,
humble, and obedient wife, ever conformable to your will and
pleasure; that never said or did anything to the contrary thereof,
being always well-pleased and contented with all things wherein
you had any delight or dalliance; whether it were in little or much,
I never grudged in word or countenance, or showed a visage or
spark of discontentation. I loved all those whom ye loved, only for
your sake, where I had cause or no, and whether they were my
friends or my enemies. This twenty years I have been your true wife,
and by me ye have had divers children, although it hath pleased God
to call them out of this world, which hath been no default in me.

'And when ye had me at the first, I take God to be my judge,
I was a true maid without touch of man; and whether it be true or
no, I put it to your conscience. If there be any just cause by the law
that ye can allege against me, either of dishonesty or any other
impediment to banish and put me from you, I am well content to
depart to my great shame and dishonour: and if there be none, then
here, I most lowly beseech you, let me remain in my former estate
and receive justice at your hands.

'The King, your father, was in the time of his reign of such estimation through the world for his excellent wisdom, that he was
accounted and called of all men the second Solomon; and my father
Ferdinand, King of Spain, who was esteemed to be one of the wittiest
princes that reigned in Spain, many years before, were both wise
and excellent kings in wisdom and princely behaviour. It is not
therefore to be doubted, but that they elected and gathered as wise

counsellors about them as to their high discretions was thought meet. Also, as meseemeth, there was in those days as wise, as well learned men, and men of as good judgment as be at this present in both realms, who thought then the marriage between you and me* [to be] good and lawful.

'Therefore it is a wonder to hear what new inventions are now invented against me, that never intended but honesty, and cause me to stand to the order and judgment of this new court, wherein ye may do me much wrong if ye intend any cruelty; for ye may condemn me for lack of sufficient answer, having no indifferent counsel but such as be assigned me, with whose wisdom and learning I am not acquainted.

'Ye must consider that they cannot be indifferent counsellors for my part, which be your subjects and taken out of your own council before, wherein they be made privy, and dare not for your displeasure disobey your will and intent, being once made privy thereto. Therefore I most humbly require you in the way of charity and for the love of God, who is the just Judge, to spare me the extremity of this new court until I may be advertised what way and order my friends in Spain will advise me to take. And if ye will not extend to me so much indifferent favour, your pleasure then be fulfilled, and to God I commit my cause!'

And with that she rose up, making a low courtesy to the King, and so departed from thence. [Many] supposed that she would have resorted again to her former place; but she took her way straight out of the house, leaning (as she was wont always to do) upon the arm of her General Receiver, called Master Griffith. And the King being advertised of her departure, commanded the Crier to call her again, who called her by the name of 'Katherine, Queen of England, come into the court, etc.' With that, quoth Master Griffith, 'Madam, ye be called again.' 'On, on,' quoth she, 'it maketh no matter, for it is no indifferent court for me; therefore I will not tarry. Go on your ways.' And thus she departed out of that court without any further answer at that time, or at any other, nor would never appear at any other court after.

The King perceiving that she was departed in such sort, calling to his Grace's memory all her lament words that she had pronounced before him and all the audience, said thus in effect:

'Forasmuch', quoth he, 'as the Queen is gone, I will in her absence declare unto you all, my lords, here presently assembled, she hath been to me as true, as obedient, and as conformable a wife as I could in my fantasy wish or desire. She hath all the virtuous qualities that ought to be in a woman of her dignity, or in any other of baser estate. Surely, she is also a noble woman born, if nothing were in her but only her conditions will well declare the same.'

With that quoth my lord Cardinal, 'Sir, I most humbly beseech your Highness to declare me before all this audience, whether I have been the chief inventor, or first mover of this matter unto your Majesty. For I am greatly suspected of all men herein.'

'My lord Cardinal,' quoth the King, 'I can well excuse you herein.'

'Marry,' quoth he, 'ye have been rather against me in attempting or setting forth thereof. And to put you all out of doubt, I will declare unto you the special cause that moved me hereunto: it was a certain scrupulosity that pricked my conscience upon divers words that were spoken at a certain time by the Bishop of Bayonne, the French King's Ambassador, who had been here long upon the debating for the conclusion of a marriage to be concluded between the Princess, our daughter Mary, and the Duke of Orleans, the French King's second son.

'And upon the resolution and determination thereof, he desired respite to advertise the King, his master, thereof, whether our daughter Mary should be legitimate, in respect of the marriage which was sometime between the Queen here and my brother, the late Prince Arthur. These words were so conceived within my scrupulous conscience that it bred a doubt within my breast: Which doubt pricked, vexed, and troubled so my mind and so disquieted me that I was in great doubt of God's indignation; which, as seemed me, appeared right well for that He hath not sent me any issue male; for all such issue male as I have received of the Queen, died incontinent after they were born; so that I doubt not the punishment of God in that behalf.

'Thus being troubled in waves of a scrupulous conscience and partly in despair of any issue male by her, it drove me, at last, to consider the estate of this realm and the danger it stood in for lack of issue male to succeed me in this imperial dignity. I thought it good, therefore, in relief of the weighty burden of [my] scrupulous conscience and the quiet estate of this noble realm to attempt the law therein, and whether I might take another wife in case that my first copulation with this gentlewoman were not lawful; which I intend not for any carnal concupiscence nor for any displeasure or mislike of the Queen's person or age [and] with whom I could be as well content to continue during my life, if our marriage may stand with God's laws, as with any woman alive: in which point consisteth all this doubt that we go now about to try by the learned wisdom and judgment of you, our prelates and pastors, of this realm here assembled for that purpose; to whose conscience and judgment I have committed the charge according to the which, God willing, we will be right well contented to submit ourself and to obey the same for our part.

'Wherein after I once perceived my conscience wounded with the doubtful case herein, I moved first this matter in confession to you, my lord of Lincoln, my ghostly father. And forasmuch as then yourself were in some doubt to give me counsel, moved me to ask further counsel of all you, my lords: wherein I moved you first, my lord of Canterbury, asking your license, forasmuch [as] you were our Metropolitan, to put this matter in question; and so I did of all you, my lords, to the which ye have all granted by writing under all your seals, the which I have here to be showed.'

'That is truth if it please your Highness,' quoth the Bishop of Canterbury, 'I doubt not but all my brethren here present will affirm the same.'

'No, Sir, not I,' quoth the Bishop of Rochester, 'ye have not my consent thereto.'

'No! ha' thee!', quoth the King. 'Look here upon this. Is not this your hand and seal?' And [he] showed him the instrument with seals.

'No, forsooth, Sire,' quoth the Bishop of Rochester, 'it is not my hand nor seal.'

To that, quoth the King to my lord of Canterbury, 'Sir, how say ye? Is it not his hand and seal?'

'Yes, Sir', quoth my lord of Canterbury.

'That is not so,' quoth the Bishop of Rochester, 'for indeed you were in hand with me to have both my hand and seal as other of my lords had already done; but then I said to you that I would never consent to no such act, for it were much against my conscience; nor my hand and seal should never be seen at any such instrument, God willing, with much more matter touching the same communication between us.'

'You say truth,' quoth the Bishop of Canterbury, 'such words ye said unto me; but, at the last, ye were fully persuaded that I should for you subscribe your name and put to a seal myself, and ye would allow the same.'

'All which words and matter,' quoth the Bishop of Rochester, 'under your correction, my lord, and supportation of this noble audience, there is nothing more untrue.'

'Well, well,' quoth the King, 'it shall make no matter; we will not stand with you in argument herein, for you are but one man.' And with that the court was adjourned until the next day of this session.

The next court day the cardinals sat there again. At which time the counsel on both sides were there present. The King's counsel alleged the marriage not good from the beginning because of the carnal knowledge committed between Prince Arthur, her first husband, the King's brother, and her. This matter being very sore touched and maintained by the King's counsel; and the contrary defended by such as took upon them to be on that other part with the good Queen. And to prove the same carnal copulation, they alleged many coloured reasons and similitudes of truth. It was answered again negatively on the other side, by which it seemed that all their former allegations [were] very doubtful to be tried, so that it was said that no man could know the truth.

'Yes,' quoth the Bishop of Rochester, '*Ego nosco veritatem*, I know the truth.'

'How know you the truth?' quoth my lord Cardinal.

'Forsooth, my lord,' quoth he, '*Ego sum professor veritatis* [I profess the truth]; I know that God is truth itself, nor He never spake but truth who saith, *Quod Deus conjunxit, homo non separet*[1] [What therefore God hath joined together, let not man put asunder]. And forasmuch as this marriage was made and joined by God to a good intent, I say that I *know* the truth; the which cannot be broken or loosed by the power of man upon no feigned occasion.'

'So much doth all faithful men know,' quoth my lord Cardinal, 'as well as you. Yet this reason is not sufficient in this case; for the King's counsel doth allege divers presumptions to prove the marriage not good at the beginning: *Ergo*, say they, it was not joined by God at the beginning, and therefore it is not lawful: for God ordaineth nor joineth nothing without a just order. Therefore, it is not to be doubted but that these presumptions must be true, as it plainly appeareth; and nothing can be more true in case these allegations cannot be avoided; therefore to say that the matrimony was joined of God, ye must prove it farther than by that text which ye have alleged for your matter: for ye must first avoid the presumptions.'

'Then,' quoth one Doctor Ridley, 'it is a shame and a great dishonour to this honourable presence that any such presumptions should be alleged in this open court which be to all good and honest men most detestable to be rehearsed.'

'What,' quoth my lord Cardinal, '*Domine Doctor, magis reverenter*' [My lord doctor, (speak) more reverently].

'No, no, my lord,' quoth he, 'there belongeth no reverence to be given to these abominable presumptions; for an unreverent tale would be unreverently answered.' And there they left, and proceeded no farther at that time. . . .

[The King demanded that Cardinals Wolsey and Campeggio interview Queen Katherine in private, 'to persuade her by their wisdoms, advising her to surrender the whole matter unto the King's hands by her own will and consent'. She would then suffer less humiliation than if she fought the divorce, and the court should side against her. Cavendish does not give the Queen's reply, though he infers she refused.]

[1] Mark x. 9.

Thus went this strange case forward from court-day to court-day until it came to the judgment, so that every man expected the judgment to be given the next court-day. At which day the King came thither and sat within a gallery against the door of the same that looked unto the judges where they sat, whom he might both see and hear speak, to hear what judgment they would give in his suit: At which time all their proceedings were first openly read in Latin. And that done, the King's learned counsel at the bar called fast for judgment.

'With that', quoth Cardinal Campeggio, 'I will give no judgment herein until I have made relation unto the Pope of all our proceedings, whose counsel and commandment in this high case I will observe. The case is too high and notable [and] known throughout the world, for us to give any hasty judgment, considering the highness of the persons and the doubtful allegations; and also whose commissioners we be, under whose authority we sit here. It were, therefore, reason that we should make our Chief Head [the Pope] counsel in the same, before we proceed to judgment definitive.

'I come not so far to please any man for fear, meed, or favour, be he king or any other potentate. I have no such respect to the persons that I will offend my conscience. I will not for favour or displeasure of any high estate or mighty prince do that thing that should be against the law of God. I am an old man, both sick and impotent, looking daily for death. What should it then avail me to put my soul in the danger of God's displeasure, to my utter damnation, for the favour of any prince or high estate in this world? My coming and being here is only to see justice ministered according to my conscience, as I thought thereby, the matter either good or bad.

'And forasmuch as I do understand, and having perceivance by the allegations and negations in this matter laid for both parties, that the truth in this case is very doubtful to be known, and also that the party defendant will make no answer thereunto [but] doth rather appeal from us, supposing that we be not indifferent, considering the King's high dignity and authority within this his own realm which he hath over his own subjects; and we, being his subjects and having our livings and dignities in the same, she thinketh that we cannot minister true and indifferent justice for fear of his displeasure. Therefore to avoid all these ambiguities and obscure doubts, I intend not to damn my soul for no prince or potentate alive. I will therefore, God willing, wade no farther in this matter, unless I have the just opinion and judgment with the assent of the Pope and such other of his counsel as hath more experience and learning in such doubtful laws than I have.

'Wherefore I will adjourn this court for this time according to the order of the court in Rome from whence this court and jurisdiction is derived. And if we should go further than our commission doth warrant us, it were folly and vain and much to our slander and blame; and [we] might be accounted, for the same, breakers of the order of the higher court from whence we have, as I said, our original authorities.' With that the court was dissolved, and no more pleas holden.

THE CARDINAL'S ORATION

With that stepped forth the Duke of Suffolk from the King, and by his commandment spake these words, with a stout and hault[1] countenance, 'It was never merry in England', quoth he, 'whilst we had cardinals among us.' Which words were set forth both with such a vehement countenance, that all men marvelled what he intended; to whom no man made answer. Then the Duke spake again in great despite.

To the which words my lord Cardinal, perceiving his vehemency, soberly made answer, and said, 'Sir, of all men within this realm, ye have least cause to dispraise or be offended with cardinals: for if I, simple Cardinal, had not been, you should have had at this present no head upon your shoulders, wherein you should not have a tongue to make any such report in despite of us who intend you no manner of displeasure; nor have we given you any occasion with such despite to be revenged with your *hault* words. I would ye knew it, my lord, that I and my brother here intendeth the King and his realm as much honour, wealth, and quietness as you or any other, of what estate or degree soever he be, within this realm, and would as gladly accomplish his lawful desire as the poorest subject he hath....

'Wherefore, my lord, hold your peace and pacify yourself and frame your tongue like a man of honour and of wisdom, and not to speak so quickly or reproachfully by your friends; for ye know best what friendship ye have received at my hands, the which I yet never revealed to no person alive before now, neither to my glory nor to your dishonour.'

And therewith the Duke gave over the matter without any words to reply, and so departed and followed after the King who was gone into Bridewell at the beginning of the Duke's first words.

George Cavendish, *The Life of Cardinal Wolsey*, ed. S. W. Singer (London, 1825), 2 vols.

---

[1] *hault*, haughty.

JOHN BOUGE
fl. 1536

When Dan John Bouge, the Carthusian monk, wrote to Dame Katheryn Manne advising her concerning the Oath of Royal Supremacy, he mentioned Sir Thomas More and unwittingly supplied biographers with a few intimate details of the Chancellor's life. More was a member of the London parish of which Bouge, as a secular priest, had been rector.

Facts in Bouge's life are few. He left his London parish to join the Carthusian order a few years prior to 1526, after which date his name appears on the records of several Charterhouses in England. His letter to Dame Katheryn, in 1535, was sent from the Charterhouse near Axholm, Lincolnshire, of which the Prior, Augustine Webster, together with two other Carthusian priors, John Houghton and Robert Lawrence, had been recently martyred by Henry VIII for refusing to take the Oath.

The Axholm Charterhouse was suppressed by the king's order on 18 June 1538, but Bouge's fate is not known.

Letter to Katheryn Manne

A Letter sent to Dame Katheryn Manne from Dan John Bouge
Jesus, Maria.
a. Salvatoris 1535

O devoted Madame, dear daughter in Our Lord God, in the spirit of meekness and of all humility I have me commend unto you:

The cause of my writing to you at this time, one, is to thank you for your token, you sent by Sir Richard Hewson. But I would have been more glad if you had sent me a little bill of three lines, scribbled with your own hand, how and in what case you stand in in this time of tribulation and calamity of this wretched world. The second cause of my writing is to thank you that you be at a due and true concordance with my lover and old friend Sir R. Hewson.

Witness the gospel *Beati pacifici*[1] [Blessed are the peacemakers]; wherefore I have exhorted him and now you of both your parts that you be perseverant and due continuance in the same. For if any person intend to please God in a good beginning and if he ceaseth and be not perseverant unto the end, his body may have pleasure for a little while, but his soul shall be tormented in pains infernal.

[1] Matt. v. 9.

And to this holy purpose saith Saint Augustine, 'Every man and woman and as they be found at the hour of death, when they depart out of this world, so they shall be rewarded in that state, either into pain or unto glory': Witness this: Saint Augustine *ubi inquit, Qualis unusquisque hinc egreditur talis in judicio praesentabitur.** [St Augustine where he says, In whatever state a man departs from this world, in that state he will present himself for judgment.]

*Item. Idem Augustinus de paenitencia: Qualem te Dominus invenerit cum vocat, talem pariter et judicat.** [The same Augustine *on penance*: Just as the Lord finds a person when He calls him, just so He will judge him.] These be great and terrible sentences to be had in memory, insomuch that holy Saint Jerome saith, 'In all my actions, whether that I eat or drink or pray or study or in any other holy pastime, evermore my mind is on four things: first, that my days be short; second, death draweth near; third, mine end is dubitable and doubtful; the fourth, my departing, painful, and my reward, pain or joy.'

Now, moreover, another lesson is to be noted by you, and it is this: how to order yourself in the time of the great schism in the Church of God: how to honour Our Lord God most principal to His pleasure and what person next in degree. Of this matter I will not greatly entreat because I showed my good godson Sir Thomas Halle, well and properly learned, desiring to keep in him these two articles: the first is the due understanding of this article, *Credo in sanctam ecclesiam catholicam** [I believe in the holy Catholic Church]; the second [is] the fourth commandment which is *Honora patrem tuum et matrem aut honora parentes* [Honour thy father and mother or honour thy parents].

In these, with their appertainings, I advise you, good daughter, soberly, devoutly, and discreetly, [to] pray you to Almighty God for grace and leave you to discreet and taught fathers, such as Doctor Boknam and Doctor Warner, my good friends and masters for to answer in these aforesaid articles; it is my study night and day. If any man or person will reason with you what name of person take you next Almighty God, say you no more but *Credo ecclesiam sanctam catholicam* [I believe in the holy Catholic Church]; I pray Jesu, help, and Our Lady, to worship all things that is admitted by our Mother Holy Church except other devout doctors pass my learning, *quia non est discipulus supra magistrum*[1] [because the disciple is not above his master].

[You are] as a prisoner arraigned at the bar, there standing betwixt two judges, having two naked swords—one of death of body for a little while, but the other of life and death in pain everlasting. And this was the answer Master More, knight, [made] to Master Crom-

[1] Luke i. 40.

well when he came from the Tower toward his place of execution. This was his answer: 'I had rather put my life of body to suffer pain for a little season than my sely soul to perish forever, etc.'

Now, good lady, daughter, you shall understand that I was familiar in acquaintance of two honourable persons, that is to say, for the spirituality, my lord Bishop of Rochester [John Fisher], by this token that we were scholars together in Cambridge, of one form and of one parish. And for a little pastime I might speak to him out of my chamber window into his chamber window. We were Bachelors of Art together and Masters of Art together, and both of one day.

Item. As for Sir Thomas More, he was my parishioner at London. I christened him two godly children. I buried his first wife, and within a month after, he came to me on a Sunday, at night late, and there he brought me a dispensation to get married the next Monday without any banns asking. And, as I understand, she is yet alive.

This Master More was my ghostly child. In his confession to be so pure, so clean, with great study, deliberation and devotion, I never heard many such. He was a gentleman of great learning, both in law, art, and divinity, having no man like now alive of a layman; *item.* a gentleman of great sobriety and gravity, once chief of the King's Council. *Item.* a gentleman of little refection and marvellous diet. He was devout in his divine services, and what more, keep you this privily to yourself, he wore a great hair shirt next his skin insomuch that my mistress [More's wife, Dame Alice] marvelled where his shirts were washed. This mistress, his wife, desired me to counsel him to put off this hard and rough shirt of hair; and yet it is very long, almost a twelve month, ere she knew this haburyon[1] of hair. It tamed his flesh till the blood was seen on his clothes, etc. Wherefore you may perceive that a wretch as I am, should not disdain to attenuate my sinful carrion and carcass, etc.

The residue of my purpose I shall write partly in Sir Hewson's letter and a part in my godson's letter. And thus fare-you-well and pray for us, me and my brethren, for as yet we live in fear and dread. There be but two ways: one, for pleasure of body, and that is the common way great peril, but the other, for the soul, that is the point.

To my good lady and madam, Dame Katheryn Manne, from your lover and friend and father, Dan John Bouge. He dwells in the Charterhouse of Axholm beyond Hull.

[From the manuscript in the library of the Parkminster Charterhouse, Horsham, England.]

---

[1] *haburyon,* garment.

NICHOLAS HARPSFIELD

1519–1575

Though Nicholas Harpsfield is best known as a biographer of Sir Thomas More, he was also an historian, theologian, and authority on canon law. With his elder brother John, he worked to uphold the failing cause of Catholicism during the reigns of Mary I and Elizabeth I. Nicholas was born in London on 16 May 1519, son of 'John Harpsfeld of London, gentleman'. After finishing his studies at Winchester school, he followed his brother to New College, Oxford, in 1535. Within two years both were made perpetual Fellows. In 1544 Nicholas received the degree of Bachelor of Canon Law, and was ordained to the priesthood. The Harpsfields remained at Oxford until 1550. Nicholas became the university's first Regius Professor of Greek.

Though Nicholas Harpsfield was not molested during the religious persecutions of Henry VIII, he was forced to flee to Belgium in 1550, after Edward VI came to the throne. In the Low Countries he joined other English exiles, particularly the families of William Roper, John Clement, and William Rastell. Their enthusiasm for the Catholic martyrs encouraged Harpsfield to write the life of Sir Thomas More.

At the accession of Mary I in 1553, Harpsfield returned to England, resuming his studies at Oxford. In the next year he took the degree of Doctor of Canon Law. It was at this time that the friendship began between Harpsfield and Cardinal Pole, who found him ready and eager to support the Catholic cause; before Pole's arrival in England as Cardinal Legate, he gave Harpsfield extraordinary powers to absolve all those under his jurisdiction who had taken the Oath of Royal Supremacy.

During the next four years Pole relied heavily on Harpsfield, whom he appointed Dean or Judge of the Ecclesiastical Court of Appeals for Canterbury and a canon of the Cathedral. As a member of the commission for the suppression of heresy in the diocese of Canterbury, Harpsfield was accused by John Foxe as having an 'unmerciful nature and agrest[1] disposition' toward heretics. Harpsfield refuted this, and historians have confirmed his statements.

When Elizabeth I came to the throne, the Harpsfields once again faced exile or submission to the English Church. Both brothers had gained fame as preachers, John especially as archdeacon of St Paul's Cathedral. When they refused to take part in the election of Matthew Parker as Archbishop of Canterbury and to subscribe to the Queen's Injunctions and the 'Book of Religion', they were heavily fined and sentenced to the Fleet. After twelve years they were released because of poor health, but were required to report 'every Star Chamber day' to show that they had neither

[1] *agrest*, brutal.

done nor said anything 'contrarie to the laws established in this realme for causes of Religion'. It is believed that Nicholas predeceased his brother, and died 18 December 1575 at Exeter College, Oxford.

The two extant English works written by Nicholas Harpsfield and printed posthumously are A Treatise on the Pretended Divorce between Henry VIII and Catherine of Aragon *(1875) and* The Life and Death of Sir Thomas More, Knight *(1931). The first work is a reply to the Universities that sanctioned the King's divorce, proving by canon law that his marriage to Katherine was valid. The* Life and Death of Sir Thomas More *is the first formal English biography and the most authentic of the several early lives of the Chancellor because Harpsfield had access to More's letters and papers through the courtesy of the Rastell and Roper families. Out of gratitude, he dedicated the* Life *to William Roper.*

The most important of Harpsfield's Latin works are Historia Anglicana Ecclesiastica *(1622);* Historia Haeresis Wicliffianae, *which was printed in the same volume; and* Dialogi Sex Contra Summi Pontificatus, *etc., written in prison and printed in Antwerp in 1566.*

A manuscript in Lambeth Palace Library, bearing the title 'The Life of our Lorde Jesus Christe, written in Latin by Nicolas Harpsfield, Doctor of Civill Lawe, faythfully translated', is considered authentic.

Life of Sir Thomas More

The Life and Death of Sir Thomas More, Knight, sometime Lord High Chancellor of England

MORE INDICTED OF TREASON

Sir Thomas More, being brought to Westminster Hall to his arraignment at the King's Bench before fifteen commissioners, appointed for that purpose, after that his indictment was read, as well the Lord Chancellor [Sir Thomas Audley] as the Duke of Norfolk [Thomas Howard] said to him: 'Sir Thomas More, ye see that ye have heinously offended the King's majesty: howbeit, we are in very good hope (such is his great bounty, benignity, and clemency) that if you will forethink and repent yourself, if you will revoke and reform your wilful, obstinate opinion that you have so wrongfully maintained and so long dwelt in, that ye shall taste of his gracious pardon.'

'My lords,' quoth Sir Thomas More, 'I do most humbly thank your Honours of your great good will toward me. Howbeit, I make this my boon and petition unto God, as heartily as I may, that He will vouchsafe this my good, honest, and upright mind to nourish, maintain, and uphold in me even to the last hour and extreme moment that ever I shall live. Concerning now the matters you charge and challenge me withal, the articles are so prolix and long that I fear, what for my long imprisonment, what for my long lingering disease, what for my present weakness and disability, that neither my wit nor my memory nor yet my voice will serve to make so full, so effectual and sufficient answer as the weight and importance of these matters doth crave.'

When he had thus spoken, sustaining his weak and feeble body with a staff he had in his hand, commandment was given to bring him a chair: wherein being set, he commenced his answer much after this sort and fashion:

'Touching the first article, wherein is purposed that I, to utter and show my malice against the King and his late marriage, have ever repined and resisted the same, I can say nothing but this: that of malice I never spake anything against it, and that whatsoever I have spoken in that matter, I have none otherwise spoken but according to my very mind, opinion, and conscience. In the which, if I had not, for discharging of my conscience to God and my duty to my Prince, done as I have done, I might well accompt myself a naughty, unfaithful, and disloyal subject. And for this mine error (if I may call it an error, or if I have been deceived therein) I have not gone scot-free and untouched, my goods and chattels being confiscated, and myself to perpetual prison adjudged, where I have now been shut up about fifteen months.

'Whereas now farther in this article is contained that I have incurred the danger and penalty of the last Act of Parliament,* made since I was imprisoned, touching the King's Supremacy, and that I have as a rebel and traitor gone about to rob and spoil the King of his due title and honour: and, namely, for that I am challenged for that I would not answer Master Secretary and others of the King's Privy Council, nor utter my mind unto them, being demanded what I thought upon the said statute, either in liking or [dis]liking but this only, that I was a man, dead and mortified toward the world and to the thinking upon any other matters than upon the Passion of Christ and passing out of the world: Touching, I say, this challenge and accusation, I answer that for this my taciturnity and silence, neither your law nor any law in the world is able justly and rightly to punish me, unless you may besides lay to my charge either some word or some fact in deed.'

To this the King's attorney occurring:[1] 'Marry,' quoth he, 'this very silence is a sure token and demonstration of a corrupt and perverse nature, maligning and repining against the statute; yea, there is no true and faithful subject that being required of his mind and

[1] *occurring*, opposing.

opinion touching the said statute, that is not deeply and utterly bound without any dissimulation to confess the statute to be good, just, and lawful.'

'Truly,' quoth Sir Thomas More, 'if the rule and maxim of the civil law be good, allowable, and sufficient that *Qui tacet, consentire videtur** [He that holdeth his peace seemeth to consent], this my silence implieth and importeth rather a ratification and confirmation than my condemnation of your statute. For as for that you said, that every good subject is obliged to answer and confess, ye must understand that in things touching conscience every true and good subject is more bound to have respect to his said conscience and to his soul than to any other thing in all the world besides, namely, when his conscience is in such sort as mine is, that is to say, where the person giveth no occasion of slander, of tumult and sedition against his Prince, as it is with me; for I assure you that I have not hither[to] to this hour disclosed and opened my conscience and mind to any person living in all the world.'

The second article did enforce also the foresaid accusation of transgressing the foresaid last statute, touching the King's Supremacy; for that Sir Thomas More (as it was pretended) wrote divers letters to [John Fisher] the Bishop of Rochester, willing him in no wise to agree and condescend to the said statute. 'Would God', quoth Sir Thomas More, 'that these letters were now produced and openly read; but forasmuch as the said Bishop, as ye say, hath burned them, I will not stick truly to utter myself, as shortly as I may, the very tenors of the same. In one of them there was nothing in the world contained but certain familiar talk and recommendations, such as was seemly and agreeable to our long and old acquaintance. In the other was contained my answer that I made to the said Bishop, demanding of me what thing I answered at my first examination in the town upon the said statute. Whereunto I answered nothing else but that I had informed and settled my conscience, and that he should inform and settle his. And other answer, upon the charge of my soul, made I none. These are the tenors of my letters upon which ye can take no hold or handfast by your law to condemn me to death.'

After this answered, he [went] to the third article, wherein was laid to his charge that at such time as he was examined in the Tower, he should answer that the statute was like a two-edged sword, the which if any man would keep and observe, he should thereby lose his soul; and in case any man did not observe it, he should lose his corporal life. 'The very same answer', said they, 'the Bishop of Rochester made, whereby [it] doth evidently appear that it was a purposed and a set matter between you by mutual conference and agreement.'

To this, Sir Thomas More answered that he did not precisely, but conditionally answer that in case the statute were like to be a double-edged sword, he could not tell in the world how a man should demean and order himself but that he should fall into one of the dangers. 'Neither do I know what kind of answer the Bishop made; whose answer, if it were agreeable and correspondent to mine, that happened by reason of the correspondence and conformity of our wits, learning, and study; not that any such thing was purposely concluded upon and accorded betwixt us. Neither hath there at any time any word or deed maliciously escaped or proceeded from me against your statute; albeit, it may well be that my words might be wrongfully and maliciously reported to the King's Majesty.'

And thus did Sir Thomas More easily cut and shake off such and like criminations: and, among other things, said that he would upon the indictment have abidden in law but that thereby should have been driven to confess of himself the matter in deed, that was the denial of the King's Supremacy, which he protested was untrue. Wherefore he thereto pleaded not guilty, and so reserved to himself advantage to be taken of the body of the matter after verdict to avoid the indictment. And, moreover, added, that if these only [odious] terms, 'maliciously, traitorously, and diabolically', were put out of the indictment, he saw therein nothing justly to charge him.

Wherefore, for the last cast and refuge, to prove that Sir Thomas More was guilty of this treason, Master [Richard] Riche was called for to give evidence to the jury upon his oath, as he did. Against whom thus sworne, Sir Thomas More began in this wise to say: 'If I were a man, my lords, that did not regard an oath, I needed not, as it is well known, in this place, at this time, nor in this case to stand here as an accused person. And if this oath of yours, Master Riche, be true, then pray I that I never see God in the face, which I would not say were it otherwise to win the whole world.' Then recited he to the court the discourse of all their communication in the Tower, according to the truth, and said: 'In good faith, Master Riche, I am sorrier for your perjury than for mine own peril. And you shall understand that neither I nor any man else to my knowledge ever took you to be a man of such credit as in any matter of importance (I, or any other) would at any time vouchsafe to communicate with you. And I, as you know, of no small while have been acquainted with you and your conversation, who have known you from your youth hitherto; for we long dwelled in one parish together, where, as yourself can well tell (I am sorry you compel me so to say), you [were] esteemed very light of your tongue, a common liar, a great dicer, and of no commendable fame. And so in your house at the Temple, where hath been your chief bringing up, were you likewise accompted.

'[Can] it, therefore, seem likely to your honourable lordships that I would, in so weighty a case, so unadvisedly overshoot myself as to trust Master Riche (a man of me always reputed for one of so little trust, as your lordships have heard) so far above my sovereign lord, the King, or any of his noble councillors that I would unto him utter the secrets of my conscience touching the King's Supremacy, the special point and only mark at my hands so long sought for—a thing which I never did, nor never would, after the statute thereof made, reveal either to the King's Highness himself or to any of his honourable councillors, as it is not unknown to your honours, as sundry several times sent from his Grace's own person unto the Tower to me for none other purpose? Can this in your judgments, my lords, seem likely to be true? And yet if I had so done indeed, my lords, as Master Riche hath sworn, seeing it was spoken but in familiar talk, nothing affirming, and only in putting of cases without other displeasant circumstances, it cannot justly be taken to be spoken maliciously, for where there is no malice, there can be no malicious offence.

'And never think, my lords, that so many worthy bishops, so many honourable personages, and so many other worshipful, virtuous, wise, and well learned men as at the making of that law were in the Parliament assembled, ever meant to have any man punished by death in whom there could be found no malice,* taking *malitia* for *malevolentia*; for [if[*malitia* be generally taken for sin, no man is there then that thereof can excuse himself: *Quia si dixerimus quod peccatum non habemus, nosmet ipsos seducimus, et veritas in nobis non est.*[1] [If we say that we have no sin, we deceive ourselves, and the truth is not in us.] And only this word "maliciously" is in this statute material, as this term "forcibly" is in the statute of forcible entry. By which statute if a man enter peaceably and put not his adversary out forcibly, it is no offence; but if he put him out forcibly, then by that statute it is an offence, and so shall [he] be punished by this term, "forcibly".

'Besides this, the manifold goodness of the King's Highness himself that hath been so many ways my singular good lord and gracious sovereign, that hath so dearly loved and trusted me (even at my very first coming unto his noble service with the dignity of his honourable Privy Council, vouchsafing to admit me), and to offices of great credit and worship most liberally advanced me, and, finally, with that weighty room of his Grace's High Chancellor (the like whereof he never did to temporal man before), next to his [own] royal person the highest officer of this his noble realm, so far above my merits or qualities able and meet therefor, of his incomparable benignity honoured and exalted me, by the space of twenty years

[1] John i. 8.

and more, showing his continual favour toward me and (until at mine own poor humble suit it pleased his Highness, giving me license with his Majesty's favour to bestow the residue of my life for the provision of my soul in the service of God, of his special goodness thereof to discharge and disburden me) most benignly heaping honours continually more and more upon me—all this his Highness's goodness, I say, so long thus bountifully extended towards me, were in my mind, my lords, matter sufficient to convince this slanderous surmise by this man so wrongfully imagined against me.'

Master Riche, seeing himself so disproved and his credit so foully defaced, caused Sir Richard Southwell and Master [Thomas] Palmer, that at the time of their communication were in the chamber with them, to be sworn what words had passed betwixt them. Where-upon Master Palmer upon his desposition said that he was so busy about the trussing up of Sir Thomas More's books in a sack, that he took no heed [to] their talk. Sir Richard Southwell likewise, upon his deposition, said that because he was appointed only to look to the conveyance of his books, he gave no ear unto them.

After this were there many other reasons, not now in my remem-brance, by Sir Thomas More in his own defence alleged to the dis-credit of Master Riche's foresaid evidence, and proof of the clearness of his own conscience. All which, notwithstanding, the jury found him guilty. And incontinent upon their verdict, the Lord Chancellor. for that matter, chief commissioner, beginning to proceed in judgment against him, Sir Thomas More said unto him: 'My Lord, when I was toward the law, the manner in such case was to ask the prisoner before judgment, why judgment should not be given against him.' Whereupon the Lord Chancellor, staying his judgment wherein he had partly proceeded, demanded of him what he was able to say to the contrary; who in this sort most humbly made answer:

'Seeing that I see ye are determined to condemn me (God knoweth how), I will now in discharge of my conscience speak my mind plainly and freely, touching my indictment and your statute withal.

'And forasmuch as this indictment is grounded upon an Act of Parliament directly repugnant to the laws of God and His Holy Church, the supreme government of which, or [of] any part whereof, may no temporal prince presume by any law to take upon him, as rightfully belonging to the See of Rome, a spiritual pre-eminence by the mouth of Our Saviour Himself, personally present upon earth, only to St Peter and his successors, bishops of the same See, by special prerogative granted, it is therefore in law, amongst Christian men, insufficient to charge any Christian man.'

And for proof thereof, like as among divers other reasons and authorities, he declared that this realm, being but one member and small part of the Church, might not make a particular law disagreeable with the general law of Christ's universal Catholic Church, no more than the city of London, being but one poor member in respect of the whole realm, might make a law against an Act of Parliament to bind the whole realm. So further showed he, that it was contrary both to the laws and statutes of our own land yet unrepealed, as they might evidently [perceive] in Magna Charta,* (*Quod ecclesia Anglicana libera sit, et habeat omnia iura sua integra, et libertates suas illaesas*) [that the Church of England shall be free, and have her whole rights and her liberties inviolable] and also contrary to the sacred oath which the King's Highness himself and every other Christian prince, always with great solemnity, received at their coronations; alleging, moreover, that no more might this realm of England refuse obedience to the See of Rome than might the child refuse obedience to his own natural father. For, as St Paul said [of] the Corinthians: I have regenerated you, my children in Christ;[1] so might St Gregory, Pope of Rome,* of whom by St Augustine, his messenger, we first received the Christian faith, of us Englishmen truly say: 'You are my children, because I have given to you everlasting salvation, a far higher and better inheritance than any carnal father can leave to his children, and by regeneration made you my spiritual children in Christ.'

Then was it by the Lord Chancellor thereunto answered, that seeing all the bishops, universities, and best learned men of the realm had to this Act agreed, it was much marvel that he alone against them all would so stiffly stick thereat and so vehemently argue there against. The which reason, in effect, the Bishop of Westminster [William Benson] also made against him, when he appeared before the commissioners at Lambeth.

To this Sir Thomas More replied, saying that these seven years seriously and earnestly he had beset his studies and cogitations upon this point chiefly, among other, of the Pope's authority. 'Neither as yet', said he, 'have I chanced upon any ancient writer or doctor that so advanceth as your statute doth, the supremacy of any secular and temporal prince. If there were no more but myself upon my side, and the whole Parliament upon the other, I would be sore afraid to lean to mine own mind only against so many. But if the number of bishops and universities be so material as your lordship seemeth to take it, then see I little cause, my lord, why that thing in my conscience should make any change.

'For I nothing doubt but that, though not in this realm, yet in Christendom about, of these well learned bishops and virtuous men that are yet alive, they be not the fewer part that are of my mind therein. But if I should speak of those that are already dead, of whom

[1] I Cor. iv. 15.

many be now holy saints in heaven, I am very sure it is the far greater part of them that all the while they lived, thought in this case that way that I think now; and therefore am I not bound, my lord, to conform my conscience to the council of one realm against the general council of Christendom. For of the foresaid holy bishops I have, for every bishop of yours, above one hundred; and for the council or Parliament of yours (God knoweth what manner of one), I have all the councils made these thousand years; and for this one kingdom, I have all other Christian realms.'

Then answered the Duke of Norfolk: 'We now plainly perceive that ye are maliciously bent.' 'Nay, nay,' quoth Sir Thomas More, 'very and pure necessity, for the discharge of my conscience, enforceth me to speak so much. Wherein I call and appeal to God, whose only sight pierceth into the very depth of man's heart, to be my witness. Howbeit, it is not for this Supremacy so much that ye seek my blood as for that I would not condescend to the marriage.'

When now Sir Thomas More, for the avoiding of this indictment, had taken as many exceptions as he thought meet, and many more reasons than I can now remember alleged, the Lord Chancellor, loth to have the burden of that [judgment] wholly to depend upon himself, there openly asked the advice of the lord [Sir John] Fitzjames, then Lord Chief Justice of the King's Bench, and joined in commission with him whether this indictment were sufficient or not. Who like a wise man answered: 'My lords all, by St Julian (that was ever his oath), I must needs confess that, if the Act of Parliament be lawful, then the indictment is good enough.' Whereupon the Lord Chancellor said to the rest of the lords: 'Lo, my lords, you hear what my Lord Chief Justice saith.' And so immediately gave [he] judgment against him.

After which ended, the commissioners yet further courteously offered him if he had anything else to allege for his defence, to grant him favourable audience. Who answered: 'More have I not to say, my lords, but that like as the blessed Apostle St Paul, as we read in *The Acts of the Apostles*, was present and consented to the death of St Stephen and kept their clothes that stoned him to death,[1] and yet be they now both twain holy saints in heaven, and shall continue there friends together forever, so I verily trust, and shall therefore right heartily pray, that though your lordships have now here in earth been judges to my condemnation, we may yet hereafter in heaven merrily all meet together to our everlasting salvation. And thus I desire Almighty God to preserve and defend the King's Majesty, and to send him good counsel.'

Thus much now concerning his arraignment. After the which he departed from the bar to the Tower again, led by Sir William

[1] Acts vii. 56–9.

Kingston, a tall, strong and comely knight, Constable of the Tower, and his very dear friend. Who when he had brought him from Westminster to the Old Swan toward the Tower, there with an heavy heart, the tears running down by his cheeks, bade him farewell. Sir Thomas More, seeing him so sorry, comforted him with as good words as he could, saying: 'Good Master Kingston, trouble not yourself, but be of good cheer, for I will pray for you and my good lady, your wife, that we may meet in heaven together, where we shall be merry forever.'

When Sir Thomas More came from Westminster to the Towerward again, his daughter, Master William Roper's wife, desirous to see her father, whom she thought she would never see in this world after, and also to have his final blessing, gave attendance about the Tower wharf where she knew he should pass by before he should enter into the Tower, there tarrying for his coming. Whom as soon as she saw, after his blessing upon her knees reverently received, she hasteing toward him, and without consideration or care of herself pressing, in among the midst of the throng and company of the guard, that with halberds and billies went round about him, hastily ran to him, and there openly in the sight of them all embraced him, took him about the neck and kissed him most lovingly. Who well liking her most natural and dear daughterly affection toward him, gave her his fatherly blessing and many godly words of comfort beside: telling her that whatsoever he suffered, though he suffered as an innocent, yet did he not suffer it without God's holy will and pleasure. 'Ye know', quoth he, 'the very bottom and secrets of my heart: And ye have rather cause to congratulate and to rejoice for me that God hath advanced me to this high honour and vouchsafed to make me worthy to spend my life for the defence and upholding of virtue, justice, and religion than to be dismayed or to be discomforted.'

O noble and worthy voice of our noble, new Christian Socrates! The old Socrates, the excellent virtuous philosopher, was also unjustly put to death; whom when his wife, at that time following, outrageously cried, 'Shall such a good man be put to death?' 'Peace, good wife,' quoth he, 'and content thyself: it is far better for me to die a good and a true man than as a wretched malefactor to live.'

Nicholas Harpsfield, *The Life and Death of Sir Thomas More, Knight.* Ed. by E.V. Hitchcock, Early English Text Society, orig. ser. 186 (1932).

PART V

ROMANCES AND TALES

ROMANCES AND TALES

INTRODUCTION BY H. S. BENNETT

TUDOR PRINTERS AND 'THE NOBLE ACTS OF CHIVALRY'

As our early English printers looked about them for matter to print that would interest the growing reading public which the fifteenth century had done so much to encourage, it was inevitable that the romance and the tale should attract their attention. Although the great days of romance compilation were long since over, and many of the romances were but degenerate and corrupt versions of earlier stories, yet the desire for a good story, for adventure, for marvels, and all the trappings of medieval chivalry and the graphic incident of life long ago remained. The Wars of the Roses also were over, Henry VII and his successors were on the throne, and their agents, Empson and Dudley, Wolsey and Cromwell, were in power. 'Lancelot was dead', indeed: yet in men's hearts and imaginations, he was still alive, and 'the matter of England, France, and of Rome the great'—the staple of medieval romances—still provided an inexhaustible source of material, long the domain of the minstrel as he passed from hall to hall, telling of the English virtues of Havelock, or of the exploits of Arthur, or of Charlemagne, or of the fairy world of Oberon, but now to become more readily available as romance after romance was printed by Caxton, de Worde, or Copland. Caxton was the first printer of the romances, *Godfrey of Boulogne*, *Charles the Great*, *Paris and Vienne*, *Blanchardyn and Eglantine*, *The Four Sons of Aymon*, and *Morte Darthur*. Other narrative works—*The Recuyell of the Histories of Troy*, *The History of Jason*, and *Eneydos*—contained much from classical myth and story, while the favourite beast fable was represented by *Reynard the Fox* and *The Fables of Aesop*. Nor was Caxton's pupil, Wynkyn de Worde, backward in following his example. No less than fifteen romances came from de Worde's press, and of these, twelve appear in print for the first time under his imprint, while little volumes of fables or tales, such as *The Frere and the Boye*, continued the work begun by Caxton. By the time of de Worde's death, early in 1535, all the romances and tales included in this anthology were in print, and a number of them had been several times reprinted—a testimony to their continued popularity.

TRADITIONAL PATTERN OF THE MEDIEVAL ROMANCE

Among all the forms of medieval story-telling none had greater prestige than the romance. To the modern reader with the great body of the English novel to draw on, these lengthy prose romances make but small appeal, although at the time of their writing, and for long afterwards, it was otherwise. Their very length, which is so deterrent to us, was a positive advantage in the eyes of their first audiences. Length seems to have been welcomed almost for its own sake. At the worst, it could be argued that the minstrel's droning chant helped to while away 'the longe nyghtes blak', for what was there to be done in many a castle or hall once the tables had been cleared and there were yet some hours before bed?

So for most medieval people the romances were full of interest. Within their lengthy convolutions there was much that was dear to this relatively simple audience. To begin with there was endless adventure. The hero, whatever else he encountered, was certain to ride forth into a world in which every kind of happening could occur. He not only took part in tourneys and mêlées, but constantly ventured out on quests where he met and conquered other knights, dragons, sorcerers, wild beasts, and sundry monsters. He was at times himself overcome (generally by magic), or was misled, but ultimately was triumphant. From end to end, the romances are crammed with adventure, made the more exciting since magic and necromancy exercise their potent spells. By such means marvellous escapes are effected; magic castles and enchanted ladies are met with; mythical birds or monstrous creatures of every kind make opportune or inopportune appearances—all helping to sustain the excitement and interest as the romance progresses.

For often this is all that the story does—hence much modern criticism. But the medieval audience was not too greatly concerned with the niceties of construction; 'the well-made tale' meant little or nothing to them. So long as there was plenty of incident, a strong love interest, a last-moment triumph of good over bad, a final drawing together of the threads, with a lovers' reunion and wedding—all was well. Poetic justice reigned: the good were rewarded; the wicked punished. In such a world of make-believe, the harsh realities of everyday life were momentarily forgotten. As he listened to the minstrel in the castle hall, the page dreamed of what might be, even as the varlet hoped as he heard of the scullion who turned out to be a lord's son, and eventually married his master's daughter. Just as today millions seek and find relief in the various worlds which the motion-pictures create for them, so the medieval audience delighted to hear of feasts, consisting of many courses, at which minstrels with every variety of instrument could be heard, and where the beauty of the ladies, the gorgeous elaboration of their dresses, and the diverse ceremonial of chivalric life were depicted in great detail.

THE PERENNIALLY POPULAR 'AMOR COURTOIS'

But there were other things than these which held the medieval listener, and, later, the Tudor reader, and kept him faithful to the romance for so many generations. Foremost among these was love —the *amor courtois*, or 'courtly love', that is at the heart of romance: for as the saying went, 'A knight cannot be of worship unless he is a lover', and it was the love of ladies, and of one lady in particular, that led the knight to valorous deeds—to rescue the beloved from the court of the King of India, or to pluck a hair from the beard of the Sultan of Babylon. It was her image that sustained him in the moments of danger, and her smile and approbation that were his greatest reward. For her sake he undertook the most desperate of adventures and suffered the greatest of hardships. As the servant of love he conformed to a type, and we must not expect to find in him much pyschological complexity. Model hero and model lover, he goes through a conventional series of actions and emotions. He is superlatively brave, hardy, adventurous and skilled in the arts of war, and at the same time courteous, debonair, chivalrous, and loyal to all, especially to his lady.

As for the ladies, we need not go as far as Léon Gautier—panegyrist of chivalry though he was—and speak of them 'for the most part as shameless little monsters', but we must allow that they were often something less than perfect. They are frequently depicted as beautiful to a fault, but aware of their beauty and of the superior position that their lover had given to them, so that at times they could be harsh, capricious, and domineering. Many a lover must have echoed Lancelot's words when Guinevere had 'ben wrothe with hym causeles'. '"Thys ys nat the firste tyme", seyde Sir Launcelot, "that ye have ben displese with me causeles. But, madame, ever I muste suffer you, but what sorrow that I endure, ye take no forse."'

As with Lancelot and Guinevere, the union between the two lovers is often an illegitimate one, or if not that, one that demands the greatest secrecy. Parents and husbands are the mortal foes of *amor courtois*: it therefore behoves lovers to act with caution. Their meetings are furtive and fraught with danger; the confidante or go-between is a necessity; the fear of discovery or of the lady being pledged elsewhere by her parents if she is unmarried always haunts the imagination. In these circumstances the lover is humble yet ardent; hopeful, yet well aware of the odds against him; full of anxiety lest the prize elude his grasp; deeply conscious of how much

is risked by the lady in loving him, and so on. Love in this fashion
is an elaborate art, a science with rules and conventions the more
binding since they are matters of conscience and honour rather than
of law. The romances depict in elaborate detail the progress and
fortunes of love, and for this alone must have been listened to eagerly
as the adventures resulting from lovers' unions and partings were
related.

THE IMPRINT OF CHIVALRY ON TUDOR NATIONAL LIFE

Thus the romances did more for the Tudor reader than just ward
off monotony. They showed him how the *preux chevaliers* of the
past had conducted themselves in love and in war, and how the
deeds of these mythical heroes were studied, their behaviour copied
and their emotions followed by countless aspirants to honour. For
the world they lived in was the world of chivalry; and although men
knew by the days of the Tudors that in essentials this world had
passed, yet it was still near enough to them to be seen, not as we see
it as through a glass darkened by the dust of centuries, but as something that happened only yesterday.

And yesterday, all that went into the making of a knight—love
of ladies, tourneys, adventures, feasting, and ceremonial—had
absorbed the interest of audiences to whom these things were part
of their everyday life, so that they scrutinized every detail with
expert skill. As they listened to the minstrel tell of the arming of the
knight, or of the etiquette of the feast, or describe the sufferings of
the rejected lover, or tell of the tactics of a battle, he was followed
from point to point by an eager audience.

Viewed in this way, the romances taught while they amused, and
inculcated a way of life which was far from easy and preached a
doctrine difficult to accept in the rough and troublesome Tudor age.
Caxton realized all this clearly enough when he closed the preface
to his edition of the *Morte Darthur* with these words, which have
never been bettered:

> Noble men may see and lerne the noble actes of chyvalrye, the
> jentyl and vertuous dedes that somme knyghtes used in tho dayes,
> by whyche they came to honour, and how they that were vycious
> were punysshed and ofte put to shame and rebuke; humbly
> bysechyng al noble lordes and ladyes wyth al other estates, of
> what estate or degree they been of, that shal see and rede in this
> sayd book and werke, that they take the good and honest actes in
> their remembraunce, and to folowe the same; wherin they shalle
> fynde many joyous and playsaunt hystoryes and noble and re-
> nomed actes of humanyte, gentylnesse, and chyvalryes. For herein
> may be seen noble chyvalrye, curtosye, humanyte, frendlynesse,

hardynesse, love, frendshyp, cowardyse, murdre, hate, vertue, and synne. Doo after the good and leve the evyl, and it shal brynge you to good fame and renommee.

This is the background against which the Tudor prose romances must be seen. They come at a moment when credulity is waning. Caxton warns his readers that 'for to pass the time this book shall be pleasant to read in, but for to give faith and belief that all is that is contained therin, ye be at your liberty'. And similarly Jean d'Arras and Lord Berners realize, as the latter says, that their 'strange and wonderful adventure, by plain letter as to our understanding should seem in a manner to be supernatural'. Romance has had its day, but it has contributed so much that later writers were to build on. As Lord Ernle has put it:

> The influence which these romances exercised on the national life of the country was prodigious. We cannot exaggerate it. They had no rivals in newspapers; with the exception of a very small number of persons, they had no competitors in the shape of schools or colleges. They coloured the medieval and Tudor conception of history and biography, of science, of geography, of natural history. They opened to the unlearned the treasures of classical literature. They helped to sweep us with the Latin nations into the movement of the early Renaissance.... They elevated the manners, they inspired the ideals, they fired the enthusiasm of successive generations. They have enriched the popular currency of our thought by characters who live as typical representatives of vices or virtues.

THE TALE AS A MORAL WEAPON

Romance, however, was but one branch of literature that the early Tudor reading public had provided for them in printed form. Throughout the Middle Ages tales and stories of a religious and moralistic nature had flowed ceaselessly from the quills of writers, intent, in Wesley's phrase, 'not to let the Devil have all the best tunes'. Morality was inculcated by means of homilies and legends, while pious tales and stories of the saints abounded. The Miracles of the Virgin may serve as an example of the *genre*: writers never tired of telling of this or that miracle worked by the Virgin, and collections such as those contained in the Vernon Manuscript (1370–80) show clearly enough the variety of this form of story. Similarly, the legendary Lives of the Saints provided a mass of material, rich beyond compare in its variety of interest and strangeness of setting, and great compilations of these existed in an English form in manuscripts such as the Southern Legend Collection in verse, or in the fifteenth-century translation of the great *Legenda Aurea* in prose. It was in the main from this version that Caxton made his own magnificent collection, a task which he tells us left him 'hafe desperate to have accomplissed it'.

There were also smaller collections and translations, such as that made by John Capgrave and others, which was printed by Richard Pynson, in 1516, under the title of *The Kalendre of the New Legende of Englande*, while even single lives in prose or in verse were thought to be worth printing, and indeed in most cases proved to be so popular that they were well-nigh thumbed out of existence. For example, an edition of Capgrave's translation of *The Lyfe of Joseph of Arimathy*, printed by Wynkyn de Worde, about 1511, was a little quarto of twelve pages, of which crude woodcuts of the Crucifixion and of the tree of Jesse occupy three pages and de Worde's device a fourth, while the legend itself is related in the remaining eight pages. Pictures and text were evidently eagerly conned, so that only two copies of it are now known to exist.

Part of the legend of Joseph of Arimathaea is to be found embedded in 'The Quest of the Holy Grail', a story which forms a section of the compilation generally known as the *Morte Darthur*. Medieval literature has nothing more striking than the dramatic change that comes over Malory's narrative when he turns from knights and war to the visions and ardours which are the lot of those seeking the Grail. Chief among them is the peerless knight, to whom the vision is denied, for as he says:

> My synne and my wyckednes hath brought me unto grete dishonoure! For whan I sought worldly adventures for worldely desyres I ever encheved them and had the bettir in every place, and never was I discomfite in no quarell, were hit ryght, were hit wronge. And now I take uppon me the adventures to seke of holy thynges; now I se and undirstonde that myne olde synne hyndryth me and shamyth me, that I had no power to stirre nother speke whan the holy bloode appered before me.

What was denied to Lancelot was vouchsafed to Galahad alone, so that here in the heart of romance those values which for generations had been so lauded, are shown to be inferior when weighed *sub specie aeternitatis*. A Christian overlay, in short, for this part of the story gives to it a quality which is quite out of keeping with most of the romance, and which is left behind as Malory in his last books sweeps forward to tell with great brilliance and magnificence the immortal story of Lancelot and Guinevere, and the downfall of the whole world of Arthur and the Round Table.

Moralists, while not always using Biblical story or sacred legend, contrived to indicate morality by the relation of a tale such as *Mary of Nemmegen.* This well related story keeps the reader constantly on the alert: the harsh behaviour of the aunt, the appearance of the devil and the compact he makes with Mary, her repentance, her journey to Rome, and her expiation are all matters of absorbing interest, so that it is a hard-hearted reader who requires the author's admonition with which he closes the story:

All this in this boke conteyned is for a trewth, and if that ye wyll nat beleve me that was the fyrst maker of this boke, if that it fortune ony of you for to goo into the lande of Flanders to a towne called Mastryche and goo to the Nonry of the converted synners, there ye shall see Emmekyns [Mary's] grave and also ye yron rynges hangyng there; and undernethe wrytyn hyr lyvynge and also hyr pennaunce.

SATIRE AND HUMOUR FROM THE CONTINENT

Representative of another branch of story-telling is the *Historye of Reynart the Foxe*, translated from the German by William Caxton in 1481. The beast fable, of which this is one of the best examples, had a wide Continental popularity, for under the guise of animals much shrewd social satire and humorous comment was possible. Reynard, like Tyll Howleglass, was a rogue, but an engaging rogue, and as has been said (with a little exaggeration), 'every district had its Noble, its Isengrim and its Bruin, and all the villagers who suffered from their cruelty felt sympathetic interest in the triumph of Reynard over them'.

At a lower level there was the secular tale. English writers had never indulged in this form to the extent that their French confreres did, so that most of the tales which have survived come to us in an English dress, but originated in France or Germany. The *fabliaux* were largely aimed at a middle-class audience: they deal with burgesses and traders; they are concerned with the relations between people, often involving illicit sex relations; they are full of references to everyday affairs and things, and are couched in a simple direct narrative form with plenty of action, rude farce, homely speech— in short, are designed to interest a large, popular audience. They inevitably have elements in them which causes Chaucer to speak of them as 'churl's tales', and to apologize for some of their more unsavoury incidents.

In *Tyll Howleglass* we have a variety of this *genre*, where the tale takes the form of a number of episodes all deriving from the personality of the hero and gaining its effect from the verbal quips, the discomfiture of those in authority, the playing of practical jokes, and the recreation of the everyday scene. The telling of these stories kept the audience on tiptoe throughout until the denouement of each of them was reached. The prologue to *Tyll Howleglass* may well claim that the stories 'renewe ye mindes of men and women of all degrees fro ye use of sadnesse to passe the tyme with laughter or myrthe'.

THE OLD STORY-TELLER'S ART

So much for the subject-matter and the background against which it should be seen. The reader will soon find for himself that 'the light reading of our ancestors' is not without literary merit. While quite naturally and properly we have learnt much about form and style since Tudor days yet, given their premises, these old tellers of tales were not wholly unacquainted with the art of story-telling. They made full use of those staples of all narrative art—love, war, the supernatural, the unknown. They carried the reader along with a story crammed with adventure and episode, and made the more acceptable by the use of homely phrase and arresting image.

Who could resist, for example, the sympathetic *frisson* as they heard of the departure of Melusine,

transfigured lyke a serpent, grete and long in fifteen foote of lengthe...flyeing thre tymes about the place, passed foreby the wyndowe gyvyng at everyche tyme an horryble cry and pyteous that caused them that beheld her to wepe for pyte, for they preceyved wel that loth she was to departe fro the place, and that it was by constraynte. And thenne she toke her way toward Lusynen, makyng in th'ayre by her furyousnes suche horryble crye and noyse that it semed al th'ayer to be replete with thundre and tempeste.

This and many other passages might be quoted to show the force and expressiveness of these writers. The reader, however, has only to turn to the extracts which follow to see for himself the many virtues of these old tellers of tales.

'PARIS AND VIENNE'

The romance of Paris and Vienne, *developed probably from Italian folk-lore of the eighth or ninth century, is a chivalric tale laid in Viennois, a district in southern France settled by the Catalans, who were of Italian descent. There is a slight resemblance in plot to that of* Romeo and Juliet, *particularly the parental opposition to the lovers' union. But in* Paris and Vienne *the objection is based on inequality of social rank rather than a long-standing feud between families as in the play. Lending some weight to its Italian origin is the fact that the oldest extant version is in Italian, printed in Treviso in 1482.*

Pierre Sippade gives the earliest known account of the romance in the preface to his French version, made in 1459 though not printed until 1487 by Gerard Leeu in Antwerp. He relates that during all his life he took pleasure in reading romances—Lancelot, Tristan, Florimond, Guy of Warwick—so he 'selected a writing in the Provençal language which was drawn from another book in the Catalan tongue', giving the life of Godfrey Dalencon, Duke of Viennois and proud father of Vienne.

It is most probable that Caxton used a manuscript of Sippade's text, or a non-extant printed copy of it, for his translation issued from his West-minster press in 1485. As W. C. Hazlitt remarks in his edition of the romance for the Roxburghe Club, Caxton's translation 'is far more interesting and valuable to us as exhibiting the romance in something like its pristine shape and simplicity'. Paris and Vienne *never becomes, as Hazlitt says, 'involved or irksome'. There is none of the usual romance paraphernalia, such as enchanted fountains, faeries, and giants; emphasis is rather on characterization, and Vienne emerges as one of the most natural and charming of the pre-Renaissance heroines. Though MacEdward Leach, who is preparing an edition of the romance for the Early English Text Society, doubts that there is any strong tie between it and* Romeo and Juliet, *since the motive in each is different, yet he points out that there is a similarity in the role of the friar whose well-intentioned services in the play and the romances are an integral part of the climax of each. Also, there is a womanly dignity about these girl heroines, Juliet and Vienne, that makes them, if not intimately, at least closely akin.*

The popularity of Paris and Vienne *in England is reflected in a passage in Gawin Douglas's* The palis of honoure *(1533?) where the lovers are listed among those in Venus's train:*

> Of France, I saw Paris and Vienne.

And Skelton, after comparing the great lovers of the world in The boke of Phyllyp Sparowe *[1545?], adds,*

> And of the love between
> Paris and Vienne.

During the reign of Elizabeth I, the romance was dramatized by an anonymous author, whose play has unfortunately been lost, and was presented at court by the child players of Westminster on Shrove Tuesday night in 1571, before the queen.

Paris and Vienne was equally popular on the Continent, where many editions were printed in Italian, French, German, and Dutch. A Latin translation was made by Jean de Pino, Bishop of Rieux, who considered it a 'wholesome and moral story', for the sons of his friend Antoine Dupray, Chancellor under Francis I. His translation was printed in 1516 in Venice, where the bishop was serving as the French ambassador.

SYNOPSIS

The city of Viennois is the scene of the major portion of the story. When it opens, Vienne, daughter of Godfrey Dalencon, the Dauphin of Viennois, is secretly loved by Paris, son of Monsieur Jacques, a wealthy baron. Because he is 'not of so hyghe lynage', Paris fears to tell his love, but serenades Vienne, playing and singing nightly under her window. Abashed at the thought of meeting her, he nevertheless enters tournaments and wins jewels and trophies in her honour.

Unsuspecting that Paris loves his daughter, the Dauphin sends his wife and Vienne to visit his friend Monsieur Jacques, who is seriously ill. Paris is away from home for the day. While Madame Jacques is showing her royal visitors through the castle, Vienne notices that the trophies won in her honour at the jousts have a conspicuous place in his private chapel. She immediately suspects his love for her and determines to test it by taking with her some of the jewels he has won and a white banner. When she confides her plan to Isabeau, her friend and constant companion, Vienne is incensed at her disparaging remarks regarding Paris's inferior social rank. After upbraiding Isabeau, she hides the trophies under her mantle when they leave the chapel.

When Paris discovers the loss, he is distressed. But the jewels are soon traced to Vienne. As she hoped, it effects a meeting with him during which she insists that he ask his father to seek the Dauphin's consent to their marriage. Hesitantly, Monsieur Jacques agrees to see the Dauphin. He is sternly rebuffed by Dalencon, who declares his daughter must marry a man of her own rank. To forestall clandestine meetings, Paris is banished from the realm and his father is imprisoned.

The lovers discuss their plight in a balcony scene on the night previous to Paris's departure from Viennois. Fearless of her father's wrath, Vienne determines to elope with Paris, exacting a promise 'that ye touche not my body unto the tyme that we be lawfully maryed'. On the following night she and Isabeau, clad in 'man's array' and with 'money and of all other thinges' necessary for the journey, steal from the palace to meet Paris and his servant George.

They have gone but a short way when a storm overtakes them and George is drowned fording a stream on horseback. More trouble comes to them when they learn that the Dauphin has sent out a party of men to arrest them. Realizing that their separation is imminent, Paris threatens suicide. Vienne pleads with him to seek refuge in some distant country, and she gives him a ring as a token of her love. Paris starts off for Genoa.

After Vienne is brought back to her parents, she is scolded and imprisoned by her father until she agrees to marry a man of royal birth. Through a ruse and the aid of Isabeau, who shares her imprisonment, she convinces several prospective husbands, chosen by her father, that she is too ill to marry, and lives in the hope of hearing from Paris.

The device of mistaken identity brings the story to a climax. During his exile Paris has visited Alexandria, Babylon, Jerusalem and the land of Prester John, where he adopts the Moslem garb. Though he never changes his Christian faith, he manages to make his way into the good graces of the Sultan. During this time, the Dauphin undertakes a pilgrimage to Jerusalem and is captured by the Moors. Paris learns of his presence in Alexandria and visits the city. He influences the Sultan to release him. Unaware of Paris's identity, the Dauphin offers him his daughter as a reward for his aid, and the offer is readily accepted.

When they return to Viennois, Paris continues to wear his Moorish garb. The Dauphin sends him with a friar to visit Vienne in prison. She recognizes him through the ring that she had given him. They decide to tell her father that she will accept the 'Moor'. Though he approves of their marriage before he learns of Paris's identity, he does not withdraw his consent. In a sub-plot Isabeau marries Edward, Paris's faithful friend.

The History of the noble right valiant and worthy Knight Paris and of the fair Vienne, the Dauphin's daughter of Viennois

TRANSLATED BY WILLIAM CAXTON

HOW DIANE AND VIENNE, HER DAUGHTER, WENT TO VISIT THE FATHER OF PARIS, THE WHICH WAS SICK

Now it happened that during this time that Paris and Edward dwelt in Brabant, the father of Paris fell into a sickness of fever or access. And the cause came of the thought that he had of his son Paris. And he being sick, the Dauphin went on a day to see him, and demanded the cause of his malady, and comforted him the best wise that he could. And, after, returned home and said to his wife that it were well done that she should go see and visit Monsieur Jacques which was sick. And forthwith, incontinent, my lady Diane, her daughter Vienne, and Isabeau, her damsel, with a great company, went to the castle of Sir Jacques and saluted him much nobly, as it well appertained and the best wise that they might.

And when they were in the chamber where Monsieur Jacques was and lay, Dame Diane demanded him of his sickness. And Monsieur Jacques said that all his disease came for his son Paris because he lost so his time. And that he went always with the Bishop of Saint Lawrence. 'Whereof I fear me that he shall become a man of religion. I have no more children but him; I wote not what I shall do with the goods that God hath given to me.'

And my Lady Diane comforted him and said that his son was much well beloved of the Dauphin; and that he had much great amity of many great lords, barons, and knights. And, also, she said that among all things he should ordain for his health. And after all this, the mother of Paris prayed her that it might please her to come see the castle. And she answered that she much desired it.

Then the mother of Paris showed her all the castle, and led her into a hall all full of arms and habiliments of war for to fight in battle. After, she led her into another hall whereas were many hawks, falcons, and many other fowles of [the] chase. And, after, into many other halls and chambers richly arrayed, which were over long to rehearse. And, after, the mother of Paris showed unto her the chamber of Paris, where that he slept, wherein were many habiliments which should well suffice the chamber of a great prince. And in the said chamber were two great standards covered after the guise of France. That one was full of cloth of gold and silk, and that other, of harness and of many other things.

Then said Vienne to Isabeau, 'By my faith, fair sister, I have no great marvel of this young knight Paris though of him be made great mention. For the ordinance of these things show well that he is of great valour.' And in beholding of these things, she saw a coverture of a horse, all white. And her seemed that it was the same that the knight bore that won the prize of the jousts that was made in the city of Viennois, and that had the shield of crystal and the garland; which she told to Isabeau.

And Isabeau answered to her, 'Never think ye so. For all[1] day been made semblable covertures and tokens white, whereof ye may well be deceived.'

Vienne enforced always herself to take better heed: and of the great joy that she had, she said to her mother, 'Madame, I am a little crazed and suddenly taken. Wherefore if it please you, I would fain rest a little in this chamber. And let me be all alone with my sister Isabeau, for I will have none other.'

[1] *all*, every.

And anon each body voided out of the chamber, and Isabeau did shut the door that none might come in.

Then said Vienne, 'Now we shall see if we may find any thing that we may have better knowledge of. For mine heart saith, "Yes".'

After that they had searched and visited all the chamber, they came on a side of the chamber where they found a little door of which hung a little key by a thong; and, anon, they opened the door and entered therein. And there was a little chamber which was twelve foot long; and was an oratory whereas was the majesty of Our Lord Jesus Christ upon a little altar, and at each corner was a candlestick of silver. And thither came Paris for to make his sacrifice when he arose and when he went to his bed.

And there were the three banners that the noble knight Paris had won in the city of Paris; and the three jewels of the three damoiselles aforesaid. And in the same place was also the shield of crystal and the garland that Vienne delivered to him when he won the prize at the jousts in the city of Viennois. And all these he kept secret in that place.

And when Vienne saw these things, she was sure that Paris was he whom she had so much desired to know, and that so much honour had done to her. And for the great joy that she had, she sat her down on the ground and there abode a great while and could not speak a word. And, after, she spoke to Isabeau and said, 'My sweet sister, blessed and praised be Our Lord of this good journey, for, methinketh, I should never depart out of this chamber. Alas, I have so long abiden to know who he was that so sweetly played in his instruments so nigh unto me; and now he is so far.'

And then Isabeau began to reprove her and said to her, 'Sweet lady, I pray you that ye say nor do anything which might turn you to folly; and be ye ruled by wisdom and reason. For notwithstanding that Paris have so much good and virtues, yet ye ought to consider that he is not equal to you in lineage nor in estate. For I know well that many noble and puissant lords have demanded you in marriage and love you and do great things for you: and, also, the honour of Paris, which is your vassal and subject, is not equal nor worthy unto you.'

Then Vienne was much angry on Isabeau, and began to say, 'Aye, very God, I am well discomforted and deceived by thee that thus again saith me of him that I so long have desired to know. Alas, I had supposed that in nothing ye would have despised me. And, in good faith, I say to thee that this man I will love and demand. And I promise thee, in good faith, that if thou any more gainsay me, I shall slay myself; and then thou shalt be cause of my death. For I will not lose him, I have so long loved; but I say to thee, for truth, that if thou ever say to me such words of my friend Paris, that thou shalt never after have space to say them again another time. For if thou considerest well his noble conditions and customs, thou shouldst praise him better than thou dost. And knowest thou not well that the King of France would that it had cost him half his realm that his son Louis were as valiant as Paris is. And also there be many notable lords that desire to know his name and to have his amity.

'Then take heed and behold, by my faith, if ever thou saw man that might be compared to him! Certainly, all virtues been in him. And since that fortune hath brought me to his love, he is worthy to have my love and yet more than is in me. And have I not reason and cause then to love him which hath done to me so great good and honour, and doubting no peril of his person: and is it not well great worship to my father to have for vassal and subject, the best knight that is in all the world. For in all the world is no knight that I would forsake Paris for; no one that hath done so much for me.'

And thus to speak of the feats of Paris, she did not stint. Then came two damoiselles knocking at the chamber door, saying, 'Vienne, ye must come to my lady.' And Isabeau sprang out, saying that she should come anon.

And Vienne, seeing that she must needs depart from thence, said to Isabeau, 'My sister, since we must depart hence, let us take some of these jewels; and we shall keep them secretly till that Paris be comen, and we shall see what countenance he shall make in himself.' Then they took the collar and the white banner of Vienne and other jewels and hid them under their clothes and went into the chamber of Monsieur Jacques.

But Vienne desired greatly to speak with Paris, and thought [how] long or he came home. And, in the meanwhile, Monsieur Jacques recovered of his malady and became all whole; whereof Vienne had great joy, but she durst not show it.

HOW MONSIEUR JACQUES DEMANDED OF THE DAUPHIN HIS DAUGHTER VIENNE IN MARRIAGE FOR HIS SON PARIS

[Vienne is determined to have a formal meeting with Paris and makes a confidant of the bishop, a friend of both. He promises to call at the Dauphin's palace with Paris. At this meeting Paris reveals that he is the one who sang under Vienne's window and won tournaments in her honour, but because of his inferior rank could not hope to marry her. In spite of his protests, Vienne makes him promise to have his father Monsieur Jacques visit her father, requesting his permission for them to marry. The Dauphin vigorously opposes the marriage.]

...Then Paris did so much that he spake unto Vienne on a dark night at a low window whereas they might well say what they would.

'I am certain', said Vienne, 'that my father hath willed to hurt you, whereof I live in great melancholy. For in all the world is nothing that I love so much as you; and if, by adventure, ye die, I will not live.'

Then said Paris, 'Honourable lady, it seemeth me best that I depart from hence a certain time till my lord, your father, be more appeased and hath passed his evil will. Howbeit, that it shall be to me a much sorrowful thing to withdraw me from you. For my life shall be much heavy. Nevertheless, I shall accomplish your will in all that ye shall command me, whatsoever come thereof.'

And Vienne, seeing the good will of Paris after many words, she said to him, 'Paris, my friend, I know well the great love that ye bear to me, and since it so is, I swear to you, by my faith, that ye shall never depart from this city without that I go with you, for it is my will. Wherefore as soon as ye may, make you ready of all things necessary, and find ye the manner that we may escape out of the realm of France; and that we may go into some other lordship whereas we may live joyously and surely. Nevertheless, before or we depart from hence, I will that ye promise two things: the first is, that ye touch not my body unto the time that we be lawfully married; the second is, that Isabeau [have] part in all the goods that we shall have: and other thing will I not, as for this present time, but that only our departing may be shortly. And I shall purvey some jewels and money for our necessity.'

And all this Paris promised to her; and each departed from other for to address such things as to them should be necessary.

HOW PARIS LED AWAY VIENNE AND ISABEAU BY NIGHT

When Paris was purveyed of money and of all other things being to them necessary, he went alone the secretest wise that he might, and came to the place emprised[1] at the hour taken. And he made a token which Vienne knew. And, anon, came Vienne and Ysabeau clad in man's array and leapen out of [the] castle by a *fauce porte*:[2] and so came these two damoiselles to the place whereas Paris was alone [and] which awaited upon their coming. And, incontinent, they departed and went whereas their horses were; whom they took and rode as fast as they might. And George rode always before because to know well the way.

And while they thus rode, arose a storm with a great rain which endured till the morn [and] at night. And then they arrived nigh

---

[1] *emprised*, arranged. [2] *fauce porte, faux porte*(?), secret passageway.

unto a little town, but they entered not because they would not be known: and [they] went and lodged them in a little church nigh unto the town, where they found a chaplain which received them gladly; the best wise he might. And then when the night came, Paris and the chaplain slept in a little house adjoining to the church. George, Paris's servant, slept in the stable with the beasts. And Vienne and Isabeau slept in the church.

And in the morning early they went lightly to horseback, and rode till they came nigh unto a river which was risen high because of the rain that had fallen. Then Paris was much angry because he saw well that it was much perilous; and [he] said to George that he should search and advise some good place where they might pass over. And George withdrew him a little from them and chose a place, which thought him good, and took the river with his horse. And when he was in the middle of the stream, his horse failed him [so] that he was drowned and his horse, also. Paris, seeing that George was drowned, was much sore abashed, and durst make no semblant because that fair Vienne should have no melancholy.

And, after, Vienne demanded of Paris where George was become. And Paris answered to her that he had sent him for to search some good passage, and they would turn into the church again till George were come. And Vienne answered to him that it pleased her well so to do, for she had great doubt and fear for to pass the water. And when they were in the church, Paris was much afraid to abide long in that place, for he saw that it was not sure. Wherefore he demanded the chaplain if they might in any wise pass that water. And the chaplain said not in three days till the water were receded and avaled.[1]

And Paris said to him that he should go into the town to search and see if he might find any men that would make a bridge so that they might pass: and that he should spare no money. 'For', said he, 'I shall pay to them as much as they will have.' And the chaplain said that he should do his best. Thus did Paris nothing but think how they might pass the river. Now leave we Paris, and turn to the Dauphin, which had lost his fair daughter, Vienne.

HOW THE DAUPHIN DID SEARCH AND SEEK VIENNE BY HIS SERVANTS

On the morn that Vienne was lost and departed from the house of her father, and that the Dauphin knew it, he [was] supposed to have gone out of his wits: and all the court was troubled; and [he] sent hastily men on horseback and afoot by divers parties, the most

----

[1] *avaled*, diminished.

secretly that he might, and prayed them that they should bring home to him Vienne, quick or dead.

It happed, by adventure, that one of his men afoot, that was sent to fetch Vienne, came into the town whereas the chaplain was come to seek men to make the bridge. The footman demanded every man if they had seen two damoiselles which were fled from the Dauphin's court. Then the chaplain said to him that it was not long since such twain departed with other men. The man supposed that the said chaplain had said it in jape or in mocking, and said that the Dauphin was much angry and had sworn that if any man or woman knew where they were and showed it not, that he should make them to lose their heads. And when the chaplain heard these words he remembered him of them that were hid in his house. And in great dread said to him, that he should tarry there a little, and that for 'the love of my lord Dauphin', he would gladly search for them: and as soon as he might find tidings of them, he should let him wite.

And so [the chaplain] departed from thence and returned home again; and told all this to Paris, and what he had heard in the town, saying, also, that he doubted that it was for them of his company. Wherefore he said to him, 'Furthermore, Sir, I pray you that ye depart from hence, and suffer not that I lose my life; but take ye the best counsel ye can, for there be fifty men on horseback that seek you.'

When Paris heard him say this, it needeth not to demand if he were heavy and melancholy: and for the great sorrow that he had, he changed all his colour. And he said to the chaplain, 'I pray you that ye tarry a little, and I shall make you an answer.'

And then Paris went to Vienne for to tell to her all this feat. And when Vienne saw him enter and so changed in his colour, [she] said to Paris, 'What tidings bring ye which are so pale and your colour changed? I pray you, as heartily as I can, that it please you to tell me.'

Then Paris said to her, 'The tidings that I bring be evil for you and for me. For shortly shall be accomplished our adventure; and therefore I will slay myself.' And also he said complaining, 'O God, how my life is sorrowful and heavy to have brought this excellent lady, as ye are, in such danger. O good God, why gave Thou not to me the death before or that I fetched her out of her father's house! O, alas, my father and my mother, what shall befall of you when the Dauphin shall know that I have stolen from him his daughter! O my good fellow Edward, why counseleth not I with thee before or I had done this folly!' And after he returned to Vienne saying, 'And what shall fall of you, my lady, when your father shall see you? Certes, I think that [no matter] how cruel that he be, when he shall see your noble person, his heart shall not suffer to do you any harm. O God Almighty, do to me that grace that I only may bare the pain of this *fait* and none other. O lady, unhappy was that day for you and for me when first ye had acquaintance of me!'

And when Paris had finished his complaint, he told to Vienne all that the chaplain had said to him. And forthwith, as a person despaired, [he] took his sword and would have riven it through his body.

And Vienne as virtuous and valiant took him to her heart and took the sword from him and comforted him, and said, 'O free knight, my joy, my life, and my solace, what will ye do? Know ye not well that who that slayeth himself wittingly, slayeth the soul and the body: and if ye die, I assure you, I shall die also; and so shall ye be [the] cause of my death as well as of your own. Aye, Paris, where is your wisdom and your prowess? Now when ye should have most strength [and] most virtuous courage, ye be afraid! O my knight, this is no new thing that the persons that live in this world have tribulation of whatsoever lineage they be. Certes, this is not the courage of one so valiant a knight as ye be. For now whom that ye ought to comfort, she must now comfort you. And, therefore, my fair brother and friend, I pray you, as much as ye may, that incontinent ye depart from hence; and that ye go your way. And if ye do not so, I shall slay myself with your sword. For your departing is as grevious to me as mine shall be to you, but it behoveth to eschew of two evils the worse. And, also, ye ought to consider one thing, that notwithstanding the great fault and trespass that I have made to my father, yet, therefore, he shall not put me to death, considering the great love he hath always had toward me. And if ye were taken, I wote well that ye and I should both die. And yet I have good hope that mine intention shall come unto a good end. For be ye sure though he never pardon me, I shall never have other husband but you: And that I promise you, by my faith. But always of one thing I pray you, that for one other lady, ye forget not me. And when ye shall be in another country, write unto me of your adventure. And to the end that ye the better remember me, lo, here is a ring of gold with a diamond, the which I pray you that ye will keep for the love of me.'

HOW VIENNE WAS FOUND IN THE CHURCH BY A FOOTMAN, AND HOW SHE WAS BROUGHT AGAIN TO HER FATHER

[Vienne is found in the church and taken back to her father.]

...After, the Dauphin took Vienne by the hand, in reproving her much greatly, and led her into her mother's chamber with Isabeau, for her mother was sick of the great sorrow that she had for her daughter. And there the mother blamed them both two. And

Isabeau said that Vienne was as pure and clean of her body as she was the day that she departed.

'Alas,' said the Dauphin, 'thou hast put us in the most greatest shame of the world. And I promise that all they that have consented thereto shall be well punished, and in especial that evil traitor Paris which is cause of all thy *fait*. And if ever I may have him, I shall make dogs devour him; and also both ye twain shall suffer therefore great penitence.'

Then said Vienne weeping, 'I see well and know that ye have intention to do me much grief and harm; and I see well that my life shall not long endure. Therefore I swear to you in good faith, that there is no man in the world that I so much love as I do him whom ye so menace and threaten. For in him I have my thought and courage without ever to fail him. And if ye shortly give to me my penance, so much shortly shall be my death: And if ye suffer me to endure it long, so much more shall I bear it, and my soul shall be the more sure before Almighty God. And know ye for certain that for him and his love, I am ready to die.'

Then the Dauphin issued out of the chamber in great indignation, and commanded that the father of Paris should be put in an evil prison. And that all his goods be taken from him. And also that Vienne and Isabeau should be enclosed in a chamber, and that well little meat should be given to them. And much he menaced and threatened them. And thus they abode a long time in that chamber, and continually Vienne dreamed of Paris.

HOW PARIS CAME TO SEE VIENNE IN THE PRISON, AND HOW SHE KNEW HIM

[Disguised as a Moor, Paris returns from his long exile during which time he befriended Vienne's father. The Dauphin is still unaware of his identity.]

And on the morn, betimes Paris clad him much more richly than he had been accustomed and gird him with a much rich sword. And he came to the prison with the Friar. And the Friar said to her, 'Madame, we been returned for to know your good answer and your intention'.

And Vienne answered, 'Lords, mine intention is that I shall never break my promise that I have made. For I have avowed that I shall never take husband, nor go out of this prison but dead, save him to whom I have promised. Therefore return ye in good time.'

Then said the Friar, 'By my faith, I wote not what to say, for it is great damage that ye suffer so much sorrow and pain. And since it is thus your will and that ye will none otherwise do, nevertheless, the Moor prayeth you that it may please you to do to him so much grace, that since ye will not take him in marriage that ye will wear this ring for the love of him.'

Now this ring was the same ring that Vienne gave to Paris when he departed from her in the house of the chaplain. And Vienne, because they should no more come again, took the ring.

And when she had received the ring, Paris said to the Friar, 'I pray you that ye tarry a little without, for I will see what countenance she will make of the ring'.

And the Friar said, 'Gladly.' Nevertheless, he marvelled much. And incontinent the Friar went out, and Vienne began to behold the ring. When Paris saw that Vienne beheld the ring so strongly, he began to speak in his plain tongue, and said, 'O much noble lady, why be ye so much admarvelled of that ring?'

Then said Vienne, 'Certes, to my seeming, I saw never a fairer.'

Then said Paris, 'Therefore, I pray you that ye take therein pleasure. For the more that ye behold it, the more ye shall praise it.'

When Vienne heard the Moor thus speak, then she was more admarvelled than before; and [she] was as a person all abashed, and said, 'Alas, am I enchanted! What is this that I see and hear speak?' And in saying these words, she would have fled for fear out of the prison, because she heard the Moor so speak.

Then said Paris, 'O much noble lady Vienne, marvel ye nothing, nor have ye no doubt. Lo, here is Paris, your true servant.'

Vienne was then abashed more than before. 'Certes,' said she, 'this may not be but by work enchanted.'

Paris said, 'Noble lady, it is none enchanted work. For I am your servant Paris, which left you with Isabeau in such a church. And there ye gave me the diamond which now I have delivered to you; and there ye promised to me that ye would never take husband but me. And be ye nothing admarvelled of the beard nor of the vesture that I wear, for they take away the knowledge of me.'

Many other words said Paris to Vienne, by which she knew clearly that he was Paris. And for the sovereign love that she bare to him and for the great joy that she had, she began to weep in his arms and to embrace and kiss him much sweetly. And there they comforted each other with sweet words, and so abode [a] long time. Vienne could not enough kiss him and embrace him. Also, Paris demanded of her adventure; and she told him all.

And of all this, Isabeau had nothing heard of, for she was fast asleep because she had watched all the night before. And for the great joy and sweetness that Paris and Vienne demeaned between them, she awoke. And when she saw Vienne embraced with the Moor, she said, 'Madame, what is this that ye do? Have ye lost your wits, that [ye] so embrace this Moor? Hath he enchanted you, that ye suffer him so familiar with you? Is this the faith ye keep to Paris for whom ye have suffered so much pain and sorrow?'

And Vienne said, 'Sweet sister, say ye no such words, but come and take your part of the solace that I have, for also well have ye found good adventure as I have. See ye not here, my sweet Paris, whom so much we have desired.'

Then Isabeau approached near to him and beheld him well and saw that it was Paris. She went and kissed him, and [there] demeaned so much great joy between them three, that there is no person in the world that might say nor think it; but so [they] abode a great while in this solace and joy, till at last Paris spoke, 'Sweet Vienne, it behoveth that we go hence before my lord, the Dauphin, your father. For now, from henceforth, it is necessary that he know all our *fait*. Nevertheless, I pray you to say nothing till I desire you.'

All three came out of the prison, and found the Friar which marvelled greatly. And all they together went to the Dauphin, which had sovereign pleasure when he saw them. Nevertheless, he was much abashed how his daughter was so come.

Then Paris said to the Friar, 'Say ye to the Dauphin that I have converted his daughter to his will and to mine, and that it please him that she be my wife.'

And the Friar said so.

Then the Dauphin said to his daughter, 'Will ye take this man for your husband which hath delivered me out of prison in great peril of his person?'

Then demanded Vienne of Paris if he would that she should speak. And Paris said, 'Yea.'

And then Vienne said to the Dauphin, 'My father, I am ready to do your commandment and his; and [I] pray you to pardon me and give to me your benediction.'

When she said thus, her father pardoned her and gave her his blessing and kissed her. Then said Vienne, 'Lo, here is my good friend Paris whom I have so much desired, and for whom I have suffered so much pain and sorrow. Father, this is he that so sweetly sang and floyted[1] and that won jousts in this city and bare with him the shield of crystal and my garland. Also, this is he that won the jousts in the city of Paris, and won there the three banners with the three jewels, and went away with them without knowing of any man. And also he hath delivered you out of prison, putting his life in jeopardy for you.'

When the Dauphin understood all this, he was marvellously glad and joyous.

After all this, Paris went to his father. When he saw him and knew that he was his son Paris, whom he had so long desired to see, he

---

[1] *floyted*, played the lute.

embraced him and kissed him; and for the joy that he had, he could not speak a word. And all the other lords and knights ran for to embrace and kiss him.

After this joy Paris's father said to the Dauphin, 'My lord, please it you that I may borrow my son home to my house for to see his mother and his fellow Edward'?

Then said the Dauphin, 'It pleaseth me right well only for this day, for tomorrow I will that the marriage of him and my daughter be made and solemnized here.'

And then Monsieur Jacques went with his son unto his house. And when he was there, verily, his father and his mother and his fellow Edward wist not where they were for joy and pleasure that they had. And that was no wonder, for they had no more children but him; and he should wed the daughter of their lord. Also, Paris was in that time become a valiant knight and full of all beauty; and for many reasons it was no marvel though they had in him great joy and pleasure. Edward demanded of him of his adventure and many other things; and he recounted and told him all.

HOW PARIS ESPOUSED AND WEDDED VIENNE; AND OF THE FEAST THAT WAS THERE MADE

Then, on the morn, the Dauphin gave his daughter in marriage to Paris. And, after, the feast was much noble and sumptuous; for much people were come thither for to see the feast. And it endured fifteen days. And the pleasure and solace which was done for the love of Paris and of Vienne was so great that uneth[1] it may be believed.

Paris and Vienne lived together a great while in right great consolation and pleasure. But after the accomplishment of the marriage, the father and mother of Paris lived not long after in this world. Paris had by Vienne, his wife, three children, that is to wit, two sons and one daughter. And the Dauphin ordained for them much noble matrimony.

And Paris, after the death of his father and his mother, would that Edward, his dear fellow, should be inheritor of all the goods that his father left. And [he] gave to him Isabeau to his wife; which lived together long time in great love and concord.

And soon after, the Dauphin and his wife died. Then was Paris Dauphin and had the possession of all the seigniory; the which lived with Vienne in this world forty years: and led a good and holy life, insomuch that after the entendement[2] of some men, they be saints in Heaven. They died both in one year.

And semblably Edward and Ysabeau died both twain in one year.

---

[1] *uneth*, scarcely.   [2] *entendement*, mind, opinion.

Therefore let us pray unto Our Lord that we may do such works in this world, that in suchwise we may accompany them in the perdurable glory of heaven. Amen.

Thus endeth the story of the noble and valiant Knight Paris and the fair Vienne, daughter of the Dauphin of Viennois: translated out of French into English by William Caxton at Westminster. . . . 1485.

'HUON OF BORDEAUX'

The fifteenth-century prose romance Huon of Bordeaux *owes its main interest to the hero's friend, the dwarf-king Auberon or Oberon, who takes his name from the famous German dwarf Alberon. But, as Professor Roger Loomis has pointed out, he most likely sprang from the Welsh pigmy ruler Beli, and so bears a close relationship to other faëry kings, Pelles, Belinor, and Wauchier's Petit Chevalier and Chrétien de Troyes' Guivret. Like the others, Oberon has a family tie with the fabulous Morgain la Fée, but he claims a mortal father, Julius Caesar. His magic wares—a cup, an ivory horn, and a golden rod—were the customary gear of the dwarf king. Oberon's gift of these articles to his mortal friend Huon and the latter's daring use of them during his adventures keep the tale in the romance genre.*

Several manuscripts of medieval metrical versions of Huon *are extant in French, Italian, German, and Spanish. Among the earliest of these is an anonymous fourteenth-century French poem* Chanson d'Huon *discovered at Turin. It is the direct source of* Huon of Bordeaux, *which was written in 1454 at the request of Charles, Seigneur de Rochfort, a noble at the court of Charles VII. The English translation, made by Lord Berners and printed in 1534, retains the charm of the long rambling tale of adventure that begins in France and takes the reader to Babylon and Jerusalem, then back to the court of Charlemagne in Paris. The story is one of the later group of* chansons de geste *that grew up around the emperor, showing him as an ailing and aged monarch. He is, however, all but forgotten except in the initial and closing incidents.*

Oberon retained his popularity even in the Renaissance, finding his way into the works of Spenser, Greene, and Shakespeare.

SYNOPSIS

When the romance opens, the brothers Huon and Gerard rule over a small district in France, inherited from their father Seguin, Duke of Bordeaux. Though he had been dead four years, the Duke's sons had neglected to pay allegiance to Charlemagne. They were called rebels by the Earl of Amaury,

who is anxious to have them killed so as to obtain their lands. The Earl
plots with the Emperor's eldest son Charlot, said to resemble Charles the
Bald, to kill the brothers while they are on their way to obey his command
to appear at Court. The plot is unsuccessful. After wounding Gerard,
Charlot is killed by Huon, who is unaware of his identity.

When Charlemagne learns of his son's death, he vows vengeance on the
murderer, who Amaury declares is Huon. The latter's uncle, the Abbot of
Cluny, pleads with the Emperor to spare Huon's life, declaring that Amaury
is a traitor. He denies the Abbot's charge, and to prove his innocence offers
to let Huon 'come into the field' against him. Amid the splendid pageantry
of the times, the knights meet on a field outside Paris. Amaury is knocked
from his horse and killed; and Charlemagne then determines to banish
Huon from France until he has undertaken a journey to Babylon and killed
the Admiral Gaudys. To prove his prowess, Huon must return with hairs
from the Admiral's beard and 'four of his greatest teeth'.

Huon accepts the task and is aided by his father's old friend Gerames,
who tells him of the Faëry King Oberon, whose dominion lies between
Jerusalem and Babylon. The young knight meets the Faëry King and
through his aid performs marvellous feats, including the killing of Gaudys.
After marrying the Admiral's daughter Esclaramonde, who becomes a
Christian, Huon returns to France with Oberon to seek a reconciliation
with the Emperor. New difficulties arise for Huon, but he is helped by
Oberon who proclaims him heir to the throne of Faëryland.

Huon of Bordeaux

TRANSLATED BY JOHN BOURCHIER, LORD BERNERS

[HOW HUON DEPARTED FROM BRANDYS]

How Huon of Bordeaux departed from Brandys and Garyn
his uncle with him; and how he came to Jerusalem, and from
thence into the deserts, where he found Gerames; and of
their devices.[1]

When Huon had heard Gerames, then he demanded further of him
if he could go to Babylon. 'Yea, sir,' quod Gerames, 'I can go thither
by two ways. The most surest way is hence a forty [days'] journey;
and the other is but fifteen days' journey. But I counsel you to take
the long way; for if ye take the shorter way, ye must pass throughout a wood sixteen leagues of length; but the way is so full of the
faëry and strange things that such as pass that way are lost, for in that
wood abideth a King of the Faëry named Oberon. He is of height
but of three feet, and crooked shouldered, but yet he hath an angel-

[1] Chapter XXI.

like visage, so that there is no mortal man that seeth him but that taketh great pleasure to behold his face. And ye shall no sooner be entered into that wood, if ye go that way, he will find the manner to speak with you. And if ye speak to him, ye are lost forever. And ye shall ever find him before you, so that it shall be, in manner, impossible that ye can scape from him without speaking to him, for his words be so pleasant to hear that there is no mortal man that can well scape without speaking to him.

'And if he see that ye will not speak a word to him, then he will be sore displeased with you; and or ye can get out of the wood, he will cause rain and wind, hail and snow, and will make marvellous tempests with thunder and lightening so that it shall seem to you that all the world should perish. And he shall make to seem before you a great running river, black and deep. But ye may pass it at your ease; and it shall not wet the feet of your horse: for all is but fantasy and enchantments that the dwarf shall make to the intent to have you with him. And if ye can keep yourself without speaking to him, ye may then well 'scape. But, Sir, to eschew all perils, I counsel you take the longer way, for I think ye can not 'scape from him; and then be ye lost forever.'

When Huon had well heard Gerames, he had great marvel; and he had great desire in himself to see that dwarf King of the Faëry and the strange adventures that were in that wood. Then he said to Gerames that for fear of any death he would not leave to pass that way, since he might come to Babylon in fifteen days: for in taking the longer way, he might, peradventure, find more adventures; and since he was advertised that with keeping his tongue from speaking, he might abridge his journey. And he said that surely he would [go] that way whatsoever chance fell.

'Sir,' quod Gerames, 'ye shall do your pleasure; for whichsoever way ye take, it shall not be without me. I shall bring you to Babylon to the Admiral Gaudys. I know him right well; and when ye be come thither, ye shall see there a damsel, as I have heard say, the most fairest creature in all Inde and the great and most sweetest and most courteous that ever was born. And it is she that ye seek, for she is daughter to the Admiral Gaudys.'

[OF THE MARVELS THAT OBERON SHOWED TO HUON]

Of the great marvels that Oberon showed to Huon and of the adventures that fell.[1]

When Huon had well heard Oberon, he had great marvel, and demanded if it were true that he had said.

[1] Chapter xxv.

'Yea, truly,' quod Oberon, 'of that make no doubt.'

'Sir,' quod Huon, 'I have great marvel for what cause ye have always pursued us.'

'Huon,' quod Oberon, 'know well, I love thee well because of the truth that is in thee, and therefore naturally I love thee: and if thou wilt know who I am, I shall show thee. True it is, Julius Caesar engendered me on the lady of the Privey Isle,[1] who was sometime well beloved of the faëry Florimont of Albany. But because that Florimont, who as then was young, and he had a mother who did [spy] so much that she saw my mother and Florimont together in a solitary place on the seaside, when my mother perceived that she was espied by Florimont's mother, she departed and left Florimont, her lover, in great weepings and lamentations and never saw him after. And then she returned into her country of the Privey Isle, the which now is named Chyfalonnye, whereas she married after and had a son who, in his time after, was King of Egypt, named Neptanabus. It was he, as it is said, that engendered Alexander the Great who after caused him to die. Then after a seven year, Caesar passed by the sea as he went into Thessaly where he fought with Pompey. In his way he passed by Chyfalonnye where my mother fetched him, and he fell in love with her because she showed him that he should discomfort Pompey, as he did. Thus I have showed you who was my father.

'At my birth there was many a prince and baron of the faëries and many a noble lady that came to see my mother while she travailed of me. And among them there was one [who] was not content because she was not sent for as well as the other. And when I was born, she gave me a gift, the which was that when I should pass three years of age, I should grow no more, but thus as ye see me now. And when she had thus done and saw that she had thus served me by her words, she repented herself and would recompense me another way. Then she gave me another gift; and that was, that I should be the fairest creature that ever nature formed, as thou mayst see me now. And another lady of the faëry named Transline gave me another gift; and that was, all that ever any man can know or think, good or ill, I do know it. The third lady, to do more for me and to please my mother the better, she gave me, that there is not so fair a country but that if I will wish myself there, I shall be there incontinent with what number of men as I list; and, moreover, if I will have a castle or a palace at mine own devise, incontinent it shall be made, and as soon gone again as I list. And what meat or wine that I will wish for it I shall have it incontinent. And, also, I am King of Momur, the which is four hundred thousand leagues from hence; and if I list incontinent, I can be there.

[1] *lady of the Privey Isle*, Morgain la Fée, who ruled Avalon.

'Know for truth that thou hast had but small sustenance, but I shall cause thee to have enough. I demand of thee whether thou wilt have meat and drink here in this meadow or in a place or in a hall? Command where, as thou wilt; and thou shalt have it for thee and thy company.'

'Sir,' quod Huon, 'I will follow your pleasure and never do nor think contrary.'

'Huon,' quod he, 'as yet I have not showed all the gifts that were given me at my birth. The fourth lady gave me, that there is no bird nor beast, be they never so cruel, but if I will have them, I may take them with my hand: and, also, I shall never seem older than thou seest me now. And when I shall depart out of this world, my place is apèrreled[1] in paradise, for I know that all things created in this mortal world must needs have an end.'

'Sir,' quod Huon, 'such a gift ought to be well kept.'

'Huon,' quod Oberon, 'well ye were counselled when ye spake to me. Ye had never before so fair adventure. Show me, by thy faith, if thou wilt eat; and what meat thou wilt have, and what wine thou wilt drink.'

'Sir,' quod Huon, 'so that I had meat and drink, I care not what it were so that I and my company were filled and rid from our famine.'

Then Oberon laughed at him, and said, 'Sirs, all ye sit down here in this meadow, and have no doubt but all that I will do is done by the puissance of Our Lord God.' Then Oberon began to wish, and said to Huon and his company, 'Sirs, arise up quickly.'

The which they did. Then they regarded before them and saw a fair and a rich palace garnished with chambers and halls, hanged and bedded with rich cloths of silk, beaten with gold, and tables ready set full of meat. When Huon and his company saw the rich palace before them, they had great marvel. Then Oberon took Huon by the hand and with him mounted up into the palace.

When they came there, they found servants there ready, bringing to them basins of gold, garnished with precious stones. They gave water to Huon. Then he sat down at the table, the which was furnished with all manner of meat and drink that man could wish. Oberon sat at the table's end on a bank of ivory richly garnished with gold and precious stones, the which seat had such virtue given to it by the faëry that whosoever by any subtle means would poison him that should sit there on, as soon as he should approach near to the seat he should fall down stark dead.

King Oberon sat thereon richly apparelled; and Huon, who sat near to him, began to eat a great pace, but Gerames had small appetite to eat, for he believed that they should never depart thence.

When Oberon saw him, he said, 'Gerames, eat thy meat and

[1] *apèrreled*, appointed.

drink. For as soon as thou hast eaten, thou shalt have leave to go when thou list.'

When Gerames heard that, he was joyful. Then he began to eat and drink, for he know well that Oberon would not do against his assurance. All the company did well eat and drink. They were served with all things that they could wish for.

When Huon saw how they were all satisfied and replete and had well dined, he said to King Oberon, 'Sir, when it shall be your pleasure, I would ye should give us leave to depart.'

'Huon,' quod Oberon, 'I am right well content so to do, but first I will show you my jewels.' Then he called Clariand, a knight of the faëry, and said, 'Friend, go and fetch to me my cup.' He did his commandment. And when Oberon had the cup in his hand, he said to Huon, 'Sir, behold well. Ye see well, this cup is void and empty.'

'That is true, sir', quod Huon.

Then Oberon set the cup on the table and said to Huon, 'Sir, behold the great power that God hath given me, and how that in the faëry I may do my pleasure'. Then he made over the cup the Sign of the Cross three times. Then incontinent the cup was full of wine. And then he said, 'Lo, sirs, ye may well see that this is done by the grace of God. Yet I shall show you the great virtue that is in this cup. For if all the men in the world were here assembled together, and that the cup were in the hands of any man being out of deadly sin, he might drink thereof his fill; but whosoever offer his hand to take it being in deadly sin, the cup should lose his virtue. And if thou mayst drink thereof, I offer to give thee the cup.'

'Sir,' quod Huon, 'I thank you, but I am in doubt that I am not worthy nor of valor to drink thereof nor to touch the cup. I never heard of such a dignity as this cup is of. But, sir, know for truth, I have been confessed of all my sins, and I am repentant and sorrowful for that I have done. And I do pardon and forgive all the men in the world whatsoever injury hath been done to me. And I know not that I have done wrong to any creature, nor I hate no man.' And so he took the cup in both his hands and set it to his mouth and drank of the good wine, that was therein, at his pleasure.

[OF THE GIFTS THAT OBERON GAVE TO HUON]

Of the great gifts that Oberon gave to Huon, as his horn of ivory and his cup. The which were of great virtues: and Huon, after, thought to prove the virtue of them, whereby he was in great peril of death.[1]

When Oberon saw that, he was right glad, and came and embraced Huon, seeing how he was a nobleman. 'I give thee this cup as it is

[1] Chapter XXVI.

in the manner as I shall show thee in anywise for anything. For the dignity of the cup be thou ever true and faithful; for if thou wilt work by my counsel, I shall aid thee and give thee succour in all thine affairs. But as soon as thou makest any lie, the virtue of the cup will be lost and lose his bounty. And besides that, thou shalt lose my love and aid.'

'Sir,' quod Huon, 'I shall right well beware thereof: and now, Sir, I require you suffer us to depart.'

'Abide yet', quod Oberon. 'Yet I have another jewel the which I will give thee because I think there be truth and nobleness in thee. I will give thee a rich horn of ivory, the which is full of great virtue, the which thou shalt bear with thee. It is of so great virtue that if thou be never so far from me as soon as thou blowest the horn, I shall hear thee and shall be incontinent with thee with a hundred thousand men of arms for to succour and aid thee. But one thing I command thee, on the pain of losing of my love and on jeopardy of thy life, that thou be not so hardy to sound thy horn without thou hast great need thereof; for if thou do otherwise, I avow to God that created me, I shall leave thee in as great poverty and misery as ever man was, so that whosoever should see thee in that case should have pity of thee.'

'Sir,' quod Huon, 'I shall right well beware thereof. Now I desire you let me depart.'

'I am content,' quod Oberon, 'and God be thy guide.'

Then Huon took leave of King Oberon and trussed up all his baggage and did put his cup in his bosom and the horn about his neck. Thus they all took their leave of the King. Oberon, all weeping, embraced Huon who had marvel why he wept, and said, 'Sir, why do you weep?'

'Friend,' quod Oberon, 'ye may well know ye have with you two things that I love dearly. God aid you. More I cannot speak to you.'

Thus the fourteen knights departed; and so they rode forth about fifteen leagues or more. Then they saw before them a great deep river, and they could find no guide nor passage to pass over; and so they wist not what to do. Then suddenly they saw pass by them a servant of King Oberon, bearing a rod of gold in his hand; and so without speaking of any word, he entered into the river and took his rod and struck the water therewith three times. Then incontinent the water withdrew to both sides in suchwise that there was a path that three men might ride afront. And that done he departed again without speaking of any word.

Then Huon and his company entered into the water, and so passed through without any danger. When they were past, they beheld behind them and saw the river close again and run after his old course.

'By my faith,' quod Huon, 'I think, we be enchanted. I believe surely King Oberon hath done this. But seeing we be thus 'scaped out of peril, I trust from henceforth we shall have no doubt.'

Thus they rode forth together singing and oftentimes spake of the great marvels that they had seen King Oberon do. And as they rode, Huon beheld on his right hand and saw a fair meadow well garnished with herbs and flowers and in the midst thereof a fair, clear fountain. Then Huon rode thither and alighted and let their horses to pasture. Then they spread a cloth on the green grass and set there up such meat as King Oberon had given them at their departing. And there they did eat and drink such drink as they found in the cup.

'By my faith,' quod Huon, 'it was a fair adventure for us when we met Oberon, and that I spoke to him. He hath showed me great tokens of love when he gave me such a cup. If I may return into France in safeguard, I shall give it to Charlemagne who shall make great feast therewith. And if he cannot drink thereof, the barons of France will have great joy thereof.' Then again he repented him of his own words, and said, 'I am a fool to think or say thus. For as yet I cannot tell what end I shall come to. The cup that I have is better worth than two cities, but as yet I cannot believe the virtue to be in the horn as Oberon hath showed nor that he may hear it so far off. But whatsoever fortune fall, I will assay it if it hath such virtue, or not.'

'Aye, sir,' quod Gerames, 'beware what ye do. Ye know well when we departed what charge he gave you. Certainly, you and we both are lost if ye trespass his commandment.'

'Surely,' quod Huon, 'whatsoever fortune fall, I shall assay it.' And so took the horn and set it to his mouth and blew it so loud that the wood rang.

Then Gerames and all the other began to sing and to make great joy.

Then Garyn said, 'Fair nephew, blow still.'

And so Huon blew still with such force that Oberon who was in his wood about fifteen leagues off heard him clearly, and said, 'Alas, my friends, I hear my friend blow whom I love best of all the world. Alas, what man is so hardy to do him any ill? I wish myself with him with a hundred thousand men of arms.'

When Huon and his company heard the host coming and saw Oberon come riding on before, then they were afraid. It was no marvel, seeing the commandment that Oberon had given them before.

Then Huon said, 'Aye, sirs, I have done ill. Now I see well we cannot escape, but that we be likely to die.'

'Certainly', quod Gerames, 'ye have well deserved it.'

'Hold your peace', quod Huon. 'Dismay you not. Let me speak to him.'

Therewith Oberon came to them, and said, 'Huon, of God, be thou cursed. Where are they that will do thee any ill? Why hast thou broken my commandment?'

'Aye, sir,' quod Huon, 'I shall show you the truth. We were sitting right now in the meadow and did eat of that ye gave us. I believe, I took too much drink out of the cup that ye gave me; the virtue of the which we well assayed. Then I thought to assay also the virtue of the rich horn, to the intent that if I should have any need that I might be sure thereof. Now I know for truth that all is true that ye have showed me. Wherefore, sir, in the honour of God, I require you to pardon my trespass. Sir, here is my sword. Strike off my head at your pleasure. For I know well without your aid, I shall never come to achieve mine enterprise.'

'Huon,' quod Oberon, 'the bounty and great truth that is in thee constraineth me to give thee pardon, but beware; from henceforth be not so hardy to break my commandment.'

'Sir,' quod Huon, 'I thank you.'

'Well,' quod Oberon, 'I know surely that thou hast as yet much to suffer, for thou must pass by a city named Tormont wherein there is a tyrant Macaire, and yet he is thine own uncle, brother to thy father, Duke Seguin. When he was in France he had thought to have murdered King Charlemagne, but his treason was known. And he had been slain, and[1] thy father Duke Seguin had not been alive, so he was sent to the Holy Sepulchre to do his penance for the ill that he had done. And so, afterward, there he renounced the faith of Our Lord God and took on him the paynim's law, the which he hath kept ever since so sorely that if he hear any man speak of Our Lord God, he will persue him to the death. And what promise that he maketh, he keepeth none. Therefore I advise thee trust not on him, for surely he will put thee to death if he may. And thou canst not scape if thou go by that city. Therefore I counsel thee, take not that way if thou be wise.'

'Sir,' quod Huon, 'of your courtesy, love, and good counsel, I thank you. But whatsoever fortune fall to me, I will go to mine uncle. And if he be such one as ye say, I shall make him to die an ill death; if need be I shall sound my horn, and I am sure at my need, ye will aid me.'

'Of that ye may be sure,' quod Oberon, 'but of one thing I defend[2] thee: be not so hardy to sound the horn without thou be hurt; for if thou do the contrary, I shall so martyr thee that thy body shall not endure it.'

'Sir,' quod Huon, 'be assured your commandment I will not break.' Then Huon took leave of King Oberon who was sorry when Huon departed.

---

[1] *and*, if. [2] *defend*, forbid.

'Sir,' quod Huon, 'I have marvel why ye weep. I pray you, show me the cause why ye do it.'

'Huon,' quod Oberon, 'the great love that I have in thee causeth me to do it, for as yet hereafter thou shalt suffer so much ill and travail that no human tongue can tell it.'

'Sir,' quod Huon, 'ye show me many things not greatly to my profit.'

'Sure,' quod Oberon, 'and yet thou shalt suffer more than I have spoken of, and all by thine own folly.'

[Huon goes to the city of Tormont: after fulfilling his boast to kill his uncle, he learns of the giant Angolafer who lives near the sea in the castle of Dunother, erected by Julius Caesar, and whom none can resist. Against Oberon's advice Huon steals into the castle and determines to kill the giant. By a ruse he puts on Angolafer's armour.]

[HOW HUON SLEW THE GREAT GIANT]

How Huon slew the great giant; and how he called Gerames and his company to him; and of the joy that they made for the death of the giant.[1]

When Huon understood the paynim, he said, 'Aye, thou fell and false deceiver, know for truth if all the preachers between the east and west preached to me a whole year and that thou wouldst give me all that thou hast and thy ring therewith, I would not render again the good harness that is now on my body. First, I shall slay thee; and then as for thy ring that thou praisest so sore, then I will have it, whether thou wilt, or not.'

When the Giant had well heard Huon and saw that he in no wise could get again his harness, he was then sorrowful; and also he saw how Huon reproved him. Therewith he was so sore displeased that his eyes seemed like two candles burning. Then he yet demanded of Huon if he would do none otherwise.

'No, truly,' quod Huon, 'though thou be great and strong, I have no fear of thee since I have on this good harness. Therefore in the Name of God and of His divine puissance, I defy thee.'

'And I, thee', quod the Giant. 'For all thy harness, thou cannot endure against me.'

Then the Giant approached to Huon and lifted up his falchion, thinking to have struck Huon. But he failed. The stroke glent,[2] and the falchion lit upon a pillar and entered into it more than two feet. Then Huon who was quick and light beheld the marvellous stroke: quickly he stepped forth with his good sword in his hands [and],

[1] Chapter XXXIV.   [2] *glent*, glanced.

regarding how the Giant had his falchion sticking fast in the pillar, he struck the Giant on both the arms near to his hands in such wise that he struck off both his hands, so that they with the falchion fell down to the earth.

When the Giant felt himself so sore hurt, for pain thereof he gave a marvellous cry so horrible as though all the tower had fallen to the earth. Whereof the damsel Sybil, being in her chamber was sore abashed. She went out of her chamber and found a staff by the way. She took it up in her hands and came to the palace where she heard the cry and met the Giant fleeing away to save himself. But the damsel, well advised when she saw that he fled, cast the staff between his legs, so that thereby he fell to the earth. And Huon who came after him with his sword in his hand, he hasted him and gave the Giant many a great stroke. And the Giant cried out so high that it was great marvel to hear him.

Then Huon lifted up his sword and gave him such a stroke in the neck that his head flew to the earth. Then Huon wiped his sword and put it up in the sheath. Then he came to the head, thinking to have taken it up to have set it on the height of the tower. But the head was so great and so heavy that he could not remove it nor turn his body. Then he smiled, and said, 'Aye, good Lord, I thank Ye of Thy Grace to have given me the puissance to slay such a creature. Would to God that this body and head were now in the palace of Paris before Charlemagne, King of France, so that he knew that I have slain him!'

Then Huon went to a window and looked out and saw where his company were. Then he said to them from high, 'Sirs, come up hither. Ye may do it surely, for this palace is won and the Giant slain!'

[HOW HUON DEPARTED FROM THE CASTLE OF THE GIANT]

How Huon departed from the castle of the giant and took leave of his company and went alone afoot to the seaside whereas he found Malabron, that faëry on whom he mounted to pass the sea.[1]

We have heard here before how Huon conquered the Giant, the which was great joy to all his company. Then the next day Huon called all his company and said, 'Sirs, ye know well the enterprise that I have taken on me to do, touching the Admiral Gaudys. Therefore it is convenient, that as shortly as I can, to do my message that I am charged by King Charles to do to the Admiral Gaudys. Wherefore I desire you all to keep good and true company with this noble

[1] Chapter xxxv.

damsel, and, also, I require you to tarry[1] me here fifteen days. And then if I return not, go you all into France and take this noble damsel with you and salute from me, King Charlemagne and all the peers of France. And show them the hard adventures that I have had and how I am gone to perform his message.'

When his company understood that he would depart, they were sorrowful, and said, 'Sir, ye desire us to tarry you here fifteen days. Know for truth, we shall tarry here for you a whole year.'

'Sirs,' quod he, 'I thank you.' Then he made him ready to depart and armed him and took his cup and horn and also the Giant's ring, the which he did put about his arm. And then he kissed his cousin and all the others, and they all made great lamentations for his departing. Then they went up into the palace and looked out at the windows after Huon, as long as they might see him.

Huon went forth till he came to the seaside, the which was not far from the castle: and there was a little haven whereas always lay some manner of ship or vessel to pass over the sea. And when Huon came thither, he had great marvel, and said, 'Aye, good Lord, what shall I do that I can find here no boat nor vessel to pass in? Alas, in an ill hour I slew Charlot whereby I am in danger. Howbeit, I did it in my defence. Great wrong King Charles hath done to banish me out of mine own country.'

Great complaints made Huon, there being alone. And he began sore to weep. And suddenly, on his right hand, he saw a great beast come swimming toward him like a bear. Huon beheld him and made on his head a Sign of the Cross and drew out his sword to defend himself, thinking the beast would have assailed him. But he did not, but went a little off from Huon and shook himself in suchwise that his skin fell off, and then he was as fair a man and as well formed as could be seen.

Then Huon had great fear and marvel. When he saw that this beast was become a man, he approached near to him and demanded what he was and whether he were a human creature, or else an ill spirit that was come thither to tempt him, and said, 'Right now, thou did swim in the sea and traversed the great waves in guise of a marvellous beast. I charge thee, in the name of God, do me no hurt and show me what thou art. I believe thou art of King Oberon's company.'

'Huon,' quod he, 'dismay thou not, I know thee right well. Thou art son to the noble Duke Seguin of Bordeaux. Noble King Oberon hath sent me to thee. Once I broke his commandment, wherefore he hath condemned me to be this thirty years like a beast in the sea.'

'Friend,' quod Huon, 'by the Lord that formed me, I will trust thee till I be passed the Red Sea.'

---

[1] *tarry*, wait for.

'Huon,' quod Malabron, 'know for truth, I am sent hither for none other thing but to bear thee whither as thou wilt. Therefore make thee ready and recommend thyself to the safeguard of Our Lord Jesus Christ, and then let me alone.' Then Malabron entered again into the beast's skin, and said to Huon, 'Sir, mount on my back.'

The Boke of Duke Huon.... Ed. by S. L. Lee. E.E.T.S. Ex. ser. 40–1; 43, 50 (London, 1882–7).

'VALENTINE AND ORSON'

The popular appeal of Valentine and Orson, *a romance of the Charlemagne cycle, has warranted seventy-four editions, including one in the nineteenth century, since its first English printing by Wynkyn de Worde not later than 1505. As H. S. Bennett points out in* English Books and Readers, 1476–1557, *the name of Henry Watson, Worde's apprentice and translator, 'first appears in connexion with a translation of* Lystoire des deux vaillons cheualier Valentin et Orson'.

This French prose tale has strong affiliations with Dutch, German, and Swedish versions of a similar romance, Valentin und Namelos. *In an exhaustive critique,* Valentine and Orson, a Study in Late Medieval Romance, *Arthur Dickson suggests its immediate source is a lost fourteenth-century French poem to which the author of the prose version added considerable new material. This latter came from a wide variety of sources— 'not only from* chansons *and* romances', *Professor Dickson notes, 'but also from the Bible, saints' legends, history, and contemporary events'. The finished work is a narrative so laden with events that it is difficult to follow. Nevertheless, it is fascinating and unrivalled among the chivalric romances as a study in villainy and the magic arts.*

The 'wild man Orson' is a familiar figure in English literature. He is mentioned as a character in a pageant that was held to celebrate the coronation of the boy king Edward VI. Professor Dickson sees a parallel between the plot of the brothers Haufray and Henry to assassinate Pepin and the murder of Duncan in Macbeth, *especially the studied effort in each case to place the knife so that the guilt is shifted to an innocent person.*

Perhaps the most famous reference to the romance in modern literature is in Dickens's A Christmas Carol *when Scrooge, recalling the stories of his childhood, imagines he sees the famous pair. 'Valentine and Orson! There they go!' he cries.*

SYNOPSIS

When the story opens Bellisant, a sister of King Pepin and wife of Alexander, Emperor of Constantinople, is exiled from court because of malicious gossip. She flees to Orleans, and in a wood outside of the city gives birth to twin sons, Valentine and Orson. A bear carries off Orson; and while his mother goes on a fruitless search for him, Pepin finds Valentine by chance. Unaware of his identity, the King takes him to court and educates him.

When Valentine reaches young manhood, he goes hunting one day and sees Orson, whom he believes is a 'wild man of the forest'. Valentine subdues him and takes him back to Pepin's court. In the months that follow, the brothers become fast friends, but do not discover their relationship until later in the story. As Orson gradually takes on civilized ways, he becomes a favourite at court, especially with Pepin. This causes jealousy between him and the King's illegitimate sons, Haufray and Henry, who attempt to kill Pepin and place the blame on Orson.

Valentine and Orson eventually leave the French court; and their adventures take them to Rome, Constantinople, Jerusalem, and India, to the tomb of St Thomas the Apostle, the only account in romance literature of the Indian shrine. Their journeys are filled with experiences that are common to the Arthurian tradition: the brothers fall in love with beautiful princesses; subdue a Green Knight; struggle with the Giant Ferragu to release their mother whom he has imprisoned; a brazen head speaks to them, revealing their true identity; they make friends with the dwarf Pacolet, who lends them his wooden horse that can fly, and it takes them to India. When occasion demands, they use sleeping charms and magic potions; and dreams foretell imminent disasters.

There are a number of minor characters; the most important of them is Pepin. His pilgrimage to Jerusalem with his twelve peers furnishes several colourful incidents.

──────────

Valentine and Orson

TRANSLATED BY HENRY WATSON

[HOW HAUFRAY AND HENRY IMAGINED GREAT TREASON AGAINST ORSON]

How Haufray and Henry imagined great treason against Orson by the aid and consenting of twain of their nephews.[1]

There was none that had to do with the King that sought other mean[2] than Orson, for the which thing Haufray and Henry, that

---

[1] Chapter LVI.   [2] *mean*, go-between.

I have made mention of tofore, had so great envy against the good Orson—so great that they imagined mortal treason against him with all their puissance. And said the one to the other, it was too great a reproach unto them and too grievous when that Orson was elevated more in honour than they.

'By God,' said Haufray unto his brother Henry, 'well ought we to praise our puissance little when we cannot take vengeance of Orson: For if he reign long, we shall see the time that by him we shall be cast out of the realm of France.'

'Brother,' said Henry, 'you have said truth. Now we be but two brethren-german[1] and [owe[2]] to comfort the one the other, and help against our enemies.'

'But upon this matter I cannot tell what to think, Henry', said Haufray. 'Understand my reason: we have two nephews that are the sons of our eldest sister, that is for to wit, Florente and Garniere, the which are much hardy and fierce. And methinketh that by them twain, a treason should be soon conspired and made sooner than by us.' For they knew well for a truth that the King loved them not, and that he would give sooner credence unto others than them. 'On the other part, the one is butler of the King, and the other is usher of the chamber that he sleepeth in. And by the means of them twain, we may enter into the chamber of King Pepin, our father, and slay him in his bed; and everybody will say that it hath been Orson. For above all the other he is the chief guard of his body and trusteth most in him. And by this mean the said Orson shall be condemned to death and the realm shall be wholly in our hands. For our brother Charles is not yet puissant enough for to govern us.'

'Haufray,' said Henry, 'you have right well devised, but for to accomplish this thing, it is expedient to make great diligence.'

In this wise, imagined the two false traitors the death of the noble and puissant King Pepin, the which was their natural father. And in so evil an hour he had engendered them that for the saving of their souls, they cared full little. They sent for their two cursed traitors, that is for to wit, Florent and Garniere, the which were right valiant and hardy.

And when they were come before them, Haufray took the words and said in this manner: 'Lords, understand our intention, for we are delibered,[3] my brother and I, for to do a thing that we may have all profit by and shall raise you and mount you in honour more than ever you were, the which thing I desire because that you are my propre nephews and of my propre blood, and owe more to desire your good than any other; [and] for to come to an end, I will tell you mine intention.

'You know that the King Pepin, how well that he is our father,

---

[1] *brethren-german*, full brothers.   [2] *owe*, ought.   [3] *delibered*, determined.

never loved us in his life with good heart. Ever with his puissance
he hath raised up the strangers and exalted them in honour and in all
offices and dignities more than us. Wherefore all these things con-
idered, my brother Henry and I, that are your uncle's legitimes[1]
([by] will and consent), are delibered for to make King Pepin die.

'And after his death we four shall govern and hold his land at our
own will. But it behooved that the thing be accomplished by one of
you twain. And methinketh that you, Garniere, are the most pro-
prest for to undertake this thing, for you have a convenable[2] office
for to do it more than any other, seeing that you are master usher
and principal guard of the King's chamber, and may know, both
night and day, who entereth into the said chamber; for the which
thing you may hide you in some secret place, and when the King
shall be in his bed on sleep, you shall slay him without making any
noise. And on the morrow, in the morning, when the tidings shall
be that the king is dead, the charge and the blame shall be given unto
Orson because that every night he sleepeth and resteth most nearest
his body. And so he shall be judged and condemned unto death.
And after these things we shall take the life soon from the little
Charles. And by this means the realm shall abide unto us for to
depart[3] it after our pleasures.'

'Uncle, said Garniere, 'of this feat doubt you nothing, for King
Pepin, your father, shall lose his life.'

Now was the treason ordained against King Pepin that thought
none ill by the two cursed children that had no pity to make their
father die. In an evil hour is the child born that would purchase such
a death against his father. And in an evil hour was ever engendered
Haufray and Henry when by them treason was done and many
countries marred.

By them was their nephew Garniere full of so evil will that soon
after that the treason was made, he espied a night as the King supped,
and took a sharp-pointed knife and subtly entered into the chamber
royal. And behind the hanging he hid him so secretly that he might
not be apperceived of nobody. And when the hour was come that
the King should go unto rest by the guards and chamberlains, he
was brought unto bed as the custom was. The King entered into the
bed, the which recommended him unto God much devoutly; and
all issued out of the chamber save Orson that devised[4] with the
King to sleeping time.

And when Orson saw that the King would sleep, without making
any more noise he left him: and the nearest him that he might, he
laid him down upon a couch bed.

---

[1] *legitimes*, legitimate children.
[3] *depart*, divide.

[2] *convenable*, suitable.
[4] *devised*, chatted.

How Garniere entered into King Pepin's chamber for to accomplish his cursed enterprise: and how he left the knife within the King's bedstraw.[1]

When it came toward midnight, the traitor Garniere issued out of his place; and bearing the knife in his hand, he went unto the bed of King Pepin for to achieve his enterprise; but when he was beside him and that he lifted up his arm for to have put him to death, him thought that the King would have wakened. Wherefore so great fear took him that he let himself slide down by the bedside, where he was a great while and durst not remove him.

After, he would have smitten secondly, but so great fear took him, as he would have smitten him, that all his body failed and began for to tremble in such wise that he might not achieve his enterprise, and [he] put the knife within the bed. After, he returned into his place all trembling for to hide him in abiding the day [and] so strongly afraid that he would have been a thousand miles beyond the sea.

And Orson was in his bed, that of that deed doubted nothing and dreamed a marvellous dream. For it seemeth him, in sleeping, that they would have taken away the honour of his wife Fezonne. And that beside her were two thieves that conspired treason against him. After, him thought that beside a pond he saw two great herons that fought with a hawk, and with all their puissance enforced them for to slay him. But the hawk defended him[self] so valiantly that he travailled the two herons in such wise that they had been both dead if it had not been [for] a great multitude of little birds that descended upon the hawk. And [they] would have slain him anon if there had not come an eagle that succoured him.

In this dream Orson awakened; that of this dream [he] was much marvelled and began for to say, 'Ha, very God, keep me from treason, and comfort my brother Valentine in such manner that of the noble lady Clerimond he may have certain tidings.'

At that hour the day appeared, and Orson issued softly out of the chamber for wakening of the King. When Garniere saw that Orson was gone out of the chamber, all so soon as he might, he issued out and went unto his lodgings, running full fast. And there he found the two brothers Haufray and Henry and with them Florent, the which had great desire and lust to know some tidings of their cursed and disloyal treason.

'Beware, Garniere, that you tell us the truth how our enterprise doth', [they said].

'Lords,' said Garniere, 'by the God Almighty that hath created

[1] Chapter LVII.

all the world, for all the riches of France, I would not do so much again as I have done. And as to the regard of King Pepin, know that he is yet on-live.[1] For even so as I thought for to have slain him, I was so afraid that my heart failed me and would not have had the courage for to have damaged his body for all the gold in the world. But of another treason I advised me; for I have left the knife, that I bare, in the King's bed. So I have thought that we shall accuse Orson of treason, and shall tell the King that they are four of one appointment that are delibered for to slay the King, of whom Orson is the principal. And [we] shall say also that they will make the little Charles to die for to have between them four the realm of France with the appurtenances.

'And for to prove our feat the better and be believed of this thing, we shall tell how Orson hath made ready his gear and left the knife within the bed. And if anybody demand us how we do know it, we shall say that they were in the chamber speaking of this matter; and how one of us was beside the door and understood their secret.'

'Garniere,' said Haufray, 'you are much subtle, and speaketh wisely. And if it happened that Orson would say the contrary, you and your brother shall take battle against him; and I know well for a certainty that he hath not the power for to vanquish you. And if that it happened by a venture that the worse turned upon you, my brother Henry and I shall be well garnished of men for to succour you.'

'Lords,' said Garniere and Florent, 'your deliberation is right good, and we have well the courage for to achieve the enterprise.'

Thus was the treason [for] the second time conspired against the noble knight Orson, the which of all this deed was pure and innocent. The day was clear; and the hour was come, after that the King had heard Mass, that he entered into the hall royal and set at dinner. There was Haufray and Henry that served at the table, the which showed good semblaunt unto Orson; but with their hearts they purchased him mortal treason with all their puissance.

And when Garniere saw that it was time for to speak, he entered into the hall and came before the King, the which he salved with great reverence, and said to him, 'Redoubted Sir, it is true that of your benign grace you have made me knight and given me office in your court more honester than unto me appertaineth. And because that you have done me so much honour to uphold me in your service, I ought not to be in [a] place by reason whereas your damage is purchased or mortal treason conspired. Wherefore I am come toward your noble Grace, as a true servant ought for to do, to declare unto you a treason that of late hath been conspired against your royal Majesty. And to the end that you may keep your person

---

[1] *on-live*, alive.

out of the danger, I advertise you, and that you may punish the malefactors, as reason is.'

'Garniere,' said the King, 'tell, on your courage, for with a good will I shall hear you.'

[HOW GARNIERE ACCUSED ORSON FALSELY OF TREASON]

How Garniere accused Orson falsely of treason unto King Pepin: and how the knife was found in the King's bed.[1]

'Sir,' said Garniere, 'make Orson to be holden lest he run away, for upon him shall turn the loss and damage. He is the traitor by whom the thing is begun and ought to be brought unto an end. And if that you will know the manner, wite that they are four of the most greatest of your court that are delibered for to make you die; of the which Orson is the principal that ought[2] to make you die in your bed and smite you to the heart with a knife when you shall be on sleep. And to the end that you believe me the better, today, as they made their accord together, I was in a certain place, whereas they knew me not, and have understood how Orson said unto the others that the knife that you shall be slain withal is hid within your bed. And if it please you for to go or for to send anybody, you shall find the thing veritable.'

'Sir,' said Florent that was on the other side, 'my brother saith truth. Whereof I am right sorrowful that they to whom you have done so much good, will purchase your death.'

The King was much amarvelled of those words; and in divers manners and countenances he beheld Orson in saying, 'False and disloyal man, have you had such a thought for to desire my death— I, that all the time of my life have holden you more dearer than the children that I have engendred.'

'Ha, Sir!' said Orson, 'believe not so lightly against me, for I thought never treason in my days, but am accused of this deed by their false envy.'

'Now speak no more,' said the King, 'for and the knife be found in the bed, I hold you culpable of the deed, and demand none other proof.' Then he called his barons and said to them, 'Lords, by Jesus Christ, I was never so much amarvelled as I am of this treason.'

'Sir,' said Milon d'Angler, 'I cannot tell how it goeth, but with pain may I believe that Orson would enterprise such a thing against your royal Majesty, seeing that he is your nephew.'

'Yea,' said the King, 'but and we find a knife within the bed, it is an evident sign that the thing ought to be believed.'

---

[1] Chapter LVIII.   [2] *ought*, determined.

'Now, before God,' said Milon d'Angler, 'let us go and see this experience.'

Then the King went into the chamber with divers of his barons and knights. And as they were before the bed, they found the knife as the traitor Garniere had told them.

'Alas,' said the King, 'in whom may one have trust when my propre nephew that I have holden so dear is covetous of my death and of my life envious! But since that the deeds is such, I swear and promise unto God that there shall never be a day of respite till that he be hanged and strangled.'

Then a valiant knight, the which was called Simon, ran toward Orson (for he loved him much) and said to him, 'Alas, fair sir, fly anon from hence and think for to escape, for the King hath found the knife within the bed, as Garniere had told him. Wherefore the King hath sworn that he shall make you be hanged and strangled also, soon as he shall be come.'

'Care you not,' said Orson, 'for I have good trust in God that He will keep my good right.'

Then the King entered into the hall, whereas Orson was kept straitly with fifteen strong knights, since he made to call lords and advocates for to judge Orson. But God that forgetteth not His good friends saved him from the false traitors and gave him the victory against them.

COLOPHON: Imprinted at London in Fleet Street at the sign of the Rose Garland by me, William Copland for John Walley. [1548.]

PHILIPPE CAMUS
d. 1473

The Two Brothers Legend, that is told in over a hundred versions in European folklore, is the source of the French romance Olivier de Castile et de Artus Delgarbe *(1482) which is attributed to Philippe Camus. The first to suggest Camus's authorship was R. E. Graves. In the foreword to a Roxburghe Library reprint of the earliest extant English translation of* Oliver of Castile, *made by Henry Watson and printed by de Worde in 1518, Graves states that while the French* littérateur *'modestly claims to be no more than its translator from the Latin', it is likely that he is the author. A Spanish edition of* Olivier, *printed in Madrid in 1735, makes an unfounded claim of authorship for Pedro de la Floresta, referring probably to Pedro de Florencia, a medieval Italian author of the Florentine School.*

But in the numerous translations made throughout Europe during the six-teenth century, the author remains anonymous.

It is pointed out by Professor MacEdward Leach in his introduction to Amis and Amiloun, *reprinted by the Early English Text Society, that the story of extraordinary friendship between the brothers Oliver and Arthur, even the Child Sacrifice motif, follows the former romance closely and may be an early version of it. Though a Spanish knight, Oliver's long sojourn in England keeps the romance well within the Arthurian tradition with the use of such motifs as the grateful dead, the visit to a hermit, the three-day tournament, a knight distinguished by a specific colour, and the life token.*

The moral of Oliver *is obedience. Watson emphasizes this in his pro-logue, stating that this virtue binds the friendship between Oliver and his 'loyal fellow' Arthur and makes it 'an example worthy of commendation', since these gallant knights chose 'to love better honour than consent to evil' and were 'rewarded even in this life'.*

Divided into seventy-six short chapters, the romance is marked by spirited and vivid narration, especially the description of the three-day tournament. Few chansons de geste *have a more effective scene than* Oliver *fondling his young son in his cradle while steeling himself to 'sacrifice' the child in order to cure his friend with the magic blood potion.*

Watson's English version, like the Paris edition of about 1511, which he probably used, is illustrated with many woodcuts by the French engraver Jean Trepperel.

SYNOPSIS

The opening incidents of Oliver of Castile *are laid in Spain shortly after the death of Charlemagne.* Oliver *is the son of 'many prayers' of the king of Castile and his queen. Left a widower at his son's birth, the king marries the widow of the king of Algarbe. Arthur, her son, and* Oliver *are brought up together in Castile and taught 'feats of arms' and games, such as 'tennis, leap, spring, wrastle, caste the stone, and caste the bar'. In tournaments* Oliver *always wins, though there is no jealousy between them. As* Oliver *grows into manhood, the queen's admiration for him turns into an incestuous love, and he determines to leave Spain secretly. In a letter, directed to Arthur, he describes a parting gift, a glass of clear water that will turn black if harm comes to* Oliver. *At this sign, Arthur must immediately search for him.*

Oliver *arrives in England after being shipwrecked off the coast. He saves himself and a friend, Sir John Talbot. They come ashore at Folkestone, and* Oliver *accompanies the knight to his home and cares for him, but he fails to regain his health. Talbot leaves great debts which the Spanish prince pays as well as the funeral expenses. Throughout his dealings* Oliver *disguises his identity.*

During a short stay in Canterbury Oliver *hears that the king of England 'has made a crye of a tournament', the prize being the hand in marriage of his daughter Helaine. Her husband must be a valiant man, but not necessarily a prince. Oliver is eager to enter the tournament, and as he walks from Canterbury to London, reciting St Julian's Pater Noster, the pilgrim's prayer for shelter, he is accosted by a knight who directs him to a hermitage and promises to furnish him with a horse and armour for the tournament. In return he receives Oliver's promise to give him half of all that he wins. The knight keeps his word, and Oliver enters the tournament well equipped and wearing on successive days the knight's colours, black, red, and white. After a brilliant display of arms, Oliver wins the prize. He poses as a poor knight of Spain, and the English king provides him with a large retinue. After a year in the monarch's service, winning several battles in Ireland, Oliver marries Helaine. A son, Henry, and a daughter, Clarisse, are born to them. Oliver is popular in England, and his charity to the poor so endears him to the people that they are distressed when he is treacherously captured by Irish nobles, seeking revenge for the death of their kings.*

In the meantime, Arthur has become king of Algarbe, through the death of his mother, and regent of Castile, through the death of Oliver's father. When he sees the water in the glass turn black, he knows harm has come to his half-brother, and he sets out to find him. Arriving in England, Arthur loses his way in a forest, and is attacked by a lion. An old knight binds up his wounds, and tells him where to find Oliver. But for a time he must pretend that he is not his half-brother. Having deceived the king and Helaine, Arthur leaves for Ireland where he frees Oliver. When the latter learns of his deception, particularly to Helaine, though Arthur had 'not lain with her' actually, Oliver in his wrath knocks Arthur from his horse, and the fall blinds him. Later, when Oliver learns that Helaine had not been unfaithful to him, he is repentant. Through a dream he learns that Arthur can be cured by drinking the 'blood of two innocents'. Grief-stricken, he slays his two children; and Arthur unaware of the deed drinks a vial of their blood and is cured. As a reward for Oliver's obedience, which is compared to Abraham's willingness to sacrifice Isaac, his children are miraculously restored to life. The bells of St Paul's Cathedral announce the tidings.

When Oliver learns of his father's death from Arthur, he discloses his true identity. With Helaine and his children, he returns to Castile for his coronation, accompanied by the king of England and Arthur, king of Algarbe.

Soon after Oliver has been crowned king of Castile, a White Knight arouses him from sleep early one morning, and presents his claim to half the booty which Oliver had won through the tournament and had sworn to divide with him. The knight demands that Oliver slay his wife in order to give him half of her body. Realizing that he is bound to keep his promise, Oliver prepares to kill her but is restrained by the knight, who commends his sense of honour. The knight declares that he is John Talbot, whom

Oliver had befriended in Canterbury. Leaving Oliver happy with his wife and children, the knight vanishes, returning to heaven. The story continues with the marriage of Oliver's daughter Clarisse to Arthur. Eventually, the latter is crowned king of England and Castile following the deaths of Oliver and his son, who is killed by the Turks.

The History of Oliver of Castile

TRANSLATED BY HENRY WATSON

[HOW A KNIGHT COMFORTED OLIVER]

How a knight came for to comfort Oliver, and of the promises they had together.[1]

Right so as Oliver complained him of his misadventure, there came a man to him the which plucked him by the sleeve divers times saying, 'Oliver of Castile, be nothing abashed because that I take you out of your thought.'

Oliver lifted up his head when he heard his name pronounced, and wist not whether that he had dreamed it, or not. And all abashed in making the Sign of the Cross, [Oliver] said unto him, 'I conjure thee in the Name of God that thou do me no harm, and that thou tell me who gave thee knowledge of my name.'

The man, that seemed both fair and reverent, said, 'My friend, have no doubt of me, for I am a Christian man, and believeth as well in God as thou dost; and marvel thee not if that I know thy name, for thou ought to know that "the fields hath sight and every wood hath sound".* I know that thy displeasure hath adnichilled[2] thine understanding; for and thou had thought on thy fate, thou would not have made thy complaint so high, for I have heard all that thou hast said, and how thou hast will for to go to the tournament that shall be held at London within this six days; also, how thou hast been dismounted, and lost thy money. I am beholden unto you for some service and pleasure that thy most nearest friends hath done unto me. Therefore I am he that will aid thee for to accomplish thy good and high enterprise in praying Our Saviour that He will give thee grace well for to finish it: and if it hold at thee, I shall furnish thee of armour and of horses so well that it shall suffice thee. But it shall be on such a condition that thou shalt promise me that of all that thou win, by occasion of the tournament, half if it be my pleasure to demand it and take it.'

Oliver, seeing the offer that the Knight made him, said unto him

---

[1] Chapter xx.   [2] *adnichilled*, made void.

as evil avised of afterclaps, 'My friend, if the hour be such and that my fortune will consent that thou do me this pleasure, I promise that upon the part that I trust to have of paradise, that if any good come to me by occasion of thy service, that you shalt be pertainer of the just half or of the greatest part, if it were your pleasure for to demand it.'

At these words the Knight answered, 'It sufficeth'; and prayed him that he would remember him when time would require it. And after those words were finished, the noble Knight said unto him, 'Mine own special friend Oliver, marvel thee nothing of that that thou seest, but keep alway this little path that thou findest on the right hand, and thou shalt find an hermitage, and there thou shalt have tidings of me. But I go thither; and there I shall fetch thee when time is.'

So they departed; and Oliver went on his way and prayed the Knight to remember him.

[HOW OLIVER SAW DIVERS KNIGHTS AND OTHER FOLK]

How Oliver of Castile saw come toward him divers knights and other folk in great triumph and array.[1]

So, as ye have heard, sojourned Oliver in the hermitage with the good holy man by the space of three days or four. And there was no more but two days unto the beginning of the tournament. This hermitage was within two miles of London. And when Oliver went for to disport him without the wood, he might see the city all at full and the place where the tournament should be, the which was all enclosed about. And there he saw them assay their saddles and their coursers and, in likewise, their harness. Wherein he took no great pleasure because he doubted that his Knight should forget him. And because that the time was short, he was in great doubt and repented him sore that he had believed him so lightly and that also in the meanwhile, that he had sojourned in the hermitage that he had not gone into the city for to see her for whose love so many noble men put themselves in pain and jeopardy and of whom he had heard so much good spoken of. But he durst not abandon the hermitage, lest that his Knight should not find him in default, saying that he was not there as he had appointed him to abide. And in that estate he passed the two days.

And when it came unto the day that every gentleman and lord ought for to be and find himself upon the lists, ye may imagine in what dolour was the poor Oliver. And if that his heart was sorry and displeasant, nobody ought to marvel them, for he stood afore

[1] Chapter XXII.

the door of the hermitage always hearkening if that his knight came, for there fell not a leaf but that he wende that he had come. He abode so long that he was out of all esperance and hope. And as he stood in that estate sore musing, he heard a great noise of riders among the leaves. And then Oliver thought that it was some great gentleman that rode to the tournament, as the other lords did. And then he cast his regard that way where he heard the noise, and espied to the number of fifteen gentlemen clothed in black sarsenet. And the surplus of their habiliments was of the same colour, and they were mounted on black coursers, and their coursers were trapped all in black velvet; and each of them had a spear in his hand, that was covered with black velvet. And then he saw come after them ten knights habiled in long gowns of black velvet and furred with martens, and led after them a courser morel, the which had buskings of cloth of gold up to the belly; and he was environed with fifteen pages mounted upon coursers of the same colour and buskings of the same colour. And after them was forty and four score pages of the same livery, reserved[1] that it was cloth.

[OF THE GREAT JOY THAT OLIVER HAD: AND OF THE FAIR ELAINE]

Of the great joy that Oliver had when he saw the fair steeds and the rich apparements[2] that his knight had brought to him. And how he armed him; and of the rich pavilion of the fair Helaine, the King's daughter of England; and of her beauty.[3]

His folk, clothed and habiled as ye have heard afore, rode unto the hermitage; and then everybody hoved and abode there all coy, and salved Oliver that was afore the door. And he full gently rendered to them their salute. And as he beheld that fair company, he thought that the Knight with the longest gown was the same Knight that spake unto him in the wood. Whereof he was right glad, and went for to salve him. But as soon as the Knight apperceived him coming, he alighted off his horse and came against him. And, after, he said to him, 'Oliver, good friend, these men that ye see here, I have brought them unto you. And because that we be come from far for to do you service and honour, I pray you that ye do so much at this tournament that ye have honour, and that we lose not our pain.'

Oliver answered him right courteously, 'My lord and my friend, ye do so much for me that I can never render you the guerdon. Wherefore such as I am, ye may command me, for the body is yours, and, at this time, I cannot give you no better thing. I pray to God

---

[1] *reserved*, except.   [2] *apparements*, apparel.   [3] Chapter XXIII.

that He give me grace for to deserve it against you, and that He give me strength for to do as well as I have the *volente*.'

These words finished, the Knight said to him that it was high hour for to arm him. And therefore in a fair green place that was afore the hermitage, there was a chair brought, wherein Oliver set him for to take his refection; and then after, they armed him diligently.

In the meanwhile that he armed him, the ladies came into the field and brought with them fair Helaine, daughter of the King of England, and led her into the pavilion that for her was ordained. It was hanged with tapestry of cloth of gold, right rich, and there was a chair raised upon high. In the which chair was ten steps or that they might come to the siege above, over the which was a canopy of purple velvet charged full of great pearls, orientals, and had in the midst thereof a carbuncle, that rendered so great *lumiere* that it was marvellous to behold it.

In the siege above, as I have recited to you, was set the excellent Helaine. And upon each of the foresaid steps sat two judges, that is for to know, a prince and a princess, each one after his degree. The other ladies and damsels, the which were there without number, put them in their places and scaffolds that were for them ordained and ensigned.

And, in likewise, on the other side was a great company of noble and valiant knights and lords of this realm of England. Ye may well think that it was great triumph and great solace for the men of arms for to behold so fair a company about the noble and excellent Helaine and everything so well ordained as that thing was there for her sake: the which was so richly apparelled that none cannot re-hearse the light that the precious stones rendered that were about her, the which embellished her excellent visage. Who that had seen her in that estate, he would have thought that she had been a thing of the other world. For I think that at her *naissance* and birth, nature had put all her excellence and grace. If that she was seemly of body and excellent of visage, it was nothing in comparison toward the gifts of grace wherewith she was endowed. For all excellence and bounty, honour and humbleness, doulsure[1] and sweetness, and all other virtues and good conditions that in any woman of noble lineage appertained flourished in her.

And therefore he should be right envious in this wretched world that might attain unto so high a thing as for to have for his part the flower and lyesse[2] of this world. And even thus everybody put him-self in pain for to conquer her. And there was not one but that him seemed that he would conquer her, or else die in the pain.

---

[1] *doulsure*, Fr. *douceur*, sweetness.   [2] *lyesse*, Fr. *lis*, lily.

[OF OLIVER AT THE TOURNAMENT]

Of the great marvels that Oliver did at the tournament above them all.[1]

And then the ladies were not so soon in the scaffolds, but that the four hundred knights were upon the field, ready for to withstand all comers, as ye have heard before, for the tournament should last three days. The first day was ordained for to joust. The second day, for to tourney, not as they do nowadays, but with sharp swords, and not rebated.[2] The third day was for to fight on foot; and everybody might have an axe of arms and a sword about him. And because that they were many knights and they had great place, they without had knowledge that they within were already at the lists upon the field and all the ladies ready for to behold them which should do best: and every knight put him in devoir for to joust the first.

Nevertheless, Oliver was not the first, for there were many there afore him, as the King's son of Scotland, and divers Kings of Ireland, and many other princes and great lords, the which were so mannerly clothed that it was triumph for to behold them. There was but few spears broken afore Oliver's coming. And when he was among the press, he smote his horse with the spurs, and made his horse to turn so gently that everybody looked upon him. And, in especial, it pleased the ladies much, his first entrance in, saying that the Black Knight was best in point and the fairest armed of all the place.

And, after, began the jousts; and everybody put him in pain for to do well. The Knight that was Oliver's governor said unto him, 'My friend, behold upon this scaffold the fair lady that ye shall conquer. If that it hold not at you, take good courage and think for to do well.' And then he took a spear and gave it to Oliver the which took of it no regard, for he had fixed his sight upon the excellent Helaine. And so he had his spear in the rest a great while, without any moving from one place, as he that thought nothing on it. And so as the Knight beheld him in that estate, he said unto him, 'Oliver, ye sleep.'

Then Oliver, as a person that is awaked out of his sleep, smote his horse with the spurs without avising where he went. And the first thing that he recounted with his spear, that was long and strong marvellously, was a post that held up a scaffold, and upon that scaffold was much people: and he smote it down and all them that were upon it. Then there was great laughter of them that saw it, and [they] said that it was a marvellous stroke. The ladies excused him, saying that he had not clear sight, or that his horse was not at his will.

[1] Chapter XXIV.   [2] *rebated*, dulled.

Oliver was led back to his fellows sore ashamed: and they gave him a new spear. The first that he encountered with was one of the Kings of Ireland, named Maquemor, the which was smitten down, horse and all. Then ye should have heard the heralds cry, 'See the adventurous Knight, armed in black, that with one only stroke hath smitten down a hundred persons, and with the second stroke a king! Ye shall see him do marvels of arms today!'

Oliver heard these words, wherefore he put himself in pain for to do well. And there was none that might abide him a stroke with a spear. Nevertheless everybody put himself in devoir, as well within as without, but above all Oliver bore the prize: the which did not displease the fair Helaine that said to herself, that and he were as knightly unarmed as he was armed, that he might be the flower of all them in the place.

[HOW OLIVER CAME TO THE TOURNAMENT THE THIRD TIME]

How Oliver came to the tournament the third time and had the honour above them all by his great prowess. And how the King commissioned twenty knights for to bring him afore him to know what he was.[1]

When the King was in his chamber, he inquired how many knights there had been slain: and they found dead of them within to the number of forty-six and of them without fifteen. Wherefore the King was much angry, and commanded that forty-six other knights should be put in the places of the dead knights: and if there were any hurt that might not help themself on the morrow, that they should put in other. The thing was done so. Upon the morrow the King went into his scaffold, where he dined, and the fair Helaine, also. During the dinner-time they spake of nothing but of the tournament of the day past. And the King said that he was right displeasant because that he might not see him that did so great deeds of arms. Wherefore he commanded twenty knights that they should have always regard to him, and that they should not fail to bring him to the banquet, for he would see him. He commanded also that the number of two thousand fighting men were armed for to keep the field from all debates and noises.

The meanwhile, the masters, stewards, and controllers were in the palace making all thing ready for the banquet and feast that should be at night, the which should be without comparison of all that ever had been seen in this realm. The hour approached that they should find them in the field. And the four hundred knights of

[1] Chapter XXVIII.

[those] within, with the two thousand, came into the field, whereof some of them had liefer have been commissioned to make ready the feast, for the example that the Red Knight had given them the day afore. The which already did arm him, and was come upon his horse, clothed in white—and all his folk in the same suit, and in the same manner that they came the day afore, save that they had been clothed in red, and so came into the field on horseback—and put himself beside the King's son of Scotland. And all the other alight in likewise.

And then when all were assembled, the King bade two knights for to go look how many they were without. Then they went down, and told the lords of the King's will and commandment. Then they took a girdle and made them for to pass underneath, and found that they of without were well four hundred. And a knight by the command-ment of the King said that everybody should ungirdle his sword; and said that the axe sufficed. And after that the battle was begun, the King sent men for to depart them, and bade that none were so hardy for to smite on the head with the trenchant after that time. And [he] advertised them that the prize should be given at night to him that hath deserved it. And then it was told that they might begin when it should seem to them good.

Then they began for to smite in such wise that it was a goodly sight to behold them. It was a seemly sight for to behold how Oliver demeaned him with his axe, for he smote so puissantly that he made him a way large enough. When they approached near, the one smote upon the other so impetuously that it was marvellous they might stand. Oliver dreamed not, for he gave so puissant strokes that him that he hit aright, he made him to kiss the ground: and he did so much that there durst not [any] abide afore him. So with force of smiting, his axe, that was great and long, did break. And when he saw that, he approached him to a knight and pulled his axe out of his hands by such a might and by such a chivalrous puissance and virtue and also manner, that whether he would, or not, he made him kiss the ground.

Twain of the Kings of Ireland had great envy at Oliver because they saw the prize could not escape him. And therefore by great displeasure they assailed Oliver, the which defended him so valiantly, that he clove one of them to the teeth. The King seeing that it might not endure without great debate, said that it sufficed. And so they departed whether they would, or not.

[OF THE PRIZE OF THE TOURNAMENT]

How the prize of the tournament was brought by divers lords
and ladies: and what it was.[1]

There came first many torches and officers for to make place. After,
came a king of arms richly clothed, holding on high, with both his
hands, a great and massive chain of gold, charged and enriched with
precious stones. After him came two fair ladies, clothed in like
habiliments, the which became them so well that it was a pleasant
sight to behold them. These ladies were accompanied with four
knights clothed likewise, and each of the ladies were on the right-
hand of two knights. And in such estate they came afore the King's
person, to whom they did reverence, as it appertained. And then
they demanded him if it were his good pleasure that the prize were
given. And he answered, 'Yea.'

Then they began to walk about the hall, and came to the place
where Oliver was hid among the press. To whom the King of
Arms said that he should come forth, and that it was to him that
they would speak. And after that he was come forth, the King of
Arms said to him in this wise: 'Carbuncle and gem of all prowess
and hardiness, the King, our sovereign lord, and the ladies of this
company by the great and high feats of arms that in you hath
showed and comen to their knowledge doth present to you this
noble chain in giving you the prize of the three days with triumph
and glory above all them that thither hath beem comen or found
them there....I make you no mention of my right redoubted
mistress and lady Helaine because that the King my sovereign lord
make thee a request, that is, that the right that ye can demand of her
by the cry that was published by his commandment, that it will
please you for to be content and for to defer and abide until a year be
passed. And he doth promise you that enduring that while, my lady
Helaine, his daughter, shall not be married: And then he shall do so
much toward you that ye shall be well content. For she shall be
apparelled for you, even as she should be at this present time, for he
would not take from you nothing which ye have deserved.'

Oliver with a simple voice, all rubicund, answered that he had
not deserved the honour that they presented him, but since that it
was the King's good pleasure and the lords and ladies he should be a
great fool and misproud to refuse it. As for the surplus, touching
the King's requests, he answered that his requests were commandments in praying if that he had won anything, that it should not be
taken from him. For he was well in will for to take it if it fell to
him: this, notwithstanding, he was well content that the King's will

[1] Chapter xxxiv.

were accomplished and to abide a year. And [he] thanked the King and the ladies that had made him that present; and [he] took the chain of gold and put it about his neck.

And then they demanded him his name and surname. He made himself Oliver, but he said that his surname might not be known at that present time. And because that the herald could not tell how to give his name in knowledge that the prize was given to, he began for to cry in this manner: 'To this Black, Red, and White Knight, the Flower of Chivalry, that by force of arms hath obtained the last triumph of the tournament, hath been delivered the prize!'

[HOW OLIVER SLEW HIS CHILDREN]

How Oliver for to give health and guerison[1] to his fellow [Arthur] slew his two children for to have the blood that Arthur might drink it.[2]

When Oliver had made thus his complaint to the Virgin Mary and that he had had divers imaginations, as well of the love that he had to his children as that which he had to his fellow, he concluded for to slay his two children for the love of his fellow, saying that he had nothing more dear than his fellow, and that the love that he loved his two children with was nothing for to compare to that the which he loved his fellow with.

Wherefore he departed from his chamber and came into that of his two children. And when he was entered, he commanded all the ladies for to void out, the which did his commandment. And when he found himself alone, he shut the chamber door and bore a basin and a naked sword in his hand unto the bed of his two children the which slept and were not yet risen. When he approached the bed, he lifted up the coverlet and found them sleeping right sweetly. The little son, that was of the age of five years, awaked and incontinent as he saw Oliver, nature taught him for to make him cheer and in smiling named him, 'Father.' The daughter, that was the younger, never left sleeping.

When Oliver saw them, he considered which of them two he should slay first; and because that the son began for to speak to him, he had so great pity in his heart that he recoiled aback, and for all the world he would not have smitten them. And then he said to himself, 'How may nature fail so much for to suffer the father for to slay his child. Nor how may there be so much cruelty in a man for to consent to murder. Alas, ye fair and good Helaine what piteous tidings shall come unto your ears! When that ye shall know that I have slain your children, what shall ye say! Certainly your piteous

---

[1] *guerison*, healing.   [2] Chapter LXVII.

heart may not endure it. And with that that ye lose your children, ye shall lose your husband also, for he dare not abide in this realm for the fear of your father that shall put him to death—for he is well worthy. And, certes, the dumb beasts hath more reason than I have, unto whom nature doth teach for to keep their fruit to the death; and, truly, I ought for to resemble unto them. I ought to put me in peril of death for to save my children, but thus it shall not go.'

And in saying this, he approached to the bed and yet lift up the coverlet again and drew him by the arm and said, 'Unhappy children, ye ought well for to curse your father and his life when he hath engendered you and put you in this world from which you must depart.' Thus saying full dolorously, with the tears descending along his face and the sword in his hand ready for to smite, nature and reason put afore him that it should be too great damage and cruelty. And liberality said to the contrary, that for to render health to his fellow, he could not do too much, the which he believed. And, in putting all fears behind, with one stroke he smote off both their heads. Then he put the basin underneath and received as much blood as he might have; and then he laid them in their bed again and the heads in their places so as they had been alive. He took a mantle with which he covered it [the basin], and so bore it in locking the door after him. And [he] took the key with him to the end that none should enter to know what was done.

[HOW THE KNIGHT HAD PITY ON OLIVER]

How the Knight had pity on Oliver, having knowledge of his loyalty and quited him all. And then he made him to be known to him and told him what he was.[1]

[The White Knight appears to Oliver and his wife Helaine and demands half of Oliver's possessions, including his wife and children. After dividing his money and jewels with the Knight, Oliver is about to sacrifice his wife to fulfil his promise when the knight restrains him.]

... 'I am the same [White] Knight, and that same that served thee at the tournament of England, and because that thou hast done me pleasure, I render to thee all thy money and all wholly thy finance that thou hast given me. And, in like wise, I render to thee thy son and quite thee in likewise the half of thy wife: that which I have done hath been for to assay thee and thy franchise.

'To the surplus I shall tell thee wherefore at the first of the tournament, I clothed thee in black, that was significance of the obscurity that I was in. The second day, that was in red, signified my

[1] Chapter LXXIV.

pains in purgatory. The last day in white, signified my salvation; for white is virgin, for it was never soiled by staining; whereby it is pure and clean. In likewise I am so at this present time, for by thee and by [thee] the cause, I am alleged of all my dolour, and now I go into the holy glory of paradise to see the presence of my Creator that is the rejoicing of the saved.

'Wherefore I take leave of thee, for there as I go, thou mayst not come yet; but be thou sure that I shall pray for thee.'

Then he vanished away, and in their presence he mounted into heaven gloriously casting the beams of his clearness upon the window that the King and Queen leaned upon. The which, in a little while, was out of their sight. Then they set them upon their knees in rendering graces to their Creator; and after that they had made their orisons in thanking God, they began for to make, the one to the other, right piteous acquaintance, so much and by such manner as if the Queen had been arisen from death at that same hour.

The King of Castile [Oliver] that never had received one goodness but that he had received ten evils against it, lived in joy with his right well beloved wife and had never displeasure after that, save all joys unto the hour of his death.

COLOPHON: Here endeth the History of Oliver of Castile and the fair Helaine, daughter unto the King of England. Imprinted at London in Fleet Street at the Sign of the Sun by Wynkyn de Worde.... 1518.

JEAN D'ARRAS
fl. 1365

Melusine *is the first full-length romance based on the ancient legend of the serpent faëry—the mermaid or sea-nymph of Hebrew, Greek, and Indian mythology. This prose tale was written about 1365 by Jean d'Arras, secretary to the sovereign Duke of Berri, son of King John II of France. Supposedly based on an old manuscript found in the royal archives, the romance was intended to entertain the Duke's sister Mary, Countess of Bar, and to chronicle the fabled rise of the Poitiers family of Lusignan, the sovereign Counts of Foret or Forest, relatives of the French royal family.*

The legend was also told in a long poem, Mellusine *(1401), by the French poet Couldrette. His version was followed by* Le Liure de Melusine *en Francoys, written in prose by an anonymous author and printed, in 1478, in Geneva. After this first printed edition,* Melusine *was translated before 1600 into German, Spanish, Bohemian, Swedish, Dutch, and Danish. A Middle English translation of Jean's* Melusine *was made about 1500. A copy of it is extant in a MS. in the British Museum and was edited by A. K. Donald in 1895. The same version may have been used by Wynkyn de Worde, who printed an English translation, in 1510, of which only a fragment remains.*

Whatever was the common source of the legends that tell of the faëry serpent, Jean's version is closely associated with the Arthurian tradition, borrowing such motifs as a fay-haunted fountain, a sparrow-hawk castle which is kept by a fay, an enchanted mountain that encloses a treasure hoard, and marriage between a mortal and a fay. As a water-nymph, Melusine is related to those of eastern folklore as well as to numerous western faëry mistresses of lakes, wells, and fountains and to the Celtic banshee who give their distressing cry to foretell a dire happening.

The influence of Melusine on English literature is perhaps slight though there is a hint of the water-fay in Ariel whom Prospero bids

'Go, make thyself like a nymph o' the sea.'

And going about his tasks, Ariel is invisible as is Melusine after her transformation into the serpent faëry nor does the change hinder her from building monasteries and churches. Keats's serpent faëry Lamia, like Melusine, seeks a union with a mortal. But the poet claims to have found Lamia's prototype in Philostrato's De Vita Apollonii.

SYNOPSIS

In constructing the story of Melusine, Jean combined two similar legends, namely, the romance of the fay Pressyne and King Elyneos and that of Melusine and Raymondyn. The story opens with the love affair between Elyneos, King of Albany, and the beautiful fay Pressyne, whom he finds singing beside a fountain. She consents to marry him provided he promises not to visit her when her children are born. After their marriage Pressyne gives birth to three daughters, Melusine, Melior, and Palatine. In his excitement Elyneos forgets his vow and hurries to see his wife. The penalty for his broken promise is the loss of Pressyne, who vanishes, taking the infants with her to the court of her sister, a queen on the Isle of Perdu or Avalon.

When Melusine is fifteen years old, she learns of her father's act and inveigles her sisters to use the magic their mother has taught them and punish him. They determine to chain Elyneos in the heart of a mountain called Brombelyoys. Pressyne is angry at her daughters for taking revenge on their father and places a curse on each of them. Every Saturday Melusine will be transformed into a mermaid or serpent faëry. If she finds a lover who will marry her and promise never to see her on that day, the curse will be gradually removed. But if he breaks his word, she will keep the form of a serpent during the rest of her life.

Following the same pattern as her mother's romance, Melusine meets

Raymondyn, an impoverished member of the Lusignan family, at the Fountain of Soif, whither he had come on horseback after leaving a hunting party during which he had killed his uncle. Infatuated with Melusine's beauty, Raymondyn asks her to marry him, agreeing never to see her on Saturday. After their marriage Melusine uses her magic powers to make Raymondyn wealthy and the lord of several great castles which she designs. They have ten children. Each of them has some abnormal feature, but this does not disturb the happiness of the pair.

After a time jealousy prompts Raymondyn to spy on his wife on Saturday. Melusine at once realizes that her mother's curse is imminent. After making her will, she takes sorrowful leave of her husband and children, and as a lamia flies out of a window of the castle, lamenting her fate. Doomed to wander about the countryside until Judgment Day, Melusine's cry is always associated with pending disaster, particularly to the family of Lusignan.

After the flight of Melusine, Jean relates the adventures of several of her children, including Geoffrey of the Great Tooth.

Melusine

HOW MELUSINE AND HER TWO SISTERS SHOWED THEM TO RAYMOND AT THE FOUNTAIN OF SOIF OR THIRST[1]

The history saith to us, that when the King [Elyneos] had lost Pressyne, his wife, and his three daughters, he was so woeful and so abasshed that he wist not what he should do or say. But it was by the space of seven years that he did none other thing but complained and sighed and made great plaints and piteous lamentations for love of Pressyne, his wife, which he loved of lawful love. And the people in his land said that he was assoted.[2] And indeed they gave and betook the government over them and of all the land to Nathas, his son, which governed valiantly, and held his father in great charity.

And then the barons of Albany gave to him unto his wife, a gentlewoman, which was lady of Yeris. And of these two issued Florymond which afterward took much of pain and travail. Nevertheless, our history is not enterprised nor begun for him, and therefore we shall hold our peace of him, and we shall return to our history.

The history saith that when Pressyne departed and yede[3] with her three daughters, she went into Avalon that was named the Isle Lost because that although had a man been there many times, yet should

---

[1] Chapter I.   [2] *assoted*, infatuated.   [3] *yede*, went.

not he can nere[1] [sic] return thither himself alone but by hap and great adventure. And there she nourished her three daughters unto the time that they were fifteen years of age. And [she] led them every morning on a high mountain which was named, as the history saith and recounteth, Elyneos, which is as much for to say in English as 'flourished hill'.

For from thence she saw enough the land of Albany. And [she] often said to her three daughters, waymenting[2] and sore weeping: 'See, my fair daughters, yonder is the land where ye were born, and ye should have had your weal and honour nor had been the damage of your father that both you and me hath put in great misery without end unto the Day of Doom, when God shall punish the evil folk, and the good he shall enhance in their virtues.'

Melusine, the oldest daughter, demanded of her mother Pressyne, 'What falsehood hath done our father, whereby we must endure so long this grief and sorrow?'

Then the lady, their mother, began to tell and show unto them all the manner of the *fait*, so as ye have heard tofore. When Melusine had heard her mother and that she understood all the *fait* or deed, she turned the talk of her mother and demanded of her the commodities of the land—the names of the cities, towns, and castles of Albany. And rehearsing these things, they all descended down from the hill and returned to the Isle of Avalon.

And then Melusine drew apart her two sisters, that is to wit, Melior and Palatine, and said to them in this manner: 'My dear sisters, now look and behold we the misery wherein our father hath put both our mother and us all that should have been so well at ease and in so great worship in our lives. What think you good, of your best advice, for to do? For, as for my part, I think to avenge me thereof. And as little mirth and solace that he hath impetred[3] to our mother by his falsehood, as little joy I think to purchase unto him.'

Then her two sisters answered to her in this manner: 'Ye be our oldest sister; we shall follow and obey you in all that ye will do and shall ordain thereof.'

And Melusine said to them, 'Ye show good love and to be good and lawful to our mother. For, by my faith, ye have said right well. And I have advised, if it seemeth you good, that we shall close or shut him on the high mountain of Northumberland, named Brombelyoys, and in misery he shall be there all his life.'

'My sister,' said either of both sisters, 'let us now hie us for to do this. For we have great desire to see that our mother be avenged of the unlawfulness that our father did show unto her.'

Then the three daughters did so much that by their false condition

---

[1] *can nere*, ever be able to.   [2] *waymenting*, lamenting.
[3] *impetred*, obtained by entreaty.

they took their father and closed or shut him on the said mountain. And after that they had so done, they returned to their mother, and to her they said in this manner, 'Mother, ye neither ought to reach[1] nor care more of the unlawfulness and falsehood of our father. For thereof he hath received his payment. For never he shall issue nor depart from the mountain of Brombelyoys, whereon he is closed and shut by us. And there he shall waste his life and his time with great dolour and woe.'

'Ha! Ha! Alas!' said their mother Pressyne to them. 'How durst you so do, evil-hearted daughters and without pity! Ye have not done well when he that begot you on my body ye have so shamefully punished by your proud courage. For it was he of whom I took all the pleasure that I had in this mortal world, which ye have taken from me. Therefore, know ye well that I shall punish you of the merit after your desert. Thou, Melusine, that art the oldest and that oughtest to have been the most knowing, all this is come and done through thy counsel. For well I wot that this prison hath been given to thy father by thee, and therefore thou shalt be she that shall be first punished thereof.

'For notwithstanding the unlawfulness of thy father, both thou and thy sisters he should have drawn to him, and ye should shortly have been out of the hands of the nymphs and of the faëries, without to return any more. And from henceforth I give to thee the gift that thou shalt be every Saturday turned unto a serpent from the navel downward. But if thou find any man that will take thee to his wife, and that he will promise to thee that never on the Saturday he shall see thee nor that shall declare nor rehearse thy *fait* or deed to no person, thou shalt live thy course natural and shall die as a natural and human woman. And out of thy body shall issue a fair line which shall be great and of high prowess.

'But if by hap or some adventure thou shouldst be seen and deceived of thine husband, know thou for certain that thou shouldst return to the torment and pain whereas thou were in afore: and ever thou shalt abide therein unto the time that the right High Judge shall hold His Judgment. And thou shalt appear by three days before the fortress or castle (which thou shalt make and thou shalt name it after thy name) at every time when it shall have a new lord and, likewise, also when a man of thy line shall die.

'And thou, Melior, to thee I give a castle in the great Armenia which is fair and rich where thou shalt keep a sparrow-hawk unto the time that the great Master shall hold His Judgment. And all noble and worthy knights descended and come of noble line that will go watch there the day before the eve, and the eve also of St John Baptist, which is on the twentieth day of June, without any sleep,

---

[1] *reach*, worry.

shall have a gift of thee of such things that men may have corporally, that is to wit, of earthly things without to demand thy body nor thy love by marriage nor otherwise. And all those that shall demand thee without cease and that will not forbear and abstain them thereof, shall be infortunate unto the ninth line and shall be put from their prosperities.

'And thou shalt be closed, Palatine, and shut on the mountain of Guygo with all the treasure of thy father unto the time that a knight shall come of our line which shall have all that treasure to help therewith for to get and conquer the land of promission[1] and shall deliver thee from thence.'

Then were the three sisters full heavy of heart and sorrowful, and departed from their mother. And Melusine went and took her way alone through the forest and thick bushes. Melior also departed, and yede toward the Sparrow-hawk Castle* in the great Armenia. And Palatine also went to the mountain of Guygo, where many a man hath seen her: and I myself heard it said of the King of Aragon and of many other of his realm.

And be not you displeased if I have recounted unto you this adventure. For it is for to adjust more of faith and for to verify the history. And from henceforth I will enter into the matter of the very and true history. But first I shall tell to you how the King Elyneos finished his days in this world; and how Pressyne, his wife, buried him within the said mountain in a much noble tomb, as ye shall hear hereafter.

Long time was the King Elyneos on the said mountain, insomuch that death, which bringeth ever person to an end, took him. Then came there Pressyne, his wife, and buried him there. And on him made to be set one so noble and so rich a tomb that never before nor since that time was seen none such nor so rich. For on the tomb were riches without comparison, as of precious stones and other jewels, and about it were great and high candlesticks, of fine gold, and lamps and torches which burned both day and night continually. And on the said tomb stood upright a statue or image of alabaster carved and made after the length, likeness, and form of King Elyneos. And the said image held in her hands a table of gold whereon was written the foresaid adventure.

And there the Lady Pressyne established a strong giant to the safeguard of the treasure before said. The which giant was wondrous fierce and horrible, and all the country thereabout he held under his subjection. And also after him many other giants kept it unto the time and coming of Geoffrey with the Great Tooth of the which ye shall more hear hereafter. Now have ye heard of the King Elyneos

---

[1] *promission*, promise.

and of Pressyne, his wife. And from henceforth I will begin and show the truth of the history of the marvels of the noble castle of Lusignan in Poitiers....

HOW RAYMOND CAME TO THE FOUNTAIN OF SOIF WHERE HE FOUND MELUSINE AND TWO OTHER LADIES WITH HER[1]

The history saith that so long bare the horse Raymond thus pensefull and heavy of heart of the mishap that was come to him, that he neither wist where he was nor whither he went nor in no manner he led his horse; but his horse led him where that he would. For Raymond touched not the bridle, and heard nor saw nought, so sore was his wit troubled.

And thus he passed before the fountain where the ladies were, without having any sight of them. But the horse that saw them was suddenly afraid and fled thence, running much fast. And then she that was the greatest lady of them three said in this manner: 'By my faith, he that rode now and passed before us seemeth to be a much gentleman, and, nevertheless, he maketh of it no semblant, but he showeth the semblant of a villain or kerle[2] that hath passed so before ladies without to have saluted them.'

And all this said she feigningly, to the end that the others should not perceive to what thing she tended. For she wist and knew well how it was with him, as ye shall here say in the history hereafter. And then she began to say to the others: 'I go to make him speak, for he seemeth to be asleep.'

She departed from the other two ladies and yede to Raymon and took the horse by the bridle and made him to stand still; and [she] said in this manner: 'By my faith, sir vassal, it cometh to you of great pride or of great rudeness for to pass before any ladies without speaking or some salutation, howbeit that both rudeness and pride may be in you.'

And the lady ceased as then of her words, but Raymond heard nor understood nor answered her not. And she, as angry and wroth, said once again to him. 'And how, sir musarde[3], are ye so dispiteous that ye deign not answer to me?' And yet he answered never a word. 'By my faith,' said she within herself, 'I believe none other but that this young man sleepeth upon his horse, or else he is either dumb or deaf: but, as I trow, I shall make him well to speak if he ever speak before.'

And then she took and pulled strongly his hand, saying in this manner: 'Sir vassal, ye sleep.'

Then Raymond was astonished and afraid, as one is when another

---

[1] Chapter VI.   [2] *kerle*, churl.   [3] *musarde,* dawdler.

awaketh him from sleep, and took his sword, weening to him that it had been his uncle's meiny[1] that would have taken and slain him.

And the lady then perceived well that he yet had not seen her, and, all laughing, began to say to him: 'Sir vassal, with whom will you begin the battle? Your enemies been not here. And know you, fair sir, that I am of your party or side?'

And when Raymond heard her speak, he beheld her and perceived the great beauty that was in her and took of it great marvel. For it seemed to him that never before he had not seen none so fair. And then Raymond descended from his horse and bowed his knees and made reverence unto her, and said, 'My dear lady, pardon to me mine ignorance and villainy that I have done toward you. For certainly I have mistaken overmuch anenst[2] your noble person. And, nevertheless, I neither saw nor heard never what ye have said till that ye took me by the hand. And know ye, that I thought much at that time on a thing that sore lieth nigh to my heart. And unto God, I pray devoutly that amends I may make unto you, and that of His grace I may at mine honour be out of this pain which hurteth mine heart sore.'

'By my faith,' said the lady, 'it is well said. For as for to begin any thing, the name of God must first be called to man's help. And I believe you well that ye heard not what I have said. But, fair sir, whither go you at this time of night? Tell it hardily to me; if goodly, ye may discover it. And if you know not the way well, I shall dress you to it. For there is neither way nor path but that I know it well, and thereof ye may trust me hardily.'

'By my faith,' said Raymond, 'Gramercy, lady, of your courtesy. And ye shall know it, my dear lady, since that your desire is for to know it, I have lost the highway since almost yesterday noon unto now, and I no wot where I am.'

Then perceived she that he kept his *fait* secret from her, and said to him: 'By God, fair friend Raymond, ye should not hide nothing from me, for I wot well how it standeth with you.'

And then when Raymond heard that she named him by his own name, he was so abashed that he wist not what he should answer.

And she that saw well that he was shameful of that she had named him and that she wist so much of his secret and counsel, said to him in this manner: 'Forsooth, Raymond, I am she, after God, that may best counsel thee and that may further and enhance thee in this mortal life. And all thine adversities and misdeeds must be turned into weal; naught availeth to thee for to hide them from me. For well I wot that thou hast slain thy lord as much by mishap as wilfully, howbeit that at that hour thou supposest not to have done

---

[1] *meiny*, household servants.   [2] *anenst*, in regard to.

it. And I wot well all the words that he told unto thee of the art of astronomy, wherein during his life he was right expert.'

When Raymond heard this he was more abashed then he was tofore, and said to the lady, 'Right dear lady, ye tell to me the truth of all things that ye say, but much I marvel me how ye may so certainly know it, and who told it so soon to you?'

And she answered to him in this manner: 'Be not thou abashed thereof, for I know the full truth of thy *fait*. And wene nor suppose thou not that it be fantasy or [the] devil's work of me and of my words. For I certify thee, Raymond, that I am of God, and my belief is as a Catholic belief ought for to be. And I lete thee, to wit, that without me and my counsel, thou mayst not come to the end of thy *fait*. But if thou wilt believe steadfastly all that thine Uncle Emerye said unto thee, it shall be profitable to thee with the help of God and of me. And I say so much that I shall make thee for to be the greatest lord that ever was of thy lineage and the greatest and best livlihood man of them all.'

When Raymond understood the promise of the lady, he remembered the words that his lord told unto him. And considering within himself the great perils wherein he was exiled and banished out of his country and from his friends, said [to himself] that he should take the adventure for to believe the lady of all that she should do or say to him. For but once, as he said, he should pass the cruel pace of the death. And to the lady he answered full humbly in this manner: 'My right dear lady, I thank you much of the promise that ye do and proffer to me. For ye shall see and know that this shall not abide or tarry by me for no travail that ye can advise, but that I shall ever do your pleasure if it be possible to be done and that a Christian man may or ought to do with honour.'

'By my faith, Raymond,' said the lady, 'that is said of free heart. For I shall not say nor counsel you nothing but that good and weal shall come thereof. But first of all', said she, 'ye must promise to me that ye shall take me to your wife. And make you no doubt of me, but that I am of God.'

And then Raymond yede and began to say and swore in this manner: 'Lady dear, by my faith, since that ye insure me that it is so, I shall do after my power all that ye will command me for to do. And, indeed, I lawfully promise you that so shall I do.'

'Yet, Raymond,' said she, 'ye must swear another thing.'

'What it is, my lady,' said Raymond, 'I am ready if it be a thing that goodly I may do.'

'Yea,' said she, 'and it may not turn you to no damage, but to all weal. Ye must promise to me, Raymond, upon all the sacraments and oaths that a man very Catholic and of good faith may do and swear that never while I shall be in your company, ye shall not pain nor force yourself for to see me on the Saturday; nor by no manner ye shall not inquire that day of me nor the place where I shall be.'

And when she had thus said to Raymond, he yet again said to her in this manner: 'On the peril of my soul I swear to you that never on that day I nere shall do nothing that may hinder nor adamage you in no manner of wise.'...

'Then', said the lady, 'I shall now tell how ye must do; doubt you not of nothing, but go forthwith unto Poitiers. And when ye shall come there, many one ye shall find coming from the chase that shall ask to you tidings of the Earl, your uncle. And to them ye shall answer in this manner: "How is he not yet come again?" And they shall say, "Nay". And then ye shall say, "I never saw him since that the chase was at the strongest, and when he lost him." And semblant ye must make to be abashed more than any other.

'And soon after shall come the hunters and others of his meiny and shall bring with them the corpse within a litter; and his wounds shall seem to every man's advice to be made by the wild boar's teeth. And they shall say all that the wild boar hath slain him. And yet they shall say that the Earl killed the said boar; and many one shall hold it for a hardy and valiant deed. Thus the dolour and woe shall begin to be much great.

'The Earl Bertrand, his son, and his daughter Blanche, and all other of his meiny, both less and great together, shall make great sorrow, and so shall ye do with them. And ye shall put on you the black gown as they shall. And after this nobly done and the term assigned and taken when the barons shall come for to do their obeissance and homage unto the young Earl, ye shall return hither to me the day before the lords and barons make their homage. And that time at this same place, ye shall find me.'

Then as Raymond would have departed from Melusine to have taken his leave of her, she said to him in this manner, 'Hold, my redoubted friend, for to begin and assemble our love, I give you these two rings of which the stones been of great virtue. For the one hath such appropriate[1] that he to whom it shall be given by paramour or lover shall not die by no stroke of no manner of weapon nor by none arms as long as he shall bear it on him. And the other is of such virtue that he that beareth it on him shall have victory of all his evil willers or enemies, albeit pleading in courts or fighting in fields or else wheresoever it be. And thus, my friend, ye may go surely.'

Then took Raymond leave of the lady and embraced and kissed her sweetly and much friendly as she on whom his hope was laid. For he was then so much apprized of her love that all that she said doubtless he held it for truth. And the reason it was, ye shall hear hereafter in this story....

[1] *appropriate*, special function.

HOW MELUSINE MADE HER TESTAMENT[1]

[Melusine and Raymond were married and live happily until one day through jealousy, he breaks his promise not to see her on Saturday. Though Raymond is sorry for his deed, 'God would never suffer' her to abide with him. Bewailing 'false Fortune', both fall in a swoon. When Melusine recovers she tells him what he must do after she leaves him. She foretells that after his death 'no man will hold your land in peace'. Through folly his heirs will lose their inheritance. Their son Geoffrey will prove valiant and must stay with his father. She promises to take care of their three other sons. A fifth son Horrible is to be put to death. She warns that no one will ever again see her in woman's form.]

... 'My sweet love,' said Raymond, 'there shall be no fault of it, but, for God's love, have pity on yourself and will [to] abide with me.'

And she said to him, 'My sweet friend if it were possible, so would I fain do, but it may not be. And wit it well, that my departing from you is more grievous and doubtous[2] a thousand times to me than to you: but it is the will and pleasure of Him that can do and undo all things.' And with these words she embraced and kissed him full tenderly saying, 'Farewell, mine own lord and husband! Adieu, mine heart and all my joy! Farewell, my love and all mine weal! And yet as long as thou livest, I shall feed mine eyes with the sight of thee, but pity I have on thee of this, that thou mayst never see me but in horrible figure.' And therewith she leapt upon the window that was toward the fields and gardens against Lusignan.

HOW MELUSINE IN FORM OF A SERPENT FLEW OUT AT A WINDOW[3]

In this part, saith the history, that when Melusine was upon the window, as before is said, she took leave sore weeping; and her commanded to all the barons, ladies, and damoiselles that were present; and, after, said to Raymond: 'Here be two rings of gold that be both of one virtue; and wit it for truth that as long as ye have them, or one of them, you nor your heirs, that shall have them after you, shall never be discomforted in plea nor in battle if they have good cause: nor they that have them shall not die by no deed of arms.'

And immediately he took the rings. And after began the lady to make piteous regrets and grevious sighings, beholding Raymond right piteously. And they that were there wept always so tenderly that each of them had great pity, they sighing full piteously.

---

[1] Chapter XLV.   [2] *doubtous*, fearful.   [3] Chapter XLVI.

Then Melusine in her lamentable place where she was upon the window, having respection toward Lusignan, said in this wise, 'Ha, thou sweet country! In thee have I had so great solace and recreation! In thee was all my felicity! If God had not consented that I had been so betrayed, I had been full happy. Alas! I was wont to be called Lady, and men were ready to fulfil my commandments; and now not able to be allowed a simple servant, but assigned to horrible pains and torments unto the day of final judgment. And all they that might come to my presence had great joy to behold me, and from this time forth they shall disdain me and be fearful of mine abominable figure. And the lusts and pleasures that I was wont to have, shall be reverted in tribulations and grievous penances.'

And then she began to say with a high voice, 'Adieu, my lusts and pleasures! Farewell, my lord, barons, ladies, and damoiselles! And I beseech you, in the most humble wise, that ye vouchsafe to pray to the good Lord devoutly for me that it please Him to minish my dolorous pain. Notwithstanding, I will let you know what I am and who was my father to the intent that ye reproach not my children that they be not born but of a mortal woman, and not of a serpent nor as a creature of the faëry: And that they are the children of the daughter of King Elynas of Albany and of the Queen Pressyne; and that we be three sisters that by predestination are predestinate to suffer and bear grievous penances. And of this matter I may no more show nor will.'

And therewith she said, 'Farewell, my lord Raymond, and forget not to do with your son called Horrible this that I have you said, but think of your two sons Raymond and Theodoric.' Then she began to give a sore sigh and therewith flew into the air out of the window, transfigured like a serpent, great and long in fifteen foot of length. And wit it well, that on the base-stone of the window appeareth at this day the imprint of her foot serpentinous.

Then increased the lamentable sorrows of Raymond and of the barons, ladies, and damoiselles, and, most in especial, Raymond's heaviness above all others. And forthwith they looked out of the window to behold what way she took. And the noble Melusine so transfigured, as it is aforesaid, flying three times about the place, passed foreby the window, giving at each time a horrible cry and piteous that caused them that beheld her to weep for pity. For they perceived well that loth she was to depart from the place, and that it was by constraint.

And then she took her way toward Lusignan, making in the air by her furiousness such horrible cry and noise that it seemed all the air to be replete with thunder and tempest.

Thus, as I have showed, went Melusine like a serpent, flying in the air toward Lusignan, and not so high but that the men of the country might see her; and she was heard a mile in the air, for she made such noise that all the people was abashed. And so she flew to Lusignan three times about the fortress, crying so piteously and lamentably like the voice of a mermaid.

Jean d'Arras, *Melusine*. Ed. by A. K. Donald. E.E.T.S. Ex. ser. 71 (London, 1895).

'PONTHUS AND SIDONE'

An anonymous French author of the early fifteenth century wrote Ponthus and the Fair Sidone *as a tribute to the Tour Landry family of Anjou for their aid in expelling the Saracens from France and Spain. The English version, made in 1450 by an anonymous translator, was followed by Henry Watson's translation, printed by de Worde in 1501 and 1511. The earlier version, extant in the Oxford MS. Digby 185, printed in 1897, is more coherent and its style less florid than Watson's text.*

When the Breton conteur *related the fortunes of Ponthus, he retained only a tenuous link with the Arthurian romance. Ponthus represents the new knight, the man of action and diplomacy, less conscious of social degree and with none of the mystical qualities of his early medieval forbears, yet he is drawn with sufficient courtesy to keep within the traditional pattern of chivalry. Sixteenth-century readers found the romance entertaining, and demanded many French and German editions of it.*

There is some borrowing from Arthurian romance, especially from Chrétien de Troyes' Yvain whose hero, like Ponthus, seeks adventure in the famous Forest of Broceliande. And Guenelet, who during Ponthus's absence at the battlefront seduces his wife Sidone, is akin to the Arthurian Mordred. Among those incidents which bring the romance closer to the more realistic fiction of the Renaissance are: Ponthus's first visit to England just 'to see it bycause of the grete renoune' of its king and his sons; the battle of Couleigne, after which Ponthus is crowned king of Galicia in the presence of his aged mother and relatives; his interest in getting his cousin Pollides married to the English king's daughter; and the homily that he delivers, instructing his cousin, who is not of royal birth, how to be 'a great kyng' when he will one day succeed to the throne. The symbolic use of thirteen, the number of children saved from capture by the Turks, was a frequently used medieval device, forshadowing tragedy. In Ponthus, *one of the thirteen children, grown to manhood, betrays the hero.*

SYNOPSIS

As a framework for his story, the author used the old Anglo-Norman romance, Horn et Rimel, *changing the locale and names. When the story opens, King Brodas, the son of the sultan of Babylon, and his army have invaded the city of Couleigne or Corunna in Galicia, a province in the north-west of Spain, and they kill King Tibur. His queen and her maid flee to the country and live like hermits to avoid capture. Their son Ponthus and his cousin Pollides with thirteen other children, sons of barons, are hidden in a cave by a monk, Dom Denis. Hunger forces them to give themselves up. When brought before the sultan's son, he is tricked by a Christian knight into believing they have accepted the Mohammedan law, and they are released in the latter's custody. He procures a ship, and sends them to Vannes in Brittany.*

In France, Ponthus and Pollides are educated by a baron named Herland, seneschal to the king. After a few years, a romance that had begun between Ponthus and Sidone, the daughter of Huguell, king of Brittany, is interrupted when word comes that the Saracens will invade France. Ponthus leads Huguell's army and defeats them after severe fighting. The king knights him and makes him Constable, and he is well liked for the way he 'kept the ryght of Bretayn withoute dooyng wrong to any man'. But while Ponthus was away fighting, he finds that his love for Sidone has been challenged by Guenelet, one of the thirteen sons of the Spanish barons who had fled with him to France. To prove his right to Sidone's love, Ponthus holds a series of tournaments in the Forest of Broceliande and emerges the victor.

Guenelet is embittered when Sidone marries Ponthus, and he determines to have revenge. While Ponthus is again away from Brittany, aiding the English king in his wars with Ireland and, later, fighting the Saracens in Spain, Guenelet turns Huguell against his son-in-law and forces Sidone to marry him, telling her that her husband is dead. Through a dream Ponthus is warned that Sidone is in danger. He returns hastily to Vannes, arriving the day that she marries Guenelet. Disguised as a minstrel, Ponthus attends the wedding feast and kills him.

Before the story ends, Ponthus succeeds Huguell as king of Brittany, having renounced his right to the Spanish throne in favour of his uncle the Earl of Destrue. Ponthus's last task is to fulfil a promise that he had made some years before to Guenever, the king of England's daughter. He had met her while on an unofficial visit to the country, and she fell in love with him. He explains to her that he is happily married, but he will bring her a husband, his cousin Pollides. Ponthus keeps his word. After attending their wedding in England, he returns to Sidone and enjoys a peaceful reign.

King Ponthus and the fair Sidone

TRANSLATED BY HENRY WATSON

[HOW BRODAS TOOK COULEIGNE AND A
KNIGHT SAVED PONTHUS]

How Brodas, son to the Sultan, took Couleigne and slew the
King Tiber; and how a Christian knight named Patrick, saved
Ponthus and the thirteen children in a ship.[1]

So it happened, as fortune would, that one of the children of the
Sultan came as the wind drove him and his navy by great torment,
[so] that he passed Spain, in Galicia, and took land nigh to a great
city that was called Couleigne: And he went to land in a balangere,[2]
he and twenty-one men with him, and took of the people thereabout
the landing. And when he asked who was lord of that land, they
answered and said that it was the realm of Spain, and that King
Tiber was king of that land. Then asked the Sultan's son, what law
they held. And they answered and said, the law of Jesus Christ.

Then he made to withdraw his navy as though he would withdraw
him from the country. And he took two and twenty ships and sent
them to the port of Couleigne: and he charged them to make[3] them
as merchants of cloth of gold, of silk, and of spices; and that they
should, in the evening, go into the town and lug them forty men of
arms with halberds under their gowns; and, in the morrow early,
that they should come upon the walls at the water-gate; and that
they should get the gate; and they should assay to scale the wall and
to come up into the town. And as they devised, it was so done.

So came the twenty-two vessels; and they made them merchants
of Cyprus, and sold their merchandise good cheap. And after that
the forty men that were lugged in the town as merchants, nigh to
the water-gate, they made their hosts to eat and drink with them
that none ingyne[4] should be thought. And when they had disported
them, they went and had taken their advice to be upon the gate on
the dawning and to go about and devise their doing.

And when it came to the hour, they went upon the wall; and at
the same hour, the son of the Sultan, that was called Brodas, came
to the foot of the wall with a great navy[5] of ladders. And some went
on them on high; and they that were above, pulled up them that
were beneath so that within awhile there was a thousand or more
upon the walls: and [they] won the water-gate: And so they entered
into the town without any gainstanding.[6] And they made great

---

[1] Chapter II.
[2] *balangere*, large row-boat.
[3] *make*, pose.
[4] *ingyne*, trap or plot.
[5] *navy*, 'number' in other editions.
[6] *gainstanding*, opposition.

martyrdom of the people; and forthwith they assailed the castle in the which the King Tiber was, and they took him by strength, notwithstanding the King defended himself and would not be taken. And so he was slain.

And the Queen went out privily into the woods. And the King's son Ponthus and thirteen children, which were lords' sons, and a good priest that took them went out privily and hid them in a rock in a garden. And there they were two days without meat or drink. And the good priest, which was called Dom Denis, had so great dread when the children would go out of the cave, he wened to have died for them. And [he] said, 'Go ye not out but if ye will die.' So he kept them two days therein.

But on the third day Ponthus said to his master, 'It is better to die on the sword than for to die with hunger, for then we shall be cause of our own death; and if we go out, we may, by the grace of God, happily find some remedy.'

And the good priest said he had liefer die for hunger than go into their hands; and [he] trembled greatly for fear.

But fierce Ponthus and his cousin-german Pollides and all the others leapt out of the rock, and anon they were espied and all taken and led to the town to the King Brodas, that made himself king of the land. And when the King saw the thirteen children, they seemed to him right fair. So he asked whose children they were. And Ponthus answered and said they were children which the King nourished for the love of God and for their service when they should be men.

'And of what service?' said the King Brodas.

'Sir,' said the children, 'some to keep his greyhounds and his chases,[1] and some to keep hawks of the tower, and some to keep griffins,[2] and others to do service in hall and in chamber.'

'What!' said the King Brodas. 'Clothed he his servants so worthily as ye be? For by your clothes that ye wear, ye seem to be great lords' sons.'

'Sir,' said Ponthus, 'we be the children but of small gentlemen.'

'By Him that I serve,' said the King, 'I cannot see what ye be, but of beauty and of fair speech thou failest none; but ye must leave your law that is naught worth and take the law that we live on; and I shall do you much good. And if ye will not, I shall make you for to die; and so choose you whether that ye will.'

'Truly,' said Ponthus, 'of the death, ye may well ordain to your pleasure, but for to leave our law and to take yours, we will not for to die therefor.'

'No!' said the King. 'Then shall ye die an evil death.'

And then came a knight Christian that had taken their law for

---

[1] *chases*, coursing hounds(?).   [2] *griffins*, falcons.

dread of death (the which always had his heart and thoughts unto Jesus Christ), the which the King loved much, and [he] said unto the King, 'Deliver them to me, for if they will not believe upon our law, I shall ordain in suchwise that they shall never do harm unto your law.'

'I pray you,' said the King, 'and I give them unto your governance.'

Then trowed Ponthus and his fellows to be dead. The Knight led them to his house and monished them sore before the Saracens; and when the Saracens were withdrawn, he said to assay them, 'Ye must believe on Mohammed, or else ye must die.'

And they answered they would not, but rather to die. And when he saw them so steadfast, he had great joy in his heart: and he asked them if they had ought eaten of late time. And they said, 'Not these three days have we neither ate nor drank.' Then he made them to eat and drink. And as they ate, one of them said to his fellows, 'Wherefore eat we, when we shall die anon?'

'Say ye not so,' quod Ponthus. 'In the grace of Our Lord been many remedies. If it like Him, we shall live; if it like Him, we shall die, for all lieth in Him. So let us have good hope in Him, and He will save us.' And so they ate and prayed to God to have mercy on them.

The Knight heard what Ponthus said, and praised him much in his heart. And [he] said, 'It were too great pity to let so fair children die.' And so he went from them, and sought a ship and by night stuffed it with victuals for a month. And early in the morrow he led the children to ship and put therein a shipman with them that was a Christian man, and put them in the bottom of the ship. And when the children were in the bottom of the ship, they pulled up the sail, and the ship sailed into the high sea.

Then the shipman came up from beneath and took the governail[1] of the ship: and [he] asked them whither they would go. Then Ponthus said, 'Since God has sent you unto us, fair friend, lead us to the coast of France.' And he said, he would; and bade them not be feared nor dreading, for they had victuals enough for a month. And [he] told them how the Knight had put them in the bottom of the ship and the victuals with them by night.

Then said Ponthus, 'Fair sir, kneel we all down, and thank we God of the great goodness that He hath sent to us; and pray we all to be His pleasance.' So did the children night and day upon their knees and elbows, praying to God full devoutly, and [had] only their trust and steadfast belief in Almighty God.

[1] *governail*, tiller.

[OF THE GREAT FEAST AT VANNES]

Of the great feast at Vannes; and how Sidone bade Herland
bring her Ponthus, that was his norye;[1] and he brought her
first Pollides for dread of evil speech; and when Ponthus was
brought, Sidone began for to love him without any point of
villany, and chose him as for her knight. How tidings came
that the Saracens were landed in the Isle of Brest.[2]

After, it happed that the term of three years was come up and that
the King held a great feast in the Whitsuntide at Vannes, and he sent
gowns of one suit to the thirteen children; and [he] sent to them
that they should come to the feast: And each baron should bring his
child. And Herland brought Ponthus and the Lord de La Vale
brought his cousin-german Pollides that was most fair, most goodly,
and best in behaving of them all except Ponthus.

When Ponthus was come every man beheld him. And when the
King saw him, he had great joy and prayed to God to save him and
to send him much worship. And [he] said that he should serve him
of his cup at the feast.

The King made his feast with his barons and his knights in one
part, and his daughter in another part. Great was the feast and the
joy and the great sports. Sidone, that heard the great speech of the
beauty that was in Ponthus and of his demeaning, was day and night
in great thought how she might find a way with her worship to
speak with him, for dread of much speech with men.

And when she had thought enough, she sent for Herland, the
seneschal. And when he was come, she gave him a right fair palfrey,
and she made him right great cheer. Herland marvelled of the great
cheer, bethinking him what she meant, and doubted.

And afterward she said all, 'Aye, fair seneschal, fair and sweet
friend, we pray you that we might see your norye Ponthus that is
well taught and rightwise, as men say. I pray you, bring us him this
night that we may see him; for men say that he can dance and sing.'

'Madame,' said the Seneschal. 'I shall bring him to you, since that
it like you that I do so.'

'Then go,' said she, 'and I shall see if he [be] such one as men say,
or not.'

The Seneschal took his leave and went on his way....

[The Seneschal fearing that Sidone would be so enamoured of
the handsome Ponthus and insist on marrying him, decided to
substitute his cousin Pollides. When Sidone discovered that she had
been deceived, she made the Seneschal promise to bring Ponthus.]

---

[1] *norye*, foster (adopted) child.   [2] Chapter VI.

The seneschal went his way to fetch him [Ponthus]. Sidone went into her warderopp[1] to look at the window if she might see him come. So she said to Ellyous, her best beloved damsel, 'Give me my mirror, and see that I be well.'

'Certainly, madame,' she said, 'ye be right well.'

Then said she, 'Look ye, if that he come.'

And so they looked oft if they might see him coming. So at the last Ellyous went running to her lady, and said, 'Madame, see ye where he cometh, the fairest of the world!'

And Sidone leaped up and came running, and saw him come and the Seneschal with him. So she saw him fair, sanguine, brown, and high, of fair stature, so that she had of him great marvel. Then she said to Ellyous, 'Damsel, meseems, he is marvellous fair.'

'Madame,' said Ellyous, 'he is no man, he is an angel. I saw never so fair an earthly creature. God made him with His own hands.'

'By my faith,' said Sidone, 'ye say very truth. I trow she that be taken with his love be fortunate.' And so she went down into her chamber to her ladies and gentlewomen.

And, anon after, Ponthus and the Seneschal came up into the chamber. And so Ponthus went forth toward Sidone with full low courtesy, salveing her and her ladies. Sidone took him by the hand and welcomed him goodly and prayed him to sit down by her.

And he said, 'Madame, it is not for me to do so'.

So they made great courtesy.

Then said she, 'Wherefore make ye all this courtesy? Be not ye the King's son of Spain?'

'Yes, Madame,' said Ponthus, 'but yet I be not like you, for ye be daughter to a great King and a mighty, and I be a King's son disherit;[2] and so I have naught but by the goodness of my lord, your father, that so much good has done to me.'

'Aye, Ponthus,' said she, 'leave these words, for God has not made you, such as nature shows you, but for to do for you: for ye be made and formed to have as much worship and good, and more, than ever your father had—the which God send you.'

'Madame, I am not in that way, but in the mercy of God is all.'

'Now sit ye,' said she, 'I you pray and command.'

So he sat a little beneath her.

Then said she to the ladies, 'I pray you of some disports to the Seneschal and to the Knight, and that we may hear Ponthus sing and see him dance.' And Sidone that much desired to talk with Ponthus put him in demand of many things. So she thought him passing wise of his age. Among all other things she said, 'Ponthus, ye have been long time in Brittany without seeing of us.'

---

[1] *warderopp*, closet.　　　　[2] *disherit*, disinherited.

'Madame, I be in governance, and so me ought to obey.'

'It is reason,' said she, 'but I demand you, have ye envy to see us and our ladies that be here?'

'Madame, nay, forsooth, for here is a full fair company to see.'

'I you demand,' said she, 'have ye any will to any lady or gentlewoman to be her knight?'

'Forsooth, Madame, nay, for the service of me is but little worth.'

'Ponthus,' said she, 'save your grace; ye be of the place to be of worship to serve the greatest lady and the fairest of all Brittany.'

So they had enough of divers demands between them, insomuch that she said, 'I will that ye take the state of knighthood and that ye be held as for my knight. And when I hear that ye do yourself worship, I will have joy of you.'

'Madame,' said he, 'God thank you, and God send me grace to do that may please you and all your ladies; for the deeds of a poor man be little worth.'

'Yet', said she, 'I would well that ye wit how that I hold you as for my knight; and when that ye do better than any of my knights, I shall love you for the best, and ye shall want nothing that I have. And I would that ye made surement[1] to serve me above all other in worship; and think ye not but that I think worship.'...

Then she gave him a ring with a diamond, and she said that he should bear that for the love of her.

'Madame,' said he, 'God thank you.' So he took it and put it upon his finger.

And, after that, she led him to dance: and, after, she prayed him to sing. And so he did her commandment as he that felt himself taken with love. So he sang so good and so sweet a song that it was marvellous to hear. Then he was looked upon with ladies and gentlewomen and greatly praised. And each of them desired in their heart the fellowship of him and said among them, she was full happy that him list for to love and cherish.

And after that they had danced, there came forth spices and wine; and so Sidone gave to the Seneschal a cup of gold full of wine: And the Seneschal thanked her much. And when they had well disported them, the Seneschal said, 'Madame, we beseech you of leave, for it is time that we go to the King.'

So she gave them leave, and she prayed the Seneschal that he should come oft and see her. And he said that he should. So she and Ponthus looked full amorously at their departing, but she kept her as covert as she might....

The feast endured three days with great joy and welfare and all manner of disports. So it happened there came marvellous tidings

---

[1] *surement*, certain.

that said that the Saracens were landed in the Isle of Brest and were more than twenty thousand. The court was greatly troubled, so that they could make no cheer.

[HOW PONTHUS WAS CROWNED KING]

How Ponthus [having returned to his native Galicia to fight the Saracens] was crowned king. And how at the feast he knew his mother among the thirteen poor people; and how he made the Earl of Destrue and Sir Patrick to be keepers of his realm and to obey unto the queen, his mother.[1]

Ponthus made leeches[2] to be sought for to heal the people that were wounded and hurt in battle: and himself did visit them oft times, and made to be brought to them all things that they needed. He feasted the lords and all his fellowship, and give them gifts. And also he found in a tower the great treasure of the King Brodas, the which was a great thing to tell. And when he had over ridden the country and cleansed it of the misbelievers, he found much people and the land well laboured both of vines and corn.

From all the countries the people came running to see their rightwise lord, and as it had been to miracles. And they loved him well for his great renown and worthiness, his bounty and courtesy; for there was none so simple nor so poor but that he would speak to them and hear them meekly. He was right piteous of the poor people; he loved God and Holy Church.

And when he had done this deed, he came to Columpne; and [he] made there a great feast, and was crowned by the hands of a holy bishop. And thither came to him the King of Aragon, his uncle, that was brother to his mother, the which had great joy to see him and of his victory. And he told him how the King Brodas had warred upon him, and how there was taken a treaty between them to a certain day—unto the time that God would set a remedy—'and through His grace, He has right well purveyed of His pity by you'. Thus complained the King to his nephew, and yet he told him how that he abode the coming of the King of France and the King of Spain that should have come this summer, 'but it is no need'.

The feast was great of the King's coronation, and there were made many strange things. The great lords of the country came and did their homage. And also the fair ladies had great joy that they were come out of hell and of servage[3] whereas they had lived in sorrow and in heaviness; and now they be brought into joy and into mirth and into paradise, as they seemeth. They liked well their King, insomuch that they had great joy to look upon him. And all manner

---

[1] Chapter xxx.   [2] *leeches*, doctors.   [3] *servage*, servitude.

of people thanked God devoutly of their deliverance. Between the courses the ladies did sing; and there were many vows to the pope, the which were long to tell. And the King did bring and present by twelve fair ladies and twelve old knights, great gifts and jewels—some of fair coursers, and some of fair cups of gold and of silver, of fair cloths of gold and of silk, and of many other great jewels—to the knights and to the chieftains, so that all men were amarvelled of his great largess. He was a man right pleasant and of great courtesy and of good conditions.

So there fell a great marvel of the custom that was that time used; for it was so, that before the King, should be served thirteen poor men for the love of God and His Apostles. So it befell that the Earl of Destrue, the King's uncle, went visiting the tables: and, as God would, he beheld the table of the poor people and saw a woman looking upon the King. And as she beheld him, the tears fell down from her eyes. The Earl looked wisely upon her and avised[1] her so well that by a token that she had in her chin, he knew well that it was the Queen, mother unto Ponthus.

And when he saw her in so poor estate, that her gown was all clouted and rent, he might not keep him from weeping. So his heart swam for pity to see her in so poor degree. And when he might speak, he thanked God and went behind the King, his nephew, and said unto him, 'Sir, here be a great marvel'.

'Whereof?' said the King.

'The best and holiest lady that I know, my lady the Queen, your mother, is herein.'

'Where be she?' said he.

And he for great pain might not tell him for pity. And when he might speak, he told him in counsel, and said, 'Sir, see ye, her sits yonder with the thirteen poor at the first end of the table.'

And Ponthus beheld her, and he perceived her cheer. And, anon, she put her hood before her eyes and wept: And the King had great pity in his heart. Then he said unto his uncle, 'Make no semeland,[2] that none espy it, but when we be up from the table, I shall into my warderopp and bring ye her privily to me.' And so it was done.

When the tables were taken up and grace given to God, the King departed privily and went into his warderopp. And the Earl, his uncle, brought thither his mother privily. And when Ponthus saw her, he kneeled down before her and took off his crown and set it on her head; and she took him up all weeping and kissed him and halsed[3] him. And sore they wept, she and her son and the Earl.

And when they might speak, Ponthus said unto her, 'Aye, Madame, so much poverty and disease as ye have suffered and endured!'

'Aye, my sweet Knight and son,' said she, 'I am come out of the

---

[1] *avised*, scrutinized.   [2] *semeland*, display(?).   [3] *halsed*, embraced.

pains of hell: and God has given me great paradise when it has pleased Him to give me so long life that I may see you with mine eyes, and that I see vengeance for the death of my lord, your father, which the tyrants put to death; and also that I see the country voided out of the misbelief and the holy law of Jesus Christ to be served. And I wot well that this sorrow and trouble has endured this thirteen years as by a chastising of God [for] the great delights and lusts that were used in this realm. So meseems, now, that God has mercy of His people; that He has kept you and sent you to deliver the country of the misbelief.' Right well spake the Queen and wisely as an old lady, as she was.

'Now, I pray you,' said the King, 'tell me how ye escaped and how ye were saved.'

'My fair son, I shall tell you. When the cry was in the morning in the town and your father slain, I was in my bed: And he armed him with no more than a halberd and his helmet, and [he] ran forth without any more abiding as the hardest knight that was, as men said. When he was departed and when I heard the cry, I was sore afraid and took one of my women's gowns and went my way with my lavender:[1] and I found, of adventure, the postern-gate open, that some people had opened, and so I went out and went into the wood fast by the lands whereas dwelled a holy hermit, the which had a chapel and a well and a lug[2] at the woodside. So I abode there.

'And my chamberlain, which was well-aged, came every day to fetch alms at the King's house. And thereby we lived—the hermit, she, and I. And so ye may see that God has saved me.'

'In good faith,' said the King, her son, 'ye led a holy life.'

And so she did, for she wore the hair [shirt] and went gird with a cord; and [she] fasted much and was a full holy lady.

The King had great joy and great pity of his mother. Then he sent for his tailor; and [he] did shape for her kirtles, gowns, and mantles, both blue and purple, and made them to be furred with ermine and sables. And when she was so arrayed, her seemed a full fair lady. And when they came to supper, they brought in the Queen richly arrayed. And when the King of Aragon, her brother, saw her, he took her in his arms and kissed her, for he wened she had been dead. The lords and ladies of Galicia had great joy of the Queen: and they did her much worship, for they held her for a good and an old lady and were all amarvelled from whence she came, for they went[3] all that she had been dead.

Her brother, the King of Aragon, was set at supper at the table end and, after, the Queen, and then her son Ponthus, for the day of his coronation he must keep his estate. The Queen was of goodly port, and seemed well to be a great lady. She was right humble and

---

[1] *lavender*, washerwoman.   [2] *lug*, hut(?).   [3] *went*, believed.

had right great joy of the worship and goodness that she saw in her son. Then she said to her son, 'Fair son, I have great desire to see our daughter, your wife, for the great goodness that I have heard of her.'

'Madame,' said he, 'ye shall see her hastily if it be pleasing to God.'

That day passed with great joy and disports of ladies and dancing and singing and of other manner of plays....

[Ponthus left his mother in charge of the realm with his uncle and Sir Patrick as aids while he sailed to Brittany to bring back Sidone. He dreamed that 'a bear had devoured' her, and he interpreted the dream as a sign that she was 'in great trouble'.]

And then he went and heard three Masses; and sent his dinner to ship, and took leave of his mother, the Queen. And [he] said unto her [in] hearing [of] all men, 'Madame, I leave you the realm and the treasure that I have, all in your demean and governance. I have commanded and command all men to obey you as they would do to mine own person. And for the better, I leave you mine Uncle and Sir Patrick, my good Knight, the which I have made constable and Seneschal of my realm, and mine uncle, my Lieutenant.'

So he took leave weeping. And she prayed him to come again in short time, for she would fain see his wife. And he took his leave of the lords and ladies of the country, and went to the ships.

[THE MARRIAGE OF POLLIDES]

Here follows of the marriage of Pollides and of [the] King's daughter of England.[1]

...Great was the feast and great were the jousts, the which began the morrow after the day of the marriage; for the King Ponthus said that he would not accord that there should be any deeds of arms done the day of the marriage, and that he said was because the King of Burgone died the day of his marriage. For to say of all the good jousts it were too long to tell, but over all Ponthus jousted well, for he was without any pity or peer. Right well jousted Pollides and the King of Ireland, the Lord de Lusignan, the Lord de la Tour, the Lord Mountford of Brittany—these had all the voice of the well jousters. It were long to tell all, so I let it pass lightly; for it were a great thing to tell of the great feast, of the ordinance, and of the services, and of the prize that was given, and of all the disports. The feast endured from the Monday unto the Friday.

After meat, the King Ponthus took his leave of the King and of the Queen, but with great pain they gave him leave. Guenevere con-

[1] Chapter XXXIV.

veyed him well two miles, and they had much good talking together, and she said unto him how she loved her lord Pollides much the more because that she had loved him covertly before, and she praised him the more because that he [Ponthus] had kept truly his first love. Ponthus smiled, and said that there no wile but that women knew and thought.

So they spake enough of divers things; and then he made her to turn [back] again with great pain, and said unto her, 'My lady and my love, I be your knight, and shall be as long as I live; so ye command me what it please you, and I shall fulfil it at my power.' And then he said before Pollides, 'My fair lady and my love, I will that my cousin here love you and obey you, and that he have no pleasance to none so much as to you. And if there be any fault, do me to wit, and I shall correct him.'

'Sir,' said she, 'he shall do as a good man ought to do.'

'God grant it', said he. So he took his leave and departed.

Then the King of Scots, the King of Ireland, and the King of Cornwall would have conveyed them, that is to say, Ponthus and his fellowship, unto the port, but Ponthus would not suffer them. But there was heaviness and courtesy at their departing. And, after, they took their leave at him, and turned again to the King's house.

And the King Ponthus came to the port and called to him his cousin Pollides aside, and said unto him, 'Thanked be God, ye owe great guerdon unto God, for ye be in the way to be [by] right a great king and mighty of arms and of behaviour and of notableness, and great lords, your subjects; so ye owe[1] to thank God highly, and, therefore, it behooves you to have four things if ye will rejoice all in peace and to live peaceably:

'The first, it behoves that ye be a very true man, that is to wit, love God over all thing with all your heart, and dread to disobey Him; if ye love Him, ye shall fare the better, and He shall help you and sustain you in all your needes. Love and worship Holy Church, and all the commandments thereof truly keep. This be the first service that men should yield to Almighty God.

'The second be, that ye should bear worship and service to them that ye be comen of and to them of whom ye have and may have worship and riches; that is to say, love to serve your father and your wife, whereof much worship shall befall you. Be to him a very right son; keep you that ye anger them not; suffer and endure what language and words that shall be said unto you or of what tales shall be reported unto you—some to please you and some to flatter you. or else for malice covert of such men as would not the peace between you and them; for, fair cousin, he that will suffer of his better and of his greater, he overcomes him. It is a great grace of God and of the

_____
[1] *owe*, ought.

world, a man toward himself to have sufferance, for divers reasons, the which should be long to tell.

'The third reason is, for to be meek and amiable, large and free, after your power, to your barons and to your knights and squires, of whom he shall have need; and if ye may not show them largess and freedom of your goods, at the least, be to them courteous and debonair, both to the great and to the little. The great shall love; the little shall praise you over all of your good cheer: and so it shall greatly avail you—so much ye shall be praised over all.

'And also it is to understand that ye should be courteous and gentle unto your wife afore any other, for divers reasons; for by worship and by courteous bearing to her, ye shall hold the love of her bond unto you; and for to be diverse and rude unto her, she might happenly change, and the love of her, so should ye worse rejoice; and, peradventure, she then might give it to another; whereas she might take such pleasance whereof, ye might be right sorry, and that ye should not withdraw it when ye would. And so there be great peril and great mastery to keep the love of marriage. And also beware that ye keep selven[1] true unto her, for it be said in [the] Gospel that ye should change her for none other. And if ye do thus as I say, God shall increase you in all good wealth and worship. If ye see her angry, appease her by fairness; and when she comes again to herself, she shall love you much the more; for there be no courtesy done to a good heart but that it is given again; and when a heart be fell and angry, and men wrath it more, it imagines things whereof many harms may fall.

'The fourth reason be, that ye should be piteous of the poor, the which that shall require right of the rich or of the mighty that would grieve them; for thereto be ye set and ordained—and all other that has great lordships—for ye come into the world as poor as they did, and as poor shall ye be at the day of your death; and ye shall have no more of the earth, save only your length, as the poor shall have; and ye shall be left in the earth alone as the poor shall be. And therefore shall ye have no lordship, but for to hold rightwiseness without blemishing or doubt of any great master or reprieve, neither letting for the love nor for the hate, for thus commands God.

'Every Friday, in especial, hear the clamour of the poor people, of women and of widows. Put not their right in respite nor dilation, nor believe not always your officers of everything that they shall tell you; inquire before the truth; ror some of them would do it to purchase damage to the poor for hate, and some for covetous to have their goods when they see that they may not do so with them as they would. So if they come with false report, it is a perilous thing for a great lord to be light of belief.'

[1] *selven*, very.

He taught and showed many good examples. And Pollides thanked him, and said unto him, 'Sir, I know well your love; and of your goodness ye have purchased me the worship and the welfare that I have; therefore, I pray you by the way of charity that we may every year meet and common together; for that shall be my comfort, all my sustenance and joy.'

'I grant thereto,' said Ponthus.

And after, when they had spoken and talked of many things, they took their leave each of other and halsed and kissed together; and neither of them had power to speak one word, for marvellously they loved together.

When the King Ponthus had his heart somewhat cleared that he might speak, he took his leave of the lords of England, and offered himself much unto them.

King Ponthus and the Fair Sidone. Ed. by F. J. Mather, Jr. P.M.L.A. vol. xii, no. 1 (Baltimore, 1897).

JOHN CAPGRAVE

1393–1464

The legend which makes Joseph of Arimathaea the apostle of Christianity to England appears first in twelfth-century English chronicles, particularly in the addition to William of Malmesbury's On the Antiquity of the Church of Glastonbury *(c. 1125). Historical facts about this citizen of Arimathaea, who out of friendship offered his tomb for Christ's burial, cease with the Biblical account. But through the centuries Joseph of Arimathaea has attracted many biographers. The first to write his life was the author of the apocryphal* Gospel of Nicodemus *in which Joseph acquires a wife and two sons. Later biographers, principally the English chroniclers, William of Malmesbury, John Capgrave, and John of Glastonbury, tell of Joseph's departure from Jerusalem, after 'the Assumption of the Blessed Virgin Mary', and his voyage to England with twelve disciples at the request of St Philip the Apostle. After years of fruitful preaching, Joseph is said to have been buried at Glastonbury in the chapel which he built in honour of the Virgin Mary, and where legend claims that his staff was planted and grew and became known as the Glastonbury Thorn that blooms at Christmas.*

In the History *of the* Abbey, *John of Glastonbury claims that King Arthur is a direct descendant of Joseph of Arimathaea. And Giraldus Cambrensis identifies Glastonbury as the Isle of Avalon where Arthur was buried.*

Both Wynkyn de Worde and Pynson printed prose lives of Joseph of

Arimathaea. The material for each was taken principally from Capgrave's Kalendre of the newe Legende of Englande, *based on Nicodemus's* Gospel *and the* Legenda Aurea. *Pynson printed the* Kalendre *in 1516, and his* De Sancto Joseph ab Arimathia *is a condensed version of Capgrave's account.*

These lives of Joseph of Arimathaea, simply and plainly told, gave a pseudo-authenticity to the legend of the Grail that writers of romance linked inseparably with the tales of Arthur's court.

De sancto Joseph ab Arimathia

When Our Lord Jesus Christ was crucified, Joseph of Arimathaea asked Pilate [for] the body of Our Lord and laid it in a clean sendal[1] and put it in a sepulchre that no man had been buried in, as the Evangelist testifies.[2] And the Jews hearing thereof put him in a dark prison that had no window; and Annas and Caiaphas locked the doors. And after, when they had thought to have put him to death, they sent for him to the prison: and before their coming on the Saturday at night, Our Lord appeared to him with a great brightness as he was in prayer. And four angels lifted up the house that he was in. And Our Lord said to him, 'I am Jesus whom thou hast buried.'

And then Joseph said, 'Lord, if Thou be He, show me the monument that I put Thee in.'

And Our Lord took him by the hand and led him to the sepulchre; and from thence brought him into his house at Arimathaea. After, the Jews sent for him and asked of him how he came out of prison. And he told them, as before appeareth. And then they let him go, and he became a disciple to St Philip; and of him, he and his son Joseph were baptized.

And he was a messenger from Ephesus betwixt St John Evangelist and Our Lady, and was at her departing with other disciples. He was a constant preacher of the Word of God, as he had heard it of Our Lord and of Our Lady; and he converted much people.

After, he with his son Joseph went into France to St Philip. And he sent Joseph and his son with ten others into Britain. And, at last, they came to a place then called Inswytryn, now called Glastonbury. And these verses be made at Glastonbury of their coming:

> *Intrat Avalloniam duodena caterva virorum,*
> *Flos Arimathiae Joseph est primus eorum.*
> *Josefes ex Joseph, genitus patrem comitatur,*
> *Hiis aliisque decem, jus Glastoniae propriatur.*

---

[1] *sendal*, a thin silk material.   [2] John xix. 38–41.

[A group of twelve men come to Avalon,
Joseph, the pride of Arimathaea, is the leader of them.
Joseph from Joseph, son is joined with father,
To them and the other ten, are given the rights of Glastonbury.]

And, after, by monition of the Archangel Gabriel, they made a church or oratory of Our Lady. And there they lived a blessed life in vigils, fastings, and prayers. And two kings [Arveragus and Coillus], seeing their blessed life, though they were paynims, gave to each of them a hide[1] of land which to this day be called 'the twelve hides'. And there they died; and Joseph was buried nigh the said oratory.

Title-page: *The kalendre of the newe Legende of England....*
R. Pynson, 1516.

'REYNARD THE FOX'

The old beast-epic Hystorie van Regnaert, *a Low German prose tale based on Æsop's fable, was first printed, in 1479, by the Flemish printer Gerard Leeu. Caxton's English translation,* The hystorye of reynart the foxe (1481), *is vigorously told with an occasional borrowing from the Dutch language, which he learned during his stay in Bruges.*

From the fable's first appearance in European literature in Fredegar's Chronicle (612?), *where it is mentioned as a* rustica fabula *of the Lion, the Fox, and the Stag, Reynard is always the wily hypocrite, denying his guilt in the Lion's court. He does not change in a twelfth-century French version of the fable, only a fragment of which remains. But in the fourteenth century the German poet Willem exposed Reynard's cunning and exiled him from court in the satirical poem* Reinard. *As social conditions became worse in the next century, Reynard's hypocrisy was again allowed to triumph, as it does in Caxton's* Reynart, *a book, he warns in his preface, 'for nede and prouffyte of alle god folke' so that every man may 'kepe hym from the subtle false shrewis', and not be deceived.*

With the intent to urge religious and political reforms through the fable's satire, Caxton again warns his readers, in an epilogue to the second edition, against Reynard's treacheries. The fox, he believes, deserved to be hung 'for he was a shrewde and felle theefe and deceived the king'. And if all traitors would be 'honged by their Neckis', Caxton felt that he 'should be therewith weel apayd' for his pains in printing the fable.

---

[1] *hide*, a measure of land, estimated at between 60 and 120 acres.

The History of Reynard the Fox

TRANSLATED BY WILLIAM CAXTON

CAXTON'S PREFACE

Here beginneth the History of Reynard the Fox

In this history be written parables, good learning, and divers points to be marked; by which points men may learn to come to the subtle knowledge of such things as daily be used and had in the counsels of lords and prelates, ghostly[1] and worldly, and also among merchants and other common people. And this book is made for need and profit of all good folk, as far as they, in reading or hearing of it, shall mowe[2] understand and feel the foresaid subtle deceits that daily be used in the world; not to the intent that men should use them, but that every man should eschew and keep him from the subtle false shrews, that they be not deceived.

Then who that will have the very understanding of this matter, he must oft and many times read in this book, and earnestly and diligently mark well that he readeth; for it is set subtly, like as ye shall see in reading of it; and not once to read it, for a man shall not with once over reading, find the right understanding nor comprise it well; but oft-times to read it, shall cause it well to be understood. And for them that understandeth it, it shall be right joyous, pleasant, and profitable.

HOW THE LION, KING OF ALL BEASTS, SENT OUT HIS COMMANDMENTS THAT ALL BEASTS SHOULD COME TO HIS FEAST AND COURT[3]

It was about the time of Pentecost or Whitsuntide, that woods commonly be lusty and gladsome, and the trees clad with leaves and blossoms, and the ground with herbs and flowers sweet-smelling, and also the fowls and birds, singing melodiously in their harmony, that the Lion, the noble King of all Beasts, would, in the holy days of this Feast, hold an open court at state; which he did to know[4] over all in his land: and commanded by straight commissions and commandments that every Beast should come thither, in suchwise that all the Beasts, great and small, came to the court save Reynard the Fox, for he knew himself faulty and guilty in many things against many Beasts that thither should come, [and] that he durst

---

[1] *ghostly*, spiritual.   [2] *mowe*, more fully.
[3] Chapter I.   [4] *did to know*, caused to be known.

not adventure to go thither. When the King of Beasts had assembled all his Court, there was none of them all but that he had complained sore on Reynard the Fox.

THE FIRST COMPLAINT MADE BY ISEGRIM THE WOLF ON REYNARD[1]

Isegrim the Wolf, with his lineage and friends, came and stood before the King, and said, 'High and mighty Prince, my lord the King, I beseech you that through your great might, right, and mercy, that ye will have pity on the great trespass and the unreasonable misdeeds that Reynard the Fox hath done to me and to my wife: that is to wit, he is come into my house against the will of my wife, and there he hath bepissed my children whereas they lay, in such wise as they thereof be waxen blind.

'Whereupon was a day set, and [it] was judged that Reynard should come and have excused him hereof, and have sworn on the holy saints that he was not guilty thereof. And when the book with the saints was brought forth, then had Reynard bethought him otherwise, and went his way again into his hole, as he had naught set thereby. And, dear King, this is known well by many of the Beasts that now be comen hither to your Court. And yet hath he trespassed to me in many other things. He is not living that could tell all that I now leave untold. But the shame and villainy that he hath done my wife, that shall I never hide nor suffer unavenged, but that he shall make to me large amends.'

THE COMPLAINT OF COURTOYS THE HOUND[2]

When these words were spoken, so stood there a little Hound and was named Courtoys, and complained to the King how that in the cold winter in the hard frost he had been sore forwintered,[3] in suchwise as he had kept no more meat than a pudding, which pudding Reynard the Fox had taken away from him.

THEN SPAKE TYBERT THE CAT

With this so came Tybert the Cat with an ireous mood, and sprang in among them, and said: 'My lord the King, I here hear that Reynard is sore complained on, and here is none but that he hath enough to do to clear himself. That Courtoys here complaineth of, that is passed many years gone; howbeit, that I complain not; that pudding was mine, for I had won it by night in a mill. The miller lay and slept. If Courtoys had any part hereon, that came by me, too.'

---

[1] Chapter II.   [2] Chapter III.
[3] *forwintered*, reduced to hardship by winter weather.

Then spake the Panther, 'Think ye, Tybert, that it were good that
Reynard should not be complained on? He is a very murderer, a
rover, and a thief; he loveth no man so well, not our lord the King
here, but that he well would that he should lose good and worship,
so that he might win as much as a leg of a fat hen. I shall tell you
what I saw him do yesterday to Cuwart the Hare, that here standeth
in the King's peace and safeguard. He promised to Cuwart, and said
he would teach him his *Credo*, and make him a good chaplain. He
made him go sit between his legs, and sang and cried loud, "Credo!
Credo!"

'My way lay thereby, that I heard this song. Then went I near
and found Master Reynard that had left that he first read and sang
and began to play his old play. For he had caught Cuwart by the
throat; and had I not that time come, he should have taken his life
from him, like as ye here may see on Cuwart the Hare the fresh
wound yet. Forsooth, my lord the King, if ye suffer this unpunished,
and let him go quit[1] that thus has broken your peace, and will do no
right after the sentence and judgment of your men, your children
many years hereafter shall be misprised and blamed therefor.'

'Sikerly,[2] Panther,' said Isegrim, 'ye say [the] truth. It were good
that right and justice were done, for them that would fain live in
peace.'

HOW GRYMBART THE DASSE,[3] THE FOX'S SISTER'S SON, SPAKE FOR REYNARD AND ANSWERED BEFORE THE KING[4]

Then spake Grymbart the Dasse, and [he] was Reynard's sister's son,
with an angry mood. 'Sir Isegrim, that is evil said. It is a common
proverb, "an enemy's mouth saith seld well". What lie ye, and wite[5]
ye mine eme[6] Reynard. I would that ye would adventure that who of
you twain had most trespassed to others should hang by the neck as a
thief on a tree. But and if he were as well in this court and as well
with the King as ye be, it should not be thought in him that it were
enow that ye should come and ask him forgiveness; ye have bitten
and nipped mine uncle with your fell and sharp teeth many more
times than I can tell. Yet will I tell some points that I well know.
Know not ye, how ye misdealed on the plaice[7] which he threw down
from the car, when ye followed after from afar: and ye ate the good
plaice alone, and gave him no more than the grate or bones which
ye might not eat yourself. In likewise, did ye to him also of the fat
flitch of bacon which savoured so well that ye alone ate it in your
belly, and when mine eme asked his part, then answered ye him

---

[1] *quit*, acquitted.   [2] *sikerly*, surely.   [3] *dasse*, badger.
[4] Chapter IV.   [5] *wite*, blame.   [6] *eme*, uncle.
[7] *plaice*, a species of fish.

again in scorn, "Reynard, fair youngling, I shall gladly give you part"—but mine eme gat nor had nought nor was not the better, notwithstanding he had won the flitch of bacon with great dread, for the man came and threw him in a sack that he scarcely came out with his life.

'Such manner things hath Reynard many times suffered through Isegrim. O ye lordes, think ye that this is good? Yet is there more. He complaineth how that Reynard, mine eme, hath much trespassed to him because of his wife. Mine eme hath lain by her, but that is well seven years tofore, ere he wedded her; and if Reynard for love and courtesy did with her his will, what was that? She was soon healed thereof. Hereof, by right, should be no complaint; were Isegrim wise, he should have believed that he doth to himself no worship thus to slander his wife. She plaineth not. Now maketh Cuwart the Hare a complaint, also. That, thinketh me, a *vis-a-vis*. If he read nor learned aright his lesson, should not Reynard his master beat him therefor? If the scholars were not beaten nor smitten and reprised[1] of their truancy, they should never learn.

'Now complaineth Courtoys that he with pain had gotten a pudding in the winter, at such time as the cost[2] is evil to find. Thereof, him had be better to have held his peace, for he had stolen it. *Male quaesisti et male perdidisti*: It is right that "it be evil lost that is evil won". Who shall blame Reynard if he have taken from a thief stolen goods. It is reason: Who that understandeth the law and can discern the right and that he be of high birth, as mine eme Reynard is, knoweth well how he shall receive stolen goods. Yet all,[3] had he Courtoys hanged when he found him with the menour,[4] he had not much misdone nor trespassed, save against the Crown, that he had done justice without leave. Wherefore for the honour of the King, he did it not; all hath he but little thanks. What scathed it him that he is thus complained on?

'Mine eme is a gentle and true man. He may suffer no falsehood. He doth nothing but by his priest's counsel. And I say you, since that my lord the King hath proclaimed his peace, he never thought to hurt any man; for he eateth no more than once a day; he liveth as a recluse; he chastiseth his body, and weareth a shirt of hair; it is more than a year that he hath eaten no flesh. As I yesterday heard say of them that came from him, he hath left and given over his Castle Maleperduys and hath builded a cluse;[5] therein dwelleth he and hunteth no more nor desireth no winning, but he liveth by alms and taketh nothing but such as men give him for charity, and doth great penance for his sins, and he is waxen much pale, and lean of praying and waking, for he would be fain with God.'

---

[1] *reprised*, reprehended.   [2] *cost*, price.   [3] *all*, withal.
[4] *with the menour, in manu*, vernacular for 'in the act'.   [5] *cluse*, cell.

Thus as Grymbart, his eme, stood and preached these words, so saw they coming down the hill to them Chanticleer the Cock, and brought on a bier a dead hen of whom Reynard had bitten the head off, and that must be showed to the King for to have knowledge thereof.

HOW THE COCK COMPLAINED ON REYNARD[1]

Chanticleer came forth and smote piteously his hands and his feathers; and on each side of the bier went twain sorrowful hens, that one was called Cantart and that other good hen, Crayant; they were two the fairest hens that were between Holland and Ardennes. These hens bare each of them a burning taper which was long and straight. These two hens were Coppen's sisters, and they cried so piteously, 'Alas and weleaway!' for the death of their dear sister Coppen. Two young hens bare the bier, which cackled so heavily and wept so loud for the death of Coppen their mother, that it was far heard. Thus came they together before the King.

And Chanticleer then said, 'Merciful lord, my lord the King, please it you to hear our complaint and abhor the great scathe that Reynard hath done to me and my children that here stand. It was so that in the beginning of April ,when the weather is fair, as that I (as hardy and proud of the great lineage that I am come of, and also had, for I had eight fair sons and seven fair daughters which my wife had hatched, and they were all strong and fat) went in a yard which was walled round about, in which was a shed wherein were six great dogs which had totore[2] and plucked many a beast's skin, in such wise as my children were not afraid. On whom Reynard the Thief had great envy because they [Reynard's children] were so sure that he could none get of them; how well oft-times hath this fell thief gone round about this wall and hath laid for us in suchwise that the dogs have been set on him and have hunted him away; and once they leapt on him upon the bank, and that cost him somewhat for his theft. I saw that his skin smoked. Nevertheless, he went his way. God amend it!

'Thus were we quit of Reynard a long while. At last came he in likeness of an hermit, and brought to me a letter for to read, sealed with the King's seal, in which stood written that the King had made peace over all in his realm, and that all manner Beasts and Fowls should do none harm nor scathe to any other. Yet, said he to me more, that he was a cloisterer or a closed recluse become, and that he would receive great penance for his sins. He showed me his slavyne and pylche[3] and an hair shirt thereunder; and then said he, "Sir Chanticleer, after this time be no more afraid of me nor take no heed, for

[1] Chapter v.　　　　　　　　[2] *totore*, torn to pieces.
[3] *slavyne and pylche*, old shoes and skincoat, raiment worn by medieval pilgrims.

I now will eat no more flesh. I am forthon[1] so old that I would fain remember my soul. I will now go forth, for I have yet to say my *sext*, *none*, and mine evensong.[2] To God, I betake you." Then went Reynard thence, saying his *Credo*; and laid him under an hawthorn.

'Then I was glad and merry, and also took none heed, and went to my children and clucked them together, and went without the wall for to walk: whereof is much harm come to us, for Reynard lay under a bush and came creeping between us and the gate, so that he caught one of my children and laid him in his male.[3] Whereof we have great harm; for since he hath tasted of him there might never hunter nor hound save nor keep him from us. He hath waited by night and day in such wise that he hath stolen so many of my children that of fifteen I have but four; in such wise hath this thief forslongen[4] them. And yet, yesterday was Coppen my daughter, that here lieth upon the bier, with the hounds rescued. This complain I to you, gracious King; have pity on mine great and unreasonable damage and loss of my fair children!'

HOW THE KING SPAKE TOUCHING THIS COMPLAINT[5]

Then spake the King:

'Sir Dasse, hear ye this well of the recluse of your eme. He hath fasted and prayed, that if I live a year he shall abye[6] it. Now hark, Chanticleer, your plaint is enough. Your daughter that lieth here dead, we will give to her the death's rite. We may keep her no longer; we will betake her to God. We will sing her vigil and bring her worshipfully on earth; and then we will speak with these lords and take counsel how we may do right justice of this great murder, and bring this false thief to the law.'

Then began they, *Placebo domino*,* [I will please the Lord][7] with the verses that to-longen,[8] which if I should say, were [for] me too long. When this vigil was done, and the commendation, she was laid in the pit: and there upon her was laid a marble stone polished as clear as any glass, and thereupon was hewen in great letters in this wise: *Coppen, Chantekler's Daughter, Whom Reynart the Fox Hath Byten, Lyeth Hier Under Buryed; Complayne Ye Her Ffor, She is Shamefully Comen to Her Death.*

After this, the King sent for his lords and the wisest of his council for to take advice how this great murder and trespass should be punished on Reynard the Fox. There was concluded and appointed

---

[1] *forthon*, now.
[2] *sext, none, and evensong*, three of the eight canonical hours observed in the Church by special prayers.
[3] *male*, bag.   [4] *forslongen*, destroyed.   [5] Chapter VI.
[6] *abye*, pay for.   [7] Ps. cxiv. 9.   [8] *to-longen*, belong.

for the best, that Reynard should be sent for; and that he [be] left not for any cause, but he come into the King's court for to have what should be said to him; and that Bruin the Bear should do the message.

The King thought that all this was good and said to Bruin the Bear, 'Sir Bruin, I will that ye do this message; but see well, too, for yourself, for Reynard is a shrew and fell,[1] and knoweth so many wiles that he shall lie and flatter, and shall think how he may beguile, deceive, and bring you to some mockery.'

Then said Bruin, 'What, good lord, let it alone! Deceiveth me, the Fox, so have I ill learned my *casus*![2] I trow, he shall come too late to mock me.' Thus departed Bruin merrily from thence; but it is to dread that he came not so merrily again.

COLOPHON: Praying all them that shall see this little treatise to correct and amend where they shall find fault: For I have not added nor minished, but have followed, as nigh as I can, my copy which was in Dutch and, by me William Caxton, translated into this rude and simple English in the Abbey of Westminster. ...1481.

'MARY OF NEMMEGEN'[3]

A 'Miracle of the Virgin' is the source of the anonymous late fourteenth-century Dutch play, A very marvellous story of Mary of Nemmegen *who for more than seven years lived and had ado with the Devil. This miracle play was turned into an English narrative by a translator in the employ of Jan van Dvesborch, who printed it in 1520. H. S. Bennett in* English Books and Readers, 1475–1557, *suggests that this English version,* A lyttel story of a mayde that was named Mary of Nemmegen, *may be the work of Laurence Andrewe, who translated several works for van Dvesborch. In the prologue to Hieronymus von Braunschweig's* The vertuose boke of Distyllatyon *(1527), Andrewe declares that he has translated 'dyvers and sondry small volumes and tryfles of myrth and pastaunce, some newly composed and some translated and of late finished'.*

Whether the narrative is the work of Andrewe or some other translator, he lacked the literary talent necessary to convert a play into a prose tale and retain its dramatic lustre. Though in craftsmanship the play is far superior to the English version with its awkward phrasing, they differ only slightly in the main points of the plot. Each begins with Mary's despair when her aunt unjustly accuses her of immoral conduct with the young men

---

[1] *fell,* cruel.   [2] *casus,* cases; a reference to the subtlety of casuists.
[3] *Nemmegen,* Nijmegen in the Netherlands.

of the village. The girl had come to pay her aunt a short visit while in Nemmegen on a shopping tour for her uncle Sir Ghysoryche, the devout parish priest with whom she lived. Despondent over the false rebuke, she leaves her aunt's house not caring 'whether the devil or God' comes to help her. The devil appears and seduces her. Finally, after seven years she is converted.

Mary's prototype is Beatrice, the legendary Brabant nun, who left her convent, but was not missed during her seven-year absence because the Virgin Mary took her place. In both the play and the narrative, Mary's paramour is not a handsome youth as in the legend, but the devil in the likeness of a man. This 'one-eyed' demon-lover strengthens the moral, namely, the way of least resistance is the way to hell. But Mary's seduction lacks reality as it is accomplished without any mental struggle. There is, however, great emphasis placed on her repentance for sin, and, especially in the play, the power of Mary, the Mother of God, to aid those who pray to her. This latter point is stressed in the play-within-the-play which Mary attends in Nemmegen, remembering that her uncle once told her, 'a play is better than a sermon to some folks'. She is moved to repent, watching the plot unfold a situation similar to her own.

There is an affinity between Mary and Marlowe's Faustus that gives the narrative considerable interest in the history of English Renaissance drama, and especially its affiliation with German literature.

Mary of Nemmegen

TRANSLATED BY LAURENCE ANDREWE

Here beginneth a little story that was of a truth done in the land of Gelders of a maid that was named Mary of Nemmegen that was the devil's paramour by the space of seven years long.

In the time when Duke Arent was taken of his son Adolfe and his host, [at] the same time dwelled in the land of Gelders, three miles from Nemmegen, a devout priest called Sir Ghysoryche. And he had a young maid with him that was his cousin[1] that was named Mary; and this Mary did all that was to do in her uncle's house.

It befell on a time that Sir Ghysoryche sent Mary to Nemmegen to the market to buy that he needed, and said, 'The days be short, if it be late ere ye have done, abide with your aunt, my sister, at Nemmegen, for it is ill for a maid for to go alone in the night.'

Then departed Mary to Nemmegen. When she was come there, she went about her business. It fortuned that same day that her aunt

---

[1] *cousin*, may also mean niece.

had chided her against four or five women for the Duke of Gelders' sake, Adolfe, that had taken his father that they attseemed[1] mad; and [they] seemed more to be devils than women. For Mary's aunt hylde on[2] the young Duke's party, and, afterwards, murdered herself when she knew that the old Duke was conveyed out of prison by the jailor thereof, as more plainly hereafter followeth.

HOW MARY CAME TO HER AUNT; AND HOW HER AUNT SPOKE TO HER KNAPYSHLY[3] AND ANGRILY

When that Mary had bought all things, it was very late. Then thought she for to tarry all night there. Then went she unto her aunt, and prayed her that she might have a bed there for the night. Then answered her aunt angrily, 'What have ye to do to tarry all night here? Wherefore go ye not home again?'

Then said Mary, 'My uncle sent me unto the market to buy that he needed. And now should I go home, [but] it is very late; and oftentimes by night is a maid espied and taken and ravished. And therefore am I afraid to go home.'

Then said her aunt, 'Alas, poor maid, ye need not to fear that, for ye know well enough how that ye should lie: and ye have been at the taverns and drunk so much that ye be drunk. For I know well that the young men of villages can teach maidens the night dances in the corn when that it is high. And that have ye well proved, for in your village dwell many young fellows.'

Then said Mary, 'Good aunt, wherefore lie ye so?'

Then said her aunt, 'A double tongue, it will not tell the truth. But I know well that ye have danced many a dance where there were no minstrel. And ye be a maid still to[4] your belly were great.'

Then said Mary, 'Why cast ye me in the teeth, good aunt, with such things, and I am thereof guiltless. But, I pray you, aunt, show unto me it that I shall have a bed here for tonight.'

Then said the aunt, 'Nay, I had liefer that you lay in the river than in my house.'

When Mary heard her aunt say so, she departed from her with a heavy heart.

HOW MARY DEPARTED FROM HER AUNT

As Mary had these answers of her aunt, she departed from her with a heavy heart out of the town of Nemmegen in the evening; and, at the last, she went so long till she came to a thick hedge where that she sat her down weeping: And giving herself unto the devil, and said, 'Woe be to thee, my aunt! This may I thank thee for. Now

---

[1] *attseemed*, judged or considered.   [2] *hylde on*, sided with.
[3] *knapishly*, brusquely.   [4] *to*, until.

care I not whether that I kill myself or whether that I go drown me; and I care not whether the devil or God come to me and help me: I care not whether of them two it be.'

HOW THE DEVIL CAME LIKE A MAN UNTO MARY WHEN THAT SHE SAT UNDERNEATH THE HEDGE

The devil, that is at all times ready for to hawk after damned souls, hearing these words of Mary turned him into the likeness of a man. But he had but one eye. For the devil can never turn him in likeness of a man, but he hath some feint.[1] And then said he to himself, 'Now will I go sugar my words for to speak unto this maid that I displease her not, for men must speak sweetly to women.' And with those words said he to Mary, 'O fair maid, why sit you here thus weeping? Hath there any man that hath displeased you, or done you wrong? If that I knew him, I should be a wreaken on him.'

Then Mary hearing his voice looked beside her and saw a man stand by her whereof she was afraid, and said, 'Help God, I am waited.'[2]

The devil said unto Mary, 'Fair maid, be not afraid, for I will not do unto you no manner of harm, but do you good. For your fairness men must love you; and if that ye will consent unto me, I shall make you a woman above all other women, for I have more love unto you than I have to any other woman now living.'

Then said Mary, 'I sit here half mad in despair. I care not whether that I give myself to God or to the devil, so that I were out of this thraldom and misery. But, I pray you, show unto me who that ye be.'

The devil answered to her, 'I am a master of many sciences; for that I take on me to do, I bring in unto an end. And if that ye will be my paramour, I shall teach to you all the foresaid sciences so that there is no woman in the world shall pass you.'

Then said Mary to the devil, 'I pray you show unto me what ye be, and what your name is.'

Then said the devil, 'When reckoneth you, what I be. I am not the best of my kin, and ye will not be displeased. My name is Satan with the One Eye that is well known among good fellows.'

Then said Mary, 'Now perceive I well that ye be the devil.'

'That is all one who I be, for I bear unto you good love.'

Then said Mary, 'I would not be afraid of him if that it were Lucifer himself.'

Then said the devil to Mary, 'Fair maid, will ye be my love? I shall teach you all the sciences aforesaid; and I shall give unto you

---

[1] *feint,* fault.   [2] *waited,* spied upon.

many other costly jewels, and also money at your pleasure so that ye shall lack nothing at all: and you shall have all your own pleasure to do that thing that ye will desire, so that there is no woman shall have the pleasure that ye shall have.'

Then said Mary to the devil, 'Or that ye lie with me, ye shall teach to me the foresaid sciences.'

Then said the devil, 'I am content. Ask what that ye will, and ye shall have it.'

Then said Mary, 'I will have necromancy for one, for I have an uncle that hath a book thereof, and when that he lyst, he will bind thee find[1] therewith.'

Then said the devil, 'O fair maid, what ye desire, ye shall have; but I occupy not that science myself, for it is so dangerous. For when that ye begin to conjure and if ye miss one letter in reading, the guest that ye call for will break your neck. And therefore I counsel you not to learn that science.'

Then said Mary, 'If that it be so, that science will I not learn.'

Then was the devil glad and said to himself, 'Now have I turned her mind from that science, for if she could [learn] necromancy, then when she were angry with me then would she bind me therewith.'

Then said the devil to Mary, 'I shall teach to you all the sciences aforesaid; and ye shall speak all manner of languages that ye will desire, wherewith ye should be exalted.'

Then said Mary, 'Now put I away all sorrow through your words, and put me all whole to your will.'

Then said the devil, 'O fair maid, I desire ye of one thing, that ye will change your name. For I love not to hear that name, for by one Mary, I and all my fellowship fare the worse. And therefore shall I never love that name; and if that ye will change your name, I shall make you a woman above all women. And choose you whether that ye will be called, Leiskin, Metken, or Gretenin.'

Then said Mary unto the devil, 'What grieveth you [in] my name, for Mary cometh of Maria, the sweetest name that can be; and for all the good in the world would not I change my name nor be called other than Mary. For of Maria was Our Lord born.'

When the devil heard her speak in that manner then said he to himself, 'Now is all my labour lost and cast under thy foot, for I cannot change her name.' Then said he to Mary, 'My sweet love, if that we two should go together, ye must change your name; and, also, whatsoever ye hear or say, ye must say nothing, or else we two must needs depart.'

Then said Mary, 'To keep your counsel, I am content; but for to change my name, I will never while I live; for Maria is all my

[1] *find*, fast.

comfort and help in all my need: and, also, I serve her daily with a prayer that I did learn in my youth, and therewith will I serve her as long as I live, though that I am here now in the wild field, sitting here comfortless.'

Then said the devil to Mary, 'While that ye be set wholly on that name, I desire and I am content that ye hold the first letter of your name that is M; and ye shall be called Emmekyn, for there be many women and maidens in your land that be called so.'

Then said Mary unto Satan, 'If that ye will not be content with my name, yet for all that will not we two depart, for I am content to be called Emmekyn, yet were I very loath to do it.'

Then was the devil glad in his mind that she had forsaken her name, and said, 'Good love, let us go to Antwerp; and or that ye come there, ye shall have learned all manner of languages and also the seven free sciences.* And also if that ye will abide with me any-time, ye shall see that we two will work marvels, and ye shall drink no other drink but wine, both muscatel, bastard,[1] romney,[2] and all manner of other wines at your own will.'

And when that Satan had spoken these words, then was Emmekyn's heart glad; and she arose and went with the devil to 's Hertogen-bosch. And when they were come there, they took their inn and abode there a great while; and [they] made good cheer with revel-ling and dancing, and paid for every man that came in their company that eat and drank with them, and would not let them spend a half penny.

HOW EMMEKYN WOULD GO AND SEE HER FRIENDS IN THE LAND OF GELDERS

Then took Satan leave and departed to Nemmegen in the land of Gelders. And when they were come to Nemmegen, it fortuned on the same [day] that it was the dedication of a church. And when they were within the town then said Emmekyn to Satan, 'Let us go see how my aunt doth.'

Then said Satan, 'Ye need not to go to her, for she is dead more than a year ago.'

Then said Emmekyn, 'Is it truth?'

Then said Satan, 'Yea.'

Then said Emmekyn to the devil, 'What do all yonder folks that be yonder gathered?'

Then said the devil, 'They play a play that is wont every year to be played.'

Then said Emmekyn, 'Good love, let us go hear it, for I have

---

[1] *bastard*, a sweet Spanish wine.   [2] *romney*, romany(?).

heard my uncle say oftentimes that a play were better than a sermon to some folk.'

Then said the devil to Emmekyn, 'What lie ye on me to see the play? Let us go to the tavern and make good cheer.'

Then said Emmekyn, 'Good Satan, let us go hear it.'

Then said Satan, 'While that ye would so fain hear it, go thither and hear it: But tarry no longer than I shall call you.'

Then went Emmekyn and heard the play; and the play was of sinful living. And there she saw her living played before her face. Then she began to be sorry and take repentance. Then called the devil her, for he would have her hear it not out. But she would not come. For by the play she was all whole turned from her misliving, and said, 'O good Lord, have mercy on me, poor wretch and sinner! I am not worthy to tread upon the earth, and I am afraid that I have run too far.'

Then said the devil to himself, 'All my labour is lost; she taketh unto her whole repentance.' And he said unto Emmekyn, 'What ails ye now? Be ye mad? Let be your weeping and sorrow, and let us go to the tavern and make good cheer and put away your sorrow.'

Then said Emmekyn, 'Go from me, thou false fiend! Woe be to thee, that ever thou came to me! And I repent me that ever I chose thee for my paramour, for by ye I am utterly damned without the more mercy of God.'

Then arose the devil from the ground, and said, 'Hold your peace and be still, or else I shall bear thee with me to everlasting pain.'

Then said Emmekyn, 'O good Lord, have mercy on me, and defend me from the hands of the devil that he do to me no harm!'

Then said the devil unto her, 'I see, it will be no better.' Then took he Emmekyn in his claws and carried her up into the air more higher than any steeple [so] that her uncle and all the people marvelled thereat how come it came that she was carried so suddenly up....

HOW SIR GHYSORYCHE HER UNCLE DEPARTED TOWARD COLOGNE WITH EMMEKYN. AND HOW HE TOOK THE HOLY SACRAMENT WITH HIM THAT THE DEVIL SHOULD HAVE NO POWER OF THEM

When that Emmekyn and her uncle could get no comfort in Nemmigen, then on the morrow did Sir Ghysoryche sing Mass; and when that Mass was done then took he the Holy Sacrament in his hands and bade that his cousin Emmekyn should go with him to Cologne for to seek remedy. And Emmekyn said, 'With a good will, uncle, I am ready.' Then they departed both toward Cologne, her uncle bearing in his hand the Holy Sacrament. And the devil followed them all the way, but he durst not come near them to do them any harm by the virtue of the Holy Sacrament.

But in the way, as he went, he broke trees and cast after them for to have broken their necks: but our good Lord, that is ever merciful, would not suffer him to have the power for to do them any harm therewith, for they both were wont for to worship daily Our Blessed Lady with a certain prayer that they had learned.

And at the last they went so long that they came unto Cologne. And when they were there, then went they unto the Bishop and confessed her to him. And when that he had heard all her confession, he was sorry for her and said, 'Aye, good daughter, your sins be so grievous that I dare not absolve you, wherefore I am sorry.' This hearing, her uncle took his leave of the Bishop and then departed.

HOW EMMEKYN AND HER UNCLE TOOK THEIR JOURNEY TO
ROME TO THE POPE FOR TO BE ABSOLVED OF HER SINS:
AND HOW THE DEVIL FOLLOWED THEM FOR TO
HAVE DONE SOME HARM UNTO THEM

Then went Mary and her uncle to the Pope. And when they were come before him, then kneeled they down. And then desired Emmekyn, the Pope, for the love of God, that she might be confessed of him. And he answered with a good will. Then sat Emmekyn and the Pope down. Then began Emmekyn for to show unto the Pope her sins, and said, 'O most Holiest Father, the earth beareth not now a more sinfuller person than I am.'

Then said the Pope, 'Good daughter, why say ye so? Tell to me the cause wherefore.'

Then said Emmekyn, 'O Holy Father, I have been the devil's paramour by the space of seven years, and have done all things that he commanded me for to do.'

The Pope said, 'Wist ye well that he was the devil when that he came unto you and spake to you?'

Then said Emmekyn, 'Yea, well enough; that me sore repenteth.'

Then said the Pope to Emmekyn, 'How could ye consent to him while that ye knew for a certain that it was the devil?'

Then said Emmekyn to the Pope, 'O Holy Father, the great gifts that he gave unto me, both of silver and of gold, and also the pleasure that I had with him daily, both in dancing and playing, and had all that I desired; for that cause did I agree unto him. And also for my sake hath there more than two hundred persons been murdered, which sore repenteth me.'

Then said the Pope, 'O good daughter, for that thing may ye be right heavy.'

Then said Emmekyn, 'That I am heavy therefore as any woman may be, and I desire you, Holy Father, that ye will for the love of God and Our Lady, give unto me penance for my sins, how great soever it be.'

Then said the Pope unto her, 'Alas, good daughter, your sins be so grievous that I cannot give you penance nor absolve you without that God give unto me some grace to give me some manner of knowledge; and I will pray unto Him therefore.' Then kneeled the Pope on his knees and prayed God that he would put in his mind some penance that were for her sins. And when he had prayed awhile, then came into his mind a penance for her, whereof he was glad. Then bade he Emmekyn that she should call her uncle, and then should he give unto her her penance. Then went Emmekyn to her uncle and bade that he should go with her to the Pope. Then went her uncle with her unto the Pope.

And when that they were come, then said the Pope unto him, 'I would be sorry that any man or woman should be lost by the fault of me.' Then took he three rings in his hand, and said, 'Take these three great iron rings and make a smith set them on, and ye shall put the greatest about your neck and the other two about your arms as fast as ye may for falling off. And then let them alone thereon till the time that they fall off by theirself and be all consumed. And when they be consumed and gone, then be your sins forgiven you and Our Lord hath mercy on you.'

Then said her uncle to the Pope, 'My Holy Father, if it please you, that thing is a thing impossible; for if that it were possible for her to live by the space of two hundred years, yet for all that they should not consume and fall off from her.'

Then said the Pope unto her uncle, 'O sir, the mercy of God is great; for she may pray so much unto Our Lord God that through her prayer Our Lord God may have mercy on her and take her to His grace, and by a miracle cause the iron rings for to fall from her.'

And as the Pope spoke these words and had given unto her this penance, then took they their leave of the Pope and prayed him that he would pray for her. And the Pope said to them that he would with a good will. But he said to her, 'Take good heed that ye abide still in the mind that ye be in. And think steadfastly that ye shall be saved, and fall not in despair for all that I have given you; for by your penance and by your great contrition may God forgive you and give unto you everlasting blessing.'

Then thanked Emmekyn and her uncle the Pope; and so departed when that Emmekyn had these rings to her penance. Then went her uncle and she to a smith and caused him for to smite on the rings— the greatest on her neck and on each of her arms one fast, that never while she had lived should have fallen off but by a miracle.

HOW AN ANGEL CAME FROM HEAVEN AND PUT OFF
THE IRON RINGS FROM EMMEKYN

As Emmekyn was thus shorn into the nunnery, she fasted and prayed so much that at the last Our Lord had mercy on her and forgave her all her sins. And on a time as she was a praying in herself, she fell asleep: and in her sleep appeared an angel and undid the iron rings from her. And she thought in her sleep how that she was in hell, and how that there came an angel and brought her into heaven. And that there were a great many doves came to her and with their wings smote off her iron rings.

And when that she had had that vision, then awaked her, and saw the rings lie before her and were undone. Whereof Emmekyn was right glad and fell upon her knees and thanked God that He had showed unto her, a poor sinner, that great miracle and had mercy on her. And after said, 'O, all ye people, take an ensample of me: and while that ye have leisure and space, do penance for your sins; and amend your wretched living while ye may have leisure, for now may ye see how merciful that God is by me. And therefore do penance and pray unto our Blessed Lady that she may pray for you that ye may come unto the joy that is without ending, to the which joy bring both you and me. Amen.'

The Conclusion

COLOPHON: Printed by Jan van Dvesborch in Antwerp in 1518.

'TYLL HOWLEGLASS'

Tyll Eulenspiegel, believed to be the son of Claus Eulenspiegel and his wife Anne Wortbeck, is said to have lived in Brunswick in the early part of the fifteenth century. The family name, Eulenspiegel, appears in the city's records during this time, and contemporary chroniclers describe Eulenspiegel's tomb at Möllen, where a gravestone, surmounted by an owl and a mirror, bears his name.

The universal popularity of the adventures of the wily German country boor is shown by the hundred-and-five editions that have been printed of the German chapbook since the first extant edition of 1519. These editions include translations in Dutch, French, English, Polish, Danish, and Hebrew.

The first English version of Tyll's experiences, Howe Howleglass served a taylor, is the work of an anonymous translator. It was printed about 1510 by Jan van Dvesborch, but only a fragment remains. Forty-

six, or half the number of the adventures in the 1519 German edition, are contained in the English translation Here beginneth a merye jest of a man that was called Howleglass, *printed by William Copland about 1528. Like the German chapbook, it begins with the birth of Tyll and describes his 'three baptisms'—in church, in the mud, and in hot water. Then follow the many practical jokes that he played on the gullible townspeople and innkeepers as he grew to manhood and finally to old age.*

Though his wit is less sharp, this 'Gothic Diogenes' is the prototype of the Elizabethan fools, Touchstone, Launcelot Gobbo, Toby Belch, Falstaff, Verges, and Dogberry. Their blunt quipping, like his, is meant for 'a merry jest and a laugh thereat'. Ben Jonson acknowledges a debt to Tyll in The Poetaster, The Alchemist, *and the* Masque of the Fortunate Isles.

While German critics are almost unanimous in rejecting Thomas Mürner as the author of Eulenspiegel, *tradition has persisted in attributing the work to the Franciscan friar who was born in Strasbourg in 1475. After studying and lecturing at various universities, including Paris, Cracow, Vienna, and Prague, Mürner began to write in support of the Catholic cause against Luther. On a visit to England in 1519, he was befriended by Sir Thomas More, who wrote to Cardinal Wolsey recommending a gratuity for him and describing Mürner as 'a Doctor of Divinity and of both Lawes and a man for wrytyng and preching of great estimation in his cuntre'. Mürner's tract,* Is The King of England a liar, or is Luther? *won favour for him at the English court.*

Like Sebastian Brant, Mürner aimed his satire at the social ills of the time, particularly the injustice to the poor tolerated by persons of high rank in church and state. The most noted of his satires are: Schelmen Zunft *(1512)* [Knave Corporation]; Narrenbeschwörung *(1518)* [Conjuration of Fools]; *and* Gauchmatte *(1519)* [Fools' Meadow].

Tyll Howleglass

Here beginneth a merry jest of a man that was called Howleglass And of many marvellous things and jests that he did in his life in Eastland and in many other places.

PREFACE

FOR the great desiring and praying of my good friends, and I, the first writer of this book might not deny them, thus have I compiled and gathered much knavishness and falseness of one Howleglass, made and done within his life: Which Howleglass died the year of Our Lord God, 1450.

Now I desire to be pardoned, both before ghostly and worldly, afore high and low, afore noble and unnoble. And, right lowly, I require all those that shall read or hear this present jest, my ignorance to excuse. This fable is not only to renew the minds of men or women of all degrees from the use of sadness to pass the time with laughter or mirth, and forbecause the simple knowing persons should beware if folks can see.

Methink it is better [to] pass the time with such a merry jest and laugh thereat and do no sin, than for to weep and do sin.

HOW THAT HOWLEGLASS WOULD FLY FROM THE TOWN HOUSE OF MAYBROUGH[1]

After that, came Howleglass to Maybrough where he did many marvellous things that his name was there well known. Then bade the principal of the town that he [Howleglass] should do something that was never seen before. Then said he that he would go to the highest [part] of the Council House and fly from it. And anon that was known through all the town, that Howleglass would fly from the top of the Council House in such that all the town was there assembled and gathered in the market place to see him.

Upon the top of the House stood Howleglass with his hands waving as though he would have flown. And then the people looked when he should have flown. Whereat he laughed and said to the people, 'I thought there had been no more fools but myself. But I see well that here is a whole town full. For had ye altogether said that ye would have flown, yet I would not have believed you. And now ye believe one afore that saith that he will fly, which thing is impossible, for I have no wings: and no man can fly without wings.'

And then went he his way from the top of the Council House, and left the folk there standing. And then departed the folk from thence, some blaming him and some laughing, saying, 'He is a shrewd fool, for he telleth us the truth.'

HOW HOWLEGLASS HAD MANY AND GREAT DISPUTATIONS WITH ALL THE NOBLE DOCTORS OF PRAGUE IN BOHEMIA[2]

Then departed Howleglass from the land of Hesse. And then came he to Prague in Bohemia where was a university of schools and students of doctors and bachelors. Then made Howleglass bills and set them upon every church door. And he wrote that he would answer to all manner of questions that were laid upon him, and give answer thereto.

[1] Adventure XIV.   [2] Adventure XXXI.

And as he had set up the bills, then came the scholars of the university and read them. And when they had read them and found therein that he should give an answer to all that was asked him, then took they a bill and went to the rector and showed him that there was one come that has 'set us these letters upon the church doors, and he saith therein that he will give answer to all manner of questions that are put to him'.

The rector hearing this sent a scholar to the place where Howleglass was lodged and charged the host of the house that he should tomorrow bring with him the man that had set up the bills, upon pain that should fall thereafter. And then the host answered, he would. Then departed the scholar home.

On the morrow came Howleglass and his host to the university with two or three of his neighbours. And when they were come, then was Howleglass taken by the arm and set in a chair. And then came the rector with many doctors; and shortly they were set about him. Then asked he him, how many gallons of water was in the sea?

Then answered Howleglass, 'Do stop all the rivers that run therein, and then I shall mete[1] it, and then shall I show you how many there be.'

Then, thought the rector, that was impossible to do; but he was content with the answer. Then asked he Howleglass the second answer, 'How many days be past since Adam [to] this time?'

And then answered Howleglass to the rector, 'It is eight days past and more. For when the week is done then beginneth again the next week seven other days, and so forth to the end of the world.'

Then said the rector, 'Tell me, now, the third answer.'

And Howleglass bade him say what he would. Then asked the rector him, where was the middle of all the world.

And then answered Howleglass to the rector, 'That is here in the midst of this house. For and you believe not me, then take a cord and mete it; and if it lack a straw breadth, then will I be counted for an unlearned man.'

And then the rector had liefer give him the mastery than he would mete it. But then he waxed angry and asked him, 'How far is the earth from heaven?'

Then answered Howleglass, 'That is hereby. For let men sing never so softly, but it is heard in heaven. And ye will not me believe? Then take a ladder and go up into heaven; and I shall here speak softly, and if ye hear it not, then will I lose the prize.'

Then the rector said to Howleglass, 'How wide is all heaven; and how broad is it?'

Then answered Howleglass to the rector, and said, 'It is twelve thousand miles broad and ten thousand miles wide. And if ye will not me believe, then must ye take the sun and the moon and all the

---

[1] *mete*, measure.

stars of heaven, and then go mete them. And if you find it not as I say, then will I give the mastery to you, and I will be overcome.'

Then the rector and the doctors knew not what they should say more to Howleglass, but they said that he was so subtle for them: and then they gave him the victory and praise. And then departed he out of the place, for he was afraid that they would have done to him some unhappiness.

HOW HOWLEGLASS CAME TO THE TOWN OF BAMBERG: AND HOW HE DID EAT FOR MONEY[1]

Upon a time came Howleglass from Nürnberg to Bamberg where he entered into a lodging where was a merry hostess that bade Howleglass oftentimes welcome, for she saw by his clothing that he was a merry guest. And as dinner-time came, the hostess asked him if that he would go to dinner: and she asked him also if it pleased him to be at the twelve-penny table.

Then answered Howleglass, and said to his hostess, 'I am but a poor man. I pray you, for God's sake, to give me my dinner.'

Then said the hostess, 'The baker and the butcher will not be so paid. And therefore must I have money, for there is none in my house but they eat and drink all for money.'

Then answered Howleglass, 'For money do men eat and drink! In good faith, so will I.'

Then answered the woman to him, 'What table will you be at? For at the lords' table they give me no less than two shillings; and at the merchant's table sixteen pence; and my household servants give me twelve pence.'

Then answered Howleglass to his hostess, 'Since I must needs eat and pay money, then give me the best meat that you have.' And then he set him down at the lords' table.

And then his hostess brought to the table the best meat and drink that she had; and she bade him make good cheer. She said oft, 'Much good do it you, gentle sir.'

Howleglass thanked his hostess many times. He ate and drank and made him well at ease. And he ate so much of the good meat that he sweat again. When that he had made him well at ease, and eaten and drunken all that he would, then bade he his hostess to void the table, for he said he must depart from thence. And right shortly, at his commandment, the table was voided. And so he arose and stood by the fire; and when he was through warm, he took his leave with his hostess, and would have departed. That seeing, the hostess took him by the sleeve and bade him to give her two shillings for his dinner.

[1] Adventure xxxiii.

Then answered he, 'God thank you! For you have remembered me, I must have two shillings of you. For you said to me that there come no manner of persons within your house but that they eat for money. And when you had told me that, I sat me down and said I would do the same. And I ate so much that I sweat again. And therefore you give *me* money.'

Then said his hostess, 'Must I give thee money to eat my meat and drink my drink? Such guests I may have great plenty. Pay me my money shortly, for the bakers and brewers will not be so answered.'

Then answered Howleglass to his hostess. 'Give *me* money. For thinkest thou that I will eat so much and labour myself so sore as I did, not to be paid for my labour? Yet I had much liefer never to have seen thee nor thy house. For I have eaten so much for money that my belly is like to burst. Would you that I should have such great labour and not to pay [me] therefor? I have other things to do than to stand chatting here with thee. And therefore come oft lightly and give me my money and let me be gone, for I have right well deserved it.'

Then said his hostess to him, 'Sir, you have eaten my meat and drunk my drink; and by my fire you have had your ease, and all at your own desire. Wherefore, I pray you, give me money.'

And he answered right angrily, 'Would ye have me to pay money, and I did eat therefor, the which is to my great harm?'

Then she answered to Howleglass, 'If your eating do you harm, I am not the cause thereof: but your eating is to my loss; not only that, I have lost more than that cometh to.' And then she said, 'Depart thou from my house. And never after this, that thou be so bold once to enter within my doors.'

Then said Howleglass, 'Will you on your conscience take my labour for nothing? Well, farewell.'

And then departed Howleglass. And he was glad that he had so scaped from her; and she was glad that she was so delivered of him.

COLOPHON: Imprinted at London in Lothbury by me William Copland. [1528?]

NOTES

PART I

PAGE 18

salted cake. The *mola salta* which the Romans sprinkled over the sacrificial victim.

PAGE 27

the Emperor and the Swiss speed well. The joint attack of the Emperor Maximilian and the Swiss on Milan occurred in March 1516. It was financed by gold from the English Treasury.

PAGE 28

the Prior...had changed his mind. Fox purchased the property for the site of his college from John Burton, prior of the Austin canons of St Frideswide's some time after 1513.

ye shall receive the Foundation. The Foundation Statutes here referred to by Fox are not extant. Corpus Christi College possesses the copy 'new writen' with the Founder's seal intact and dated 1 March 1516/17. This copy gives the names of the masters, bachelors, and six fellows among whom is Thomas Fox, diocese of London, 'my pore kyndesman'.

PAGE 30

the great tempest. A severe epidemic of the sweating sickness at this time caused the death of 400 students at Oxford in one week. Though Claymond was among those who were stricken at Corpus Christi College, he recovered.

PAGE 40

Childermas Day come to Paul's Church. On the feast of St Nicholas, 6 December, it was the custom in European cities for a young boy to dress as a bishop and preach from the pulpit of the cathedral. His address was called the boy-bishop sermon.

PAGE 43

Melius est habundare. A saying found in old Latin school-books. Its origin is unknown according to G. Fumagalli in *Chi l'ha detto?* (Milan, 1946), p. xiii.

Tot capita. Cf. Terence, *Phormio*, III, 2. The old Latin proverb *Quot capita, tot sententiae.*

Trahit sua. *Eclog.* II, 65.

Nescia mens. *Aeneid*, x, 501.

as Aesop says. Cf. 'Man and the two wives', no. xlv.

PAGE 45

Ptolomeus was a rich man. Locher's marginal note, which Watson printed, reads, 'Ptolemy Philadelphus (309–246 B.C.) whom [Flavius] Josephus mentions in [*Antiquities of the Jews* (A.D. 93)] Bk. XII.' The twelfth book of Josephus deals with the Maccabean wars.

PAGE 46

You students, that wear long gowns. Locher's marginal notes, printed by Watson, refer the reader to Ecclus. 2, 7, 8, 12, 16, 44; St Paul's Epistles; Heb. V; II Tim. iii; and *Epistles* of Seneca, XVII, XXXVII.

PAGE 54

repute themselves, kings. Horace, *Satires*, II, 3.

PAGE 60

all heavy and glooming…from Trophonius' cave or Saint Patrick's Purgatory. Trophonius was the son of Erginus, the fable King of Boeotia. For his crimes he was believed to have been swallowed up in the earth. A cave near Delphi became known as Trophonius's cave where he was consulted as an oracle. The suppliant always emerged from the cave pale and dejected. St Patrick's Purgatory refers to a cave on an island in Loch Derg in Donegal, Eire. The saint is said to have spent there long periods of severe fasting and prayer. Since earliest times the place has been frequented by pilgrims. Marie of France is credited with *L'Espurgatoire Seint Patriz* (1190?), a translation of a Latin work by her contemporary Henri de Saltrey.

PAGE 62

Demosthenes who, following Archilochus. Archilochus is described in Plutarch's *Instituta Laconica* as a pacifist whom the Spartans ordered to leave their country when they found he had written against war.

PAGE 63

he had seen a wolf at unaware. Prof. Hoyt Hudson points out in the notes to his translation of *The Praise of Folly* (Princeton, 1941), that 'the Latin expression *lupus in fabula* or *lupus in sermone* corresponds to our "talk of the devil", and indicates that since the person being talked about appeared, the speaker breaks off in embarrassment'.
Which Quintilian interpreteth. *Institutiones Oratoriae* (A.D. 90?), XI, i, 43–4 (Loeb, vol. IV).
worthy saw of Plato's. *Republic*, V, 473.

PAGE 75

Aristotle asketh a question. Prof. Richard McKeon has kindly identified this passage. 'It is doubtless from the pseudo-Aristotelian *Problemata*, bk. xxx, ch. 10 (Loeb Classical Library, vol. II). The passage runs in the Oxford translation in terms sufficiently similar to that of the English translation of Vives's work to justify the identification: "Why are theatrical artists generally persons of bad character? Is it because they partake but little of reason and wisdom, because most of their life is spent in the pursuit of the arts which provide their daily needs, and because the greater part of their life is passed in incontinence and often in want, and both these things prepare the way to villainy?"'

PAGE 76

the poet Martial writeth. Epigrams, x, 35.
the four daughters of Queen Isabella. Isabella, the wife of Emmanuel, King of Portugal; Maria, who married Emmanuel after her sister's death; Joanna, wife of Phillip, King of Austria; Katherine, wife of Henry VIII, King of England.

PAGE 77

the daughters of S.T.M.Kn. Sir Thomas More, Knight, and his daughters, Margaret, Emily, Cecily, and their foster-sister, Margaret Giggs.
Saint Jerome writing unto Laeta. Laeta, the daughter of Paula, his convert, wrote to St Jerome, asking how to educate her daughter Paula. Vives quotes from St Jerome's lengthy reply to her letter. See *Select Letters of St Jerome*, trans. by F. A. Wright (Loeb Classical Library), Epistle CVII.

PAGE 85

with comment of Futtiratius. Research has failed to discover the identity of Futtiratius. In answer to an inquiry Prof. Paul Oscar Kristeller suggests that 'it may be a distortion of Eustratius (fl. 1100) who wrote a famous and widely used commentary on the *Ethics*. He wrote in Greek and his work was known in Latin translations by Grosseteste and presumably later ones. Eustratius enjoyed equal authority with the ancient Greek commentators on Aristotle and was republished in the *Commentaria in Aristotelem Graeca* of the Prussian Academy.' As Archbishop of Nice, Eustratius was widely known for his scholarship. Besides Grosseteste, St Albertus Magnus and St Thomas Aquinas translated his commentary on the *Ethica Nicomachea*.

PAGE 87

Oeconomicus. Translated by Raffaele Maffei, the Italian humanist, and appended to his *Commentariorum Urbanorum* (1511). Lupset's translation of *Oeconomicus* is not extant. However, an English version was made by his friend Gentian Hervet and printed in 1532. It is thought to be the first English translation made direct from Greek.

comment of Simplicius. Simplicius, a fifth-century neo-Platonist, was the author of several commentaries on the works of Greek philosophers. *The Interpretation of the Enchiridion of Epictetus,* written in Greek, was first printed in Venice in 1528.

PAGE 90

Plato affirmeth. Republic, bk. IV, 423 E.

PAGE 91

by the example of Artaxerxes. Plutarch, *Lives,* 'Artaxerxes', 5.
retained with him the poet Cherilus. Plutarch, *Lives,* 'Alexander'.

PAGE 93

What is so furious…as a vain sound of words. De Oratore, bk. I, 12.

PAGE 94

Tusculan Disputations, I, bk. I, 26.
Horace, Epistles, bk. II, *Ad Augustum.*

PAGE 97

Quintilian's opinion. Institutiones Oratoriae, bk. X, i, 40.

PAGE 100

a man's personality is reflected in his speech. Cf. Cicero, *Tusc. Disp.* V, 47. Also Seneca, *Epist. Mor.* 114, 1.
some rare sort of creature. Cf. Juvenal, *Satires,* XIII.

PAGE 101

a choice bite suddenly snatched from their jaws. Cf. Terence, *Heaut.* IV, 2.
Plato, in the Cratylus. 418, B–D.
a statement of Aristotle. Cf. *Organon De Interpretatione.* I–II.

PAGE 103

as Horace puts it. Ars Poetica, ll. 358–60.
the reply which Erasmus gave to Philip Melanchthon. This correspondence is probably lost as the reference is not found in any of the collected editions of the letters of Erasmus and Melanchthon.

PAGE 104

Pammachius. This play by Thomas Kirchmeyer, German adherent of Martin Luther, concerns an imaginary pope named Pammachius. He is in league with Satan and overthrows the Roman Empire. It implied that the Pope again sought complete domination of the Holy Roman Empire and England.

PAGE 105

caput audacie impunitatis spes. Cf. *Pro Milone*, XVI, 43 : *quis ignorat maximam illecebram esse peccandi impunitatis spem?*

PAGE 139

to be a good orator. Cox's qualifications for a good orator and the 'four kinds of oration' parallel Cicero's *De Oratore*. Cf. chap. 31 for the latter. For Cox's use of Aristotle's *Ethics* regarding justice, see bk. v, 1, 7, 10; also the *Rhetoric*, bk. II, 22, 'for the handling of a theme simple'.

PAGE 150

the mother of neediness or poverty. Palsgrave's marginal note refers the reader to Plautus's *Trinummus*. Cf. Prologue, a dialogue between Luxuria and Inopia.

PAGE 151

Out upon this light. The marginal note refers to Seneca, possibly his *Oedipus*. Cf. I, 926: *Qui poenas*, etc.

It irketh me. The marginal note refers to Virgil's *Aeneid*, IV, 450: '*Tum vero infelix fatis*', etc. Cf. *Hamlet*, II, 2: '...it goes so heavily with my disposition', etc.

PART II

PAGE 179

to the Diet hither. The Diet of Worms was held in 1521 in the Bischerhof in Worms, where Martin Luther was examined for heresy.

clementines. A collection of decretals and constitutions of Pope Clement V. They were published about 1308.

PAGE 179

declaration he put in print. This declaration was drawn up by Luther after the burning of the decretals on 10 December 1520, in front of the University of Wittenberg. In it Luther appealed from the Pope to a general council to hear the charge of heresy that was brought against him.

PAGE 179 *(cont.)*

I send your grace [*a copy*]. This is perhaps Luther's appeal *To the Christian Nobility of a German Nation* (1520).

goeth to Rome for annates. The profit paid from the first year's revenue of a parish benefice was called annates. It was demanded of each new incumbent and had to be paid to the papal treasury. After the English Reformation Henry VIII ordered the annates to be paid to the English treasury.

They say it is in Dutch. The German translation *Von der Babylonischen gefengknuss der Kirchen* (Augsburg, 1520) is attributed to Thomas Mürner, Franciscan friar and opponent of Luther. His reason for translating it was, he said, to let the people know the falsity of Luther's arguments against the Catholic faith.

PAGE 180

bull of his condemnation. The bull *Decet Romanum* was issued by Clement VII on 15 May 1520.

a treatise to justify his opinions. Luther's *Epistola Lutheriana ad Leonem Decimum Summum Pontificem: Liber de Christiana libertate, continens summam Christianae doctrinae* (1521). [Luther's Letter to the Supreme Pontiff (Leo X): A Book concerning Christian freedom, containing a summary of Christian doctrine.]

Ban Imperial. A ban imperial was signed against Luther and his followers by Charles V on 26 May 1521.

PAGE 203

The Book of the Moralities of the Chess. The original work, *Liber de moribus hominum et officiis nobilium ac popularium super ludo scachorum* (1275?) was written by Jacobus de Cessolis. The author likens life to a game of chess, using chessmen to explain social degree. William Caxton made the first English translation, *The game and playe of the chesse* (1476?), using the French versions made independently by Jean Faron and Jehan de Vignay. In Caxton's dedication to Clarence, Duke of Warwick, he states that it is 'full of holsom wysdom and requysyte unto every astate and degree'. Cf. reprint of Caxton's edition edited by W. E. Axon (London, 1883).

PAGE 204

gutta cavat lapidem... legendo. Ovid, *Ex Ponto*, IV, x, 5.

PAGE 205

quod melior est... philosophorum. In the 1598 edition of the *Book of Husbandry*, 'newlie corrected', this passage reads: 'For there is an auncient saying, & authenticall, of wondrous good authority, "That the practice or knowledge of a husbandman well proued, is better than the Science of Philosophy unexperimented."'

Sanat, sanctificat, ... mane. There is no text similar to this in the Bible. In *Oeconomica*, bk. I, vi, 3–6. Aristotle writes, 'It is likewise well to rise before daybreak; for this contributes to health, wealth, and wisdom.'

PAGE 208

The Knight of the Tower. The French romance known as *Le Livre* by Geoffrey de la Tour Landry who wrote it 'pour l'enseigne-ment de ses filles'. The romance was translated into English by William Caxton and printed in 1484. See E.E.T.S., orig. ser. 33, edited by Thomas Wright.

Adhibe curam; quod otiosus non gaudebit... inferno, and *tene mensuram.* These have not been found in the writings of Solomon. In the 1598 edition this passage reads, 'have doone your diligence, and endeuour, according unto the first article of the Philosopher, which is this: Take heede to your charge; and also wel recordest the wisedome of Salomon, that idlenes hath no part with the elect in heauen, but shall mourne eternallie without time with the reprobate in hell; then you must remember and keepe in minde, the second article', etc.

PAGES 208–9

Juxta facultates faciendi ... consumat. This saying attributed to St Paul has not been found in his writings. A similar idea is expressed in Xenophon's *Oeconomica*, VII, 36. 'And beware that that which was appointed to be spent in a twelve month, be not spent in a month.'

PAGE 209

Eat within thy tether. In the 1598 edition this is called 'an old English proverb which albeit rude, yet is it very significant and alludeth to matter of profit'.

PAGE 211

of the five Orders. The four orders usually referred to are the Carmelites, Augustinians, Dominicans, and Franciscans. Fish added the Crossed or 'crowched' friars, introduced into England in 1244 and suppressed in 1656.

PAGE 211

angels. Gold coins, bearing the image of the Archangel Michael. They were valued at six shillings and eightpence.

fifteens. The fifteenth part of a citizen's personal estate; and taxes were computed in the number of 'fifteens' that he owned.

PAGE 213

warmoll or *wardmote quest*. A regular meeting called by an alderman of a district to settle disputes and claims of the citizens living in his ward.

premunire. The Statute of *Premunire* was designed by the king and parliament of England to check evasions of existing statutes against provisors, i.e. persons appointed to English benefices or dignities by papal provision. Violation of the statute incurred severe punishment. See 'Premunire', in *A Catholic Dictionary*, ed. W. E. Addis and T. Arnold (London, 1917).

PAGE 215

one paid five hundred pounds. See Sir Thomas More's answer in *Supplication of Souls*, bk. i, to Fish's charge. More replies at length to Fish's discussion of the Hunne case in *The Dialogue against Tyndale* (1528), *Works*, ed. W. E. Campbell (London, 1924–31), bk. iii, ch. xv.

PAGE 220

syphogrants. Superiors or 'elders'. One was chosen by every thirty families to rule over them.

PAGE 223

Nephelogetes. 'Children of the mist.'
Alaopolitans. Those who dwelt in the city of the blind.

PAGE 227

bead-roll. The list of the dead kept in each parish church, and regularly prayed for.

PAGE 228

limiter. A friar who was licensed to beg within certain limits.
quarterage. Alms that were paid quarterly.

PAGE 229

The great Turk. Solyman the Magnificent who, in 1526, at the head of an army of 100,000 Turks, defeated the Hungarians at Mohacs.

PAGE 234

Aesop's ape. Cf. fable of Zeus and the monkey; also John Heywood's *Proverbs*, pt. ii, 4.

PAGE 235

as Horace saith of Homer. *Ars Poetica*, ll. 356–60.

PAGE 236

the brotherhood speak much less of him. More refers to the reformers, John Frith, Simon Fish, Thomas Bilney, and Thomas Cranmer. Owing to Stephen Gardiner's influence, Barnes did not openly attack the Holy Eucharist as did the other Reformers.

PAGE 238

he gathered out of John Gerson. Gerson's tract *Declaratio defectuum virorum ecclesiasticorum* (*c.* 1415) was intended to correct the laxity in Church discipline. The work was first printed in 1486.

PAGE 240

if a man be ex officio brought before the ordinary for heresy. The Pacifier objects to the law whereby bishops are permitted to call up one suspected of heretical leanings and force him to abjure even though no witnesses will step forward to accuse the suspected man and give evidence of his heresy. (Cf. *A Treatise concerning a Division*, etc., ed. I. Taft, E.E.T.S. 1933.) More says that he sees nothing wrong with such a law, neither he 'nor those wyse men neyther that made the lawe'. He goes on to say that 'those wyse men' were many, and not just *one*. For he says though that law is found in the *extravagant. de haereticis cap. ad abolendam*, yet was that law made in general council. This law refers to the *Decretalia* of Gregory IX. More's exact reference may be found in the *Corpus Juris Canonici*, ed. A. Frieberg (Leipzig, 1861), vol. II, p. 780. The decretals are a collection of ecclesiastical laws drawn up by Raymond of Pennafort by order of Gregory IX (1227–41) and completed about 1234. The chapter '*De Haereticis*' is a verbatim reproduction of a decree of Pope Lucius III (1181–5) and had been incorporated into the decrees of the Fourth Lateran Council (1215). Hence it was the work, as More says, of many 'wise men'. Further information on these early decretals and the origin of the word 'extravagant', i.e. 'decretals that are not to be found in the official collections', is given by F. W. Maitland, *Canon Law in the Church of England* (London, 1898) and Amleto Cicognani, *Canon Law* (Westminster, Maryland, 1934).

PAGE 243

when I was Chancellor. More was accused of cruelty to heretics while he was Chancellor. But in that office he presided over a court of equity and not a criminal court. He answers his critics in the *Apology* in chapter xxxvi: 'And of all that ever came in my hand for heresy, as help me God, saving as I said, the sure keeping of them (and yet not so sure neither but that George Constantine [a Reformer] could steal away) else had never any of them any stripe or stroke given them, so much as a fillip on the forehead.'

PAGE 251

a writ of excommunicato capiendo. Such legal phrases as *excommunicato capiendo* [seizure of the excommunicated] and *excommunicato deliberando* [freeing of the excommunicated] belong to court procedure in use as early as the Middle Ages. In England when a person was excommunicated by the bishop or the Church, he was obliged to retract within forty days. If the time elapsed and the excommunicated person had not made any retraction, the bishop communicated this fact in writing to the King's chancery. The chancellor of the kingdom then wrote a brief or letter, *breve de excommunicato capiendo*, to the bailiff or to the King's court, obliging the bailiff to confiscate all the belongings *mobilia et immobilia* of the excommunicated person. And if the excommunication was incurred because of errors against the faith of the Church, the excommunicated person was put in jail. If he retracted after the *breve de excommunicato capiendo*, he was set free and his property restored by virtue of another letter from the chancellor, namely, *breve de excommunicato deliberando*. If the person refused absolutely to retract, all his belongings that had been seized by the court were sold. When involved in heresy, the excommunicated person was sent to the civil court for examination and failing to retract was burnt in the public square. Cf. C. Du Cange, *Glossarium Mediae et Infimae Latinitatis*, 'Excommunicatio.'

as appeareth in clementinis. This law is in the *Corpus Iuris Canonici*, Leipzig, 1879–81, vol. II, p. 1182 ff. It begins: '*Multorum quaerela sedis apostolicae pulsavit auditum, quod nonnulli inquisitores per sedem eandem contra pravitatem haereticam deputati metas sibi traditas excedentes*', etc. [Many complaints have been brought to the notice of the Holy See that some inquisitors sent by this same See to investigate heretical disorders have gone beyond the limits prescribed for them.]

PAGE 260

unlucky marriage. The marriage of Henry VIII to Anne Boleyn.

greatest and highest counsel of two noble realms. Robert Shirburn, Bishop of Chichester, was the special ambassador of Henry VII to request a dispensation from Pope Julius II for the proposed marriage of Katherine of Aragon, widow of Prince Arthur, and Arthur's brother Prince Henry. The justification of the Pope's ruling was inadvertently brought out in a study of the validity of marriages involving consanguinity made by the Dominican Cardinal, Thomas de Vio Cajetan, in 1517, prior to the divorce proceedings and independent of them. The treatise is a commentary on a section of St Thomas Aquinas's *Summa Theologica*. See *Opera*

Omnia, vol. x, Rome, 1899, pp. 238–42. Cf. Philip Hughes, *The Reformation in England* (London, 1950), vol. I, pp. 168–77.

PAGE 279

medicine alterative. Medicine that produces a change in the system from a morbid state to or toward one of health.

medicine consolidative. Medicine that has the power of healing in the system.

PAGE 280

flowers of women. Menses.

PAGE 281

St Anthony's fire. This is an old term used for several diseases, including erysipelas.

A vein made in the water. This passage may refer to the 'distilled' water mentioned on p. 280.

PAGE 286

Vapors capinoso. The term is probably from the Greek καπνίζω, meaning to turn into smoke or become smoky. In Dalton's *Doctrines of Circulation*, he states that 'according to Galen these substances were excreted by the arterial system through its terminal branches in the skin and other membranous surfaces on the one hand and through the *arteria venalis* (pulmonary vein) in the lungs on the other. They consisted mainly of "fuliginous vapours", that is, volatile products like those from burning fuel.'

PAGE 287

castoreum. Mucilaginous substance found in beavers.

PAGE 290

eight and thirtieth aphorism. This is probably a reference to the frequently quoted *Aphorisms* of Hippocrates. The thirty-eighth aphorism of his seventh book reads *Distillationes in ventrem supernum in viginti diebus suppurantur* [Distillations in the upper belly suppurate in twenty days]. Cf. *Genuine Works of Hippocrates*, trans. and ed. Francis Adams (London, 1849), 2 vols., vol. I, p. 767.

PAGE 292

bole armoniac. An astringent earth found in Armenia and widely used in medieval medicine.

sanguis draconis or *dragon's blood.* A resin that exudes from various trees and so called from its red colour.

sarcocolla. A gum resin found in Ethiopia.

PAGE 293

a compendious doctrine for the curing of sickness. Cf. *Methodus Medendi*,
bk. I [Method of Curing], *Omnia Claudii Galeni...Opera*, ed.
H. Gemusaeus (Basel, 1542), 8 vols., vol. VI. 'Galen's *Methodus
Medendi* may be regarded as a partial consideration of Galen's
Practice of Physic, as far as medicine is concerned', according to
John R. Coxe, M.D., who also remarks that the Greek physician's
entire 'writings point out how greatly he depended on diet'.
Galen's patron and friends exhorted him to write on the Practice
of Physic and in the foreword of the *Methodus Medendi* he claims,
'I truly desire to do [so], both to gratify him and to benefit
posterity. Yet, I always delayed and that on many accounts; the
chief of which was that I feared I should write in vain since
scarcely any of this period paid attention to the seeking after truth.
Money, civil power, and voluptuousness alone took the lead, and
all who pursued knowledge were regarded as madmen!' See
Writings of Hippocrates and Galen, trans. and ed. by John R.
Coxe, M.D. (Philadelphia, 1846), pp. 643–5.

PAGE 294

euphorbium. An acrid poisonous green resin that flows from the
tree known botanically as *euphorbia offeninarum*.

lysimachia. Loosestrife, a species of primrose.

scordium. A plant that smells like garlic, according to its Latin name.
It is probably the water germander.

the whole study of Salerno. The poem *Regimen Sanitatis Salernitanum*
[*The Rule of Health of Salerno*], which in its longest version consists
of 352 lines, exists in many manuscripts, and three hundred editions
of it were printed before 1846. Some historians believe that it was
composed about 1100 for Robert, Duke of Normandy, son of
William the Conqueror. Elyot evidently held to the old tradition
that it was written for the latter since he says that it was made 'at
the request of a king of England'. The first English translation
*Schola Salernitana: Regimen sanitatis Salerni: This boke techyng al
people to gouerne them in helthe* (1528) 'was made by Thomas
Paynell' who thought it 'a fruitful book and very expedient at
sometymes for the welthe of unlerned persons to busy my selfe
therein'. After nine editions the work was again translated by Sir
John Harington, who titled it: *The Englishmans doctor. Or the
Schoole of Salerne* (1607). Cf. F. R. Packard, *The School of Salernum,
Regimen Sanitatis Salernitanum, the English version by Sir John
Harington* (New York, 1920).

PAGE 295

Introduction into grammar. See above, 'Tudor Grammars' by Eloise
L. Pafort.

PAGE 296

the nature of honey. In his *Natural History* Pliny describes the hippo-centaur. Cf. bk. VIII, 3; the story of Romulus and the Emperor Augustus is told in Pliny's *History*, bk. XXIII, 53, 'Honied Wine: Six Remedies'.

PAGE 297

as Aristoxenus writeth. Cf. Athenaeus, *Deipnosophists*, trans. Chas. B. Gulick (London, 1921–41), 7 vols., vol. I, p. 31.

PAGE 300

in their state. Probably means the critical stage of this illness when the humours become saturated with infection and the body attempts to relieve the condition by vomiting, etc.

PAGE 301

three sorts and kinds of spirits. Galen's physiological scheme of the workings of the human body included three types of spirits: natural spirits, formed in the liver and distributed in the veins; the vital spirits, formed in the heart and distributed by the arteries; and the animal spirits, formed in the brain and distributed by the nerves. Cf. Galen, *On the Natural Faculties*, trans. Arthur J. Brock (London, 1916). See Introduction.

PART III

PAGE 327

The Hill of Perfection. Many of Alcock's quotations in *The Hill of Perfection* cannot be found in the works of those authors to whom he attributes them. The editor is indebted to Mother St Miriam of the Temple, C.N.D., for the following notes, which are taken from her proposed edition of Alcock's sermons.

PAGE 329

blood red, 'bis cocte'. St Jerome does not make this statement. Cf. *Speculum Sacerdotale*, ed. Edw. H. Weatherly, E.E.T.S., old ser. 200 (London, 1936), p. 53. 'For Jerom seyth that mylk is nouȝt ellis but flesche meltid þrou chaungynge of colowre of the blode.' The editor gives as reference *Adversus Jovinianum*, II, *PL.* 23, col. 308.
approving the habit of your religion. This tradition concerning Christ's blessing of the Carthusian habit is given in a history of the Order. See E. Margaret Thompson, *The Carthusian Order in England* (London, 1930), pp. 217–18.

PAGES 329-30

Saint Bernard saith, '*Who loses obedience...devilish man*'. According
to a Cistercian scholar there is no exact equivalent of this passage
in any of the treatises where Saint Bernard treats of obedience.

Therefore saith Saint Ambrose, '*I, having so good a Lord...fear not to
die*'. Alcock quotes directly from the Latin. Cf. Paulinus
Notarius, *Vita Sancti Ambrosii, PL.* 14, col. 45: 'Non ita inter
vos vixi, ut pudeat me vivere: nec timeo mori: quia Dominum
bonum habemus.' See also *Legenda Aurea*, ed. Thomas Graesse
(Leipzig, 1850), p. 577. Alcock has added the phrase 'obedyent to
my superior' to make the citation pertinent.

The Abbot Pambo said to them all four, '*The virtue...himself a bondman*'.
Cf. St Jerome, *De Vitis Patrum*, lib. v, '*Verba Seniorum*', *Libellus*
xiv. *PL.* 73, col. 949.

PAGE 331

them that suffereth longer martyrdom. St Jerome, *Epistolae*, cviii,
'*Epitaphium Sanctae Paulae*', *CSEL*, LV, 349.

as Saint Nicholas, that is named sacerdotum honor. Nicolaus Clarae-
Vallensis, *Sermo in Festo S. Nicolai Myrensis Episcopi, PL.* 184,
col. 1055, 1.

PAGE 337

The clerk Orpheus marvelleth. Cf. *The Mythi-Hymns Of Orpheus*,
trans. Thos. Taylor (London, 1896), 'To Night', p. 10.

PAGE 349

The clear springs of the Holy Scripture. Hervet refers to the third edition
of Erasmus's Latin translation of the New Testament, *Novum
Instrumentum* (1527). The Philistines are Luther and Tyndale and
their followers.

PAGE 352

The ancient poets feigned there rose a strife. Jupiter's war with
Typhoeus. See Ovid, *Metamorphoses*, Bk. I, ll. 151-55.

PAGE 367

Triumph or *ruff* is a card game that resembles whist.

PAGE 374

by a late proclamation. In May 1555 a royal proclamation was issued
prohibiting the sale of all books, Latin and English, that contained
'any heretical, erroneous or slanderous doctrines'. They were
to 'be destroyed and burnt throughout the realm'. *The Book of
Common Prayer*, 'set forth by Parliament', was to be delivered up

to be burned or disposed of in some other way. See Strype's *Ecclesiastical Memorials*, vol. III, pt. I, p. 417.

PAGE 382

let them ever keep the preachings rather than the Mass. Whytford's advice to the laity to attend the Sunday sermon rather than Mass on that day, if one must choose between them, may probably be explained by the fact that the sermon in some places in rural England was not delivered during Mass, but at a later time, generally in the afternoon. Remembering that the tasks of the rural parishioner might, on occasion, prevent his attendance at both services, Whytford urged him at least to attend the later one—the 'preaching'. The laity's obligation to attend Sunday Mass is mentioned in the writings of English theologians as early as the seventh century. Then Bishop Theodore of Canterbury imposed penalties on those who failed to attend Mass on Sunday. In the fifteenth century John Myrc, in *Liber Festialis*, stressed the same obligation. See E. L. Cutts, *Parish Priests and their People in the Middle Ages in England* (London, 1898); also F. A. Gasquet, *Parish Life in Medieval England* (London, 1922), ch. vii.

PAGE 386

And where be the emperors...estates. The author here follows St Anselm of Canterbury, who enlarges on the words of the Prophet Baruch. In St Anselm's *Exhortatio ad Contemplatum*, etc., he asks, '*Dic ubi sunt reges? Ubi principes? Ubi imperatores?*' etc., *Opera* (Bonn, 1721), p. 190.

saith Saint Augustine. This direct quotation has not been found. The thought is inferred in *The City of God*, ed. Whitney J. Oates (New York, 1948), 2 vols., vol. II, ch. x, 'That the Saints lose nothing in losing temporal goods'.

saith Saint Anselm. This quotation has not been found in St Anselm's writings, but the thought is frequently inferred in his *Contemptu Mundi*.

PAGE 389

these three virtues. Poverty, chastity, and obedience are the three vows taken by all those who enter the monastic life.

PAGE 391

Saint Godric said. St Godric, born at Walpole in Norfolk, lived as a hermit at Finchale, near Durham, where he died in 1170. He is the author of several hymns, one especially to the Blessed Virgin which according to John Capgrave, in *Nova Legenda Aurea*, was dictated to him by Mary herself. She recommended its use as a solace in pain or temptation. The poem is one of the most ancient

specimens of English poetry. The following version is from one of
the earliest manuscripts:

> Saint Mary [chaste] Virgin,
> Mother of Jesus Christ of Nazareth,
> Take, shield, help, thy Godric;
> Take, bring him quickly with thee into God's kingdom.
> Saint Mary, Christ's chamber,
> Purity of a maiden, flower of a mother,
> Destroy my sin, reign in my mind,
> Bring me to dwell with the only God.

See Joseph Ritson, *Bibliographia Poetica* (London, 1802), pp. 1–4.

PAGE 395

abominable great pocks. An account of the 'great pocks' is given
by Thomas Paynell, who, in 1539, translated *Of the Wood called
Gualacum, that Healeth the French Pockes* from Sir Ulric Hutten's
De Morbo Gallico (1519). Paynell remarks in his preface that the
success of his translation of *Regimen Sanitatis Salernitanum* and the
urging of his printer, Thomas Berthelet, caused him to translate
Hutten's work. In the first chapter Hutten remarks, 'It hath
pleased God that in our tyme sycknesses shuld aryse which were
to our forefathers (as it may well be coniectured) unknowen. In
the yere of Christ 1493, or there about, this foule and most
greuous disease began to spredde amonge the people, not in
France but first at Naples in the Frenchman's hoste, whereof it
took his name (which kept warre vnder the Frenche kynge
Charles) before hit appered in any other place.' Hutten describes
it as a 'sickness that is no other thinge but a postumation and
rotting of unpure blood, the which after it begynneth to drye
turnethe into swellyngs and hard knobbes; the which thing pro-
cedeth of the lyuer corrupte'.

PAGE 402

Saint Augustine saith. St Augustine, Epistle *Ad Probam*, cxxx, 9.
PL. 33, col. 501.

PAGE 409

In Babylonica where ye write this sentence. Martin Luther, *First
Principles of the Reformation or Three Primary Works of Martin
Luther*, trans. H. Wace and C. A. Buchheim (Philadelphia, 1885),
On the Babylonish Captivity of the Church, 'On Baptism', ch. 3, p. 185.

PAGE 426

it was well said of Bias (Magistratus virum ostendit). This statement is
credited to Pittaci, another of the Seven Sages. Cf. *Magistratus*

quale cujusque ingenium sit ostendit, in *Apophthegmata, Fragmenta Philosophorum Graecorum*, ed. G. A. Mullachius (Paris, 1860), vol. I, p. 224.

PAGE 446

in Seville and Portugal, too, so go there all the slaves. More's remarks concerning slavery in Hungary refer to the aftermath of the army's defeat by Solyman the Magnificent at Mohacs, on 29 August 1526, when thousands of Hungarians were taken captive by the Moslems. Negro slavery in Portugal and Spain flourished in More's day, having begun about 1442 when Anton Gonçalves, serving under the Portuguese Prince Henry the Navigator, traded Negroes along the African coast.

PAGE 461

For St Austin saith. Cf. *On Predestination*, ch. xxix, 'God's dealing does not depend upon any contingent merits of men', and ch. xxxiv, 'The special calling of the Elect is not because they have believed, but in order that they may believe.' *Basic Writings of St Augustine*, ed. Whitney J. Oates (New York, 1948), vol. I.

PAGE 462

Lucian. Frith's reference to Lucian relates to the translation of Lucian's *Dialogues*, especially the *Tyrannicida*, which More and Erasmus made during the latter's second visit to England in 1506.

St Austin addeth. Cf. *On Grace and Free Will*, ch. xvii, 'The Faith that he kept was the free gift of God.' *Basic Writings*, vol. I.

But why He chooseth the one...inquire not. On the Pre-destination, etc., ch. xvi, 'Why the gift of Faith is not given to all'. *Basic Writings*, vol. I.

PAGE 464

Invitatory. The psalm, generally the *Venite, exultemus Domino* (Ps. xciv), recited at the beginning of matins.

PAGE 465

Use. The name given to the ritual followed in church services in certain dioceses, as for example the Sarum Use, compiled by St Osmund, Bishop of Salisbury, *c.* 1078–99.

PART IV

by counsel of Neot or Notus. According to the life of King Alfred by his friend Asser, whom he refers to as 'my Bishop', and from William of Malmesbury's *De Gestis Regum*, St Neot, the English hermit, acted not only as his sovereign's adviser in spiritual affairs but also those of the kingdom. These early chroniclers declare that it was on St Neot's advice that Alfred established several grammar schools, one of which was at Oxford and has led to the more or less legendary beginnings of the University by the King. An account of this Anglo-Saxon foundation is given by Anthony à Wood in *The History of Oxford*, vol. II, pp. 1–25, also, Asser, *De Rebus Gestis Aelfredi*, ed. W. H. Stevenson, who printed the *Annals of St Neot's*, an anonymous twelfth-century chronicle.

and translated many laws, as Mercian law and others. Alfred's Dooms or laws were compiled by him about 893. The document consists of an historical introduction, showing his interest in Mosaic law and a second introduction revealing how the early Church synods influenced English jurisprudence. With regard to the scope of his laws, he writes, 'I then, King Alfred, gathered these laws together and caused them to be written down, selecting many which pleased me from among those ordained by my predecessors.... But whenever I found in the laws passed in the days of my kinsman Ine, or of Offa, King of Mercia, or of Ethelbert, the first English convert to Christianity, anything that seemed to me to be most justly decided, such laws I gathered in, and the others I left out.' Offa I is credited with having written the Mercian code. See *The Legal Code of Alfred the Great*, edited with an introduction by Milton H. Turk (Halle, 1890); also, *Political History of England*, ed. William Hunt and Reginald Poole (London, 1905–21), 12 vols., vol. I (by Thomas Hodgkin), ch. xvii, pp. 299–305.

But how he had his pilgrim in mind...church. The early chroniclers, especially Symeon of Durham, agree on Alfred's devotion to St Cuthbert, Bishop of Lindisfarne in Northumbria. Symeon tells how in 876 the Saint's uncorrupt body was disinterred by Edred, Abbot of the monastery at Carlisle. With the Abbot's aid Bishop Eardulf moved it from place to place in northern England for fear of the Danes. After eight years the guardians of the Saint's remains were given sanctuary by Alfred. Through the converted Danish leader Guthred, son of Harthacnut, Alfred gave them 'all the land between Wear and Tyne for a perpetual possession', and he contributed to the church erected at the old Roman station, Chester-le-Street, near Durham, where the Saint's body was re-interred. It was removed to the church at Durham in 995. See Symeon of Durham, *History of the Church of Durham*, ed. T. Arnold, Rolls Ser. (London, 1882–5), 2 vols.

PAGE 484

the first charter that ever they had. The charter reads, 'William, King, greets William, Bishop, and Gosfregth, Portreeve, and all the burgesses within London, French and English, friendly. And I give you to know that I will that ye both be worthy of all those laws that ye were of in King Edward's day. And I will that every child be his father's heir after his father's day, and I will not suffer that any man offer you any wrong. God keep you.' See W. de G. Birch's *Historical Charters and Constitutional Documents of the City of London* (London, 1887); also M. Bateson, 'A London Municipal Collection of the Reign of John', *English Historical Review*, vol. XVII, pp. 480 ff. and 707 ff.

PAGE 492

in every eyelet the needle. According to Mr Kingsford, this may be a reference to the Prince's stay at Queen's College, Oxford, since it has an ancient New Year's day custom of presenting each student in the dining hall with a silk-threaded needle, bidding him, 'Take this and be thrifty'. The needles are supposed to be emblematical of diligence toward one's duty.

PAGE 496

as the common fame is. In the early accounts of Henry's life, especially those in Thomas Walsingham's *Historia Anglicana* and Caxton's *Chronicles of England*, there are stories of the Prince's riotous youth. Walsingham remarks how on becoming king 'he was changed suddenly into another man', and in Caxton's *Chronicles*, he is described as 'a noble prince after he was King and crowned'.

PAGE 497

that thing that is written of the Archbishop of Canterbury. The Arch-bishop referred to may be Thomas à Becket. An anonymous life, written by a contemporary of the prelate, describes him after his consecration as Archbishop of Canterbury, as '*moxque divina cooperante gratia mutatus in virum alterum, veterem hominem cum actibus exuit*', etc. [and presently, by the help of divine grace, was changed into another man; in all of his acts, he cast off the 'old man' and assumed the 'new' in justice and sanctity]. Cf. *Materials for the history of Thomas Becket*, ed. J. C. Robinson and J. B. Sheppard (London, 1875–85), 7 vols.; vol. IV, ch. 22, p. 79.

PAGE 498

he commandeth to edify his royal manor.   When Queen Anne, wife of
Richard II, died in the royal manor house at Sheen on the south
bank of the Thames, out of grief the King had the place demolished.
In 1414 Henry V rebuilt it, erecting a 'curious and costly building'
that was known then as the manor of Sheen. Fire destroyed it in
1494, and Henry VII rebuilt it on a magnificent scale. The structure
became known as Richmond Court.

He also founded two monasteries.   Besides building and endowing
the Carthusian house at Sheen, Henry V founded the famous
monastery of Syon for the Brigittines, an order to which both
men and women belonged. Richard Whytford, one of the most
noted English members of the order, lived at the Syon monastery.

whom King Henry the Fourth had intimulate in the Friars of Langley.
Richard II is said to have been buried first in the Black Friars
priory church in King's Langley, Hertfordshire. On 4 December
1413 Henry V brought the king's body from Langley and interred
it in Westminster Abbey.

PAGE 509

the commons in the west country arose and slew the bishop of Salisbury.
According to the *English Chronicle*, on 29 June [1450], the feast
of St Peter and Paul, Bishop William Aiscough 'was slayn of his
owen parisshens and peple at Edyngdoun aftir that he hadde said
masse, and was drawe fro the auter and led up to an hille ther
beside in his awbe [alb] and his stole aboute his neck; and there
thay slow him horribly, thair fader and thair bishoppe, and
spoillid him unto the nakid skyn and rente his blody shirte in to
pecis and baar thaym away with thaym and made bost of their
wickidnesse'. *English Chronicle* (Rich. II to Henry VI), ed. J. S.
Davies, Camden Soc. no. 64; also Mabel E. Christie, *Henry VI*
(London, 1922), p. 201.

PAGE 510

Armenica.   A corruption of 'America', which name was first used
to designate the New World by Martin Waldseemüller on the
world map that he published with his *Cosmographiae Introductio*
(1507).

PAGE 514

as writeth Gemma Frisius.   Cf. Gemma Frisius, *De principiis
astronomiae et cosmographiae*; *deque usu globi ab eodem editi. Item:
de orbis divisione, et insulis, rebus nuper inventis* (1530), ch. xxx,
'*De America*'. [Concerning the principles of astronomy and
cosmography; and of the use of the globe published by him.

Item: Of the division of the world, and tidings concerning the islands recently found]. Eden quotes almost directly from Frisius's description of the wealth of the country and the friendly natives that inhabited '*Terra Florida et Bacalearium*'.

PAGE 515

Damian a Goes writeth. Eden refers to Goes's statement, '*sed cum Erasmo Roterdamo meis literis egi*', etc. [I have also pleaded with Erasmus of Rotterdam in my letters that he should write about these conditions]. Cf. Damian a Goes, *Fides, religio, moresque Aethiopum...De deploratione Lappianae gentis*, etc. (1544) [The beliefs, religion, and customs of the Aethiopians...Concerning the lament for the people of Lapland], p. 524.

And these be the very words...to the Bishop of Rome, Paul the Third. Cf. Damian a Goes's dedicatory epistle to Pope Paul III prefixed to *Fides...Aethiopum*, p. 453

PAGE 516

Impiger extremos...per ignes. Horace, *Odes*, I, i, 45.

PAGE 518

as writeth Haytho. Hetoun or Hayton, Prince of Gorigos, was an exiled member of fourteenth-century Christian Armenian royalty. He wrote the *Historia Orientalis* (1529) of which '*De Societate*', is Chapter LX.

PAGE 539

the Blackfriars. A district in London, located in the vicinity of old St Paul's Cathedral. In medieval times the property had belonged to the Dominicans or Blackfriars, as they were called.

PAGE 541

the marriage between you and me. See Part II, Reginald Pole's letter to Cuthbert Tunstall.

PAGE 548

Witness this: Saint Augustine 'ubi inquit...presentabitur'. This passage has not been found in St Augustine's works, but it is almost identical with one in the *Dialogi* of Pope Gregory I: *Qualis hinc quisque egreditur, talis in judicio praesentatur* [In whatever state one departs hence, just so is he received for judgment]. *PL.*, vol. 77, lib. 4, c. 39, col. 396A. The closest parallel in the writings of St Augustine is found in his letter to Hesychius, *Epistola* cxcix, caput I, sec. 2: '*In quo enim quemque invenerit suus novissimus dies, in hoc eum comprehendet mundi novissimus dies; quoniam qualis in die isto quisque moritur, talis in die illo judicabitur.*' [In whatever state a man's own last day shall find him, in such a state shall the last day of the world take him; for as a man dies on the former day, so shall he be judged on the latter.] *PL.*, vol. 33, col. 905.

Idem Augustinus, de poenitencia...judicat. St Augustine has no specific work on penance, though various of his epistles deal with it. A spurious work, *De vera et falsa penitentia ad Christi devotam*, contains no passage similar to that quoted by Bouge. However, in St Augustine's letter to Hesychius, quoted above, a passage approximates the thought in Bouge's reference: *Tunc enim unicuique veniet dies ille, cum venerit ei dies ut talis hinc exeat, qualis judicandus est illo die. Ac per hoc vigilare debet omnis christianus, ne imparatum inveniat eum Domini adventus. Imparatum autem inveniet ille dies, quem imparatum invenerit suae vitae hujus ultimus dies* [That (i.e. the Judgement) day will come to every man when the day comes on which he must leave this world in the same state as he will be judged on the judgement day. Wherefore every Christian ought to watch lest the coming of the Lord find him unprepared. That day shall find unprepared whomsoever the last day of his own life finds unprepared]. Ibid., col. 906.

credo in sanctam ecclesiam catholicam. This is an approximation to the ninth article of the Apostles' Creed.

PAGE 552

danger and penalty of the last Act of Parliament. More refers to the Act of Succession, which encompassed the Oath of Royal Supremacy, passed in 1534. It was made a test of loyalty and approval of all the King had done and chose to do.

PAGE 553

Qui tacet,...consentire videtur. Decretals, bk. v, ch. 12, sec. 43.

PAGE 555

that so many worthy bishops...ever meant to have any man punished by death in whom there could be found no malice. According to William Rastell, nephew of Sir Thomas More, an eye-witness at the trial, whose *Life* of More is lost except for some fragments, Parliament purposely inserted the word 'malicious' in the Act of Supremacy. In his *Life* of More, Rastell states that the word 'malicious' made it 'highe treaso[n] to do or speke againste *the kynges* supreamacey and other thing[es]. Note dilligently here, *that the* bill was earnestly *with*stode, *and* could not be suffered to passe, vnlese *the* rigor of it were qualified *with* this worde "[ma]liciusly"; *and* so not eueri one spekinge againste the supreamacey [to be trea]son, but onlei maliciusly spekinge, *and* so for more p[layne declarac]ion thereof, *the* word "maliciusly" was twise put into *the* [acte, and yet afterwardes] in puttinge the acte in execucion againste [Bushope Fisher, Sir Thomas Moore, the Car]thusians *and* others,

the word "malici[usly" playnely expressed in the act was adiudged]
by *the* k[ynges commissioners, before whome they were arrayned,
to be voyed].' 'Rastell Fragments', Nicholas Harpsfield's *Life Of
Sir Thomas More*, ed. Elsie V. Hitchcock, E.E.T.S. orig. ser. 186,
App. I, pp. 228–9.

PAGE 557

as they might evidently [perceive] in Magna Charta. More quotes from
the first article of Magna Charta.

So might St Gregory, Pope of Rome. There is no similar passage in
the works of St Gregory the Great. The words put on his lips by
More are perhaps not an actual statement of the Pope's, but rather
one that he might well have made, in view of his role in bringing
about the evangelization of England. Cf. Bede's *Ecclesiastical
History of the English Nation*, bk. II, ch. i. This account probably
inspired the invention of the statement.

PART V

PAGE 607

the fields hath sight and every word hath sound. An English proverb,
'Wode has erys, felde has sigt.' See *King Edward and the Shepherd*
(*c.* 1300).

PAGE 622

the Sparrow-hawk Castle. The legend of the sparrow-hawk in
English literature is of Welsh origin, dating from the early times
when the bird was given as a prize to a knight for his prowess
in arms. He in turn presented the hawk to the most beautiful lady
of the realm. In *Melusine* the Sparrow-hawk Castle, presided over
by Melior, is located in Armenia, possibly in deference to the
connection of the Lusignan family with Little Armenia, where
Guy de Lusignan ruled as king in 1342. For the story of Melior as
told by Jean d'Arras see the edition of *Melusine* ed. by A. K.
Donald for E.E.T.S. (London, 1895), pp. 363–8. A discussion of
the sparrow-hawk adventure is given in Loomis's *Arthurian
Tradition and Chrétien de Troyes* (New York, 1949). Also cf.
'A Bibliography of the Melusine legend', compiled by A. Van
Gennep, *Manuel de folklore français* (Paris, 1938), IV, p. 651.

PAGE 651

Placebo Domino. The antiphon of the first vespers in the Church's
Office for the Dead.

PAGE 657

The seven free sciences. These, also known as the seven liberal arts,
are grammar, rhetoric, logic, arithmetic, music, geometry, and
astronomy.

BIBLIOGRAPHIES

Modern Humanities Research Association. *Annual Bibliography of English Language and Literature*, ed. A. Macdonald and H. J. Pettit (Jr.). 'XVI Century.' (Cambridge.)

The Year's Work in English Studies. The Renaissance, compiled by F. S. Boas. (Oxford.)

Publications of the Modern Language Association, ed. W. R. Parker. 'Renaissance and Elizabethan Literature', compiled by A. G. Chester and M. A. Shaaber. (New York.)

Progress of Medieval and Renaissance Studies in the United States and Canada, S. H. Thomson. (Univ. of Colorado, Boulder, Colo.)

Studies in Philology. 'Recent Literature of the Renaissance', compiled by H. Craig; 'Neo-Latin Literature of the Renaissance', compiled by D. C. Allen. (Univ. of N.C., Chapel Hill, N.C.)

Modern Language Quarterly. 'A Bibliography of critical Arthurian Literature', compiled by J. J. Parry. (Univ. of Washington, Seattle, Wash.)

Renaissance News, ed. Josephine W. Bennett. 'Projects and News', and 'Renaissance Books', compiled by E. J. Schlochauer. (New York, N.Y.)

SUGGESTED READING

PART I: TUDOR HUMANISTS

ALLEN, P. S. *The Age of Erasmus*. (Oxford, 1914.)

—— *Erasmus's Services to Learning*. Brit. Acad. Lecture. (London, 1925.)

AURNER, N. *Mirror of Fifteenth-century Letters* [Caxton]. (Boston, 1926.)

BENNETT, H. S. *English Books and Readers: 1475–1557*. (Cambridge, 1952.)

BENNETT, JOSEPHINE W. 'On the Causes of the Renaissance.' *Ren. News*, II, 5–6.

BOLGAR, R. R. *The Classical Heritage*. (Cambridge, 1954.)

BÜHLER, C. F. 'Sir John Paston's *Grete Boke*: A Fifteenth-century Best-seller.' *Mod. Lang. Notes*, LVI, 345–51.

—— 'Aldus Manutius: The First Five Hundred Years.' Trumbull Lecture at Yale, 1950. *Bibl. Soc. Amer.* XLIV, 205–15.

BURROWS, M. 'Memoir of William Grocyn.' *Collectanea*, second ser., pt. VI, etc. (Oxford Hist. Soc. 1890.)

BUSH, D. 'Tudor Humanism and Henry VIII.' *Univ. Toronto Quart.* VII, 162–77.

—— *The Renaissance and English Humanism*. (Univ. Toronto Press, 1939.)

—— 'Julius Caesar and Elyot's Governour.' *Mod. Lang. Notes*, LII, 407–8.

—— 'The Humanist Critic.' *Kenyon Rev.* XIII, 81–92.

CAMPBELL, W. E. 'Erasmus in England.' *Dublin Rev.* 211, 36–49.

CHAMBERS, R. W. *Thomas More*. (London, 1935.)

—— *The Place of St Thomas More in English Literature and History*. (London, 1937.)

—— 'On the Continuity of English Prose.' Introduction to Harpsfield's *Life and Death of Sir Thomas More* (E.E.T.S., orig. ser., no. 186, 1932).

CLARK, D. L. 'Ancient Rhetoric and English Renaissance Literature.' *Shakespeare Quart.* II, 195–204.

CRANE, W. G. *Wit and Rhetoric in the Renaissance*. (Columbia Univ. Press, 1937.)

CRAWFORD, R. M. *The Renaissance and other Essays*. (Melbourne Univ. Press, 1945; reissued 1947.)

EINSTEIN, LOUIS D. *The Italian Renaissance in England*. (New York, 1902.)

ELLIS, A. J. *On Early English Pronunciation*. Chaucer Soc., 2nd ser. 5, vols., nos. 1, 4–5, 11, 25 (London, 1896–89.).

ERASMUS, D. Letters of Erasmus, trans. F. M. Nichols, 2 vols. (London, 1901–18.)

—— *The Praise of Folly*, trans. H. H. Hudson. (Princeton Univ. Press, 1941.)

FERGUSON, WALLACE K. *The Renaissance in Historical Thought: Five Centuries of Interpretation*. (Cambridge, Mass., 1948.)

FLYNN, VINCENT J. 'The Grammatical Writings of William Lily.' *Bibl. Soc. of America*, XXXVII, 85–113.

FOWLER, THOMAS. *The History of Corpus Christi College*. (Oxford, 1873.)

GEE, JOHN A. *Life and Work of Thomas Lupset*. (Yale Univ. Press, 1928.)

GILMORE, MYRON P. *The World of Humanism, 1453–1517: (The Rise of Modern Europe*, ed. Wm. L. Langer, vol. II.) (New York, 1953.)

GOLDSCHMIDT, E. P. *The Printed Book of the Renaissance*. (Cambridge, 1950.)

GUTTMAN, SELMA. 'Alexander Barclay: A Product of his Age.' *Papers of Mich. Acad. Arts and Letters*, vol. XXXV, 317–328.

HAYDN, HIRAM C. *The Counter Renaissance*. (New York, 1950.)

KITTREDGE, GEORGE L. *English Grammars of Five Centuries*. (Boston, 1913.)

KREY, A. C. 'Padua in the English Renaissance.' *Huntington Lib. Quart.* X, 129–34.

KRISTELLER, PAUL O. 'The Place of Classical Humanism in Renaissance Thought.' *Jour. Hist. Ideas*, VI, 59–63.

—— *Essays on Renaissance Thought and Letters*. (Rome, 1953.)

MACKENZIE, KATHLEEN. 'John Colet of Oxford.' *Dalhousie Rev.* XXI, 15–28.

MARRIOT, SIR J. A. R. *The Life of John Colet*. (London, 1933.)

McDONNELL, M. F. J. *History of St Paul's School*. (London, 1909.)

MULLINGER, J. BASS. *The Schools of Charles the Great and the Restoration of Education in the Ninth Century*. (The English classical scholar Alcuin and the court school at Aachen.) (Cambridge, 1877.)

PAFORT, E. L. 'A group of Early Tudor School Books.' *Bibl. Soc., The Library*, Fourth ser., vol. XXVII, no. 7, 227–61.

—— 'Notes on the Wynkyn de Worde editions of *The Boke of St Albans*.' *Bibl. Soc. Univ. Va.* vol. V, 43–52.

PEARCE, T. M. & MACMANAWAY, J. G. 'The Vernacular Tongue in English Education.' *Ren. News*, IV, 11–12.

PHILLIMORE, J. S. 'Blessed Thomas More and the Arrest of Humanism in England.' *Dublin Rev.* CLIII, 1–26.

POMPEN, AURELIUS, O. F. M. *The English Versions of The Ship of Fools: A Contribution to the History of the Early French Renaissance in England*. (London, 1925.)

RAJEWSKI, SISTER MARY ALVARITA. *Sebastian Brant*. (Cath. Univ. of Amer. Press, 1944.)

ROGERS, ELIZABETH F. *The Correspondence of Sir Thomas More*. (Princeton Univ. Press, 1947.)

SCOTT-CRAIG, T. S. K. 'Thomas More's 1518 Letter to the University of Oxford.' *Ren. News*, I, 17–24.

SELLERY, GEORGE CLARK. *The Renaissance, its Nature and Origins*. (Univ. of Wis., 1950.)

SIMONINI, R. C. (jr.) 'Italian-English Language Books of The Renaissance.' *Romanic Rev.* XLII, 241–4.

SLEDD, JAMES. 'A Note on the use of Renaissance Dictionaries.' *Mod. Phil.* XLIX, 10–15.

STARNES, D. T. 'Shakespere and Elyot's Governour.' *Univ. Texas Stud. in Eng.* no. 7, 112–33.

STENBERG, THEODORE. 'Sir Thomas Elyot's Defense of Poets.' *Univ. Texas Studies in Eng.* no. 6, 121–46.

TILLYARD, E. M. W. *English Renaissance: Fact or Fiction?* (London, 1952.)

WARREN, LESLIE. 'Patrizi's *De Regno et Regis Institutione* and the Plan of Elyot's *The Boke named The Governour.*' *Jour. Eng. and Ger. Phil.* XLIX, 67–77.

WATSON, FOSTER. *English Grammar Schools to 1660.* (Cambridge, 1908.)

—— *Luis Vives, el gran Valenciano: 1492–1540.* (Oxford, 1922.)

WEISS, ROBERTO. *Humanism in England during the Fifteenth Century.* (Oxford, 1941.)

—— 'England and the decree of the Council of Vienne on the teaching of Greek, Arabic, Hebrew and Syriac.' *Bibliothèque d'Humanisme et Renaissance*, vol. XIV, 1–9. (Geneva, Switzerland.)

PART II: THE POLITICAL AND SOCIAL ORDER

ALLEN, DON CAMERON. *The Star-Crossed Renaissance: the Quarrel about its Influence in England.* (Duke Univ. Press, 1941.)

ALLEN, J. W. *A History of Political Thought in the Sixteenth Century.* (London, 1928.)

AMES, RUSSELL. *Citizen Thomas More and his Utopia.* (Princeton Univ. Press, 1949.)

ARBER, AGNES. *Herbals.* (Cambridge, 1912.)

BAUMER, FRANKLIN LE VAN. 'Thomas Starkey and Marsilius of Padua.' *Politica*, II, 188–205.

—— *The Early Tudor Theory of Kingship.* (New Haven, 1940.)

BENNETT, H. S. *The Pastons and their England.* (Cambridge, 1922.)

BINDER, JAMES. 'More's *Utopia* in English: A Note on Translation.' *Mod. Lang. Notes*, LXII, 370–6.

BUKOFZER, MANFRED F. *Studies in Medieval and Renaissance Music.* (New York, 1950.)

'Courtly Music of the Renaissance' (record disc). Fogg Art Museum, Cambridge, Mass.

DWYER, JOSEPH G. 'The *Pro Ecclesiasticae Unitatis Defensione* of Reginald Pole: A Translation with Historical Introduction and Critical Commentary' (micro-cards). (Fordham Univ. 1950.)

FORTESCUE, JOHN. *De Laudibus Legum Angliae*, ed. S. B. Chrimes. (Cambridge, 1942.)

GRACE, WILLIAM J. 'The Conception of Society in More's *Utopia.*' *Thought*, XXII, 282–96.

HARVEY, JOHN. *An Introduction to Tudor Architecture.* (London, 1949.)

HEXTER, J. H. *More's Utopia: the Biography of an Idea.* (Princeton Univ. Press, 1951.)

HIND, A. M. *Engraving in England in the Sixteenth & Seventeenth Centuries.* Part I, The Tudor Period. (Cambridge 1952.)

HOGREFE, PEARL. 'The Life of Christopher Saint German.' *Rev. Eng. Stud.* XLII, 398–404.

MAITLAND, F. W. *English Law and the Renaissance.* (Cambridge, 1901.)

MCNALTY, SIR ARTHUR SALISBURY. *The Renaissance and its Influence on English Medicine, Surgery, and Public Health.* (London, 1946.)

PARKS, GEORGE B. 'More's *Utopia* and Geography.' *Jour. Eng. and Ger. Phil.* XXXVII, 224–36.

—— *English Traveller in Italy,* 2 vols. (Rome, 1953.)

PICKTHORN, KENNETH. *Early Tudor Government: Henry VIII.* (Cambridge, 1934.)

POWER, SIR D'ARCY. 'The Place of the Tudor Surgeons in English Literature.' *Proceedings of the Royal Soc. Med.,* Mar. 1927, XX; section on 'The History of Medicine', 1075–79.

REINHARD, J. R. 'Burning at the Stake in Medieval Law and Literature.' *Speculum,* XVI, 186–209.

RICHARDSON, W. C. *Tudor Chamber Administration: 1485–1547.* (Baton Rouge, 1952.)

ROHDE, E. S. *The Old English Herbals.* (London, 1922.)

SALZMAN, LOUIS FRANCIS. *Building in England down to 1540: a Documentary History.* (Oxford, 1952.)

SARTON, GEORGE. 'The Quest for Truth: An Account of Scientific Progress during the Renaissance, 1350–1600.' *Renaissance, a Symposium.* (Metropolitan Mus. of Art, 1953.)

SCHENK, WILHELM. *Reginald Pole: Cardinal of England.* (London, 1950.)

SCHOECK, R. J. 'Two Notes on Margaret Gigs Clement, Foster-Daughter of Sir Thomas More.' *Notes and Queries,* CXCIV, 532–3.

—— 'Thomas Gygges, Tudor Lawyer.' *Notes and Queries,* CXCV, 267–71.

SMITH, CARLETON SPRAGUE. 'Religious Music and the Lute.' *Guitar Review,* vol. II, no. 9, 31–35.

SURTZ, EDWARD, S. J. 'Logic in *Utopia*.' *Phil. Quart.* XXIX, 389–401.

—— 'Thomas More and Communism.' *P.M.L.A.* LXIV, 549–64.

TALBER, ERNEST. 'The Notebook of a Fifteenth-century Practising Physician.' *Univ. Texas Stud. in Eng.* 1942.

TAYLOR, E. G. R. *Tudor Geography 1485–1583.* (London, 1930.)

Tudor Economic Documents, ed. by R. H. Tawney and Eileen Power. (London, 1924.)

Under God and Law. Papers read before Thomas More Law Soc. of London. (Oxford, Blackwell, 1949.)

WILSON, ROBERT H. 'Caxton's Chess Book.' *Mod. Lang. Notes,* LXII, 93–102.

ZEEVELD, W. GORDON. 'Richard Morison, Official Apologist for Henry VIII.' *P.M.L.A.* LV, 406–25.

—— 'A Tudor Defense of Richard III.' *P.M.L.A.* LV, 956–7.

—— *Foundations of Tudor Policy.* (Harvard Univ. Press, 1948.)

PART III: SERMONS AND RELIGIOUS TREATISES

AVELING, DOM HUGH. 'Tudor Westminster.' A Sketch of John de Feckenham, last Abbot of Westminster Abbey under Mary I. *Ampleforth and its Origins,* ed. Abbot Justin McCann and Dom Columba Cary-Elwes. (London, 1952.)

BATESON, MARY. 'Robert Aske's Narrative of the Pilgrimage of Grace.' *Eng. Hist. Rev.* V, 330–45.

BRIDGETT, T. E. *Life of Blessed John Fisher.* (London, 1902.)

BUTTERWORTH, CHAS. C. 'Bishop Tunstall and the English *Hortulus*.' *Lib. Chron. Univ. Pa.* XVI, 37–45.
—— *The English Primers, 1529–1545: their Publication and Connection with the English Bible and the Reformation in England.* (Univ. Penn. Press, 1952.)
CAMPBELL, W. E. *Erasmus, Tyndale and More.* (London, 1949.)
CHAMBERS, R. W. *Man's Unconquerable Mind.* (London, 1939.)
CHESTER, ALLAN G. 'Robert Barnes and the Burning of the books.' *Huntington Lib. Quart.* XIV, 211–21.
—— 'Hugh Latimer at Cambridge.' *Crozier Quart.* XXVIII, 306–18.
—— *Hugh Latimer: A Critical Biography.* (Univ. Penn. Press, 1953.)
CHEW, SAMUEL C. *The Crescent and the Rose: Islam and England during the Renaissance.* (Oxford, 1937.)
Cloud of Unknowing, ed. Dom Justin McCann. (London, 1941.)
CONSTANT, GUSTAVE. *The Reformation in England.* (London, 1939.)
CUNNINGHAM, THOMAS W. 'St John Fisher's *A Godlie Treatisse Declarying The Benefites and Great Commodities of Prayer*' (micro-cards). (Fordham Univ. 1950.)
GAIRDNER, JAMES. *The English Church in the Sixteenth Century.* (London, 1920.)
GASQUET, F. A. *Henry VIII and the English Monasteries.* (London, 1925.)
—— *Henry VIII and the Reformation.* (London, 1927.)
—— *Cardinal Pole and his Early Friends.* (London, 1927.)
GEE, JOHN A. 'Margaret Roper's English Version of Erasmus's *Precatio Dominica*.' *Rev. Eng. Studies*, XIII, 257–71.
GRAY, CHAS. M. *Hugh Latimer and the Sixteenth Century.* (Harvard Univ. Press, 1950.)
GREEN, V. H. H. *Renaissance and Reformation.* (New York, 1952.)
HUGHES, PHILIP. *Rome and the Counter-Reformation in England.* (London, 1942.)
—— *The Reformation in England*, vol. I (London, 1950); vol. 2 (1953); vol. 3 (1954.)
HYMA, ALBERT. *Renaissance to Reformation: a Critical Review of the Spiritual and Temporal Influences on Medieval Europe.* (Grand Rapids, Mich. 1951.)
JANELLE, PIERRE. *The Catholic Reformation.* (Milwaukee, 1949.)
JOURDAN, C. V. *The Movement of Catholic Reform in the Early Sixteenth Century.* (London, 1914.)
KLEIN, EDW. J. *The Imitation of Christ: from the First Edition made, c. 1530, by Richard Whytforde.* (New York, 1941.)
KNOWLES, DOM DAVID. *The Religious Orders in England.* (Cambridge, 1948.)
MAYNARD, THEODORE. *The Crown and the Cross: a Biography of Thomas Cromwell.* (New York, 1950.)
MESSINGER, C. E. *The Reformation, the Mass, and the Priesthood.* (London, 1936–7.)
MORE, SIR THOMAS. *The Last Letters of Blessed Thomas More.* Introduction by Cardinal Gasquet, ed. by W. E. Campbell. (London, 1924.)
—— *The English Works of Sir Thomas More.* Ed. by W. E. Campbell, vols. I and II. (London, 1927–31; reissued 1953.)
MOZLEY, J. F. *William Tyndale.* (New York, 1937.)
MULLER, JAMES A. *Stephen Gardiner and the Tudor Reaction.* (New York, 1926.)
O'NEIL, J. L., O.P. *Jerome Savonarola: a Sketch.* (Boston, 1898.)
OWST, G. R. *Literature and Pulpit in Medieval England.* (Cambridge, 1933.)
PARKER, T. M. 'Was Thomas Cromwell a Machiavellian?' *Jour. Eccles. Hist.* I, 63–75.
PERRY, EDITH WEIR. *Under Four Tudors: Being the story of Matthew Parker, Archbishop of Canterbury.* (London, 1940.)

REID, W. STANFORD. 'Clerical Taxation: the Scottish Alternative to Dissolution of the Monasteries, 1530–1560.' *Cath. Hist. Rev.* no. 2, XXXV, 129–53.

RICE (Jr.), EUGENE F. 'Erasmus and the Religious Tradition: 1495–1499.' *Jour. Hist. Ideas*, XL, 387–411.

SCHENK, WILLIAM. 'The Erasmian Idea.' *Hibbert Jour.* XLVIII, 257–65.

SCOTT, SISTER ST MIRIAM, C.S.N.D. 'The English Sermons of John Alcock' (micro-cards). (Fordham Univ. 1947.)

SEEBOHM, F. *The Oxford Reformers*, (London, 1867, reissued 1938.)

STURGE, CHARLES. *Cuthbert Tunstal*. (London, 1938.)

SULLIVAN, FRANK and M. P. *Moreana: a preliminary Check list (1478–1945)*. (Kansas City, 1946.)

SURTZ, EDWARD. L., S. J. '"Oxford Reformers" and Scholasticism.' *Stud. in Philology*. XLVII, 547–56.

SWEET, ALFRED H. 'John de Feckenham and the Marian Reaction.' *Persecution and Liberty: Essays in Honour of George Lincoln Burr*. (New York, 1931.)

WHITE, HELEN C. *Social Criticism in Popular Religious Literature of the Sixteenth Century*. (New York, 1944.)

—— *The Tudor Books of Private Devotion*. (Univ. of Wis. Press, 1951.)

PART IV: CHRONICLES AND HISTORIES

BOAS, F. S. *Shakespeare and his Predecessors*. (London, 1896; reissued 1910.)

BUFORD, ALFRED H. 'History and Biography: The Renaissance Distinction.' *George Coffin Taylor Studies*. (Univ. N.C. Press, 1952.)

DEAN, LEONARD F. *Tudor Theories of History Writing*. (Univ. of Mich. Press, 1947.)

HAY, DENYS. *Polydore Vergil, Renaissance Historian and Man of Letters*. (Oxford, 1952.)

Lyfe of Syr Thomas More, sometymes Lord Chancellor of England. Ed. by E. V. Hitchcock and P. E. Hallett. E.E.T.S., orig. ser., no. 222. (London, 1950.)

MAGOUN (Jr.), F. P. 'Brutus and English Politics: the Emphasis placed on the Trojan Foundation of Britain in Early Annals.' *Jour. Eng. Lit. Hist.* XIV, 176–218.

MATTINGLY, GARRETT. *Catherine of Aragon*. (Boston, 1941.)

ROPER, WILLIAM. *The Lyfe of Sir Thomas More, Knight*, ed. James M. Cline. (New York, 1950.)

TRIMBLE, WALTER R. 'Early Tudor Historiography: 1485–1548.' *Jour. Hist. Ideas*, XI, 30–40.

WOLF, EDWIN. 'Edward Hall's *The Union of the Two Noble and Illustre Famelies of Lancastre and Yorke* and its Place among English Americana.' *Bibl. Soc. of America,* vol. XXXIII, 40–54.

ZEEVELD, WILLIAM. *The Influence of Hall on Shakespeare's English Historical Plays*. (Baltimore, 1937.)

PART V: ROMANCES AND TALES

BOURDILLON, F. W. 'Huon de Bordeaux and Melusine.' *Bibl. Soc., The Library*, Fourth ser., I, 20–39.

BROWN, ARTHUR C. *The Origin of the Grail Legend*. (Harvard Univ. Press, 1943.)

CRANE, RONALD S. *The Vogue of Medieval Chivalric Romance during the English Renaissance*. (Menasah, Wis., 1919.)

DICKSON, ARTHUR. *Valentine and Orson: A Study in late Medieval Romance*. (New York, 1929.)

DUNLOP, J. *History of Prose Fiction*. (London, 1888.)

ESDAILE, A. J. *A List of English Tales and Prose Romances printed before 1740*. (London, 1921.)

FINLAY, SISTER GERMAINE MARY, S.S.J. 'Joseph of Arimathea and the Grail' (microcards). (Columbia Univ. 1951.)

GIST, M. A. *Love and War in the Middle English Romances*. (Univ. Penn. Press, 1947.)

HIBBARD, LAURA A. *Medieval Romance in England*. (Oxford, 1924.)

HOLMES (jr.), U. T. 'New Interpretation of Chrétien's *Conte del Graal*: its source, St Paul's Epistle to the Hebrews.' *Stud. in Philology*, XLIV, 453–76.

HOUSMAN, JOHN E. 'Higden, Trevisa, Caxton, and the beginning of Arthurian Criticism.' *Rev. Eng. Stud.* XXIII, 209–17.

LANCASTER, C. M. *Saints and Sinners in Old Romance*. (Vanderbilt Univ. Press, 1942.)

LOOMIS, ROGER S. *Celtic Myth and Arthurian Romance*. (New York, 1927.)

—— *Arthurian Legends in Medieval Art*, Pt. II, in collaboration with Laura Hibbard Loomis. (*Mod. Lang. Assoc.* monograph ser., 1938), 3 vols.

—— *Arthurian Tradition and Chrétien de Troyes*. (Columbia Univ. Press, 1949.)

McSHANE, MOTHER EDITH ELIZABETH. 'Tudor Opinions of the Chivalric Romances: An Essay in History and Criticism' (microcards). (Catholic Univ. of Amer., 1950.)

RIEDEL, F. C. *Crime and Punishment in Old French Romances*. (Oxford, 1938.)

ROEMANS, ROB. *Analylische Bibliographie van Mariken van Niemmeghen*. A full bibliography of articles and books on Mary of Nemmegen. (Antwerp, 1951.)

The following supplementary references came to my attention while this book was in the press.

PART I

BUSH, DOUGLAS. *Classical Influences in Renaissance Literature*. Martin Classical Lectures. (Harvard Univ. Press, 1952.)

CONKLIN, GEORGE N. *Aspects of Renaissance Culture*. (Wesleyan Univ. Press, 1953.)

JONES, RICHARD F. *The Triumph of the English Language*. (Stanford Univ. Press, 1953.)

MORE, SIR THOMAS. *The Latin Epigrams of Sir Thomas More*. Edited with Translations and Notes by Leicester Bradner and C. Arthur Lynch. (Chicago, 1953.)

SCHOECK, R. J. 'Sir Thomas More's Schooldays.' (London, Supplement to *The Times*, 18 Dec. 1953.)

SIMONINI, R. C. (JR.). 'Italian scholarship in Renaissance England.' *Stud. in Comp. Lit.* no. 3. (Univ. N.C. Press, 1952).

SURTZ, EDWARD, S.J. 'Thomas More and the Great Books.' *Phil. Q.* XXXII, 43–57.

TAYLOR, E. G. R. *The Mathematical Practitioners of Tudor and Stuart England*. (Cambridge, 1954.)

PART II

CASPARI, F. *Humanism and the Social Order in Tudor England.* (Univ. of Chicago Press, 1954.)

ELTON, G. R. *The Tudor Revolution in Government.* (Cambridge, 1953.)

READ, CONYERS. *Social and Political Forces in the English Reformation.* Rockwell Lectures. (Houston, 1953.)

SARTON, GEORGE. *Galen of Pergamon.* (Univ. of Kansas Press, 1954.)

SCHOECK, R. J. 'Rhetoric and Law in Sixteenth-century England.' *Stud. in Phil.* no. 1, 110–27.

SURTZ, EDWARD, S.J. 'St Thomas More and his Utopian Embassy of 1515.' *Cath. Hist. Rev.* XXXIX, Oct. 1953.

WILLIAMSON, JAMES A. *The Tudor Age.* (New York, 1953.)

PART III

BROMILEY, GEOFFREY W. *Nicholas Ridley: a biography.* (London, 1953.)

COULTON, G. G. *Art and the Reformation.* (Oxford, 1928; reissued, Cambridge, 1954.)

DOYLE, SISTER TERESA ANN, O.S.B. 'Classical and Baroque Elements of Spirituality in Medieval Didactic Works for Women' (microcards). (Fordham Univ., 1948.)

DUHAMEL, P. ALBERT. 'The Oxford Lectures of John Colet.' *Jour. Hist. Ideas,* XIV, 493–510.

PRESCOTT, HILDA F. M. *Mary Tudor.* (New York, 1953.)

SMITH, LACEY B. *Tudor Prelates and Politics,* Princeton Stud. in Hist., VIII. (Princeton Univ. Press, 1953.)

SULLIVAN, FRANK. *Syr Thomas More* (bibliographical notebook). (Los Angeles, 1953.)

PART IV

CEPRESS, SISTER MARY CELESTINE. 'Thomas Stapleton's *Vita Mori:* critical analysis' (microcards). (Catholic Univ. of Amer., 1953.)

PAUL, LESLIE. *Sir Thomas More.* (London, 1953.)

PENROSE, BOIES. *Travel and Discovery in the Renaissance, 1420–1620.* (Harvard Univ. Press, 1952.)

POLLARD, A. F. *Wolsey.* (New York, 1929; reissued 1953.)

SCHOECK, R. J. 'Another Renaissance Biography of Sir Thomas More.' *Eng. Stud.* XXXIV, 115–17.

STEUERT, HILARY. 'Cavendish's *Life of Cardinal Wolsey*.' *Downside Rev.*, Exeter, Jan. 1939.

WALSH, WILLIAM T. *Philip II.* (New York, 1953.)

PART V

King Ponthus and the Fair Sidone: a critical edition. Ed. by Edith S. Krappe (microfilm). (Univ. Penn., 1953.)

INDEX